90

D1757164

Charles Seale-Hayne Library
University of Plymouth
(01752) 588 588
LibraryandITenquiries@plymouth.ac.uk

Interference
and Inhibition
in Cognition

Interference
and
Inhibition
in Cognition

Edited by

Frank N. Dempster
Department of Educational Psychology
University of Nevada, Las Vegas
Las Vegas, Nevada

Charles J. Brainerd
Department of Educational Psychology
The University of Arizona
Tucson, Arizona

ACADEMIC PRESS
San Diego   New York   Boston   London   Sydney   Tokyo   Toronto

This book is printed on acid-free paper. ∞

Copyright © 1995 by ACADEMIC PRESS, INC.

Academic Press, Inc.
A Division of Harcourt Brace & Company
525 B Street, Suite 1900, San Diego, California 92101-4495

United Kingdom Edition published by
Academic Press Limited
24-28 Oval Road, London NW1 7DX

Library of Congress Cataloging-in-Publication Data

Interference and inhibition in cognition / edited by Frank N.
    Dempster, Charles J. Brainerd.
        p.   cm.
    Includes bibliographical references and index.
    ISBN 0-12-208930-8
        1. Cognition.   2. Interference (Perception)   3. Inhibition.
    I. Dempster, Frank N.   II. Brainerd, Charles J.
    BF323.I52I57   1994
    153.7--dc20   94-5430
                                                             CIP

PRINTED IN THE UNITED STATES OF AMERICA
94   95   96   97   98   99   QW   9   8   7   6   5   4   3   2   1

Contents

I
Historical Perspective

1 Interference and Inhibition in Cognition: An Historical Perspective
Frank N. Dempster

II
Developmental Perspectives

2 Interference Effects in Memory and Reasoning: A Fuzzy-Trace Theory Analysis
Valerie F. Reyna

3 Interference or Facilitation in Infant Memory?
Carolyn Rovee-Collier and Kimberly Boller

III
Adult Perspectives

7 Selective Attention and the Inhibitory Control of Cognition

W. Trammell Neill, Leslie A. Valdes, and Kathleen M. Terry

10 Catastrophic Interference in Neural Networks: Causes, Solutions, and Data

Stephan Lewandowsky and Shu-Chen Li

11 Inhibitory Processes in Cognition and Aging

Joan M. McDowd, Deborah M. Oseas-Kreger, and Diane L. Filion

12 New Perspectives on Interference and Inhibition in Cognition: Final Comments

Frank N. Dempster and Charles J. Brainerd

Contributors

Numbers in parentheses indicate the pages on which the authors' contributions begin.

David F. Bjorklund (141), Department of Psychology, Florida Atlantic University, Boca Raton, Florida 33431.

Kimberly Boller (61), Department of Psychology, Rutgers University, New Brunswick, New Jersey 08903.

Charles J. Brainerd (105, 401), Department of Educational Psychology, The University of Arizona, Tucson, Arizona 85721.

Frank N. Dempster (3, 401), Department of Educational Psychology, University of Nevada, Las Vegas, Las Vegas, Nevada 89154.

Mark Faust (295), Department of Psychology, Washington University, St. Louis, Missouri 63130.

Diane L. Filion (363), Department of Psychology, Pomona College, Claremont, California 91711.

Morton Ann Gernsbacher (295), Department of Psychology, University of Wisconsin—Madison, Madison, Wisconsin, 53706.

Katherine Kipp Harnishfeger (141, 175), Department of Psychology, University of Georgia, Athens, Georgia 30602.

Stephan Lewandowsky (329), Department of Psychology, University of Oklahoma, Norman, Oklahoma 73019.

Shu-Chen Li[1] (329), Department of Psychology, University of Oklahoma, Norman, Oklahoma 73019.

Joan M. McDowd[2] (363), Department of Psychology, Pomona College, Claremont, California 91711.

W. Trammell Neill (207), Department of Psychology, Adelphi University, Garden City, Long Island, New York 11530.

Deborah M. Oseas-Kreger (363), Department of Psychology, University of Southern California, Los Angeles, California 90089.

Valerie F. Reyna (29, 263), Department of Educational Psychology, The University of Arizona, Tucson, Arizona 85721.

[1]Present address: Department of Psychology, McGill University, Montreal, Quebec, Canada H3A 1B1.
[2]Present address: Kansas University Medical Center, Occupational Therapy Education, Kansas City, Kansas 66160.

Carolyn Rovee-Collier (61), Department of Psychology, Rutgers University, New Brunswick, New Jersey 08903.

Kathleen M. Terry (207), Department of Psychology, Adelphi University, Garden City, Long Island, New York 11530.

Allison L. Titcomb (263), Department of Educational Psychology, The University of Arizona, Tucson, Arizona 84721.

Leslie A. Valdes[3] (207), Department of Psychology, Adelphi University, Garden City, Long Island, New York 11530.

[3]Present address: Department of Psychology, Saint Cloud State University, St. Cloud, Minnesota 56301.

Preface

An important new development in the study of human cognition is the reemergence of the concepts of interference and inhibition, which played a prominent role in early theories of learning and forgetting. Although these concepts were once confined largely to specific paradigms, such as the A–B, A–C transfer task and the Brown–Peterson task, they are now being applied in much broader ways. This has spawned theories that are truly global in character and that offer a fresh approach to the age-old problems of cognition. These theories, as well as the findings they have generated, have sharpened our understanding of how the mind works, how it develops, and what goes wrong when it malfunctions.

The present volume is designed to achieve three goals. First, it presents some of the most recent theoretical and empirical work on interference and inhibition phenomena in human cognition. This work has fomented reinterpretations of existing evidence and has generated new programs of experimentation that have significantly altered the current theoretical landscape.

Second, the volume serves as a forum for a variety of perspectives on interference and inhibition. Such a forum is much needed because research on these topics continues to resemble a cottage industry, with scientists representing different domains and orientations working in relative isolation from each other. Accordingly, although this volume contains chapters from researchers who represent a variety of disciplines, their work is united by their common interest in interference and inhibition.

Third, the volume suggests new directions for research on interference and inhibition. In this connection, we trust that the following chapters will serve as a catalyst for new research and help shape the direction of future work in the area.

In Chapter 1, Dempster gives an historical introduction to the volume, showing how the roots of modern research can be traced to the rise and fall of classical interference theory. According to Dempster, the modern era was fueled primarily by four key developments, with the basic process movement in cognitive developmental research, rather than mainstream adult research, leading the way.

The next five chapters present developmental perspectives on interference and inhibition in cognition. In Chapter 2, Reyna presents evidence suggesting that some of the empirical complexities associated with the relation between memory and reasoning, including the memorial basis of reasoning errors, can be explained only in terms of interference. More specifically, recent findings reveal that memory and reasoning can and often do interfere with one another, especially in young children, in contrast to the longstanding assumption that memory enables reasoning and reasoning shapes memory. As Reyna notes, such findings have become the basis of fuzzy-trace theory. This theory assumes that there are multiple representational systems and predicts that the ability to resist interference from alternative representations, gist or verbatim, increases with age. In Chapter 3, Rovee-Collier and Boller present evidence indicating that the memories of infants as young as 3 months are highly susceptible to interference effects, in sharp contrast to much of the earlier research in this area. However, they also demonstrate that new information, encountered either prior or subsequent to learning, can facilitate retention as well as impair it. The fate of an infant's memory, it turns out, depends not only on the nature of the interpolated information but also on when the infant encounters the information. In Chapter 4, Brainerd focuses on the counterintuitive tendency for free recall to alternate between words with stronger memory representations and words with weaker memory representations, beginning with recall of some of the weaker words. This pattern, which he refers to as cognitive triage, is not an epiphenomenon but reflects processes designed to optimize recall by minimizing output interference. Further, the optimization explanation suggests that developmental improvements in unconstrained recall are governed in considerable part by age changes in production of and sensitivity to this and possibly other forms of interference. In Chapter 5, Bjorklund and Harnishfeger offer the provocative thesis that inhibitory processes played a major role in human evolution by enabling our ancestors to defer and delay potentially disruptive sexual and emotional responses, abilities that were essential for success in the social organization of early humans. Over time, the neural machinery, especially the prefrontal cortex, that was initially responsible for inhibiting these behaviors became recruited for other purposes, including reflection, planning, and an increase in the ability to resist interference from task-irrelevant information. Bjorklund and Harnishfeger, along with a growing number of other behavioral scientists, believe that contemporary human thought can be better understood through an understanding of its evolution, just as cognitive developmental research informs our understanding of adult cognition. In Chapter 6, Harnishfeger reviews evidence suggesting that inhibitory processes become more efficient between early childhood and adulthood. In addition, she highlights some of the differences between cognitive and behavioral inhibition and shows how inhibition and its counterpart, resistance to interference, figure in recent theories of cognitive development. Her chapter concludes with an appeal for an integrated theory that encompasses different forms of inhibition.

The next five chapters present adult perspectives on interference and inhibition in cognition. In Chapter 7, Neill, Valdes, and Terry review evidence relative to the crucial role of inhibitory mechanisms in selective attention, focusing on negative priming. In addition, they provide a thorough theoretical analysis of negative priming and clarify the ramifications for cognition. They argue that inhibition of irrelevant processing is a major function of selective attention. In Chapter 8, Titcomb and Reyna review the extensive literature on misinformation effects in event memory, noting the strong resemblance between the misinformation procedure and classical interference paradigms. As they point out, some of the same issues surrounding classical interference effects have also arisen in the study of misinformation effects, including the storage versus retrieval controversy and controversies regarding the interpretation of factors that determine the size of these effects. Following a discussion of major explanations of misinformation effects, the authors argue that a new theoretical perspective that makes specific predictions about interference—namely, fuzzy-trace theory—can encompass the findings. In Chapter 9, Gernsbacher and Faust propose that comprehension is highly susceptible to interference from inappropriate information and that successful suppression (i.e., inhibition) is a prerequisite for skilled comprehension. To back up this proposal, they describe a series of studies demonstrating that skilled comprehenders are more successful than less-skilled comprehenders in suppressing potentially interfering information. Finally, they present data indicating that successful suppression is influenced by the likelihood that inappropriate information will be activated. In Chapter 10, Lewandowsky and Li discuss the tendency of neural network models to display disproportionate or catastrophic interference, a phenomenon that seriously challenges the status of these models as being realistic of human cognition. Worse, catastrophic interference is not merely an analog of classical interference effects between competing stimuli, but represents a fundamental aspect of the nature of learning in connectionist networks. As Lewandowsky and Li demonstrate, however, properly modified networks can overcome catastrophic interference and be successfully applied to forgetting paradigms, including those in which either normal or accelerated forgetting (e.g., as in schizophrenia) has been observed. In Chapter 11, McDowd, Oseas-Kreger, and Filion review evidence from several paradigms that have been used to assess selective attention in the elderly. These authors conclude that diminished inhibitory processes are characteristic of normal aging and have important implications for overall cognitive functioning, although there are significant gaps in the evidence. For example, direct linkages between this decline and other cognitive deficits associated with cognitive aging have not been satisfactorily demonstrated.

Finally, in Chapter 12, Dempster and Brainerd identify and discuss two themes that the chapters in this volume have in common. In addition, they note some unresolved issues that suggest directions for future research.

Frank N. Dempster
Charles J. Brainerd

I

Historical Perspective

1

Interference and Inhibition in Cognition
An Historical Perspective

Frank N. Dempster

The purpose of this chapter is to set the stage for the chapters that follow by providing a historical introduction to the volume. In this context, I hope to convey some of the excitement and potentially revolutionary nature of modern work on interference and inhibition in cognition. This is strictly an interpretive history and it is by no means an exhaustive account. For example, I make no mention of Pavlov's writings on inhibition. Rather, I focus only on the heritage of earlier ideas and findings that pertain more or less directly to the present volume.

As an organizational device, I divide research on interference and inhibition into the classical period, the neoclassical period, and the modern period, much as various cultural and literary phenomena are divided into periods. The classical period began in the late-nineteenth century and ended in the mid-1960s. It was during this period that the verbal learning tradition dominated the study of learning and memory. The defining characteristic of the neoclassical period or transition period is an approach that is part classical interference theory and part cognitive theory. In some sense, this period represents a revival of interest in interference and inhibition following a decline late in the classical period. By contrast, the signature characteristic of the modern period is that it makes only passing reference to classical interference theory, tending instead to conceptualize interference and inhibition in purely cognitive terms. The transition from the neoclassical period to the modern period was precipitated largely by four critical developments, namely, the discovery that the concepts of interference and inhibition were highly relevant to the study of individual and developmental differences in cognition, the growing partnership between the behavioral sciences and the brain sciences, neural network models, and the growing impact of selective attention research on the field of cognition. Each of these influences is discussed toward the end of the chapter.

THE CLASSICAL PERIOD

Classical interference theory began to take shape in the late-nineteenth century. By appropriate coincidence, published studies of interference began to appear exactly 100 years ago. In 1894, Bergström reported experiments that explored the effects of interference on the execution of experimentally acquired habits. The bulk of early research on interference, however, was inspired by G. E. Muller, a German scientist, who with Schumann in 1894 published the first of a series of empirical contributions to the study of interference phenomena. Using techniques that reveal the influence of Ebbinghaus, Muller and Schumann observed that the learning of a second list of items interfered with memory of the first list. For example, items occupying the same serial position on the two lists were often confused. This observation was extended and studied in greater detail by Muller and Pilzecker (1900) and the phenomena was called "retroactive inhibition" (cf. Murray, 1976).

Much of the early work on interference was carried out by German investigators (cf. Schacter, 1982) who, like Muller, seemed anxious to apply the theoretical assumptions of British associationism. In many ways, classical interference theory was a product of a long tradition of British philosophical thought and German empirical science. The British philosophers, particularly Hobbes and Locke, provided a congenial conceptual framework for the study of interference and the Germans provided the laboratory.

After the First World War, the venue for research on interference shifted more and more from Germany to America where the study of verbal learning and retention was gathering momentum. Verbal learning research, which was strongly rooted in functionalism, which in turn was biased toward associationism, focused on the acquisition, retention, and recall of rote-learned verbal material under a standard set of controlled conditions. In this environment, the study of interference was a natural, and by 1932, the year of McGeoch's highly influential formulation of interference theory, literally dozens of studies of retroactive interference had been published. By then, McGeoch (1932) could confidently conclude that retroactive interference was a significant cause of forgetting.

In the early literature on interference, there was much less emphasis on proactive interference than on retroactive interference. Although Muller had demonstrated what we now would refer to as "proactive interference," it was not considered particularly important. Then in the late 1950s, the significance of proactive interference was enhanced considerably by the appearance of a major paper by Underwood (1957). In that paper, Underwood demonstrated that proactive interference makes a much greater contribution to forgetting than had previously been believed. In fact, this and subsequent research, much of which exploited the newly minted Brown–Peterson short-term memory paradigm (Peterson & Peterson, 1959), suggested that proactive interference was at least as potent as retroactive interference. This new interest in proactive interference was clearly warranted because there is normally much more old information available to interfere with new learning than there is new information available to interfere with old learning.

In many respects, the work of the classical interference theorists was the most remarkable achievement of the once fashionable verbal learning tradition in psychology. Two potent sources of interference were identified and a variety of experimental variables were examined in order to determine their influence on proactive and retroactive interference. Two of these, (1) similarity and (2) degree of learning, were studied extensively and both were found to have substantial effects on interference. Similarity, which was eventually manipulated along a variety of dimensions (e.g., formal, semantic, taxonomic), tended almost invariably to increase the amount of observed interference as did degree of interpolated learning. On the other hand, interference was found to be an inverse function of degree of original learning. In short, a rich set of observations and ideas were effectively explored and catalogued by the many investigators who studied interference in the classical tradition.

The Decline of Classical Interference Theory

As recently as 1960, interference theory was the dominant approach to the study of memory (Postman, 1961). By 1970, however, classical interference theory, as well as published reports of proactive and retroactive interference, began to decline. The problems posed by the study of interference never completely died out, but the area was to undergo a rapid transformation during the next two decades.

There were many reasons for the decline of classical interference theory, but they can probably be reduced to perceived shortcomings in the theoretical analysis of interference effects in the face of increasing competition from more cognitive views of learning and memory and questions about its relevance to everyday life. Each of these is worth examining in some detail.

Theoretically, classical interference theory was beset by two problems. First, it was not very effective in explaining the facts of interference. Following McGeoch (1932), most investigators used the term "inhibition" to refer to the observed decrement in the retention of the original material and the term "interference" to refer to the direct cause of the decrement, namely, the interpolated (task irrelevant) material. Although many accounts were offered and systematically investigated (e.g., response competition and unlearning), there was little agreement on the mechanisms responsible for the forgetting. As a consequence, prominent investigators in the field soon came to believe that much of what ailed classical interference theory was due to internal inconsistencies and theoretical complications (Crowder, 1976; Postman, 1976).

In addition to this difficulty, classical interference theory was largely an association theory, a tradition that by the late 1960s was rapidly giving way to an approach, broadly known as cognitive psychology, that made more complex assumptions about the nature of thinking. Associationism is essentially an attempt to reconstruct the human mind with minimal theoretical assumptions, including the simple idea that learning could be regarded as the formation of associations or bonds between previously unrelated events. Further, associationism is defined at least as much by its empiricist methodology and by its insistence that theory should not stray too far from immediate sense data. In the hands of the functionalists, that meant little more than observing the relationship between the conditions of learning and the resulting changes in performance. Associationism, and with it classical interference theory, fell out of favor in part because it did not encourage a systematic account of how individuals bring their cognitive equipment to bear on the information-processing demands of the task.

The second major reason for the decline of classical interference theory was that it had difficulty in demonstrating its relevance to the everyday operation of the human mind. In contrast to the many demonstrations of proactive and retroactive interference using traditional verbal learning materials (e.g., random unrelated words) and procedures (e.g., paired associates learning), a number of early investigators were unable to demonstrate interference when prose or connected discourse was used as the material to be learned and recalled (Ausubel, Robbins, & Blake, 1957; Ausubel, Stager, & Gaite, 1968; Hall, 1955; McGeoch & McKinney, 1934). For instance, Ausubel et al. (1957), found that a passage about Christianity did not interfere (proactively or retroactively) with retention of a passage about Buddhism (compared to an appropriate control). At a time when researchers were becoming increasingly sensitive to the practical implications of their work, these findings raised serious questions about the role of interference in everyday life and suggested to some that further research in the area would produce little of practical value (e.g., Ausubel, 1963; Neisser, 1982; see also Chapter 8 by Titcomb & Reyna, this volume).

Although other studies were more successful, even these did little to challenge the claim that when meaningful connected discourse is normally comprehended, the laws of interference do not apply. A case in point is a series of studies by Slamecka (1959, 1960, 1961), who noted that failures to obtain interference in connected discourse occurred under atypical conditions. Rather than present an entire passage, as Ausubel and his colleagues had done, Slamecka used the serial anticipation method of presenting one word at a time. As a result, the same sort of interference effects that had been found with traditional verbal learning materials were obtained. Nevertheless, this simply demonstrated that if the subject can treat the material as a random list of elements, connected discourse was also susceptible to both proactive and retroactive interference (see also Entwisle & Huggins, 1964; King & Cofer, 1960; King & Tannenbaum, 1963).

Another successful strategy was to use sentences or passages that conform to the classical A–B, A–C paradigm and to test for the original details (B) with A. In this case, subjects in the A–B, A–C condition retained fewer changed details than did subjects in the control group or subjects in an A–B, C–D condition (e.g., J. R. Anderson & Bower, 1973; R. C. Anderson & Carter, 1972; R. C. Anderson & Myrow, 1971; Bower, 1974; Crouse, 1971; M. J. A. Howe & Colley, 1976; Mehler & Miller, 1964). For example, several studies found that memory for specific details about a fictitious poet was reduced following the presentation of two or more short biographies about other fictitious poets, each of whom had a different name, a different date and place of birth, fathers with different occupations, and so forth.

By the mid 1970s, therefore, interference using relatively natural materials had been detected only under rather restricted conditions, namely those in which subjects could engage in word-for-word processing or when subjects were tested for changed details. As a consequence, many researchers concluded that proactive and retroactive interference were primarily "verbal learning" or "behaviorist" phenomena with little application to real life. In their reviews of the literature on learning and memory, for example, M. J. A. Howe (1980) suggested that retroactive interference is "too weak" to be of much practical significance and Klatzky (1980) concluded that retroactive interference occurs only under rather "constrained" circumstances. At the same time, it was not uncommon for textbooks designed for prospective teachers to advise that interference was of little practical importance (Miller, Belkin, & Gray, 1982, p. 135; Mouly, 1982, p. 328; Woolfolk & McCune-Nicolich, 1984, p. 213).

From a historical perspective, it is ironic that interference theory came to be seen as largely irrelevant to everyday life given that the intellectual roots of functionalism were nurtured by pragmatism. It was the seductive appeal of "relevance" that attracted American psychologists; associationism was adopted by functionalism because it was expected to meet the needs of educators (J. R. Anderson & Bower, 1973). By the mid 1970s, however, this promise was still unfulfilled.

THE NEOCLASSICAL PERIOD

With the decline of classical interference theory, research on interference, though less plentiful than earlier, increasingly began to take on the flavor of cognitive psychology. The promise of cognitive psychology, as Mayer (1981) noted, is that it offered a new perspective, "a way of looking at human behavior from the inside" (p. xiv). Whereas the functionalists were inclined to inquire about the conditions of acquisition, retention, and recall, the new *Zeitgeist* produced investigators who were much more likely to formulate their experimental questions with reference to the theoretical stages of encoding, storage, and retrieval as well as the theoretical structures of short- and long-term memory.

Two of the most important catalysts of the new wave of interference research were books. Perhaps the most influential book was Ulric Neisser's *Cognitive Psychology*, published in 1967. While Neisser dealt mainly with research on perception, he presented a general information-processing model consisting of distinct memory stores and processes that provided a framework for cognitive research in all areas of psychology. Another book that stimulated renewed interest in interference was *Human Associative Memory* (J. R. Anderson & Bower, 1973). *Human Associative Memory* (HAM) provided what classical interference theory did not, a systematic theory about the structure of human memory and language comprehension. HAM departed from the associationist–verbal learning tradition in two other important ways. First, it was neo-associationist in that it represented a mixture of methodological rationalism and empiricism, and second, it provided a propositional interpretation of the major findings from verbal learning research including interference data. Its focus on propositions as the fundamental units of memory, as opposed to word-to-word associations, helped set the stage for cognitive analyses of interference effects.

These and other less recognizable publications had the effect of opening up several new lines of inquiry that were part classical interference theory and part cognitive theory. An especially important research program focused on the so-called "fan effect," a phenomenon that was first reported in an experiment published in the mid 1970s (J. R. Anderson, 1974). In that experiment, subjects learned a long list of propositions, each of which involved a person and place, until they knew it, more or less perfectly. At that point, they were given a new set of propositions and asked to indicate whether these had been a member of the previous set. The more frequently the person and place had appeared in the previous set of propositions, the longer it took the subjects to determine whether the person and place had appeared together in the first set. According to Anderson, this increase in reaction time was related to an increase in the fan of facts emanating from the network representation of the concept.

The fan effect is really an interference effect, inasmuch as additional information about a concept interferes with memory for a particular piece of information. Unlike traditional measures of interference, however, fan effects were measured by recognition time. Although the fan effect was understood in terms of an explicit model of the retrieval process, the way in which items were paired with one another (e.g., the same person to multiple locations) is reminiscent of the classical interference paradigm.

Another line of inquiry of this sort culminated in an article revealingly entitled, "Evolution of cognitive structures and processes" (Hayes-Roth, 1977). Although its title puts the article firmly within the cognitive mainstream, it made frequent reference to classical interference theory and the new findings presented were largely consistent with earlier studies. For example, Hayes-Roth was able to show that proactive interference between two related propositions is most likely if the first-learned proposition has been moderately well learned. By contrast, minimally learned and overlearned first- learned propositions resulted in either no net transfer or proactive facilitation. Nevertheless, at least some of the theoretical assumptions from which her predictions were derived had a decidedly cognitive flavor, not the least of which was the idea that the unit of cognition changes over the course of experience.

From the present perspective one of the most important consequences of these efforts is that they helped to place interference within a contemporary cognitive framework. They did not, however, do much to dispel doubts about the relevance of interference to everyday life. Although propositions are clearly an improvement on nonsense syllables and unrelated words, few everyday situations require people to rote-learn sets of related sentences.

The possibility that interference might play a significant role in everyday memory received a substantial boost from the work of Loftus, and subsequently other investigators, on misinformation effects that might occur in the course of eyewitness testimony (see Chapter 2 by Reyna, and Chapter 8 by Titcomb & Reyna, this volume). In her seminal study, by now something of a classic, Loftus and Palmer (1974) had subjects watch a film of a car crash. They were later asked various questions about the incident including how fast the cars were going when they hit each other. All the subjects were asked the same question except that for some the word "hit" was replaced by either "contacted," "bumped," "collided," or "smashed." The particular word used influenced the estimated speed, with the word "smashed" associated with the highest average speed and the word "contacted" evoking the lowest average speed. When questioned further a week later and asked if there was any evidence of broken glass, those that had been tested using the word "smashed" were consistently more likely to incorrectly report the presence of broken glass.

Although the interfering effects of subsequent questioning on eyewitness testimony has been known since the work of Munsterberg (1908), the full force of these retroactive effects has only recently been discovered. Even so, the theoretical controversy that still rages over these data is strongly reminiscent of the response competition–unlearning controversy that divided classical interference theorists many years ago. As it was then, a key issue is whether an original memory that is disrupted by interference is permanently erased or whether, under appropriate conditions, it can be recovered. For a more complete discussion of this issue and misinformation effects, see Titcomb and Reyna, Chapter 8, this volume.

For many, however, the jury on retroactive interference and its application to real life was still out, despite the encouraging line of inquiry initiated by Loftus. What was lacking was a convincing demonstration of retroactive interference in naturalistic prose, but without the limitations of the earlier work. This prompted a series of three experiments that seemed to suggest that retroactive interference is an important factor in memory for material similar to what students frequently encounter in school (Dempster, 1988). (For other work on the role of retroactive interference in prose comprehension, see Gernsbacher & Faust, Chapter 9, this volume.)

The general procedure consisted of exposing experimental groups to two presentations of the target passage followed by written recall and two presentations of the second passage followed by written recall. The control group was exposed to two presentations of the target passage followed by written recall and an unrelated interpolated activity. In two of the three experiments, all written subjects received a previously unannounced written recall test of the target passage 24 h later and in one experiment a 24-h recall was followed by a cued-recall test.

What distinguishes these experiments most from previous efforts to extend the principles of retroactive interference to realistic prose were three design characteristics. First, the passages were not written in strict A–B, A–C fashion. Second, except for the one cued-recall test, the method of testing was free recall. According to J. R. Anderson and Bower (1973), who reviewed much of the earlier research, this deviation should not have produced retroactive interference. In HAM, interference is only expected if the subject is probed with the repeated portion of the proposition and asked for recall of the portion that is not repeated. Third, a simple classificatory scheme was introduced that divided each passage into four meaning structures, two at the paragraph level and two at the sentence level. At the paragraph level are the main ideas corresponding to the main topic or category (e.g., learning) and the subtopic or subject (e.g., positive reinforcement). At the sentence level are the sentence themes (e.g., the first sentence in one of the target passages concerns the effect of positive reinforcement on desired conduct) and sentence details (e.g., the first sentence in that same passage reads that positive reinforcement causes an "increase" in desired conduct). This scheme was valuable in helping to identify the conditions leading to retroactive facilitation. In some of the earlier research, the failure to distinguish between conditions that lead to facilitation and conditions that lead to interference may have been responsible for failures to obtain retroactive interference (e.g., Ausubel et al., 1957).

Several of Dempster's findings are of special interest. First, significant retroactive interference was detected only when the two passages shared the same main topic. Second, significant retroactive interference was found only when passages contained different subtopics (e.g., positive reinforcement; negative reinforcement), at least some sentence themes that were different (e.g., the effect of positive reinforcement on desired conduct; the effect of punishment on self concept), and different sentence details (e.g., an "increase" in desired conduct; may result in "low" self-concept). Significantly, retroactive interference was not confined to the recall of changed details; the significant overall differences between experimental and control groups were due to reduced retention of both themes and details. Finally, the cued-recall results suggest that the loss of themes were due to forces operating to block retrieval. No evidence was found for response unavailability.

As was the case with retroactive interference, it took some time before the relevance of proactive interference to everyday life was convincingly demonstrated. Much of the research on proactive interference conducted after 1965 made use of the Brown–Peterson procedure in which subjects participate in a series of recall trials, three or four of which ordinarily occur in rapid succession. Further, the stimuli used on each trial are usually similar to each other in terms of some salient dimension; and each trial includes a distractor-filled delay interval interposed between presentation and recall. The popularity of this task was based primarily on three considerations. First, Brown–Peterson performance was thought to be mainly a measure of short-term memory, a hypothetical construct that was investigated exhaustively by the new cognitive psychologists. Second, it was soon established, to almost everyone's satisfaction, that forgetting in this task was due almost entirely to interference as opposed to decay (for a review, see Crowder, 1989). Third, the "release from proactive interference" effect (a reduction in interference associated with the use of distinctive items on the final trial) first reported by Wickens, Born, and Allen (1963), led to numerous analytical investigations of the conditions most favorable to that release (see also Chapter 4 by Brainerd, this volume). For example, if the final Brown–Peterson trial consisted of three words instead of three numbers on each of the previous trials, performance on the final trial was almost as high as performance on the first trial. Although the effects of distinctiveness or similarity on performance in this task are consistent with classical interference theory, this procedure helped sustain interest in interference phenomena.

Although there were countless demonstrations of proactive interference in the Brown–Peterson task with unrelated words and other traditional verbal learning materials, it was not until the late 1970s that Brown–Peterson interference was demonstrated with realistic materials (Blumenthall & Robbins, 1977; Gunter, Clifford, & Berry, 1980). In the study by Gunter et al. (1980), the material consisted of television news items that subjects listened to while they viewed a videotape of the same events. Subjects heard three items during each trial and attempted to recall them after a 1-min delay. The control group received items about the same topic (either politics or sports) over a series of four trials. By contrast, the experimental group received items about the same topic over the first three trials and then were shifted to items about the other topic on the fourth trial. The results were similar to those found with less realistic materials. The proportion of correct responses declined over the first three trials for both the control group and the experimental group, from roughly 85% on the first trial to about 55% on the third trial. On the fourth trial, however, the control group recalled 43% and the experimental group recalled 74%.

By the late 1980s, therefore, there were reasons to believe that both proactive and retroactive interference played an important role in everyday learning and memory. In retrospect, the analysis of interference effects in eyewitness testimony and the discovery of interference in realistic materials using older interference paradigms were good news to those who would argue that classical interference theory died a premature death. With the exception of the work on eyewitness testimony, however, these developments have not had much of an impact on contemporary approaches to interference and inhibition. For example, indications are that Dempster's (1988) work in retroactive interference has been largely ignored. Thus, while these developments help to legitimize the recent ground swell of interest in these concepts, they are not directly responsible for it.

THE MODERN PERIOD

The transition from the neoclassical period to the modern period was fueled largely by four developments. The single most significant event was the discovery by developmental psychologists, and to a lesser extent psychologists interested in individual differences, that the concepts of interference and inhibition were highly relevant to their respective disciplines (see especially Chapter 5 by Bjorklund & Harnishfeger and Chapter 6 by Harnishfeger, this volume). In part, this realization was precipitated by growing disenchantment with traditional explanations of developmental and individual differences. These include knowledge-based explanations inspired by Piaget's work as well as activation resource and strategic explanations associated with the computer-inspired information-processing perspective.

A second major development has been the rapidly growing partnership between the behavioral sciences and the neurosciences. This trend has helped to place the recent interest in interference and inhibition on a firm biological foundation. As neuroscientists have known for some time, the human brain contains inhibitory mechanisms as well as excitatory mechanisms and at least one function of inhibition is to control interference.

A third and related development that has contributed to the resurgence of interest in interference and inhibition is the advent of neural networks, also known as connectionist or PDP models, in which inhibitory processes are frequently implemented in terms of activation/suppression weights (Sejnowski & Rosenberg, 1988). These models have generated a great deal of excitement in recent years and their ability to provide elegant accounts of certain aspects of human cognition is due, in part, to their implementation of inhibition (see Lewandowsky & Li, Chapter 10, this volume).

A fourth factor is the increasing impact of selective attention research on the field of cognition. Whereas theories of selective attention have always assumed the presence of irrelevant stimuli, it is only recently that research has shown that a critically important function of selective attention is the inhibition of irrelevant stimuli. Each of these developments will be considered separately.

Developmental and Individual Differences

For years, the dominant themes in the study of cognitive development were inspired by Piaget. What developed, according to Piaget, were certain forms of knowledge, such as an appreciation of the significance of objects distinct from action and logical operations that enabled adults to understand the world differently than children. Although Piaget's account of cognitive development is still popular, it is gradually giving way to more interferenced-based interpretations. Consider, for example, two key developmental milestones from the Piagetian repertoire, the infant A-not-B search task and two bench marks of the transition between preoperational thought and concrete operational thought, conservation and class inclusion.

Piaget observed that 8- to 12-month-old infants can find a hidden object at an initial location (A). However, after several successful searches at A, many infants continue to search there when an object is hidden at a different location (B), even though the displacement is visible and the infant watches as the object is hidden.

For Piaget, these errors ("A-not-B" errors) were regarded as critical evidence of his once widely held view that the infant's understanding of objects and spatial relationships is fundamentally different from that of adults. According to Piaget, 8- to 12-month-old infants search for the object at A because the object's existence and position in space are linked to or are partially defined by the infant's action; in effect, the object exists for the infant as the "object that I find at location A." Thus, for the infant, the object remains "at disposal in the place where the action has made use of it" (Piaget, 1954, p. 50).

Given the critical role played by the "A-not-B" error in Piaget's theory of how the child acquires knowledge of the external world, it is not surprising that this error has been studied extensively and that alternative accounts have been suggested. But it was not until much later that the first systematic interference-type arguments appeared (Harris, 1973, 1975). Basically, Harris suggested that young infants were especially vulnerable to proactive interference from the initial location and that it was this interference that was primarily responsible for their errors.

Although Harris (1975) quickly abandoned this hypothesis, at least as a generalized account of infant search errors, in favor of Piaget's discontinuity thesis, recent research casts serious doubts upon this thesis. Although there is still no agreed-upon interpretation of this phenomenon, certain findings suggest that Harris's earlier hunch was essentially correct, and that infants younger than 12 months of age are extremely susceptible to the effects of proactive interference generated by their initial search(es) at A. First, infants of this age display nearly perfect recall on trials not preceded by similar, potentially interfering, activities (Schacter, Moscovitch, Tulving, McLachlan, & Freedman, 1986). Second, the spatial similarity or closeness of the alternative location to the currently correct location of the object appears to be a primary determiner of whether that location will be the locus of any incorrect search attempt (E. L. Bjork & Cummings, 1984). Third, the results of a study using a nonsearch variant of this task call into serious question attempts at explaining infants' search errors in terms of faulty memory mechanisms per se (Baillargeon, DeVos, & Graber, 1989); however, they are consistent with the hypothesis that infants are unable to suppress a previously correct solution. Finally, eye movements suggest that infants sometimes seem to "know" the correct location, but cannot resist repeating a behavior (i.e., reaching) that is no longer appropriate (Diamond, 1991).

Although older children make fewer errors on search tasks than do infants, the errors they do make often involve searching in the location where the object was found on the preceding trial (Sophian, Larkin, & Kadane, 1985). Errors of this sort continue to occur as late as 4½ years of age (Sophian & Wellman, 1983). Thus, there is a developmental shift from relatively error-prone search performance during infancy to predominately correct search patterns during early childhood; however, the types of errors are remarkably similar.

In short, these findings suggest that the search behaviors of infants and young children are united by a common but increasingly more efficient process, namely, resistance to interference. While it is no doubt true that infants and young children acquire an increasingly sophisticated understanding of objects and space, that knowledge can be applied only if inappropriate responses can be inhibited (see Rovee-Collier & Boller, Chapter 3, this volume). As Diamond (1991) noted, "Cognitive development can be conceived of, not only as the progressive *acquisition* of knowledge, but also as the enhanced *inhibition* of reactions that get in the way of demonstrating knowledge that is already present" (p. 67).

Conservation and class inclusion, on the other and, are just two of the many childhood reasoning problems that Piaget introduced that were supposed to pit reliance on "logic" against reliance on "perception." Although Piaget argued that it was the absence of logical operations rather than visual confusion that was the culprit in these tasks, a handful of skeptics quickly drew renewed attention to the misleading structure of these tasks and showed that task difficultly could be profoundly influenced by adding or subtracting misleading, potentially interfering, information (Bruner, 1966; Gelman, 1969; Wallach, Wall, & Anderson, 1967; Zimiles, 1963). For example, Gelman (1969) showed that preconservers could "conserve" if they were taught to ignore the irrelevant features of the task, such as changes in size, shape, and color. Although these findings did little, at the time, to temper enthusiasm for Piaget's account of cognitive development, they spawned a persistent line of inquiry suggesting that conservation and class inclusion have more to do with the ability to resist interference than they do with the child's ability to grasp their underlying "logic" (Brainerd & Reyna, 1991; Dempster, 1992). In class inclusion problems, for example, Brainerd and Reyna (1991) argue that reasoning errors are by-products of interference between two types of gist that are extracted from background inputs: numerical gist ("more", "less") and inclusional gist ("everything here is an animal").

Another perspective that once offered rarely challenged accounts of developmental and individual differences is the information-processing perspective. Among its most pervasive legacies is the belief that activation resources (i.e., working memory capacity and activation rate) can explain a wide range of data. From this perspective, then, the burden of explanation has fallen heavily on the number of cognitive units that can be activated simultaneously and the speed with which these units can be activated. Despite persistent measurement problems (Dempster, 1985b; Flavell, 1978; Navon, 1984), activation resources have been invoked to explain age-related improvements in intellectual ability (e.g., Bjorklund, 1987; Halford, 1982), cognitive aging (e.g., Craik & Byrd, 1982; Salthouse, 1982, 1988), as well as individual differences in cognition and general intelligence (e.g., Jensen, 1989).

After an idea has become so fashionable that it is commonplace, it is often reevaluated. In recent years this has been the fate of activation resource theory. Although most investigators apparently believe that activation resources are useful theoretical constructs, a growing number are suggesting that inhibitory processes have been unduly neglected and that they are at least as important as excitatory processes (for a sample, see M. L. Howe & Pasnak, 1993). Perhaps the most influential critique of activation resources was offered by Hasher and Zacks (1988) who suggested that age differences (between young and old adults) in working memory capacity were due, in substantial part, to age deficits in inhibitory functioning. In addition, Hasher and Zacks reported data showing that a minimum of two independent resources had to be postulated to account for age- related declines in comprehension, a finding that is difficult to reconcile with a generic resource approach. In this and subsequent work, their data have generally shown that older adults tend to have a less efficient inhibitory system than younger adults (e.g., Hasher, Stoltzfus, Zacks, & Reyna, 1991). Reduced ability to resist interference in the elderly is also implicated in studies and reviews by Dempster (1990, 1992), McDowd and Oseas-Kreger (1991), McDowd, Oseas-Kreger and Filion (Chapter 11, this volume), and Tipper (1991).[1]

It is in the fields of cognitive development and intelligence, however, that activation resources have had their greatest impact. As Brainerd and Reyna (1989) observed, the resources hypothesis was for some time ". . . the preeminent metatheoretical principle of cognitive development" (p. 1). In the field of intelligence, speed of information processing has been virtually synonymous with psychometric g, the general ability factor (e.g., Jensen, 1989; Vernon, 1987), even though it does not come close to accounting for all the variance in that factor.

Although there is still heavy reliance on activation resources in these areas of study, there is growing evidence that resistance to interference and its counterpart, the efficiency of inhibition, contribute to both cognitive development and individual differences in cognition (Bjorklund & Harnishfeger, 1990; Chapter 5, this volume; Dempster, 1985a, 1985b, 1989, 1991, 1992; Harnishfeger, Chapter 6, this volume; Harnishfeger & Bjorklund, 1993). Moreover, as this idea gains acceptance, it is likely that inhibitory constructs will prove useful to resource theorists. For example, it might help to explain why there is only a haphazard correlation between indices of capacity utilization and performance (Mitchell & Hunt, 1989). If the pool of activated representations contains unsuppressed irrelevant representations, at least a portion of the capacity resource will be misdirected, leading to a decrement in performance. As Bjorklund and Harnishfeger (1990) suggested, a model that includes inefficient inhibition ". . . may serve as neutral ground for both resource and non resource theorists, regardless of what the field may decide about 'resources'" (p. 67).

---

[1]The notion that elderly adults are more susceptible to interference than are younger adults is not new. At about the time that the verbal learning approach peaked, it was the most frequent explanation for age-related declines in performance (Arenberg, 1967; Botwinick, 1973; Jerome, 1959; Welford, 1958). Specifically, it was proposed that proactive and retroactive interference disrupted the processes of learning and memory more easily in older adults than in younger adults. By the mid 1970s, however, this view gave way to the prevailing ideas of the times and it largely declined in favor of activation resource and strategic explanations of cognitive aging (see Arenberg, 1980).

From an information-processing perspective, strategies such as rehearsal and organization are control processes that govern the movement of information through the component stores of the system. Strategic explanations of individual and developmental differences in cognition became extremely popular during the 1970s (Flavell, 1971; Kail & Hagen, 1977; Newell & Simon, 1972; Ornstein, 1978). Nowhere was this more apparent than in the area of memory development, where strategies were widely believed to be "what develops" (Flavell, 1971).

While strategic explanations of ability differences have inspired a great deal of optimism, they have failed to live up to their earlier promise (Bjorklund, 1985, 1987; Dempster 1985b, 1992; Brainerd & Reyna, 1991). Research on memory span is a case in point. Much of that research has focused on the contribution of strategic variables to span differences. However, individual as well as developmental differences in strategies such as chunking, grouping, and rehearsal have been found to account for only modest amounts of intersubject variability in span (Dempster, 1981, 1985b; Dempster & Zinkgraf, 1982). Another instructive example is Bjorklund's demonstration that the development of taxonomic organization is controlled more by primitive nonstrategic associative and knowledge base processes than by organizational strategies (Bjorklund, 1985, 1987).

As a consequence, some investigators began to shift theoretical attention away from strategies to nontraditional, nonstrategic approaches to ability differences. This development, which began in the early 1980s, has been referred to as the "basic process" movement (Brainerd, 1990). One of its core beliefs is that strategies should not serve as the basic unit of analysis in memory research but that they should have more of a peripheral explanatory role (Brainerd & Reyna, 1991).

Among the beneficiaries of this movement are the concepts of interference and inhibition. For example, having determined that strategies did a poor job of predicting individual and developmental differences in span, Dempster (1981, 1985b; Dempster & Cooney, 1982) suggested that susceptibility to interference might be an important factor in span differences as well as differences in other traditional short-term memory tasks (see also Harnishfeger, Chapter 6, this volume). Similarly, Brainerd (Chapter 4, this volume) has concluded that strategic processes have little to do with the development of recall, arguing instead that it is controlled largely by age-related changes in sensitivity to interference.

In short, developmental and individual differences research, rather than mainstream adult research, has led the way in fomenting a new theoretical orientation. But the most impressive aspect of recent developmental research on interference is that it has produced three new theories that are unusually global and integrative in character; inefficient inhibition theory (Bjorklund & Harnishfeger, 1990; Chapter 5, this volume; Harnishfeger, Chapter 6, this volume; Harnishfeger & Bjorklund, 1993); fuzzy trace theory (Brainerd &

Reyna, 1991, 1993; Reyna, Chapter 2, this volume), and resistance to interference theory (Dempster, 1985b, 1990, 1992). Unlike most adult theories,
which tend to be tied to specific paradigms such as negative priming, these
three theories seek to explain and have achieved some success in explaining a
range of otherwise disparate phenomena. Although these theories were motivated by somewhat different considerations (inefficient inhibition theory grew
out of need to deal with all of the empirical challenges to resource theory,
fuzzy trace theory was motivated by findings demonstrating that the relationship between memory and cognitive development is more often one of utter
independence or outright competition than one of facilitation; and resistance
to interference theory arose as a response to the various empirical and theoretical shortcomings of activation resources and strategies), each implement
interference concepts to explain age-related shifts in performance.

The Impact of the Neurosciences

The reemergence of interference/inhibition-based ideas in the study of
human cognition can also be traced to the rapidly growing impact of the neurosciences on almost every area of psychology. To some extent, the weight of
this impact can be measured in terms of the sheer number of relatively new
multidisciplinary journals that focus on the relation between the brain and
behavior. Examples include *Behavioral Neuroscience, Brain and Cognition,*
and the *Journal of Cognitive Neuroscience.* Another, less tangible, indicator is
the ever-increasing preference among cognitive psychologists for the brain
metaphor as opposed to the computer metaphor, which for at least two
decades probably discouraged interest in inhibitory processes (R. A. Bjork,
1989; Dempster, 1991, 1993; Harnishfeger & Bjorklund, 1993).

As a result of a growing awareness of the relevance of the brain sciences
to their work, many cognitive psychologists have developed theories consistent with information known about cerebral structure and function. For example, some researchers have suggested that developmental changes in myelination (which is normally not complete until late adolescence) (Yakovlev &
Lecours, 1967) are associated with increased speed of processing (Bjorklund
& Harnishfeger, 1990; Case, 1985; Dempster, 1985b). From the present perspective, however, the most significant marriage between the neurosciences
and the behavioral sciences relates the frontal cortex (i.e., frontal lobes) to resistance to interference and inhibition. Although the frontal cortex has long
been implicated in the ability to resist interference (e.g., Fuster, 1989; Luria,
1966), it is only recently that this region of the brain has been called upon to
help validate interference-based theories of cognitive development, aging,
and individual differences (see also Chapters 5 and 6 by Bjorklund &
Harnishfeger and Harnishfeger, respectively this volume).

There are three critical links in this chain of reasoning. First, young children, older adults, and individuals with frontal lobe lesions demonstrate a

similar pattern of performance deficits in a wide range of interference-sensitive tasks, including the Wisconsin Card Sorting Test, measures of field dependence, illusions of judgment (e.g., conservation), selective attention tasks, the Brown–Peterson Task, and text processing (see Dempster, 1992, for a review). In the Wisconsin Card Sorting Test, for example, frontal lobe patients, young children, and elderly adults make significantly more perseverative errors (errors that reflect an inability to inhibit a previously established response set) than normal young adults. Second, the frontal lobes are the last region of the brain to develop and they appear to be the first to undergo involution later in life (for reviews, see Dempster, 1992, 1993). Finally, the frontal lobes are relatively fragile (Weinberger, 1987) and their neuropsychological properties vary considerably across individuals of the same or similar ages (Terry, DeTeresa, & Hansen, 1987).

Biologically determined changes and differences in the brain, including the frontal cortex, manifest themselves in a variety of ways. For example, synaptic density increases during infancy and reaches a maximum at 1 or 2 years of age when it is about 50% of the adult mean (Huttenlocher, 1979). Following this period of synapse accumulation, some, presumably excess, synapses are progressively eliminated, a process that continues throughout childhood and adolescence (Goldman-Rakic, 1987; Huttenlocher, 1979). Further decreases in synaptic density occur in the elderly and there are marked individual differences in synaptic profiles associated with the frontal cortex (Huttenlocher, 1979).

Although it is not understood exactly what intellectual implications these and most other variations in the human nervous system have, there are reasons to believe that they are associated with age-related and individual differences in processing efficiency, including the efficiency of inhibitory processes. For example, it may be that a critical mass of synapses is a necessary condition for the emergence of some abilities (e.g., elimination of errors in the "A-not-B" task), but not a sufficient condition for adult competence (Goldman-Rakic, 1987). Because synapse elimination is consistent with the general principle of competitive elimination in the mammalian central nervous system and is associated with the removal of unproductive axons (La Mantia & Rakic, 1984), a high level of adult competence may depend on an optimal level of synapse pruning. It may not be coincidental, therefore, that in some instances of mental retardation low synaptic densities have been reported in the frontal cortex (Goldman-Rakic, 1987), whereas in others, relatively high synaptic densities have been reported (Cragg, 1975). Although the relation between synaptic density in the frontal lobes and resistance to interference in most interference-sensitive tasks is speculative, there is compelling evidence that elimination of errors in the "A-not-B" and related tasks is made possible partly by maturational changes in the frontal cortex and its neural connections (Diamond, 1988, 1991; Harnishfeger, Chapter 6, this volume).

In the domain of individual differences, some of the impetus for interference-based interpretations can be traced to the results of studies of certain atypical populations in which frontal lobe dysfunction is implicated. These include the learning disabled (Lazarus, Ludwig, & Aberson, 1984), attention-deficit-disordered children (Chelune, Ferguson, Koon, & Dickey, 1986), schizophrenics (Weinberger, 1987), and Korsakoff patients (Parkin & Leng, 1987), all of whom perform poorly on the Wisconsin Card Sorting Test or some other interference-sensitive task. Although these are atypical populations, it is reasonable to assume that the efficiency of frontal lobe function varies in the normal population and that these variations, however small, have important intellectual consequences.

Neural Network Models

A third source of new interference and inhibition-based ideas in cognition is the advent of neural network models, which, unlike most information-processing models, bear at least some abstract resemblance to how the brain operates. In these models, as in connectionist models in general, simple processing units at varying levels of complexity are in continual interaction, each unit being able to send excitatory and inhibitory signals to other units via the connections among them.

Another, albeit unintentional, feature of neural network models that has refocused attention on inhibitory mechanisms is their susceptibility to "catastrophic interference," the nearly instantaneous forgetting of existing information during the acquisition of new material (McCloskey & Cohen, 1989). As might be expected, this has led to various efforts to reduce or eliminate catastrophic interference (for a full discussion, see Lewandowsky & Li, Chapter 10, this volume). Nevertheless, this discovery has reminded cognitive psychologists that interference and a means of resisting it must be a component of any realistic theory of human cognition.

Selective Attention Research

The impact of selective attention research has been felt at two levels, theoretical and methodological. At the theoretical level, recent advances in selective attention research indicate that inhibitory mechanisms have profound implications for general cognitive functioning. In part, this is the result of an increasingly compelling body of data suggesting that young children and older adults are less able than are young adults to inhibit irrelevant stimuli in selective attention tasks (for reviews, see Dempster, 1992, 1993; Lane & Pearson, 1982). At the methodological level, recently popular ways of measuring inhibition, such as the negative priming paradigm (McDowd, Oseas-Kreger, & Filion, Chapter 11, this volume; Neill, Valdes, & Terry, Chapter 7, this volume; Tipper, 1985), have become the tools of choice for many researchers in other specialty areas, including cognitive development and cognitive aging.

SUMMARY

The concepts of interference and inhibition played an important part in early theories of learning and forgetting. In many respects, the work of the classical interference theorists was the most remarkable achievement of the once-fashionable verbal learning tradition in psychology. Yet, classical interference theory was not effective in either explaining the facts of interference or in showing how interference applies to everyday life. It was partly for these reasons that interference theory, as well as published reports of proactive and retroactive inhibition, began to decline in the early 1970s.

Another limitation of classical interference theory was that it was largely an association theory, a tradition that by the late 1960s was rapidly giving way to more complex assumptions about the human mind. This approach, broadly known as cognitive psychology, went beyond the associationists' claim that ideas are connected through the action of an association and focused instead on mental processes and structures. Cognitive psychology, which has been dominated by the computer-inspired information-processing perspective, has been largely responsible for the popularity of "activation resource" (e.g., working memory capacity, speed of information processing) explanations of empirical data. On the other end of the hardware–software dimension, this approach, coupled with the Piagetian tradition in developmental psychology, has been largely responsible for the still-prevalent view that much of human information processing is strategic in nature. In short, the influence of classical interference theory waned in the face of increasing competition from more cognitive views of learning and memory.

Of late, however, there has been a renewed interest in the time-honored concepts of interference and inhibition. Ironically, this renewal reflects a growing disenchantment with many of the same information-processing perspectives (e.g., activation resources and strategies) that supplanted the verbal learning approach in the first place. But while classical interference theory was largely irrelevant to the everyday operation of the human mind, recent work has shed important new light on complex human behaviors. It has become increasingly clear that many, if not most, intellectual tasks are interference sensitive. Research on a wide variety of psychological processes, including attention, perception, learning and memory, psycholinguistics, cognitive development, aging, learning disabilities, and neuropsychology, suggests that resistance to interference, and by implication the capacity for inhibition, is a critically important dimension of cognition. Thus, many of the phenomena and issues studied by cognitive psychologists have been framed in a new way, one that has far-reaching implications for understanding the human mind.

ACKNOWLEDGMENT

I thank Alice Corkill Dempster and Chuck Brainerd for their assistance and encouragement in the preparation of this chapter.

REFERENCES

Anderson, J. R. (1974). Verbatim and propositional representation of sentences in immediate and long-term memory. *Journal of Verbal Learning and Verbal Behavior, 13,* 149–162.
Anderson, J. R., & Bower, G. H. (1973). *Human associative memory.* Washington, DC: Winston.
Anderson, R. C., & Carter, J. F. (1972). Retroactive inhibition of meaningfully-learned sentences. *American Educational Research Journal, 9,* 443–448.
Anderson, R. C., & Myrow, D. L. (1971). Retroactive inhibition of meaningful discourse. *Journal of Educational Psychology, 62,* 81–94.
Arenberg, D. (1967). Age differences in retroaction. *Journal of Gerontology, 22,* 88–91.
Arenberg, D. (1980). Comments on the processes that account for memory declines with age. In L. W. Poon, J. L. Fozard, L. S. Cermak, D. Arenberg, & L. W. Thompson (Eds.), *New directions in memory and aging* (pp. 67–71). Hillsdale, NJ: Erlbaum.
Ausubel, D. P. (1963). *The psychology of meaningful verbal learning.* New York: Grune & Stratton.
Ausubel, D. P., Robbins, L. C., & Blake, E. (1957). Retroactive inhibition and facilitation in the learning of school materials. *Journal of Educational Psychology, 48,* 250–255.
Ausubel, D. P., Stager, M., & Gaite, A. J. H. (1968). Retroactive facilitation in meaningful verbal learning. *Journal of Educational Psychology, 59,* 250–255.
Baillargeon, R., DeVos, J., & Graber, M. (1989). Location memory in 8-month-old infants in a non-search AB task: Further evidence. *Cognitive Development, 4,* 345–367.
Bergström, J. A. (1894). The relation of interference to the practice effect of an association. *American Journal of Psychology, 6,* 433–442.
Bjork, E. L., & Cummings, E. M. (1984). Infant search errors: Stage of concept development or stage of memory development. *Memory & Cognition, 12,* 1–19.
Bjork, R. A. (1989). Retrieval inhibition as an adaptive mechanism in human memory. In H. L. Roediger, III & F. I. M. Craik (Eds.), *Varieties of memory and consciousness* (pp. 309–330). Hillsdale, NJ: Erlbaum.
Bjorklund, D. F. (1985). The role of conceptual knowledge in the development of organization in children's memory. In C. J. Brainerd & M. Pressley (Eds.), *Basic processes in memory development: Progress in cognitive development research* (pp. 103–142). New York: Springer-Verlag.
Bjorklund, D. F. (1987). How age changes in knowledge base contribute to the development of children's memory: An interpretive review. *Developmental Review, 7,* 93–130.
Bjorklund, D. F., & Harnishfeger, K. K. (1990). The resources construct in cognitive development: Diverse sources of evidence and a theory of inefficient inhibition. *Developmental Review, 10,* 48–71.
Blumenthal, G. B., & Robbins, D. (1977). Delayed release from proactive interference with meaningful material: How much do we remember after reading brief prose passages? *Journal of Experimental Psychology: Human Learning and Memory, 3,* 754–761.
Botwinick, J. (1973). *Aging and behavior.* New York: Springer-Verlag.

Bower, G. H. (1974). Selective facilitation and interference in retention of prose. *Journal of Educational Psychology, 66,* 1–8.

Brainerd, C. J. (1990). Issues and questions in the development of forgetting. *Monographs of the Society for Research in Child Development, 55*(3–4, Whole No. 222).

Brainerd, C. J., & Reyna, V. F. (1989). Output- interference theory of dual-task deficits in memory development. *Journal of Experimental Child Psychology, 47,* 1–18.

Brainerd, C. J.,& Reyna, V. F. (1991). Fuzzy-trace theory and children's acquisition of mathematical and scientific concepts. *Learning and Individual Differences, 3,* 27–59.

Brainerd, C. J., & Reyna, V. F. (1993). Memory independence and memory interference in cognitive development. *Psychological Review, 100,* 42–67.

Bruner, J. S. (1966). On the conservation of liquids. In J. S. Bruner, R. R. Olver, & P. M. Greenfield et al. (Eds.), *Studies in cognitive growth.* (pp. 183–207). New York: Wiley.

Case, R. (1985). *Intellectual development: Birth to adulthood.* New York: Academic Press.

Chelune, G. J., Ferguson, W., Koon, R., & Dickey, T. O. (1986). Frontal lobe disinhibition in attention deficit disorder. *Child Psychiatry and Human Development, 16,* 221–234.

Cragg, B. C. (1975). The density of synapses and neurons in normal, mentally defective and aging human brains. *Brain, 98,* 81–90.

Craik, F. I. M., & Byrd, M. (1982). Aging and cognitive deficits: The role of attentional resources. In F. I. M. Craik & S. Trehub (Eds.), *Aging and cognitive processes* (pp. 191–211). New York: Plenum.

Crouse, J. H. (1971). Retroactive interference in reading prose materials. *Journal of Educational Psychology, 62,* 39–44.

Crowder, R. G. (1976). *Principles of learning and memory.* Hillsdale, NJ: Erlbaum.

Crowder, R. G. (1989). Modularity and dissociations in memory systems. In H. L. Roediger, III & F. I. M. Craik (Eds.), *Varieties of memory and consciousness* (pp. 271–294). Hillsdale, NJ: Erlbaum.

Dempster, F. N. (1981). Memory span: Sources of individual and developmental differences. *Psychological Bulletin, 89,* 63–100.

Dempster, F. N. (1985a). Proactive interference in sentence recall: Topic similarity effects and individual differences. *Memory & Cognition, 13,* 81–89.

Dempster, F. N. (1985b). Short-term memory development in childhood and adolescence. In C. J. Brainerd & M. Pressley (Eds.), *Basic processes in memory development: Progress in cognitive development research* (pp. 209–248). New York: Springer-Verlag.

Dempster, F. N. (1988). Retroactive interference in the retention of prose: A reconsideration and new evidence. *Applied Cognitive Psychology, 2,* 97–113.

Dempster, F. N. (1989). Reflections on the nature and sources of individual differences in learning. *Learning and Individual Differences, 1,* 1–6.

Dempster, F. N. (1990, November). *Resistance to interference: A neglected dimension of cognition.* Presented at the annual meeting of the Psychonomic Society, New Orleans, LA.

Dempster, F. N. (1991). Inhibitory processes: A neglected dimension of intelligence. *Intelligence, 15,* 157–173.

Dempster, F. N. (1992). The rise and fall of the inhibitory mechanism: Toward a unified theory of cognitive development and aging. *Developmental Review, 12,* 45–75.

Dempster, F. N. (1993). Resistance to interference: Developmental changes in a basic processing mechanism. In M. L. Howe & R. Pasnak (Eds.), *Emerging themes in cognitive development: Vol. 1. Foundations* (pp. 3–27). New York: Springer- Verlag.

Dempster, F. N., & Cooney, J. B. (1982). Individual differences in digit span, susceptibility to interference, and aptitude/achievement test scores. *Intelligence, 6,* 399–416.

Dempster, F. N., & Zinkgraf, S. A. (1982). Individual differences in digit span and chunking. *Intelligence, 6,* 201–213.

Diamond, A. (1988). Abilities and neural mechanisms underlying A $\bar{\text{B}}$ performance. *Child Development, 59,* 523–527.

Diamond, A. (1991). Neuropsychological insights into the meaning of object concept development. In S. Carey & R. Gelman (Eds.), *The epigenesis of mind: Essays on biology and cognition* (pp. 67–110). Hillsdale, NJ: Erlbaum.

Entwisle, D. R., & Huggins, W. H. (1964). Interference in meaningful learning. *Journal of Educational Psychology, 55,* 75–78.

Flavell, J. H. (1971). First discussant's comments: What is memory development the development of? *Human Development, 14,* 272–278.

Flavell, J. H. (1978). Comments. In R. S. Siegler (Ed.), *Children's thinking: What develops?* (pp. 97–105). Hillsdale, NJ: Erlbaum.

Fuster, J. M. (1989). *The prefrontal cortex* (2nd ed.). New York: Raven Press.

Gelman, R. (1969). Conservation acquisition: A problem of learning to attend to relevant attributes. *Journal of Experimental Child Psychology, 7,* 167–187.

Goldman-Rakic, P. S. (1987). Development of cortical circuitry and cognitive function. *Child Development, 58,* 601–622.

Gunter, B., Clifford, B. R., & Berry C. (1980). Release from proactive interference with television news items: Evidence for encoding dimensions within televised news. *Journal of Experimental Psychology: Human Learning and Memory, 6,* 216–223.

Halford, G. S. (1982). *The development of thought.* Hillsdale, NJ: Erlbaum.

Hall, J. F. (1955). Retroactive inhibition in meaningful material. *Journal of Educational Psychology, 46,* 47–52.

Harnishfeger, K. K., & Bjorklund, D. F. (1993). The ontogeny of inhibition mechanisms: A renewed approach to cognitive development. In M. L. Howe & R. Pasnak (Eds.), *Emerging themes in cognitive development: Vol. 1. Foundations* (pp. 28–49). New York: Springer-Verlag.

Harris, P. L. (1973). Perseverative search at a visibly empty place by young infants. *Journal of Experimental Child Psychology, 18,* 535–542.

Harris, P. L. (1975). Development of search and object permanence during infancy. *Psychological Bulletin, 82,* 332–344.

Hasher, L., Stoltzfus, E. R., Zacks, R. T., & Rypma, B. (1991). Age and inhibition. *Journal of Experimental Psychology: Learning, Memory, and Cognition, 17,* 163–169.

Hasher, L., & Zacks, R. T. (1988). Working memory, comprehension, and aging: A review and a new view. In G. H. Bower (Ed.), *The psychology of learning and motivation: Advances in research and theory* (Vol. 22, pp. 193–224). San Diego: Academic Press.

Hayes-Roth, B. (1977). Evolution of cognitive structures and processes. *Psychological Review, 84,* 260–278.

Howe, M. J. A. (1980). *The psychology of human learning.* New York: Harper & Row.

Howe, M. J. A., & Colley, L. (1976). Retroactive interference in meaningful learning. *British Journal of Educational Psychology, 46,* 26–30.

Howe, M. L., & Pasnak, R. (Eds.). (1993). *Emerging themes in cognitive development: Vol. 1. Foundations.* New York: Springer-Verlag.

Huttenlocher, P. R. (1979). Synaptic density in human frontal cortex—Developmental changes and effects of aging. *Brain Research, 163,* 195–205.

Jensen, A. (1989). The relationship between learning and intelligence. *Learning and Individual Differences, 1,* 37–62.

Jerome, E. A. (1959). Age and learning—experimental studies. In J. E. Birren (Ed.), *Handbook of aging and the individual: Psychological and biological aspects* (pp. 655–699). Chicago: University of Chicago Press.

Kail, R. V., Jr., & Hagen, J. W. (Eds.). (1977). *Perspectives on the development of memory and cognition.* Hillsdale, NJ: Erlbaum.

King, D. J., & Cofer, C. N. (1960). Retroactive interference in meaningful material as a function of the degree of contextual constraint in the original and interpolated learning. *Journal of General Psychology, 63,* 145–158.

King, D. J., & Tanenbaum, S. (1963). Comparison of two procedures in the study of retroactive interference in connected meaningful material. *Journal of Experimental Psychology, 65,* 420–421.

Klatzky, R. L. (1980). *Human memory: Structures and processes* (2nd ed.). San Francisco: Freeman.

La Mantia, A., & Rakic, P. (1984). The number, size, myelination and regional variations in the corpus callosum and anterior commissure of the developing rhesus monkey. *Society of Neuroscience Abstracts, 10,* 1373.

Lane, D. M., & Pearson, D. A. (1982). The development of selective attention. *Merrill-Palmer Quarterly, 28,* 317–337.

Lazarus, P. J., Ludwig, R. P., & Aberson, B. (1984). Stroop color-word test: A screening measure of selective attention to differentiate LD from non LD children. *Psychology in the Schools, 21,* 53–60.

Loftus, E. F., & Palmer, J. C. (1974). Reconstruction of automobile destruction: An example of the interaction between language and memory. *Journal of Verbal Learning and Verbal Behavior, 13,* 585–589.

Luria, A. R. (1966). *Higher cortical function in man.* New York: Basic Books.

Mayer, R. E. (1981). *The promise of cognitive psychology.* San Francisco: Freeman.

McCloskey, M., & Cohen, N. J. (1989). Catastrophic interference in connectionist networks: The sequential learning problem. In G. H. Bower (Ed.), *The psychology of learning and motivation* (Vol. 24, pp. 109–164). San Diego: Academic Press.

McDowd, J. M., & Oseas-Kreger, D. M. (1991). Aging, inhibitory processes, and negative priming. *Journal of Gerontology, 46,* 340–345.

McGeoch, J. A. (1932). Forgetting and the law of disuse. *Psychological Review, 39,* 352–370.

McGeoch, J. A., & McKinney, F. (1934). The susceptibility of prose to retroactive inhibition. *American Journal of Psychology, 46,* 429–436.

Mehler, J., & Miller, G. A. (1964). Retroactive interference in the recall of simple sentences. *British Journal of Psychology, 55,* 295–301.

Miller, D. R., Belkin, G. S., & Gray, J. L. (1982). *Educational psychology: An introduction* (2nd ed.). Dubuque, IA: Wm. C. Brown.

Mitchell, D. B., & Hunt, R. R. (1989). How much "effort" should be devoted to memory? *Memory & Cognition, 17,* 337–348.

Mouly, G. J. (1982). *Psychology for teaching.* Boston: Allyn & Bacon.

Muller, G. E., & Pilzecker, A. (1900). Experimentelle beiträge zur Lehre vom gedächtmis [Experimental contributions to the study of memory]. *Zeitschrift für Psychologie, Erganzunosband, 1,* 1–288.

Muller, G. E., & Schumann, F. (1894). Experimentelle beiträge zur untersuchung des gedächtmisses. *Zeitschrift für Psychologie, 6,* 81–90.

Munsterberg, H. (1908). *On the witness stand.* New York: Doubleday, Page.

Murray, D. J. (1976). Research on human memory in the nineteenth century. *Canadian Journal of Psychology, 30,* 201–220.

Navon, D. (1984). Resources—A theoretical soup stone? *Psychological Review, 91,* 216–234.

Neisser, U. (1967). *Cognitive psychology.* New York: Appleton-Century- Crofts.

Neisser, U. (Ed.). (1982). *Memory observed: Remembering in natural contexts.* San Francisco: Freeman.

Newell, A., & Simon, H. A. (1972). *Human problem solving.* Englewood Cliffs, NJ: Prentice-Hall.

Ornstein, P. A. (Ed.). (1978). *Memory development in children.* Hillsdale, NJ: Erlbaum.

Parkin, A. J., & Leng, N. R. C. (1987). Aetiological variation in the amnesic syndrome. In M. M. Gruneberg, P. E. Morris, & R. N. Sykes (Eds.), *Practical aspects of memory: Current research and issues* (Vol. 2, pp. 16–21). Chichester, UK: Wiley.

Peterson, L. R., & Peterson, M. J. (1959). Short-term retention of individual verbal items. *Journal of Experimental Psychology, 58,* 193–198.

Piaget, J. (1954). *The construction of reality in the child.* New York: Basic Books.

Postman, L. (1961). The present status of interference theory. In C. N. Cofer (Ed.), *Verbal learning and verbal behavior* (pp. 152–179). New York: McGraw-Hill.

Postman, L. (1976). Interference theory revisited. In J. Brown (Ed.), *Recall and recognition* (pp. 157–181). London: Wiley.

Salthouse, T. A. (1982). *Adult cognition: An experimental psychology of aging.* New York: Springer-Verlag.

Salthouse, T. A. (1988). Resource-reduction interpretations of cognitive aging. *Developmental Review, 8,* 238–272.

Schacter, D. L. (1982). *Stranger behind the engram: Theories of memory and the psychology of science.* Hillsdale, NJ: Erlbaum.

Schacter, D. L., Moscovitch, M., Tulving, E., McLachlan, D. R., & Freedman, M. (1986). Mnemonic precedence in amnesiac patients: An analogue of the AB error in infants? *Child Development, 57,* 816–823.

Sejnowski, T. J., & Rosenberg, C. R. (1988). Learning and representation in connectionist models. In M. S. Gazzaniga (Ed.), *Perspectives in memory research* (pp. 135–178). Cambridge, MA: MIT Press.

Slamecka, N. J. (1959). Studies of retention of connected discourse. *American Journal of Psychology, 72,* 409–416.

Slamecka, N. J. (1960). Retroactive inhibition of connected discourse as a function of similarity of topic. *Journal of Experimental Psychology, 60,* 245–249.

Slamecka, N. J. (1961). Proactive inhibition of connected discourse, *Journal of Experimental Psychology, 62,* 295–301.

Sophian, C., Larkin, J. H., & Kadane, J. B. (1985). A developmental model of search: Stochastic estimation of children's rule use. In H. M. Wellman (Ed.), *Children's searching* (pp. 185–214). Hillsdale, NJ: Erlbaum.

Sophian, C., & Wellman, H. M. (1983). Selective information use and perseveration in the search behavior of infants and young children. *Journal of Experimental Child Psychology, 35,* 369–390.

Terry, R. D., DeTeresa, R., & Hansen, L. A. (1987). Neocortical cell counts in normal adult aging. *Annals of Neurology, 21,* 530–539.

Tipper, S. P. (1985). The negative priming effect: Inhibitory priming by ignored objects. *Quarterly Journal of Experimental Psychology, 37A,* 571–590.

Tipper, S. P. (1991). Less attentional selectivity as a result of declining inhibition in older adults. *Bulletin of the Pyschonomic Society, 29,* 45–47.

Underwood B. J. (1957). Interference and forgetting. *Psychological Review, 64,* 49–60.

Vernon, P. A. (Ed.). (1987). *Speed of information-processing and intelligence.* Norwood, NJ: Ablex.

Wallach, L., Wall, A. J., & Anderson, L. (1967). Number conservation: The roles of reversibility, addition-subtraction, and misleading perceptual cues. *Child Development, 38,* 425–442.

Weinberger, D. R. (1987). Implications of normal brain development for the pathogenesis of schizophrenia. *Archives of General Psychiatry, 44,* 660–669.

Welford, A. T. (1958). *Aging and human skill.* London: Oxford University Press.

Wickens, D. D., Born, D. G., & Allen, C. K. (1963). Proactive inhibition and item similarity in short-term memory. *Journal of Verbal Learning and Verbal Behavior, 2,* 440–445.

Woolfolk, A. E., & McCune-Nicolich, L. (1984). *Educational psychology for teachers* (2nd ed.). Englewood Cliffs, NJ: Prentice-Hall.

Yakovlev, P. I., & Lecours, A. R. (1967). The myelogenetic cycles of regional maturation of the brain. In A. Minkowski (Ed.), *Regional development of the brain in early life* (pp. 3–70). Oxford: Blackwell.

Zimiles, H. (1963). A note on Piaget's concept of conservation. *Child Development, 34,* 691–695.

II

Developmental Perspectives

2

Interference Effects in Memory and Reasoning
A Fuzzy-Trace Theory Analysis

Valerie F. Reyna

INTRODUCTION

Recently, theories of cognitive development have turned a historical corner. Greater emphasis is now being placed on basic memory processes, such as interference, that were neglected in the wake of the cognitive revolution (Brainerd, Chapter 4, this volume; Dempster, 1992; Harnishfeger, Chapter 6, this volume; Reyna & Brainerd, 1991a). Basic processes were neglected because theorists believed that they were ill suited to explaining the complexities of higher cognition (Dempster, Chapter 1, this volume). In this paper, I argue the opposite: that interference allows us to explain some of the complexities of classic phenomena of cognitive development. In particular, a collection of cognitive phenomena will be brought together, each of which has been explained by different theories, that have interference as a common denominator. These include inferential remembering, source confusions, suggestibility and autosuggestibility, and reasoning errors in a variety of paradigms (e.g., class inclusion).

29

The chapter proceeds as follows. In the following section, I introduce the general issue of the relationship between memory and reasoning, as it has been traditionally construed. Then, I discuss new findings that challenge that interpretation, but which can be explained by distinguishing between gist and verbatim memories. In the next section, I discuss how these multiple verbatim and gist memories can lead to interference, and introduce a taxonomy of interference effects that organizes the remainder of the chapter. The taxonomy is used to explore commonalities among apparently disparate phenomena, such as gist-based interference in memory and reasoning, as well as interactions with age and delay. Finally, the implications of interference for constructive memory and for conceptions of reasoning competence are discussed.

RELATIONSHIPS BETWEEN MEMORY AND REASONING

Traditional Views of the Memory–Reasoning Interface

The phenomena discussed in this chapter involve the relationship between memory and reasoning. Traditionally, memory and reasoning were thought to reinforce one another. After all, it seems only logical that accurate reasoning would require, at a minimum, an accurate representation of problem information; accurate memory for problem facts must be sustained long enough to apply reasoning operations to those facts. For example, if reasoners are given the two premises *Harry is taller than Fred* and *Fred is taller than Bill*, it seems irrefutable that they must remember who is taller than whom in order to infer that Harry is taller than Bill. Thus, it has long been assumed that the accuracy of memory constrains the accuracy of reasoning. This memory "necessity" assumption, that memorial accuracy acts as a lower bound on reasoning accuracy, is a feature of both Piagetian and information-processing theories of reasoning (e.g., see Bjorklund, 1989; Reyna & Brainerd, 1990).

Although Piagetian theorists assumed that memory for problem facts was necessary for accurate reasoning, little emphasis was placed on developmental changes in memory per se (as distinct from reasoning's effects on memory). Memory development, however, has been a central concern in information-processing theories. Developmental improvements in reasoning have been attributed to advances in memory capacity, organization, retrieval, and so on (Bjorklund, 1989; Siegler, 1991). For example, Trabasso (1977), summarizing the extensive literature on transitive reasoning in children, argued that, because reasoning improved when memory for the premises was trained, inadequate memory for the premises largely explained why young children performed poorly on transitive reasoning tasks.

Constructivists (and many schema theorists) have made the further assumption that accurate reasoning facilitates accurate memory (Paris &

Lindauer, 1976, 1977; Perner & Mansbridge, 1983; Prawatt & Cancelli, 1976). Perner and Mansbridge, for instance, found that memory for transitively related sentences (e.g., *Harry is taller than Fred; Fred is taller than Bill*) improved with age as transitive reasoning presumably improved. This improvement was not observed for unrelated sentences. It was inferred that adults do not treat related sentences as an arbitrary list, but instead are able to use their understanding that the sentences form a linear ordering to organize their memory. Although there has been some dispute about the exact locus of the effect of reasoning on memory (see Alba & Hasher, 1983, and Liben, 1977, for excellent reviews), the constructivist claim that the way we understand the world influences our memory has enjoyed wide influence (e.g., Bransford, Barclay, & Franks, 1972; Piaget & Inhelder, 1973; Prawatt & Cancelli, 1976; Schwartz & Reisberg, 1991).

In sum, two claims that have traditionally been made about the relationship between memory and reasoning are that memory enables reasoning and that reasoning shapes memory. Either view, however, leads to the prediction that measures of memory and reasoning will be dependent: some portion of the variation in memory and reasoning measures must be shared. (Of course, if there is no variation in memory at all, dependency cannot be measured [Brainerd & Reyna, 1992].) Memory failure should result in lower probabilities of correct reasoning, and reducing memory failures should enhance reasoning, given that children are capable of sometimes reasoning correctly. In addition, changes in reasoning should produce changes in memory (e.g., Prawatt & Cancelli, 1976). Therefore, whether memory enables reasoning or reasoning shapes memory, the long-standing assumption has been that the two operate in tandem. The idea that memory and reasoning might be oppositional, that one might interfere with the other, is antithetical to this assumption. New findings, however, indicate that memory and reasoning can interfere with one another, and this leads to a reformulation of the theoretical relationship between them.

New Findings

Before discussing possible relationships between memory and reasoning, it is important to clarify these two terms. It is not surprising that those theorists who assume dependency find it difficult to draw a definite line between memory and reasoning. Some writers contrast memory in the "narrow sense" with memory in the "broad sense" (e.g., Piaget & Inhelder, 1973; Siegler, 1991). Memory in the broad sense is influenced by reasoning. However, dependency entails that such boundaries are indistinct. In other words, if memory and reasoning interact, there can be no memory in the narrow sense. Other theorists have taken an intuitive approach, defining memory as whatever limits reasoning. Rabinowitz, Howe, and Lawrence (1989), for instance, formulated a model of class-inclusion reasoning that turned on the concept of limited working-memory capacity. Memory, however, was never measured. Reasoning errors were simply assumed to reflect memory limitations.

Recently, however, experiments have been conducted to examine the relationship between memory and reasoning directly (for a review, see Reyna, 1992). The results of these studies have led to sharper distinctions between memory and reasoning. First, these studies have indicated that memory and reasoning function independently. In particular, memory for verbatim aspects of presented information is typically independent of reasoning (when reasoning is based on memory for gist). Verbatim memory and gist appear to be represented separately (i.e., they do *not* appear to be integrated in long-term memory), and children avoid relying on verbatim memory in reasoning tasks, especially as they get beyond the preschool years. So, rather than explaining reasoning in terms of memory, and rather than assuming that memory is shaped by reasoning, these results suggest that memory and reasoning are dissociated (e.g., Reyna & Kiernan, 1994).

For instance, in a series of studies of children's reasoning in classic developmental paradigms (e.g., conservation, class inclusion, probability judgment, transitive inference), reasoning accuracy was found to be independent of memory for crucial problem information (Reyna, 1992; Reyna & Brainerd, 1990); similar findings have been obtained with adults (Fisher & Chandler, 1991; Klapp, Marshburn, & Lester, 1983; Lim, 1993). Such findings have become the basis of a new approach to cognitive development, fuzzy-trace theory, which incorporates the assumption of multiple representational systems that develop at different rates, and can be called on in different cognitive contexts (Reyna & Brainerd, 1991a, 1992).

This same research indicates that these multiple representations are not simply copies or different versions of events that are, nevertheless, similar in kind. Instead, the nature of information preserved in multiple representations differs. One kind of representation, verbatim memory, incorporates episodically coded surface details of stimuli (though these representations are symbolic, rather than literal copies of reality). Gist representations, on the other hand, capture the overall sense of information. In Perner and Mansbridge's (1983) study of memory for transitively related sentences, for example, the gist of the inputs is the sense of an overall linear ordering, without precise specification of *exactly* where Harry or Fred were located (i.e., the global pattern). "Gist" and "verbatim" memory, therefore, are interpreted as they usually are in psycholinguistics (e.g., Clark & Clark, 1977; Glucksberg & Danks, 1975), except that they have been extended to refer to representations of numerical, as well as verbal, information (Reyna, 1991; Reyna & Brainerd, 1991a, 1993).

Merely assuming that there are multiple memories for presented information (without positing gist vs. verbatim memories) is insufficient to account for the effects of specific manipulations, such as the effect of varying instructions. Reyna and Kiernan (1994) have shown, for instance, that memory independence and memory dependency can both be created in a sentence recognition task by varying whether subjects are instructed to base their responses on either verbatim or gist representations. When subjects used a common gist representation to recognize presented and unpresented true sentences (those consistent with the meaning of presented sentences), dependency resulted. For the *same* sentences, however, instructions to base recognition of presented sentences on *verbatim* memory produced independence between presented and unpresented (gist recognized) true sentences (see Table 1 for illustrative sentences).

Thus, when judgments based on verbatim and gist representations, respectively, were related to one another, independence was found, but when gist was related to gist, dependency was found. The circle is complete if earlier findings are added showing that two judgments that both relied on verbatim memory were positively dependent (Reyna, 1992). Thus, dependency be-

TABLE 1.   Types of Gist and Verbatim Interference Errors[a]

Presented Sentences

The cat is on the sofa.
The birds are in the cage.
The cage is under the table.
The birds have yellow feathers.

Misinformation

The birds have green feathers.

Verbatim Recognition Question

Interference Errors

Verbatim: Say "no" to *The birds have yellow feathers* because retrieve *The birds have green feathers.*

Gist: Say "yes" to *The birds are under the table* because retrieve inferential gist.

Gist Recognition Question

Verbatim: Say "no" to *The birds are under the table* because retrieve *The birds are in the cage.*

Gist: Say "yes" to *There are more birds than animals* because retrieve the gist that there are more birds than cats.

---

[a]For verbatim recognition questions, subjects should say "yes" only if the exact sentence was presented. For gist recognition questions, subjects should say "yes" only to true sentences. "Misinformation" refers to paradigms in which subjects are misled about information that was presented in order to determine whether such misinformation impairs original memory (e.g., Loftus, 1979). The assignment of "yes" responses to gist errors (and "no" to verbatim) represents phenomena actually studied; this does not preclude, however, the possibility that there could be gist errors that involve saying "no" and verbatim errors that involve saying "yes."

tween judgments turns on consultation of common representations, either verbatim in both cases or gist in both cases (but see Reyna, 1992, and Reyna & Brainerd, 1990, for boundary conditions on dependency). As suggested earlier, specific evidence points to gist being preferred for answering reasoning questions, whereas verbatim memory is more often required to answer memory questions (e.g., Cooney & Swanson, 1990; Marx, 1985, 1986; Reyna, 1992; Reyna & Brainerd, 1991b; Swanson, Cooney, & Brock, 1993), which accounts for the typical pattern of independence between memory and reasoning. In short, memory in the strict sense, as a record of experience (rather than an interpretation of experience), has been found to be dissociated from reasoning in a variety of tasks: from judgments of meaning (Reyna & Kiernan, 1994), of probability (Reyna, 1991; Reyna & Brainerd, 1991b, in press), of physical quantities (e.g., Chapman & Lindenberger, 1992; Reyna & Brainerd, 1990), and so on. According to fuzzy-trace theory, then, these dissociations between memory and reasoning are really dissociations between verbatim and gist memory.

How Multiple Verbatim and Gist Memories Can Lead to Interference

Generalizing the discussion a bit further, it is possible to distinguish two classes of questions that a subject might be asked, verbatim or gist, and two classes of representations the subject might use to answer those questions. By a "verbatim" or "gist" question I mean a question that stipulates a more versus less exact response, respectively, such as recalling the precise number of presented objects in a category versus selecting the "biggest" category without specifying its numerosity. (Actually, questions and representations can be more finely characterized along a fuzzy-to-verbatim continuum, although I shall refer to a gist–verbatim dichotomy here for the sake of exposition [but see Reyna & Brainerd, 1992]). In principle, therefore, it is possible for a gist representation to interfere with answers to a verbatim question, and vice versa. That is, a subject might misidentify gist as verbatim (presented) information, or a subject's response might be limited to verbatim information, though the question calls for gist (e.g., an inference).

In fact, a number of familiar phenomena can be classified in just these ways. For example, given the presented sentences shown in Table 1, subjects could either be instructed to say "yes" just to sentences that had been presented (a verbatim judgment) or to say "yes" to all true sentences (that are consistent with the gist of the presented sentences). As indicated in Table 1, in the verbatim task, subjects can err by saying "yes" to true inferences (or by saying "yes" to any sentence that is consistent with semantic gist, but was not actually presented). This kind of error, saying "yes" to true inferences in a memory task, or "inferential remembering," has been well documented among children and adults (e.g., Bjorklund, 1989; Clark & Clark, 1977; Glucksberg & Danks, 1975; Schwartz & Reisberg, 1991; Siegler, 1991). As will be shown, inferential remembering, as well as many other phenomena (e.g., source confusions), can be analyzed as gist responses to verbatim questions.

Conversely, subjects can err in the gist task by rejecting true inferences because they were not presented. That is, subjects might interrogate verbatim memory, fail to find a match, and exit rather than consult gist memory. Evidence for such a verbatim–exit bias in young children has been obtained in a story comprehension task, the details of which are discussed below (e.g., Brainerd & Reyna, 1993). These kinds of errors—giving a gist response to a verbatim question, or a verbatim response to a gist question—essentially involve giving a correct answer to the wrong question. In other words, the gist and verbatim responses might reflect perfectly accurate representations in themselves, but correct gist is still irrelevant to a verbatim question (and vice versa). Of course, subjects can also err by accessing[1] the wrong verbatim representation to answer a verbatim question (saying that $9 \times 9 = 18$ because $9 + 9 = 18$), or the wrong gist to answer a gist question (saying that birds are more numerous than animals because birds are more numerous than cats, as in a class-inclusion task; see Table 1). These, too, are in some sense correct answers to wrong questions, and their analysis as interference errors has implications for developmental assumptions about cognitive competence (Reyna, 1991). In toto, then, there are four categories of errors to be discussed: giving an inappropriate gist or verbatim response to a verbatim question, or giving an inappropriate gist or verbatim response to a gist question.

It should be noted that this classification scheme implies certain theoretical commitments. Such an analysis would not make sense if memory were a single, integrated system. If memory were integrated, misrecognition of gist in the verbatim task, for example, would *entail* poor verbatim memory for what had actually been presented. Misrecognition of gist could occur for a variety of reasons, because verbatim details had become integrated with gist (e.g., Bransford & Franks, 1971; Paris & Carter, 1973), or because verbatim memory was lost or inaccessible (e.g., Clark & Clark, 1977; Jarvella, 1971). Whatever the mechanism, however, if memory were a single system, misrecognition of gist would reflect the contents of verbatim memory.

If gist and verbatim representations are independent, however, subjects (witnesses, students) can commit errors by accessing the wrong representation *despite* having an accurate alternative (e.g., verbatim) representation in storage. Thus, misrecognition of gist need not imply that verbatim memory has

---

[1]Throughout, I use the terms "access" and "retrieve" (as in "accessing the wrong representation") in order to underline the fact that interference effects do not necessarily imply storage failure. However, this should not be taken to imply that storage failure has been ruled out. On the contrary, two models of suggestibility are presented in Figure 2, one that assumes storage failure and one that assumes retrieval failure. In this chapter, therefore, "inaccessibility" simply refers to a failure to retrieve, either because memories are inaccessible (but stored) or because memories are not stored.

been degraded or modified. Indeed, responses based on gist memory have been found to be completely independent of responses based on verbatim memory (see above). This kind of interference is a basic process because it is not the result of conscious strategic or deliberative processes—subjects are not consciously trying to misrecognize gist. Similarly, reliance on verbatim memory does not necessarily imply that children are incapable of accessing gist, such as inferences. Rather than oversimplifying complex cognitive phenomena, interference allows us to differentiate among different kinds of performance failures. Children may perform poorly in a memory task *simply* because their memory is poor, or because alternative gist or verbatim representations interfere. They may reason poorly *simply* because they are unable to reason, or because they access the wrong gist or verbatim representations. It is to these forms of interference that I now turn.

VERBATIM INTERFERENCE

Output Interference

Verbatim interference occurs when the accuracy of verbatim memory performance is degraded by the presence of some factor (relative to its absence). The simplest kind of verbatim interference occurs as a function of outputs of processing (Brainerd, Chapter 4, this volume; Reyna & Brainerd, 1989). That is, verbatim memory is especially susceptible to output interference (more so than gist) that occurs as a result of reasoning. Consider a procedure in which sentences are presented, and subjects are later asked verbatim questions (Was this exact sentence presented?) as well as questions about gist (Is this a true inference, based on the presented sentences?). In addition, assume that the order of verbatim and gist questions varies; sometimes verbatin questions come first, and sometimes gist questions come first.

Even within short periods of time after stimulus presentation, verbatim accuracy declines if subjects respond to reasoning questions prior to answering verbatim questions (Brainerd & Reyna, 1993; Schwartz & Reisberg, 1991). For example, Brainerd and Reyna (1993) reported three experiments with preschoolers and second graders in which children were presented sentences much like those in Table 1 (misinformation was not presented). Verbatim memory (i.e., acceptance of a memory target such as *The birds are in the cage,* Table 1) declined as a function of the number of prior reasoning questions, and this decline was greater in younger than in older children. The latter result—that younger children are more sensitive to interference—has been found for a variety of tasks (Dempster, 1992). Younger children answered prior reasoning questions correctly; in each of the three experiments, the unconditional probability of accepting true inferences was significantly above chance. Thus, if memory were constructive (i.e., if verbatim memory were integrated with gist), accurately accessing the gist of presented information should have improved memory performance. Instead, prior reasoning questions interfered with memory performance.

Output interference is nonspecific, however, and need not be caused by prior reasoning questions (Reyna & Brainerd, 1989). Answering a series of memory questions also produces decrements in performance on subsequent memory questions, but such decrements are not seen for questions about gist after the same number of interpolated outputs (Brainerd & Reyna, 1993). Moreover, output interference occurs for verbatim questions regardless of whether prior reasoning questions were solved correctly or incorrectly. Prior reasoning errors, which might have been expected to demand greater intellectual effort or greater working memory capacity, did not produce more verbatim memory errors. Again, it does not seem to be anything *specific* about prior processing that interferes with verbatim memory.

Output interference also explains critical phenomena that have been used to argue for effects of working-memory capacity on reasoning (Bjorklund & Harnishfeger, 1990; Reyna & Brainerd, 1989). In mental arithmetic tasks, for example, subjects are sometimes asked to add numbers to a starting number, and then to recall that original number. Verbatim recall of the original number declines as the number of interpolated addends increases (e.g., Reyna, 1992). Therefore, if reasoners are forced to process exact information without mnemonic supports (e.g., to mentally add specific numbers; to recall arbitrary assignments of colors to items), processing will be disrupted by irrelevant outputs generated by concurrent tasks (e.g., Bjorklund & Harnishfeger, 1990; Hasher & Zacks, 1988; Hitch, 1978; Reyna, 1992; Reyna & Brainerd, 1989).

Constructive Memory: Misrecognizing Gist

The greater sensitivity of verbatim memory to output interference is perhaps one reason why subjects prefer to rely on gist (cf. the fuzzy-processing preference, Reyna & Brainerd, 1991a, 1991b). All other factors being equal, gist is more likely to be accessible than verbatim memory (e.g., less affected by interference), especially over time (Clark & Clark, 1977; Glucksberg & Danks, 1975; Kintsch, Welsch, and Schmalhofer, and Zimny, 1990). There are numerous demonstrations of gist supplanting verbatim memory, including the classic sentence recognition experiments of Bransford and Franks (1971), which have been replicated with children (e.g., Liben & Posnansky, 1977; Paris & Carter, 1973). In such experiments, subjects are asked to give strictly verbatim judgments of sentences (indicate only whether sentences are old or new). Adults and older children (Liben & Posnansky, 1977), however, tend to report having seen sentences that are consistent with the meaning of presented sentences. Thus, semantic gist can be said to interfere with correct verbatim recognition. Some researchers have gone so far as to claim that such misrecognition is evidence of advanced reasoning, predicting that misrecognitions will increase with developmental level (e.g., Prawatt & Cancelli, 1976).

The standard interpretation of such experiments (see Bjorklund, 1989) is that subjects' memories have become modified so that the original verbatim memories are lost (e.g., Jarvella, 1971) or cannot be retrieved apart from a semantically integrated representation of presented information (e.g., Alba & Hasher, 1983). Memory, therefore, is said to be constructive in the sense that experienced events are integrated with inferences and other elaborations that go beyond direct experience (McKoon & Ratcliff, 1992). This view of memory implies that it is difficult, perhaps impossible, to know what we have actually experienced (e.g., Schwartz & Reisberg, 1991). Although constructivists have emphasized the benefits of going beyond the literal level of experience (e.g., Paris & Lindauer, 1976, 1977), the claim that original experience is nonrecoverable has troubling implications in certain contexts, such as eyewitness testimony, psychotherapy, and classroom instruction (Reyna, 1992). It is especially troubling when one considers that subjects claim memory for many inferences that follow only loosely from presented premises (e.g., pragmatic inferences, Ackerman, 1992).

In contrast, fuzzy-trace theory assumes that verbatim memories are independent of semantic gist and, so, are not modified or integrated with gist. Therefore, despite interference from gist, fuzzy-trace theory does not imply that original experience is nonrecoverable. Reyna and Kiernan's (1994) results illustrate this distinction between interference from alternative gist representations and supposedly constructive memory in which gist is held to be integrated with verbatim memories. Reyna and Kiernan found evidence of significant interference from gist in their "verbatim" task, replicating earlier findings such as Paris and Carter's (1973). That is, true inferences that were never presented were indeed misrecognized as having been presented. Unlike prior studies of constructive memory, however, Reyna and Kiernan analyzed the stochastic dependency between verbatim recognition of presented sentences and misrecognition of gist (e.g., true inferences), and found that they were independent. Thus, subjects were not misrecognizing gist because they forgot exactly what was presented (this would have produced negative stochastic dependency), but because they were retrieving gist representations when cued with a true inference.

The relationship between recognition of presented sentences and true inferences could be manipulated, however, by changing the retrieval conditions, such as asking subjects to base all judgments on gist (which produced dependency) or, in the verbatim condition, by testing after a delay, which increased the rate of misrecognition based on gist and also increased dependencies. Thus, interference from gist was attributable to factors affecting the type of representation that was retrieved, such as instructions (gist vs. verbatim), delay (immediate vs. delayed tests), and the retrieval cue supplied by the recognition sentence itself (e.g., presented sentences were more likely to cue verbatim representations).

Memory for the Sources of Information

Errors of misrecognizing gist in verbatim tasks are reminiscent of the say/mean confusions investigated by Beal (1990a, 1990b). Beal found that younger children were more likely to misattribute inferences to the presented story than to themselves (the actual source of inferences). However, as in Reyna and Kiernan's (1994) study, even the youngest children usually attributed inferences correctly. In addition, as in Reyna and Kiernan's study, misattributions varied directly with the accessibility of gist representations (e.g., clues or invitations to an inference increased source errors). Ackerman and colleagues, in several recent studies (e.g., Ackerman & McGraw, 1991; Ackerman, Paine, & Silver, 1991), have shown that inferences are most likely when gist information is accessible in memory.

Lindsay and Johnson (1991) also showed that an emphasis on gist increased source errors. They presented adults with words printed on 3 × 5 cards; words were presented either on the right or on the left. One group was instructed to make up a sentence with each word, and the other group counted the number of *E*'s in each word. Thus, subjects in the first group were processing words semantically (i.e., processing gist), whereas the second group was processing at a verbatim level. Subsequently, half of the subjects in each orienting condition was given an old/new recognition test (circle the words that had been presented) and the other half was given a source monitoring test (circle the words that had been presented on the right).

For the old/new judgments, gist versus verbatim processing elicited the typical finding that semantic processing produced better word recognition. The fact that an advantage was found for meaningful processing suggests that gist was more helpful than verbatim memory in discriminating old from new words. This makes sense because old words differed in meaning from new words (though they obviously also differed in surface form; memory for meaning, or gist, however, is generally retained better than memory for surface form). The surprising result was that although an emphasis on gist improved word recognition, source judgments were impaired. That is, verbatim processing produced better memory for source than did gist processing (83% correct vs. 65% correct). Thus, an emphasis on gist was not uniformly beneficial (as some constructivists have suggested). On the contrary, a crossover was observed such that gist and verbatim emphases had opposite effects on source and item judgments, which, in turn, is evidence that source memory is associated with verbatim memory for "episodically coded surface details of stimuli," as might be expected.[2]

---

[2]It should be noted that Lindsay and Johnson (1991) argue that levels of processing theory account for the old/new memory results, but that source memory results are accounted for by the fact that the orienting task (counting *E*'s) provided a cue that differentiated words presented on the right from those presented on the left. Although effects of the distinctiveness of cues are not incompatible with the account given here, Lindsay and Johnson's explanation raises a number of questions, including why distinctiveness would fail to improve old/new judgments and why

A number of studies has indicated that children as young as six perform quite well in identifying the source of memories (e.g., Foley, Durso, Wilder, & Friedman, 1991; Foley, Johnson, & Raye, 1983; Lindsay, Johnson, & Kwon, 1991). Foley et al. (1983), for example, found that 6-year-olds were as accurate as adults when discriminating between words they had imagined saying and words that they had heard another person say. They were also able to discriminate which of two other people had said particular words (see also Foley et al., 1991). Children's generally good memory for source is consistent with evidence from other tasks that verbatim memory (e.g., source memory) develops rapidly, and completes its development in childhood (whereas memory for gist develops slowly, and completes its development in adulthood, Reyna, 1992).

There are, however, conditions in which older children should outperform younger children on verbatim tasks. First, younger children are less likely to dissociate gist from verbatim memory (Reyna & Kiernan, 1994). Therefore, memory for source should be worse for younger children when gist is emphasized (see discussion of Ackerman, 1992, below). Younger children seem less able to inhibit accessible, but inappropriate, gist (Dempster, 1992; Reyna & Brainerd, 1991a). Second, younger children do not encode verbatim details as efficiently as older children do (though developmental differences are even bigger for gist encoding). Given identical study or exposure time, older children will have encoded more verbatim details than younger ones (Brainerd & Reyna, 1988; Brainerd, Reyna, Howe, & Kingma, 1990). Therefore, if sources are highly similar in terms of verbatim details, younger children should be more likely than older children to confuse them.

In those instances in which developmental differences have been found, details about sources were, in fact, more similar (compared to conditions in which differences were not found; Foley et al., 1983, 1991; Lindsay et al., 1991). Children were more likely than adults to be confused about which things they had done and which things they had imagined doing, when self was the source in both cases, but not when the sources were self versus other, or two different others (see above). Lindsay et al. attributed these developmental patterns to similarity between sources (i.e., that children are more susceptible to confusion between similar sources), and, in their own experiments, unconfounded "self versus other" with similarity. They showed that children were more confused about similar sources even when the sources were both external. As in the prior studies, however, *verbatim* similarity was varied, such as the physical appearance of speakers or the verbatim similarity of sentences spoken by different people. Hence, developmental differences in source

---

"deep" or semantic processing would fail to facilitate memory for source information. The explanation suggested here for these contradictory results is that the effects of different manipulations (e.g., distinctiveness) depend on whether they involve gist or verbatim memory.

memory would be expected under conditions in which gist was emphasized and in which sources shared verbatim characteristics.

Ackerman (1992) examined the effects of gist versus verbatim emphasis on children's memory for source. Based on the idea that verbatim and gist representations are encoded in parallel (Reyna and Brainerd, 1992) and that episodic details about the source of information are part of verbatim representations (Lindsay & Johnson, 1991), he presented stories that invited inferences and subsequently tested both inference judgments and source memories. He proposed that source errors would be more likely when gist representations were more accessible, and systematically varied degree of accessibility. Children were asked about causal inferences that followed from presented stories immediately prior to being asked about the source of those inferences (i.e., whether they had been directly stated in the stories or were inferred). Accessibility was manipulated by local cues (e.g., mentioning a key object involved in an inference) and global cues (e.g., providing a title that mentioned the key object).

Consistent with Ackerman's (1992) predictions, correct inferences were more likely with increasing numbers of cues. Moreover, conditions associated with the most inferences were also associated with the highest number of source errors, except for the oldest children (fourth graders). Thus, Ackerman concluded, incorrect source attributions appear to "reflect gist attributions" (p. 100). In subsequent experiments, Ackerman investigated developmental trends in source errors. Using an instructional manipulation similar to the one used by Reyna and Kiernan (1994), children focused either on meaning or on the verbatim form of stories. Reyna and Kiernan had argued that although older children are more likely to base inferences on gist, there is also greater *dissociation* between verbatim and gist representations with age. Thus, despite higher rates of inferential reasoning, older children should be more resistant to interference from gist (and have fewer source errors) in all conditions. Because verbatim memory and gist are more likely to be associated for younger children, however, they should make both fewer inferences *and* fewer source errors in the verbatim focus condition.

Results were consistent with these predictions. Presumably, by making verbatim memory for source *more* accessible, younger children were less likely to base source judgments on gist representations (which included inferential information). In another experiment, Ackerman (1992) made verbatim memory *less* accessible by introducing a delay between presentation and test. Reyna and Kiernan's (1994) results had indicated that verbatim judgments were more accurate for older children on immediate tests. However, they also found that verbatim memory became inaccessible for both younger and older children after a delay, despite better initial performance by older children. Thus, if source errors depend on the relative accessibility of gist as opposed to verbatim memory, then developmental differences should shrink after a delay because verbatim memory will be relatively inaccessible for both age groups (see Figure 1). Indeed, Ackerman found that misattributions increased for older children after a delay, making their performance comparable to that of younger children (who did not change).

Both Beal's (1990a, 1990b) and Ackerman's (1992) data (as well as earlier studies by Foley and colleagues, 1983, 1991) show that elementary schoolers are generally capable of making accurate source judgments. However, the accuracy of source judgments—verbatim judgments about whether sentences have been presented (as opposed to inferred)—are affected by the accessibility of gist, but only for younger children. Thus, younger children made better source judgments when gist had not been cued. These results imply that source confusions are at least partly due to gist interference, rather than a complete inability to judge the source of inferences. Although this evidence indicates that source confusions are gist-to-verbatim interference effects, this does not rule out any role for conceptual confusions (as Beal has claimed). Indeed, younger children might be more prone to access gist *because* they fail to fully understand the say/mean distinction. Under favorable conditions, however, young children can access "say" (verbatim) representations that do not incorporate inferences.

Suggestibility and Autosuggestibility

Many of the issues involved in say/mean confusions and source errors are relevant to the analysis of suggestibility effects, in particular the issue of interference between gist and verbatim memories (see also Titcomb & Reyna, Chapter 8, this volume). As in studies of memory for source, subjects in sug-

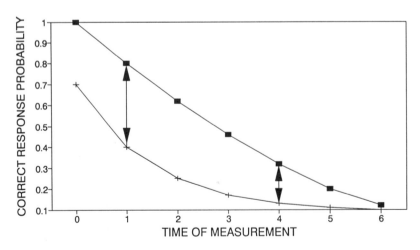

FIGURE 1. Predicted convergence of age differences in retention. Older subjects, ■; younger subjects, +.

gestibility experiments may have to distinguish between two external events (e.g., what they actually experienced vs. what others have told them about the experience) or between external and internal events (what they actually experienced vs. what they have inferred). After Binet (1900), I will use the term "suggestion" to refer to influences of another person (an external influence), and the term "autosuggestion" to refer to influences within the individual (an internal influence). In this scheme, say/mean confusions and inferential remembering, which I have already reviewed, would both be classified as autosuggestibility; in such cases, subjects confuse internally generated inferences with what was presented. For both suggestion and autosuggestion, however, subjects are influenced to misreport actual experience. These are true interference effects because performance improves in the absence of suggestions.

According to Ceci and Bruck (1993), autosuggestibility may reflect the interfering effects of prior knowledge, such as semantic or script-based knowledge about typical events. Thus, children erroneously recall events that are consistent with their prior knowledge but inconsistent with what they actually saw (e.g., Ceci, Caves, & Howe, 1981; Ceci, Leichtman, & White, in press). Thus, autosuggestibility effects occur because subjects are induced to "infer script-relevant details that were omitted from the actual event or to integrate postevent information with the original event" (Ceci & Bruck, 1993, p. 416). Of course, this is the same constructivist argument made in the sentence recognition literature.

Consistent with the constructivist account, Lindberg (1991), for example, found that sixth graders and college students made more false attributions than third graders about an ambiguous event. When subjects were erroneously told that the film they were viewing depicted cheating, older subjects tended to report ambiguous acts (e.g., speaking to another student) as cheating. Younger children, who did not understand that speaking to another student provides an opportunity for cheating, were less likely to make false reports. Thus, whether suggestions derive from prior knowledge about what usually occurs in the target situation or from external suggestions, or both, the subject's understanding of the event (the gist of what occurred) is misreported as the verbatim event. The mere fact of finding such effects has been interpreted, in the constructivist vein, as evidence for inferential remembering or semantic integration (as the Ceci and Bruck quote, above, illustrates). As has been shown, however, this does not necessarily follow. Instead, the same subjects can exhibit what appear to be inferential remembering and semantic integration effects, and yet independently access verbatim memory (Reyna & Kiernan, 1994).

Autosuggestibility effects are modulated by a number of factors, including age, prior knowledge, and delay. They are generally greater in children than in adults (but see Ceci & Bruck, 1993, for exceptions). Thus, the developmental trend is similar to that observed in Beal's (1990a, 1990b) and Ackerman's (1992) studies and other studies of source monitoring in which actions that children have performed are confused with actions that they imagined themselves performing (Foley et al., 1983, 1991). Delays also exacerbate autosuggestibility effects. For example, Ceci et al. (1981) found that, on an immediate test, children were able to answer questions correctly about incongruous characters in stories (i.e., characters with implausible combinations of features, based on everyday knowledge). However, after a three-week delay, when verbatim memory was no longer so accessible, children made systematic errors that were consistent with everyday knowledge.

Delay is also important in obtaining suggestibility effects (see Rovee-Collier & Boller, Chapter 3, this volume). In a typical suggestibility study, subjects first view an event (e.g., slides of a car accident, including a slide showing a stop sign). They then receive information about the event, some of which is misleading (e.g., that a yield sign appeared). Subjects who were misinformed are less likely to correctly recognize the original information (the stop sign) compared to a nonmisinformed control group (e.g., Loftus, 1979; Loftus & Hoffman, 1989). (In fact, there is considerable debate about measuring suggestibility, or misinformation, effects; see Titcomb & Reyna, Chapter 8, this volume.) Belli, Windschitl, McCarthy, and Winfrey (1992), for example, have shown that suggestibility effects in adults are more robust when there is a delay between presentation of the original stimulus and presentation of misinformation. Similarly, developmental studies that introduce a delay between original presentation and misinformation tend to elicit suggestibility effects (Cassel & Bjorklund, 1993; Ceci, Ross, & Toglia, 1987; Ceci, Toglia, & Ross, 1988), whereas those with little delay tend not to find significant effects (e.g., Zaragoza, Dahlgren, & Muench, 1992). As in the source memory literature, developmental *differences* in suggestibility are subtle, but they have been obtained (see Ceci & Bruck, 1993).

Age also interacts with delay. For instance, age differences after moderate delays should converge after long delays. This is because forgetting curves are negatively accelerated, and so (verbatim) memories should become relatively inaccessible for both age groups after a sufficiently long delay (see Figure 1). Convergence should ultimately be observed regardless of whether forgetting rates are the same for different age groups (and regardless of whether initial learning is equated, e.g., Brainerd et al., 1990). Ornstein, Gordon, and Larus (1992), for example, found that 6-year-olds were initially less suggestible than 3-year-olds. As in the Reyna and Kiernan (1994) and the Ackerman (1992) studies, however, the older children's accuracy on misleading questions declined during a long retention interval, and the difference between the two age groups disappeared.

Although it is clear empirically that delay affects suggestibility in important ways, it is not clear what the underlying mechanism is (Titcomb & Reyna, Chapter 8, this volume). For instance, it might be that, on immediate tests, verbatim memories for both original information and misinformation are accessible, whereas, after a delay, accessibility differs because of the gap between the original experience and the misinformation that was presented last. In this interpretation, misinformation enjoys a recency advantage in a competition between verbatim memories for misinformation and for original experience.

Alternatively, suggestibility effects might reflect a competition between gist and verbatim memory. As noted earlier, it is well known that verbatim memory becomes inaccessible more rapidly than memory for gist. Therefore, after a delay, subjects would tend to retrieve gist (Cassel & Bjorklund, 1993; Ceci & Bruck, 1993). There are at least two plausible ways in which this could create suggestibility (or autosuggestibility) effects. First, gist-based intrusions (e.g., script- or schema-relevant intrusions or semantic representations integrating multiple sources of information) could occur because verbatim memories of the *original experience* were not accessed. (This would be autosuggestion because the gist-based intrusions would originate within the individual.) Second, suggestibility could depend on the inaccessibility of verbatim memories for *source* (Lindsay, 1990). Subjects would remember what had been presented (probably, after a delay, by remembering gist), but not where it had been presented (cf. Lindsay & Johnson, 1991). Having forgotten where they learned the misinformation, subjects might assume (or guess) that it was part of the original experience. Thus, at one level of analysis, effects of delay on suggestibility and autosuggestibility can be explained by the relative accessibility of gist and verbatim memories.

Although I use the term "accessibility," I do not intend to prejudge the issue of whether suggestibility effects indicate that original memories are inaccessible versus unavailable. (For further discussion of the availability vs. accessibility issue see Titcomb & Reyna, Chapter 8, this volume.) Original memories might be less accessible *in extremis* due to storage failure. This would produce negative dependencies between memory for the original stimulus and acceptance of misinformation. On the other hand, suggestibility, like autosuggestibility (Brainerd & Reyna, in press; Reyna & Kiernan, 1994), might be independent of memory for the original stimulus (Howe, 1991). Unfortunately, stochastic dependencies between original memories and misrecognitions or misrecalls have not been reported.

In the absence of data, Figure 2 presents the two kinds of suggestibility I have discussed, verbatim–verbatim interference and gist–verbatim interference, under assumptions of either storage failure or retrieval failure for original information. (Such possibilities as blending and blocking are omitted, and, here, retrieval is conceived to be primarily under the control of cues.) As Figure 2 indicates, if suggestibility occurs because of storage failure for original memories, then negative dependency should be observed. This would provide evidence for a trace-strength hypothesis, that suggestibility occurs to the extent that original memories fail (Howe, 1991). Suggestibility might also occur because either gist or verbatim misinformation was retrieved, in lieu of original memories, and this would result in independence. The parallels be-

TYPES OF INTERFERENCE

ERRONEOUS MEMORY	ORIGINAL MEMORY	STORAGE FAILURE	RETRIEVABILITY: CUE CONTROL
VERBATIM	VERBATIM	NEGATIVE DEPENDENCY	INDEPENDENCE
GIST	VERBATIM	NEGATIVE DEPENDENCY	INDEPENDENCE

FIGURE 2. Predicted relationships between original and competing memories in suggestibility and autosuggestibility given different assumptions about the state of original memories.

tween verbatim–verbatim interference and gist–verbatim interference (also shown in Figure 2) indicate that gist and verbatim memories for the same experience are separate representations that can operate much like memories for different experiences (e.g., original experience and misinformation).

Autosuggestibility in the Class-Inclusion Paradigm

Autosuggestibility has also been investigated in the context of problem solving, and there, too, it has been analyzed as gist interference with verbatim memory (Brainerd & Reyna, in press). Again, the effect is called autosuggestibility because, in contrast to suggestibility effects, misleading information is supplied by subjects' own mental representations, in this case as a result of class-inclusion reasoning. In the class-inclusion paradigm, subjects are presented with two or more subsets from the same superordinate set (say, 10 animals, 7 cows and 3 horses). Ostensibly, the class-inclusion question has to do with relative numerosity; children are asked about the relative numerosity of the subsets compared to the superordinate set (Are there more cows or more animals?). The typical finding is that, until the surprisingly advanced age of about 10, children judge the more numerous subset as larger than the superordinate set (Reyna, 1991; Winer, 1980).

The autosuggestibility effect is the further curious finding that children make systematic errors in answering memory questions about the numerosities of the various sets. So, if the child is asked how many cows there were, 7 or 10, the child tends to select 10. In control conditions involving the same numbers, but distinct sets, children's memory for such numbers is highly accurate. Therefore, memory questions in the context of the class-inclusion paradigm elicit a systematic pattern of errors in which numbers belonging to the superordinate set (e.g., animals) and the larger subset (e.g., cows) are confused. Memory performance, in fact, is below chance. Rather than guess, children tend to reject the correct numbers, and select the largest number for the subset (e.g., 10) and the intermediate number (e.g., 7) for the superordinate set.

The pattern of memory errors mirrors the pattern of reasoning errors: When asked which set is bigger, children claim the subset is larger than the superordinate (e.g., that there are more cows than animals). However, when stochastic dependencies between errors in reasoning and in memory were computed (i.e., contingencies within subjects and within problems were aggregated so that reasoning was related to memory with respect to the same problem), there was no relationship between memory errors on a particular problem and reasoning errors on that problem. Put another way, subjects' memories were no more likely to be distorted if they had made the reasoning error. It should be noted that appreciable variation in reasoning and in memory occurred; memory questions about the same sets were stochastically dependent on one another, and reasoning questions involving the superordinate set were dependent on one another. Therefore, the finding of independence between reasoning and memory cannot be due to insufficient variation for either memory or reasoning.

Because memory errors were not related to reasoning errors, the constructivist assumption that reasoning affected memory (e.g., Siegler, 1991) is untenable. Thus, any model that purports to explain autosuggestibility effects in class-inclusion reasoning must take into account the fact that memory and reasoning errors are independent. One model of autosuggestibility that has been proposed assumes that the variance in errors for memory versus reasoning questions comes from different sources. Reasoning errors are due to reliance on an inappropriate gist (the relative magnitude of subsets) that is salient and easy to process (reasoning errors in class inclusion are discussed in detail below). Memory errors, on the other hand, are due to a two-stage process in which the first stage contributes almost all of the variance. In the first stage, the disparity or distinctiveness of the numbers determines whether children access verbatim memory. If numbers are distinctive (say 10 and 3), responses are based on verbatim memory. If numbers are not distinctive (say, 10 and 7), children access gist. The highly salient gist that "cows are the big set" tends to be accessed, leading to systematic errors in the direction of identifying the larger subset with the larger number (and other sets with smaller numbers). Note that there is negligible variation in the accessibility of the salient gist (it remains highly accessible) and therefore *variations* in gist salience can contribute little to shared variance between memory and reasoning. Instead, the distinctiveness of numbers, which determines whether verbatim or gist judgments are made, controls variations in memory performance. Moreover, gist interference occurs because an inappropriate gist serves as the basis for memory responses when numbers are not distinctive.

Thus, although the same salient gist undermines performance for both memory and reasoning questions, the factors that affect whether that gist is used differ for memory and reasoning questions (and this leads to independence between memory and reasoning). For memory questions, the numbers in the memory question cue either verbatim memory or gist. For reasoning, the class-inclusion question cues the gist of relative magnitudes from the outset (e.g., that cows are the big set), and retrieval of the correct reasoning principle and difficulty in processing it determine whether the inappropriate gist is used. When memory errors occur, they reflect the nature of the inappropriate gist, the gist of relative magnitudes of subsets. Hence, they can be referred to as gist interference. But the tendency to make memory errors is not controlled by the degree to which gist is compelling in this paradigm, and seems to be due instead to the distinctiveness of verbatim cues.

Summary

There are a number of paradigms and literatures that can be grouped under the general heading of "gist-to-verbatim interference." These include Bransford and Franks' (1971) classic findings of misrecognition of gist (and their analogues in the developmental literature, e.g., Liben and Posnansky, 1977; Paris & Carter, 1973). There are two interpretations of these findings, the well-accepted constructivist view (including many schema theories) that verbatim inputs are semantically integrated, so that memory reflects the gist of experiences, not just the surface form of inputs; and fuzzy-trace theory, which differs fundamentally in assuming nonintegration of gist and verbatim memory. On this point, critical evidence was provided by Reyna and Kiernan (1994) who replicated the key "constructivist" findings (i.e., misrecognition of gist) but showed that gist and verbatim memory were, nevertheless, independent.

The distinction between gist and verbatim memory has proved useful in accounting for some aspects of source errors, as well. The data of Lindsay and Johnson (1991), for example, suggest that source is a verbatim detail; memory for source is improved when subjects focus on surface features of stimuli. In contrast, memory for content—such as recognizing words—is improved by focusing on gist. This distinction between verbatim memory for source and the gist of presented information (e.g., inference) explains variation in say/mean confusions. For example, source errors in say/mean tasks, in which subjects must distinguish inferences from text (Beal, 1990a, 1990b), increase when inferences are made more accessible, and also increase when verbatim memory is made more inaccessible, such as after a delay (Ackerman, 1992). Thus, autosuggestibility effects (e.g., inferential remembering; say/mean confusions) are analyzed as gist-to-verbatim interference, whereas suggestibility effects are analyzed as either verbatim-to-verbatim interference (competing verbatim memories are supplied by an external source) or gist-to-verbatim interference (verbatim source memories fade allowing memory for the gist of misinformation to intrude). Like autosuggestibility, suggestibility also increases with delay but decreases with age. Effects of such moderating variables as age and delay are explained by developmental differences in susceptibility to interference with verbatim memory, dissociation between gist and verbatim memories, and changes in the relative accessibility of gist and verbatim memories over time.

GIST INTERFERENCE

Verbatim-to-Gist Interference

There are two kinds of documented interference with gist: gist-to-gist interference, in which competition derives from alternative but inappropriate gist representations, as in class-inclusion reasoning, conservation, and probability judgment; and verbatim-to-gist interference, gist interference in which gist is not consulted, and subjects instead rely inappropriately on verbatim representations. The latter has been identified in the sentence comprehension paradigm discussed earlier (Brainerd & Reyna, 1993). In that task, children were instructed to say "yes" to sentences that either had been presented or could be inferred, based on presented sentences (see Table 1). They were to say "no" to sentences that were false (all false sentences, of course, had not been presented).

Second graders showed the pattern discussed earlier in the context of the Reyna and Kiernan (1994) study, namely, independent recognition of presented sentences and true inferences. Presumably, for these children, presented sentences tended to cue verbatim memory, whereas recognition of true inferences, since it could not be based on verbatim memory, was based on semantic gist. Therefore, the two judgments were independent: remembering the verbatim sentences was unrelated to reasoning (i.e., to recognizing the true inferences that followed from the presented sentences).

For preschoolers, however, the two judgments were negatively dependent. The more likely young children were to remember the presented sentences, the *less* likely they were to accept the true inferences. In addition, manipulations that increased the memorability of the presented sentences decreased the probability that the corresponding true inferences (derived from the presented sentences) would be affirmed. For example, in one experiment, information was presented pictorially rather than verbally. Pictures had the usual effect of enhancing memory for presented information. However, pictures apparently made it easier to reject information, including true inferences, that had not been presented. The relationship between memory and reasoning became more strongly negative for preschoolers, and reached significance for second graders as well. For both age groups, then, enhancing memory had the paradoxical effect of harming reasoning.

These (and other) results can be accounted for by a simple three-process model. The first process is a superficial novelty check. Because presented sentences (memory items) and true inferences both contained words that were presented, they would pass such a novelty check. The other two processes involve verbatim similarity judgments and constructive gist processing, respectively. For memory items, test sentences can be accepted without processing their meaning by making verbatim similarity judgments about their surface forms. For true inferences, verbatim similarity matches will not be possible, and such sentences should be subjected to gist processing.

There are two reasons to expect that younger children might have a verbatim-exit bias, that they might be tempted to reject true inferences on grounds of verbatim dissimilarity. First, such children may have poorly developed gist-processing abilities. Not coincidentally, they might also have a general verbatim-processing preference; young children may be more familiar with identifying a verbatim match, as opposed to making complex judgments about inferences. (Liben and Posnansky, 1977, found such a preference for young children. There is evidence for both of these possibilities, namely, that younger children have more difficulty processing gist and that, once subjects are capable of both types of processing, the tendency to engage in gist processing increases over time (the so-called verbatim-to-gist shift, e.g., Reyna, 1991, 1992; Reyna & Brainerd, 1991a).

A verbatim-exit bias among young children would account for the result that judgments of memory items and of true inferences were negatively dependent. If subjects exited after consulting verbatim memory only, high levels of acceptance of memory targets (which would signal good verbatim memory) would be detrimental to true inferences because, obviously, the indicated response would be "reject." Conversely, poor verbatim memory (e.g., guessing) would be bad for memory items, but it would be better for inferences because they could not be definitively ruled out. This account of negative dependency also explains why increases in memorial accuracy (as opposed to guessing) would strengthen the dependency.

Thus, the gist- and verbatim-processing preferences are not invoked as strategic responses to individual problems, but are global approaches (during certain periods in development) to problems in general (Reyna & Brainerd, 1991a, 1992). Although verbatim traces are more susceptible to interference than gist traces, younger children are more likely to rely on them. Their verbatim-processing preference could explain, at least in part, why younger children are more susceptible to interference than older children. Interference would still be a basic process, however, because the verbatim-processing preference is not strategic. Children who exhibit such a preference are well below the age at which conscious strategies are used (e.g., Bjorklund, 1989; Siegler, 1991).

Gist-to-Gist Interference

Although traditional theories of cognitive development stress increasing emphasis on precision with age, the account of sentence processing that I have presented suggests that an emphasis on superficial precision is detrimental to reasoning. The more exact memory became, the more tempting it was to ignore the gist of the sentences' meaning. For adults, fortunately, it does not appear that a gist versus verbatim emphasis is an either–or proposition, as it appears to be in preschoolers. Adults can engage in both types of processing, and they are more likely to be dissociated in adults than in children. However, there are occasions in which, even for adults, an emphasis on exact memory for what was presented leads to reasoning difficulties. One example is the class-inclusion paradigm.

"Class inclusion" is somewhat of a misnomer because, as noted earlier, reasoners are not asked about inclusion relationships among classes. In fact, Piaget assumed that many children who failed class inclusion knew the relevant class relations, and explicitly distinguished such knowledge from class-inclusion reasoning. Reasoners are actually asked about the relative numerosities of sets, wherein lies the difficulty. Children who respond on the basis of relative numerosities tend to get the question wrong. The salience of the relative numerosity of subsets, combined with the ambiguity of the question, leads to systematic misreporting of irrelevant gist (e.g., that cows are the big set). So, when asked about the relationship between cows and animals, for example, subjects tend to report the relationship between cows and horses.

Although some studies have reported that adults make errors on class-inclusion questions, most studies find correct responses, but long latencies to respond (e.g., Rabinowitz et al., 1989). Adults clearly know the correct answer to such questions, but their long latencies suggest that they are experiencing interference. For children, too, superior performance for the same concept can be demonstrated when the "class-inclusion" question is asked outside the class-inclusion paradigm. If children are asked directly whether there are more cows than animals, or more people in Tucson or in Arizona, they are able to answer correctly. Moreover, in an interesting parallel to the sentence comprehension experiment discussed earlier, presenting a visual display of the problem information (e.g., pictures of 7 cows and 3 horses) *decreases* reasoning performance relative to a display-absent condition (Brainerd & Reyna, in press). Making the irrelevant gist more salient (e.g., that cows are the big set) merely smoothes the garden path to an erroneous solution. For these reasons, class-inclusion reasoning has been analyzed elsewhere as an interference paradigm (Reyna, 1991; Reyna & Brainerd, 1991a).

Correct conservation reasoning has been similarly analyzed as the result of, at least in part, the development of resistance to salient, but irrelevant, magnitude relationships (Reyna & Brainerd, 1991a, Table 2). For example, in conservation of number, two sets of objects are counted, A and B, which the subject agrees are identical in number. Next, A is transformed (e.g., spread out) to form A'. The experimenter then asks about the relationship between A' and B. The typical conservation error is to deny that A' and B are identical in number, arguing instead that A' has more because it is longer. Length is a competing, but irrelevant, cue: children are presumably swayed by the fact that A' does "have more," but it has more length as opposed to numerosity. Even adults fall prey to salient length cues, for example, misalphabetizing a last name such as "Simon" before "Simmons" because it is shorter (e.g., Reyna, 1991). However, the ability to inhibit responses to misleading cues develops with age (Dempster, 1992). Reyna and Brainerd (1991a), for example, have argued that the presence of interference separates the two developmental paradigms in which children do well—transitivity and probability judgment—from the two in which they have more difficulty—conservation and class inclusion. Of course, the "easier" tasks have harder versions, but many of the latter take advantage of interference (see, e.g., Reyna & Brainerd, 1990, for a discussion of resistance to visual illusions in the development of transitive inference).

Probability judgment provides interesting examples of both interference and noninterference versions. The easier version referred to above is one in which subjects need only compare the magnitudes of targets, or targets versus nontargets, across samples (shown in Figure 3). In a one-sample task, for instance, a subject might be shown an opaque container into which 7 toy cows and 3 toy horses are tossed. After the container is shaken, subjects are asked to predict which toy will be drawn from the container. In a two-sample task, the subject might have to pick which of two containers to draw from in order to obtain a target toy (e.g., one with 7 targets and 3 nontargets, or 5 targets and 5 nontargets). Because the total frequency does not vary across samples, ratios of targets to total frequency need not be computed. Therefore, the

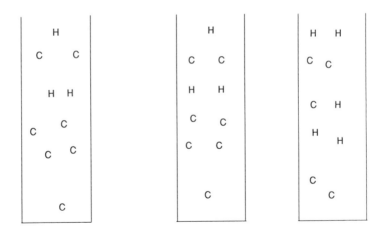

Which animal will be drawn?   Which container would you
                                          pick to draw a cow?

FIGURE 3. Noninterference versions of probability judgment, one- and two-sample tasks.

"big" set (the most numerous set) is also the more probable set.

There is ample evidence that children and adults tend to make simple magnitude comparisons in such situations, rather than compute ratios (Reyna & Brainerd, in press). However, the task can be altered in various ways to make relative magnitudes a misleading cue (shown in Figure 4). As in class inclusion, once relative magnitude becomes a misleading cue, errors increase and persist into middle childhood (e.g., Callahan, 1989; Offenbach, Gruen, & Caskey, 1984; Reyna & Brainerd, in press; Surber & Haines, 1987). For example, in a two-sample task, if totals in each sample are unequal, the number of targets can be larger in the *less* probable sample; 5 targets out of 10 objects altogether is less probable than 3 targets out of 4 objects (see Figure 4). Again, adults and older adolescents are not entirely immune to these kinds of interference effects (Callahan, 1989; Offenbach et al., 1984). When probabilities are equal in the two-sample task, for instance, children and adults are biased in favor of the sample with more targets (Acredolo, O'Connor, Banks, & Horobin, 1989; Reyna & Brainerd, 1993; in press). The presence of such effects in mature reasoners suggests that these are indeed interference effects rather than simply reasoning difficulties.

Summary

Although adults sometimes mistake gist for verbatim memory, they are unlikely to do the opposite. Adults are biased in favor of processing gist, as opposed to verbatim details (Reyna & Brainerd, 1992). Young children, however, are subject to both kinds of errors, gist-to-verbatim interference and ver-

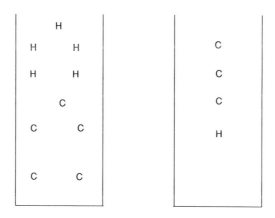

Which container would you pick to draw
a cow?

FIGURE 4. Interference version of probability judgment.

batim-to-gist interference. In both cases, errors increase when alternative representations are made more salient, for example, when gist was more accessible in Ackerman's (1992) verbatim task, and when pictures enhanced verbatim memory in Brainerd and Reyna's (1993) comprehension task. The ability to resist interference from alternative representations, gist or verbatim, increases with age (e.g., Dempster, 1992; Reyna, 1991; Reyna & Brainerd, 1991a).

Although the ability to dissociate alternative representations is part of children's problem in gist tasks, their greater tendency to rely on verbatim memory might also stem from difficulties in processing gist. In each of the cases I have reviewed (verbal inference, class inclusion, conservation, probability judgment), young children's performance is above chance in noninterference versions of the tasks. This suggests that children (at least children as young as those who have been tested) do not lack basic reasoning competence in these domains. For example, when the correct principle is cued in class inclusion (although its application to the task is not explained), performance improves substantially. Children know the correct principle, but they do not necessarily recognize its relevance spontaneously (Reyna, 1991).

In addition, interference versions of the tasks have a garden-path quality to them that is reflected in longer latencies and higher initial errors, even for older subjects who ultimately solve the problems correctly. For example, adolescents will initially make errors on interference versions of probability problems, but will "catch on" and compute ratios after multiple problems (Callahan, 1989; Offenbach et al., 1984; Reyna & Brainerd, in press). Competence cannot be defined as the invariant application of knowledge wherever it is relevant because no reasoner, child or adult, would ever satisfy such a stringent criterion. However, children who have basic competence in a domain may differ, nonetheless, in their ability to process the gist of any given problem (Reyna & Brainerd, 1990, 1991a).

GENERAL DISCUSSION

It is perhaps obvious that there are fewer documented cases of gist interference than verbatim interference. This is exactly what would be predicted if gist is less vulnerable than verbatim memory to interference. In particular, there are few cases of verbatim memory usurping gist judgments, except in the very young (e.g., the preschoolers in Brainerd & Reyna, 1993). It appears that children learn to extract a variety of representations, gist and verbatim, rather early, and they can make both gist and verbatim judgments under favorable conditions. However, these differing representations tend to interfere with each other, especially in the young. Autosuggestibility, in which self-generated gist is reported as though it had been directly experienced, is somewhat easier to induce than suggestibility, in which an external source misinforms witnesses about what they have experienced. As Reyna and Kiernan's (1994) data show, however, gist-based errors do not necessarily entail anything about the state of original verbatim memories. Witnesses who misreport gist as experienced can independently access verbatim memories with a high degree of accuracy.[3]

Interference with gist, on the other hand, seems to signal more fundamental problems. It could be argued that children who are susceptible to gist interference really do not understand the task. Why else would children reject inferences just because they had not been presented, or rely on magnitude in a probability judgment task, rather than ratios? Is it that subjects just do not get it? Indictment of children's reasoning competence, however, must be tempered by the realization that children can often perform these tasks when interference is reduced, or eliminated. Also, adults are subject to qualitatively similar interference effects (Reyna & Brainerd, in press). The conjunction fallacy in adults, in which a hypothetical woman characterized as a social activist is judged to be more likely to be a feminist bank teller than just a bank teller, is analogous to children's class-inclusion errors (see Reyna, 1991). Despite the fact that bank tellers *includes* all feminist bank tellers, adults often persist in feeling that their fallacious judgments were somehow true. Of course, in one sense, they are true. Linda is "more similar" to a feminist bank teller than to a plain bank teller, just as the longer array in number conservation "has more" than the shorter one. In both cases, however, the moreness is on the wrong dimension, so reasoners respond incorrectly.

As I intimated earlier in connection with sentence processing, weak gist processing might be an impetus to avoid reasoning. Children might have stuck with verbatim verification because they were less familiar with inferential processing. The fact that adults can be induced to display cognitive illusions in the domain of probability (Reyna & Brainerd, 1991b, 1993) and even with conservation of physical quantities (Winer, Craig, & Weinbaum, 1992) might reflect our tenuous grasp of probability and of physics. There is a difference, however, between reasoning correctly by chance alone versus consistently reasoning at high levels in one context, but not in another. It may be more useful to think of reasoning competence in a more differentiated way, as both the ability to solve the problem correctly and, for high levels of competence, the ability to inhibit interference.

[3]How this dissociation is consciously experienced is an important question, but one that is beyond this discussion. However, it has not proved necessary to invoke consciousness to explain memorial confusions, and, in some cases, it has been clearly ruled out (e.g., in the verbatim-exit bias). This contrasts with other theoretical approaches that place a heavy emphasis on conscious deliberation to explain memory interference effects (e.g., Gardiner & Java, 1991; Johnson, Hashtroudi, & Lindsay, 1993).

REFERENCES

Ackerman, B. P. (1992). The sources of children's source errors in judging causal inferences. *Journal of Experimental Child Psychology, 54*, 90–119.

Ackerman, B. P., & McGraw, M. (1991). Constraints on the causal inferences of children and adults in comprehending stories. *Journal of Experimental Child Psychology, 51*, 364–394.

Ackerman, B. P., Paine, J., & Silver, D. (1991). Building a story representation: The effects of early concept prominence on later causal inferences by children. *Developmental Psychology, 27*, 370–380.

Acredolo, C., O'Connor, J., Banks, L., & Horobin, K. (1989). Children's ability to make probability estimates: Skills revealed through application of Anderson's functional measurement methodology. *Child Development, 60*, 933–945.

Alba, J., & Hasher, L. (1983). Is memory schematic? *Psychological Bulletin, 93*, 203–231.

Beal, C. R. (1990a). The development of text evaluation and revision skills. *Child Development, 61*, 247–258.

Beal, C. R. (1990b). Development of knowledge about the role of inference in text comprehension. *Child Development, 61*, 1011–1023.

Belli, R. F., Windschitl, P., McCarthy, T., & Winfrey, S. (1992). Detecting memory impairment with a modified test procedures: Manipulating retention interval with centrally presented event items. *Journal of Experimental Psychology: Learning, Memory, and Cognition, 18*, 356–367.

Binet, A. (1900). *La suggestibilité*. Paris: Schleicher Frères.

Bjorklund, D. F. (1989). *Children's thinking: Developmental and individual differences*. Pacific Grove, CA: Brooks/Cole.

Bjorklund, D. F., & Harnishfeger, K. K. (1990). The resources construct in cognitive development: Diverse sources of evidence and a theory of inefficient inhibition. *Developmental Review, 10*, 48–71.

Brainerd, C. J., & Reyna, V. F. (1988). Memory loci of suggestibility development: Comment on Ceci, Ross, and Toglia. *Journal of Experimental Psychology: General, 117*, 197–200.

Brainerd, C. J., & Reyna, V. F. (1992). The memory independence effect: What do the data show? What do the theories claim? *Developmental Review, 12*, 164–186.

Brainerd, C. J., & Reyna V. F. (1993). Memory independence and memory interference in cognitive development. *Psychological Review, 100*, 42–67.

Brainerd, C. J., & Reyna, V. F. (in press). Autosuggestibility in memory development. *Cognitive Psychology*.

Brainerd, C. J., Reyna, V. F., Howe, M. L., & Kingma, J. (1990). The development of forgetting and reminiscence. *Monographs of the Society for Research in Child Development, 53* (3–4, Whole No. 222).

Bransford, J. D., Barclay, J R., & Franks, J. J. (1972). Sentence memory: A constructive versus interpretative approach. *Cognitive Psychology, 3*, 193–209.

Bransford, J. D., & Franks, J. J. (1971). The abstraction of linguistic ideas. *Cognitive Psychology, 2*, 331–380.

Callahan, P. (1989). *Learning and development of probability concepts: Effects of computer assisted instruction and diagnosis*. Unpublished doctoral dissertation, University of Arizona, College of Education, Tucson.

Cassel, W. S., & Bjorklund, D. F. (in press). Developmental patterns of eyewitness memory and suggestibility: An ecologically-based short-term longitudinal study. *Law and Human Behavior*.

Ceci, S. J., & Bruck, M. (1993). Suggestibility of the child witness: A historical review and synthesis. *Psychological Bulletin, 113*, 403–439.

Ceci, S. J., Caves, R., & Howe, M. J. A. (1981). Children's long term memory for information incongruent with their knowledge. *British Journal of Psychology, 72*, 443–450.

Ceci, S. J., Leichtman, M., & White, T. (in press). Interviewing preschoolers: Remembrance of things planted. In D. P. Peters (Ed.), *The child witness: Cognitive, social, and legal issues.* Dordrecht, The Netherlands: Kluwer Academic Publishers.

Ceci, S. J., Ross, D. F., & Toglia, M. P. (1987). Suggestibility in children's memory: Psycholegal implications. *Journal of Experimental Psychology: General, 116,* 38–49.

Ceci, S. J., Toglia, M. P., & Ross, D. F. (1988). On remembering . . . more or less: A reply to Brainerd and Reyna. *Journal of Experimental Psychology: General, 117,* 201–202.

Chapman, M., & Lindenberger, U. (1992). Transitivity judgments, memory for premises, and models of children's reasoning. *Developmental Review, 12,* 124–163.

Clark, H. H., & Clark, E. V. (1977). *Psychology and language.* New York: Harcourt Brace Jovanovich.

Cooney, J. B., & Swanson, H. L. (1990). Individual differences in memory for mathematical story problems: Memory span and problem perception. *Journal of Educational Psychology, 82,* 570–577.

Dempster, F. (1992). The rise and fall of the inhibitory mechanism: Toward a unified theory of cognitive development and aging. *Developmental Review, 12,* 45–75.

Fisher, R. P., & Chandler, C. C. (1991). Independence between recalling interevent relations and specific events. *Journal of Experimental Psychology: Learning, Memory, and Cognition, 17,* 722–733.

Foley, M. A., Durso, F. T., Wilder, A., & Friedman, R. (1991). Developmental comparisons of explicit versus implicit imagery and reality monitoring. *Journal of Experimental Child Psychology, 51,* 1–13.

Foley, M. A., Johnson, M. K., & Raye, C. L. (1983). Age-related confusion between memories for thoughts and memories for speech. *Child Development, 54,* 51–60.

Gardiner, J. M., & Java, R. I. (1991). Forgetting in recognition memory with and without recollective experience. *Memory* & Cognition, 19, 617–623.

Glucksberg, S., & Danks, J. (1975). *Experimental psycholinguistics: An introduction.* Hillsdale, NJ: Erlbaum.

Hasher, L., & Zacks, R. T. (1988). Working memory, comprehension, and aging: A review and a new view. In G. H. Bower (Ed.), *The psychology of learning and motivation* (Vol. 22, pp. 193–224). San Diego: Academic Press.

Hitch, G. J. (1978). The role of short-term working memory in mental arithmetic. *Cognitive Psychology, 10,* 302–323.

Howe, M. L. (1991). Misleading children's story recall: Forgetting and reminiscence of the facts. *Developmental Psychology, 27,* 746–762.

Jarvella, R. J. (1971). Syntactic processing of connected speech. *Journal of Verbal Learning and Verbal Behavior, 10,* 409–416.

Johnson, M. K., Hashtroudi, S., & Lindsay, D. S. (1993). Source monitoring. *Psychological Bulletin, 114,* 3–28.

Kintsch, W., Welsch, D., Schmalhofer, F., & Zimny, S. (1990). Sentence Memory: A theoretical analysis. *Journal of Memory and Language, 29,* 133–159.

Klapp, S. T., Marshburn, E. A., & Lester, P. T. (1983). Short-term memory does not involve the "working memory" of information processing: The demise of a common assumption. *Journal of Experimental Psychology: General, 112,* 240–263.

Liben, L. S. (1977). Memory in the context of cognitive development: The Piagetian Approach. In R. V. Kail & J. W. Hagen (Eds.), *Perspectives on the development of memory and cognition* (pp. 297–331). Hillsdale, NJ: Erlbaum.

Liben, L. S., & Posnansky, C. J. (1977). Inferences on inference: The effects of age, transitive ability, memory load, and lexical factors. *Child Development, 1977, 48,* 1490–1497.

Lim, P. (1993). *Meaning versus verbatim memory in language processing: Deriving inferential, morphological, and metaphorical gist.* Unpublished doctoral dissertation, University of Arizona, Tucson.

Lindberg, M. (1991). A taxonomy of suggestibility and eyewitness memory: Age, memory, and focus of analysis. In J. Doris (Ed.), *The suggestibility of children's recollections* (pp. 47–55). Washington, DC: American Psychological Association.

Lindsay, D. S. (1990). Misleading suggestions can impair eyewitnesses' ability to remember event details. *Journal of Experimental Psychology: Learning, Memory, and Cognition, 16,* 1077–1083.

Lindsay, D. S., & Johnson, M. K. (1991). Recognition memory and source monitoring. *Bulletin of the Psychonomic Society, 29,* 203–205.

Lindsay, D. S., & Johnson, M. K., Kwon, P. (1991). Developmental changes in memory source monitoring. *Journal of Experimental Child Psychology, 52,* 297–318.

Loftus, E. F. (1979). *Eyewitness testimony.* Cambridge, MA: Harvard University Press.

Loftus, E. F., & Hoffman, H. G. (1989). Misinformation in memory: The creation of new memories. *Journal of Experimental Psychology: General, 118,* 100–104.

Marx, M. H. (1985). Retrospective reports on frequency judgments. *Bulletin of the Psychonomic Society, 23,* 309–310.

Marx, M. H. (1986). More retrospective reports on event-frequency judgments: Shift from multiple traces to strength factor with age. *Bulletin of the Psychonomic Society, 24,* 183–185.

McKoon, G., & Ratcliff, R. (1992). Inference during reading. *Psychological Review, 99,* 440–466.

Offenbach, S. I., Gruen, G. E., & Caskey, B. J. (1984). Development of proportional response strategies. *Child Development, 55,* 963–972.

Ornstein, P. A., Gordon, B. N., & Larus, D. (1992). Children's memory a personally experienced event: Implications for testimony. *Applied Cognitive Psychology, 6,* 49–60.

Paris, S. G., & Carter, A. Y. (1973). Semantic and constructive aspects of sentence memory in children. *Developmental Psychology, 9,* 109–113.

Paris, S. G., & Lindauer, B. K. (1976). The role of inference in children's comprehension and memory for sentences. *Cognitive Psychology, 8,* 217–227.

Paris, S. G., & Lindauer, B. K. (1977). Constructive aspects of children's comprehension and memory. In R. V. Kail & J. W. Hagen (Eds.), *Perspective on the development of memory and cognition* (pp. 35–60). Hillsdale, NJ: Erlbaum.

Perner, J., & Mansbridge, D. G. (1983). Developmental differences in encoding length series. *Child Development, 54,* 710–719.

Piaget, J., & Inhelder, B. (1973). *Memory and intelligence.* New York: Basic Books.

Prawatt, R. S., & Cancelli, A. (1976). Constructive memory in conserving and nonconserving first graders. *Developmental Psychology, 12,* 47–50.

Rabinowitz, F. M., Howe, M. L., & Lawrence, J. A. (1989). Class inclusion and working memory. *Journal of Experimental Child Psychology, 48,* 379–409.

Reyna, V. F. (1991). Class inclusion, the conjunction fallacy, and other cognitive illusions. *Developmental Review, 11,* 317–336.

Reyna, V. F. (1992). Reasoning, remembering, and their relationship: Social, cognitive, and developmental issues. In M. L. Howe, C. J. Brainerd, & V. F. Reyna (Eds.), *Development of long-term retention* (pp. 103–127). New York: Springer-Verlag.

Reyna, V. F., & Brainerd, C. J. (1989). Output interference, generic resources, and cognitive development. *Journal of Experimental Child Psychology, 47,* 42–46.

Reyna, V. F., & Brainerd, C. J. (1990). Fuzzy processing in transitivity development. *Annals of Operations Research, 23,* 37–63.

Reyna, V. F., & Brainerd, C. J. (1991a). Fuzzy-trace theory and children's acquisition of mathematical and scientific concepts. *Learning and Individual Differences, 3,* 27–59.

Reyna, V. F., & Brainerd, C. J. (1991b). Fuzzy-trace theory and framing effects in choice: Gist extraction, truncation, and conversion. *Journal of Behavioral Decision Making, 4,* 249–262.

Reyna, V. F., & Brainerd, C. J. (1992). A fuzzy-trace theory of reasoning and remembering:

Paradoxes, patterns, and parallelism. In A. Healy, S. Kosslyn, & R. Shiffrin (Eds.), *From learning processes to cognitive processes: Essays in honor of William K. Estes* (Vol. 2, pp. 235–259). Hillsdale, NJ: Erlbaum.

Reyna, V. F., & Brainerd, C. J. (1993). Fuzzy memory and mathematics in the classroom (pp. 91–119). In R. Logie & G. Davies (Eds.), *Everyday memory*. Amsterdam: North-Holland Publ.

Reyna, V. F., & Brainerd, C. J. (in press). The origins of probability judgment: A review of data and theories. In G. Wright & P. Ayton (Eds.). *Subjective probability*. New York: Wiley.

Reyna, V. F., & Kiernan, B. (1994). The development of gist versus verbatim memory in sentence recognition: Effects of lexical familiarity, semantic content, encoding instructions, and retention interval. *Developmental Psychology, 30*, 178–191.

Schwartz, B., & Reisberg, D. (1991). *Learning and memory*. New York: Norton.

Siegler, R. S. (1991). *Children's thinking*. Englewood Cliffs, NJ: Prentice-Hall.

Surber, C. F., & Haines, B. A. (1987). The growth of proportional reasoning. *Annals of Child Development, 4*, 35–87.

Swanson, H. L., Cooney, J. B., & Brock, S. (1993). The influence of working memory and classification ability on children's word problem solution. *Journal of Experimental Child Psychology, 55*, 374–395.

Trabasso, T. (1977). The role of memory as a system in making transitive inferences. In R. V. Kail, Jr. & J. W. Hagan (Eds.), *Perspective on the development of memory and cognitive* (pp. 333–336). Hillsdale, NJ: Erlbaum.

Winer, G. A. (1980). Class-inclusion reasoning in children: A review of the empirical literature. *Child Development, 51*, 309–328.

Winer, G. A., Craig, R. K., & Weinbaum, E. (1992). Adults' failure on misleading weight-conservation tests: A developmental analysis. *Developmental Psychology, 28*, 109–120.

Zaragoza, M., Dahlgren, D., & Muench, J. (1992). The role of memory impairment in children's suggestibility. In M. L. Howe, C. J. Brainerd, & V. F. Reyna (Eds.), *Development of long-term retention* (pp. 184–216). New York: Springer-Verlag.

3

Interference or Facilitation in Infant Memory?

Carolyn Rovee-Collier and Kimberly Boller

The nature of forgetting has been a major area of inquiry throughout this century (for reviews, see Crowder, 1976; Kimble, 1956; Postman, 1971). In traditional research on interference, experimental subjects first study one type of material and then study a second type, while controls study only one. When test performance on the original material is impaired by having studied the second type, this is called *retroactive interference*. When test performance on the second type is impaired by what was studied initially, this is called *proactive interference*. In general, interference is determined by the similarity of the interfering material and the material to be retained (Spear, 1978; Dempster, Chapter 1, this volume). In adults, the effects of retroactive interference on forgetting are usually stronger after shorter retention intervals, while the effects of proactive interference are stronger after longer ones. The interference of new learning with old is an active process and not merely the result of decay. Jenkins and Dallenbach (1924), for example, found that periods of sleep interpolated between learning and testing resulted in less forgetting than if subjects stayed awake during the retention interval. Ekstrand (1967), controlling for the total number of lists learned during study, confirmed their findings. In general, awake subjects are thought to learn something during the retention interval that interferes with their memory of original learning, although Underwood (1957) has argued that proactive interference is of far greater significance than retroactive interference.

Historically, research using visual attention procedures has found little evidence that infants are susceptible to interference of either type during the first year of life. Using different procedures, however, we have found that memories of infants as young as 3 months are highly susceptible to interference effects. In the present chapter, we review theories of interference and problems associated with measuring interference in infants, as well as prior infant research on interference. Finally, we present our own work on proactive and retroactive interference. We conclude that the effects of new information depend critically on its timing and that new information can facilitate performance on a retention test as well as impair it.

THEORIES OF INTERFERENCE: A BRIEF OVERVIEW

McGeoch (1942) placed the source of interference at retrieval: The interpolated stimulus inhibited recall of the original one, and different responses that were associated with the target stimulus competed at the time of testing (see also Brainerd, Chapter 4, this volume). By his account, new learning did not weaken the original stimulus–response association. Today, this view is referred to as a multiple-trace interpretation of interference in which competition among traces at the time of retrieval is the cause of forgetting.

Melton and Irwin (1940) introduced a two-factor theory to explain their finding that the amount of measured interference did not reflect the total amount of interference. Their subjects had learned an initial list of nonsense syllables and then had studied a second list for 5, 10, 20, or 40 trials. During testing for savings 1 day later, the number of incorrect responses increased with the amount of interpolated learning but only up to 10 interpolated trials; thereafter, retroactive interference in the form of intrusions from the other list decreased. Melton and Irwin attributed intrusions to response competition between the two lists—a retrieval-based mechanism, explaining the decrease in intrusions after more interpolated trials in terms of subjects' improved ability to differentiate list membership. They attributed the fact that total retroactive interference remained high, however, to unlearning the associations on the first list as a result of learning new associations on the second. Their unlearning factor, a storage-based mechanism of interference, has survived as a changed-trace view of interference.

Howe and Brainerd (1989) concluded that the current formulation of forgetting as either storage based or retrieval based is incorrect and proposed a trace-integrity model, which attributes interference in long-term memory to both mechanisms. In their account, long-term retention is thought to result from retrieval failures *and* storage failures, both of which are aspects of a single memory factor, trace integrity. Storage is viewed as a dynamic process, and performance on a long-term retention test reflects the strength of the memory trace. Trace strength refers to the degree of *integration* between the elements of the memory trace, which apparently results from rehearsal. Trace integrity, thus, is determined by the degree of disintegration that has occurred and results in a continuum between trace *availability* and trace *accessibility* (see this distinction by Tulving, 1972). Disintegration occurs as a result of unavailability caused by storage-based forgetting, inaccessibility caused by retrieval-based forgetting, or a combination of these two. Storage-based forgetting is not an absence of the memory trace but a decrease in integration strength. It can also result from a trace change caused by adding information to or deleting information from the trace. In a similar vein, Brainerd, Reyna, Howe, and Kingma (1990) have defined "trace integration" as the extent to which contextual information is integrated with the core semantic gist to produce a coherent representation. In their formulation, retrieval results in further integration. They attribute integration to both storage and retrieval; over time, as trace integration decreases, forgetting and amnesia occur. (The availability versus accessibility issue is also considered by Reyna and Titcomb & Reyna, Chapters 2 and 8, respectively, this volume.)

Another recent approach to interference theories has involved the use of computer models. Modeling interference by implementing gradual unlearning has met with mixed results using distributed memory models (for reviews, see Lewandowsky, 1991; Lewandowsky & Chen-Li, Chapter 10, this volume). Models such as TODAM (Murdock, 1983) produce the unlearning of first-list associations seen in human retroactive interference; however, some connectionist models produce complete forgetting of first-list associations after only a few trials on the second list (McCloskey & Cohen, 1989). Lewandowsky (1991) suggested that parallel distributed processing models could be adapted slightly to account for the gradual unlearning seen in the human data. The significant issue for this review is the *placement* of the source of interference in these models. As summarized by Shiffrin and Murnane (1991), some models place the source of interference at storage, whereas others place interference at retrieval. According to Anderson (1981), models that place interference at retrieval can account for differences in list strength that models emphasizing storage cannot.

These approaches have been applied with some success to account for forgetting by adults, but their generality for animals and prelinguistic infants is less clear. Spear (1978) has cited two factors that complicate extrapolation from interference theories developed with adults to studies with nonverbal animals—concerns that apply equally well to prelinguistic infants. First, there is the problem that nonverbal subjects cannot be instructed regarding what response to give. As a result, their retention depends not only on the mechanisms of interference that have been described by adult interference theory, but also on (1) their tendency to do the last thing they learned, and (2) the contextual similarity between the learning and retention test. Second, the content of experimentally induced memories differs from adults to infants and animals. Whereas tasks with nonverbal organisms typically involve a single discrete response signaled by a single cue, most tasks with adults involve verbal lists. Yet, interference theory has had great difficulty accounting for interference with a single response within a list (Postman & Underwood, 1973). In addition, the materials learned by adults are usually familiar, whereas those learned by animals and young infants are novel. Despite these complications, the accumulating data on interference suggest that nonverbal organisms are subject to many of the same types of interference effects as adults. These effects are reviewed below.

INTERFERENCE IN INFANT SHORT-TERM MEMORY

Visual Attention Measures

The paired-comparison procedure (Fagan, 1970) and the habituation-discrimination procedure (Cohen & Gelber, 1975) have been used to study retention in infancy. Fagan (1970) combined the "test–train–test" procedure of Saayman, Ames, and Moffett (1964) with the multiple-novel-stimuli procedure used by Fantz (1964). In the resulting procedure, he first familiarized infants with a target stimulus for 2 min and then exposed them to that same target paired first with one novel stimulus and then with another (side position counterbalanced). Each problem set, thus, consisted of three stimuli, one familiarization stimulus and two novel test stimuli, and infants were presented with all stimuli in all orders over 3 days, usually in sessions 24 h apart. The mean duration of fixation to novel relative to familiar stimuli was the dependent variable. If more than 50% of an infant's total looking time was on *novel* stimuli, then the infant was presumed to remember the previously exposed target; the higher the mean percent of time spent looking at the novel stimulus of the test pair, the better his/her recognition memory for the familiar target. The group mean percent novel looking time was then tested against a hypothetical value of 50% (no difference, or chance) using a directional *t* test.

In the habituation procedure, infants are presented with a slide of a simple stimulus for a fixed number of trails or until a proportional criterion for decreased looking time is met (for review, see Cohen & Gelber, 1975). Trials typically last 10–15 s each or, when the infant-control procedure is used (Horowitz, Paden, Bhana, & Self, 1979), until the infant diverts his/her gaze from the stimulus for a given period. The duration of visual fixation, which is measured on each trial, declines over successive stimulus presentations. At the end of the habituation series, the infant is presented with either the same (control group) or a novel (experimental group) stimulus. Fixations in the no-shift control group remain stable or continue to decline, while those in the experimental group recover, the degree of recovery presumably reflecting the degree of perceived novelty. The response measure is the percent of looking at the novel stimulus relative to either the control stimulus or, when no control group is run, the habituation stimulus on the immediately preceding preshift trial.

Underlying both the paired-comparison and habituation procedures is the assumption that the extent to which infants selectively fixate a novel stimulus relative to a previously exposed one reflects the extent of retention of the prior stimulus. This assumption is based on Sokolov's (1963) classic model of the habituation of the orienting reflex in which an internal representation or *memory engram* of an external stimulus is presumably constructed and embellished each time the organism encounters that same stimulus in the same context. Once the engram matches the external stimulus, then attention to the familiar stimulus is inhibited, and the infant orients elsewhere, at novel stimuli. By this account, what infants fixate depends on the status of the memory engram for the previously exposed (familiar) stimulus; fixation of a novel stimulus is taken as evidence that they still have a memory engram of the prior one.

This assumption has been questioned by those who view the response-to-novelty as a perceptual processing mechanism, devoid of implications for memory (Fagen & Rovee-Collier, 1982; Jeffrey, 1976; Olson, 1976; Rovee-Collier & Hayne, 1987). For example, we have argued elsewhere that orienting to a novel stimulus need not imply identification of a familiar one (for discussion, see Fagen & Rovee-Collier, 1982, p. 71). In fact, the response-to-novelty is analogous to the nonmatching-to-sample paradigm that has been used to study short-term memory (STM) with pigeons (Grant, 1975), rats (Roberts, 1974), and primates (Jarrard & Moise, 1970). From this perspective, it is not surprising that infants, like animals tested in these procedures, typically fail to recognize the familiar stimulus after delays greater than 5 to 15 s (Cohen & Gelber, 1975; Sherman, 1985; Stinson, 1971, in Werner & Perlmutter, 1979; but see Bomba & Siqueland, 1983), although amount of study time is a key variable (A. J. Caron, Caron, Minichiello, Weiss, & Friedman, 1977; Olson, 1979). Similar delays have defined the limits of short-term memory in studies with adults (Brown, 1958; Norman, 1970; Peterson & Peterson, 1959). Finally, although infants' performance on habituation tasks, like their performance on paired-comparison tasks, correlates in the .40s with IQ on standard tests at 3–4 years, duration of first fixation on the initial habituation trial is a stronger predictor than is habituation rate (A. Slater, personal communication, February, 1993). This result indicates that the infant's ability to *selectively attend* to a discrepant stimulus, and not inhibition or learning factors, is the basis for this correlation. Given that selective attention is fundamental for both encoding and retrieval at all ages, the magnitude of the correlation is understandable.

Retroactive Interference in Delayed Recognition

Fagan was the first to explore systematically whether the similarity between previously studied and interpolated material influenced infants' delayed recognition at 5–6 months. In the initial article, Fagan (1971) presented infants with a series of three problems. After each, he administered an immediate visual recognition test, and after the entire set, he repeated each test in its original order, with the resulting delay between immediate and delayed tests ranging from 4 to 7 min. Despite the large opportunity for interference from the interpolated material, infants' delayed recognition was not disrupted. Subsequently, however, Fagan (1973) observed that infants failed to recognize face masks after a 3-h delay. He hypothesized that encounters during the delay with human faces, which somewhat resembled the masks, might have retroactively interfered with infants' delayed recognition.

To test the similarity hypothesis, he exposed infants for 2 min to facial photos, administered an immediate retention test, and then exposed them for three 10-s periods to novel paired stimuli that were either high (upright photos), medium (rotated photos), or low (line drawings) in similarity to the familiarized photos. A second recognition test with the original and novel photos followed the immediate one by approximately 1 min. A comparison of delayed with immediate recognition performance indicated that retention was disrupted only by the intervening exposure to material of medium similarity. Fagan again exposed the medium-similarity photos either immediately after the immediate recognition test or just before the 3-h delayed recognition test. When the exposure was immediate, delayed recognition was disrupted as before, but when it was delayed, the interpolated material had no effect; delayed recognition (i.e., attention to novelty) was excellent.

In 1977, back-to-back studies of retroactive interference were published from three laboratories that used variations of the paired-comparison (Fagan, 1977) and habituation (Cohen, DeLoache, & Pearle, 1977; McCall, Kennedy, & Dodds, 1977) procedures. Unless otherwise indicated, Fagan exposed infants to a pair of targets for a 2-min familiarization period, to a pair of intervening targets for 20 s, and then to the original target and a completely novel one for two 10-s test periods (left–right positions reversed). In his first study, Fagan varied the similarity of the interpolated material to the familiarized material and the duration of familiarization time. Infants required more study time to recognize a previously studied stimulus as the perceptual similarity of the interpolated to the familiar material increased. Moreover, photos of different faces were more similar to each other than were rotated and upright photos of the same face, and line drawings were most different from the studied photos.

In his second study, Fagan exposed the initial material for either 40 or 120 s and tested for delayed recognition 1 min later with one of the three kinds of distractors interpolated for either 20 or 40 s between familiarization and the delayed recognition test. This time, only the distractor *most similar* to the familiarization stimulus (i.e., an upright photo of another face) disrupted retention. Additional exposure to the familiarization stimulus during the retention interval, however, offset the interference effect. In his final study, Fagan presented the upright photo distractor for either 20 or 40 s, either immediately or 1 min after familiarization; subjects who viewed the distractor immediately had a 60-s delay prior to retention testing. There were no effects of the intervening material. These results suggested that the loss of recognition due to upright photo distractors in the preceding studies was transient. Fagan concluded that the type of distractor was an important source of interference but that the effects of interpolated distractors were short-lived and preventable.

Prior to the Cohen et al. (1977) study, the interfering effects of intervening material on infants' retention of habituation were unclear. Both Pancratz and Cohen (1970) and DeLoache (1976) had obtained evidence of retroactive interference, but others had not (R. F. Caron & Caron, 1969; Gelber, 1972; Martin, 1975). In the DeLoache study, 4-month-olds were habituated first to a set of four differently colored geometric shapes and then to another set that were either high, medium, or low in similarity. The second habituation series continued until either an individual habituation criterion was reached or for 8 trials. On the delayed recognition test that ensued, infants failed to recognize the first set of shapes, indicating that the intervening set had disrupted retention. Cohen and Gelber (1975) had hypothesized that interference might be seen only if interpolated material was presented sufficiently long as to be encoded in long-term memory, forming a competing memory engram. In the DeLoache study, this presumably occurred.

Using 4-month-olds as subjects, Cohen et al. (1977) tested the exposure-duration hypothesis by presenting stimuli of varying similarity to the original habituation stimulus during the retention interval. Whether or not an intervening stimulus entered long-term memory was assessed in terms of whether or not infants habituated to it during the retention interval. Although infants discriminated between the original and the intervening stimuli and habituated to both, no evidence of retroactive interference was found in any condition. Also, infants who habituated to the intervening stimuli were no more likely to exhibit interference than those who did not. They concluded that, ". . . infant visual memory is a relatively robust phenomenon, an outstanding characteristic being its persistence even after a variety of potentially interfering circumstances" (p. 96).

A similar finding was obtained by McCall et al. (1977) with 3-month-olds. Instead of using a proportional habituation criterion or a fixed number of trials, however, they used an absolute criterion that required infants to fixate the stimulus for less than 4 s on 2 consecutive trials. Distracting stimuli were then presented for 5 trials at 5 s each and were of either graded similarity or totally dissimilar to the habituation stimulus. McCall et al. assumed that infants who initially habituated more rapidly would encode the distractor differently than those who habituated more slowly; however, this was not the case. Nor was there an effect of similarity on retention during the delayed recognition test with the original stimulus.

Taken together, the preceding research suggests that infant short-term memory is relatively immune to retroactive interference.

Proactive Interference in Delayed Recognition

Tyrell, Snowman, Beier, and Blanck (1990) have recently explored the role of proactive interference in infant recognition memory using a procedure similar to that of Fagan (1973, 1977). Infants 25 weeks old were presented with three exposures to interfering stimuli *prior* to a familiarization period with a black-and-white photograph of a human face. An interference trial lasted until each infant had accumulated 10 s of looking time. Two familiarization trials then followed, with presentation of the stimulus continuing until each infant had accumulated 20 s of looking time per trial. Therefore, infants experienced a total interference time of 30 s over three trials and a total familiarization time of 40 s over two trials. Preference for novelty was tested by presenting the familiarized stimulus and a novel photograph during two periods of 10 s each.

The authors predicted that the similarity of the interfering stimulus and the familiarization stimulus would differentially affect recognition memory. Similarity was manipulated by presenting either inverted line drawings of faces (dissimilar), correctly oriented photos of faces (highly similar), or inverted photos of faces (moderately similar) during the initial proactive interference phase. Interference was inferred from a *decrease* in infants' preference for the novel stimulus. Based on Fagan's (1973) earlier retroactive interference results, Tyrell et al. (1990) predicted a preference for novelty when either the dissimilar or highly similar stimulus was presented during the interference phase but a chance distribution of looking when the moderately similar (most interfering) stimulus was presented.

Tyrell et al. found evidence of significant proactive interference, however, when *either the highly similar or the moderately similar stimulus* was presented during the interference phase but not when the dissimilar stimulus was presented. This study demonstrates that proactive interference does affect infant short-term recognition memory. Infants may have responded, however, to a dimension of the stimulus (e.g., brightness) other than its content. In addition, the authors raised the possibility that infants may have experienced the dissimilar stimulus as a member of a different category than the target stimulus, thereby causing a release from proactive interference in this group.

The only other study of proactive "interference" effects has recently been reported by Needham (1992). Using Baillargeon's impossible-task paradigm, in which infants gaze longer at an event that is surprising, she exposed some infants for 2 min to a vertical box placed on the dresser in their bedrooms. Twenty-four h later, she brought the infants into the laboratory and allowed them to view either a garden hose moving horizontally and contiguously with the same box or the garden hose moving away from the box by itself. Infants who had been preexposed to the box gazed longer at the box moving with the hose, suggesting that they found the contiguous movement of the two objects surprising. In contrast, infants with preexposure to the box gazed equally at both events, indicating that they did not perceive the hose and the box as discrete objects and, hence, they did not perceive the contiguous movement of the hose and the box as unusual. These data reveal that preexposing an object for as brief a period as 2 min can affect the distribution of infants' attention to events in which that object participates 24 h later in a completely different context. Whether this effect is actually *interference,* however, is arguable.

INTERFERENCE IN INFANT LONG-TERM MEMORY

The role of interference in infant long-term memory (LTM) has not been widely studied. The results, however, stand in sharp contrast to those obtained using visual attention measures of interference in the preceding section. First, let us review the general procedure that has been followed in all of this work.

Mobile Conjugate Reinforcement Procedure

Because prelinguistic infants lack a verbal response to indicate what they remember about an event, they must be taught a motoric one. In our work, we teach infants to perform an operant response, a foot kick, to activate a crib mobile on which we have displayed particular visual information. After a delay, we show infants either the original mobile or one on which we have altered the visual information and ask them to tell us whether or not they recognize it. If they do, then they indicate "yes" by kicking at a rate above baseline; if they do not recognize it, then they withhold kicking, indicating "no." In studies of interference, the question of interest is whether information that infants encounter either prior to or following training produces either proactive or retroactive interference, respectively.

At 3 months, infants typically receive two 15-min training sessions separated by 24 h in their home cribs (Figure 1A & B) and a test session 1 or more days later. The pattern of training for 2 sessions and testing with the same mobile in a third session is represented as AA/A, with the letters before the slash indicating the training mobile in each session, and the letter after the slash indicating the test mobile; thus, AA/B refers to training with one

mobile for two sessions and testing with another. Each training session begins with a 3-min nonreinforcement period (Figure 1A). Note that the ribbon
and the mobile are suspended from different hooks, so that kicks cannot activate the mobile. Kicking during this phase provides an index of infants' un-

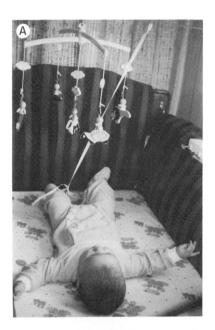 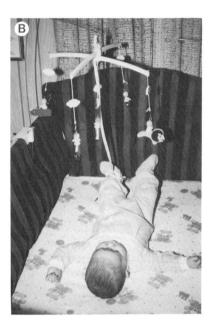

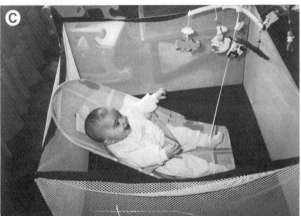

FIGURE 1. (A) A 3-month-old during a nonreinforcement phase in which the ribbon attached
to the infant's ankle is attached to the stand without the mobile; in this arrangement kicks do
not move the mobile; (B) the same infant during a reinforcement phase in which the ribbon is attached to the stand holding the mobile; in this arrangement kicks move the mobile; (C) a
6-month-old in the apparatus.

learned activity level *(baseline)*. Next follows a 9-min reinforcement phase *(acquisition)*, when the ribbon and the mobile are suspended from the same hook, and kicks activate the mobile (Figure 1B). Within minutes, infants learn to control the mobile by kicking, doubling or tripling their baseline rate. We have previously shown that their increase in response rate is solely a result of the contingency and not behavioral arousal (Hill, Borovsky, & Rovee-Collier, 1988; Rovee & Rovee, 1969; Rovee-Collier, Morrongiello, Aron, & Kupersmidt, 1978). At the end of acquisition, we leave the mobile in place but return the ribbon to the empty stand for 3 min. Kicking during this phase at the end of session 2 provides an index of the infant's final level of training and retention after zero delay *(immediate retention test)*. After a delay, we measure retention for 3 min under these same conditions *(delayed recognition test)*. At 6 months, sessions are one-third shorter and take place in a playpen supplied by the experimenter (Figure 1C).

If a group's kick rate is significantly higher during the delayed recognition test than during the baseline phase (baseline ratio > 1.00), then the group exhibited retention; if its test rate has returned to the baseline rate, however, then they showed none. If a group's kick rate during the delayed test did not decline from its rate during the immediate retention test at the end of training (i.e., the retention ratio ≥ 1.00), then the group showed perfect retention. Because long-term retention is tested only during the nonreinforcement phase at the outset of a distant session, the infant's retention performance reflects *only* what he or she remembers from previous sessions and *not* new learning at the time of testing. Measuring retention in this way involves a heavier memory load than a savings measure, which requires only that the infant relearn more rapidly. Moreover, because infants learn much more rapidly when they are older, conclusions regarding retention after long delays would be compromised by a savings measure. Because retention is enhanced by repeated testing, however, all of our work unless otherwise specified involves independent groups of infants tested only once.

Our work capitalizes on the fact that infants' memories are highly specific. If a retrieval cue does not almost exactly match the information that infants originally encoded, then it does not retrieve the memory. Infants as young as 3 months, for example, typically exhibit perfect retention of their training mobile 24 h later, but if the test mobile contains *more than a single novel object*, they exhibit none (Hayne, Greco, Earley, Griesler, & Rovee-Collier, 1986). They also fail to recognize the original training mobile in a test *context* that differs even slightly from the context in which they were trained. This is seen 3 days after training at 3 months of age (Butler & Rovee-Collier, 1989; Rovee-Collier & DuFault, 1991) and only 1 day after training at 6 months of age (Borovsky & Rovee-Collier, 1990; Rovee-Collier, Schechter, Shyi, & Shields, 1992; Shields & Rovee-Collier, 1992). We have exploited the specificity required of effective retrieval cues to study whether and how new information affects the original training memory.

Retroactive Interference in Delayed Recognition

Despite the considerable specificity of infants' memories for both the mobile and the context, their training memory can subsequently be modified or updated by other mobiles or contexts. For example, Fagen, Morrongiello, Rovee-Collier, and Gekoski (1984) found that when training was *variable,* that is, a *different* mobile was present during each training session (group AB/C), infants evidenced excellent performance when tested with yet another novel mobile. In contrast, infants whose training was *constant,* that is, the *same* mobile was present during each training session (group AA/C), performed at baseline when tested with a novel mobile. The difference in these results suggested that variably trained infants had learned to respond to a *class* of mobiles instead of to a *particular* mobile—a suggestion that was subsequently confirmed (Hayne, Rovee-Collier, & Perris, 1987). However, Fagen et al. (1984) also found that retention of variably trained infants was *impaired* when they were tested with the *original* mobile (group AB/A)—a retroactive interference effect. A similar result was obtained when infants were trained in different contexts during each session and were tested in yet another novel one. At both 3 months (Rovee-Collier & DuFault, 1991) and 6 months (Amabile & Rovee-Collier, 1991), variable training *facilitated* recognition of the original mobile in a novel test context but *impaired* its recognition in the *original* context.

A number of possibilities could account for these results. First, stimuli present during the second training session could have overwritten those represented in the memory of the first. Overwriting is the strong case of the storage-based interference hypothesis. Amabile and Rovee-Collier (1991), however, rejected this possibility because overwriting the session-1 context (*context A*) would have left only a representation of the second context (*context B*) and would have resulted in a recognition failure in the novel test context (*context C*), that is, group AB/C would have functionally been converted into group BB/C, yet infants' retention in completely novel context C was, in fact, excellent. A second possibility is the weaker case of the storage-based interpretation that the memories of session 1 and session 2 were blended, creating a new memory with components of both prior experiences (Loftus & Hoffman, 1989). We have recently obtained evidence that rejects this interpretation as well (Rovee-Collier, Borza, Adler, & Boller, 1993). Three-month-old infants who were trained with a different mobile in each session were tested with a composite mobile containing equal numbers of elements from the session-1 and session-2 mobiles. These infants, however, failed to respond at a rate above baseline during the 24-h test. A third possibility, that the most recently presented stimulus has a privileged status in memory, has also been discounted (Boller & Rovee-Collier, 1992a). Further, a recency hypothesis makes no predictions about novel stimuli, hence cannot explain why infants showed excellent retention in a completely novel test context.

We favor a fourth account, an interference hypothesis that retrieval based on the still-remembered details of the session-1 mobile (or context) competes with retrieval based on relevant general features of the test stimulus. Presumably, infants learned in session 2 that the details of the mobile (or context) were nonpredictive or irrelevant; competition arose, however, because of infants' strong propensity to match still-remembered details when they are detected with details stored in LTM. Such an interpretation also predicts the infants' excellent retention in a completely novel test context, where such competition does not exist. If this account is correct, then interference effects should no longer be seen after retention intervals sufficiently long that infants have forgotten the details of their original training stimulus.

Retroactive Interference in Memory Reactivation

After delays so long that infants no longer recognize the mobile, we use a *reactivation paradigm* to recover the forgotten memory. This is a priming paradigm in which the infant is briefly (2–3 min) and passively exposed to a retrieval cue (a "reminder") from the original situation (the mobile, the context, or both) well in advance of the long-term test. During the reactivation treatment with the mobile, the ankle ribbon is disconnected (Figure 2). The reminder presumably primes or reactivates the dormant or latent memory, increasing its accessibility. Later, we use a standard long-term retention test

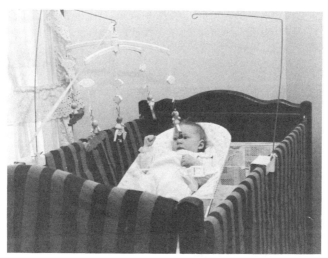

FIGURE 2. A 3-month-old infant during a reactivation treatment. The mobile and the ribbon are attached to the same stand, but the ribbon is drawn and released by the experimenter (not shown).

to confirm whether or not the memory was recovered. At 3 months, a single reminder presented after a delay as long as 1 month restores the forgotten memory to full strength, at which point the reactivated memory is then reforgotten at the same rate that it was forgotten originally. The recovery of a forgotten or "dormant" memory by a reactivation treatment, or reminder, is all-or-none, unaffected by the interval between training and reminding, although ultimately, a point is reached after which a single reminder is not effective. Three-month-olds, for example, exhibit perfect retention 24 h after a reminder whether it was exposed 2, 3, or 4 weeks after training. Finally, the magnitude of a newly acquired memory is affected by the amount of training (number of trials, session time), but the magnitude of a reactivated memory is not. In general, memory reactivation can be viewed as a purely automatic, perceptual identification process.

Usually, a brief (2 min) exposure to the original training mobile completely alleviates forgetting if the reminder is presented in the original training context (Hill et al., 1988; for review, see Rovee-Collier & Hayne, 1987); however, if it is presented in a different one, it is completely ineffective, and the memory remains forgotten (Borovsky & Rovee-Collier, 1990; Shields & Rovee-Collier, 1992). Amabile and Rovee-Collier (1991), however, found that training 6-month-old infants in a different context during each session (variable training) impaired memory reactivation in any context. They were unable to recover the forgotten memory 3 weeks after training when the original mobile was presented as a reminder in either the original training context or in a completely novel one.

We attribute this failure to recover the forgotten memory to competition between activated memories at the time of retrieval (see also Shiffrin & Murnane, 1991; Brainerd, Chapter 4, this volume). Ackerman (1987) views the role of context as facilitating identification of the appropriate memory or set of memories to be retrieved, much as we use luggage tags to identify which suitcases are ours. By this account, both memory representations matched the reminder context equally, hence neither was retrieved in the time allotted.

Finally, it is noteworthy that the process of retrieving a forgotten memory is apparently facilitated by sleep, which *removes* all sources of potential interference. Fagen and Rovee-Collier (1983) trained 3-month-olds for two sessions and allowed them to forget the mobile task for 2 weeks. Thirteen days later, the baseline performance of a control group who was tested with the original mobile confirmed that the memory had, indeed, been forgotten. At this point, they exposed infants to an effective reminder (the original mobile) for 3 min and then tested them, as usual, with that mobile either 15 min, 1 h, 8 h, 24 h, or 72 h later. They found that retention following the reactivation treatment was an increasing monotonic function of time since reactivation, with the first signs of significant recovery emerging after the 8-h delay and recovery finally peaking 72 h later. More important for present purposes, assuming that external interference from activity interpolated between the reactivation treatment and the retention test would be reduced during sleep, they asked the mothers of the eight infants in the 8-h test group to record the amount of time their infants slept in that interval. The resulting correlation between the percentage of sleep during the delay and the resulting retention ratio ($r = +.75$) was significant, suggesting that sleep reduced interference and allowed greater cognitive effort to be allocated to the retrieval process, increasing its efficiency.

INTERFERENCE AS A RESULT OF PASSIVE EXPOSURE

The Passive-Exposure Paradigm

The passive-exposure paradigm exploits the fact that infants pick up new information in their environment through mere observation. In the passive-exposure paradigm, infants are trained as usual and then are allowed to view a novel event for either 2 min (6-month-olds) or 3 min (3- month-olds). Later, they are presented with either the new information or the original information as a retrieval cue during either a delayed recognition test or a reactivation treatment. The interpolated event may be either the original mobile moving in a novel context, a stationary mobile suspended in a novel context, or a novel context with no mobile present at all (Boller & Rovee-Collier, 1992a). Because the infant is not permitted to activate the mobile him- or herself on those occasions that it is present but can merely observe it, we refer to this as a *passive-exposure* procedure.

Retroactive Interference in Delayed Recognition

If 6-month-olds are trained with a given mobile on 2 successive days in one context and, immediately after session 2, are exposed for only 2 min to the training mobile in a novel context (or for that matter, to a novel context with no mobile present at all), then they will recognize the training mobile in that novel exposure context 1 day later (Boller & Rovee-Collier, 1992a). Moreover, they behave as if they had been *explicitly trained* in that novel context (see Amabile & Rovee-Collier, 1991). Recall that infants otherwise fail to recognize the original training mobile in a novel context. Likewise, if 3-month-old infants are trained for two sessions with a particular mobile and then are passively exposed for only 3 min to a novel mobile being moved noncontingently at the end of session 2, then they will behave as if they had actually been trained with the novel exposure mobile and will respond vigorously to it during testing 1 day later (Rovee-Collier, Borza et al., 1993).

In this instance, the *functional* similarity between the novel exposure mobile and the training mobile is the critical factor that integrates the novel mobile with the prior training memory (Grabelle & Boller, 1992; Greco, Hayne, & Rovee-Collier, 1990). If infants do not observe the novel mobile moving as the training mobiles had moved, then it cannot cue retrieval of the training memory during the long-term test. This is true at 6 months as well as at 3. Note that in order for the novel exposure mobile (or context) to cue retrieval of the training memory, it must have somehow become integrated with, or modified, that memory representation.

We have shown that this retroactive memory modification is *not* a simple recency effect. Even when infants are passively exposed to a novel context immediately after session 1 instead of after session 2, they still recognize their original mobile in the novel exposure context as well as in a completely novel one 24 h after the conclusion of training (Boller & Rovee-Collier, 1992a).

Proactive Interference in Delayed Recognition

We originally thought that infants' memories were relatively immune to proactive interference via passive exposure. When we had exposed infants to a mobile moving noncontingently in a novel context immediately *after* training session 1, then they had subsequently recognized their training mobile in that novel exposure context (Boller & Rovee-Collier, 1992a). When we had exposed them to either a novel mobile (Grabelle & Boller, 1992) or to the original mobile in a novel context (Boller & Rovee-Collier, 1992a) immediately *before* training session 1, however, then infants did *not* respond to the novel mobile or in the novel context during the 1-day test, even though the exposure in each instance was as temporally contiguous with training before session 1 as after it. These results suggest that infants' memories are organized in terms of *meaningful or significant events*. Before infants have learned that they can kick to move a mobile in a particular context, mobiles and contexts have no particular significance for them. Once the memory of training has been encoded, however, then mobiles and contexts are meaningful, and there is a significant event with which subsequently encountered mobiles and contexts can be associated.

The preceding results, however, may not reflect a failure of the novel mobile or context to interfere with the training memory because it was exposed prior to training but because the exposure occurred as a part of the training episode. An alternative account is that infants' memory of the mobile or the context was recoded in terms of the mobile or context they saw *last* during the first session. From this perspective, the novel mobile or context that was passively exposed *prior* to training would have been recoded in terms of the training context. Evidence for this account has been obtained by K. Boller (unpublished data). When infants were exposed to a novel context for only 2 min *24 h prior to session 1*, instead of immediately before it, then they did respond in the preexposed novel context during the delayed recognition test 24 h after training was over, despite the fact that testing did not occur until 3 days after the exposure.

Thus, proactive exposure to a component of the subsequent event (the context) can affect long-term retention of that event once infants have acquired an explicit response by which to *express* what they originally encoded. More specifically, these data confirm that contextual information pertaining to a given session is recoded by the context last encountered within that session. Once the session has ended and a memory returns to the long-term store, however, it appears to be buffered against future recoding.

Retroactive Interference in Memory Reactivation

The relative ease with which infants' newly acquired memories are modified or updated by information to which infants are only briefly and passively exposed subsequent to training led us to wonder whether their training memories are equally susceptible to modification over the long term. To answer this, we let the original memory be forgotten for 3 weeks and then used a reactivation procedure to recover it, thereafter attempting to modify the reactivated memory via the passive-exposure procedure (Boller & Rovee-Collier, 1994). Recall that infants who are exposed to the original training mobile in the original training context for 2 min as a reminder typically show perfect retention 1 day later. However, if they are exposed to the original mobile in a novel context, then their training memory is not reactivated, and they exhibit no retention whatsoever during testing the next day. Likewise, if reactivated in the original context but tested in a novel one, they also show no retention (Borovsky & Rovee-Collier, 1990). The reactivated memory is not expressed in a novel context. It was this contextual specificity of the reactivated memory that we sought to change.

In the typical reactivation paradigm with 6-month-olds, 20 days after training, when the memory is forgotten, we present the reactivation treatment. This consists of returning infants to their original training context and showing them, for 2 min, the mobile being moved noncontingently at the same rate that the same infant had moved it during the last 2 min of acquisition in session 2. Twenty-four h later, we assess retention by hanging the original training mobile, now stationary, in front of the infant. The playpen is again draped with a distinctive context (either the original one or a novel one, depending on the group). If the memory has been reactivated, infants will kick, indicating that they again recognize the original mobile. Our problem in designing the present study was this: Because infants' memories can be reactivated only in the original context and not in a novel one, when should infants be passively exposed to the novel context? When we had modified the original, newly acquired memory, it had been in an active state at the time; but a forgotten memory obviously is not. Thus, it seemed clear that we would first have to present an effective reminder in order to *initiate* the process of retrieving the forgotten memory before we could present the passive-exposure treatment to modify it. This, then, was our initial strategy. We started the memory recovery process by showing infants the original mobile in the original context, and then we attempted to "slip in" the novel context immediately afterward, during a passive-exposure treatment. The results are shown in Figure 3.

The first column in Figure 3 confirms that the reactivation treatment was indeed effective. Group AA-A/A, who was reminded and tested in the original context, exhibited significant retention during the 3-week delayed recognition test in the original context. The second group (second column from the left) displayed the typical result that a reactivated memory is not retrieved in a novel context. The remaining columns in Figure 3 are data from passive-exposure groups who were exposed to a novel context immediately after reminding and tested in that novel context 1 day later. None exhibited retention.

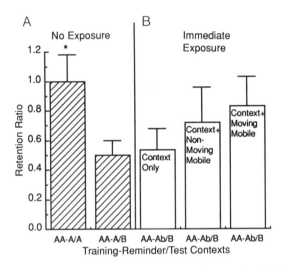

FIGURE 3. Mean retention ratios of independent groups of 6-month-olds who were trained, reminded, and tested in context A or context B. The first two letters represent the training context. The letter after the dash represents the reactivation context and the letter after the slash, the test context. The lowercase letter represents the exposure context. (A) One no-exposure control group (AA-A/A) exhibited retention when there was no context shift between training, reminding, and testing. The other displayed a retention deficit when trained and reminded in one context but tested in a novel one. (B) Three passive-exposure groups who were trained and reminded in the same context but were passively exposed to a novel context immediately after the reminder. The three groups differed in the number and type of cues present during the passive-exposure treatment (context only, the context + the nonmoving mobile, or the context + the moving mobile). In all three cases, there was no evidence of retention. The asterisk indicates that only group AA-A/A exhibited significant retention (i.e., M baseline ratio significantly > 1.00). Vertical bars indicate ± 1 SE.

We were surprised by these data. If the memory was reactivated but not modified, then perhaps the memory must be in an active state to be modified, as some researchers have suggested (Lewis, 1979). On the other hand, if infants did not detect that the presentation of the original and novel contexts at the time of the reactivation treatment was *sequential,* then perhaps the memory was never reactivated in the first place. Recall that a memory cannot be reactivated in a novel context (Borovsky & Rovee-Collier, 1990; Shields & Rovee-Collier, 1992).

In our next study, therefore, we increased the time between the reactivation treatment and the passive-exposure treatment. Boller, Rovee-Collier, Borovsky, O'Connor, and Shyi (1990) had previously found that reactivated memories take less time to be recovered following a reactivation treatment at 6 months than at 3 (cf. Fagen & Rovee-Collier, 1983). This is illustrated in Figure 4. Independent groups of infants were trained, reminded, and tested with the same mobile in the same context. As at 3 months, no infant exhibited significant retention immediately after the reminder. The first evidence of significant retention began to emerge, however, after 1 h, and all infants exhibited robust retention after 4 h, when recovery peaked. Despite the day-end glitch 8 h after reminding, infants continued to exhibit significant retention 24 h later.

In our next study, therefore, we distanced the passive-exposure treatment from the reactivation treatment by either 15 min, 1 h, or 4 h in order to

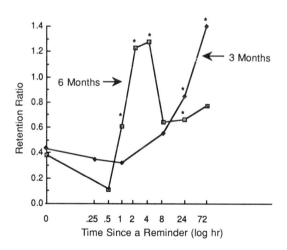

FIGURE 4. Mean retention ratios of independent groups of 3- and 6-month-old infants trained, reminded, and tested in the same context. Groups differ by the amount of time between the reminder and the long-term test. Retention peaked after 4 h at 6 months and after 3 days at 3 months. Asterisks indicate that a group exhibited significant retention (i.e., M baseline ratio significantly > 1.00). (From Boller et al., 1990).

determine whether it was necessary for the memory to be active in order for it to be modified. As shown in Figure 5, however, it did not matter when the passive-exposure treatment was presented. As before, none of the groups exhibited any evidence that they recognized the mobile in the novel test context. Thus, we concluded that even when the memory reactivation treatment was effective, the status of memory recovery at the time of the passive-exposure treatment did not affect whether the memory could be modified or not.

At this point, it appeared that reactivated memories might be impervious to modification. Our final strategy, therefore, was to allow infants to *actively participate* in the original event once more during a partial training trial. This experience occurred immediately after the reactivation treatment. Instead of merely passively observing the mobile in motion for 2 min in a novel context, infants were *hooked up* to the mobile in the novel context and allowed to move the mobile for themselves for the 2 min—an *active-exposure treatment*. Controls received identical training and the 2-min active-exposure treatment but no reactivation procedure in the original context.

This time, trained infants who received both the reactivation treatment and the active-exposure treatment exhibited significant retention when tested in the novel context 24 h later. In contrast, infants who were originally trained in context A but received no reactivation treatment in that context prior to their active exposure in novel context B displayed no retention in the

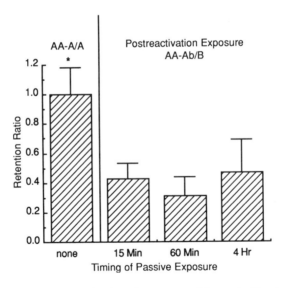

FIGURE 5. Mean retention ratios of independent groups of 6-month-olds who were trained, reminded, and passively exposed to a novel context either 15 min, 60 min, or 4 h after the reminder. Testing occurred 24 h later in the exposed context. The asterisk indicates that only group AA-A/A exhibited significant retention (i.e., *M* baseline ratio significantly > 1.00). Vertical bars indicate ± 1 *SE*.

novel test context. This indicates that the reactivation treatment in the original context was necessary in order to initiate the recovery process. A 2-min active exposure treatment in a novel context was not sufficient to reactivate the memory that had originally been acquired in context A, just as a typical 2-min reactivation treatment with the original mobile in a novel context will not reactivate the original memory (see Figure 6; an X indicates the absence of a training or reactivation treatment prior to the active-exposure treatment). In Figure 6, the far-right column depicts the test performance of the no-training control group which received only the reactivation treatment in context A and the 2-min active exposure treatment in context B. As can be seen, the latter group also exhibited no retention.

These data demonstrate that *both* original training in a particular context *and* the memory reactivation treatment in the original context are necessary in order for a partial training trial in a novel context to facilitate retention in a novel context 24 h later. The fact that infants did respond in the novel exposure context suggests that the immediacy of the passive-exposure treatment to the reactivation treatment in the first series of experiments was

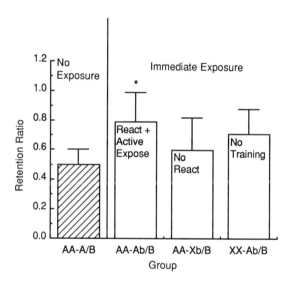

FIGURE 6. Mean retention ratios of independent groups of 6-month-olds. Group No Exposure was trained and reminded in context A and tested in novel context B. Group React+Active Expose was trained and reminded in context A and then immediately received a 2-min active exposure treatment in context B (i.e., their kicks activated the mobile). Group No React and No Training were control groups. Group No React also received an active exposure treatment in context B but no reactivation treatment. Group No Training received the reactivation and active exposure treatment in context B but no prior training. The asterisk indicates that only the group receiving both the reactivation treatment in context A and the active exposure in context B exhibited significant retention (i.e., M baseline ratio significantly > 1.00). Vertical bars indicate ± 1 SE.

not the factor that had precluded memory reactivation; rather, *passively* exposing infants to the original mobile in the novel context was simply insufficient to modify their memory of prior training. The present study also demonstrates that a memory need not have yet returned to an active state in order to be modified. Similar results have been reported by Rovee-Collier, Adler, and Borza (in press), who found that infants' newly acquired memory for the details of their training mobile can be modified by new details they subsequently encounter once the original details (but not the general features) have been forgotten.

In summary, although infant memories are highly susceptible to interfering information presented while the training memory is still active, infants are able to reject interfering information when it is presented after a reactivation treatment. This ability to prevent the corruption of memories over the long term may be adaptive for infants, allowing memories to be preserved for extended periods and updated when infants actively participate in an event themselves, not merely through passive observation.

In our final analysis of the interfering effects of passively exposed information on memory reactivation, we consider the observation that at 3 months, the original mobile can neither retrieve the training memory after 24 h nor reactivate it once it is forgotten if infants were trained with one mobile but passively exposed to a novel one immediately after training (Rovee-Collier, Borza et al., 1993). Boller and Rovee-Collier (1992a), using a passive-exposure procedure with 6-month-olds, had obtained identical results when infants were trained in the same context in each of two sessions and were merely exposed to the mobile in a novel context for 2 min at the end of training session 2. Those infants subsequently recognized their training mobile in a completely novel context 24 h after training but failed to recognize it in the original, session-1 training context! Also, the 6-month-olds failed to be reminded in either the session-1 context or the novel one 3 weeks later. Recall that Ackerman (1987) had proposed that the context is the means by which subjects identify which memory to access in which situation. Perhaps the forgotten memory of training was not retrieved by the mobile reminder because the particular memory in which the reminder mobile was represented could not be readily identified. It might have been represented in two different contexts, each in a different memory, both of which competed for retrieval access at the time of reminding.

If this were the case, then passively exposing infants to the novel context at the end of *each* training session might recode each session in terms of that novel context and thereby eliminate the original context from both memory representations. This, in turn, should eliminate competition between memories and permit the memory to be retrieved in the novel reactivation context. In fact, this was the case. When infants were briefly exposed to a novel context at the end of both training sessions, then the original mobile was an effective reminder in that novel exposure context but not in the actual training context 3 weeks later (K. Boller & C. Rovee-Collier, unpublished observations).

DEVELOPMENTAL CHANGES IN INHIBITORY PROCESSES

Most studies of discrimination learning are based on the theoretical assumption that discrimination results from the buildup of inhibition. The physiology of inhibition is by no means clear-cut; however, most researchers assume that the physiological immaturity of inhibitory mechanisms makes it impossible for young infants to withhold responding, for example, to an S– or during an extinction phase. On the surface, this conclusion appears to be confirmed by the different patterns of extinction of younger and older infants: 2-month-old infants continue to increase responding monotonically during a 6-min extinction phase rather than decrease it; 3-month-olds initially increase and then decrease responding; and 6-month-olds decrease responding within 1–2 min (Hill et al., 1988; Rovee-Collier & Gekoski, 1979). To demonstrate extinction, however, a subject must detect a change in the reinforcement contingency. Therefore, the more rapid decline in responding at the older age may result from their more rapid detection of the contingency change rather than from a superior ability to withhold responding.

Whether responding is withheld in the presence of an S–, on the other hand, also depends on the nature of the response. Newborn infants whose high-amplitude sucks previously produced reinforcement may not refrain from sucking altogether when the contingency is reversed, for example, but their rate of high-amplitude sucks may significantly decline (Siqueland, 1968a, 1968b, 1969). (Sucking is virtually obligatory for a young infant with a nipple in his/her mouth.) Likewise, at 1.5–3 months, arm and leg movements that do not produce reinforcement in the mobile conjugate reinforcement paradigm may cease completely in some limbs but continue in others as a passive reflection of lateralized activity (Rovee-Collier et al., 1978).

In a free-operant discrimination study of behavioral contrast with 3-month-olds, Rovee-Collier and Capatides (1979) reinforced kicks in the presence of one mobile (S+: white blocks with blue patterns) and withheld reinforcement in the presence of another (S–: yellow blocks with green patterns). Reinforcement was mobile movement, and mobiles (counterbalanced across reinforcement conditions) were alternated every 2 min. In Experiment 1, responses to *both* mobiles were reinforced in session 1; in sessions 2–4, however, the discrimination contingency was introduced, and reinforcement was withheld during S– but was available during S+. As is characteristic of this procedure, response rates increased sharply during S+ in sessions 2–4 and remained reliably higher than the rates of controls who continued to be reinforced by both mobiles. Infants' response rates in S–, however, *did not decline* despite the fact that infants had obviously discriminated that reinforcement was no longer forthcoming during S– by virtue of their altered responding in S+, in which the contingency had *not* changed. In Experiment 2, the training procedure was varied, and some infants did inhibit responding to S–; however, their response patterns were relatively unstable and highly individualistic. From these data, we conclude that whether or not inhibition of free-operant responding during the first 3 months can be demonstrated depends as much on the nature of the response as on the age of the infant. Even so, it is not a robust phenomenon.

We have recently completed a series of studies of visual pop-out effects in 3- and 6-month-old infants. Visual pop-out is the phenomenon wherein a unique stimulus in an array of otherwise homogeneous stimuli stands out or calls attention to itself (the "familiar face in a crowd" phenomenon). In perceptual identification studies with both adults (Treisman, 1988; Wolfe, Cave, & Franzel, 1989) and infants (Chazin, Bhatt, & Rovee-Collier, 1992), pop-out is relatively unaffected by the number of distractors in which the unique stimulus is embedded. There are differences, however, in the degree to which infants are affected by the unique character in 24-h delayed recognition tests at 3 and 6 months, and these differences appear to reflect the differential extent to which infants at each age can inhibit responding to the unique item that had engaged their attention. At 3 months, infants who have been trained with, for example, a mobile containing seven pink blocks displaying black "*L*"s will exhibit perfect retention of that same mobile 24 h later, kicking vigorously during the long-term test; if they are tested with a pink-block mobile displaying black "+"s, however, they will respond at their baseline level, indicating no recognition. If the test mobile contains six "*L*"s and one "+," however, infants also will not respond, treating the entire mobile as if it were composed of "+"s. Conversely, if the test mobile contains six "+"s and one "*L*," then infants will respond, treating the entire mobile as if it were composed of "*L*"s, that is, as if it were their training mobile! In each instance, the unique character popped out and determined whether or not infants recognized the test mobile (Rovee-Collier, Hankins, & Bhatt, 1992).

At 6 months, in contrast, infants trained with "*L*"s and tested with either a single novel "+" amidst six "*L*"s or with a single "*L*" amidst six "+"s recognize both test mobiles. Because the familiar "*L*" popped out from the array of six "+"s, we presume that the single "+" did also, as it did at 3 months; however, responding by these older infants is less constrained by the purely perceptual features displayed on the test mobile. Even though the novel "+" popped out, they can inhibit attention to that compelling single novel cue and sample the other cues on the test mobile, all of which predict reinforcement. As a result, they kick vigorously during the 24-h delayed recognition test (Bhatt, Rovee-Collier, & Weiner, 1994).

THE TIMING OF INTERPOLATED INFORMATION:
THE TIME WINDOW

Interference in Delayed Recognition Tests

In an earlier section, we saw that if infants are explicitly trained with a discriminably different mobile or in a different context in each session, then they will respond to another novel mobile or in another novel context during a long-term retention test (Amabile & Rovee-Collier, 1991; Boller & Rovee-Collier, 1992a; Hayne et al., 1987; Rovee-Collier & DuFault, 1991; Shields & Rovee-Collier, 1992). Thus, explicit variable training overrides the retention deficit otherwise seen when infants are trained with only a single mobile (Hill et al., 1988) or in only a single context (Borovsky & Rovee-Collier, 1990; Butler & Rovee-Collier, 1989; Shields & Rovee-Collier, 1992). Even so, if 3-month-old infants are trained with yellow-block mobiles that display alphanumeric characters *(A or 2)* in a different color each day, then during the 1-day test, they will respond to a mobile with the *same* character in another novel color, but they will not respond to a mobile with a *different* character in another novel color. Nor will they generalize after any delay to a novel object, such as a stained-glass and metal butterfly windchime, that is highly physically dissimilar to the yellow-block training mobiles (Greco et al., 1990). However, when we passively exposed the 3-month-olds to the moving butterfly for only 3 min immediately after the end of training, it was integrated with their previously established training memory and could cue responding 1 day later. Also, as before, the integration was accomplished through functional similarity. If the butterfly was *stationary* when infants viewed it, then it was *not* integrated with the training memory and did *not* cue responding during the 1-day retention test (Greco et al., 1990; Rovee-Collier, Borza et al., 1993).

In the preceding studies, new information was integrated with old when infants were allowed merely to view a novel mobile or novel context *immediately* after a training session—a time when the prior memory was still active. To explore whether the timing of the new, postevent information affects its integration or interference with the prior memory, we delayed infants' exposure to the butterfly for different numbers of days after training and tested their retention 1 day after the delayed exposure (Rovee-Collier, Greco-Vigorito, & Hayne, 1993).

As shown in Figure 7, infants who were exposed to the butterfly after delays as long as 4 days exhibited significant retention when tested with the butterfly 24 h later, but infants exposed after delays of 5 days and longer exhibited none, even though they remembered the training exemplars for longer than a week.

These data reveal that postevent information can be integrated with the

infants' prior training memory over an unexpectedly long period—on the order of several days. There was, however, a fixed time window within which
this could occur. The width of this time window was particularly surprising
in that infants had observed the postevent information only passively, only
briefly, and only once. Presumably, when infants encountered functional information about the highly physically dissimilar novel object that matched
functional information in their memory representation of training, the training memory was retrieved into short-term memory, where the new information was integrated with it. Notably, the common functional information
(*movement*) that was responsible for integrating the novel mobiles or the
butterfly with the prior memory of training was never physically present at
the time of testing. Recall that infants were always tested with a *stationary*
mobile or butterfly.

Muzzio (1994) attempted to modify 6-month-olds' memory of their
training mobile by exposing them to a novel mobile in motion after delays
ranging from 1 to 13 days, the period over which infants of this age typically
discriminate a novel mobile from the training one (Borovsky & Rovee-
Collier, 1990; Hill et al., 1988). Infants were trained for 2 days with mobile
A and then were allowed to view mobile B passively for 2 min. Twenty-four
h later, they were tested with either mobile A or mobile B. Unlike infants
whose passive exposure immediately followed training in session 2 and who
responded to all test mobiles, both old and new, on the following day, these
infants responded only to mobile B and not to mobile A during all succeed-
ing tests administered as long as 8 days after training. Thereafter, they re-

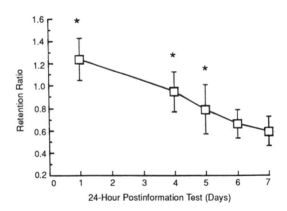

FIGURE 7. Mean retention ratios of independent groups of 3-month-olds during a transfer
test with the stationary butterfly 24 h after they were passively exposed to it in motion for 3
min. The passive-exposure procedure occurred either 0 (immediately), 1, 3, 4, 5, or 6 days after
category training; the retention test occurred 1, 4, 5, 6, or 7 days after training. Asterisks indicate that a group exhibited significant retention (i.e., M baseline ratio significantly > 1.00).
Vertical bars indicate ± 1 SE. (From Rovee-Collier, Greco-Vigorito, & Hayne, 1993.)

sponded to neither mobile. Because infants usually remember the details of their training mobile for as long as 14 days, exposing them to the novel mobile even 13 days after training clearly impaired retrieval of the original training memory.

This conclusion was confirmed when Muzzio was unable to reactivate the original memory 20 days after training with mobile A for infants who had been briefly exposed to novel mobile B 1 week earlier (13 days after training). Had mobile B not affected infants' memory for mobile A when mobile B was exposed after a 13-day delay, then the original memory once more would have been retrieved by mobile A during the 3-week test. In contrast, both mobiles A and B were effective reminders when the exposure to mobile B had occurred only 1 day after training, despite the fact that exposure to mobile B had also rendered mobile A ineffective as a retrieval cue during a delayed recognition test 1 day later. This result indicated that mobile A was still in the memory representation following exposure to mobile B but simply could not be accessed at the time of the delayed recognition test, perhaps as a result of temporary interference. If this were the case, then the interference should dissipate after longer exposure–test delays, and at some point we would expect infants to resume responding to mobile A during the delayed recognition test as well (cf. Chandler, 1991). This, however, remains to be tested.

Why the training memory was not reactivated by the original mobile when the novel mobile was exposed 13 days after training is unclear. We currently think that the single memory trace with which the more recent representation of mobile B was integrated must have competed successfully for retrieval with the two memory tokens of mobile A (i.e., one from session 1 and one from session 2) at the time of reminding.

A similar effect was found using the passive-exposure procedure to update contextual information. To explore the time window in which facilitation and interference occurred, K. Boller (unpublished observations) trained infants in context A and then passively exposed them to context B either 1 day or 6 days after the completion of training. In both cases, infants were tested with the mobile in the presence of either the exposed or the original training context 24 h later. There was no evidence of retention in the two groups tested in the original training context, and infants who were exposed to the novel context 1 day after training did not exhibit retention in that context. When the exposure treatment was presented after 6 days, however, there was evidence of retention in the novel exposure context. Thus, the original memory was highly susceptible to the interfering effects of the passively exposed novel context whether the exposure occurred at a shorter or longer delay after training. However, the facilitatory effect of the passive-exposure treatment was seen only when it occurred after a longer time period.

Finally, we have recently considered the impact of successive training trials that occur either within the time window or outside of it. Presumably, information even from a complete training trial will not be integrated with that of a prior trial if the second trial does not occur within the critical time interval defined by the time window (Rovee-Collier, in press). To explore this possibility, we trained 3-month-old infants for two successive training sessions and tested their delayed recognition 8 days after the initial session. Groups differed, however, in the spacing between their first and second sessions—either 1, 2, 3, or 4 days. When the second session occurred within 3 days of the first, infants showed significant retention during the 8-day test (see Figure 8). When the second session occurred 4 days after the first, however, infants performed no better than a control group who had received only a single session 8 days earlier (Rovee-Collier, Evancio, & Earley, in press). These data suggest that there is a time window within which any subsequently encountered information can be integrated with a prior memory representation. If the subsequent information is not encountered within that span, then it is not associated with what came before and is, effectively, like a first-time occurrence.

These results are reminiscent of the well-documented massed-distributed learning distinction, which has also been demonstrated in infants

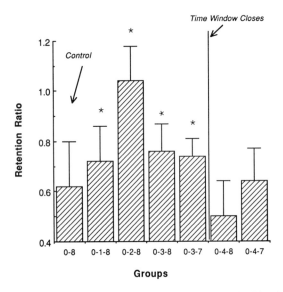

FIGURE 8. Mean retention ratios of independent groups of 3-month-olds whose second training session followed their first after a delay of either 1, 2, 3, or 4 days. These groups were tested either 7 or 8 days after their initial session. The control group received no second session and was tested 8 days later. Asterisks indicate that a group exhibited significant retention (i.e., M baseline ratio significantly > 1.00). Infants exhibited no retention when the time between session 1 and session 2 exceeded 3 days. Vertical bars indicate ± 1 SE. (From Rovee-Collier, Evancio, et al. in press).

(Vander Linde, Morrongiello, & Rovee-Collier, 1985). Different accounts have been offered for this distinction, including the greater variation in contextual cues that are likely to accompany greater intersession delays (Coulter, 1979) and the fuller processing that information in a later session may receive as a result of the greater effort required to retrieve the original memory (Bjork, 1975). For whatever reason, however, the finding that there is a fixed period within which a prior memory can be retrieved and integrated with current information and after which it cannot is genuine.

Interference in Memory Reactivation Tests

If postevent information has truly been incorporated with the training memory when it is passively exposed within a given time window, then it should also be able to prime the prior training memory in a reactivation paradigm once the training memory has been forgotten. Recall that, unlike the simple delayed recognition procedure in which subjects are *tested* with the potential retrieval cue (e.g., a novel mobile or in a novel context), the reactivation procedure is a prior-cuing procedure in which the potential retrieval cue is presented as a reminder *substantially in advance of* the long-term retention test, and subjects are tested with the original training mobile or in the original training context.

In our initial test of this hypothesis, Rovee-Collier, Greco-Vigorito, and Hayne (1993) passively exposed infants for 3 min to the moving butterfly windchime either 4 days after training with the yellow-block mobiles (inside the putative time window) or 6 days afterward (outside the time window). Thirteen days later, they were again exposed to the moving butterfly windchime for 3 min as a *reminder* for the training memory; 24 h later, all infants were tested with another exemplar of the yellow-block training mobiles. Recall that infants who had been passively exposed to the butterfly within a 4-day time window had exhibited excellent retention during a delayed recognition test 24 h later, but those who had encountered the butterfly after delays longer than 4 days had exhibited none. Recall that only a component of the original training memory can effectively reactivate that memory once it has been forgotten. We hypothesized, therefore, that if the butterfly had truly been integrated with the prior training memory within a 4-day time window, then it would be an effective reminder for the forgotten training memory only if it had originally been exposed within 4 days of training. Conversely, it should not be able to reactivate the training memory if it had been exposed 6 days afterward.

This hypothesis was confirmed. As shown in Figure 9, the butterfly was indeed an effective reminder, but only if infants had been exposed to the moving butterfly within the time window (group Expose 4); infants who were exposed to the butterfly outside the time window (group Expose 6) exhibited no retention during the 2-week test. Their performance was no better

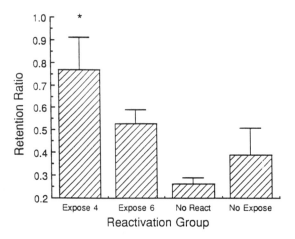

FIGURE 9. Mean retention ratios of independent groups of 3-month-olds who were passively exposed to the butterfly windchime during a postevent-information procedure that occurred either inside (group Expose 4) or outside (group Expose 6) of the time window (4 days or 6 days after category training, respectively). All infants were reminded with the butterfly in a reactivation paradigm 20 days after category training. Its efficacy as a reminder was assessed during a retention test 1 day later (21 days after training) with a novel category member. Also shown are control groups who received either the postevent information procedure on day 4 but no reminder (group No React) or a reminder but no interpolated postevent-information procedure (group No Expose). Asterisks indicate that a group exhibited significant retention (i.e., M baseline ratio significantly > 1.00). Vertical bars indicate $\pm$ 1 SE. (From Rovee-Collier, Greco-Vigorito, & Hayne, 1993.)

than that of infants who had been exposed to the butterfly 4 days after training but had received no reactivation treatment or of infants who had been reminded with the butterfly without previously having been exposed to it. These data indicate that postevent information was integrated with the prior memory representation within a 4-day time window and demonstrate that the memory modification is relatively permanent.

The same hypothesis was tested with infants in the Rovee-Collier, Evancio, et al. (in press) study whose second training session had occurred either inside the time window (2 days after the first session) or outside of the time window (4 days after their first training session). Three-month-olds trained in one of these conditions received a reactivation treatment with the original mobile 14 days after their initial session and were tested with that same mobile 1 day later. As in the study with different time of exposure to the butterfly, infants whose second session had occurred within the time window exhibited excellent retention during the long-term test, but infants whose second session had occurred outside the time window exhibited none (Rovee-Collier, Evancio, et al., in press). These results confirm the validity of the construct of a time window for the integration of successively encountered information. The time window for postevent information was longer in the example of exposure to the butterfly than in the example of the second training session because of the different strengths of the original memory in each instance; in the first example, infants had received three initial training sessions prior to the butterfly's exposure, whereas in the second example, they had received only one prior training session.

In some regards, the time-window construct appears to resemble classic consolidation theory, which argued that the consolidation of neural traces shortly after learning is essential for long-term memory. By this view, immediately after an event, memory traces are unstable and only become permanent or "consolidated" after some period of time. Duncan (1949), for example, trained rats in an active-avoidance task at the rate of one trial per day. After each trial, independent groups received an electroconvulsive shock (ECS) treatment either 20 s, 40 s, 60 s, 4 min, 15 min, 1 h, 4 h, or 14 h after each trial. Acquisition was significantly slowed by ECS presentations closer in time to training; after delays of 1 h and longer, however, rats receiving ECS treatments performed at control levels. Duncan's findings suggested that memory is gradually consolidated over time; the more it is consolidated, the less vulnerable it is to disruption by events (e.g., ECS) that break up the electrical activity in the brain. This account has also been invoked to explain retrograde amnesia in humans: people who sustain head injuries and lose consciousness usually fail to remember events that occurred immediately prior to the injury.

In a classic experiment, however, Miller and Springer (1972, 1973) demonstrated that ECS impairs retrieval but does not destroy the memory. They trained rats in a passive-avoidance task with foot shock, followed immediately by ECS. Several days later, as predicted by consolidation theory, rats exhibited no memory of their training, responding like controls who had never been trained in the first place. If the rats then received a reminder (a brief foot shock in a novel apparatus) in a reactivation paradigm, however, the original memory was recovered, and the rats once again exhibited the acquired passive-avoidance response in the original test box. Because controls who received the reminder procedure without original training did not exhibit the passive-avoidance response, the ECS treatment had not destroyed the original memory but merely rendered it more difficult to retrieve. This and other experimental challenges to consolidation theory have led neuropsychologists to conclude that if consolidation occurs at all, it is so rapid as to be virtually unmeasurable by current technology.

The work on time-window phenomena that is described below similarly challenges a consolidation account. Briefly, this work demonstrates that the effects of manipulations that modify memories are most dramatic when they are introduced at the *end* of the time window rather than immediately after the original event occurred (see Reyna, Chapter 2, this volume for similar conclusions about memory suggestibility). Moreover, the effects seem to increase over retention intervals that follow the original experience by several *days*.

Differential Timing of Interpolated Information within the Time Window

We wondered whether differences in the timing of postevent information even *within the time window* might also affect infants' retention. To this end, we passively exposed infants to the butterfly either at the beginning of the time window, immediately after training, or at the end of the time window, 4 days afterward, and then tested them with the butterfly after different delays in a simple delayed recognition paradigm.

The results confirmed that interpolating new information at different times within the time window had differential effects on retention. When the butterfly was exposed immediately after training, it was an effective retrieval cue for 4 days. In contrast, when its exposure was delayed until the end of the time window (4 days after the end of training), it continued to cue retrieval for an additional 10 days, or for at least 2 weeks after training (see

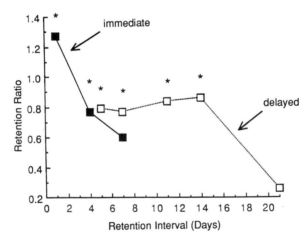

FIGURE 10. Mean retention ratios of independent groups of 3-month-olds during a transfer test with the stationary butterfly. Infants in the immediate-exposure condition (■) were passively exposed to the butterfly for 3 min immediately after the end of category training (day 0) and were tested either 1, 4, or 7 days after training. Infants in the delayed-exposure condition (□) were passively exposed to the butterfly for 3 min 4 days after the end of category training and were tested either 1, 3, 7, 10, or 17 days later (5, 7, 11, 14, or 21 days after training, respectively). Asterisks indicate that a group exhibited significant retention (i.e., *M* baseline ratio significantly > 1.00). Vertical bars indicate ± 1 *SE*. (From Rovee-Collier, Greco-Vigorito, & Hayne, 1993.)

Figure 10). Particularly striking was the fact that delaying infants' exposure to the butterfly appeared to *arrest* forgetting at the level characteristic of the delay when it was encountered (4 days) and to sustain performance at that level for a relatively protracted period.

One account for the retention enhancement in the delayed-exposure condition relates to the process by which postevent information is integrated with the prior training memory. When the postevent information is presented after zero delay, the prior training memory is already active and does not have to be retrieved into short-term memory. When the postevent information is encountered after a 4-day delay, however, the training memory must be retrieved into short-term memory via a match between memory attributes that the postevent information shares with attributes represented in the training memory. Once the old and new information simultaneously cohabit STM, their representations are integrated.

The preceding data are consistent with findings from tests with adults (Belli, Windschitl, McCarthy, & Winfrey, 1992; Loftus, Miller, & Burns, 1978) and children (Brainerd & Reyna, 1988) that delaying exposure to postevent information increases the likelihood that subsequent memory performance will be affected by the interpolated exposure (see also Titcomb & Reyna, Chapter 8, this volume). Loftus et al., for example, found that postevent information was remembered better when it was introduced at the end of a retention interval than when it was introduced immediately after the original episode. They concluded that memories are more readily modified when the original memory trace is weaker—a conclusion supported by the preceding data. Brainerd and Reyna suggested that memory retrieval by a relevant exemplar during a postevent-information procedure constitutes a functional study trial for the target memory, thereby enhancing later memory performance.

Bjork (1975) had similarly argued that any retrieval from long-term memory facilitates later retrievals. He had proposed that (1) the effectiveness of retrieval for later retention increases as a function of the difficulty of retrieval, and that (2) retrieval difficulty increases with the retention interval. By this account, the retention advantage of delaying exposure to the butterfly for 4 days resulted not only because the memory had to be retrieved but also because the retrieval was relatively difficult.

In our study of the interval between successive training trials (Rovee-Collier, Evancio, et al., in press) described earlier, we had also found a differential effect of timing within the original time window; however, in this instance, performance was superior when the second training session had occurred 2 days after the first. Even though we defined the time window as closing 3 days after the initial session, infants in the 3-day group had exhibited only partial retention 8 days after their first session. In examining the basis for this effect, we discovered that some infants in the 3-day group had already forgotten the effects of the first session by the time of their second session. For these infants, then, the time window had already closed by the outset of their second session.

Taken together, the preceding data confirm the following general principle: Retrieving a prior memory at the end of the time window has a greater impact on retention than retrieving it earlier in the same time window; a prior memory cannot be retrieved after the time window has closed, however. Information encountered after the time window has closed will be treated as unique and will *not* be integrated with a prior experience. Restated, the *timing* of interpolated information, therefore, determines whether interference or facilitation will occur as well as its extent.

POSTEVENT INFORMATION AND EYEWITNESS TESTIMONY

Research on adult eyewitness testimony has revealed that postevent information has two effects. First, *it can increase the likelihood that subjects will treat the new information as if it had been part of the original memory,* and second, *postevent information can impair retention of the original memory* (for a fuller discussion of this literature, see Titcomb & Reyna, Chapter 8, this volume). We have already reviewed considerable evidence that the first of these effects occurs in infancy as well: At both 3 and 6 months of age, infants who are exposed to a novel mobile once training is complete will treat that novel mobile as if they had been trained with it. To test whether the second effect also occurs in infancy, Rovee-Collier, Greco-Vigorito, and Hayne (1993) exposed 3-month-old infants to the butterfly at the end of the time window and tested them with a component of the original training memory—a yellow-block mobile—after the longest delay at which the infants had previously recognized a yellow-block mobile in the absence of postevent information. As can be seen in Figure 11, infants who were *not* exposed to the butterfly after training continued to recognize a yellow-block mobile for 11 days after the end of training, but infants who *were* exposed to the butterfly at the end of the time window no longer recognized a yellow-block mobile after that delay. Muzzio's (1994) findings similarly suggest that exposing 6-month-olds to a novel mobile over a period of 13 days after training can impair their subsequent retention of the original mobile with which they had been trained for two entire sessions. We conclude, therefore, that both of the effects of postevent information that have been reported in studies with adults also are found in studies with young infants.

Considerable controversy has arisen in the adult literature concerning the fate of the original memory trace—whether it is overwritten or displaced (Loftus, 1981; Loftus & Loftus, 1980; McCloskey & Zaragoza, 1985), whether a new memory is formed that consists of a blend of old and new attributes (Loftus & Hoffman, 1989), or whether the original memory and a memory of the postevent information coexist (Christiaansen & Ochalek,

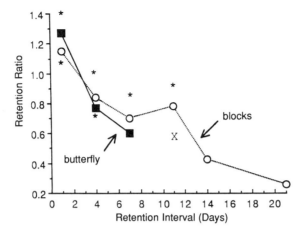

FIGURE 11. Mean retention ratios of independent groups of 3-month-olds who were tested with a novel yellow-block category exemplar at different delays after the end of category training. Infants either received no interpolated exposure to the butterfly and were tested 1, 4, 7, 11, 14, or 21 days after the end of category training (○) or were passively exposed to the butterfly for 3 min 4 days after the end of training and tested 7 days later, 11 days after the end of category training ("X"). Also shown is the performance of infants who were exposed to the butterfly immediately after category training and tested either 1, 4, or 7 days later (■). Asterisks indicate that a group exhibited significant retention (i.e., M baseline ratio significantly > 1.00). Vertical bars indicate ± 1 SE. (From Rovee-Collier, Greco-Vigorito, & Hayne, 1993.)

1983). Recall that infants who were exposed to the butterfly after a 4-day delay had exhibited excellent retention in a reactivation paradigm when reactivated with a yellow-block mobile 3 weeks after training (Rovee-Collier, Greco-Vigorito, & Hayne, 1993). Greco et al. (1990) obtained identical results when they had exposed infants to the butterfly immediately after training with a series of yellow-block mobiles for 3 days. These data, then, indicate that the delayed postevent exposure to the butterfly did *not* overwrite the yellow-block components of the original memory. These data also eliminate overwriting as a basis for the poor performance of infants who were exposed to the butterfly after a 4-day delay and tested 11 days after training with a yellow-block mobile (Rovee-Collier, Greco-Vigorito, & Hayne, 1993). Instead, their exposure to the butterfly seems merely to have *hastened* forgetting of the original memory component.

We have found other evidence that access to the original memory is impaired by postevent information. Three-month-olds fail to recognize their *original* training mobile or context 1 day later, for example, if they are passively exposed to a novel mobile or context immediately after training. Such a memory impairment does not occur, however, if a day elapses between training and exposure to the novel mobile. Moreover, because infants can still be reminded by the original mobile 3 weeks later when the exposure was delayed by 1 day (Rovee-Collier, Borza et al., 1993) or when it is immediate but infants received three training sessions (Greco et al., 1990; Rovee-Collier, Greco-Vigorito, & Hayne, 1993) indicates that a memory of the original training mobile must still be intact.

These observations raise significant questions regarding the mechanism that underlies whether and how a prior memory is altered. The fact that memory impairment does not occur if a day elapses between training and exposure to the novel mobile suggests that the memory representation that is retrieved at the time of the novel exposure is only a *copy* of the memory of a prior session and that the original representation in LTM remains intact. Old information in the retrieved copy, however, is replaced or updated by the new information that is physically present in the current session and that conflicts with it, thereby creating a new memory *token*. This new memory token is *not a blend* of old and new elements: Recall that when infants were trained with one mobile and then were exposed to another, they did not recognize a test mobile composed of equal numbers of old and new objects (Rovee-Collier, Borza et al., 1993), as a memory-blend hypothesis would predict. When a retrieval cue accesses an equal number of competing memory tokens, memory retrieval is impaired. When there are unequal numbers of competing tokens, however (and, perhaps, when there are equal numbers of competing tokens but one is considerably more *recent* than another), then memory retrieval can proceed relatively unimpeded.

FACILITATING EFFECTS OF INTERPOLATED MATERIAL

We have suggested that postevent information retrieves a prior memory and creates a new memory in which the postevent information is represented. Interpolated information thus establishes another *token* of the same *type* of event. Although we have demonstrated that in infants, as in adults, this process has two effects, we now argue that it actually has *three*. In addition to *interfering* with retrieval of the original memory and increasing the probability that the postevent information will be treated as if it had been part of the original event, the new memory token can also facilitate the recognition of *completely novel stimuli* whose features match those represented in both the old and new memory tokens. After being trained with mobile A and then exposed to mobile B, for example, both 3- and 6-month-old infants will also respond to a completely novel mobile, mobile C, which they otherwise would have discriminated (Fagen et al., 1984; Grabelle & Boller, 1992; Greco et al., 1990). This third effect will be recognized as *categorization*: Successive experience with multiple category exemplars facilitates responding to novel category members that are subsequently encountered. In studies of adults' eyewitness testimony, this third effect has not been seen because no researchers have given adult subjects forced-choice tests between *two novel objects,* one which is a category member and one which is not.

In addition, information to which infants are only passively exposed may be encoded but not expressed until a later occasion when infants have an *opportunity* to express what they previously noticed (Boller & Rovee-Collier, 1992b; Needham, 1992). Such proactive pickup of information is as likely to be facilitatory as inhibitory. More important, this phenomenon reveals most clearly the important distinction between the *acquisition* and *expression* of knowledge. This distinction is unlikely to be reserved for infants, but it may be particularly problematic for younger subjects.

CONCLUSIONS AND IMPLICATIONS

There is little evidence from studies with infants that short-term memory is susceptible to retroactive interference. In contrast, there is considerable evidence that infants' long-term memory is highly susceptible to retroactive interference after even the briefest exposure to novel information that is interpolated between original encoding and retention testing. At 3 months, for example, infants may actively encounter the original information for a total of 30 min over 2 days of training; at 6 months, they may encounter it twice for a total of 18 min; in contrast, the novel information may be exposed only passively, only briefly (e.g., for either 3 or 2 min, respectively), and only once. Yet, at both ages, recognition of the original information may be severely impaired. In addition, recent research has revealed evidence of significant attentional bias as a result of information that is encountered proactively early in development. Whether information encountered proactively interferes with or facilitates subsequent performance, however, depends on the nature of the subsequent task. Because one cannot know what infants do or do not encode of information that they only passively view until they are given an explicit opportunity to demonstrate it, the impact of *proactive* exposure to potentially conflicting information continues to be difficult to evaluate.

In addition, findings from research on eyewitness testimony with adults parallel findings from research on postevent information with infants. Because infants are not subject to the task or social demands or instructional misinterpretations that plague experiments with older children and adults, we believe that they are actually the subjects of choice for research on the basic mechanisms that underlie memory modification. At a minimum, research with infants can inform research with children and adults regarding critical variables that influence retroactive interference and other postevent information effects. In addition, research with infants has revealed facilitatory effects of interpolated information that have not previously been studied with adults. *Categorization* is one such case. It has also revealed that there is a *time window* within which subsequently encountered information can be integrated with, or affect the retention of, information previously encoded. Presumably a similar time window affects the subsequent retrieval of proactively encountered information.

Given the ubiquity of interference effects during infancy, susceptibility to the impairing *and* facilitating effects of proactive and retroactive sources of conflicting information may be an adaptive mechanism in early development, when more information is novel than is not and when the infant's niche is changing rapidly (see also Bjorklund & Harnishfeger, Chapter 5, this volume for a discussion of the adaptive significance of inhibition mechanisms in adulthood). Clearly, updating information under these conditions is crucial for young organisms, and it would be inefficient were it necessary for infants to experience every new situation in order to acquire its significance. Moreover, attaching new events to tokens of old memories permits infants to expand the range of events to which they will have both a ready response and expectations about potential outcomes. That this updating process becomes easier after longer delays is also of functional value. After delays so long that the original memory has been forgotten, however, modification of a reactivated memory is constrained by the requirement that the critical elements defining the original event (in our task, e.g., the contingency) continue to predict the event after a long delay. In this way, long-held memories appear to be protected against adventitious modification and against evocation in potentially inappropriate circumstances. Finally, although old information is in jeopardy of loss when memories are recoded or through disuse when new memory tokens containing conflicting information are formed, the fate of the original information or memory token may be impossible to determine.

The data demonstrate that whether information encountered either prior or subsequent to learning will interfere with that learning or will facilitate performance in a subsequent test depends on what is asked and what is being measured. If the question is whether the postevent information expands the range of situations for which a subject has an appropriate response, that is, will treat interpolated information as if it were part of the original memory, then we will seek examples of facilitation effects. Categorization is such an example. If one is interested in the impact of new information on the original memory, then we may seek examples of inhibitory effects. Greater complexity is added to the analysis when one considers that the timing of postevent information also affects interference and facilitation. For example, delaying the presentation of interpolated material until the end of the time window can prolong retention of the new material while impairing retention of the old. Clearly, it is a mistake to consider only the potentially *interfering* effects of interpolated information without considering potential *facilitatory* effects as well.

These finding have major implications for the development of memory, growth of the knowledge base, and the emergence of individual differences. Whether or not a memory of an early event will be perpetuated through significant periods of behavioral transition, as well as its specificity, for example, depends not only on *what* new information infants encounter subsequent to that event but *when* they encounter the information. Future access to the memory could be strengthened, impaired, or unaffected, depending on whether or not the new information is encountered within the time window for integration, and what is remembered could be expanded, narrowed, or selectively distorted depending on whether the new information is encountered early or late within the time window. Because the width of the time window for integrating new information with old progressively broadens as a function of the number of times the memory has previously been retrieved, the experiential history of each individual will determine the particular effect of the new information on the subsequent access to and quality of a given memory. It is important to recognize that during the course of their normal commerce with their environment, new information that infants only *chance* to view within the time window can retrieve a prior memory and be integrated with it if the new information is physically and/or functionally similar to information they previously encoded. Insofar as the effect of the new information on their prior memory representation will depend on when in the time window it is encountered, however, individual differences in memory development as well as in the development of the knowledge base will be inevitable, limitless, and largely unpredictable.

REFERENCES

Ackerman, B. P. (1987). Developmental differences in episodic retrieval: The role of differences in concept representations in semantic memory. *Developmental Psychology, 23,* 31–38.

Amabile, T. A., & Rovee-Collier, C. (1991). Contextual variation and memory retrieval at six months. *Child Development, 62,* 1155–1166.

Anderson, J. R. (1981). Interference: The relationship between response latency and response accuracy. *Journal of Experimental Psychology: Human Learning and Memory, 7,* 326–343.

Belli, R. F., Windschitl, P. D., McCarthy, T. T., & Winfrey, S. E. (1992). Detecting memory impairment with a modified test procedure: Manipulating retention interval with centrally presented event items. *Journal of Experimental Psychology: Learning, Memory, and Cognition, 18,* 356–367.

Bhatt, R., Rovee-Collier, C., & Weiner, S. (1994). Developmental changes in the interface between perception and memory retrieval. *Developmental Psychology, 30,* 151–162.

Bjork, R. A. (1975). Retrieval as a memory modifier. In R. L. Solso (Ed.), *Information processing and cognition: The Loyola symposium* (pp. 123–144). Hillsdale, NJ: Erlbaum.

Boller, K., & Rovee-Collier, C. (1994). Contextual updating of reactivated memories. *Developmental Psychobiology, 27,* 241–256.

Boller, K., & Rovee-Collier, C. (1992a). Contextual coding and recoding of infants' memories. *Journal of Experimental Child Psychology, 53,* 1–23.

Boller, K., & Rovee-Collier, C. (1992b, November). *Sensory preconditioning and learned irrele-*

vance in infants. Paper presented at the meeting of the International Society for Developmental Psychobiology, Newport Beach, CA.

Boller, K., Rovee-Collier, C., Borovsky, D., O'Connor, J., & Shyi, G. C.-W. (1990). Developmental changes in the time-dependent nature of memory retrieval. *Developmental Psychology, 26,* 770–779.

Bomba, P. C., & Siqueland, E. R. (1983). The nature and structure of infant form categories. *Journal of Experimental Child Psychology, 35,* 294–328.

Borovsky, D., & Rovee-Collier, C. (1990). Contextual constraints on memory retrieval at six months. *Child Development, 61,* 1569–1583.

Brainerd, C. J., & Reyna, V. F. (1988). Memory loci of suggestibility development: Comment on Ceci, Ross, and Toglia. *Journal of Experimental Psychology: General, 117,* 197–200.

Brainerd, C. J., Reyna, V. F., Howe, M. L., & Kingma, J. (1990). The development of forgetting and reminiscence. *Monographs of the Society for Research in Child Development, 55* (3–4, Serial No. 222).

Brown, J. A. (1958) Some tests of the decay theory of immediate memory. *Quarterly Journal of Experimental Psychology, 10,* 12–21.

Butler, J., & Rovee-Collier, C. (1989). Contextual gating of memory retrieval. *Developmental Psychobiology, 22,* 533–552.

Caron, A. J., Caron, R. F., Minichiello, M. D., Weiss, S. J., & Friedman, S. L. (1977). Constraints on the use of familiarization-novelty method in the assessment of infant discrimination. *Child Development, 48,* 747–762.

Caron, R. F., & Caron, A. J. (1969). Degree of stimulus complexity and habituation of visual fixation in infants. *Psychonomic Science, 14,* 78–79.

Chandler, C. C. (1991). How memory for an event is influenced by related events: Interference in modified recognition tests. *Journal of Experimental Psychology: Learning, Memory, and Cognition, 17,* 115–125.

Chazin, S., Bhatt, R. S., & Rovee-Collier, C. (1992, April). *Perceptual pop-out with variable distractors at 6 months.* Paper presented at the meeting of the Eastern Psychological Association, Boston, MA.

Christiaansen, R. E., & Ochalek, K. (1983). Editing misleading information from memory: Evidence for the coexistence of original and postevent information. *Memory & Cognition, 11,* 467–475.

Cohen, L. B., DeLoache, J. S., & Pearle, R. A. (1977). An examination of interference effects in infants' memory for faces. *Child Development, 48,* 88–96.

Cohen, L. B., & Gelber, E. R. (1975). Infant visual memory. In L. Cohen & P. Salapatek (Eds.), *Infant perception: From sensation to cognition* (Vol. 1, pp. 347–403). New York: Academic Press.

Coulter, X. (1979). The determinants of infantile amnesia. In N. E. Spear & B. A. Campbell (Eds.), *The ontogeny of learning and memory* (pp. 245–270). Hillsdale, NJ: Erlbaum.

Crowder, R. L. (1976). *Principles of learning and memory.* Hillsdale, NJ: Erlbaum.

DeLoache, J. S. (1976). Rate of habituation and visual memory in infants. *Child Development, 47,* 145–154.

Duncan, C. P. (1949). The retroactive effect of electroshock on learning. *Journal of Comparative and Psysiological Psychology, 42,* 32–44.

Ekstrand, B. R. (1967). The effect of sleep on memory. *Journal of Experimental Psychology, 75,* 64–72.

Fagan, J. F., III. (1970). Memory in the infant. *Journal of Experimental Child Psychology, 9,* 217–226.

Fagan, J. F., III. (1971). Infants' recognition memory for a series of visual stimuli. *Journal of Experimental Child Psychology, 11,* 244–250.

Fagan, J. F., III. (1973). Infants' delayed recognition memory and forgetting. *Journal of Experimental Child Psychology, 16,* 424–450.

Fagan, J. F., III. (1977). Infant recognition memory: Studies in forgetting. *Child Development, 48*, 68–78.

Fagen, J. W., Morrongiello, B. A., Rovee-Collier, C., & Gekoski, M. J. (1984). Expectancies and memory retrieval in 3-month-old infants. *Child Development, 54*, 394–403.

Fagen, J. W., & Rovee-Collier, C. (1982). A conditioning analysis of infant memory: How do we know they know what we know they knew? In N. E. Spear & R. Isaacson (Eds.), *The expression of knowledge* (pp. 67–111). New York: Plenum.

Fagen, J. W., & Rovee-Collier, C. (1983). Memory retrieval: A time-locked process in infancy. *Science, 222*, 1349–1351.

Fantz, R. L. (1964). Visual experience in infants: Decreased attention to familiar patterns relative to novel ones. *Science, 146*, 668–670.

Gelber, E. R. (1972). *The effect of time and intervening items on the recovery of an habituated response.* Unpublished master's thesis, University of Illinois, Urbana, IL.

Grabelle, M., & Boller, K. (1992, April). *The functional plasticity of infant memory.* Paper presented at the meeting of the Eastern Psychological Association, Boston, MA.

Grant, D. S. (1975). Proactive inhibition in pigeon short-term memory. *Journal of Experimental Psychology: Animal Behavior Processes, 104*, 207–220.

Greco, C., Hayne, H., & Rovee-Collier, C. (1990). Roles of function, reminding, and variability in categorization by 3-month-old infants. *Journal of Experimental Psychology: Human Learning and Memory, 16*, 617–633.

Hayne, H., Greco, C., Earley, P., Griesler, P., & Rovee-Collier, C. (1986). Ontogeny of early event memory: II. Encoding and retrieval by 2- and 3-month-olds. *Infant Behavior and Development, 9*, 441–460.

Hayne, H., Rovee-Collier, C., & Perris, E. E. (1987). Categorization and memory retrieval in 3-month-olds. *Child Development, 58*, 750–767.

Hill, W., Borovsky, D., & Rovee-Collier, C. (1988). Continuities in infant memory development. *Developmental Psychobiology, 8*, 33–39.

Horowitz, F. D., Paden, L., Bhana, K., & Self, P. (1979). The infant-control procedure. *Developmental Psychology, 7*, 90.

Howe, M. L., & Brainerd, C. J. (1989). Development of children's long-term retention. *Developmental Review, 9*, 310–340.

Jarrard, L. E., & Moise, S. L. (1970). Short-term memory in the stumptail macaque: Effect of physical restraint of behavior on performance. *Learning and Motivation, 1*, 267–275.

Jeffrey, W. E. (1976). Habituation as a mechanism for perceptual development. In T. J. Tighe & R. R. Leaton (Eds.), *Habituation: Perspectives from child development, animal behavior, and neurophysiology* (pp. 279–296). Hillsdale, NJ: Erlbaum.

Jenkins, J. G., & Dallenbach, K. M. (1924). Oblivescence during sleep and waking. *American Journal of Psychology, 35*, 605–612.

Kimble, G. A. (1956). *Principles of general psychology.* New York: Ronald Press.

Lewandowsky, S. (1991). Gradual unlearning and catastrophic interference: A comparison of distributed architectures. In W. E. Hockley & S. Lewandowsky (Eds.), *Relating theory and data: Essays on human memory in honor of Bennett B. Murdock* (pp. 445–476). Hillsdale, NJ: Erlbaum.

Lewis, D. J. (1979). Psychobiology of active and inactive memory. *Psychological Bulletin, 86*, 1054–1083.

Loftus, E. F. (1981). Mentalmorphosis: Alterations in memory produced by the mental bonding of new information to old. In J. Long & A. Baddeley (Eds.), *Attention and performance IX* (pp. 417–434). Hillsdale, NJ: Erlbaum.

Loftus, E. F., & Hoffman, H. G. (1989). Misinformation and memory: The creation of new memories. *Journal of Experimental Psychology: General, 118*, 100–104.

Loftus, E. F., & Loftus, G. R. (1980). On the permanence of stored information in the human brain. *American Psychologist, 35*, 409–420.

Loftus, E. F., Miller, D. G., & Burns, H. J. (1978). Semantic integration of verbal information into a visual memory. *Journal of Experimental Psychology: Human Learning and Memory, 4,* 19–31.

Martin, R. M. (1975). Effects of familiar and complex stimuli on infant attention. *Developmental Psychology, 11,* 178–185.

McCall, R. B., Kennedy, C. B., & Dodds, C. (1977). The interfering effect of distracting stimuli on the infant's memory. *Child Development, 48,* 79–87.

McCloskey, M., & Cohen, N. J. (1989). Catastrophic interference in connectionist networks: The sequential learning problem. In G. H. Bower (Ed.), *The psychology of learning and motivation* (Vol. 24, pp. 109–164). San Diego: Academic Press.

McCloskey, M., & Zaragoza, M. (1985). Misleading postevent information and memory for events: Arguments and evidence against memory impairment hypotheses. *Journal of Experimental Psychology: General, 114,* 1–16.

McGeoch, J. A. (1942). *The psychology of human learning: An introduction.* New York: Longmans, Green.

Melton, A. W., & Irwin, J. M. (1940). The influence of degree of interpolated learning on retroactive inhibition and the overt transfer of specific responses. *American Journal of Psychology, 53,* 173–203.

Miller, R. R., & Springer, A. D. (1972). Induced recovery of memory in rats following electro-convulsive shock. *Physiology & Behavior, 8,* 645–651.

Miller, R. R., & Springer, A. D. (1973). Amnesia, consolidation, and retrieval. *Psychological Review, 80,* 69–79.

Murdock, B. B. (1983). A distributed memory model for serial-order information. *Psychological Review, 90,* 316–338.

Muzzio, I. A. (1994). *Integrating information with a prior memory: Timing effects.* Unpublished master's thesis, Rutgers University, New Brunswick, NJ.

Needham, A. (1992, May). *Young infants use memories in object perception.* Paper presented at the International Conference on Infant Studies, Miami, FL.

Norman, D. A. (Ed.). (1970). *Models of human memory.* New York: Academic Press.

Olson, G. M. (1976). An information processing analysis of visual memory and habituation in infants. In T. J. Tighe & R. R. Leaton (Eds.), *Habituation: Perspectives from child development, animal behavior, and neurophysiology* (pp. 239–277). Hillsdale, NJ: Erlbaum.

Olson, G. M. (1979). Infant recognition memory for briefly presented visual stimuli. *Infant Behavior and Development, 2,* 123–134.

Pancratz, C. N., & Cohen, L. B. (1970). Recovery of habituation in infants. *Journal of Experimental Child Psychology, 9,* 208–216.

Peterson, L. R., & Peterson, M. J. (1959). Short-term retention of individual verbal items. *Journal of Experimental Psychology, 58,* 193–198.

Postman, L. (1971). Transfer, interference, and forgetting. In J. W. Kling & L. A. Riggs (Eds.), *Woodworth and Schlosberg's experimental psychology* (pp. 1019–1132). New York: Holt, Rinehart, & Winston.

Postman, L., & Underwood, B. J. (1973). Critical issues in interference theory. *Memory & Cognition, 1,* 19–40.

Roberts, W. A. (1984). Spaced repetition facilitates short-term retention in the rat. *Journal of Comparative and Physiological Psychology, 86,* 164–171.

Rovee, C. K., & Rovee, D. T. (1969). Conjugate reinforcement of infant exploratory behavior. *Journal of Experimental Child Psychology, 8,* 33–39.

Rovee-Collier, C. (in press). Time windows in cognitive development. *Developmental Psychology.*

Rovee-Collier, C., Adler, S. A., & Borza, M. A. (in press). Substituting new details for old? Effects of delaying postevent information on infant memory. *Memory & Cognition.*

Rovee-Collier, C., Borza, M. A., Adler, S. A., & Boller, K. (1993). Infants' eyewitness testimony:

Effects of postevent information on a prior memory representation. *Memory & Cognition, 21,* 267–279.

Rovee-Collier, C., & Capatides, J. B. (1979). Positive behavioral contrast in 3-month-old infants on multiple conjugate reinforcement schedules. *Journal of the Experimental Analysis of Behavior, 32,* 15–27.

Rovee-Collier, C., & DuFault, D. (1991). Multiple contexts and memory retrieval at 3 months. *Developmental Psychobiology, 24,* 39–49.

Rovee-Collier, C., Evancio, S., & Earley, L. A. (in press). The time window hypothesis: Spacing effects. *Infant Behavior and Development.*

Rovee-Collier, C., & Gekoski, M. J. (1979). The economics of infancy: A review of conjugate reinforcement. In H. W. Reese & L. P. Lipsitt (Eds.), *Advances in child development and research* (Vol. 13, pp. 195–255). New York: Academic Press.

Rovee-Collier, C., Greco-Vigorito, C., & Hayne, H. (1993). The time window hypothesis: Implications for categorization and memory modification. *Infant Behavior and Development, 16,* 149–176.

Rovee-Collier, C., Hankins, E., & Bhatt, R. (1992). Textons, visual pop-out effects, and object recognition in infancy. *Journal of Experimental Psychology: General, 121,* 436–446.

Rovee-Collier, C., & Hayne, H. (1987). Reactivation of infant memory: Implications for cognitive development. In H. W. Reese (Ed.), *Advances in child development and behavior* (Vol. 20, pp. 185–238). San Diego: Academic Press.

Rovee-Collier, C. K., Morrongiello, B. A., Aron, M., & Kupersmidt, J. (1978). Topographical response differentiation in three-month-old infants. *Infant Behavior and Development, 1,* 323–333.

Rovee-Collier, C., Schechter, A., Shyi, G. C.-W., & Shields P. (1992). Perceptual identification of contextual attributes and infant memory retrieval. *Developmental Psychology, 28,* 307–318.

Saayman, G., Ames, E. W., & Moffett, A. (1964). Response to novelty as an indicator of visual discrimination in the human infant. *Journal of Experimental Child Psychology, 1,* 189–198.

Sherman, T. (1985). Categorization skills in infants. *Child Development, 56,* 1561–1573.

Shields, P. J., & Rovee-Collier, C. (1992). Long-term memory for context-specific category information at 6 months. *Child Development, 63,* 245–259.

Shiffrin, R. M., & Murnane, K. (1991). Composition, distribution, and interference in memory. In W. E. Hockley & S. Lewandowsky (Eds.), *Relating theory and data: Essays on human memory in honor of Bennett B. Murdock* (pp. 445–476). Hillsdale, NJ: Erlbaum.

Siqueland, E. R. (1968a). Reinforcement patterns and extinction in human newborns. *Journal of Experimental Child Psychology, 6,* 431–432.

Siqueland, E. R. (1968b, March). *Visual reinforcement and exploratory behavior in infants.* Paper presented at the meeting of the Society for Research in Child Development, Worcester, MA.

Siqueland, E. R. (1969). *Further developments in infant learning.* Paper presented at the meeting of the 19th International Congress of Psychology, London.

Sokolov, E. N. (1963). *Perception and the conditioned reflex.* New York: Macmillan.

Spear, N. E. (1978). *The processing of memories: Forgetting and retention.* Hillsdale, NJ: Erlbaum.

Treisman, A. (1988). Features and objects: The fourteenth Bartlett memorial lecture. *Quarterly Journal of Experimental Psychology, 40A,* 201–237.

Tulving, E. (1972). Episodic and semantic memory. In E. Tulving & W. Donaldson (Eds.), *Organization of memory* (pp. 382–403). New York: Academic Press.

Tyrell, D. J., Snowman, L. G., Beier, J. A., & Blanck, C. M. (1990). Proactive interference in infant recognition memory. *Bulletin of the Psychonomic Society, 28,* 188–190.

Underwood, B. J. (1957). Interference and forgetting. *Psychological Review, 64,* 49–60.

Vander Linde, E., Morrongiello, B. A., & Rovee-Collier, C. (1985). Determinants of retention in 8-week-old infants. *Developmental Psychology, 21,* 601–613.

Werner, J. S.,& Perlmutter, M. (1979). Development of visual memory in infants. In H. W. Reese & L. P. Lipsitt (Eds.), *Advances in child development and behavior* (Vol. 14, pp. 2–56). New York: Academic Press.

Wolfe, J., Cave, K., & Franzel, S. (1989). Guided search: An alternative to the feature integration model for visual search. *Journal of Experimental Psychology: Human Perception and Performance, 15,* 419–433.

4

Interference Processes in Memory Development
The Case of Cognitive Triage

Charles J. Brainerd

A quarter of a century ago, the late W. F. Battig, M. Allen, and A. R. Jensen (1965; see also Battig, 1965) reported a remarkable finding about how words' memory strengths are related to their order of articulation during unconstrained recall. Whereas common sense and theories of retrieval forecast that words with stronger memory representations will come to mind before words with weaker representations, Battig et al.'s studies seemed to show the opposite. On free-recall tests, the mean output positions of words classified as weak were *earlier* than those of words classified as strong. This datum was made all the more puzzling by the fact that Battig et al. had used a highly sensitive empirical measure of strength, recall accuracy, that eliminated noise from intersubject variability in the strengths of individual words. This measure is also well correlated with standard normative indexes of words' memory strengths (e.g., concreteness, familiarity, meaningfulness).

Given their apparent conflict with fundamental theoretical ideas, it is hardly surprising that Battig et al.'s (1965) studies were challenged on various grounds. For instance, some investigators proposed that early retrieval of weak words might be a statistical artifact of serial position effects (e.g., Postman & Keppel, 1968). Ultimately, opinion coalesced around the notion that this finding was some quirk of the labyrinthine strategies that college students use during free recall (e.g., Roberts, 1969) and that it therefore was not probative with respect to the underlying relationship between memory strength and retrieval order. This resolved the conflict between theory and data, but only at the cost of trivializing the data. Naturally, such a resolution discouraged further investigation. Eventually, knowledge of Battig et al.'s studies passed out of the literature, with the last mention of them in a primary journal article occurring more than a decade ago (Friedman & Gildemeister, 1980).

Recently, my colleagues and I rediscovered Battig et al.'s (1965) finding in a series of developmental experiments (Brainerd, Olney, & Reyna, 1993; Brainerd, Reyna, Harnishfeger, & Howe, 1993; Brainerd, Reyna, & Howe, 1990; Brainerd, Reyna, Howe, & Kevershan, 1990, 1991). Actually, it would be more accurate to say that we observed a complex strength-ordering pattern in which Battig et al.'s result figured as a component effect. That pattern, which we call *cognitive triage* because of its resemblance to the battlefield surgical technique of treating the most difficult cases first, consists of five basic effects:

1. Weak Priority—When performance on Trial 1 or any subsequent precriterion trial is used to split words that are recalled on the *next* trial into high versus low strength (high = recalled, low = not recalled), the mean output positions of low-strength words are earlier than those of high-strength words. This is merely Battig et al.'s (1965) original result (Figure 1).

2. Nonmonotonic Emergence—When words recalled on any precriterion Trial i that comes after Trial 2 are assigned to *graded* strength categories on the basis of their complete performance history up to that point (strongest = $i - 1$ prior successes, next-strongest = $i - 2$ prior successes, . . . , weakest = 0 prior successes), a nonmonotonic weaker → stronger → weaker ordering emerges as trials proceed (Figure 2).

3. Criterion Nonmonotonicity—When *criterion* recall positions are plotted against graded experimental strength measures (total errors to criterion, trial number of the last error, etc.), the weaker → stronger → weaker sequence is again observed (Figure 3). Other nonmonotonic sequences have been observed in certain studies (e.g., Brainerd, 1990; Brainerd & Reyna, 1993), but they have been more complex concatenations of weaker → stronger → weaker (cf. below).

4. Intertrial Sharpening—Findings 1 and 2 tend to be more pronounced on later precriterion trials than on earlier ones.

5. Developmental Sharpening—Findings 1–3 become more marked as development proceeds, but all of them occur in children as young as age 6 (Figures 1–3).

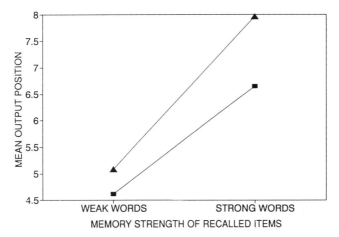

FIGURE 1. Relationship between output positions in free-recall queues and dichotomous memory-strength measures. Younger children, -■-; older children, -▲-. These plots are based on data reported in Brainerd, Olney, and Reyna (1993).

Although all of these findings are surprising, the last one is particularly informative because it challenges the "strategic quirk" explanation of Battig et al.'s (1965) studies. The developmental literature on recall contains extensive work on strategic development (for reviews, see Bjorklund, 1985; Bjorklund & Muir, 1988). According to this literature, age 6 is far below the level at which children spontaneously use mnemonics as simple as one-word re-

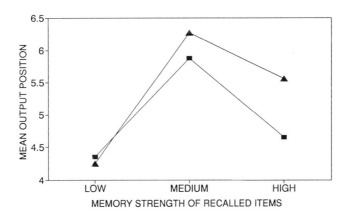

FIGURE 2. Relationship between output positions in free-recall queues and trichotomous memory-strength meaures. Younger children, -■-; older children, -▲-. These plots are based on data reported in Brainerd, Reyna, Howe, and Kevershan (1991).

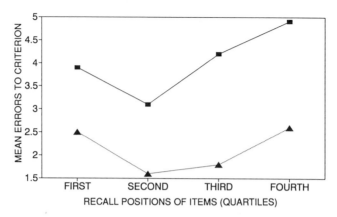

FIGURE 3. Relationship between output positions in criterion free-recall queues and continuous memory-strength measures. Younger children, ■; older children, ▲. These plots are based on data reported in Brainerd, Reyna, Howe, and Kevershan (1991).

hearsal. Such children appear to output words in whatever order they come to mind, which means that cognitive triage cannot be dismissed as a mere eccentricity of strategic intervention. On the contrary, the data seem to argue that it is a basic feature of retrieval throughout the life-span and, therefore, worthy of theoretical interpretation (Brainerd, Reyna, Howe, & Kevershan, 1990).

To date, there have been two basic lines of attack on the problem of how to interpret the triage pattern. The purpose of this chapter is to review them and to assess their relative credibility. One approach, the *distortion hypothesis,* assumes that stronger → weaker is the true underlying relationship, but that plotting output sequences as functions of recall accuracy measures somehow distorts its expression. Specific process models are then formulated that explain how Findings 1–5 could occur if the true relationship is stronger → weaker. Such models are examined in the first section below. The other approach, the *interference hypothesis,* accepts the triage pattern at face value as invalidating the stronger → weaker relationship and assumes that the observed relationships are due to interference processes that operate during output. Models are then formulated that show how these processes could deliver the component effects of the triage pattern. A model of this sort is reviewed in the second section below.

THE DISTORTION HYPOTHESIS

The initial objective of any theoretical interpretation of the triage pattern is to somehow reconcile its component effects with the stronger → weaker relationship favored by common sense and traditional conceptualizations of retrieval. It is prudent to begin with the hypothesis that this relationship is actually correct, but its expression is distorted when output order is plotted against accuracy measures in free-recall experiments. To date, four models that implement this working hypothesis (the serial-position model, the metamnemonic model, the strength-reordering model, and the continuation model) have been formulated and studied. I now explore these models, along with relevant experimental results.

The Serial-Position Model

The oldest and simplest account of why free-recall queues do not conform to the stronger → weaker ordering is that the expression of this ordering is distorted by *recency effects*. An unbuffered free-recall design was used in Battig et al.'s (1965) original experiments and in most other free-recall studies of that era. That is, the words on the target list were presented one at a time for study, and free recall began immediately after the final word had been studied. In such designs, the last few words studied on Trial i are recalled more accurately than other words (the recency effect), *and* they tend to be articulated at the start of recall. Postman and Keppel (1968) pointed out that, statistically, there must be a reverse recency effect for those same words on the immediately preceding trial (Trial $i - 1$), that is, recall of these same words must have been lower than average on the preceding trial.

Although this reverse recency effect may seem highly counterintuitive, the reason for it is easily seen by considering the orders in which words are presented during the study phases of Trials $i - 1$ and i. If recency effects are present, words recalled on Trial $i - 1$ will have been studied disproportionately at recency positions on that trial, and words that are not recalled will have been studied disproportionately at *non*recency positions. If performance on Trial $i - 1$ is then used to classify items as to memory strength (weak = not recalled, strong = recalled), words studied at recency positions will receive higher average strength classifications than words studied at nonrecency positions. Because presentation orders are randomized between trials, the average Trial i presentation position of Trial $i - 1$ recency words (high strength classifications) will *regress toward the mean,* while the average Trial i presentation position of Trial $i - 1$ nonrecency words (low strength classifications) will *increase toward the mean.* So, relative to words that were recalled on Trial $i - 1$, words that were not recalled and not studied at recency positions on Trial $i - 1$ have an increased probability of being studied at recency positions and being recalled on Trial i. Because, as mentioned, words studied at recency positions also tend to be output first during free recall, the initial words that subjects recall will have lower strength classifications than words that are recalled later. This is the weak priority effect (Figure 1).

Thus, unbuffered designs can make it appear as though weaker words are read out first, when in fact it is recency words that are read out first (regardless of their underlying memory strength). Some slight extensions of this analysis allow the other four components of the triage pattern to be explained. Concerning nonmonotonic emergence and criterion nonmonotonicity (Figures 2 and 3), suppose that after the initial burst of recency words, subjects switch to retrieving further words in a stronger → weaker direction. These two processes, a burst of recency words at the start followed by a stronger → weaker sequence yields an overall weaker → stronger → weaker ordering on precriterion and criterion tests, which explains nonmonotonic emergence and criterion nonmonotonicity. The remaining two components of the triage pattern, intertrial sharpening and developmental sharpening, can then be explained by merely assuming that these processes become more well established across trials and with age.

Although I have thus far confined attention to recency effects, note that parallel explanations of the triage pattern can be constructed using primacy effects. Specifically, if there are primacy effects (the first few words studied are recalled more accurately than other words) and if there is also a correlation between study positions and recall positions such that output consists of an initial burst of primacy items followed by a stronger → weaker sequence, then Findings 1–5 can be explained in the same manner as before.

Experimentally, the serial-position model makes straightforward predictions about the relationship between the presence–absence of primacy and recency effects and the presence–absence of the triage pattern. If, as the model supposes, the triage pattern is an artifact of recency or primacy effects, it must disappear when these effects are eliminated. This possibility was examined in Experiments 1–6 of Brainerd et al. (1991), where the free recall of 7- and 12-year-olds was studied using a buffered-recall procedure. Consistent with other findings in the literature (Bjorklund & Muir, 1988), interpolating an irrelevant buffer activity (30 sec of letter shadowing) between the study and test phases of each trial eliminated both primacy and recency effects in 7-year-olds. Nevertheless, these children exhibited weak priority, nonmonotonic emergence, and intertrial sharpening. (Criterion nonmonotonicity was not studied because the experiments were noncriterion designs.) In 12-year-olds, who also exhibited these three findings, the buffer activity eliminated recency effects but not primacy effects. Although primacy effects could therefore potentially explain these findings, we have seen that the explanation presumes that there is a correlation between presentation positions and output positions such that words occupying the first few output positions were presented for study at primacy positions. This was not the case. When rank-order correlations were computed between presentation positions and output positions on adjacent study and test cycles, the correlation coefficients ranged from −.02 to .05. Thus, these experiments failed to show that the triage pattern was due to serial-position effects in either younger or older children.

The Metamnemonic Model

To memory researchers, the notion that the triage pattern is somehow a by-product of metamnemonic activity is probably the explanation that comes most readily to mind. The assumption is that subjects understand, at an abstract level, that some of the target words have weaker memory representations than others and therefore will always be harder to recall. The errors that subjects make on free-recall tests are used to diagnose such words. On a given study cycle, the weak words that are easiest to identify are those that have most often produced recall failures in the past, particularly words for which recall has failed on the immediately preceding test. Because subjects understand that these words are difficult to recover from long-term memory, they retain some of them in short-term memory. It is these words that are read out at the start of the next test. Once short-term memory has been exhausted, subjects fall back to retrieving traces from long-term memory in a stronger → weaker order.

Thus, the metamnemonic model implies that the overall order of read-out during free recall is weaker → stronger → weaker, which explains both nonmonotonic emergence and criterion nonmonotonicity, although the order of readout from *long-term memory* is stronger → weaker. Weak priority is then explained as follows. If words recalled on Trial i are split into those that were and were not recalled on Trial $i - 1$, words in the latter category are far more likely to have been held in short-term memory (and read out at the start of the test) than to have been retrieved from long-term memory. Finally, intertrial sharpening is explained by assuming that metamnemonic control improves across trials, and developmental sharpening is explained by assuming that metamnemonic control and/or short-term memory capacity improves with age. (However, developmental studies of short-term memory argue against the capacity-increase assumption [see Bjorklund & Muir, 1988].)

The metamnemonic model suffers from both general implausibility and specific disconfirmations. The implausibility problem arises from the fact that the postulated form of metamnemonic insight is quite sophisticated. Although it might seem reasonable to attribute such insight to college students, it seems far fetched in the case of young children, who display only limited understanding of the most elementary metamnemonic principles (for a review, see Schneider & Pressley, 1989).

Direct disconfirmations of the metamnemonic model have come from two sources: buffered free-recall studies and strategy questionnaire studies. The former are pertinent to the metamnemonic model as well as to the serial-position model because of the assumption that weak words are intentionally held in short-term memory for immediate readout on the next test. If so, interpolating a short-term memory emptying buffer activity between study and test cycles should eliminate or drastically curtail the triage pattern. It does not. Several buffered recall experiments have been reported in which all five components of the triage pattern were obtained in children, adolescents, and adults (Brainerd, Reyna, & Howe, 1990; Brainerd, Reyna, Howe, & Kevershan, 1990). In questionnaire studies, I have administered instruments to large samples of college students that inquired about the strategies they implemented during free recall (Brainerd, 1989, 1990; Brainerd, Reyna, Howe, & Kevershan, 1990). College students seem to be unaware of the particular principle postulated in the metamnemonic model. They also state that they do not deliberately adopt output strategies that are based on the perceived difficulty of different words.

The Strength-Reordering Model

This model assumes that (1) recall order as observed in Trial i and recall accuracy as observed on earlier trials are *both* monotonically related to memory strength (i.e., the stronger → weaker relationship is correct), but that (2) learning events intervene between Trial $i - 1$ and Trial i such that the order measurements taken on the latter trial are nonmonotonic functions of the accuracy measurements taken on earlier trials (Brainerd, Reyna, & Howe, 1990). The events in question are selective increments in the memory strengths of weaker words that are induced by error priming.

Unlike the serial-positioning and metamnemonic models, this model does not treat the strength of a word's long-term memory representation as a functional invariant. Instead, it assumes that initial memory-strength orderings are shuffled repeatedly across trials. Error priming is the postulated shuffling mechanism. When words are not remembered on a free-recall test, their memory representations are assumed to be placed in states of high activation, which makes them particularly sensitive to the words' appearance on the next study trial. With some probability, the study trial generates special processing activity that converts such representations into the strongest traces in the target set. Because the strength-ordering relationship is stronger → weaker, these particular traces are retrieved first on the next recall test. Because recall *failures* initiate special processing, the strengths of initially weak traces (high failure rates) will be selectively enhanced, relative to the strengths of initially strong traces.

This scenario explains nonmonotonic emergence and criterion nonmonotonicity on the ground that error-driven special processing is imperfect; it produces selective strength increments in some weak traces but not in all. Thus, the model's interpretation of the weaker → stronger → weaker surface ordering is that words occupying early output positions correspond to *initially* weak traces that have been transformed by special processing, whereas words occupying intermediate and terminal output positions correspond to initially strong and weak traces, respectively, whose positions on the strength dimension have not been permuted by special processing. Weak priority, intertrial sharpening, and developmental sharpening are then explained by adding three further assumptions. First, concerning weak priority, special processing is assumed to succeed more often than it fails, which means that the traces of most of the items recalled on Trial i that were not recalled on Trial $i - 1$ will have been converted to the strongest ones in the target set. Second, concerning intertrial sharpening, it is assumed that, as trials accumulate, special processing becomes more effective at enhancing memory strength. Third, concerning developmental sharpening, it is assumed that special processing also becomes more effective as development proceeds. In the latter connection there is, of course, ample evidence of age improvements in mnemonics that might be used for special processing (e.g., Baker-Ward, Ornstein, & Holden, 1984; Ornstein, Baker-Ward, & Naus, 1988).

Like the metamnemonic model, the strength-reordering model suffers from both general implausibility and specific disconfirmations. Regarding implausibility, the memory representations that determine the initial strength orderings of words in free-recall experiments are based on literally thousands of prior episodic contacts. It seems improbable that the few additional contacts that occur during the course of an experiment could affect these representations sufficiently to permute their strength orderings. Some experiments by Dagenbach, Horst, and Carr (1990) bear directly on this point. Dagenbach et al. studied the amount of episodic contact, in the sense of numbers of study opportunities and experimental sessions, that was necessary to produce changes in the memory representations of familiar and unfamiliar words. Their basic procedure was to present words for study together with new episodic information about those words (e.g., definitions). They found that five weeks of spaced experimental sessions were required before there was any evidence that new episodic information had been incorporated into words' memory representations.

Turning to direct experimental tests, the strength-reordering model makes predictions about (1) the relationship between words' output positions at criterion and words' subsequent forgetting rates and about (2) recall accuracy for primed versus unprimed words *following* error priming. Concerning (1), Brainerd, Reyna, and Howe (1990) noted that because performance is errorless on a criterion free-recall test, the output sequence on such a test is necessarily a *final ordering* of words with respect to memory strength. If the strength-reordering model is correct in claiming that this ordering is stronger → weaker, subsequent forgetting should be a monotonic-increasing function of criterion output position. That is, under the standard assumption that forgetting rates are higher for words with weaker memory representations than for words with stronger representations (e.g., Brainerd, Reyna, Howe, & Kingma, 1990), forgetting rates should increase as words' criterion recall positions increase. This is not what Brainerd, Reyna, and Howe (1990) found, however. In experiments with children and adolescents, they observed a nonmonotonic higher → lower → higher relationship between words' criterion recall positions and their forgetting rates across a two-week retention interval: words that were recalled at the initial and terminal positions on criterion trials of acquisition sessions were retained more poorly across two weeks than words that were recalled at intermediate positions (see Figure 4).

Concerning Prediction (2), the strength-reordering model postulates that error-driven special processing selectively enhances the strengths of unrecalled items; failing to recall a word makes that word especially likely to have its memory representation converted into one of the strongest ones on the next study trial. If so, then once error priming has occurred, primed words should be easier to recall than unprimed words. More explicitly, if words recalled on Trial i are split into those that were and were not primed on Trial $i - 1$, the former should produce better recall on subsequent trials. Brainerd, Olney, and Reyna (1993) investigated this prediction in a series of trial-by-trial analyses. Using data from criterion free-recall experiments with children and adolescents, they classified words as primed or unprimed on a given free-recall test, accordingly as an error or a success occurred on that test. Next, they plotted recall accuracy on subsequent trials as a function of words' priming status. The results are shown in Figure 5. In Figure 5A, recall accuracy from Trial 3 onward is shown for words classified on the basis of Trial 1 recall. In Figure 5B, recall accuracy from Trial 4 onward is shown for words classified on the basis of Trial 2 recall. It can be seen that, contrary to the strength-reordering model, recall was poorer for primed than for unprimed words at both age levels.

Brainerd, Olney, and Reyna (1993) also conducted a series of supplementary analyses that were designed to determine whether error priming pro-

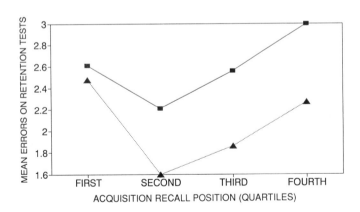

FIGURE 4. Relationship between output positions in criterion free-recall queues and recall accuracy on two-week retention tests. Younger children, ■; older children, ▲. These plots are based on data reported in Brainerd, Reyna, and Howe (1990).

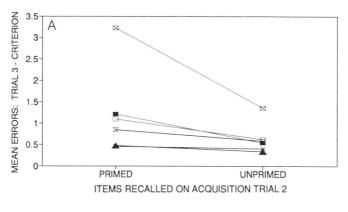

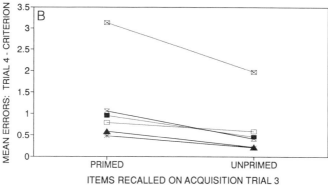

FIGURE 5. (A) Recall accuracy on Trial 3—criterion as a function of error priming on Trial 1, and (B) recall accuracy on Trial 4—criterion as a function of error priming on Trial 2. Younger 12 items, -■-; younger 16 items, -□-; younger 24 items, -⊠-; older 12 items, -▲-; older 16 items, -✳-; older 24 items, -⊗-. These plots are based on data reported in Brainerd, Olney, and Reyna, (1993).

duced any improvement at all in memory strength—improvements that were too small to premute words' initial memory-strength orders but were nevertheless detectable. They found no evidence of such improvements. Finally, they reported a developmental study that was designed to determine whether *experimentally induced* special processing of weak words could produce results that were consistent with the strength-reordering model. The manipulation was selective rehearsal of weak items. Children in a control condition received three standard free-recall trials on a list of 16 nouns. For children in a selective rehearsal condition, the procedure was different on Trials 2 and 3. During the study phase of Trial 2, words that had not been recalled on Trial 1 were presented with a thick line underneath them, whereas words that had been recalled were presented as before. The children were told that underlined words had not been recalled on Trial 1, and that each of these words should be rehearsed aloud as many times as possible when it was presented for study. The children were also told not to rehearse words that were not underlined, and compliance with these selective rehearsal instructions was monitored. The same procedure was followed on Trial 3. The magnitude of the weak priority effect was then examined for the experimental and control groups. If the strength-reordering model is correct, the weak priority effect should be larger in the experimental group because these children engaged in the sorts of activities that the model says are responsible for the effect. As can be seen in Figure 6, however, the reverse was true: selective rehearsal of weak words reduced rather than amplified the weak priority effect.

The Continuation Model

This last distortion explanation was proposed by Brainerd, Reyna, et al. (1993), although they did not test it. The continuation model assumes, first, that the order in which words are recalled on the *first trial* of a free-recall experiment is stronger → weaker. On Trial 2, however, the output sequence is not reset to stronger → weaker at the start of a free-recall test. Instead, the tail end of the stronger → weaker sequence from Trial 1 is carried over to the start of the next test, which is where the term "continuation" comes from. On Trial 1, then, the subject recalls as many words as possible from the target list following a stronger → weaker ordering. Some words will normally not be recalled, and they will be from the weak end of this ordering. When no more words can be recalled, the study phase of Trial 2 ensues. After all the words have

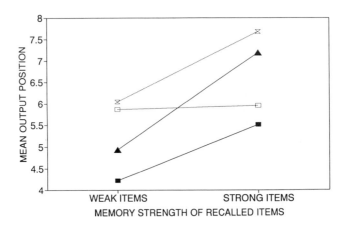

FIGURE 6. Variations in the weak priority effect as a function of selective rehearsal of weak words. Younger control, –■–; older control, –▲–; younger rehearsal, –□–; older rehearsal, –⊠–.

been restudied, the test phase is initiated. At this point, free recall simply picks up where it left off at the end of Trial 1. That is, Trial 2 recall begins with the remaining weak words that could not be remembered on Trial 1. When as many of those words have been recalled as possible, the Trial 2 output sequence is reset to stronger → weaker. It is assumed that this procedure is followed on subsequent trials.

The continuation model explains the component effects of the triage pattern as follows. To begin with, the assumption that the output sequence from Trial 2 onward is weaker → (reset ordering) → stronger → weaker obviously implies that both nonmonotonic emergence and criterion nonmonotonicity will be observed when recall orders are plotted against graded measures of recall accuracy. It also implies weak priority if one adds the assumption that a majority of the unrecalled words from Trial $i - 1$ will be articulated at the start of Trial i. Finally, intertrial sharpening and developmental sharpening can be explained by assuming that the tendency for recall orderings to be continued from the end of one trial to the start of the next increases across trials and with age.

Since no data on the continuation model have been previously reported, I conducted two experiments that were designed to test it. Experiment 1 was a developmental free-recall study in which a mixed sample of first and second graders ($N = 48$, mean age = 6 years, 11 months) and a sample of sixth graders ($N = 48$, mean age = 11 years, 9 months) were administered a list of 18 familiar concrete nouns (e.g., STAR, BOOK, TABLE) that had been drawn from the Paivio, Yuille, and Madigan (1968) norms. Experiment 2 was also a developmental free-recall study in which a sample of second graders ($N = 30$, mean age = 7 years, 8 months) and a sample of sixth graders ($N = 30$, mean age = 12 years, 2 months) were administered a list of 20 line drawings of familiar objects.

Both of these experiments used Estes (1960) type RTT designs. Specifically, each child studied the list once (R), then performed a 30-s buffer activity (letter shadowing), then performed an initial free-recall test (T_1), then performed 30 s more of the same buffer activity, and then performed a final free-recall test (T_2). In such designs, reminiscence occurs between T_1 and T_2, especially when lists are composed of pictures or concrete nouns (Payne, 1987). That is, some of the items that are recalled on T_2 will not have been recalled on T_1. The continuation model makes a clear prediction about the output positions of these reminisced items. If it is true that the T_1 sequence is stronger → weaker, items that are not recalled on T_1 are the weakest ones on the list, by definition. If recall picks up at this point on T_2, it is obvious that any newly remembered (reminisced) items should be articulated at the start of T_2. To evaluate this prediction, each item recalled on T_2 was classified in terms of whether or not it had been recalled on T_1, and the mean recall positions of reminisced and nonreminisced items on T_2 were then calculated. The results for each experiment are plotted separately by age level in Figure 7.

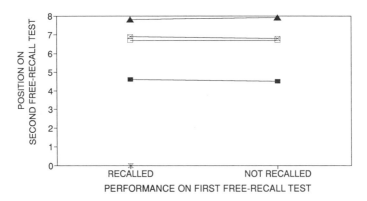

FIGURE 7. Words' recall positions on the second of two free-recall tests as a function of whether the words were recalled (reminisced items) or not recalled (nonreminisced items) on the first test. Younger words, -■-; older words, -□-; younger pix, -⊠-; older pix, -▲-.

There, it can be seen that there was no support for the continuation model's prediction. In all instances, the mean recall positions of reminisced and nonreminisced words were virtually identical.

Some data reported by Brainerd, Olney, and Reyna (1993) disconfirm another prediction of the continuation model. As we have seen, the model assumes that the output sequence on the first free-recall test is stronger → weaker. If so, there should be a monotonic relationship between words' output positions on Trial 1 and the accuracy of their recall on subsequent trials. Specifically, words that occupy initial output positions, because they are the strongest ones on the list, should exhibit higher levels of accuracy on subsequent trials than words that occupy later output positions. To evaluate this prediction, Brainerd, Olney, and Reyna plotted recall accuracy from Trial 2 onward as a function of output position on Trial 1 in the same developmental studies on which the plots in Figures 5 and 6 are based. Contrary to the continuation model, there was not a tendency for the words that children recalled at the start of Trial 1 to have lower subsequent error rates.

THE INTERFERENCE HYPOTHESIS

Encapsulating the discussion so far, the component effects of the triage pattern conflict with the hoary notion that as information is accessed during unconstrained recall, access proceeds in a stronger → weaker direction. Some plausible models have been devised that attempt to preserve this notion by assuming that the expression of the stronger → weaker sequence is distorted when output orders are plotted against on-line accuracy measures. As we have seen, however, these distortion models have not fared well in experimentation because, when tested, their key predictions have not received support. This has made the distortion approach seem far less compelling as a working hypothesis. It has also encouraged the more radical hypothesis that stored information may not be retrieved in a stronger → weaker direction, at least not during free recall.

The optimization model of fuzzy-trace theory (Brainerd et al., 1991; Harnishfeger & Brainerd, 1994) implements this latter hypothesis. I consider the optimization model in the present section. Its basic assumptions and account of the triage pattern are examined first. Next, I review experimental evidence that bears on some of its predictions.

The Optimization Model

The optimization model, like many theories, treats a word's memory strength as a composite property of features of its long-term memory representation. On one hand, the model makes the traditional assumption that memory strength is the chief determinant of a word's *overall* accuracy of recall; words with stronger representations will tend to be accessed more often *on average* than words with weaker representations. On the other hand, the model emphasizes that memory strength is not the sole determinant of accuracy on a given free-recall test; on such a test, the subject's task is to read out as many of the target words as possible, *regardless of their strength.* Just recalling the words with the strongest memory representations is not good enough.

From the subject's standpoint, then, it is essential to structure output so that even the weakest words can be accessed. The optimization model assumes that in order to do this, recall must accommodate the fact that articulating a series of words is a dynamic process in which a word's memory strength is modulated by at least two response-produced variables, one that facilitates the recall of further words *(episodic activation)* and one that inhibits the recall of further words *(output interference).* Since weaker words ought to be more sensitive than stronger ones to accumulated output interference, the objective of maximizing total recall, as opposed to recalling any particular word, can be more closely approximated by accessing weaker words whenever interference levels are low. This is a basic tenet of the optimization model. Because they have opposite effects on accuracy and because they fluctuate differently during a free-recall test, episodic activation and output interference jointly affect the relationship between memory strength and words' positions in output queues. This is another basic tenet of the model.

Episodic activation refers to the familiar idea that words' long-term memory representations form contextual connections during a free-recall experiment, and that retrieving a trace activates this episodic network, which in turn facilitates the retrieval of other traces in the network. On the hypothesis that stronger traces form richer episodic connections than weaker ones, retrieving a stronger trace releases more activation than retrieving a weaker one. So, the activation level at any point in an output sequence is controlled by the recent history of that sequence: it will be lower at the start than after the first few words have been recalled, and it will grow more slowly when weaker words are recalled than when stronger words are recalled. Moreover, since episodic activation is a response-produced process, the optimization model assumes that activation levels fall if they are not refreshed by the retrieval of additional traces.

Output interference refers to another familiar idea: the operations that access traces and pass them through motor control programs to produce articulation generate off-task noise that inhibits subsequent retrieval (Dempster, 1992; Hadley, Healy, & Murdock, 1992; Hasher & Zacks, 1988; Howe & Rabinowitz, 1989). Thus, output interference is a form of proactive inhibition inasmuch as current retrieval activities have consequences that redound to the detriment of subsequent retrieval (see also Dempster, Chapter 1, this volume). Specific examples of such consequences include *scheduling noise* from queuing up parallel memory representations for serial readout and *feedback noise* from forced recoding of item-specific information that has already been retrieved, read out, and is therefore irrelevant to subsequent recall (Brainerd & Reyna, 1989; Hadley et al., 1992; Reyna & Brainerd, 1989). According to the optimization model, the inhibitory effects of output interference vary inversely with words' memory strengths: although it is harder to access any trace when interference is high than when it is low, this is especially true for weaker traces, which means that they will tend to be retrieved when interference is low.

The model also assumes that output interference subsidies as episodic activation grows, so that the interference level will be lower following the retrieval of a series of stronger traces than following the retrieval of a series of weaker traces. Hence, there are multiple points in a free-recall sequence when interference should be minimal and access to weak traces should be less problematical, namely, at the start, before interference has begun to accumulate, and later on, following the retrieval of a series of strong traces. It should be noted, however, that the idea that interference recedes as episodic activation grows differs from the traditional belief that interference simply increases as more items are recalled from a target list. Continuing the proactive inhibition analogy, this idea is a *within-list* analogue of release from proactive inhibition. Traditionally, release from proactive inhibition has been a *between-list* concept, being defined as reductions in accumulated interference that occur after several lists of a particular type (e.g., animal names) have been recalled (e.g., Crowder, 1976; Wixted & Rohrer, 1993). However, a number of recent findings (e.g., Hadley et al., 1992; Hasher & Zacks, 1988) suggest that retrieval of certain types of items immediately reduces accumulated interference. (See Harnishfeger, Chapter 6, this volume for a related perspective on the development of retrieval inhibition in the directed-forgetting paradigm.) This suggestion has been adopted in the optimization model.

Summing up, from the perspective of maximizing output, the optimum strength-ordering relationship might be to begin by recalling some weaker words, then to rotate in progressively stronger words as interference builds, and to return to weaker words whenever interference recedes. If so, the optimization model has no difficulty accounting for nonmonotonic emergence and criterion nonmonotonicity. In both cases, output begins with some weak words because interference has not yet begun to accumulate, switches to stronger words as interference builds, and then switches back to weaker words when interference subsides. (The model also has no difficulty accounting for more complex nonmonotonic sequences because interference levels might be characterized by multiple build/recede cycles.) This explanation of nonmonotonic emergence and criterion nonmonotonicity suggests a previously unsuspected difficulty with the traditional stronger → weaker ordering. Reading words out in that order would cause episodic activation to grow rapidly at first (as stronger items are recalled) and then to recede (as weaker items are recalled). It would therefore also cause output interference to increase steadily throughout a free-recall test, rather than first increasing and then receding. At the end of a test, when the most interference-sensitive words remain to be retrieved, the system would occupy a state of high interference and low episodic activation.

A remaining theoretical problem is to identify a specific mechanism whereby words' memory strengths can be diagnosed with sufficient precision to balance the opposing influences of episodic activation and output interference during recall. It would be desirable if the mechanism relied on some objective, on-line form of information that (1) is relatively easy for subjects of all ages to discriminate and retain without the necessity of complex metamnemonic understanding and that (2) is a reliable predictor of underlying memory strength. Error–success feedback is just such an information source. Concerning (1), frequency memory, which has been demonstrated in infants and young children (Hasher & Zacks, 1979, 1984), can be exploited to store such information. As study-test cycles accumulate, so do error–success counts for individual words. Such counts are a form of information that is incidentally retained by both adults (Ekstrand, Wallace, & Underwood, 1966) and children (Brainerd et al., 1991), that is, subjects deposit such information although they are not instructed to do so. Concerning (2), because overall accuracy is monotonically related to memory strength, differentiating words in terms of their error–success histories is tantamount to differentiating them in terms of their memory strengths. Further, reliance on error–success frequencies allows memory-strength discriminations to become more precise as trials go by because the two events accumulate differentially as a function of strength.

Using error–success frequencies to order output queues explains developmental sharpening, intertrial sharpening, and weak priority. Regarding development, although error–success frequencies are retained at an early age, the ability to use such information on memory tests improves throughout childhood and adolescence (e.g., Ghatala & Levin, 1976; Marx, 1986). Regarding intertrial sharpening, the ability to use such information also improves across the trials of a memory experiment (e.g., Ekstrand et al., 1966; Estes, 1976). Regarding weak priority, at the start of a free-recall test, when it is crucial to begin with weaker items, the error–success counts that will be most salient are those that accumulated on the immediately preceding trial. Also, of the two types of events, errors are known to be memorially more distinctive than successes (e.g., Halff, 1977). Therefore, if frequency counts are processed to shape recall order in the direction of maximum output, Trial i recall is likely to begin by accessing some of the traces that could not be retrieved on Trial $i - 1$ because those traces were flagged with highly salient error information. Statistically, we know that such items will also tend to have produced errors before Trial $i - 1$, which means that they are among the weakest ones on the list. For this reason, it will be especially difficult to return to recalling *these particular items* later, after output interference has accumulated; that is, if an item from this group is not read out at the start of a test, it is unlikely to be recalled at all. Hence, if items recalled on Trial i are split into those that were and were not recalled on Trial $i - 1$, the latter will have earlier mean output positions, that is, weak priority.

Last, it is interesting to note that it is possible to use error–success feedback in this same manner outside the laboratory (Brainerd et al., 1991), which may explain why subjects rely on it in free-recall experiments. Responses to inquiries about autobiographical events are one of the most common examples of unconstrained recall in the everyday lives of children and adults. (Where did you go on your class trip? What did you do at grandma's? Who came to the birthday party?) These responses are often followed by error–success feedback if interrogators have knowledge of those events. (Didn't you go to the park, too? Didn't you bake cookies, too? Weren't Amanda and Evan there, too?) Obviously, given our vast funds of everyday experience with such feedback, one could learn to use it to structure autobiographical retrieval so as to enhance the numbers of events that are accessed.

Experimental Evidence

To date, experimentation on the optimization model has concentrated on predictions in four areas: (1) adaptiveness of triage, (2) triage-accuracy asymmetries, (3) effects of semantic relatedness, and (4) effects of preexperimental memory strength.

Adaptiveness of Triage   The model's most obvious predictions are that cognitive triage is good for recall (hence, the term "optimization") and that the strength of this relationship should increase with age. That is, recall, in the sense of total output, ought to be better when it conforms to this pattern than when it does not, and this connection should become more apparent as development proceeds. Although these predictions are central to the optimization model, it should be noted that they are not unique to it. For instance, two of the distortion models, the metamnemonic model and the strength-reordering model, imply that the triage pattern is a by-product of processes that redound to the benefit of accuracy and, hence, that age improvements in accuracy should be tied to age improvements in those processes.

To investigate triage-accuracy relationships, a measurement problem must first be solved. If the aim is to determine whether following the triage pattern enhances recall, goodness of triage must somehow be measured independently of recall accuracy; achieving a certain goodness-of-triage level must not depend on achieving a certain recall-accuracy level. Brainerd, Reyna et al. (1993) showed that an appropriate measure, actually a family of measures, can be secured by focusing on the degree of *strength grouping* in output queues. I briefly describe their measure before summarizing the results of experiments in which it has been used to study triage-accuracy relationships.

Scoring Free-Recall Protocols for Strength Grouping   Empirically, cognitive triage is just a tendency for words of similar memory strength to show up at adjacent positions in output queues. Thus, recall of a low-strength word is apt to occur in proximity to recall of other low-strength words, and recall of a high-strength word is apt to occur in proximity to recall of other high-strength words. So, to have face validity, a goodness-of-triage index should tells us *how tightly the words in an output queue are packed with respect to memory strength*. The tighter the packing, the higher the triage level. It is easy to see that this problem is isomorphic with the problem of how to measure levels of taxonomic clustering in free recall. With clustering, we seek to measure the degree to which output queues are organized into bursts of same-category words, and various statistics have been devised that assess taxonomic clustering independently of recall accuracy (e.g., Roenker, Thompson, & Brown, 1971).

Thanks to the isomorphism between measuring strength grouping and measuring taxonomic clustering, clustering statistics can be applied to the study of triage-accuracy relationships. It is only necessary to classify each word that is read out on a recall test as belonging to a *memory-strength* category rather than to a taxonomic category. Then, clustering statistics give the degree of strength grouping in an output sequence rather than the degree of taxonomic clustering. On trials after Trial 1, strength categories are generated in the normal way using words' error–success histories (i.e., strongest words = no previous errors, next-strongest words = 1 previous error, . . . , weakest words = $i - 1$ prior errors). If i is any precriterion trial after Trial 1, at least two strength categories must be available: *strong* (success on the preceding test) and *weak* (error on the preceding test). From a statistical point of view, this two-category scheme is the easiest method of strength classification because the number of categories is constant. It also takes advantage of the fact that the error–success frequency counts that accumulate on the immediately preceding trial will be more salient than those that accumulated on earlier trials.

The two-category scheme also allows one to compute strength-grouping scores separately for strong and weak words. This is an important proviso because the optimization model expects certain differences in the behavior of the two types of scores, as well as differences in their abilities to predict accuracy (see Brainerd, Reyna et al., 1993; Harnishfeger & Brainerd, 1994). To begin with, the nonmonotonic emergence and criterion nonmonotonicity effects both entail that strength grouping will be tighter for strong words than for weak words. Here, remember that strong words tend to be read out in a single cluster in the middle of a queue, and weak words tend to be read out in two clusters (at the beginning and the end). Second, experimentation (e.g., Brainerd, Reyna, Howe, & Kevershan, 1991) has shown that the latter tendency increases across the trials of a free-recall experiment, which means that strength grouping will *decrease* across trials for weak words but will increase for strong words. For these two reasons, one's goodness-of-triage measure must be sensitive to differences in the levels of strength grouping for strong versus weak words.

This rules out most standard clustering statistics because they measure only average amounts of clustering for all the taxonomic categories that are included in a list, rather than measuring it separately for individual categories. However, Brainerd, Reyna et al. (1993) noted that one standard statistic, Bousefield's (1953) ratio of repetition, measures clustering separately by taxonomic category and, hence, can be used to derive separate estimates of strength grouping for strong and weak words. They provided a worked example, which is reproduced in Table 1, of various combinations of ratios of repetition for a free-recall protocol in which 14 words were recalled, with 8

TABLE 1. Retrievability-Grouping Scores for Illustrative Free-Recall Protocols Calculated via Bousefield's (1953) Ratio of Repetition

Output sequences[a]	RR_E score	RR_H score
HHHEEEEEEEEEHHH	1.00	.80
HHEEEEEHEEHHEEH	.71	.40
EHHEEEHEHEHHEE	.43	.40
HEEHEHEEHEHEHE	.19	.00

[a]E = Easy word (recalled on previous trial); H = hard word (not recalled on previous trial).

being classified as "strong" (success on the previous trial) and 6 classified as "weak" (error on the previous trial).

Data   The ratio-of-repetition measure has been used to study triage-accuracy relationships in six experiments, five reported by Brainerd, Reyna et al. (1993) and one reported by Harnishfeger and Brainerd (1994). In Experiments 1 and 2 of Brainerd, Reyna et al. (1993), children of two age levels (7- and 11-years-olds) were administered six buffered free-recall trials using a list of 14 familiar nouns (Experiment 1), or 18 familiar nouns (Experiment 2, half the subjects) or 24 familiar nouns (Experiment 2, half the subjects). On Trials 2–6, each word that a child recalled was classified as either strong or weak accordingly as it was or was not recalled on the preceding trial. Ratio-of-repetition scores were then calculated to measure the level of strength grouping in each protocol. To measure triage-accuracy relationships, these scores were correlated with the total number of words recalled in each protocol. Averaging across trials, the mean triage-accuracy correlations for 7-year-olds were .35 (Experiment 1), .30 (Experiment 2, 18 words), and .29 (Experiment 2, 24 words). The corresponding values for 11-year-olds were .57, .44, and .43. All six correlations were reliable at or beyond the .05 level, and for each list length r-to-z transformations showed that the correlation for 11-year-olds was significantly larger than that for 7-year-olds. So, consistent with the optimization model, greater strength grouping meant better recall, in both younger and older children, and the relationship became more marked with age.

In Experiment 3 of this same article, college students were administered six buffered free-recall trials on a list composed of 16 familiar nouns. The same triage-accuracy analyses were conducted as in the two developmental studies, and the results were comparable. Across trials, the mean correlation between strength-grouping scores and recall accuracy was .49.

Triage-accuracy relationships were also investigated in the presence of certain list-difficulty manipulations in Experiments 4 and 5 of Brainerd, Reyna et al. (1993) and in Experiment 2 of Harnishfeger and Brainerd (1994). In the former case, buffered free-recall trials were administered to either 7- and 11-year-olds (Experiment 4) or to college students (Experiment 5) using lists composed of half easy words (familiar nouns or high-meaningfulness nouns) and half hard words (unfamiliar nouns or low-meaningfulness nouns). In the latter case, 7- and 11-year-olds were administered buffered free-recall trials using either lists of unrelated nouns (half the subjects) or lists of categorized nouns (half the subjects). The results were similar to those reported above. For 7-year-olds, the mean triage-accuracy correlations across trials were .28 (easy/hard lists), .27 (unrelated lists), and .39 (categorized lists). For 11-year-olds, the corresponding values were .41, .51, and .51. For college students, the mean triage-accuracy correlation was .56 with easy/hard lists. All of these correlations were reliable. In addition, each of the 7-year-old correlations was significantly smaller than the corresponding 11-year-old correlation.

Summing up, available evidence supports two obvious predictions that the optimization model makes about triage-accuracy relationships. First, higher levels of triage, as measured by strength-grouping scores, have been found to be associated with more accurate recall from early childhood through early adulthood. Second, this relationship has been found to develop with age. It appears to be weaker in younger children, where the average correlation for all the aforementioned data sets (.31) accounts for only 10% of the variation, than it is in older children, where the average correlation for these same data sets (.48) accounts for 23% of the variation.

Triage-Accuracy Asymmetries   Although the predictions examined above are fundamental to the optimization model, we saw that they are not unique to it. There are some additional proposals about triage-accuracy relationships, however, that do not follow from any of the distortion models. Those predictions are considered in the present section.

The proposals in question are concerned with potential variation in the magnitude of triage-accuracy relationships as a function of whether the two variables are measured on the *same* trial, as in the aforementioned results, or on *different* trials. These predictions violate a powerful intuition that researchers have about how simultaneity of measurement influences statistical relationships between variables. When two variables, X and Y, are measured, our intuition tells us that these measurements are more apt to be statistically related if they are taken concurrently (e.g., on the same trial of an experiment) rather than nonconcurrently (e.g., on different trials of an experiment). This statement seems ineluctable if the XY relationship is causal: if X causes Y, it is not more likely that X and Y will be found to be related if X is measured at the precise time when it is causing Y than if it is measured at some earlier or later time when it is not causing Y?

Oddly enough, the optimization model says that the answer is no for triage-accuracy relationships, and this leads to surprising predictions about the relative magnitudes of three instances of this relationship: *simultaneous* (strength grouping and accuracy measured on the same trial), *forward* (strength grouping measured on earlier trials and accuracy measured on later trials), and *backward* (strength grouping measured on later trials and accuracy measured on earlier trials). The intuitive ordering would be that simultaneous relationships should be strongest and that forward relationships should be stronger than backward relationships. However, the optimization model expects that backward relationships will be strongest, though it concurs that simultaneous relationships should be stronger than forward relationships.

The reason is that according to the model, Trial $i - 1$ accuracy exerts more direct control over Trial i strength grouping (backward triage-accuracy relationships) than Trial i strength grouping exerts over Trial i accuracy (simultaneous triage-accuracy relationships). Concerning simultaneous relationships, although strength grouping ought to translate into better recall on any trial, this is not the only factor influencing accuracy, nor is it the most important one. On the contrary, the triage pattern is viewed as the surface expression of the modulation of memory strength by on-line factors. Memory strength itself is still the most important determinant of accuracy. Concerning backward relationships, on the other hand, Trial $i - 1$ accuracy is the most important determinant of Trial i strength grouping. There are two reasons. First, at a general level, error–success counts from earlier trials, especially the immediately preceding trial, supply the informational basis for strength grouping; the cause–effect path is much more direct than it is for simultaneous relationships. Second, at a more specific level, a familiar property of frequency memory provides a direct link between Trial $i - 1$ accuracy and Trial i memory-strength ordering, namely, event frequencies are more easily discriminated if the numbers of events occupying different frequency categories are numerically unbalanced. In paradigms such as verbal discrimination learning, where the task is to respond differentially to events on the basis of their prior frequency counts, performance is better if the number of events for which different frequency counts accumulate are unequal, for example, if the number of events for which "win" outcomes accumulate is larger (or smaller) than the number of events for which "loss" outcomes accumulate. Thus, if error–success frequencies supply the informational basis for structuring output queues, prior accuracy levels will directly control subsequent levels of strength grouping: as more words from the target list are recalled, the numbers of words in the "success" and "error" categories become more unbalanced *and therefore more discriminable,* which means that higher levels of accuracy on Trial $i - 1$ (and, to a lesser extent, on earlier trials) directly affect the memorability of the error–success inputs to Trial i strength grouping.

Last, forward triage-accuracy relationships should be weaker than either backward or simultaneous relationships. If strength grouping is measured on Trial $i - 1$ and accuracy is measured on Trial i, there would be no direct cause–effect relationship between the two variables under the model. The magnitude of the observed covariation between them would then depend on (and will have as its upper bound) the relationship between strength groupings on consecutive trials. For convenience of reference, the optimization model's proposals about the ordering of simultaneous, forward, and backward relationships are summarized geometrically in Figure 8. In this parallel-

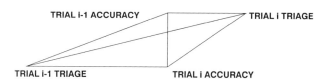

FIGURE 8. Geometric representation of variations in the strengths of triage-accuracy relationships as predicted by the optimization model.

ogram, the strengths of relationships are represented as line distances—the shorter the line, the stronger the relationship. In addition to preserving the backward > simultaneous > forward ordering, this figure builds in a strong relationship between accuracy on adjacent trials because, naturally, the numbers of words recalled on adjacent trials are highly correlated (e.g., Mazur & Hastie, 1978).

The relative magnitudes of forward, backward, and simultaneous triage-accuracy relationships were examined in the five experiments reported by Brainerd, Reyna et al. (1993). The results were consistent with the counterintuitive ordering forecast by the optimization model. In the three developmental studies, four types of triage-accuracy correlations were computed: (1) simultaneous, (2) one step forward (strength grouping measured on Trial $i - 1$ and accuracy measured on Trial i), (3) one step backward (strength grouping measured on Trial i and accuracy measured on Trial $i - 1$), and (4) two steps backward (strength grouping measured on Trial i and accuracy measured on Trial i–2). The pooled results are displayed separately by age level at the top of Figure 9. For younger children, it can be seen that the average one step backward relationship (.47) was indeed larger than the average simultaneous relationship (.31), which was in turn larger than the average one step forward relationship (.10) but the same as the average two steps backward relationship (.31). The forward relationship was not reliable. For older children, the average one step backward relationship (.64) was also larger than the average

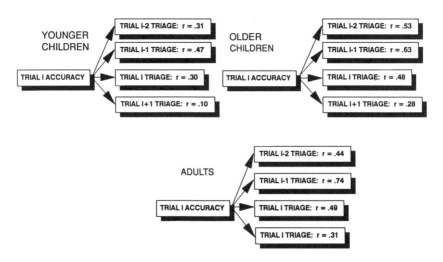

FIGURE 9. Average simultaneous, one step forward, one step backward, and two steps backward triage-accuracy correlations for younger children, older children, and adults. These values are for the pooled data of the five experiments reported by Brainerd, Reyna, Harnishfeger, and Howe (1993).

simultaneous relationship (.48), which was in turn larger than the average one step forward relationship (.26) and approximately the same size as the average two steps backward relationship (.53). The simultaneous, one step backward, and two steps backward relationships were all significantly larger in older children than in younger children. Finally, the pooled results for the two experiments with college studies appear at the bottom of Figure 9. There, it can be seen that the magnitude ordering of forward, backward, and simultaneous relationships was the same as in the developmental studies.

Effects of Semantic Relatedness   Up to this point, I have reviewed results that bear on the optimization model's predictions about triage-accuracy relationships. In the experiments that produced those results, as well as the prior literature on cognitive triage, children or adults were adminstered lists of unrelated words under standard free-recall conditions. I now consider the question of how the triage pattern might be influenced by the introduction of semantic relationships between list items.

Generally speaking, the optimization model expects that the pattern should be less pronounced when list items are semantically related. Remember that, according to the model, triage effects are by-products of the interplay between episodic activation levels and output interference levels; high levels of episodic activation tend to dispel accumulated interference and encourage the retrieval of weaker words. Thus, reliance on the network of episodic relationships that is formed during the course of an experiment is ostensibly integral to the expression of these effects. When list items are not semantically related, episodic relationships provide the principal basis for discriminating list items from words that are not on the list and, hence, recall is heavily dependent on those relationships. However, when list items are semantically related, those items can be distinguished from words that are not on the list by relying on preestablished semantic connections (e.g., all list members are either articles of furniture or gems), which reduces the need to rely on episodic connections. With taxonomically related items, in particular, the familiar tendency to group words by category during output (clustering) should compete with the tendency to group words in terms of their error–success histories (triage).

Available data on this prediction are mixed. Harnishfeger and Brainerd (1994) reported two categorized-list experiments that did not produce supportive results. In Experiment 1, the weak priority effect was studied in children of two age levels (10- and 12-year-olds). The experiment involved two sessions. During Session 1, the children rated exemplars of familiar categories for typicality using procedures developed by Bjorklund and Bernholtz (1986). During Session 2, which occurred three weeks later, the children were administered four free-recall trials with a list composed of 12 exemplars (half typical, half atypical) of one category and 12 exemplars (half typical, half atypical) of a second category. A weak priority effect was observed at both age levels, and the magnitude of the effect was comparable to that observed at the same age levels with unrelated lists. For 10-year-olds, the mean output positions were 8.48 for strong words versus 7.05 for weak words. For 12-year-olds, the corresponding means were 10.49 (strong) versus 8.31 (weak). In Experiment 2, weak priority effects were directly compared for related and unrelated lists. Children from two age levels (7- and 12-year-olds) were adminstered six free-recall trials using either a list of 16 unrelated nouns or a list of 16 nouns composed of 4 exemplars of each of 4 categories. For the younger children, the mean output positions were 6.63 (strong) versus 5.47 (weak) with categorized lists and 6.19 (strong) versus 5.26 (weak) with unrelated lists. For the older children, the mean output positions were 7.07 (strong) versus 5.25 (weak) for categorized lists and 7.04 (strong) versus 5.76 (weak) for unrelated lists. Thus, the weak priority effect was virtually identical for categorized versus unrelated lists, contrary to the optimization model.

A possible explanation of these results is that the subjects were not relying on semantic relationships to any great degree, certainly not sufficiently to override their normal reliance on episodic relationships. This is a plausible hypothesis for children, who have difficulty taking advantage of semantic relationships (e.g., Bjorklund & Muir, 1988). In experiments such as Harnishfeger and Brainerd's (1994), where only a few trials were administered, children's observed levels of clustering are typically low, and clustering scores do not usually predict recall accuracy. However, children's clustering scores increase across trials, which suggests that reliance on semantic relationships increases. If so, criterion experiments, in which children receive whatever number of trials is necessary to produce perfect recall, might reveal the predicted difference in triage effects for unrelated versus categorized lists.

To test this hypothesis, I conducted an experiment that paralleled Experiment 2 of Harnishfeger and Brainerd (1994), except that a criterion design was used. That is, a sample of second graders and a sample of sixth graders received a series of buffered free-recall trials involving either 16-item lists of unrelated nouns (half the children at each age level) or 16-item lists composed of 4 exemplars of each of 4 familiar categories (half the children at each age level). Trials continued for each child until he or she met a criterion of two consecutive errorless free-recall tests. Since reliance on semantic relationships was presumably greater on criterion trials than on initial trials, the criterion nonmonotonicity effect was used to assess variations in triage as a function of semantic relatedness. The results are shown in Figure 10, where an experimental measure of words' memory strengths (total errors to criterion) has been plotted against output positions on criterion free-recall tests. It can be seen that, as predicted, the weaker → stronger → weaker sequence was less pronounced with semantically related words than with unrelated words. Indeed, the sequence disappeared at the second-grade level (where it was much less marked to begin with). Thus, the results of this experiment suggest that the optimization model's predictions about how semantic relationships

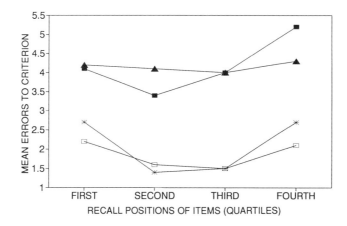

FIGURE 10. Relationship between criterion output position and on-line memory strength in younger and older children's recall of categorized and unrelated lists. Younger unrelated, -■-; younger categorized, -▲-; older unrelated, -⊠-; older categorized, -□-.

affect triage are borne out when care is taken to ensure substantial reliance on such relationships.

Effects of Preexperimental Strength   The optimization model differs fundamentally from traditional theories of memory development in that it is a basic-processes theory rather than a strategic theory. The model posits that children (and adults) automatically deposit error–success frequency counts on free-recall trials and that those memories then function as informational inputs in balancing the opposing influences of episodic activation and output interference during recall. The balancing process, like the storage of frequency information, is assumed to involve neither conscious awareness nor deliberate strategic control.

The findings assumed to support this viewpoint are subject to the possible qualification that the materials administered in triage experiments have not been such as to facilitate conscious mnemonic governance of recall order. Those materials have usually consisted of lists of unrelated words that have been carefully equated for preexperimental memory strength (e.g., lists of familiar concrete nouns). Many would argue that when list items are homogeneous with respect to preexperimental strength, subjects will be forced to rely on error–success frequencies to diagnose differences in memory strength because no other reliable information is available that could be used for this purpose. The implication is that if such information were made available, the situation would change, and subjects would use that information to gain deliberate strategic control over output order.

This hypothesis can be tested by simply relaxing the homogeneity constraint and allowing list items to vary along some standard preexperimental strength dimension (familiarity, meaningfulness, typicality, etc.). If the hypothesis is correct, analysis of free-recall protocols will show that words' preexperimental strength classifications are reliable predictors of their output positions. This assumes, of course, that subjects process preexperimental strength information during free recall. Some encouraging data on this point can be found in the literature on judgments of subjective memorability (e.g., Lovelace, 1984; Mazzoni, Cornoldi, & Marchitelli, 1990). In such experiments, subjects make subjective judgments about how difficult it will be to learn to recall individual items on a target list whose members vary on some preexperimental strength dimension. Subjects are able to make reliable judgments (i.e., their judgments correlate with words' actual positions on the relevant dimension), and when lists are administered whose words have been rated for subjective memorability, those ratings predict recall accuracy in both children and adults (Schneider & Pressley, 1989). These experiments establish, therefore, that adults and children are aware of preexperimental differences in memory strength and that they process such information on recall tasks. Consequently, they might be able to use that information to regulate output order during free recall.

This possibility has been investigated in two developmental studies (Experiment 4 of Brainerd, Reyna et al. [1993] and Experiment 1 of Harnishfeger and Brainerd [1994]) and in one study with adults (Experiment 5 of Brainerd, Reyna et al. [1993]). In each experiment, half of the list items were high on some preexperimental dimension (frequency or typicality in the developmental studies and meaningfulness in the adult study) and half were low on the same dimension. To test the conjecture that subjects shift toward strategic control of output orders when preexperimental strength information is available, four specific predictions were examined. (1) If preexperimental strength information is used to order output, strength-ordering relationships of some sort should be apparent on the first free-recall test (*before* error–success counts have begun to accumulate). (2) After Trial 1, when error–success counts have begun to accumulate, strength-ordering relationships should be present for preexperimental strength measures as well as for the usual on-line measures. (3) If the availability of preexperimental strength information produces a shift toward deliberate control of recall order, preexperimental strength should be the preferred source of information, which means that strength-ordering relationships should be more marked for preexperimental measures than for the usual on-line measures. (4) If strength-grouping scores (cf. the earlier sections of triage-accuracy relationships) are calculated for preexperimental as well as on-line strength measures, these scores should predict recall accuracy, and, indeed, they should do a better job than scores based on on-line strength.

The optimization model does not authorize any of these predictions because it does not anticipate that subjects will switch to relying on preexperimental strength information rather than on-line information. Although such a shift is certainly possible under the model, it would provide no clear advantage when it comes to maximizing recall. On-line error–success information is just as good as a memory-strength discriminator when lists are heterogeneous as when they are homogeneous, and retention of this information is still supported by developmentally primitive frequency memory systems. It can even be argued that when preexperimental and on-line strength information are both available, the latter is easier to use (because it is supported by primitive frequency-memory systems), and it is a statistically more reliable index of memory strength (because it minimizes noise from individual differences).

Consistent with the optimization model, the aforementioned experiments provided no support for any of the four predictions. Concerning Prediction (1), there was no evidence that younger children, older children, or adults used preexperimental strength to order their output on Trial 1. In Brainerd, Reyna et al.'s (1993) experiments, for example, the mean recall positions on Trial 1 of words that differed in preexperimental strength were 3.58 (strong) versus 3.33 (weak) for 7-year-olds, 6.49 (strong) versus 6.40 (weak) for 11-year-olds, and 6.60 (strong) versus 6.48 (weak) for adults. Concerning Predictions (2) and (3), words' preexperimental strength classifications also failed to predict recall order after Trial 1. As in homogeneous list experiments, however, on-line error–success history did predict recall order after Trial 1. Concerning Prediction (4), when strength-grouping scores were calculated on the basis of words' preexperimental strength classifications, those scores did not correlate with recall accuracy at any age level, and they were much lower than corresponding strength-grouping scores calculated on the basis of on-line error–success history. Finally, the latter scores, as in homogeneous list experiments, correlated with recall accuracy in younger children, older children, and adults.

To conclude, within-list variation of words' preexperimental memory strengths is an interesting manipulation theoretically. It provides subjects with the opportunity to switch from unconscious frequency-based control of output orders to conscious strategic control. Available data show that information about words' preexperimental strengths is being processed on recall tasks because both children and adults make accurate judgments of subjective memorability on the basis of such information (e.g., Lovelace, 1984; Mazzoni et al., 1990), and, in cognitive triage experiments, strength-grouping scores derived from such information are above chance. However, these same data fail to confirm that subjects shift from ordering output in terms of on-line strength information to ordering it in terms of preexperimental information: no relationship between preexperimental strength classifications and recall order has so far been reported, and although preexperimental strength-grouping scores are above chance, they have not been found to predict recall accuracy.

SUMMARY AND CONCLUSIONS

The core feature of the triage pattern is a tendency for free recall to *alternate* between words with stronger memory representations and words with weaker memory representations, rather than to follow a simple monotonic output ordering. As common sense and theories of retrieval expect, recall of stronger words tends to be followed by recall of weaker words. Counterintuitively, however, recall of weaker words tends to be followed by recall of stronger words. Most often, overall output sequences have begun with some of the weakest words (weak priority effect), continued in a weaker → stronger direction, and then reversed later on, to finish in a stronger → weaker direction (nonmonotonic emergence and criterion nonmonotonicity). Although such results have been typical, they have not been universal. For instance, Brainerd, Reyna, Howe, and Kevershan (1991) found that when young children were administered long lists, weak priority was absent on the first few trials. Similarly, Figure 11 contains illustrative data from an experiment in which the overall relationship between recall order and memory strength at criterion was weaker → stronger → weaker → stronger. In this experiment, children of two age levels learned lists of 24 nouns to a criterion of two consecutive errorless free-recall tests. As can be seen, at both age levels recall began with weaker words, continued in a weaker → stronger direction, then switched to stronger → weaker, then switched back to weaker → stronger.

Thus, memory-strength alternation, the fact that recall of weaker words sets the stage for recall of stronger words and vice versa, is the basal phenomenon to be accounted for. One approach is to treat it as an epiphenomenon; to assume that the underlying relationship between words' memory strengths

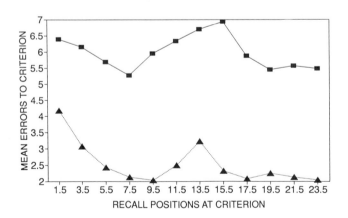

FIGURE 11. Relationship between criterion output position and on-line memory strength in younger and older children for an experiment in which the overall sequence of output was weaker → stronger → weaker → stronger. Younger children, ‑■‑; older children, ‑▲‑.

and their output positions is still stronger → weaker, but this "true" ordering is distorted when recall orders are plotted against on-line accuracy measures. Although this is a natural tack to take whenever data conflict with time-honored theoretical ideas, it has not as yet borne fruit. Four distortion models have been formulated that postulate that observed departures from the stronger → weaker ordering are caused by recency and/or primacy effects (serial-position model), or by retention of weak words in short-term memory (metamnemonic model), or by special processing of weak words (strength-reordering model), or by carrying output sentences forward from the end of one free-recall test to the start of the next (continuation model). However, findings have been reported that conflict with the assumptions of each of these models: triage effects remain when primacy and recency effects are eliminated (Brainerd et al., 1991), even college students do not exhibit conscious awareness of strength-based output strategies (Brainerd et al., 1991), special processing has not been found to selectively increase the memory strengths of weak words (Brainerd, Olney, & Reyna, 1993), and recall orders have not been found to continue from the end of one test to the start of the next (this chapter).

The other approach to explaining the triage pattern, which is represented by the optimization model, assumes that it is not an epiphenomenon. According to the optimization model, the hypothesis that output follows a stronger → weaker ordering suffers from theoretical incompleteness. Specifically, it fails to recognize that output is influenced by at least two classes of variables, namely, stable properties of words' memory representations (e.g., strength) and on-line variables whose levels fluctuate as words are recalled (e.g., output interference, episodic activation). The optimization model's central premise is that these two classes of variables must be integrated during an output sequence if recall is to be maximized. Effects such as weak priority, nonmonotonic emergence, and criterion nonmonotonicity are interpreted as manifestations of the integration process. Effects such as intertrial sharpening and developmental sharpening are interpreted as examples of improvements in the integration process. The precise reasons for these improvements remain to be ascertained. One obvious possibility is that as trials accumulate and as development proceeds, the sheer amount of output interference that is generated by retrieval decreases (e.g., Hasher & Zacks, 1988). Another obvious possibility is that as trials accumulate and development proceeds, subjects become less sensitive to given types of output interference (e.g., see Chapter 6 by Harnishfeger and Chapter 2 by Reyna, this volume).

The optimization model, unlike the distortion models, has received support from four lines of experimentation. First, studies of triage-accuracy relationships have found that when children's and adults' free-recall protocols conform more closely to the triage pattern (i.e., words are tightly packed with respect to memory strength), total recall improves (Brainerd, Reyna et al.,

1993; Harnishfeger & Brainerd, 1994). Such relationships are consistent with the model's assumption that triage effects reflect processes that maximize output. Second, studies of variations in triage-accuracy relationships as a function of the trials on which the two variables are measured have produced the counterintuitive finding that relationships are weaker when the variables are measured on the same trial than when accuracy is measured on the trial *before* goodness of triage is measured (Brainerd, Reyna et al., 1993). Such variations support the model's claim that subjects use on-line error–success feedback to discriminate memory strength. Third, fixed-trials studies with children have found that weak priority is not affected by the degree of semantic relatedness among list items (Harnishfeger & Brainerd, 1994), but criterion designs have found that criterion nonmonotonicity is less pronounced with categorized lists than with unrelated lists (this chapter). The latter result supports the model's claim that the tendency to maximize output by relying on preexisting semantic relationships (e.g., clustering by taxonomic category) should compete with the tendency to maximize output by relying on on-line information about memory strength (grouping by strength level). Fourth, studies of the effects of preexperimental versus on-line measures of memory strength have found that although children and adults group output in terms of both types of strength, only on-line strength grouping predicts recall accuracy (Brainerd, Reyna et al., 1993). The latter result is consistent with the model's claim that the process of integrating stable features of words' memory representations with dynamic factors is largely automatic.

Finally, although the optimization model has achieved some success in explaining triage effects, it must be reiterated that it is not a typical theory of memory development. Memory development research has long been characterized by theories that stress the determinative role of higher cognitive processes (mnemonic strategies, metamnemonic knowledge) in the ontogenesis of specific types of remembering (Reyna & Brainerd, 1991, 1992). Indeed, the only area of memory development research that has not been dominated by this high-cognitive approach is the study of infant memory (see especially, Rovee-Collier & Boller, Chapter 3, this volume; Rovee-Collier & Hayne, 1987), where it would simply be implausible.

In developmental studies of recall, the high-cognitive orientation has involved an almost exclusive emphasis on age improvements in organizational strategies (see Dempster, Chapter 1, this volume for an analogous perspective). For many years, developmental researchers accepted the fact that measures of organization in recall (taxonomic clustering, subjective organization) correlate with recall accuracy in adults as strong support for this orientation (Bjorklund & Muir, 1988). Lately, however, several investigators have rejected this interpretation and have concluded, on the basis of other data, that the development of recall is controlled by basic rather than strategic processes (see also Harnishfeger, Chapter 6, this volume). Three examples of such findings are that age improvements in the use of organizational strategies often fail to correlate with age improvements in recall (Bjorklund, 1985), that there is no improvement in organizational strategies within certain age ranges in which recall accuracy improves considerably (Brainerd et al., 1991), and that improving organizational strategies by training children how to use them does not produce collateral improvements in recall accuracy (DeMarie-Dreblow, 1991). Such results have prompted the alternative hypothesis that the development of recall is governed chiefly by age changes in basic processes, *especially age changes in production of and sensitivity to different forms of interference.* The optimization model, although originally formulated for the more narrow purpose of explaining the triage pattern, continues this trend toward basic-process accounts of the development of recall.

REFERENCES

Baker-Ward, L., Ornstein, P. A., & Holden, D. J. (1984). The expression of memorization in early childhood. *Journal of Experimental Child Psychology, 37,* 555–575.

Battig, W. F. (1965). Further evidence that strongest free-recalled items are not recalled first. *Psychological Reports, 17,* 745–746.

Battig, W. F., Allen, M., & Jensen, A. R. (1965). Priority of free recall of newly learned items. *Journal of Verbal Learning and Verbal Behavior, 4,* 175–179.

Bjorklund, D. F. (1985). The role of conceptual knowledge in the development of organization in memory. In C. J. Brainerd & M. Pressley (Eds.), *Basic processes in memory development* (pp. 103–142). New York: Springer-Verlag.

Bjorklund, D. F., & Bernholtz, J. E. (1986). The role of knowledge base in the memory performance of good and poor readers. *Journal of Experimental Child Psychology, 41,* 367–393.

Bjorklund, D. F., & Muir, J. E. (1988). Children's development of free recall memory: Remembering on their own. *Annals of Child Development, 5,* 79–123.

Bousefield, A. K. (1953). The occurrence of clustering in the recall of randomly arranged associates. *Journal of General Psychology, 49,* 229–240.

Brainerd, C. J. (1989, November). *Fuzzy-trace theory and children's cognitive triage.* Paper presented at the Psychonomic Society, Atlanta, GA.

Brainerd, C. J. (1990, November). *Triage 3.* Paper presented at the Psychonomic Society, New Orleans, LA.

Brainerd, C. J., Olney, C. A., & Reyna, V. F. (1993). Optimization versus effortful processing in children's cognitive triage: Criticisms, reanalyses, and new data. *Journal of Experimental Child Psychology, 55,* 353–373.

Brainerd, C. J., & Reyna, V. F. (1989). Output-interference theory of dual-task deficits in memory development. *Journal of Experimental Child Psychology, 47,* 1–18.

Brainerd, C. J., & Reyna, V. F. (1993). Domains of fuzzy-trace theory. In M. L. Howe & R. Pasnak (Eds.), *Emerging themes in cognitive-developmental theory* (Vol. 1, pp. 50–94). New York: Springer-Verlag.

Brainerd, C. J., Reyna, V. F., Harnishfeger, K. K., & Howe, M. L. (1993). Is retrievability grouping good for recall? *Journal of Experimental Psychology: General, 122,* 249–268.

Brainerd, C. J., Reyna, V. F., & Howe, M. L. (1990). Cognitive triage in children's memory: Optimal retrieval or effortful processing? *Journal of Experimental Child Psychology, 49,* 428–447.

Brainerd, C. J., Reyna, V. F., Howe, M. L., & Kevershan, J. (1990). The last shall be first: How memory strength affects children's retrieval. *Psychological Science, 1,* 247–252.

Brainerd, C. J., Reyna, V. F., Howe, M. L., & Kevershan, J. (1991). Fuzzy-trace theory and cognitive triage in memory development. *Developmental Psychology, 27,* 351–369.

Brainerd, C. J., Reyna, V. F., Howe, M. L., & Kingma, J. (1990). The development of forgetting and reminiscence. *Monographs of the Society for Research in Child Development, 53* (3–4, Whole No. 222).

Crowder, R. G. (1976). *Principles of learning and memory.* Hillsdale, NJ: Erlbaum.

Dagenbach, D., Horst, S., & Carr, T. (1990). Adding new information to semantic memory: How much learning is enough to produce semantic priming? *Journal of Experimental Psychology: Human Learning and Memory, 16,* 581–599.

DeMarie-Dreblow, D. (1991). Relation between knowledge and memory: A reminder that correlation does not imply causation. *Child Development, 92,* 484–498.

Dempster, F. N. (1992). The rise and fall of the inhibitory mechanism: Toward a unified theory of cognitive development and aging. *Developmental Review, 12,* 45–75.

Ekstrand, B. R., Wallace, W. P., & Underwood, B. J. (1966). A frequency theory of verbal discrimination learning. *Psychological Review, 73,* 566–578.

Estes, W. K. (1960). Learning theory and the new "mental chemistry." *Psychological Review, 67,* 203–227.

Estes, W. K. (1976). The cognitive side of probability learning. *Psychological Review, 83,* 37–64.

Friedman, P., & Gildemeister, J. E. (1980). A negative priority effect. *Perceptual and Motor Skills, 51,* 39–44.

Ghatala, E. S., & Levin, J. R. (1976). Children's recognition memory processes. In J. R. Levin & V. L. Allen (Eds.), *Cognitive learning in children: Theories and strategies.* New York: Academic Press.

Hadley, J. A., Healy, A. F., & Murdock, B. B. (1992). Output and retrieval interference in the missing-number task. *Memory & Cognition, 20,* 60–82.

Halff, H. M. (1977). The role of opportunities to recall in learning to retrieve. *American Journal of Psychology, 90,* 383–406.

Harnishfeger, K. K., & Brainerd, C. J. (1994). Nonstrategic facilitation of children's recall: Evidence of triage with semantically related information. *Journal of Experimental Child Psychology, 3,* 259–280.

Hasher, L., & Zacks, R. T. (1979). Automatic and effortful processes in memory. *Journal of Experimental Psychology: General, 108,* 356–388.

Hasher, L., & Zacks, R. T. (1984). Automatic processing of fundamental information: The case of frequency of occurrence. *American Psychologist, 39,* 1372–1388.

Hasher, L., & Zacks, R. T. (1988). Working memory, comprehension, and aging: A review and a new view. In G. H. Bower (Ed.), *The psychology of learning and motivation* (Vol. 22, pp. 193–224). San Diego: Academic Press.

Howe, M. L., & Rabinowitz, F. M. (1989). On the uninterpretability of dual-task performance. *Journal of Experimental Child Psychology, 47,* 32–38.

Lovelace, E. A. (1984). Metamemory: Monitoring future recallability during study. *Journal of Experimental Psychology: Learning, Memory, and Cognition, 10,* 756–766.

Marx, M. H. (1986). More retrospective reports on event-frequency judgments: Shift from multiple traces to strength factor with age. *Bulletin of the Psychonomic Society, 24,* 183–185.

Mazur, J. E., & Hastie, R. (1978). Learning as accumulation: A reexamination of the learning curve. *Psychological Bulletin, 85,* 1256–1276.

Mazzoni, G., Cornoldi, C., & Marchitelli, G. (1990). Do memorability ratings affect study-time allocation? *Memory & Cognition, 18,* 196–204.

Ornstein, P. A., Baker-Ward, L., & Naus, M. J. (1988). The development of mnemonic skill. In F. E. Weinert & M. Perlmutter (Eds.), *Memory development: Universal changes and individual differences* (pp. 31–50). Hillsdale, NJ: Erlbaum.

Paivio, A., Yuille, J. C., & Madigan, S. A. (1968). Concreteness, imagery, and meaningfulness values for 925 nouns. *Journal of Experimental Psychology Monographs, 76* (1, Pt. 2).

Payne, D. G. (1987). Hypermnesia and reminiscence in recall: A historical and empirical review. *Psychological Bulletin, 101,* 5–27.

Postman, L., & Keppel, G. (1968). Conditions determining the priority of new items in free recall. *Journal of Verbal Learning and Verbal Behavior, 7,* 260–263.

Reyna, V. F., & Brainerd, C. J. (1989). Output interference, generic resources, and cognitive development. *Journal of Experimental Child Psychology, 47,* 42–46.

Reyna, V. F., & Brainerd, C. J. (1991). Fuzzy-trace theory and children's acquisition of mathematical and scientific concepts. *Learning and Individual Differences, 3,* 27–59.

Reyna, V. F., & Brainerd, C. J. (1992). A fuzzy-trace theory of reasoning and remembering: Patterns, paradoxes, and parallelism. In A. F. Healy, R. M. Shiffrin, & S. K. Kosslyn (Eds.), *From learning processes to cognitive processes: Essays in honor of William K. Estes* (Vol. 2, pp. 235–259). Hillsdale, NJ: Erlbaum.

Roberts, W. A. (1969). The priority of recall of new items in transfer from part-list learning to whole-list learning. *Journal of Verbal Learning and Verbal Behavior, 8,* 645–652.

Roenker, D. L., Thompson, C. P., & Brown, S. C. (1971). Comparison of measures for the estimation of clustering in free recall. *Psychological Bulletin, 76,* 45–48.

Rovee-Collier, C., & Hayne, H. (1987). Reactivation of infant memory: Implications for cognitive development. In H. W. Reese (Ed.), *Advances in child development and behavior* (Vol. 20, pp. 185–238). San Diego: Academic Press.

Schneider, W., & Pressley, M. (1989). *Memory development from 2 to 20.* New York: Springer-Verlag.

Wixted, J. T., & Rohrer, D. (1993). Proactive interference and the dynamics of free recall. *Journal of Experimental Psychology: Human Learning and Memory, 19,* 1024–1039.

5

The Evolution of Inhibition Mechanisms and Their Role in Human Cognition and Behavior

David F. Bjorklund and Katherine Kipp Harnishfeger

Neural inhibition is not a new innovation in evolution. Excitatory and inhibitory circuits characterize the nervous systems of animals from the lowly aplysia to the lofty *Homo sapiens,* making inhibition a phylogenetically primitive function indeed. Yet, following Jerison (1973), when primitive functions such as attention and inhibition "are correlated with specific visual or auditory inputs and specific response patterns that had been learned in connection with those inputs, it becomes a total behavior pattern that may truly be described as 'higher order '" (pp. 415–416). Such "higher order" behavior patterns can be found in the brains and behavior of all vertebrates. However, inhibitory mechanisms began to take on modified roles in primates, contributing significantly to what are often referred to as "higher cognitive processes."

Our intent in this chapter is to provide an account of the evolution of human cognitive and behavioral inhibition mechanisms. To anticipate, we

141

propose that in hominid phylogeny pressures related to intraspecific cooperation and competition led to enlargement of the neocortex, including connections between the prefrontal lobe and the limbic system (see Figure 1). These
connections afforded greater voluntary inhibitory control over sexual and aggressive behaviors, which in turn led to enhanced social harmony. As inhibition mechanisms came increasingly under cortical control, neural circuits, initially evolved to inhibit emotional responding, were recruited for purposes of
inhibiting other social behaviors and cognitions, contributing to our current
cognitive/behavioral system. Before presenting evidence for this evolutionary
account, we will first review the role of inhibition in contemporary human
cognition and behavior, its development, and the neural basis for such inhibition.

THE ROLE OF INHIBITION IN HUMAN COGNITION
AND BEHAVIOR

Inhibition has had a checkered career in psychology (see also Dempster,
Chapter 1, and Harnishfeger, Chapter 6, this volume). Many prominent theorists have proposed inhibitory models. For example, repression was a central

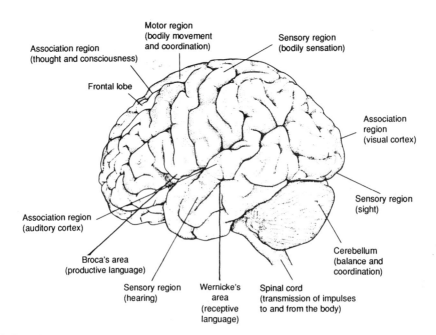

FIGURE 1. Lateral view of the human brain. Broca's area and Wernicke's area are involved in
the production and comprehension of language, respectively.

construct in Freud's psychoanalytic theory. In his model, repression was the blocking (inhibition) of thought from conscious awareness. It was an active and effortful process. Lorenz (1966) argued that higher level control of the inhibition of aggressive behavior was a central difference between humans and other species. Pavlov (1966) postulated an inhibitory form of conditioning, and Luria argued that inhibition was central to understanding development (1961) and brain functioning (1973). Following this early interest, however, inhibition lost its popularity as an explanatory construct during the heyday of behaviorism. In most early cognitive theories, inhibition continued to be neglected, perhaps because the concept appeared to be incompatible with the computer metaphor of mainstream information-processing models (see Bjork, Neill, Valdes, & Terry, Chapter 7, this volume).

Currently, the inhibitory construct is enjoying renewed interest by theorists from a wide range of theoretical and research perspectives, including developmentalists (e.g., Bjorklund & Harnishfeger, 1990; Dempster, 1992; Diamond, 1991), cognitive psychologists (e.g., Bjork, 1989; Hasher & Zacks, 1989; Tipper, 1992), neuroscientists (e.g., Dustman, Snyder, & Schlehuber, 1981; Nash & Williams, 1982; Woodward, Brown, Marsh, & Dawson, 1991), and clinicians (e.g., Enright & Beech, 1993b; Malloy, 1987; Perecman, 1987). Inhibition is a ubiquitous process in human behavior, and its value as an explanatory construct is again being investigated. Our primary interest here is on the role of inhibition in human cognition. In the following sections we will outline inhibition as it relates to basic cognitive processes (such as attention), higher level social behaviors (such as control of aggressive responses), and developmental function.

Basic Cognitive Processes

Cognitive inhibition is the suppression of previously activated cognitive contents or processes, the clearing of irrelevant actions or attention from consciousness, and resistance to interference from potentially attention-capturing processes or contents. At a basic level, inhibitory processes control the contents of consciousness as well as the operation of processing activities, restricting attention to only the relevant aspects of the environment and limiting processing to only those necessary for the task at hand.

Failure to maintain control through inhibitory efficiency may be detrimental to task performance in some contexts, such as during tests requiring speed and frequent changes in response. An extreme example of the deleterious effects of poor inhibitory control is obsessive-compulsive disorder. Individuals suffering from this psychiatric disorder are unable to keep unwanted (and often emotionally disturbing) thoughts from consciousness, which can significantly impair their normal daily functioning (e.g., Enright, Beech, 1993a, 1993b; Malloy, 1987). Conversely, inhibitory inefficiency may enhance performance in other situations, such as tests of creativity that require suspension of closure while various tangential avenues are explored (e.g., Houtz, Denmark, Rosenfield, & Tetenbaum, 1980; Tegano, 1990).

One of the clearest forms of cognitive inhibition is the suppression of attention to external stimuli that are irrelevant to current concerns. Selective attention to relevant stimuli requires efficient inhibition of wandering or captured attention. For example, in the classroom the child is expected to focus attention on the teacher's directions, not on what is happening outside the window or the latest comic book waiting in the desk.

There are many laboratory demonstrations of this type of cognitive inhibition, including speeded classification (e.g., Strutt, Anderson, & Well, 1975), selective listening (e.g., Doyle, 1973), and Stroop tests (e.g., Tipper, Bourque, Anderson, & Brehaut, 1989). One paradigm studied extensively with children is incidental learning (see, e.g., Hagen & Hale, 1973). In this paradigm, children are shown pairs of pictures, with one member of the pair being the target that children are told to remember, and the other being the distractor that children are told to ignore. Following presentation, children are asked to recall both the target and distractor stimuli. Typically, young children recall fewer of the target stimuli, but recall as many or more of the distractor stimuli as do older children and adults. These results demonstrate young children's poor inhibitory control, being unable to ignore task-irrelevant stimuli, resulting in less than optimal processing of central, task-relevant stimuli.

Inhibitory processes permit the control of internal, or endogenous distractors as well as the control of external, or exogenous distractors. For example, when engaged in an effortful cognitive task we must keep our attention limited to the task and not let our minds wander into enticing daydreams. This form of inhibition can be controlled at a high level, as in the monitoring of task performance (e.g., Zimmerman & Martinez-Pons, 1990) and the deliberate control of consciousness (e.g., Wegner, 1989). Inhibition of internal distractions can also be controlled at a low or preconscious level, such as when a child does not think about night-flying mammals while reading about bats in a baseball story (e.g., Swinney & Prather, 1989). This type of inhibition, in which the context-inappropriate meaning is activated, has been examined in both adults and children (e.g., Onifer & Swinney, 1981; Swinney & Prather, 1989; Swinney, Zurif, & Nicol, 1989). From this research, it appears that immediately following the presentation of a polysemous word, all meanings of the word are accessed. Subsequently, however, the contextually appropriate meaning is selected and contextually inappropriate meanings are suppressed or inhibited. Research using this paradigm with children has been interpreted as reflecting the development of inhibitory efficiency over the childhood years (Harnishfeger & Bjorklund, 1993).

Social Behavior

Inhibition is central to the control of social behavior. It permits us to withhold strong emotional responses (aggressive, sexual, and appetitive behaviors) while we consider the personal and social implications of our actions. It allows us to delay gratification, inhibiting an immediate response to gain a larger reward later. Inhibitory efficiency contributes to the ability to manipulate others' thoughts about and behaviors toward us; by concealing our true intentions or emotions, we deceive others.

Inhibition allows us to control social cognition as well. As noted earlier, Freud's repression construct was essentially the inhibition of thought. More recently, Wegner (1989) developed an experimental procedure that demonstrates the operation of this form of inhibition. In his paradigm, an individual is asked to generate a stream of speech about anything that comes to mind. There is one catch: the participant is to avoid thinking about a "white bear." This is difficult to accomplish. People rarely think about "white bears"—until they are told not to. Wegner demonstrated the difficulty of such thought suppression as well as a rebound effect: when participants are released from the white bear prohibition and are allowed to say anything, their discourse is filled with references to white bears! Wegner relates this experimental phenomenon to similar real-world situations in which individuals attempt to control obsessive thoughts (e.g., giving up smoking).

Cognitive Development

The efficiency of cognitive and behavioral inhibition increases with age, and this improvement likely plays a central role in qualitative changes in behavior and cognition across development (e.g., Bjorklund & Harnishfeger, 1990; Dempster, 1992, 1993; Diamond, 1991; Harnishfeger, Chapter 6, this volume; Harnishfeger & Bjorklund, 1993). In infancy, inhibitory processes contribute to developmental improvements in the ability to withhold prepotent responses (Diamond, 1988). For example, when presented with a transparent box with a toy inside, young infants attempt to reach through the box, rather than reaching around it to the opening. Inhibition of motor behavior continues to improve into childhood, and during the preschool years children become increasingly able to control their motor behavior with external as well as self-vocalized inhibitions (Luria, 1961).

Developmental improvements in inhibitory efficiency also contribute to changes in cognitive performance across childhood. Examples of this are children's increasing abilities to selectively attend to relevant information in perceptual and cognitive tasks (Lane & Pearson, 1982) and to inhibit the activation of irrelevant internal distractors (Harnishfeger & Bjorklund, 1993). Moreover, developmental changes in cognitive functioning during aging have also been proposed to be a function of inhibition mechanisms (Hasher & Zacks, 1989; see also McDowd, & Oseas-Kreger & Filion, Chapter 11, this volume).

One example of developmental differences observed both over childhood and again during aging concerns the ability to keep task-irrelevant information out of working memory. Young children's inability to moderate the contents of their working memory is reflected in their high rates of false recognition errors and intrusions in memory tasks (e.g., Brown, Smiley, Day, Townsend, & Lawton, 1977). For example, we have examined young children's cued recall for target words that were related to the cues either categorically, functionally, or acoustically (Bjorklund & Harnishfeger, 1990). We assessed children's inhibitory efficiency by computing the proportion of intrusions (i.e., words recalled that were not on the list) in their recall. The youngest children (nursery school and kindergartners) not only had greater proportion of intrusions in their recall than elementary-school-aged children, but their intrusions were also more likely to be unrelated to the task. That is, when third and sixth graders had intrusions in their recall, they were likely to be categorically, functionally, or acoustically related to the cue; this was less apt to be true for the nursery school and kindergarten children, with many of their intrusions being task irrelevant (often nonwords), reflecting a difficulty in staying "on task" and suppressing inappropriate responses. Young children's failure to keep their working memories clear of irrelevant intrusions is also evident in their free-recall performance (e.g., Harnishfeger & Bjorklund, 1993).

Failures to keep irrelevant information out of working memory are also found at the other end of the life-span. For example, Hamm and Hasher (1992) found that older adults suffered from the failure to moderate the contents of working memory during discourse-processing tasks. In their paradigm, older and younger adults read two types of passages: consistent passages, which maintained the meaning of the passage inferred in early sentences, and garden-path passages, which altered the meaning of the passage so that initial inferences were invalidated by the end of the passage. Hamm and Hasher found that the older adults maintained the invalidated inferences in working memory longer than the younger adults, and they interpreted this as a failure to inhibit the activation or maintenance of task-irrelevant information in working memory. Hasher and her colleagues have found similar developmental declines in inhibitory efficiency over later adulthood in a reading task, during which subjects attempted to ignore distractor words woven into target passages (Connelly, Hasher, Zacks, 1991).

Thus, cognitive inhibition changes with development, both early and late in life, and this change affects such other cognitive processes as recall, recognition, and text processing. Partially based on such research, inhibitory processes have recently been proposed as explanatory mechanisms of developmental change by numerous researchers (e.g., Bjorklund & Harnishfeger, 1990; Dempster, 1992, 1993; Diamond, 1991; Harnishfeger & Bjorklund, 1993). These contemporary approaches link changes in behavior and cognition. As one example, the inhibition of prepotent responding, which improves over infancy and early childhood (see, e.g., Diamond, 1991; Harnishfeger & Bjorklund, 1993), is thought to contribute to the development of self-regulation and a sense of personal control, fostering cognitive (e.g., Piaget, 1952) and social/emotional (e.g., Ainsworth, Blehar, Waters, & Wall, 1978) development and a positive sense of agency and self-concept (e.g., Bandura, 1989).

Another trend in developmental research has been to relate cognitive and behavioral inhibition mechanisms to brain function, and it is to this that we now turn. Much is known about the neuropsychology of inhibition, and we will discuss some of this research in the following section. This discussion will serve as a foundation for our later discussion of the evolution of the brain and its inhibitory functions.

THE NEURAL BASIS OF INHIBITORY MECHANISMS

Neuropsychological research has identified the associative cortex of the frontal lobes, *the prefrontal cortex,* as the primary locus of behavioral inhibition (Dempster, Chapter 1, this volume; Fuster, 1980, 1984; Luria, 1973) (see Figure 1). The prefrontal cortex is structurally defined as the part of the neocortex (cerebral cortex) that receives projections from the mediodorsal nucleus of the thalamus. It is a functionally heterogeneous area, with the various functions falling together in a pattern related to the temporal organization of behavior, including the suppression of interference, or inhibition (Fuster, 1980, 1984; Goldman-Rakic, 1987).

Much of the evidence regarding the functions of the prefrontal cortex comes from comparative research involving frontal lesions and from human research involving individual cases of brain damage. While these methods reveal a host of phenomena attributable to the prefrontal cortex, there are several reservations that must be logged. Among the problems of using brain damage research to understand brain function are: (1) brain damage can rarely be narrowed to one area; (2) brain damage frequently involves complications beyond that of simple lesions; (3) disorders following brain damage may not reveal how the brain functions normally; and (4) prefrontal lesions frequently lead to morphological and functional changes beyond that of the isolated lesion site (Fuster, 1980). Given these reservations, the comparative, clinical, and human developmental literatures can be examined and convergences noted to help illuminate the functional nature of the prefrontal cortex.

Evidence from Comparative Research

"Frontal animals," those with extensive ablation of the prefrontal cortex, show an interesting pattern of cognitive and behavioral deficits, with a central deficit involving inhibitory failures (Fuster, 1980). These animals have particular difficulty with successive discrimination tasks and "go/no go" tasks in which they must respond to some stimuli and not respond to others. In these situations, they typically respond to all stimuli, apparently unable to control the prepotent response. These animals are distractible but rigid in their perseverance to overlearned responses.

The delayed-response task is a paradigm that illuminates some of the central difficulties of frontal animals. In this procedure, an animal is presented with two objects. The animal watches as food is hidden under one of the objects. A delay is imposed during which the animal cannot reach for the food reward, although the objects may remain visible. Following the delay, the animal is permitted to reach for either of the objects and retrieve the food. If the animal correctly lifts the object hiding the food, the animal can take the food. The hiding place for the food is randomly varied across trials.

Prefrontal lesions greatly impair delayed-response performance in primates (as well as some other species, Fuster, 1980). One of the most important aspects of the task is the length of the delay between hiding and retrieval. Frontal animals may show no deficits immediately, but large deficits are seen with delays of even 1–2 seconds (Goldman-Rakic, 1987). The inability to perform the delayed-response task does not reflect a short-term memory deficit, because frontal animals are able to learn new discriminations and new tasks. Rather, it appears that the deficit is due to inhibition and response control failures, with frontal animals being unable to inhibit inappropriate or interfering responses (Fuster, 1980, 1984; Goldman-Rakic, 1987).

Frontal animals show emotional and behavioral deficits following prefrontal lesions. There may be a general hyperactivity of movement, especially to novel stimuli. The animal shows a disinhibition of behavior, with frontal animals being unable to inhibit behavioral responses and unable to inhibit attention and action to irrelevant stimuli. Further, there is frequently an inability to inhibit appetitive, aggressive, and sexual responses

Evidence from Comparative Developmental Research

The prefrontal cortex is one of the last areas of the brain to reach full maturity in ontogeny (Luria, 1973). Development of the frontal lobes in humans is rapid between birth and about 2 years of age. There is another, less pronounced growth spurt between about 4 and 7 years of age, with subsequent growth being slow and gradual into young adulthood (Luria, 1973).

Development of the frontal lobes takes several forms. First, individual neurons increase in size and complexity. Second, the process of myelination of the frontal areas begins relatively late in development (compared to myelination of the sensory and motor cortices) and is not complete until adulthood (e.g., Yakovlev & Lecours, 1967). Myelin is the fatty tissue that surrounds neurons, producing faster transmission of nerve signals and less electrical interference from surrounding neurons. This relatively late myelination of the frontal areas has been hypothesized by some to contribute to age-related changes in speed and efficiency of cognitive processing (e.g., Bjorklund &

Harnishfeger, 1990; Case, 1985; Konner, 1991) and possibly to the greater plasticity of the young relative to the older human brain (see Bjorklund & Green, 1992). Also, the density of synapses—the connections between neurons—reaches it peak in the frontal areas between 1 and 2 years of ages (Huttenlocher, 1979). This is not due to the production of *more* neurons during this time; essentially all the neurons a person will ever have are produced prenatally. Rather, the number of connections per neuron is higher now than at any other time in life, with subsequent development involving the pruning of neurons, via a process known as *selective cell death* (Goldman-Rakic, 1987). Presumably, experiences during this time determine which neurons will live and which will die, which connections will remain functional and which will become obsolete (e.g., Greenough, Black, & Wallace, 1987), and which bundle of neurons will be dedicated to which mind/brain operations (e.g., Edelman, 1987).

Likely because of its slow rate of development, damage to the frontal areas early in life often demonstrates a functional sparing, or preservation of later function (Fuster, 1980). For example, comparative research suggests that ablations of the prefrontal cortex early in young animals (such as in monkeys younger than 2 years of age) do not impede performance on frontal tasks (such as the delayed-response task), nor do they result in behavioral deficits, such as hyperactivity and appetitive disturbances (Fuster, 1980). Identical lesions later in development result in widespread functional deficits.

Recent comparative developmental research has examined the development of the frontal lobes and its relation to behavior in early life in nonhuman primates (see Goldman-Rakic, 1987). Goldman-Rakic found early prenatal development of the frontal cortex, with maximum synaptic density at about 4 months postnatally (in nonhuman primates), and with subsequent postnatal development in the form of a decline in density over several years (cf. Huttenlocher, 1979, for humans). To examine function, she compared delayed-response performance to performance on the conceptually similar Piagetian AB̄ (A-not-B) task. (For further discussions of the A-not-B task see Chapter 1 by Dempster and Chapter 6 by Harnishfeger, this volume.) In the AB̄ task, infants watch as a toy is hidden in one of two wells; infants are distracted for a delay period, after which they are allowed to retrieve a toy. Over trials, the hiding place is changed to well "B" following a series of correct retrievals in well "A." Infants much younger than 12 months cannot successfully retrieve the toy from the new hiding place, even though they saw it being hidden, and even though they may be gazing at the correct hiding place! The probability of errors increases as the delay between the hiding and searching of the object increases (Diamond, 1985). Nonhuman primates are unable to solve the delayed-response task until about 4 months of age, leading Goldman-Rakic to conclude that reaching the critical level of synaptic density is required for delayed-response or AB̄ performance, but that adult performance may be dependent on the elimination, rather than growth, of synapses.

Evidence from Cases of Brain Damage

A third line of evidence regarding the neural basis of inhibitory function comes from human neuropsychology. Humans with prefrontal damage present a set of diverse, and usually subtle, behavioral deficits (Fuster, 1980, 1984; Luria, 1973). These patients have difficulty with spontaneous behavior, with planning, and with concentration. Frontal lobe dysfunction has been implicated in some psychiatric syndromes (Perecman, 1987). For example, obsessive-compulsive disorder, a syndrome characterized by an inability to inhibit the recurrence of disturbing thoughts or ritualistic behaviors, has been linked to dysfunctions of the frontal lobes (Flor-Henry, 1983; Malloy, 1987). Specific to our interests here, these patients have particular difficulty with interference susceptibility, being highly distractable by both external and internal stimuli. Moreover, recent evidence suggests that the mental processing underlying obsessive-compulsive disorders is qualitatively similar to the processes underlying "normal" cognition. For example, Enright and Beech (1993a, 1993b) have shown that subjects with obsessive-compulsive disorder fail to show priming effects in a semantic negative-priming task. In contrast, negative-priming effects are demonstrated by subjects with all other subcategories of anxiety disorders, as they are by nondisturbed subjects (e.g., Tipper, 1992). These results suggest that the difficulty of obsessive-compulsive individuals to suppress unwanted thoughts and behaviors represents an extreme form of inhibition failure, and does not represent a qualitatively different phenomenon than the inhibition mechanisms that function in normal cognition.

Luria described the frontal lobes as being involved in the regulation of conscious attentional processes (Luria, 1973). Patients with frontal lobe damage are often unable to regulate their conscious, or speech-controlled attention. There are no deficits in involuntary attentional responses. Consequently, these patients may be unable to respond to a direct query, while being simultaneously unable to disregard attention to irrelevant stimuli. They are unable to control "their orienting reactions to irrelevant stimuli, unconnected with their intention. Such elementary forms of responses as a rule not only are undisturbed, but sometimes they may actually be more brisk or even pathologically intensified" (Luria, 1973, p. 198).

These patients also lose the ability to control verbally their behavior (Luria, 1973). When given a verbal command, they are unable to execute it and, similar to frontal animals, they may be rigid in their perseverance to overlearned response patterns. They are unable to follow a verbal command that contradicts a more salient routine. For example, when attempting to synchronize alternate movements with another person (tap once to experimenter's double taps, tap twice to experimenter's single tap), these patients are often unable to inhibit an imitative response. Furthermore, they are unable to guide their behavior with their own speech.

Luria (1973) concluded that the frontal lobes are involved in the regulation of behavior through the suppression of lower level orienting responses, perseverative or imitative responses, and impulsive response tendencies. Although the deficits are typically subtle and patients may show no deficits on intelligence tests, the damage usually does affect many cognitive processes, such as engaging in an cooperative conversation and analyzing complex scenes for meaning (Luria, 1973).

Evidence that patients with frontal lobe damage have difficulty with inhibiting prepotent responses comes from a variety of sources, including delayed-response tasks (discussed earlier) and the Wisconsin Card Sorting Test (WCST). In delayed-response tasks, subjects watch as an object is hidden, are required to wait for a specified period of time, and then are allowed to retrieve the object. The task is performed over multiple trials, with the hiding location of the object being changed on consecutive trials. This is similar to the A-not-B task of object permanence described earlier. We had already noted that animals with frontal lobe lesions perform more poorly on these tasks than nonlesioned animals (see Goldman-Rakic, 1987). Similar results are observed with humans with frontal lobe impairments (e.g., Milner, 1964; Schacter, Moscovitch, Tulving, McLachlan, & Frendman, 1986). A typical pattern of people with frontal lobe damage is to search at the location where the object was found on the previous trial, suggesting that they are unable to inhibit the memory of their prior response (Schacter et al., 1986). According to Dempster (1993), "it appears that sensitivity to proactive interference generated on previous trials is the principal source of errors on delayed response tasks and A-not-B tasks" (p. 16).

The Wisconsin Card Sorting Test consists of cards on which are depicted different objects (square, star, etc.), which vary in terms of color and number (see Figure 2). The subject's task is to sort the cards into specified categories (i.e., according to color, number, or shape), which is reinforced by the examiner. Without specifically informing the subject, the examiner then switches reinforcement to another category. For example, the initial category

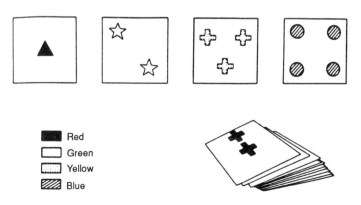

FIGURE 2. The Wisconsin Card Sorting Test (Milner, 1964).

may be number, in which case subjects would be reinforced for sorting all the target cards with four items on them under the cue card consisting of four circles, all the cards with three items on them under the cue card with the three crosses, regardless of the color or shape of the items on the cards. The examiner may then switch from number to shape, so that all target cards are now to be placed with the cue card consisting of the same shape (stars with stars, triangles with triangles, etc.), with color and number being irrelevant dimensions. Subjects are corrected after an erroneous placement, so they should presumably be able to learn a new classification scheme after only a few trials. Normal people do exactly this. However, patients with lesions in the frontal lobes do poorly on this task, often making perservative errors, finding it difficult to make new responses (Milner, 1964). Similar to the delayed-response tasks, performance of patients with frontal-brain damage on the WCST reflects an inability to inhibit a previously acquired response. Based on these and related findings, it has become clear that the frontal lobes play a central role in the selection and regulation of behavior by inhibiting previous responses and fostering resistance to interference from extraneous stimuli (see Dempster, 1993, Chapter 1, this volume; Diamond, 1991; Harnishfeger, Chapter 6, this volume; Luria, 1973).

Evidence from Human Developmental Research

A final line of evidence regarding the neural basis of inhibition comes from human developmental research. Several paradigms have been used to study frontal lobe functioning in infants, including the A-not-B task, the delayed-response task, and the object retrieval task (Diamond, 1985, 1988, 1990, 1991; Goldman-Rakic, 1987). Infants show gradual improvement in A-not-B task performance from about 7.5 months through the middle of the second year. Similar developmental improvements are seen in the delayed-response task and on the object retrieval task (in which the infant must reach around a transparent box to obtain a visible toy within it). Diamond and Goldman-Rakic each propose that improvements in these tasks are a function of frontal lobe development, and that the ability to inhibit the execution of a prepotent act is central to the ability to solve these tasks (changes in the interpretation of A-not-B task performance are discussed by Dempster, Chapter 1, this volume) Recently, Bell and Fox (1992) recorded EEG activity from the frontal lobes of 7- to 12-month-old infants performing the A-not-B tasks. They reported changes in EEG patterns as a function of age and delay, consistent with the findings from the animal work, further confirming the role of the prefrontal cortex in the development of inhibition abilities during infancy.

Developmental differences have also been found in several tasks that have been used to assess lobe damage in adult patients. For example, age differences are found on the Wisconsin Card Sorting Test, with young children performing much the way adults with frontal lesions perform (e.g., Chelune

& Baer, 1986). The ability to verbally regulate behavior also improves with age (see Luria, 1961; Vygotsky, 1962; Wozniak, 1972), with young children often displaying the same problems shown by adults with frontal lesions. For example, preschool children show the same difficulty in performing tasks in which verbal instructions contradict a more salient routine as do frontal lesion patients, such as the task in which subjects are to tap once each time the examiner taps twice, and tap twice each time the examiner taps once (Llamas & Diamond, 1991). Such developmental patterns, along with evidence of corresponding ontogenetic changes in the structure of the frontal lobes, bolster the interpretation from the clinical literature that the frontal lobes play a major role in the inhibition of prepotent responses.

THE EVOLUTION OF INHIBITION MECHANISMS

As we noted earlier, neural inhibition is not a new evolutionary invention. However, for humans, the ability to inhibit one's thoughts and emotional responses likely played an important role in the evolution of human cognition, particularly social cognition. For a highly social species such as modern (and presumably ancient) humans, the ability to keep ideas and actions to oneself in certain circumstances would seemingly provide substantial adaptive advantages, including the ability to conceal, to deceive, to reflect, and to delay gratification. Not the least benefit of enhanced inhibitive skills is the ability to control aggressive and sexual urges for reasons that are quite apparent to modern humans, but may have been great insights to our australopithecine and early hominid ancestors.

In the following sections we will explore the role of inhibitory mechanisms in human evolution. We will first take a brief look at the evolution of the human brain, examining what can be gleaned from the fossil record and comparing the neural organization of extant primates and modern humans. However, changes in neural inhibition across human evolution do not provide the level of analysis needed by the psychologist to understand either contemporary human thought or its evolution; a cognitive level of analysis is needed. In fact, Cosmides and Tooby (1987; Tooby & Cosmides, 1992) have stated that information-processing programs are what have been selected for in evolution, making cognitive analyses the "missing link" in evolutionary theory. We agree, and in a second section we examine the environmental (mainly social) pressures that may have led to enhanced inhibitory skills and the possible consequences of such inhibitive abilities.

Evolution of the Human Brain

Human brains are remarkably similar in form to those of chimpanzees and follow the general mammalian plan. Perhaps the most distinctive feature of human brains is their size (or at least parts of them) relative to expected brain size given body weight (Jerison, 1973). This increase in relative size and corresponding function occurred over what, in human perspective, is a long period of time, but which, from geological perspective, was a brief interval. From our small-brained but bipedal australopithecine ancestors, first seen in the fossil record between 3.5 and 4 million years ago, to the first evidence of archaic *Homo sapiens* about three million years later, skull capacity increased from an average of slightly over 400 cc to over 1300 cc (see Eccles, 1989) (see Figure 3).

Because *Homo sapiens* is the only living member of the hominid line, comparisons with the brains of our phylogenetic predecessors must be restricted to fossil evidence. Based on such evidence, gross brain size (or endocranial capacity) has increased from about 420 cc for the early *Australopithecus afarensis* (about 3.5 million years BP [before present]), to about 650 cc for *Homo habilis* (about 2 million years BP), to about 950 cc for *Homo erectus* (about 1.3 million years BP), to about 1350 cc for *Homo sapiens* (first seen in the fossil record about .3 million years BP) (Eccles, 1989; Tobias, 1987). Although there was a corresponding increase in body mass over this evolutionary sequence, brains generally grew faster than bodies. Using the encephalization quotient (EQ) developed by Jerison (1973) that reflects the ratio of actual brain size to the size of an average living mammal

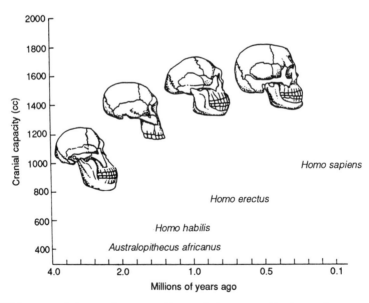

FIGURE 3. Cranial shape and capacity of hominids form *Australopithecus africanus* to *Homo sapiens*. (Adapted from Stebbins, 1982.)

with allowance for body weight (with 1.0 being the "expected" EQ), increases in brain size relative to body weight are seen from *afarensis* (EQ = 3.1) to *Homo habilis* (EQ = 4.0) to *Homo erectus* (EQ = 5.5) to *Homo sapiens* (EQ = 7.6) (data from Tobias, 1987), with the greatest increase occurring between *habilis* and *erectus*. This change is graphically presented in Figure 4 (data from Tobias, 1987).

Based on cranial endocasts, substantial and relatively unambiguous enlargement of both Broca's and Wernicke's areas, each centrally involved in language (see Figure 1), is not found until *Homo erectus*, suggesting to some that the advent of humanlike intelligence, and particularly protolanguage, was likely first seen in this species (Bickerton, 1990). Moreover, there was extreme sexual dimorphism in *habilis*, as there was for australopithecines, with males being nearly twice the size of females, suggesting a quite different social organization among *habilis* than that existing among contemporary humans and that which presumably existed among *erectus* (see Corballis, 1991). Yet, the brain of *Homo habilis* does reflect appreciably greater encephalization than that of the australopithecines, accounting for its inclusion in the genus *Homo;* and, according to Tobias (1987), *Homo habilis*'s emergence "marked the beginning of the phase of aggrandizement of the hominid brain" (p. 747).

Only so much can be learned about brain evolution by studying the limited fossil evidence from extinct species. Another way of evaluating human

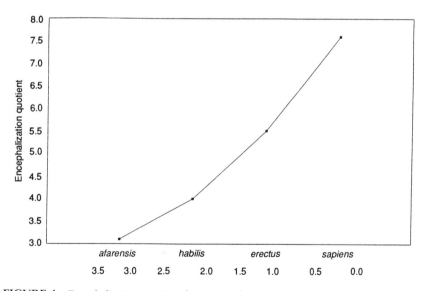

FIGURE 4. Encephalization quotient (brain size relative to expected body size) for four species of hominids. Vertical axis = encephalization quotient; horizontal axis = time in millions of years; 0.0 = present. (Figure from Bickerton, 1990; data from Tobias, 1987.)

brain evolution is by contrasting the brains of modern humans with those of extant primates, notably chimpanzees. Humans and chimpanzees share over 98% of their genetic material (with gorillas having slightly less genetic overlap with both humans and chimps, see Sibley & Ahlquist, 1984), making them closely related species. Knowing this, and estimating the rate at which mutations occur over evolutionary time, it is believed that humans and chimpanzees shared a common ancestor as recently as 5 to 8 million years ago (Sibley & Ahlquist, 1984).

Because of the genetic similarity and the relatively recent divergence of these two species, differences and similarities between the brains of chimpanzees and humans can yield insights into our evolutionary history. For example, using Jerison's (1973) encephalization quotient, both chimpanzees and humans are "brainier" than would be expected for their body weight, with the EQ being 2.3 for chimps and 7.6 for *Homo sapiens* (Jerison, 1973). This suggests that the human's substantial brain capacity is merely an extension of a pattern already established in our ancestors.

However, not all parts of the brain have expanded at comparable rates in chimpanzees and humans. Stephan and his associates (as reported in Eccles, 1989) developed the size index (SI), which is conceptually similar to Jerison's EQ measure, but which uses the most primitive living mammal, the basal insectivores, as a baseline for evaluating brain development and makes contrasts for specific brain structures. Using the SI, most major brain structures have increased in relative size in the apes and humans (the olfactory bulb and olfactory cortex being notable exceptions). The brain area that experienced the greatest increase in apes and humans, however, is the neocortex. The SI for samples of pongids (apes) for the neocortex is 61.88. Although this value is nearly three times as great as that for primitive primates (prosimians), reflecting an enormous advantage in brain power, the corresponding SI value for humans is more than three times greater again (196.41). Other areas of the brain have shown a substantial increase from apes to humans (e.g., cerebellum, diencephalon, hippocampus), but none so much as the neocortex.

The neocortex is the part of the brain that is most associated with human thought (Fuster, 1984; Luria, 1973). Specializations of the neocortex, particularly those associated with asymmetrical organization, promoted generative functions resulting, possibly, in tool use (Corballis, 1991), language (Bickerton, 1990), and self-consciousness (Eccles, 1989). Expansion of the neocortex also resulted in quantitative enhancements of cognitive skills, likely available to lesser degrees in monkeys and apes, including memory, problem solving, and control of emotional reactions. It is the latter function of the neocortex, inhibition of emotional responses, which is of paramount concern here, and which we are proposing played an important role in human social and cognitive evolution.

As we mentioned earlier, the frontal area of the neocortex has been implicated in cognitive inhibition, with damage to the prefrontal lobes resulting in loss of appropriate social and emotional inhibitions and increased distractibility and behavioral impulsivity. The prefrontal lobes of the neocortex are the last to fully develop in ontogeny, and presumably, the last to have developed phylogenetically (see Eccles, 1989; Jerison, 1973). In contrast, visual and motor areas of the neocortex are relatively well developed in apes and monkeys, suggesting that "at the outset of the evolutionary way to *Homo sapiens,* full developmental accomplishment had already been achieved in the retina and the visual pathway through the LGB [lateral geniculate body] to the primary visual cortex" (Eccles, 1989, p. 131).

With respect to inhibitions of inappropriate social/emotional responses, there are extensive neural pathways from the septal nuclei and amygdala of the limbic system through the thalamic nucleus that progress (mostly) to the prefrontal lobe (Eccles, 1989) (see Figure 5). These structures have been unambiguously implicated in both pleasurable (e.g., sexual) and aggressive (e.g.,

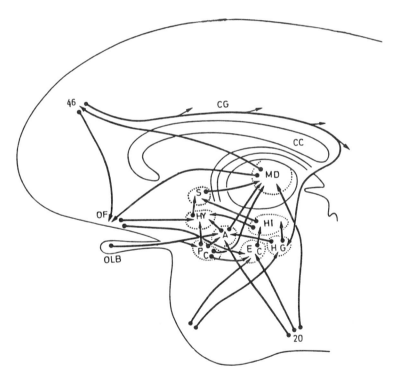

FIGURE 5. Schematic representation of the right cerebral hemisphere, showing connections between the neocortex and the mediodorsal thalamus (MD) and the limbic system. (OF = Orbital surface of prefrontal cortex; HI = hippocampus; S = septum; CC = corpus collosum; EC = entorhinal cortex; A = amygdala; CG = cingulate gyrunl; OLB = olfactory bulb; PC = piriform cortex; HG = hippocampal gyrun; HY = hypothalamus. The numbers 46 (frontal lobe) and 20 (temporal lobe) correspond to areas identified by Broadmann. (From Eccles, 1989.)

rage) emotions (see MacLean, 1990). Some have speculated that the limbic system is less evolved and plays a less important role in the human brain than in the primate brain (see Armstrong, 1991, for discussion). However, the individual components of the limbic system have actually increased in size in humans, suggesting that "the limbic structures play approximately the same role in the human brain as they do in the other primates" (Armstrong, 1991, p. 123). Moreover, structures in the limbic system, particularly the hippocampus and the amygdala, play a critical role in learning and remembering, suggesting that these structures continued to evolve in hominid evolution, rather than diminishing in importance (Armstrong, 1991). Thus, humans' apparently increased emotional control relative to other primates is not likely due to a reduction in the role of the limbic system in human behavior; we remain highly emotional animals. A more likely cause is inhibition from the prefrontal cortex.

The connections between the "thinking" (prefrontal cortex) and "emotional" (limbic system) parts of the brain have important implications for cognition and behavior. In part, the limbic system gives affective value to experiences processed by the associative areas of the brain, making some things more worth learning and retrieving than others (see Armstrong, 1991). But the important role played by the limbic system in forming, affectively evaluating, and retrieving memories in no way minimizes its role in generating emotional behavior. If the limbic system's role in processing information has expanded in evolution, there is no reason to believe that the system's role in emotionality has decreased, and, in a socially complex world, such emotionality may need to be controlled.

Critically, the inhibitory function of the prefrontal cortex permits the control of emotional expression. Signals from the limbic system are received by the prefrontal cortex and can be contrasted with signals coming from other areas of the brain. Decisions (intentional or otherwise) can then be made to vent or suppress emotional expression, based on nervous information received from different brain modules (including the limbic system) and integrated at the prefrontal cortex. This ability to inhibit emotional responses would have important implications for the survival of a social animal and may have contributed significantly to cognitive evolution, as we will argue below.

Eccles (1989) rhetorically asks why early hominids failed to develop advanced technical skills in stone culture, despite having well-developed visual and motor abilities. The answer, he proposes, is that *Homo habilis* and its predecessors, although having well-developed visual and motor cortices, lacked a sufficiently well-developed prefrontal lobe, important not only in conceptual tasks, but also in concentration. Eccles proposes that "with a still not fully developed prefrontal cortex the hominids may have been deficient in motivation and concentration" (p. 132). Concentration, as conventionally understood, refers to resistance to interference, the ability to allocate attentional resources to a task free from extraneous thoughts or undue influences from external sources. Thus, expansion of the prefrontal neocortex may have been a necessary development in human cognitive evolution, providing, among other things, the ability to control emotional responses and to block out both internal and external task-irrelevant information, resulting in an animal that could better control his or her own behavior and create culture.

Pressures Leading to Enhanced Inhibition in Hominid Social Groups

Many contemporary scholars of hominid evolution posit a central role for social factors in the origins of human intelligence (see, for example, Alexander, 1989; Byrne & Whiten, 1988; Crook, 1980; Dunbar, 1993; Humphrey, 1976). In fact, the most complex aspects of human life (and particularly of traditional peoples) are not concerned with food acquisition, avoiding predators, or developing technology, but with dealing with conspecifics. Given the physical demands of our ancestral environment (based on the life-styles of contemporary hunter/gatherers and paleological evidence), humans are far more intelligent than they need to be. Humphrey (1976) points out it is not only Bushmen who fail to use their intellectual brilliance for most mundane tasks, but a field anthropologist observing Albert Einstein from afar would probably have concurred that he, too, had a "hum-drum mind." Even chimpanzees show a keener intelligence in laboratory tasks than is seemingly required for their survival "in the wild." The key, Humphrey states, is that human genius (and perhaps ape genius as well) is displayed at rare times in artificial tasks. Even Einstein did not use his mental prowess in the everyday world of practical affairs, for he did not need to (Humphrey, 1976). We do use our impressive intellectual skills everyday (as do apes), however, for dealing with other members of our species. In all societies, from the high society of Palm Beach, Florida to the hunter/gatherer societies of the San !Kung in the Kalahari Desert, social interactions and relations are complex and the basis of human life. From this perspective, human intellect evolved to solve social problems, with civilization and advanced technology being the consequences.

Basically, social intelligence is political intelligence, or what Byrne and Whiten (1988) have referred to as Machiavellian intelligence. In hominid evolution, as social complexity increased, the pressures to cooperate and compete with other members of the group can be seen as the driving force of intelligence. Machiavellian intelligence requires controlling sexual, aggressive, and other "emotional" impulses, planning (covertly) one's "moves" and anticipating the "moves" of others, and often deceiving other group members in order to protect or garner important resources. Such intelligence is obviously complex, but one necessary component for keen social intellect is the ability to inhibit prepotent responses. If sexual or aggressive urges are not under voluntary control, for example, pandemonium could break loose in a small social group dependent on cooperation for its survival.

We are by no means the first to propose a potent role for inhibition in human cognitive evolution. For example, America's most influential philosopher of the early twentieth century, John Dewey, touted the central place of "reflective thought" in human intelligence. For Dewey, reflective thought "converts action that is merely appetitive, blind, and impulsive into intelligent action. A brute animal, as far as we know, is pushed from behind; it is moved in accordance with its present physiological state by some present stimulus" (Dewey, 1933/1964, p. 212). We are different than the animals because we can inhibit our gut responses and use reason to solve problems and ponder our nature. "If a man's actions are not guided by thoughtful conclusions, then they are guided by inconsiderate impulse, unbalanced appetite, caprice, or the circumstance of the moment. To cultivate unhindered unreflective external activity is to foster enslavement, for it leaves the person at the mercy of appetite, sense, and circumstance" (1933/1964, pp. 258, 259).

But how is it that human beings came to possess "reflective thought," freeing us from "caprice" or instinctive appetites? Reflective thought and reason require more than just an inhibition of impulse. But such withholding of appetitive or acquired responding would seem to be a necessary condition for such advanced forms of intelligence to develop. It is unlikely that the neural inhibition mechanisms responsible for contemporary *Homo sapiens*'s intellect initially evolved for that purpose. Rather, based on our knowledge of primate life, brain organization, and the fossil record, it seems that inhibition mechanisms evolved to deal with specific problems that arose as a result of the social organization of small hominid groups. Once present, the inhibition mechanisms made possible subsequent behaviors and cognitions that required withholding or delaying responses necessary for their successful completion.

Inhibition of Sexual Responses   The earliest theories positing a role for inhibition mechanisms in primate evolution centered around animals' need to suspend sexual activity (e.g., Chance, 1962; Chance & Mead, 1953; Fox, 1972). According to Chance, inhibition of aggression and sexual behavior served a major role in avoiding and handling conflict within primate social groups. In many species of mammals, including primates, there is considerable competition between males for access to females in estrus. The receptivity of females varies across species, with the period of receptivity in chimps and some monkeys being extended considerably, thus extending the amount of time males may be in conflict with one another. Also, in chimps, some mating is done when the female is not in estrus, with such couplings being attributed to social factors. Social as opposed to hormonal influences on sex reaches its apex in modern humans. Of all mammals, only the human female conceals ovulation, providing no external sign to potential mates of her impregnability. Moreover, unlike any other mammal, she presents permanently swollen mammaries, whether nursing or not, which have become constant sexual signals for males, despite their unreliability in predicting sexual receptivity or ovulation. Such deceptive body signals make it nearly impossible for a man to know when a woman is ovulating. Sexual receptivity, in both human males and females, cannot be determined by physical body signs, such as swollen genitals as in monkeys and apes. Moreover, both males and females are, in theory, continually receptive sexually, with their willingness to copulate being primarily under the control of social and not hormonal factors.

The opportunity for continuous mating would result in continuous conflict among males if some mechanisms for inhibiting sexual responses had not evolved. In baboons, for example, dominant males control a harem, with much aggression resulting when a subordinate male attempts to copulate with a female in the dominant male's presence. Male baboons who fail to inhibit their sexual advances tend to fail in their competition for access to females. Because of their uncontrolled behavior and the reactions of the dominant male to them, they fail to become integrated into the social hierarchy, holding onto the periphery of the group or leaving the group altogether (Chance, 1962; Fox, 1972). According to Chance (1962), the selection of sexual inhibitory functions would eventually pave the way "for the development of social groupings in which continuous mating behaviour, and therefore continuous suppression of mating behaviour through competition, may occur" (p. 102).

Chance proposed that inhibition of sexual responses became increasingly under cortical, and thus intentional, control in mammalian evolution. Essentially, one of the consequences of the increased size of the neocortex in mammalian phylogeny (see our discussion above) was to shift control of sexual behavior from hormonal to social factors. This relationship was recognized nearly 50 years ago by Beach (1947), who stated "that in the course of mammalian evolution as the cerebral cortex assumed a more and more dominant role in the cortical control of all complex behavior patterns, it came to exert an increasing influence over more primitive neural mechanisms which originally possessed sole responsibility for the mediation of sexual activities" (p. 310). Although sexual activity in no species is independent of hormonal influences, Beach (1947) noted that the role of hormones is particularly minimized in the anthropoid apes and humans, with the cerebral cortex playing an increasingly important role in courtship and mating.

The relationship here, of course, is a complex one. Increases in neocortex resulted in greater voluntary control of sexual and emotional behavior through an increased ability to inhibit prepotent responses. This in turn facilitated social harmony among small groups of hominids. The neural apparatus used to evaluate and sometimes inhibit emotional signals from the limbic system could then be recruited for other cognitive operations, resulting in increased resistance to interference and distractibility, and thus to enhanced concentration skills necessary for development of complex technology. For example, the circuits involved in suppressing sexual responses could seemingly be used to inhibit attention to distracting stimuli and to keep task-irrelevant information out of working memory. The cognitive and neuronal processes involved in resisting sexual temptation may not be so different than those involved in resisting attention to task-irrelevant stimuli. Both involve "putting out of one's mind" distracting stimuli and selectively attending to other task-relevant aspects of the environment. The connection may seem odd, but our ability to attend to central stimuli on incidental memory tasks (e.g., Lane & Pearson, 1982) and to keep task-irrelevant information out of working memory while reading (e.g., Hasher & Zacks, 1989), for example, may have their origins in our ability to inhibit sexual behavior when the social situations dictate that that is the appropriate thing to do.

But the relation among sexual inhibition, social pressure, and a larger neocortex is multidirectional, and it is not possible to determine which came first. However, once the cycle began, inhibition mechanisms became a powerful force in hominid social and intellectual evolution.

The Power Not to Respond   The most ambitious theory to include inhibition mechanisms in an account of human cognitive evolution was formulated by Stenhouse (1974). Stenhouse proposed four components in the evolution of human intelligence: memory store; abstraction and generalization; sensorimotor capabilities; and the power not to respond. Stenhouse referred to this last component as the Postponement factor, or P-factor, and proposed that, of the four, this was the most important factor in intellectual evolution, such that "its absence would negate the very possibility of adaptive variability in behaviour" (p. 67). (This perspective was apparently shared, although not greatly expounded on, by Harlow [1958], who wrote, "I believe that inhibition is the single process accounting for all learning" [p. 282]).

Similar to Chance (1962), Stenhouse believed that inhibition mechanisms had their phylogenetic origins in social behaviors; but rather than stressing sexual restraint, Stenhouse proposed that a tendency to withhold aggressive responses was evolved by dominant males in primate groups. Stenhouse observed that, in monkey groups, the mark of a socially dominant male is a relaxed demeanor and impassivity. By not reacting to mild provocations, the dominant male is illustrating total lack of fear, something that may further enhance his position. The possibility (and reality) of attack is always present, however. In fact, Stenhouse (1974) proposed that "the complete absence of fear itself is an implicit or latent threat" (p. 139). Following this logic, if, by being passive in appropriate contexts, the dominant male solidifies his position, it will likely result in a more stable social group, to the benefit of all members. This, in turn, may lead to greater cooperation.

Although the ability to postpone consummatory actions seems to have reached its most developed form in primates, it is not limited to these late-evolving creatures. Rats, for instance, will postpone instinctive behaviors such as feeding or mating in order to explore novel surroundings. Exploration, so characteristic of anthropoid apes and humans especially, would seem to require the withholding of virtually all alternative behaviors, except those in response to danger (see also Crook, 1980). It is through exploration, Stenhouse states, that individuals acquire information essential to storage and abstraction. According to Stenhouse, exploration implies a dissatisfaction with what one currently knows. In searching for novelty, an individual inhibits established responses and directs his or her behavior to new goals.

The ability to withhold prepotent responses so that one can approach the novel is likely important in any aspect of behavioral evolution. For example, Stenhouse suggested that the transition from quadrapedal to bipedal locomotion, first achieved in the primate line by australopithecines, required the individual "to resist the temptation to crawl and to climb trees, if he is to even begin to learn to stand and walk upon hind legs" (p. 172). Stenhouse made a similar claim for the evolution of language. For instance, some vocalizations of monkeys refer to specific situations, often specific predators. These vocalizations have a strong emotional association with them. For these "words" to develop a conceptual understanding, the individual must inhibit the old, emotional response (e.g., associating a vocalization meaning "snake" with an emotional response) and replace it with a conceptual/symbolic response.

Bickerton (1990) similarly argues, although along different lines, for the importance of vocal inhibition in the evolution of language. Although possible (see below), apes apparently have a difficult time suppressing calls associated with the presence of predators or the discovery of food. Yet an alarm call is often a double-edged sword, alerting the troop, for instance, to a predator while putting the caller at greater risk because of the noise he or she makes. According to Bickerton, the ability to suppress vocalization would have been particularly adaptive for *Australopithecus afarensis*. Because of its physical characteristics (25–35 kg body weight) and presumed life-style (spending much time on the ground instead of in the protection of trees), a noise at the wrong time might have disastrous consequences, more likely so than for a forest-living ape. Thus, proposed Bickerton, the voluntary suppression of vocalizations would have strong selection value. The neural mechanisms evolved to suppress vocalization would necessarily coexist with mechanisms to control voluntary vocalizations, an important step in the evolution of language.

The ability to suppress vocalizations may extend to the ability to verbally regulate behavior, something that Luria (1961, 1973) postulated involved a significant inhibitory role. As we noted earlier, patients with frontal lobe lesions and young children find it difficult to use language (either self-produced or instructions from others) to guide their behavior under certain situations. For example, frontal lobe patients and young children respond to the "impulsive" rather than the symbolic aspect of language (Llamas & Diamond, 1991; Luria, 1961, 1973), failing to follow instructions such as "tap twice each time the examiner taps once," or "Don't press the ball every time the examiner says 'Don't press'." Rather, young children and frontal lobe patients tap the same number of times as the examiner taps and press the ball to the verbal signal, being unable to inhibit these more dominant responses. In development, verbal regulation of behavior eventually becomes covert, with children being able to direct their problem solving without the need of overt speech (Vygotsky, 1962). Such overt-to-covert language seemingly requires the suppression of speech, something that young children find difficult or impossible to do, with overt (private) speech often being used by older children to guide their problem-solving behavior when tasks become especially difficult (e.g., Berk, 1986). Such covert-verbal thought, which adults take for granted, not only has an ontogenetic history but also has a phylogenetic history. In both cases, the ability to use covert language to guide overt behavior seemingly involves a significant inhibitory role.

Inhibition and the Evolution of Parenting   The ability to postpone emotional responding may also have had important implications for parenting (see Crook, 1980; Stenhouse, 1974). Primates in general, and humans in particular, have extended periods of youth. In humans, an infant is born helpless and cannot exist independently before the age of five or six, and then requires another decade before true independence is possible. The helplessness and considerable demands of the infant/child require a parent who is willing and able to postpone his or (and more likely) her own needs. Successful parents must inhibit their immediate emotional urges when they are awakened in the middle of the night by an aversive cry or when they are vomited on, for example. Also, the calm, reflective handling of infants is characteristic of mothers who have securely attached infants, infants who form close emotional bonds with their mothers and who, in childhood, tend to be curious, resourceful problem solvers, self-assured, and socially adept (see, e.g., Ainsworth et al., 1978; Cassidy, 1988; Cohn, 1990; Erickson, Sroufe, & Egeland, 1985).

The behaviors of children continue to try the patience of their parents as they get older. Young children greatly overestimate their abilities (e.g., Bjorklund, Gaultney, & Green, 1993), and, as a consequence, often get into dangerous, or at least awkward, situations. Aggressive responses to such childishness are frequently considered by modern parents, but also are frequently inhibited. The prolonged childhood of *Homo sapiens,* necessary for mastering the complex social world characteristic of all groups of humans, required a patient parent, one who was able to inhibit emotional responses and often delay her own gratification for the sake of her offspring.

The Need to Deceive   One consummate political skill dependent on an ability to withhold responses is deceit. Whether one is merely concealing an emotion (very valuable in playing poker, among other things) or actively misleading an opponent, deception requires inhibiting a prepotent response.

Deception is characteristic of many species, including insects that look like sticks, innocuous butterflies that mimic a noxious species, and birds who will lure predators away from their egg-filled nests. But in each of these cases, the deception is inflexible. The individual does not "choose" to deceive, but, because of its bodily appearance or a fixed-action pattern, automatically deceives its predator. Moreover, in each case, the deception is aimed at a member of another species, not a conspecific. The type of deception pertinent to our arguments here is intraspecific and involves a flexible, learned component. Thus, leading a fellow group member away from a source of food, inhibiting vocalizations during a clandestine mating, or distracting another so that a treat can be obtained all require an active withholding of a prepotent response.

There is no question that humans have the ability to deceive. Our skill at lying has resulted in the creation of such technological tools as voice-stress analyzers and polygraphs. Deception would also seem to be an important political skill for our primate cousins, who also live in complex social groups with status determined by intelligence as well as brawn. Whiten and Byrne (1988) sent questionnaires to 115 primatologists asking for evidence of deception in their subjects. Most of the responses they received (50 of a total of 79 examples of primate deception) involved concealment or distraction. Let us sketch briefly some of the more illustrative examples from the literature, some of which were also cited by Whiten and Byrne (1988):

Goodall (1986) reports that male chimpanzees would sometimes inhibit their distinctive cry during orgasms when copulating with a favorite female. In this way, they avoid having to share the female with other males.

Premack (1988) and Savage-Rumbaugh and McDonald (1988) each report evidence of deception in language-trained chimpanzees. For example, Austin and Sherman of the Yerkes laboratory have perfected ways of escaping from their cages, but have never allowed humans to knowingly watch them while doing it (Savage-Rumbaugh & McDonald, 1988). Premack (1988) reports that chimps quickly learned to distinguish between a trainer who provided them with food rewards and one who did not, and suppressed responding in the presence of the hostile trainer (or, in one case, actively misled the trainer), but not in the presence of the benign one.

In research by Menzel (1974), one chimp, Belle, was shown the location of hidden food and would then lead the small group of chimps to it. She ceased leading the group directly to the food, however, when Rock (the dominant male) was present, because Rock would kick or bite her and take the food. When Rock was present Belle would wait until Rock left before uncovering food. On a few occasions, Belle actually led the troop in the opposite direction from food, then, while Rock was searching, she doubled back to get the food. On other trials, the experimenter hid extra pieces of food in a second place. On those trials, Belle would lead Rock to this second, smaller source, and then go to the main cache. A similar observation of not retrieving or looking at a banana until after a more dominant chimp had left the area, was reported for the juvenile chimp Figan by Goodall (1971).

A female baboon approached a male baboon who had some meat, which he showed no willingness to share. The female edged up to the male and began grooming him until he lolled back, at which time she grabbed the meat and ran (Jolly, 1985).

Concealment was observed in both our close genetic relatives, the apes (including chimpanzees and gorillas), and in our more distant relatives, the monkeys (including baboons); but Whiten and Byrne (1988) commented that "there is no monkey example which matches those for gorillas and chimpanzees . . . where what is concealed is an object" (p. 221). There were reports of monkeys inhibiting their behavior (e.g., freezing) in order not to attract the attention of another, usually dominant, animal, but no cases in which concealment or distraction involved an object (such as food, as in the cases reported by Menzel and Goodall with chimps above). Whiten and Byrne suggested that monkeys can likely "inhibit attention to others whom they wish to avoid, whereas only apes inhibit attention to resources they want. . . ." They further suggested that "a simian capacity for ignoring could, nevertheless, have been an important preadaptation for evolution of the ape's more complex ability" (p. 222).

From this brief overview, it should be apparent that human deception and the associated inhibitory mechanisms have their origins in similar, though less sophisticated, mechanisms in monkeys and apes. Progressing from monkeys to apes to humans—social animals all—deceptive abilities increase along with the social complexity of the group. (We found few accounts of deception in orangutans, great apes who do not live in social groups.) Improvements of inhibition abilities alone would not make a chimpanzee a skilled poker player or a major player in the political machinations of a small government; additional cognitive skills are clearly required. For example, maintaining our poker metaphor, one has to know when to hold them and when to fold them. And there are obviously times when expressing a prepotent response will produce the most advantageous outcome. Were an animal to inhibit its sexual urges completely, for example, it would never procreate. But without the inhibitory ability to delay, more complicated decision-making skills could not develop at all.

IMPLICATIONS OF THE EVOLUTION OF INHIBITION MECHANISMS

Inhibition of prepotent, emotional, or learned responses seems to be necessary for effective life in a complex social primate group. As sexual responsiveness increases, the need to inhibit sexual and aggressive responses under certain conditions becomes critical for social cohesion. As social cohesion increases, relations among troop members become more complicated, requiring not only physical strength or dexterity for individual success, but social skills as well. These social skills involve effective communication, patient rearing of offspring, and occasionally keeping secrets or actively deceiving other conspecifics.

Successful social life in early hominid groups may have required more social skills than that, however. Social contracts play an important role in all complex human societies and involve, among other things, making deals. In many cases in contemporary human cultures, a deal will involve a trade for immediate services or resources from one individual in exchange for a promise of services or resources in the future. Such deals, which may have been critical in the formation of families and larger kinship groups, require an ability to delay gratification. They also require memory and an ability to detect cheaters (see Cosmides & Tooby, 1992), and perhaps an ability to reflect on the worthiness of the "deal." But none of these "higher" cognitive operations would be possible without an ability to first withhold responding. Promises of payoffs in the future require not only a cognitive system that can make a decision that forgoing a resource now (e.g., sharing meat) may produce other resources (e.g., roots and berries) in the future, but also a cognitive system that can delay gratification in the first place.

Similarly, the importance of deceit obviously requires inhibition, but deception often has a second component to it. Merely "keeping quiet" or distracting another troop member often has no immediate payoff. The payoff comes when the distracted individual is sufficiently off his guard so that the distractor can "make her move," such as the female baboon mentioned above who groomed a male until he was relaxed enough so that she was able to grab the meat and run. That is, inhibition in cases of social contracts and deception provides not only the ability not to respond, but also the time to generate or execute a plan. Cognitive or behavioral inhibition, then, is not directly responsible for planning, reflection, or advanced problem-solving abilities found in the anthropoid apes and humans; but inhibition is a permissive factor, providing the opportunity for these more advanced forms of cognition.

What we propose is that inhibition mechanisms became increasingly under cortical control in human evolution, initially to permit the individual greater voluntary control of sexual and aggressive behaviors. As the social complexity of the group increased, in large part due to the inhibition of these often disruptive responses, it became adaptive to gain voluntary control of other behaviors, such as sexual or predator cries, gazes toward valuable resources, and emotional expressions. The neural mechanisms were initially evolved to inhibit sexual and aggressive behaviors, but became recruited for other purposes, leading not only to the ability to deceive, but possibly also to language and Dewey's notion of reflective thought. Again, let us emphasize that we do not claim that inhibitory mechanisms are directly responsible for the complex cognitions characteristic of our species. Rather, they played a permissive role, permitting neocortical circuits to evolve to handle the demands of an increasingly complex social world and to be recruited by those circuits, when necessary, for successful task performance.

Surely performance on most laboratory tasks such as memory span, free recall, selective attention, and word recognition has not been under strong selection pressures over the past four million years. Yet the inhibitory mechanisms underlying performance on these tasks, so familiar to cognitive psychologists, have been selected for, with *Homo sapiens*'s information processing being the end result. For example, the inhibitory mechanisms needed to stay focused on a goal and to delay responding until the appropriate time also provided contemporary humans with the ability to keep task-irrelevant information out of working memory when performing a novel motor task, reading, or recalling the sequence of actions of a recent event. These basic cognitive processes are also present in our simian cousins; but, we propose, our enhanced inhibitory abilities, among other factors, resulted in an effective increase in the functional capacity of working memory by keeping irrelevant information from intruding into awareness and thus interfering with the performance of the task at hand.

If information-processing programs are the "missing link" in evolution as some have proposed (Cosmides & Tooby, 1987; Tooby & Cosmides, 1992), it is unlikely they were selected for performance of reading comprehension or Stroop tasks. Yet, performance on such laboratory tasks reflects a processing with a long history, evolved to solve important problems. As *Homo sapiens*'s technological sophistication increased, new "important problems" presented themselves, and the cognitive mechanisms initially used for inhibiting inappropriate social responses could be used to create tools, perform multistep reasoning, tell stories, and make sense of both spoken and written language. Our needs to inhibit aggressive and sexual responses, to delay gratification, and to sometimes deceive conspecifics are likely similar in nature to the needs of our ancestors. However, we have evolved new needs, and these more "cognitive" needs are served by these same, ancient inhibitory mechanisms.

EPILOGUE

Our goal in this chapter has been to demonstrate that inhibition mechanisms play a central role in human cognition, the control of social and emotional behavior, and development. The neural basis for these mechanisms is relatively well understood, having been illuminated by comparative, neuropsychological, clinical, and developmental research. This research also reflects the fact that inhibition plays a central role in the behavioral control and cognitions of species other than our own.

However, much of what is special about human cognition and social control of behavior seems to involve significant inhibitory components above and beyond that displayed by our close genetic relatives. We show greater voluntary control of our emotions, particularly our sexual behavior, than any other species; we are able to delay gratification (sometimes for years) in the quest of a goal; we can deceive others or hide our true feelings, often to our political (or simply physical) advantage. Each of these behaviors, while perhaps not unique to humans, reaches its zenith in *Homo sapiens* and contributes to our success as a species. Each also involves inhibition.

Such inhibition mechanisms, while perhaps being qualitatively similar to mechanisms found in other species, gained special status in humankind. This special status was acquired through evolution. Human evolution represents a confluence of factors, acting synergistically over millions of years, with each factor serving both as cause and consequence of a host of other factors. It is impossible to point to any single set of causes for human evolution, or even to propose one factor or set of factors as paramount. Yet we do believe it is fruitful to look at how various environmental pressures may have influenced behavioral and neural development and how these changes may have in turn resulted in a more adaptive organism.

To examine these questions, we have briefly reviewed what is known about the evolution of the human brain through fossil evidence and comparisons with extant primates Although our review was admittedly cursory, it demonstrated that gross differences in brain structures do exist between humans and both modern apes and our hominid ancestors, consistent with the proposition that there were phylogenetic differences in inhibitory mechanisms over hominid evolution. From there, we moved to a cognitive level of analysis, examining the environmental and social pressures that may have lead to enhanced inhibitory skills.

Our central argument is that we can better understand contemporary human thought through an understanding of its evolution. Further, the evolutionary evidence is consistent with the possibility that neural inhibition, selected initially to handle problems resulting from hominids' particular social organization, became available for other more "cognitive" operations, such as self-awareness, abstraction, reflection, planning, and possibly even language. We have not meant to imply that an increased ability for cognitive inhibition was the primary impetus for human intellectual evolution; merely that cognitive inhibition played a central role in such evolution, and was both a cause and a consequence of the changing human mind.

REFERENCES

Ainsworth, M. D. S., Blehar, M. C., Waters, E., & Wall, S. (1978). *Pattern of attachment: A psychological study of the strange situation.* Hillsdale, NJ: Erlbaum.

Alexander, R. D. (1989). Evolution of the human psyche. In P. Mellers & C. Stringer (Eds.), *The human revolution: Behavioural and biological perspectives on the origins of modern humans.* (pp. 455–513) Princeton, NJ: Princeton University Press.

Armstrong, E. (1991). The limbic system and culture: An allometric analysis of the neocortex and limbic nuclei. *Human Nature, 2,* 117–136.

Bandura, A. (1989). Regulation of cognitive processes through perceived self-efficacy. *Developmental Psychology, 25*, 729–735.

Beach, F. A. (1947). Evolutionary changes in the physiological control of mating behavior in mammals. *Psychological Review, 54*, 297–315.

Bell, M. A., & Fox, N. A. (1992). The relations between frontal brain electrical activity and cognitive development during infancy. *Child Development, 63*, 1142–1163.

Berk, L. E. (1986). Relationship of elementary school children's private speech to behavioral accompaniment to task, attention, and task performance. *Developmental Psychology, 22*, 671–680.

Bickerton, D. (1990). *Language and species.* Chicago: University of Chicago Press.

Bjork, R. A. (1989). Retrieval inhibition as an adaptive mechanism in human memory. In H. L. Roediger, III & F. I. M. Craik (Eds.), *Varieties of memory and consciousness* (pp. 309–330). Hillsdale, NJ: Erlbaum.

Bjorklund, D. F., Gaultney, J. F., & Green, B. L. (1993). "I Watch, therefore I can do:" The development of meta-imitation during the preschool years and the advantage of optimism about one's imitative skills. In M. L. Howe & R. Pasnak (Eds.), *Emerging themes in cognitive development* (p. 79–102 (Vol. 2). New York: Springer-Verlag.

Bjorklund, D. F., & Green, B. L. (1992). The adaptive nature of cognitive immaturity. *American Psychologist, 47*, 46–54.

Bjorklund, D. F., & Harnishfeger, K. K. (1990). The resources construct in cognitive development: Diverse sources of evidence and a theory of inefficient inhibition. *Developmental Review, 1*, 48–71.

Brown, A. L., Smiley, S. S., Day, J. D., Townsend, M. A. R., & Lawton, S. C. (1977). Intrusion of a thematic idea in children's comprehension and retention of stories. *Child Development, 48*, 1454–1466.

Byrne, R., & Whiten, A. (Eds.). (1988). *Machiavellian intelligence: Social expertise and the evolution of intellect in monkeys, apes, and humans.* Oxford: Clarendon Press.

Case, R. (1985). *Intellectual development: Birth to adulthood.* New York: Academic Press.

Cassidy, J. (1988). Child-mother attachment and the self in six-year-olds. *Child Development, 59*, 121–134.

Chance, M. R. A. (1962). Social behaviour and primate evolution. In M. F. A. Montagu (Ed.), *Culture and the evolution of man.* (pp. 84–130) New York: Oxford University Press.

Chance, M. R. A., & Mead, A. P. (1953). Social behavior and primate evolution. *Symposia of the Society for Experimental Biology, 7*, 395–439.

Chelune, G. J., & Baer, R. A. (1986). Developmental norms for the Wisconsin Card Sorting Test. *Journal of Clinical and Experimental Neuropsychology, 8*, 219–228.

Cohn, D. A. (1990). Child-mother attachment of six-year-olds and social competence at school. *Child Development, 61*, 152–162.

Connelly, S. L., Hasher, L., & Zacks, R. T. (1991). Age and reading: The impact of distraction. *Psychology & Aging, 6*, 533–541.

Corballis, M. C. (1991). *The lopsided ape: Evolution of the generative mind.* New York: Oxford University Press.

Cosmides, L., & Tooby, J. (1987). From evolution to behavior: Evolutionary psychology as the missing link. In J. Dupré (Ed.), *The latest on the best essays on evolution and optimality.* (pp. 277–306). Cambridge, MA: MIT Press.

Cosmides, L., & Tooby, J. (1992). Cognitive adaptations for social exchange. In J. H. Barkow, L. Cosmides, & J. Tooby (Eds.), *The adapted mind: Evolutionary psychology and the generation of culture.* (pp. 163–228) New York: Oxford University Press.

Crook, J. H. (1980). *The evolution of human consciousness.* Oxford: Clarendon Press.

Dempster, F. N. (1992). The rise and fall of the inhibitory mechanisms: Toward a unified theory of cognitive development and aging. *Developmental Review, 12*, 45–47.

Dempster, F. N. (1993). Resistance to interference: Developmental changes in basic processing mechanisms. In M. L. Howe & R. Pasnak (Eds.), *Emerging themes in cognitive development: Vol. 1: Foundations* (pp. 3–27). New York: Springer-Verlag.

Dewey, J. (1964). How we think: A restatement of the relation of reflective thinking to the education process. In R. D. Archambault (Ed.), *John Dewey on education.* (pp. 212–228). New York: Modern Library. (Original work published 1933).

Diamond, A. (1985). Development of the ability to use recall to guide action as indicated by infants' performance on A̅B̅. *Child Development, 56,* 868–f883.

Diamond, A. (1988). Abilities and neural mechanisms underlying A not B performance. *Child Development, 59,* 523–527.

Diamond, A. (1990). Rate of maturation of the hippocampus and the developmental progression of children's performance on the delayed non-matching to sample and visual paired comparison tasks. In A. Diamond (Ed.), *The development and neural bases of higher cognitive functions* (pp. 394–426). New York: New York Academy of Sciences.

Diamond, A. (1991). Frontal lobe involvement in cognitive changes during the first year of life. In K. R. Gibson & A. C. Petersen (Eds.), *Brain maturation and cognitive development: Comparative and cross-cultural perspectives* (pp. 127–180). New York: de Gruyter.

Doyle, A. B. (1973). Listening to distraction: A developmental study of selective attention. *Journal of Experimental Child Psychology, 15,* 100–115.

Dunbar, R. I. M. (1993). Co-evolution of neocortex size, group, size, and language in humans. *Behavioral and Brain Sciences, 16,* 681–735.

Dustman, R. E., Snyder, E. W., & Schlehuber, C. J. (1981). Life-span alterations in visually evoked potentials and inhibitory function. *Neurobiology of Aging, 2,* 187–192.

Eccles, J. C. (1989). *Evolution of the brain: Creation of the self.* London: Routledge.

Edelman, G. M. (1987). *Neural Darwinism: The theory of neuronal group selection.* New York: Basic Books.

Enright, S. j., & Beech, A. R. (1993a). Further evidence of reduced cognitive inhibition in obsessive-compulsive disorder. *Personality and Individual Differences, 14,* 387–395.

Enright, S. J., & Beech, A. R. (1993b). Reduced cognitive inhibition in obsessive-compulsive disorder. *British Journal of Clinical Psychology, 32,* 67–74.

Erickson, M. F., Sroufe, L. A., & Egeland, B. (1985). The relationship between quality of attachment and behavior problems in preschool in a high-risk sample. In I. Bretherton & E. Waters (Eds.), Growing points of attachment theory and research. *Monographs of the Society for Research in Child Development, 50* (Serial No. 209).

Flor-Henry, P. (1983). *Cerebral basis of psychopathology.* Boston: John Wright.

Fox, R. (1972). Alliance and constraint: Sexual selection and the evolution of human kinship systems. In B. Campbell (Ed.), *Sexual selection and the descent of man 1871–1971.* (pp. 282–331) Chicago: Aldine.

Fuster, J. M. (1980). *The prefrontal cortex: Anatomy, physiology, and neuropsychology of the frontal lobe.* New York: Raven Press.

Fuster, J. M. (1985). The prefrontal cortex and temporal integration. In A. Peters & E. G. Jones (Eds.), *Cerebral cortex: Vol. 4. Association and auditory cortices.* (pp. 151–177). New York: Plenum.

Goldman-Rakic, P. S. (1987). Development of cortical circuitry and cognitive function. *Child Development, 58,* 601–622.

Goodall, J. (1971). *In the shadow of man.* London: Collins.

Goodall, J. (1986). *The chimpanzees of Gombe.* Cambridge, MA: Belknap.

Greenough, W. T., Black, J. E., & Wallace, C. S. (1987). Experience and brain development. *Child Development, 58,* 539–559.

Hagen, J. W., & Hale, G. A. (1973). The development of attention in children. In A. D. Pick (Ed.), *Minnesota symposium on child psychology* (Vol. 7, pp. 117–140). Minneapolis: University of Minnesota Press.

Hamm, V. P., & Hasher, L. (1992). Age and the availability of inferences. *Psychology & Aging,* *7,* 56–64.

Harlow, H. F. (1958). The evolution of learning. In A. Roe & G. G. Simpson (Eds.), *Behaviour and evolution.* (pp. 269–290) New Haven, CT: Yale University Press.

Harnishfeger, K. K. & Bjorklund, D. F. (1993). The ontogeny of inhibition mechanisms: A renewed approach to cognitive development. In M. L. Howe & R. Pasnak (Eds.), *Emerging themes in cognitive development: Vol. 1. Foundations* (pp. 28–49). New York: Springer-Verlag.

Hasher, L., & Zacks, R. T. (1989). Working memory, comprehension, and aging: A review and a new view. In G. H. Bower (Ed.), *The psychology of learning and motivation: Advances in research and theory* (Vol. 22, pp. 193–224). San Diego: Academic Press.

Houtz, J. C., Denmark, R., Rosenfield, S., & Tetenbaum, T. J. (1980). Problem solving and personality characteristics related to differing levels of intelligence and ideational fluency. *Contemporary Educational Psychology, 5,* 118–123.

Humphrey, N. K. (1976). The social function of intellect. In P. P. G. Bateson & R. A. Hinde (Eds.), *Growing points in ethology.* (pp. 303–317) Cambridge: Cambridge University Press.

Huttenlocher, P. R. (1979). Synaptic density in human frontal cortex-developmental changes and effects of aging. *Brain Research, 163,* 195–205.

Jerison, H. J. (1973). *Evolution of the brain and intelligence.* New York: Academic Press.

Jolly, A. (1985). *The evolution of primate behavior* (2nd ed.). New York: Macmillan.

Konner, M. (1991). Universals of behavioral development in relation to brain myelination. In K. R. Gibson & A. C. Petersen (Eds.), *Brain maturation and cognitive development: Comparative and cross-cultural perspectives.* (pp. 181–223) New York: de Gruyter.

Lane, D. M., & Pearson, D. A. (1982). The development of selective attention. *Merrill-Palmer Quarterly, 28,* 317–337.

Llamas, C. & Diamond, A. (1991, April). *Development of frontal cortex abilities in children between 3–8 years of age.* Paper presented at the meeting of the Society for Research in Child Development, Seattle, WA.

Lorenz, K. (1966). *On aggression.* (Work published, 1963). (M. K. Wilson, Trans.). New York: Harcourt, Brace, & World.

Luria, A. R. (1961). *The role of speech in the regulation of normal and abnormal behavior.* New York: Pergamon.

Luria, A. R. (1973). *The working brain: An introduction to neuropsychology.* New York: Basic Books.

MacLean, P. D. (1990). *The triune brain in evolution: Role in paleocerebral functions.* New York: Plenum.

Malloy, P. (1987). Frontal lobe dysfunction in obsessive-compulsive disorder. In E. Perecman (Ed.), *The frontal lobes revisited.* (pp. 207–223) New York: IRBN Press.

Menzel, E. W. (1974). A group of young chimpanzees in a 1-acre field: Leadership and communication. In A. M. Schrier & F. Stollnitz (Eds.), *Behavior of nonhuman primates* (pp. 83–153 Vol. 5). New York: Academic Press.

Milner, B. (1964). Some effects of frontal lobectomy in man. In J. M. Warren & K. Akert (Eds.), *The frontal granular cortex and behavior.* (pp. 313–334) New York: McGraw-Hill.

Nash, A. J., & Williams, C. S. (1982). Effects of preparatory set and task demands on auditory event related potentials. *Biological Psychology, 15,* 15–31.

Onifer, W., & Swinney, D. A. (1981). Accessing lexical ambiguities during sentence comprehension: Effects of frequency of meaning and contextual bias. *Memory & Cognition, 9,* 225–236.

Pavlov, I. P. (1966). *Essential works.* New York: Bantam Books.

Perecman, E. (Ed.). (1987). *The frontal lobes revisited.* New York: IRBN Press.

Piaget, J. (1952). *The origins of intelligence in children.* New York: Norton.

Premack, D. (1988).'Does the chimpanzee have a theory of mind?' revisited. In R. W. Byrne & A. Whiten (Eds.), *Machiavellian intelligence: Social expertise and the evolution of intellect in monkeys, apes, and humans.* (pp. 160–179) Oxford: Clarendon Press.

Savage-Rumbaugh, S., & McDonald, K. (1988). Deception and social manipulation in symbol-using apes. In R. W. Byrne & A. Whiten (Eds.) *Machiavellian intelligence: Social expertise and the evolution of intellect in monkeys, apes, and humans.* (pp. 224–237) Oxford: Clarendon Press.

Schacter, D. L., Moscovitch, M., Tulving, E., McLachlan, D. R., & Frendman, M. (1986). Mnemonic precedence in amnesiac patients: An analogue of the $\overline{AB}$ error in infants. *Child Development, 57,* 816–823.

Sibley, C. G., & Ahlquist, J. E. (1984). The phylogeny of hominid primates, as indicated by DNA-DNA hybridization. *Journal of Molecular Evolution, 20,* 2–15.

Stebbings, G. L. (1982). *Darwin to DNA: Molecules to humanity.* San Francisco: Freeman.

Stenhouse, D. (1974). *The evolution of intelligence: A general theory and some of its implications.* London: Allen & Unwin.

Strutt, G. F., Anderson, D. R., & Well, A. D. (1975). A developmental study of the effects of irrelevant information on speeded classification. *Journal of Experimental Child Psychology, 20,* 127–135.

Swinney, D. A., & Prather, P. (1989). On the comprehension of lexical ambiguity by young children: Investigations into the development of mental modularity. In D. S. Gorfein (Ed.), *Resolving semantic ambiguity* (pp. 225–238). New York: Springer-Verlag.

Swinney, D. A., Zurif, E., & Nicol, J. (1989). The effects of focal brain damage on sentence processing: An examination of the neurological organization of a mental module. *Journal of Cognitive Neuropsychology, 1,* 25–37.

Tegano, D. W. (1990). Relationship of tolerance of ambiguity and playfulness to creativity. *Psychological Reports, 66,* 1047–1056.

Tipper, S. P. (1992). Selection for action: The role of inhibitory mechanisms. *Current Directions in Psychological Science, 1,* 105–109.

Tipper, S. P. Bourque, T. A., Anderson, S. H., & Brehaut, J. (1989). Mechanisms of attention: A developmental study. *Journal of Experimental Child Psychology, 48,* 353–378.

Tobias, P. V. (1987). The brain of *Homo habilis*: A new level of organization in cerebral evolution. *Journal of Human Evolution, 16,* 741–761.

Tooby, J., & Cosmides, L. (1992). The psychological foundations of culture. In J. H. Barkow, L. Cosmides, & J. Tooby (Eds.), *The adapted mind: Evolutionary psychology and the generation of culture.* New York: Oxford University Press.

Vygotsky, L. S. (1962). *Thought and language.* Cambridge, MA: MIT Press.

Wegner, D. M. (1989). *White bears and other unwanted thoughts: Suppression, obsession, and the psychology of mental control.* New York: Viking.

Whiten, A., & Bryne, R. W. (1988). The manipulation of attention in primate tactical deception. In R. W. Byrne & A. Whiten (Eds.) *Machiavellian intelligence: Social expertise and the evolution of intellect in monkeys, apes, and humans.* (pp. 211–223 Oxford: Clarendon Press.

Woodward, S., Brown, W., Marsh, J., & Dawson, M. (1991). Probing the time course of the auditory oddball P3 with secondary reaction time. *Psychophyisology, 28,* 609–618.

Wozniak, R. H. (1972). Verbal regulation of motor behavior: Soviet research and non-Soviet replications. *Human Development, 15,* 13–57.

Yakolev, P. I., & Lecours, A. R. (1967). The myelogenetic cycles of regional maturation of the brain. In A. Minkowski (Ed.), *Regional development of the brain in early life* (pp. 3–70). Philadelphia: Davis.

Zimmerman, B. J., & Martinez-Pons, M. (1990). Student differences in self-regulated learning: Relating grade, sex, and giftedness to self-efficacy and strategy use. *Journal of Educational Psychology, 82,* 51–59.

6

The Development of Cognitive Inhibition
Theories, Definitions, and Research Evidence

Katherine Kipp Harnishfeger

Several contemporary developmental theories emphasize the role of changes in inhibitory efficiency in accounting for developmental changes in other aspects of cognition and behavior (e.g., Bjorklund & Harnishfeger, 1990, Chapter 5, this volume; Brainerd & Reyna, 1993; Dempster, 1993; Harnishfeger & Bjorklund, 1993; Hasher & Zacks, 1988; McDowd, Oseas-Kreger, & Filion, Chapter 11, this volume). A central assumption of such approaches is that inhibitory mechanisms become more efficient during early development and decline in efficiency in later development. In this chapter, I examine the tenability of the hypothesis that certain forms of cognitive inhibition improve in efficiency over childhood. To begin, I discuss cognitive inhibition in the context of historical and contemporary inhibition models (see also Dempster, Chapter 1, this volume). I then examine some of the key characteristics of the cognitive inhibition construct. Here, I am primarily concerned with distinguishing between behavioral and cognitive inhibition and between inhibition and interference. In addition, I examine intentional and automatic forms of cognitive inhibition. Having distinguished interference and cognitive inhibition, I then turn to a review of recent research evidence concerning developmental changes in these variables. Evidence is reviewed from several different paradigms, with an assessment of both intentional and automatic (or preconscious) inhibitory processing.

MODELS OF INHIBITION IN DEVELOPMENTAL PSYCHOLOGY

Early Models

The inhibition construct played a minor role in early psychological theories (e.g., Ebbinghaus, 1885/1964; James, 1890). For early developmental theories, inhibitory mechanisms were more important. The level of analysis of inhibition varied, from low-level mechanisms operating in learning and conditioning (e.g., Pavlov, 1927) to higher level mechanisms operating in the control of behavior (e.g., Luria, 1961). However, this behavior was not always conscious or intentional (e.g., Freud, 1915/1957).

In Freudian theory, inhibition played two primary roles. First, there was the inhibition of unwanted thoughts or behaviors, which Freud called repression (Brenner, 1957; Freud, 1915/1957). Aleksandrowicz (1977) explained that "repression means blocking of an idea from awareness and making it inaccessible (as opposed to simple inattention). Freud pointed out that repression is not just a lack of awareness, but an active inhibitory process, requiring a constant expenditure of energy" (p. 191). The second type of inhibition, which Freud called primary repression, was the repression of experiences and memories from infancy and early childhood.

Other theories that employed inhibition as a central developmental mechanism include those of the Russian psychologists Luria and Vygotsky. Vygotsky (1962) proposed a series of stages through which children acquire the control of their behavior via internalized speech. This approach was explored and expanded on by Luria. Luria (1961) demonstrated a developmental sequence of action control via verbal regulation. Very young children are not able to guide their own behavior either through external or internal speech. That is, they are unable to follow directions that contradict more habitual or prepotent responses, and they are unable to use verbal commands to stop (or inhibit) their ongoing behaviors. Indeed, commands to "stop" frequently will lead to an intensification of the behavior (Luria, 1961; Saltz, Campbell, & Skotko, 1983). Later, toddlers become capable of using external verbal commands to direct their behavior, yet they continue to be unable to regulate their behavior with their own verbal instructions (internal or aloud). Development of the verbal control of behavior occurs from the outside in, with external verbal control being achieved before internal verbal control of behavior. This research also revealed a distinction between excitatory and inhibitory functions of speech. For young children, the excitatory mechanisms initiates action with verbal commands, and this function comes under external and internal control before the ability to inhibit action verbally develops (cf. Fuson, 1979; Luria, 1961; Wozniak, 1972).

Contemporary Models

Although inhibitory mechanisms have continued to appear in developmental theories (e.g., Fishbein, 1976, 1984), such mechanisms have not been prominent for the past 30 years or so. During this period, developmental psychology came to be dominated by information-processing models, in which inhibitory mechanisms were not seen as particularly useful (Bjork, 1989). Currently, however, inhibition is undergoing a revival as a developmental principle (cf. Dempster, 1993; Harnishfeger & Bjorklund, 1993). As in early theories, contemporary developmental theories examine inhibition at a variety of levels. In this section, I introduce several contemporary models that employ inhibitory mechanisms to account for cognitive development in childhood and aging, and for individual differences in children's social and personality development.

Inefficient Inhibition and Resource Limitations   Many contemporary cognitive theorists postulate models featuring a central, or generic, pool of mental resources that must be allocated to the various operations involved in processing, retaining, and reporting information (e.g., Hasher & Zacks, 1979; Shiffrin & Schneider, 1977). These models conceptualize cognitive processes on a continuum, with those processes that require mental capacity for their execution at one extreme, and those that do not at the other. If the operations being executed required more mental capacity than is available, performance will suffer (Navon & Gopher, 1979).

The limited resource model has been particularly useful for understanding developmental changes in children's cognitive processes. Developmental models, such as those proposed by Case (1985; Case, Kurland, & Goldberg, 1982) and Bjorklund (1985, 1987) typically postulate that the limited pool of mental resources available for the execution of cognitive operations and storage of information does not increase with age. Improvements in cognitive performance do occur, however, due to increases in the efficiency with which cognitive operations can be executed. This increased processing efficiency releases mental resources to be used for the storage of additional information or for the execution of other cognitive processes and strategies. Thus, according to these models, mental capacity is stable throughout life, with increases in processing speed or efficiency being agents of improvement in cognitive functioning.

Bjorklund and Harnishfeger (1990; Harnishfeger & Bjorklund, 1993) proposed an extension of the resources model, which emphasizes the role of inhibitory processes. Inhibition is defined as a basic cognitive suppression that contributes to task performance by keeping task-irrelevant information from entering and being maintained in working memory. If processing efficiency is conceptualized as speed of activation, such as in a semantic network, then inhibition can be conceptualized as a process that blocks the spread of activation, keeping attention focused sharply on the task at hand. Lateral inhibition, or the inhibition of concurrent cognitive processes, is also central to the efficient processing of cognitive operations.

Bjorklund and Harnishfeger (1990) proposed that inhibitory processes become more efficient with age. Young children's immature inhibitory mechanisms result in less efficient cognitive processing because their limited working-memory space is consumed with irrelevant information, leaving less mental space available for other aspects of processing. Using the resource metaphor, inefficient inhibition clogs storage space with irrelevant material, leaving less of it available for the storage of other materials or for the execution of other processes. Consistent with this hypothesis, Harnishfeger and Bjorklund (1993) found young children's poor memory performance was attributable, in part, to the irrelevant information they remembered. Harnishfeger and Bjorklund reported a series of memory experiments in which children's intrusion errors (i.e., producing a word at recall that was not on the list of to-be-remembered words) were examined. They found that preschool and kindergarten children produced more intrusions of nonlist words in their recall than did third- and sixth-grade children. Furthermore, the intrusions that the younger children produced were more likely to be task-irrelevant than were the intrusions produced by older children.

Harnishfeger and Bjorklund (1993) argued that inhibition might best be seen as an explanatory mechanism for cognitive development in general. They discussed evidence from a variety of experimental paradigms to demonstrate that inhibitory efficiency improves with age and that it affects children's behavior. For example, inhibitory control is involved in infants' object permanence, in toddler's verbal control of behavior, in young children's impulse and motor control, and in children's memory and attentional processing.

Resistance to Interference   Other theorists share Harnishfeger and Bjorklund's view of children's inhibitory inefficiency as part of a pattern of immature cognition that is characterized by susceptibility to interference (e.g., Brainerd & Reyna, 1993; Dempster, 1993). For example, Dempster argues that *resistance to interference* is a basic process that affects cognitive performance across a variety of tasks (Dempster, 1991, 1992, 1993, Chapter 1, this volume). Experimental tasks that demonstrate sensitivity to interference are those that require shifting attention or responses, competition among stimuli or responses, or shifting reinforcement contingencies. Examples include measures of field dependence, the Wisconsin Card Sorting Test, the Brown–Peterson Task, selective attention tasks, and conservation tasks.

Dempster argues that interference-sensitive tasks tap the function of the frontal lobes (Dempster, 1991, 1992, 1993, Chapter 1, this volume). The frontal lobes are involved in central executive functions, such as planning and monitoring of performance, and integrative functions, with a rich pattern of connections between sensory and motor areas meeting in the frontal cortex. One of the primary roles of this area, however, is inhibitory function (Bjorklund & Harnishfeger, Chapter 5, this volume; Fuster, 1989; Luria, 1973). There is extensive neuropsychological evidence that dysfunction of the frontal lobes leads to inhibitory deficits in action, cognition, emotion, and personality (Dempster, 1993; Fuster, 1989; Luria, 1973). More to the issue of cognitive theories of inhibition, Dempster argues that interference regulation is a key role of the frontal lobes, with frontal patients showing marked deficits on a variety of interference-sensitive tasks (Dempster, 1991, 1993).

Dempster has also documented developmental improvements across childhood and decrements in aging on these interference-sensitive tasks; he links these developmental changes to changes in the frontal lobes (Dempster, 1991, 1992, 1993). The frontal lobes are one of the last brain areas to develop, with full maturity not reached until adolescence in humans. Dempster argues that young children's difficulty with resisting interference is due to the immaturity of the frontal cortex. There is even some evidence that developmental spurts and lags in frontal lobe development map onto qualitative changes in interference sensitivity (Dempster, 1993).

According to Dempster, resistance to interference is a basic-level cognitive process that is central to our understanding of development, as well as individual differences (cf. Dempster, 1991). Dempster speculates that the construct is not unitary, but rather a family of inhibitory processes. Interference varies along several dimensions, including locus (internal or external sources), direction (forward, backward, or simultaneous interference), and psychological form (motor, perceptual, or verbal) (Dempster, 1991, 1993). Consistent with this interference framework, there is preliminary evidence that these different forms of interference sensitivity show different developmental trajectories (Dempster, 1993).

Output Interference   Fuzzy-trace theory is another contemporary cognitive developmental theory in which interference holds a key position (Brainerd & Reyna, 1989, 1990, 1993; Reyna, Chapter 2, this volume; Titcomb & Reyna, Chapter 8, this volume). Fuzzy-trace theory is a gist-driven, intuition-based model of cognition. A central assumption of this approach is that information is extracted from inputs in verbatim as well as gist (i.e., essential patterns or senses) form, with multiple forms of traces being available for cognitive processing on any particular task. For most tasks, people prefer to operate on gist, or fuzzy representations of problems. Regarding developmental change, the theory predicts a verbatim-to-gist shift in primary representation and operation, with very young children relying on verbatim representations, and facility of gist processing emerging in the early elementary school years. Verbatim trace processing is thought to peak early in life, while gist processing develops more gradually over childhood and into early adolescence.

Another construct central to fuzzy-trace theory is output interference (Brainerd & Reyna, 1989; Brainerd, Chapter 4, this volume). Interference is a central processing by-product that disrupts efficient processing. One source of interference in cognitive processing is the scheduling of responses for serial output from parallel production routines. That is, according to fuzzy-trace theory, possible responses are generated in parallel but can only be verbalized one at a time. Interference results from the cuing of these responses for verbalization. Interference is also generated by the noise or cross talk associated with the act of responding. High levels of interference during cognitive processing make it more difficult to access and activate traces, with verbatim traces being more sensitive to these disruptive effects than gist traces.

Interference sensitivity is a key developmental change, according to fuzzy-trace theory (Brainerd & Reyna, 1993). With age, children become less sensitive to disruption of performance due to interference (Brainerd & Reyna, 1989). Very young children rely more heavily on verbatim traces than on gist, and because verbatim traces are more susceptible to interference, young children's performance will be more disrupted by it than will older children's performance. Developmental changes in interference sensitivity are thought to contribute to a variety of other developmental changes in cognitive performance. For example, short-term memory becomes more reconstructive (rather than simple retrieval of verbatim traces) with age, and episodic forgetting decreases with age, both due in part to decreasing interference sensitivity (Brainerd & Reyna, 1993).

Based on developmental differences in interference sensitivity, fuzzy-trace theory makes some novel predictions about developmental changes in cognitive performance (Brainerd & Reyna, 1993). As one example, the theory predicts that balancing the facilitative effects of episodic activation against the detrimental effects of output interference results in free-recall protocols in which the maximum number of words are retrieved by patterning memory-strength ordering in recall (Brainerd, Reyna, Howe, & Kevershan, 1990). Words with a low memory strength have earlier mean output positions than high memory-strength words, and the overall structure of output queues is lower memory strength → higher memory strength → lower memory strength. Such recall production patterns have been demonstrated across numerous subject populations and age levels, with children as young as 6 years old using triage patterns to facilitate their recall (e.g., Brainerd, Reyna, & Howe, 1990; Brainerd, Reyna, Howe, & Kevershan, 1990). Developmentally, triage effects become stronger with age, as children become less sensitive to output interference. Cognitive triage is a counterintuitive phenomenon, and one that cannot be adequately explained by noninterference perspectives (Brainerd, Chapter

4, this volume; Brainerd, Reyna, Harnishfeger, & Howe, 1993; Harnishfeger & Brainerd, 1993).

Cognitive Aging   Hasher and Zacks (1988) proposed a model of cognitive change in aging that also incorporates inhibition (see also McDowd et al., Chapter 11, this volume). According to this model, inhibition gates which information will be entered into working memory, edits the contents of working memory according to current processing requirements, and limits response competition. Hasher and Zacks proposed that older adults perform more poorly on various cognitive tasks because they have less efficient inhibitory processing. This inefficiency results in irrelevant information becoming activated, being encoded in working memory, and competing with relevant information at retrieval.

Consistent with this model, Hasher, Zacks, and their colleagues have found evidence of reduced efficiency of cognitive inhibition in elderly adults (e.g., Hasher, Stoltzfus, Zacks, & Rypma, 1991). Hasher et al. examined inhibition in a negative-priming task, in which latency to name a stimulus that had not appeared in a previous trial (control condition) was compared with latency to name a stimulus that had served as a distractor on the immediately previous trial (negative-priming condition). Young adults were efficient cognitive inhibitors, with longer latencies in the negative priming than in the control conditions (see Neill, Valdes, & Terry, Chapter 7, this volume, for a detailed review of the negative-priming literature). Elderly adults were inefficient inhibitors, taking no more time to identify the stimulus when it had just served as the distractor than they took when it had not been seen on the previous trial.

Hasher and Zacks (1988) propose that older adults' inefficient inhibition will contribute to impaired performance on various cognitive tasks, including attention, memory, and linguistic processing. According to the model, older adults will be more likely to activate tangentially related or irrelevant information during cognitive processing. They will be less able to effectively monitor their activations, resulting in effortful cognitive processing being applied to irrelevant as well as relevant cognitive contents. In support of this, Connelly, Hasher, and Zacks (1991) found age differences in adults' ability to ignore distracting material embedded in text passages. Connelly et al. presented the adults with text passages that were peppered with intrusions printed in a different font than the target text. The task was to read the texts for comprehension while ignoring the intrusions. They found that the younger adults were much better able to ignore the distractors than the elderly adults. The older adults read the passages with distracting intrusions more slowly than passages with no intrusions, and their comprehension of the material was also disrupted. Thus, consistent with the Hasher and Zacks (1988) model, Connelly et al. (1991) found older adults to be more likely to activate irrelevant information during cognitive processing, and this disrupted the efficiency of their processing (for a more complete discussion of inefficient inhibition in the elderly, see McDowd et al., Chapter 11, this volume).

Social and Personality Development   Inhibition has also been investigated by researchers interested in children's social and personality development. Following Luria (1961), inhibition has been held to be central to the development of self-control (e.g., Camp, Blom, Hebert, & van Doorninck, 1977; Kopp, 1982, 1987; Schachar & Logan, 1990). For example, Kopp (1982, 1987) proposes that the ability to control behavior verbally is an early step in the development of self-control, and that later developments in symbolic thought and flexible planning contribute to a compliant, controlled child. Inhibitory mechanisms have also been invoked to explain developmental changes in social behaviors such as delay of gratification and resistance to temptation (e.g., Mischel, Shoda, & Rodriguez, 1989).

Inhibition also plays a central role in at least one developmental theory of personality (Kagan, 1989). Kagan and his colleagues propose that a central dimension of personality is the temperamental trait of *behavioral inhibition,* which they define as the tendency to be shy, timid, fearful, and inactive, especially in unfamiliar environments (Reznick, 1989). This research has unveiled a population of inhibited children who show early onset of inhibition, with a relatively high degree of stability (Kagan, Reznick, & Snidman, 1988; Reznick et al., 1986). Kagan, Rezick, and their colleagues found that children who were classified as inhibited at age 21 months are inhibited at 4.5, 5.5, and 7.5 years. These inhibited children were more timid among peers and adults, and more reluctant to engage in new activities or enter new environments (Kagan, 1989; Reznick et al., 1986). Furthermore, this trait appears to have a biological basis; inhibited children are more highly physiologically aroused by novel environments than are uninhibited children (Kagan et al., 1988).

Summary   Inhibition is receiving renewed interest from developmental theories. Harnishfeger and Bjorklund (1993) and Hasher and Zacks (1988) propose models that stress the suppression of irrelevant information during cognitive processing. These approaches use the term "inhibition," and measure intrusions in performance as an index of inhibitory efficiency. Brainerd and Reyna (1993) and Dempster (1993) propose models that stress the competition among multiple stimuli, targets, or responses. These approaches use the term "interference," and measure processing under conditions of competition (e.g., selective attention, dual tasks) to assess inhibitory efficiency. From a different perspective, theories of personality and social development are also reviving the inhibition construct. These approaches emphasize the development of self-control and behavioral responses to novel situations.

DEFINING COGNITIVE INHIBITION

Inhibition is clearly receiving widespread attention in the developmental literature. One drawback of this popularity, however, concerns the theoretical definition and empirical operationalization of the construct. Definition is indeed a problem for the inhibition construct, as reflected in the different uses of the term "inhibition" in the current literature (e.g., compare Kagan, 1989, with Connelly et al., 1991). Is there a single inhibition process that applies to all the different paradigms currently employing the term? Or are there many different and independent processes that merely share a common operating characteristic of suppression? (This issue is also addressed by McDowd et al., Chapter 11, this volume.)

One approach to the problem of multiple inhibitory constructs is to propose a family of inhibition processes. Taking this approach, several theorists have proposed that inhibition may best be conceptualized as a general process operating in different domains (e.g., Dempster, 1993; Luria, 1973; Passler, Isaac, & Hynd, 1985). For example, Luria (1966, 1973) identified various forms of inhibition resulting from frontal lobe dysfunction, including the inability to stop an ongoing repetitive behavior, the inability to commence a new pattern of behavior that is inconsistent with an overlearned stereotypic response, and the inability to plan, direct, and monitor cognitive processing. Luria also identified an attentional inhibition, with frontal patients frequently being unable to control orientation to irrelevant stimuli while simultaneously being unable to correctly orient to focal stimuli. Luria relates his experience that frontal patients " . . . do not pay proper attention to anyone speaking to them. If, however, while the patient is being tested . . . the nurse comes into the ward . . . he may actually reply involuntarily to her conversation with another patient. If the physician begins to question not [the patient] but his neighbor, the patient will at once join in this conversation, and experienced physicians know well that the best way of prompting such a patient's speech activity is by addressing his neighbor and starting a conversation with him. The patient will join in such a conversation much more easily than he will reply to direct questioning" (Luria, 1973, pp. 198–199).

Also taking the family of inhibition processes approach is Dempster (1993), who proposed a trichotomy of inhibitory processes that are functionally and developmentally distinct. Dempster argues that motor, perceptual, and linguistic inhibition are dissociated, and can be further discriminated according to the location (internal or external) and temporal operating characteristics of the interfering stimuli. Motor inhibition shows the earliest developmental change, with children becoming sensitive to perceptual and linguistic interference only later in childhood. While Dempster argues that these categories of interference sensitivity are dissociated, he notes that they all reach mature levels by early adolescence.

Thus, Luria (1973) and Dempster (1993) propose that inhibition is a general construct that affects many aspects of behavior. Another approach to the problem of defining inhibition is to propose separate processes that have different operating characteristics and that apply to different circumstances (see also Lewandowsky & Li, Chapter 10, this volume). Taking this approach, in the following sections I suggest some broad lines of demarcation, which might help to delineate the boundaries of the inhibition construct.

Distinguishing between Behavioral and Cognitive Inhibition

Inhibition mechanisms can be distinguished according to what psychological constructs (e.g., behavior, cognition) they act on. *Behavioral inhibition* involves the (potentially intentional) control of overt behavior, such as resisting temptation, delay of gratification, motor inhibition, and impulse control (e.g., Luria, 1961; Mischel et al., 1989). For example, Logan and his colleagues have examined behavioral inhibition in a stop-signal paradigm (Logan & Cowan, 1984; Logan, Cowan, & Davis, 1984; Schachar & Logan, 1990). In this procedure, subjects are primarily engaged in a cognitive task that requires some form of overt response, such as a forced-choice letter discrimination task. At the same time, they listen for an auditory signal. If a signal is heard, they attempt to inhibit or withhold the production of their overt response to the primary task. *Cognitive inhibition* involves the control of cognitive contents or processes, and can be intentional and conscious, or unintentional and unavailable for conscious introspection. Examples include: thought suppression, or the intentional control of the contents of consciousness (e.g., Wegner, 1989); the clearing of incorrect inferences from memory as the reading of a garden-path passage reveals the correct inference (e.g., Hamm & Hasher, 1992); the suppression of context-inappropriate meanings of polysemous words (e.g., Swinney & Prather, 1989); and the gating of irrelevant information from working memory during memory processing (e.g., Harnishfeger & Bjorklund, 1993).

Development of Behavioral Inhibition   Both behavioral and cognitive inhibition appear to become increasingly efficient with age. There are many examples of developmental change in behavioral inhibition in the research literature. Diamond (1988, 1990a, 1990b, 1991) has argued that the efficiency with which infants can inhibit overlearned responses improves during infancy and contributes to developmental improvements in performance on object permanence and delayed-response tasks. (Comparative data concerning the latter are reviewed by Bjorklund & Harnishfeger, Chapter 5, this volume.) For example, in the Piagetian AB task, an infant reaches into a covered well (well "A") to retrieve a hidden toy. After the infant successfully reaches a number of times into the same hiding place, the toy is hidden in full view of the infant in a different well (well "B"). Infants younger than 1 year usually continue to reach to well "A," an error Piaget attributed to a lack of object permanence. Diamond argues that the perservative error shown in this (and similar) tasks is due, in part, to inhibitory inefficiency. The development of the ability to correctly solve the AB task (i.e., always reach to the well that houses the toy) reflects the development of inhibitory control. Diamond argues that this form of inhibitory control develops over the later half of the first year (cf. Diamond, 1990a, 1990b, 1991).

In toddlers, developmental changes in behavioral inhibition are reflected by qualitative changes in the verbal control of behavior (Luria, 1961). As discussed above, Luria's research suggests that the inhibitory control of behavior through verbalization develops between toddlerhood and the early elementary-school years. The development of behavioral inhibition is not complete at this point, however. Throughout the elementary-school years children continue to struggle with self-control via behavioral inhibition; this is reflected in developmental changes in the ability to delay gratification, resist temptation, and inhibit impulsive behavior (cf. Mischel et al., 1989; Olson, 1989). Because this developing behavioral inhibition contributes to self-control and the suspension of impulsive action, it makes an important contribution to the child's developing sense of self (cf. Harter, 1983; Kopp, 1987; Mischel et al., 1989).

Development of Cognitive Inhibition   Evidence of increasingly efficient cognitive inhibition with age comes from selective-attention paradigms. (Theories of selective attention are highlighted by Neill et al., Chapter 7, this volume.) The development of selective attention, or the ability to attend to focal stimuli while simultaneously ignoring task-irrelevant distractions, has been studied experimentally with central–incidental learning tasks and dichotic listening tasks. Research using these and other selective-attention tasks has demonstrated that over the elementary school years, children become more and more efficient at inhibiting attention to irrelevant stimuli (Hagen & Hale, 1973; Lane & Pearson, 1982), although the ability to ignore incidental or irrelevant information does not peak until early adolescence (Schiff & Knopf, 1985). One experimental paradigm used to examine selective attention assesses children's ability to switch their attention between ears on a dichotic listening task (e.g., Pearson & Lane, 1991), or between left and right perceptual fields in a visual selective-attention task (e.g., Pearson & Lane, 1990). Pearson and Lane have found that children's ability to reorient to a new stimulus following a change cue in visual and auditory selective-attention tasks develops over later childhood and early adolescence (Pearson & Lane, 1990, 1991). (The development of cognitive inhibition will be examined in more detail below.)

The Relationship between Behavioral and Cognitive Inhibition   Behavioral and cognitive inhibition control different psychological constructs. Evidence that these two categories of inhibition are distinct abilities comes from patterns of individual differences, with performance on a variety of tasks being correlated within each category (i.e., behavioral or cognitive), but not across categories. For example, in the developmental literature there have been a number of attempts to assess self-control and impulsivity as general constructs. Typically, these studies have been multimethod assessments of self-control, impulsivity, motor inhibition, and conceptual tempo (i.e., Kagan's [1965] reflectivity/impulsivity dimension). These studies have found fairly low cross-measure correlations across the behavioral/cognitive category boundary, with stronger correlations occurring within either the behavior- or the cognitive-inhibition category (cf. Bentler & McClain, 1976; Bjorklund & Butter, 1973; Olson, 1989; Paulsen & Johnson, 1980; Toner, Holstein, & Hetherington, 1977). Using factor-analytic techniques, Olson (1989) found that various measures of inhibitory control cohere into three higher order factors: ability to delay gratification, motor inhibition, and cognitive inhibition. Controlling for age and IQ, Olson found a significant correlation between motor inhibition and delay of gratification, two forms of behavioral inhibition. The correlations between the behavioral inhibition factors and measures of cognitive inhibition were nonsignificant.

Although it is useful to distinguish between cognitive and behavioral forms of inhibition, the two are clearly related. One aspect of the relationship is children's use of cognitive inhibition to facilitate behavioral inhibition. For example, Mischel et al. (1989) reviewed a program of research on delay of gratification, examining the variables that affect young children's ability to inhibit impulsive responding and thereby achieve a greater reward following a delay. Behavioral inhibition in this paradigm was seen in the young children's abilities to withhold their responses long enough to achieve the greater reward. Mischel et al. found that one effective way of facilitating this behavioral inhibition was to engage in *thought suppression*. Thought suppression is the attempt to keep unwanted thoughts out of conscious awareness, and is one form of cognitive inhibition. Wegner (1989) argued that adults are best able to control the intrusion of unwanted thoughts into their conscious awareness by substituting other irrelevant thoughts. Mischel et al. found that this tactic works well for young children in delay-of-gratification situations: those children who engaged in cognitive inhibition, by thinking distracting and fun thoughts that were unrelated to the reward, or by talking or singing to themselves, were better able to withhold their behavioral response than were children who did not engage in such activities. Thus, Mischel et al.'s research suggests that efficient cognitive inhibition is used by some children in attempts to maintain behavioral control.

Control and Awareness of Inhibitory Processes

Automatic Inhibition   Much of the research on inhibition has been concerned with automatic, or preconscious, processing. This refers to attentional processing that is used to gate which information will enter consciousness (see also McDowd et al., Chapter 11, this volume). This is not usually thought of as a process that is intentionally invoked, although it may be available to reflection or introspection. One example of an experimental paradigm used to assess automatic inhibition involves the selection of context-appropriate meanings for polysemous words (Swinney & Prather, 1989). Typically, this research involves presentation of polysemous words in various contexts that prime one of the meanings of the word (e.g., "The dog gave a loud *bark* and growled." "The tree was losing its *bark* and leaves.") Subsequently, activation levels for the alternative meanings of the polysemous words are measured (see also Gernsbacher & Faust, Chapter 9, this volume). The currently favored view of lexical ambiguity resolution posits that all meanings of polysemous words are initially activated, with subsequent inhibition of context-inappropriate meanings occurring simultaneously with continued activation of context-appropriate meanings (Seidendberg, Tanenhaus, Leiman, & Bienkowski, 1982; Swinney, Zurif, & Nicol, 1989). In this paradigm, inhibition is the active suppression of a previously activated cognitive content that appears to occur automatically and without intention or awareness.

Another experimental paradigm used to assess automatic inhibition is the selective-attention task (e.g., Neill, 1977; Tipper, 1985; Tipper & Cranston, 1985). The Stroop task is one example of a selective-attention test. In this task, the subject attempts to name the color of the ink of a series of words, which are themselves color names. To measure inhibition, performance in the standard condition (ink colors and color names paired randomly) is compared with a negative-priming condition, in which the color to be named on trial n is identical to the color word on trial $n-1$. The color *word* on trial $n-1$ was an irrelevant stimulus and thus should have been ignored. Tipper (1985; Tipper & Cranston, 1985) has found that adults' performance is impaired (longer latencies to respond and higher errors) in negative-priming conditions. This supports the idea that ignored stimuli are actively inhibited, and so when those words subsequently become target stimuli, processing is impaired.(See Chapter 7 by Neill et al. and Chapter 11 by McDowd et al., this volume, for further discussions of negative priming.) As in the lexical ambiguity paradigm, this active suppression of previously activated cognitive contents appears to occur automatically and without intention.

Intentional Inhibition   Not all cognitive inhibition occurs automatically, and other researchers have been more concerned with intentional inhibition (e.g., Wegner, 1989; Bjork, 1989). This is a process deliberately invoked to deal with peripheral or irrelevant stimuli, from either internal or external sources. Examples of tasks that assess this mechanism include thought-suppression paradigms (e.g., Wegner, 1989), directed-forgetting tasks (e.g., Bjork, 1989), and the control of intrusions in memory (e.g., Harnishfeger & Bjorklund, 1993).

Intentional inhibition processes are available to conscious reflection, regardless of whether they ordinarily operate with or without awareness. However, when they operate with awareness, they are also likely available for mnemonic intervention. There have been some attempts to measure the ability to strategically control inhibition. For example, Wegner (1989) developed a procedure for thought control that involves the deliberate selection of an alternative target for conscious reflection during thought suppression. As noted above, adults who use this strategy are better able to control the contents of their consciousness (Wegner, 1989), and children who use this strategy are better able to delay gratification (Mischel et al., 1989).

The intentional control of inhibition has also been examined in studies of directed forgetting. In directed-forgetting procedures, subjects are instructed to forget previously learned target items, and their efficiency of forgetting is assessed by a surprise recall test for to-be-forgotten information (Bjork, 1989). Presentation procedures vary, with cues to forget being given either following the learning of entire portions of the target material (intralist cuing), or following each individual target item (item-by-item cuing). Intentional inhibition is measured in item-by-item cuing, because with this procedure subjects can strategically differentiate the to-be-remembered from to-be-forgotten items, and with that information they can intentionally inhibit to-be-forgotten targets.

Using an item-by-item cuing procedure, Geiselman, Rabow, Wachtel, and MacKinnon (1985) experimented with various strategies that adults could use to facilitate directed forgetting. They found that instructing adults to use an inhibitory strategy (saying "stop" after each forget cue), facilitated intentional forgetting of list items. Developmental investigations of directed forgetting have also examined the role of strategies in children's performance (e.g., Bray, Hersh, & Turner, 1985; Lehman & Bovasso, 1993). Generally, memory strategies become more efficient with age (cf. Harnishfeger & Bjorklund, 1990). Consistent with this, directed-forgetting studies have found some evidence that the development of selective rehearsal strategies facilitates intentional forgetting when forget cues are given with each target item (but see Lehman & Bovasso, 1993).

Distinguishing between Interference and Cognitive Inhibition

Inhibition and interference have often been used interchangeably in the literature; however, the construct of cognitive inhibition is not synonymous with susceptibility to interference, a point that is also stressed by Neill et al., Chapter 7, this volume. *Inhibition* refers to an active suppression process, such as the removal of task-irrelevant information from working memory (e.g., Hamm & Hasher, 1992; Harnishfeger & Bjorklund, 1993). *Interference* refers to susceptibility to performance decrements under conditions of multiple distracting stimuli, such as dual-task performance (cf. Brainerd & Reyna, 1989) or selective attention (cf. Lane & Pearson, 1982). The terms are sometimes confused because paradigms originally developed to study interference have been modified to examine inhibition. For example, the Stroop paradigm is a classic procedure for investigating susceptibility to interference from multiple stimuli (Stroop, 1935). More recently, negative-priming measures have been developed using Stroop paradigms to assess inhibition. Because negative priming conditions require the subject to disinhibit previously irrelevant dimensions, these conditions are thought to directly measure the power of inhibitory processing in the interference task (e.g., Neill, 1977; Tipper, 1985).

Inhibition and interference may also be confused because of the correlation between populations of subjects who are highly susceptible to interference and populations showing relatively poorer inhibitory efficiency. Tipper and Baylis (1987) found larger inhibition effects in a negative-priming paradigm among adults who reported greater difficulty with selective attention in everyday functioning. Similarly, Neumann and Deschepper (1992) explored the relationship between susceptibility to interference and inhibition efficiency in a negative-priming task. They found that the fastest responders in a selective-attention task (an interference measure) showed greater levels of negative priming (an inhibition measure).

While interference and inhibition are related constructs, cognitive developmental theories distinguish between them, with different approaches addressing primarily inhibition (e.g., Bjorklund & Harnishfeger, 1990; Hasher & Zacks, 1988) or interference (e.g., Brainerd & Reyna, 1993; Dempster, 1993), and with different explanations and predictions for the two concepts. Looking first at inhibition, cognitive theories define it as an active suppression process that keeps irrelevant information from entering and being maintained in working memory, and from disrupting cognitive processing in general. Deficits in inhibition impair processing, resulting in the activation, maintenance, and retrieval of irrelevant information. Measures of inhibition include negative priming, intrusions in memory, and activation of relevant and irrelevant information during cognitive processing.

Turning to the interference construct, cognitive theories define it as cognitive competition among multiple stimuli, processes, or responses. Unlike inhibition, interference does not necessarily involve the active suppression of cognitive processes or contents. Interference disrupts processing because it produces bottlenecks, during which selection procedures must isolate the processes that will be executed, and the response that will be produced. Interference also disrupts performance by making it more difficult to access low-memory-strength or verbatim traces, a point that is considered at length in Chapter 4 by Brainerd and Chapter 2 by Reyna, this volume. Interference theories do not necessarily postulate a limited processing space or the activation and maintenance of irrelevant information. Measures of interference include decrements in speed of access, speed of response, and dual-task processing.

DEVELOPMENTAL CHANGE IN INTERFERENCE AND INHIBITION

Previous reviews have addressed the nature of developmental change in inhibition and interference over childhood and in aging (Dempster, 1992, 1993; Harnishfeger & Bjorklund, 1993), but these discussions have not distinguished between inhibition and interference. There is ample evidence from the developmental literature that resistance to interference improves over childhood (cf. Dempster, 1992; Lane & Pearson, 1982). However, there is little evidence that specifically examines developmental changes in inhibition. In the following sections I review efforts to chart developmental changes in general inhibitory functioning across childhood. As noted above, there has been more success at charting developmental change in interference, and I next turn to a discussion of one area of research that has been particularly fruitful in this regard: developmental changes in memory span. Finally, I present some preliminary evidence regarding developmental change in cognitive inhibition.

Charting the Development of General Inhibitory Functioning

Current theory and evidence suggest that inhibition is linked functionally to the frontal lobes of the brain (e.g., Bjorklund & Harnishfeger, Chapter 5, this volume; Dempster, 1992, 1993; Fuster, 1989). Because of this connection, a number of attempts have been made to chart the development of inhibitory functioning by assessing developmental changes in frontal lobe functioning. A primary example of this is Luria's research, tracking developmental and clinical patterns in frontal lobe functioning. The frontal lobes are one of the last areas of the brain to develop, and neuropsychologists have proposed that functional maturity of the frontal lobes in humans is not reached until between 4 and 7 years (e.g., Luria, 1973) and 12 years of age (e.g., Golden, 1981). These researchers have typically also assumed that frontal lobe functions, such as inhibition, do not reach maturity until these ages.

Passler et al. (1985), for example, examined the development of inhibitory functioning in frontal lobe tasks with children from 5 to 12 years old. They tested children for verbal proactive and retroactive inhibition (word list learning), and nonverbal proactive and retroactive inhibition (action-series learning). Behavioral inhibition was assessed in perseveration tasks, in which the children were asked to complete a series of actions in a predetermined, rigid order. They also assessed verbal and nonverbal conflict in Luria-type tasks, by asking children to say "day" to white cards and "night" to gray cards (verbal conflict), and by asking children to tap twice with a stick to the experimenter's single-tap, and once to the experimenter's double-tap. Passler et al. were interested in assessing the developmental progression of these different frontal lobe tasks, all of which assess deficits in patients with frontal lobe damage, and all of which appear to involve some form of cognitive or behavioral inhibition. They found a developmental dissociation among the tasks, with performance on the verbal conflict tasks peaking before age six, performance on the nonverbal conflict, proactive inhibition, and perseveration tasks peaking by age eight, and full maturity on all tasks not being reached until between 10 and 12 years old.

The dissociation among the tasks did not fall into distinct behavioral and cognitive or verbal and nonverbal categories. Passler et al. concluded that the differing patterns of development are not interpretable according to category models of inhibition (e.g., Dempster, 1993; Luria, 1966, 1973), and that one measure of inhibitory function cannot predict performance on other measures of inhibition. Nevertheless, all the measures develop over the childhood years and reach maturity by late childhood or early adolescence.

Developmental Changes in Interference

One of the most robust effects in the cognitive developmental literature is the improvement of memory-span performance over the early childhood years. Between the ages of 3 and 10, children's immediate memory span increases from about three to about six items (Dempster, 1981). Adults' memory span is about seven items. Short-term memory span is a paradigm in which age change appears to be dependent on developmental changes in sensitivity of interference.

Early interpretations of this effect focused on the increasing capacity of short-term store (Pascual-Leone, 1970), and the use of mnemonic strategies to facilitate performance (Chi, 1978). Although short-term memory does show dramatic effects of deliberate strategy use, such as organization and chunking, these variables do not account for age changes in memory span (Dempster, 1981, 1985). Rather, two basic-level cognitive processes appear to be the most likely causes of developmental change in memory span: item identification speed (Case et al., 1982; Dempster, 1985) and speech rate (Baddeley, 1986; Hulme, 1986). These basic-level factors show substantial developmental change over childhood (Dempster, 1985; Kail, 1986, 1993).

Case (1985) argued that short-term memory space is a limited-capacity working area that does not increase in size with development. He proposed that the total processing space of short-term memory is allocated to two different functions: the storage of information, and the execution of cognitive operations. With age, the execution of operations becomes more efficient and therefore consumes less of the limited processing space. Thus, there is a developmental trade-off between storage and operating space, with young children using more of their processing space for operating functions, and older children and adults using a larger proportion of their processing space for storage. According to this model, memory span improves with age as children's operations become more efficient, opening up more processing space for the storage of additional items. Case et al. (1982) argued that the efficiency in processing is most likely due to decreases in item identification speed that oc-

cur with age. They demonstrated that when adults' item identification speed
was slowed to a rate comparable to that of a six-year-old, the adults' memory
span was comparable to the six-year-olds' memory span as well.

Other researchers argue that developmental changes in the rate of
speech leads to increased processing efficiency and longer memory span (e.g.,
Baddeley, 1986; Hitch & Halliday, 1983; Hulme, 1986). The word-length effect in memory span refers to the finding that memory span is affected by the
length of the words being recalled. More short words can be recalled in a
memory span task than long words, and memory span is a linear function of
the number of syllables in the to-be-remembered words (e.g., Hulme, Thomson, Muir, & Lawrence, 1984). Developmentally, children's speech rate increases with age, and their memory span increases along with speech rate. In
fact, the slope of the relationship between speech rate and memory span is
constant across age groups, suggesting that developmental changes in memory span are attributable to developmental changes in speech rate (e.g., Hitch
& Halliday, 1983; Hulme et al., 1984; Nicholson, 1979).

From the present perspective, the central issue is that identification
speed and speech rate are sensitive to interference. This argument is made explicitly by cognitive developmental theories of interference. For example,
Brainerd and Reyna (1989, 1993) argue that interference disrupts speech production through response scheduling and response feedback effects. Evidence
that speech rate is sensitive to interference comes also from the memory span
research. Manipulations that increase the level of interference significantly
impair the memory span performance of both adults and children. For example, acoustic similarity among auditorily learned list items and visual similarity among pictorially presented list items both impair memory span performance (Hitch, Halliday, Schaafstal & Heffernan, 1991; Hulme, 1984; Hulme
et al., 1984; Hulme & Tordoff, 1989). Further evidence of the interference
sensitivity of memory span is the finding that interference produced by articulatory suppression (i.e., eliminating articulation of to-be-remembered stimuli
by having subjects vocalize unrelated information during item presentation)
eliminates the word-length effect in memory span.

This research demonstrates that memory span is highly susceptible to interference effects. Children's increasing resistance to interference with age
may be a key factor responsible for developmental change in memory span
performance. Consistent with this conclusion, young children's performance
is disrupted by interference manipulations in memory span tasks (e.g.,
acoustic similarity, articulatory suppression), as is that of adults. Additionally,
there is some evidence that young children are more disrupted than older children and adults. Hitch, Halliday, and Littler (1984) found that the memory
span of eight-year-olds in an articulatory suppression condition was impaired
to a greater degree than was the memory span of 11-year-olds.

In sum, the developmental changes that have been so clearly demonstrated for children's immediate memory span may be attributable to develop-

mental changes in interference sensitivity. This suggests that resistance to interference undergoes its greatest developmental changes over the elementary school years, a conclusion that is consistent with cognitive developmental theories of interference (e.g., Brainerd, Chapter 4, this volume; Brainerd & Reyna, 1993; Dempster, 1993; Reyna, Chapter 2, this volume).

Developmental Changes in Cognitive Inhibition

I turn now to a consideration of developmental changes in inhibition. This is an area of research that has not received considerable attention, most likely because interest in this construct is fairly recent (cf. Bjork, 1989), but also because developmental changes in inhibition have implicitly been assumed to reflect developmental changes in interference sensitivity. As discussed above, this assumption is not warranted, and so developmental change in inhibition needs to be considered in its own right.

Negative Priming   Perhaps one of the most important cognitive functions of inhibition is its role in selective attention. At any given moment, we are capable of receiving an almost infinite array of stimuli. In order to function effectively, we must select critical stimuli and ignore irrelevant, distracting stimuli. Our ability to do this is a key cognitive skill and has been the focus of a large body of research (see reviews by Davies, Jones, & Taylor, 1984; Lane & Pearson, 1982; Neill et al., Chapter 7, this volume).

Several investigators have demonstrated that inhibitory processes operate in selective attention tasks (e.g., Dalrymple-Alford, & Budayr, 1966; Neill, 1977; Tipper, 1985; Tipper & Cranston, 1985). Concerning development, Tipper, Bourque, Anderson, and Brehaut (1989) examined children's inhibition with a negative-priming condition in a Stroop task. The Stroop task has traditionally been a measure of interference sensitivity, and research has demonstrated a clear age improvement in resistance to interference using the standard Stroop comparisons (i.e., randomly paired ink colors and color terms vs. ink colors paired with neutral words). Tipper et al. attempted to isolate the contribution of inhibition to developmental change in Stroop performance. They contrasted the performance of adults and second graders on both the standard Stroop task and the negative-priming task. They found evidence for inhibition only for the adults and concluded that inhibitory processes were not operational by the second grade.

My colleagues and I have extended this research to investigate the nature of developmental change in inhibitory processing across the elementary school years (Harnishfeger, Nicholson, & Digby, 1993). We tested children from the first, third, and fifth grades and college students in three Stroop conditions. In a *neutral* condition, children identified the ink colors of a list of X -strings. In a standard *Stroop* condition, children identified the ink colors of a list of color names printed in various colored inks. In this condition, the color names and ink colors of the words were unrelated. Finally, in the *negative-priming* condition, the color names and ink colors were related such that the ink color to be named on item *n* was the same as the color name on item *n–1*. Children and adults named the ink colors of 30-item series in each condition. Order of presentation (e.g., neutral-Stroop-inhibition, Stroop-inhibition-neutral) was counterbalanced across subjects.

The pattern of main effects in this study supported Tipper et al.'s (1989) general conclusion that inhibition becomes more efficient between early childhood and adulthood. Examination of the pattern of naming latencies by adults revealed significant inhibition effects. The first graders did not differ in naming time between the standard Stroop and inhibition conditions. (This difference replicates Tipper et al.'s results for second graders.) However, there was not a smooth patterning age change because third graders showed significant inhibition effects but the fifth graders did not. Thus, developmental change in inhibition does not appear to be a simple matter of quantitative improvements with age.

Indeed, there were several significant interactions suggesting a more complicated relationship between age and inhibition. In addition to the effects of primary interest (age, condition), we also examined effects of trial (children completed two trials in each condition, adults completed three trials per condition) and order of presentation. These nuisance variables interacted with age and condition. First, the significant interaction among condition, trial, and order of presentation revealed an inconsistent pattern of inhibition effects: in 2 of the 12 cells inhibition effects were significant, in 1 cell the negative-priming condition facilitated performance, and in 9 of the cells there was no difference between negative priming and standard Stroop. Second, we investigated patterns of children's performance by categorizing each subject as an "inhibitor" or "noninhibitor," based on the difference between mean negative priming and Stroop conditions. When we examined latencies for these different groups, we found significant inhibition effects for inhibitors in every age-group. There were no differences between negative priming and Stroop for the older children and adults classified as noninhibitors. However, the first grade noninhibitors showed significant *facilitation* for the negative-priming condition.

In sum, it appears that children do show some evidence of inhibition in the early grade-school years. However, their inhibition is less consistent than that shown by adults. They are influenced by trial and by the order in which they perform different tasks. With age, inhibitory processing becomes more efficient, more consistent, and more task independent.

Directed Forgetting   The directed-forgetting task is another paradigm in which cognitive inhibition has been studied. Using an intralist cuing procedure, subjects are presented with a list of items to be remembered. After the first half of the list has been presented, subjects are told that all previously presented items should now be forgotten and that only the subsequently presented items should be remembered for a later recall test. Following presentation, recall of *both* to-be-forgotten and to-be-remembered items is tested. Studies using this paradigm have found dramatic directed-forgetting effects. Typically, for adults, recall of the to-be-remembered items is high and shows no interference from the to-be-forgotten items (Bjork, 1970). Although recall of to-be-forgotten items is quite low, these items are indeed stored in memory, as demonstrated by high levels of recognition memory (e.g., Davis & Okada, 1971; Geiselman, 1974).

Bjork and Geiselman (Bjork, 1989; Geiselman, Bjork, & Fishman, 1983) propose that inhibition may be the central process responsible for directed-forgetting effects. They propose that inhibition is an active, conscious, and goal-oriented process. In the directed-forgetting paradigm "a cue to forget can initiate a process that inhibits or blocks access routes to the episodic memory traces corresponding to the [to-be-forgotten] items, making them nonretrievable at the time of recall except in the presence of prepotent retrieval cues, such as the copy cues on a recognition test" (Geiselman et al., 1983, pp. 60–61).

Bjork and Geiselman's work suggests that directed-forgetting effects occur because adults are able to inhibit the activation of to-be-forgotten stimuli. If young children are indeed poor inhibitors, we would expect them to exhibit different patterns of directed forgetting. Specifically, young children would be expected to show little difference in recall between to-be-remembered and to-be-forgotten words. As inhibitory efficiency develops, older children would show more distinction between the words, remembering more to-be-remembered than to-be-forgotten words, and showing less interference from the to-be-forgotten words.

My colleagues and I have conducted several experiments investigating the development of children's directed-forgetting performance (e.g., Harnishfeger, 1991; Harnishfeger, Digby, Scott, Nicholson, & Liberty, 1992; Harnishfeger, Scott, & Nicholson, 1993). To isolate retrieval inhibition in directed forgetting, we used an intralist cuing procedure in each study. This insures that subjects encode and attempt to store the to-be-forgotten words, because they are not expecting any forget instructions. We also manipulated the word production instructions given as recall was attempted, to examine whether children and adults differ in their ability to limit recall to what is requested (or whether they give every item stored from the task, regardless of instructions).

An initial directed-forgetting task contrasted the performance of first-, third-, and fifth-grade children and college students (Harnishfeger et al., 1992). The subjects were given the *forget* or *remember* cue halfway through a 20-item unrelated word list. Recall was assessed following a 30-s buffer clearing task. In addition to the *forget* versus *remember* cue during item presentation, a recall-instruction manipulation was included in the *forget* conditions.

Subjects were instructed to produce either all the list items at recall (the traditional directed-forgetting instructions), or only the to-be-remembered words. Thus, subjects were assigned to one of three experimental conditions: *Remember* (remember cue, produce all words), *Forget/All* (forget cue, produce all words), *Forget/All (forget cue, produce only to-be-remembered words)*. This manipulation allowed us to contrast subjects' ability to recall to-be-forgotten information with their ability to withhold this information when so directed. Young children were expected to differ little in their performance across the two *forget* conditions, because they would not be able to inhibit the production of to-be-forgotten words that were remembered (cf. Harnishfeger & Bjorklund, 1993).

The results of this experiment were consistent with the hypothesis that inhibition improves with age. For the *Remember* and *Forget/All* conditions, adult performance replicated previous research, with subjects remembering to-be-remembered words and not showing interference from to-be-forgotten words. The children, in contrast, remembered more second-half words regardless of cue or recall instruction. The patterns of recall were different between the children and adults, with the patterns becoming more adultlike with increasing age. Of particular interest was the *Forget/Only* condition, in which subjects were instructed to forget precue items, and were not told to remember them at recall. The adults were able to withhold production of these items at recall. The children were not: they produced as many second-list-half words in the *Forget/Only* condition as they did in the *Forget/All* condition. This effect replicates previous research demonstrating that young children make more intrusion errors in their recall attempts (Harnishfeger & Bjorklund, 1993).

Children showed different patterns of performance than adults, and their performance became more adultlike with increasing age. While this demonstrates developmental changes in directed forgetting, it does not give clear evidence of developmental changes in *retrievable inhibition,* because alternative explanations of the results are tenable. For example, it is possible that adults used a selective-rehearsal strategy in this task, dropping to-be-forgotten items from their rehearsal queues following the forget cue, and only rehearsing to-be-remembered items for the remainder of the task. If this strategic explanation is correct, developmental changes can be accounted for by developmental improvements in selective rehearsal.

To isolate developmental changes in inhibition, we conducted another experiment, embedding an incidental learning manipulation within a directed-forgetting task (Harnishfeger, Scott, & Nicholson, 1993). Subjects were instructed to attempt to remember only some of the words presented. Other words were learned incidentally, under the guise of a word-rating task. Differences between to-be-remembered and to-be-forgotten words that were learned intentionally were contrasted with incidentally learned words. Of particular interest were developmental differences in inhibitory efficiency, as reflected by the failure to produce to-be-forgotten and incidentally learned words when they were requested at recall, and the withholding of remembered words when they were not requested at recall.

In this experiment, adults and children from the first, third, and fifth grades were read a list of unrelated words, each preceded by an instruction either to remember the word or to indicate preference for the word (e.g., . . . remember PUZZLE . . . do you like a FORK? . . .). Following the presentation of the first half of the list, one-half of the subjects at each grade level (the *Forget* groups) were instructed to forget the previous words and only remember the subsequent words. The remaining subjects (the *Remember* groups) were instructed to continue trying to remember all the words. The second half of the word list was then presented, followed by a 30-s buffer clearing task. Then recall was assessed, with one-half of the subjects in each instruction group asked to recall only to-be-remembered words (the *Only* groups) and the remaining subjects asked to recall all the words (the *All* groups). Thus, at each age level subjects were randomly assigned to one of four conditions: *Remember/All, Remember/Only, Forget/All,* and *Forget/Only.*

Recall patterns were examined for directed-forgetting effects, differences in recall patterns for incidental and intentional words, and subjects' ability to limit recall to those items requested (i.e., intrusions in recall). Adults showed typical directed-forgetting effects for the intentional words, and they remembered more intentional than incidental words. Adults were able to limit their production at recall to only those words requested.

The fifth graders showed some aspects of efficient directed-forgetting performance: they recalled more to-be-remembered than to-be-forgotten words in the *Forget* conditions, but they did not show an advantage for first-half-words in the *Remember* conditions. Their performance differed from adults in that they recalled as many incidental as intentional words. They were not able to limit their recall to only those words requested in the *Remember/Only* condition, but were able to in the *Forget/Only* condition.

In general, the first and third graders' performance was not affected by word type or condition, with the only significant effects being higher recall of second-list-half incidental words in the forget conditions. These young children recalled as many incidental as intentional words, showed no processing advantages in the remember conditions, and did not limit their recall production to requested items.

These results confirm and extend our earlier findings concerning children's inhibition in the directed-forgetting paradigm. Children become more efficient inhibitors with age in that they are better able to inhibit words under forget instructions and withhold production of incidentally learned words during recall. These findings are consistent with the view that increased efficiency of inhibitory processing contributes to memory performance, and is a central factor in cognitive development (cf. Bjorklund and Harnishfeger, 1990; Dempster, 1992, 1993; Harnishfeger & Bjorklund, 1993).

The Development of Inhibition   The evidence reviewed here supports the hypothesis that cognitive inhibition improves over the elementary school years. In both intentional and automatic situations, children become more efficient, more consistent, and more task independent in cognitive inhibition between ages six and ten, with further improvements shown by adulthood. Developmental change is seen both in basic-level tasks (e.g., negative priming), and in higher level (e.g., directed forgetting) tasks. Across the elementary school years, children become better able to efficiently manage their inhibition, keeping irrelevant information from interfering with cognitive processing or clogging limited working memory space.

The developmental change does not appear to be one of simple capacity increase, however. Developmental changes are seen in efficiency, but changes are more dramatic in terms of consistency and task independence. This creates two possibilities. Actual inhibitory processing may develop fairly early (perhaps by second or third grade), with later developments being primarily improvements in applications of abilities or integration of inhibition with other processing components. This would explain early competence shown in some negative-priming conditions. Alternatively, inhibition may improve gradually over childhood, although improvements in task performance do not follow improvements in inhibition linearly.

CONCLUSION: TOWARD AN INTEGRATED THEORY OF INHIBITION

Currently, there is a renewed emphasis on inhibition as an explanatory mechanism of human behavior and development. Theories postulating inhibitory constructs have recently been proposed in many different literatures, including cognitive development (e.g., Dempster, 1993; Graham & Campbell, 1992; Harnishfeger & Bjorklund, 1993), cognitive aging (Hasher & Zacks, 1988), personality development (Kagan, 1989), and individual differences (e.g., Dempster, 1991). However, every model holds a slightly different definition of inhibition, and many times that definition is not clearly delineated.

One way of distinguishing the constructs is to embed them within a framework of similar ideas. Dempster (1993) proposed a typology of interference mechanisms, which distinguishes among various forms of interference sensitivity, various sources of interference, and various directions of interfering influence. Such a typology might also apply to inhibition. Above, I suggested a concern with other aspects of inhibition that appear to be functionally important. Behavioral and cognitive forms of inhibition can be distinguished, which is similar to Dempster's motor and perceptual/linguistic forms. Further, it is important to distinguish between automatic and intentional forms of inhibition, at least until it can be determined whether these qualitatively different constructs have a common underlying basis.

A primary reason to be concerned with definitions and typologies is to guard against the formation of premature conclusions about one domain on the basis of conclusions from another domain. For example, Dempster (1993) argues that different forms of resistance to interference may develop along different courses, and that generalizations cannot be made from one form to another. Similarly, it cannot be assumed that cognitive forms of inhibition will develop in the same way as behavioral forms, without an examination of each. Inhibition, as defined by cognitive developmental theories, cannot be assumed to develop at the same rate or in the same way as interference sensitivity. To examine the development of inhibition, one must study developmental changes in performance in the paradigms used to define inhibition, such as negative priming and intrusions in memory and reasoning. While there is some preliminary evidence that inhibitory efficiency develops, the exact nature of that developmental change remains an empirical question.

ACKNOWLEDGMENTS

Portions of the research reported here were supported by Faculty Research Grant #10-21-RR064-002 from the University of Georgia Research Foundation, and by a Sarah H. Moss Fellowship.

I would like to thank the students and staff of Danielsville, Ila, and South Jackson Elementary Schools for their cooperation in the execution of the negative priming and directed-forgetting experiments. I also thank David Bjorklund, Charles Brainerd, Frank Dempster, and Steffen Pope for comments on earlier drafts of this chapter.

REFERENCES

Aleksandrowicz, D. R. (1977). Are there precursors to repression? *Journal of Nervous and Mental Disease, 164,* 191–197.

Baddeley, A. (1986). *Working memory.* Oxford: Clarendon Press.

Bentler, P. M., & McClain, J. (1976). A multitrait-multimethod analysis of reflection-impulsivity. *Child Development, 47,* 218–226.

Bjork, R. A. (1970). Positive forgetting: The noninterference of items intentionally forgotten. *Journal of Verbal Learning and Verbal Behavior, 9,* 255–268.

Bjork, R. A. (1989). Retrieval inhibition as an adaptive mechanism in human memory. In H. L. Roediger, III & F. I. M. Craik (Eds.), *Varieties of memory and consciousness* (pp. 309–330). Hillsdale, NJ: Erlbaum.

Bjorklund, D. F. (1985). The role of conceptual knowledge in the development of organization in children's memory. In C. J. Brainerd & M. Pressley (Eds.), *Basic processes in memory development: Progress in cognitive development research* (pp. 103–142). New York: Springer-Verlag.

Bjorklund, D. F. (1987). How age changes in knowledge base contribute to the development of children's memory: An interpretative review. *Developmental Review, 7,* 93–130.

Bjorklund, D. F., & Butter, E. J. (1973). Can cognitive impulsivity be predicted from classroom behavior? *Journal of Genetic Psychology, 123,* 185–194.

Bjorklund, D. F., & Harnishfeger, K. K. (1990). The resources construct in cognitive development: Diverse sources of evidence and a theory of inefficient inhibition. *Developmental Review, 10,* 48–71.

Brainerd, C. J., & Reyna, V. F. (1989). Output interference theory of dual-task deficits in memory development. *Journal of Experimental Child Psychology, 47,* 1–18.

Brainerd, C. J., & Reyna, V. F. (1990). Gist is the grist: Fuzzy-trace theory and the new intuitionism. *Develomental Review, 10,* 3–47.

Brainerd, C. J., & Reyna, V. F. (1993). Domains of fuzzy trace theory. In M. L. Howe & R. Pasnak (Eds.), *Emerging themes in cognitive development: Vol 1. Foundations* (pp. 50–93). New York: Springer-Verlag.

Brainerd, C. J., Reyna, V. F., Harnishfeger, K. K., & Howe, M.L. (1993). Is memory-strength grouping good for recall? *Journal of Experimental Psychology: General, 122,* 249–268.

Brainerd, C. J., Reyna, V. F., & Howe, M. L. (1990). Cognitive triage in children's memory: Optimal retrieval or effortful processing? *Journal of Experimental Child Psychology, 49,* 428–447.

Brainerd, C. J., Reyna, V. F., Howe, M. L., & Kevershan, J. (1990). The last shall be first: How memory strength affects children's retrieval. *Psychological Science, 1,* 247–252.

Bray, N. W., Hersh, R. E., & Turner, L. A. (1985). Selective remembering during adolescence. *Developmental Psychology, 21,* 290–294.

Brenner, C. (1957). The nature and development of the concept of repression in Freud's writings. *Psychoanalytical Study of the Child, 12,* 19–46.

Camp, B. W., Blom, G. E., Hebert, F., & van Doorninck, W. J. (1977). "Think aloud": A program for developing self-control in young aggressive boys. *Journal of Abnormal Child Psychology, 5,* 157–169.

Case, R. (1985). *Intellectual development; Birth to adulthood.* New York: Academic Press.

Case, R., Kurland, M., & Goldberg, J. (1982). Operational efficiency and the growth of short-term memory span. *Journal of Experimental Child Psychology, 33,* 386–404.

Chi, M. T. H. (1978). Knowledge structures and memory development. In R. S. Siegler (Ed.), *Children's thinking: What develops?* (pp. 73–96). Hillsdale, NJ: Erlbaum.

Connelly, S. L., Hasher, L., & Zacks, R. T. (1991). Age and reading: The impact of distraction. *Psychology & Aging, 6,* 533–541.

Dalrymple-Alford, E. C., & Budayr, B. (1966). Examination of some aspects of the Stroop color-word test. *Perceptual and Motor Skills, 23,* 1211–1214.

Davies, D. R., Jones, D. M., & Taylor, A. (1984). Selective and sustained-attention tasks: Individual and group differences. In R. Parasuraman, R. Davies, & J. Beatty (Eds.), *Varieties of attention* (pp. 395–447). New York: Academic Press.

Davis, J. C., & Okada, R. (1971). Recognition and recall of positively forgotten items. *Journal of Experimental Psychology, 89,* 181–186.

Dempster, F. N. (1981). Memory span: Sources of individual and developmental differences. *Psychological Bulletin, 89,* 63–100.

Dempster, F. N. (1985). Short-term memory development in childhood and adolescence. In C. J. Brainerd & M. Pressley (Eds.), *Basic processes in memory development: Progress in cognitive development research* (pp. 208–248). New York: Springer-Verlag.

Dempster, F. N. (1991). Inhibitory processes: A neglected dimension of intelligence. *Intelligence, 15,* 157–173.

Dempster, F. N. (1992). The rise and fall of the inhibitory mechanism: Toward a unified theory of cognitive development and aging. *Developmental Review, 12,* 45–75.

Dempster, F. N. (1993). Resistance to interference: Developmental changes in a basic processing mechanism. In M. L. Howe & R. Pasnak (Eds.), *Emerging themes in cognitive development: Vol. 1. Foundations* (pp. 3–27). New York: Springer-Verlag.

Diamond, A. (1988). Abilities and neural mechanisms underlying A not B performance. *Child Development, 59,* 523–527.

Diamond, A. (1990a). The development and neural bases of memory functions as indexed by the

AB and delayed response tasks in human infants and infant monkeys. In A. Diamond (Ed.), *The development and neural bases of higher cognitive functions* (pp. 267–309). New York: New York Academy of Sciences.

Diamond, A. (1990b). Rate of maturation of the hippocampus and the developmental progression of children's performance on the delayed non-matching to sample and visual paired comparison tasks. In A. Diamond (Ed.), *The development and neural bases of higher cognitive functions* (pp. 394–426). New York: New York Academy of Sciences.

Diamond, A. (1991). Frontal lobe involvement in cognitive changes during the first year of life. In K. R. Gibson & A. C. Petersen (Eds.), *Brain maturation and cognitive development: Comparative and cross-cultural perspectives* (pp. 127–180). New York: de Gruyter.

Ebbinghaus, H. (1964). *Memory* (H. A. Ruger & C. E. Bussenius, Trans.). New York: Dover. (Original work published 1885)

Fishbein, H. D. (1976). *Evolution, development, and children's learning.* Pacific Palisades, CA: Goodyear.

Fishbein, H. D. (1984). *The psychology of infancy and childhood: Evolutionary and cross-cultural perspectives.* Hillsdale, NJ: Erlbaum.

Freud, S. (1915, 1957). The unconscious. In J. Strachey (Ed. and Trans.). *The standard edition of the complete psychological works of Sigmund Freud (pp. 159–209, Vol. 14).* London: Hogarth Press. (Original work published 1915)

Fuson, K. C. (1979). The development of self-regulating aspects of speech: A review. In G. Zivin (Ed.), *The development of self-regulation through private speech* (pp. 135–217). New York: Wiley.

Fuster, J. M. (1989). *The prefrontal cortex: Anatomy, physiology, and neuropsychology of the frontal lobe.* New York: Raven Press.

Geiselman, R. E. (1974). Positive forgetting of sentence material. *Memory & Cognition, 2,* 677–682.

Geiselman, R. E., Bjork, R. A., & Fishman, D. L. (1983). Disrupted retrieval in directed forgetting: A link with posthypnotic amnesia. *Journal of Experimental Psychology: General, 112,* 58–72.

Geiselman, R. E., Rabow, V. E., Wachtel, S. L., & MacKinnon, D. P. (1985). Strategy control in intentional forgetting. *Human Learning, 4,* 169–178.

Golden, C. J. (1981). The Luria-Nebraska children's battery: Theory and formulation. In G. W. Hynd & J. E. Obrzut (Eds.), *Neuropsychological assessment and the school aged child* (pp. 277–302). New York: Grune & Stratton.

Graham, D. J., & Campbell, J. I. D. (1992). Network interference and number-fact retrieval: Evidence from children's alphaplication. *Canadian Journal of Psychology, 46,* 65–91.

Hagen, J. W., & Hale, G. A. (1973). The development of attention in children. In A. D. Pick (Ed.), *Minnesota symposium on child psychology* (Vol. 7, pp. 117–140). Minneapolis: University of Minnesota Press.

Hamm, V. P., & Hasher, L. (1992). Age and the availability of inferences. *Psychology & Aging, 7,* 56–64.

Harnishfeger, K. K. (1991). *Converging evidence of the development of efficient inhibition.* Unpublished doctoral dissertations, Florida Atlantic University.

Harnishfeger, K. K., & Bjorklund, D. F. (1990). Strategic and nonstrategic factors in gifted children's free recall. *Contemporary Educational Psychology, 15,* 346–363.

Harnishfeger, K. K., & Bjorklund, D. F. (1993). The ontogeny of inhibition mechanisms: A renewed approach to cognitive development. In M. L. Howe & R. Pasnak (Eds.), *Emerging themes in cognitive development: Vol. 1. Foundations* (pp. 28–49). New York: Springer-Verlag.

Harnishfeger, K. K., & Brainerd, C. J. (1993). *Nonspecific facilitation of children's recall: Evidence of triage with semantically related information. Journal of Experimental Child Psychology, 57,* 259–280.

202 Katherine Kipp Harnishfeger

Harnishfeger, K. K., Digby, S., Scott, D., Nicholson, S., & Liberty, E. (1992). *Developmental changes in directed-forgetting performance: Evidence for the inefficient inhibition hypothesis.* Paper presented at the Conference on Human Development, Atlanta, GA.

Harnishfeger, K. K., Nicholson, S., & Digby, S. (1993). *Increasing inhibitory efficiency with age: Evidence from the Stroop task.* Paper presented at the Society for Research in Child Development, New Orleans, LA.

Harnishfeger, K. K., Scott, D., & Nicholson, S. (1993). *Incidental learning in a directed-forgetting task: Developmental differences in inhibition.* Paper presented at the Society for Research in Child Development, New Orleans, LA.

Harter, S. (1983). Developmental perspectives on the self-system. In E. M. Hetherington (Ed.), P. H. Mussen (Series Ed.), *Handbook of child psychology: Vol. 4. Socialization, personality, and social development* (pp. 275–385). New York: Wiley.

Hasher, L., Stoltzfus, E. R., Zacks, R. T., & Rypma, B. (1991). Age and inhibition. *Journal of Experimental Psychology: Learning, Memory, and Cognition, 17,* 163–139.

Hasher, L., & Zacks, R. T. (1979). Automatic and effortful processes in memory. *Journal of Experimental Psychology: General, 108,* 356–388.

Hasher, L., & Zacks, R. T. (1988). Working memory, comprehension, and aging: A review and a new view. In G. H. Bower (Ed.), *The psychology of learning and motivation: Advances in research and theory* (Vol. 22, pp. 193–225). San Diego: Academic Press.

Hitch, G. J., & Halliday, M. S. (1983). Working memory in children. *Philosophical Transactions of the Royal Society of London, Series B 302,* 325–340.

Hitch, G. J., Halliday, M. S., & Littler, J. (1984). *Memory span and the speed of mental operations.* Paper presented at the joint Experimental Psychology Society/Netherlands Psychonomic Foundation Meeting, Amsterdam (from Baddeley, 1986).

Hitch, G. J., Halliday, M. S., Schaafstal, A. M., & Heffernan, T. M. (1991). Speech, "inner speech," and the development of short-term memory: Effects of picture-labeling on recall. *Journal of Experimental Child Psychology, 51,* 220–234.

Hulme, C. (1984). Developmental differences in the effects of acoustic similarity on memory span. *Developmental Psychology, 20,* 650–652.

Hulme, C. (1986). Memory development: Interactions between theories in cognitive and developmental psychology. *Bulletin of the British Psychological Society, 39,* 247–250.

Hulme, C., Thomson, N., Muir, C., & Lawrence, A. (1984). Speech rate and the development of short-term memory span. *Journal of Experimental Child Psychology, 38,* 241–253.

Hulme, C., & Tordoff, V. (1989). Working memory development: The effects of speech rate, word length, and acoustic similarity on serial recall. *Journal of Experimental Child Psychology, 47,* 72–87.

James, W. (1890). *The principles of psychology.* New York: Holt.

Kagan, J. (1965). Impulsive and reflective children: Significance of conceptual tempo. In J. D. Krumholtz (Ed.), *Learning and the educational process* (pp. 133–161). Chicago: Rand McNally.

Kagan, J. (1989). Temperamental contributions to social behavior. *American Psychologist, 44,* 668–674.

Kagan, J., Reznick, J. S., & Snidman, N. (1988). Biological bases of childhood shyness. *Science, 240,* 167–171.

Kail, R. V., Jr. (1986). Sources of age differences in speed of processing. *Child Development, 57,* 969–987.

Kail, R. V., Jr. (1993). The role of a global mechanism in developmental change in speed of processing. In M. L. Howe & R. Pasnak (Eds.), *Emerging themes in cognitive development: Vol. 1. Foundations* (pp. 97–119). New York: Springer-Verlag.

Kopp, C. B. (1982). Antecedents of self-regulation: Caregivers and children. In N. Eisenberg (Ed.), *Contemporary topics in developmental psychology* (pp. 34–55). New York: Wiley.

Lane, D. M., & Pearson, D. A. (1982). The development of selective attention. *Merrill-Palmer Quarterly, 28*, 317–337.

Lehman, E. B., & Bovasso, M. (1993). Development of intentional forgetting in children. In M. L. Howe & R. Pasnak (Eds.), *Emerging themes in cognitive development: Vol. 1. Foundations* (pp. 214–233). New York: Springer-Verlag.

Logan, D. G., & Cowan, W. B. (1984). On the ability to inhibit thought and action: A theory of an act of control. *Psychological Review, 91*, 295–327.

Logan, D. G., Cowan, W. B., & Davis, K. A. (1984). On the ability to inhibit simple and choice reaction time responses: A model and a method. *Journal of Experimental Psychology: Human Perception and Performance, 10*, 276–291.

Luria, A. R. (1961). *The role of speech in the regulation of normal and abnormal behavior.* New York: Liveright.

Luria, A. R. (1966). *Higher cortical functions in man.* New York: Basic Books.

Luria, A. R. (1973). *The working brain.* New York: Basic Books.

Mischel, W., Shoda, Y., & Rodriguez, M. L. (1989). Delay of gratification in children. *Science, 244*, 933–938.

Navon, D., & Gopher, D. (1979). On the economy of the human processing system. *Psychological Review, 86*, 214–255.

Neill, W. T. (1977). Inhibitory and facilitatory processes in selective attention. *Journal of Experimental Psychology: Human Perception and Performance, 3*, 444–450.

Neumann, E., & Deschepper, B. G. (1992). An inhibition-based fan effect: Evidence for an active suppression mechanism in selective attention. *Canadian Journal of Psychology, 46*, 1–40.

Nicholson, R. (1979). The relationship between memory span and processing speed. In M. P. Friedman, J. P. Das, & N. O'Connor (Eds.), *Intelligence and learning* (pp. 179–183). New York: Plenum.

Olson, S. L. (1989). Assessment of impulsivity in preschoolers: Cross-measure convergencies, longitudinal stability, and relevance to social competence. *Journal of Clinical Child Psychology, 18*, 176–183.

Pascual-Leone, J. A. (1970). A mathematical model for the transition rule in Piaget's developmental stages. *Acta Psychologica, 32*, 301–345.

Passler, M. A., Isaac, W., & Hynd, G. W. (1985). Neuropsychological development of behavior attributed to frontal lobe functioning children. *Developmental Neuropsychology, 1*, 349–370.

Paulsen, K., & Johnson, M. (1980). Impulsivity: A multidimensional concept with developmental aspects. *Journal of Abnormal Child Psychology, 8*, 269–277.

Pavlov, I. P. (1927). *Conditional reflexes.* (G. V. Anrep, Ed and Trans.). Oxford: Oxford University Press.

Pearson, D. A., & Lane, D. M. (1990). Visual attention movements: A developmental study. *Child Development, 61*, 1779–1795.

Pearson, D. A., & Lane, D. M. (1991). Auditory attention switching: A developmental study. *Journal of Experimental Child Psychology, 51*, 320–334.

Reznick, J. S. (Ed.). (1989). *Perspectives on behavioral inhibition.* Chicago: University of Chicago Press.

Reznick, J. S., Kagan, J., Snidman, N., Gersten, M., Baak, K., & Rosenberg, A. (1986). Inhibited and uninhibited behavior: A follow-up study. *Child Development, 57*, 660–680.

Saltz, E., Campbell, S., & Skotko, D. (1983). Verbal control of behavior: The effects of shouting. *Developmental Psychology, 19*, 461–464.

Schachar, R., & Logan, G. D. (1990). Impulsivity and inhibitory control in normal development and childhood psychopathlogy. *Developmental Psychology, 26*, 710–720.

Schiff, A. R., & Knopf, I. J. (1985). The effect of task demands on attention allocation in children of different ages. *Child Development, 56*, 621–630.

Seidenberg, M. S., Tanenhaus, M. K., Leiman, J. M., & Bienkowski, M. (1982). Automatic access of the meanings of ambiguous words in context: Some limitations of knowledge-based processing. *Cognitive Psychology, 14*, 489–537.

Shiffrin, R. M., & Schneider, W. (1977). Controlled and automatic human information processing: II. Perceptual learning, automatic attending, and a general theory. *Psychological Review, 84*, 127–190.

Stroop, J. (1935). Studies of interference in serial verbal reactions. *Journal of Experimental Psychology, 18*, 643–662.

Swinney, D. A., & Prather, P. (1989). On the comprehension of lexical ambiguity by young children: Investigations into the development of mental modularity. In D. S. Gorfein (Ed.), *Resolving semantic ambiguity* (pp. 225–238). New York: Springer-Verlag.

Swinney, D. A., Zurif, E., & Nichol, J. (1989). The effects of focal brain damage on sentence processing: An examination of the neurological organization of a mental module. *Journal of Cognitive Neuropsychology, 1*, 25–37.

Tipper, S. P. (1985). The negative priming effect: Inhibitory priming by ignored objects. *Quarterly Journal of Experimental Psychology, 37A*, 571–590.

Tipper, S. P., & Baylis, G. C. (1987). Individual differences in selective attention: The relation of priming and interference to cognitive failure. *Personality and Individual Differences, 8*, 667–675.

Tipper, S. P., Bourque, T. A., Anderson, S. H., & Brehaut, J. (1989). Mechanisms of attention: A developmental study. *Journal of Experimental Child Psychology, 48*, 353–378.

Tipper, S. P., & Cranston, M. (1985). Selective attention and priming: Inhibitory and facilitatory effects of ignored primes. *Quarterly Journal of Experimental Psychology, 37A*, 591–611.

Toner, I. J., Holstein, R. B., & Hetherington, E. M. (1977). Reflection-impulsivity and self-control in preschool children. *Child Development, 48*, 239–245.

Vygotsky, L. S. (1962). *Thought and language*. Cambridge, MA: MIT Press.

Wegner, D. M. (1989). *White bears and other unwanted thoughts: Suppression, obsession, and the psychology of mental control*. New York: Viking.

Wozniak, R. H. (1972). Verbal regulation of motor behavior: Soviet research and non-Soviet replications. *Human Development, 15*, 13–57.

III

Adult Perspectives

7

Selective Attention and the Inhibitory Control of Cognition

W. Trammell Neill, Leslie A. Valdes,
and Kathleen M. Terry

INTRODUCTION

The Problem of Selective Attention

Natural environments often confront us with multiple sources of information, objects and events, that could potentially control or guide our behavior. Yet, by necessity, we respond to only some limited subset of those sources. We commonly refer to selected, goal-appropriate objects and events as "attended," while the remaining sources of information are "ignored." How we accomplish such selection has been perhaps the most contentious issue in cognitive psychology.

Much theoretical debate has focused on the extent to which we analyze ignored stimuli. Broadbent's (1958) influential "filter" theory postulated that selective attention occurs early, prior to categorization. Simple physical features of ignored stimuli would not be identified, in the sense of contacting their corresponding representations in memory. Other theorists, like Deutsch and Deutsch (1963) and Norman (1968), proposed alternative "late selection" theories, asserting that ignored stimuli are fully analyzed and identified prior to selection.

Until recently, most theories have taken for granted that attention directly facilitates processing. That is, automatic processing is assumed up to some level, early or late. Attention then intervenes, enabling selected, relevant information to receive further processing (Figure 1A). Ignored stimuli are not processed further, and their effects dissipate passively over time (Van der Heijden, 1981). However, there is a logical alternative: the mechanism of attention might instead inhibit the processing of irrelevant information (Figure 1B). Processing of relevant information would then simply proceed, unhampered by interference from irrelevant information.

Considerable evidence has accumulated in support of the latter position. Inhibition of irrelevant processing appears to be an important, if not exclusive, function of selective attention. Beyond its consequences for our theoretical understanding of attention, this new perspective has important implications for real-world cognitive functioning. In particular, subject populations that are distinguished either clinically or developmentally by cognitive deficits

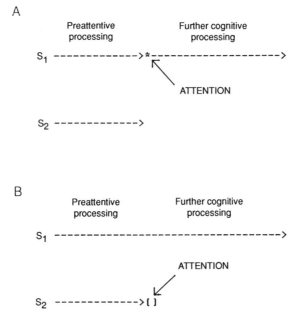

FIGURE 1. Theoretical conceptions of attention: (A) attention as facilitation; (B) attention as inhibition.

are often unable to inhibit certain kinds of distracting information. This chapter reviews the empirical evidence for inhibitory mechanisms in attention and their theoretical implications.

Negative Priming

How can we distinguish empirically between facilitation of relevant processing and inhibition of irrelevant processing? Suppose that a subject responds to an "attended" object, S_1, ignoring another object, S_2, as in Figure 1. Next, suppose that he or she must unexpectedly respond to the just-ignored object S_2, or to a new object, S_3. According to facilitation theories, the initial effects of S_2 dissipate over time. If those effects have not dissipated completely, then processing of S_2 would have a "head start" relative to S_3, yielding a "priming effect" (Neely, 1976, 1977; Posner & Snyder, 1975). If the initial effects of S_2 have already dissipated, then processing of S_2 and S_3 should simply not differ.

If, however, the processing of S_2 was inhibited in order to further process S_1, subsequent processing of S_2 must overcome any persistence of that inhibition. Consequently, S_2 should be more difficult to process than S_3. In many experiments that consider the predictions of attention as facilitation versus attention as inhibition, the latter pattern of results is obtained: subjects are slower and/or less accurate in responding to stimuli related to recently ignored stimuli. Tipper (1985) introduced the term *negative priming* to describe the inhibitory effects of ignored stimuli, to contrast with the facilitatory effects (priming) typically produced by attended stimuli. (Developmental changes in negative priming are discussed by Harnishfeger, Chapter 6, and McDowd, Oseas-Kreger, & Filion, Chapter 11, this volume.)

Dalrymple-Alford and Budayr (1966) provided the first-known demonstration of negative priming, using the Stroop (1935) color-word task. In this task, subjects try to quickly name the ink colors in which words are written. Color naming is greatly slowed if the words denote incompatible ink colors, for example, GREEN written in *red* ink. This is the well-known "Stroop Effect." Dalrymple-Alford and Budayr found that color naming was even slower for a list of Stroop words if each word named the *next* color in the list, for example, GREEN in *red* ink, followed by YELLOW in *green* ink, then BLUE in *yellow* ink, and so on. They reasoned that subjects had to suppress the response to each word in order to name the ink color; if the suppressed response was required for the next ink color, that response would be slowed.

Because of methodological difficulties inherent in the whole-list procedure, Neill (1977) replicated this effect in vocal naming latencies to single, randomized Stroop words. Thus, if the relevant color on trial n matched the irrelevant distractor word on trial $n-1$, reaction time was significantly slower than if the current Stroop word was unrelated to the previous one. In subsequent experiments, subjects learned arbitrary keypress responses to different colors; the distractor suppression effect was still obtained (Neill, 1982; Neill & Westberry, 1987). Hence, the effect does not particularly depend on response modality, vocal or manual.

GENERALITY OF NEGATIVE PRIMING

Since the initial demonstrations of negative priming in the Stroop task (see also Lowe, 1979, 1985), similar effects have been demonstrated in a great variety of other selective-attention tasks. In addition to the basic task requirements (identification, matching, localization, etc.), experiments vary widely in methodological details such as stimulus set sizes, timing of within- and between-trial events, and within- and between-subject manipulations. Some procedural variations do not appear to qualitatively affect results, while others do, and still others remain to be systematically investigated.

By convention, the term *probe* will refer to an experimental trial on which performance is measured and classified according to the relation of the critical target stimulus to a previously presented stimulus, the *prime*. Most often, this refers to two successive trials in an experiment. In some experiments, every trial is classified according to its relation to the preceding trial (e.g., Neill, 1977). Hence, each trial serves as both a probe relative to the preceding trial, and a prime relative to the next trial. In other experiments, prime and probe trials may be distinguished by different task demands (e.g., Tipper, 1985) or by presentation as temporally distinct pairs.

Identification Tasks

Picture Naming   In an influential study by Tipper (1985), subjects were shown superimposed line drawings, one (the target) drawn in red ink, the other (the distractor) in green. Subjects were instructed to remember the prime trial target, and then to quickly name the probe target. After naming the probe, subjects recalled the prime target. The critical variable was the relation of the probe target to the prime trial stimuli. In the "Ignored Repetition" condition, the probe target and prime distractor were identical (except for ink color). Naming latencies were significantly slower in this condition than when the prime and probe trials were unrelated.

In one experiment (Tipper, 1985, Experiment 3), the probe target was sometimes nonidentical, but semantically related, to the prime distractor; for example, a picture of a dog following an ignored pictured of a cat. This "Ignored Semantic" condition also produced slower naming latencies than those in the control condition. Hence, negative priming generalizes to semantic associates of ignored stimuli. On other trials, the probe target could be identical or related to the prime target ("Attended Repetition" and "Attended Semantic," respectively). These conditions produced facilitation relative to the control condition, that is, positive priming instead of negative.

In some later experiments, targets and distractors were distinguished by spatial location rather than ink color. For example, Tipper, Weaver, Cameron, Brehaut, and Bastedo (1991, Experiments 1, 2, and 6) presented target pictures at a central fixated location, while nonoverlapping distractor pictures appeared randomly to the left or right. Despite the spatial separation, ignored pictures still produced negative priming.

Word Naming   Kane, Hasher, Stoltzfus, Zacks, and Connelly (1994) used a vocal word-naming task to investigate negative priming in young and old subjects. In this task, two words were presented on each trial, above and below fixation. Subjects were instructed to pronounce the target word, specified by color (red or green). Young subjects responded more slowly to probe target words if they were identical to the word ignored on the prime trial. To anticipate later discussion, old subjects did not show this negative-priming effect.

Chiarello et al. (1993) used a "crosswords" variation of this procedure to investigate hemispheric lateralization of negative priming. Here, vertically and horizontally spelled words shared a common central letter (e.g., DOG vertically and TON horizontally). Subjects were instructed to name the horizontal word and ignore the vertical, or vice versa. Negative priming was found only when probes were presented to the left visual hemifield, suggesting a special inhibitory role for the right cerebral hemisphere, at least when *spatial* selection is required.

Letter Identification   Subjects in a series of experiments by Tipper and Cranston (1985) vocally named target letters written in red ink, ignoring overlapping green distractor letters. As in picture and word naming, letter naming was slower if the probe target letter was identical to the recently ignored prime distractor (see also Tipper, MacQueen, & Brehaut, 1988).

We have used variations of Eriksen's flanker-compatibility paradigm (B. A. Eriksen & Eriksen, 1974; Eriksen & Hoffman, 1973) to study negative priming. In one variation, the letters A, B, C, and D are assigned to different keypress responses. A target letter is flanked on the left and right by a distractor letter that is either compatible (e.g., AAA) or incompatible (e.g., BAB) with the target. Incompatible distractors produce a Stroop-type interference effect, relative to compatible flankers. Negative priming is shown by slower responses to probe targets that match the prime trial flanker (e.g., CBC following BAB).

Table 1 shows previously unpublished data from two such experiments, in which we also varied location uncertainty. In the "wobble" condition, prime triplets were unpredictably centered at fixation, or shifted to the left or right. In the "no wobble" condition, the triplets were always centered at fixa-

TABLE 1. Mean Reaction Times (in ms) for Letter Identification, as a Function of Location Uncertainty ("Wobble"), Prime Location, and Trial Type

	Prime Location		
	No wobble	Wobble	
Trial type	Centered	Centered	Off center
Prime trials			
Incongruent	659 (652)[a]	666 (665)	724 (725)
Congruent	627 (608)	618 (629)	665 (646)
Interference	32 (44)	48 (36)	59 (79)
Probe trials			
Related	663 (652)	676 (660)	687 (676)
Unrelated	642 (638)	649 (654)	656 (659)
Negative priming	21 (14)	27 (6)	31 (17)

[a]Experiment 2 reaction times are in parentheses.

tion. In Experiment 1, location uncertainty was manipulated between blocks of trials within subjects; in Experiment 2, it was manipulated between subject groups.

We assessed Stroop-type interference by varying the compatibility of flankers on prime trials. As shown in Table 1, incompatible flankers produced longer reaction times than those produced by compatible flankers. In both experiments, interference was increased for the "off-center" trials in the wobble condition. This is not surprising, because a flanker appeared at fixation in this condition, while the target was moved off fixation. In analyses of centered trials alone, "wobble" and "no wobble" conditions did not differ significantly.

Negative priming was assessed on probe trials following prime trials that had incompatible distractors. Reaction times were longer in the Ignored Repetition condition (e.g., CBC after BAB) than in the control condition (e.g., CBC after DAD). The presentation conditions also produced marginally significant interactions ($p < .10$) with negative priming. Although the patterns differ somewhat between the two experiments, it may be noted that the ordering of negative-priming effects parallels the ordering of interference effects within each experiment.

Categorization

Semantic Categorization   Tipper and Baylis (1987) required subjects to respond vocally with the superordinate category name (animal, furniture, music, tool, body) appropriate to target words, again specified by color. Although this study found negative priming, it did not generalize to another category member. For example, after ignoring the word CAT, the response "animal" was slower to the probe word CAT, but not to the probe word DOG. On the other hand, generalization of negative priming was found in a similar study by Tipper and Driver (1988).

The Tipper and Driver study is particularly important because subjects categorized both words and pictures. As much negative priming was found between stimulus domains (from word primes to picture probes, and vice versa) as within the same stimulus domain. Hence, negative priming does not depend on physical similarity between prime and probe—at least in this task. We will return to this important observation.

Lexical Decision   In a lexical-decision task, subjects must judge whether each string of letters is a word (e.g., NURSE) or a nonword (e.g., NERSE). This task has been perhaps the most commonly used tool for investigating (positive) associative priming effects (e.g., Meyer & Schvaneveldt, 1971; Neely, 1976, 1977). The typical result is that a word is recognized more quickly as a word per se if it follows a related word, for example, NURSE following DOCTOR. In most such experiments, however, the priming word is deliberately attended; the question naturally arises of whether a deliberately ignored word produces a negative priming effect. Not surprisingly (by now), it does.

In an experiment by Yee (1991, Experiment 1), subjects were required to classify geometric figures on the prime trials. The figures were flanked above or below, or both, by irrelevant distractor words. After the response to a geometric figure, a probe trial then required a word/nonword judgment for a string of letters. Lexical decision was slower for words related to a prime trial distractor (e.g., DOG after ignoring CAT).

Other studies have also demonstrated negative priming in lexical decision (e.g., Fuentes & Tudela, 1992; Marcel, 1980). Yee's study is notable in that the distractor stimuli (words) were irrelevant to the prime-trial task to classify a geometric figure. Thus, negative priming does not require that the distractors elicit responses that directly conflict with the prime-trial decision.

Matching Tasks

Letter Matching   Neill, Lissner, and Beck (1990) required subjects to judge whether the second and fourth letters of a five-letter string were same or different. Thus, subjects would respond "same" to CACAC, but "different" to CACBC. A benefit of this procedure is that the overt response can be manipulated independently of the targets' specific identity. As shown in Table 2, negative priming occurred regardless of whether the prime and probe required identical or opposite responses. (Neill and Valdes [1992] did find negative priming to vary for different response sequences, but primarily in interaction with different prime–probe delays, which induced shifts in response bias.)

**TABLE 2. Mean Probe Reaction Times (in ms) as a Function of
Prime-Trial Type, Probe-Trial Type, and Relatedness to
Prime-Trial Distractors[a]**

| | Prime trial type | |
Probe-trial type	Same (ABABA)	Different (ABAEA)
Same		
Related (DADAD)[b]	779	819
Unrelated (DCDCD)	766	803
Negative priming	13	16
Different		
Related (DADCD)	864	861
Unrelated (DFDCD)	842	849
Negative priming	22	12

[a]From Neill, Lissner, & Beck, 1990.
[b]Examples of stimuli are in parentheses.

Shape Matching   Another benefit of same–different matching is that it can
be used for unfamiliar stimuli. DeSchepper and Treisman (1991) presented
novel shapes like those in Figure 2, such that a target shape drawn in green
was superimposed on a distractor shape drawn in red. Subjects were instructed to judge whether the target shape matched a third shape, drawn in white.
Negative priming was shown by slower responses on probe trials if the target

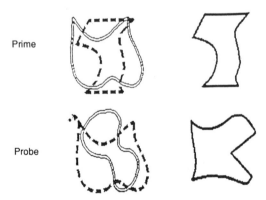

FIGURE 2.   Subjects judge whether the green (▬ ▬ ▬) and white (▬▬▬▬) figures are same or
different, ignoring the red figure (════). Negative priming occurs if the green probe figure
matches the red prime figure. (Adapted from DeSchepper & Treisman, 1991.)

shape was identical to the ignored distractor shape on the prime trial. Such results demonstrate that negative priming does not depend on a preexisting cognitive representation of the ignored stimulus (see also Treisman, 1992, for discussion).

Counting Tasks

In a task adapted from Francolini and Egeth (1980), Driver and Tipper (1989) presented arrays of eight red and black letters and digits. Subjects were instructed to count the number of red items, ignoring the black items. In one experiment, the red targets were letters on some trials, and digits on other trials. In the latter case, the subject might have to count, for example, four red 2s. Consistent with Francolini and Egeth, digit targets produced a Stroop-type interference relative to letter targets. In addition, the digits produced negative priming. For example, if the subject had to count four red 2s on the prime trial, counting *two* red items would be slowed on the probe trial.

In another experiment, the red targets were always letters, while the black distractors were digits on some trials and letters on other trials. Here, digit distractors did not produce interference, again consistent with Francolini and Egeth. Nonetheless, they still produced negative priming. Thus, if the subject ignored black 2s on the prime trial, counting *two* red items would again be slowed. The magnitude of negative priming was approximately equal in the two experiments. These experiments demonstrate that ignored stimuli may produce negative priming, regardless of whether they produce interference.

Localization Tasks

In the tasks discussed above (with possible exception of counting), subjects selected relevant stimuli by a physical attribute, such as location or color, and then based their response on the identity of the stimulus possessing that attribute. Many experiments on selective attention employ such "select-where/respond-what" tasks. Tipper, Brehaut, and Driver (1990) point out that in the natural environment, we often select objects by identity, and respond on the basis of location. For example, in reaching for a coffee cup among other objects on a desk, one must select the object by its identity (coffee cup) and then use its location to guide reaching.

Tipper et al. (1990, Experiment 1) devised a "select-what/respond-where" task, in which a target symbol (@) appears in one of four horizontally arrayed locations, and a distractor symbol (+) appears in another. Subjects are instructed to press a key corresponding to the location of the target. Negative priming is shown by slower responses to a probe target that appears in the same location as the prime-trial distractor. Hence, an irrelevant object location can be inhibited in much the same way as an irrelevant object identity.

In a variation of this task (Tipper et al., 1990, Experiment 3), subjects watched the target and distractor move vertically down the screen of a computer monitor, until they were occluded by vertical strips of tape (Figure 3). The stimuli then emerged near the bottom of the screen, each at one of four possible locations. Again, the subject was instructed to press a key corresponding to the location of the emerging target. If the target symbol emerged at the expected location of the distractor, responses were slower than if it emerged at a wholly new location. Thus, negative priming appears to "move with" the ignored object, rather than adhering to its last-seen location.

In yet another variation of this task (Tipper, Lortie, & Baylis, 1992), the subject was required to move his or her hand from a "start" button to one of nine target buttons, signaled by the onset of an adjacent red light. At the same time, a yellow light signaled an irrelevant location. The reaching response was slower if a probe-trial target location had been signaled by the distractor light on the prime trial.

A particularly important finding in the reaching experiments was that negative priming depended on the location of the distractor relative to the in-

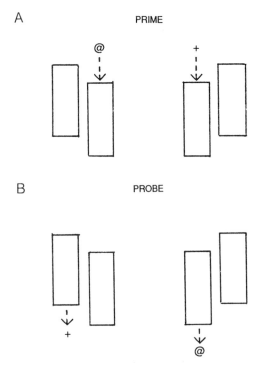

FIGURE 3. Subjects observe a target (@) and distractor (+) travel behind occluding strips (A); and respond to location of target when it emerges (B). Negative priming occurs if the target emerges at the expected distractor location. (Adapted from Tipper, Brehaut, & Driver, 1990).

tended movement. In one experiment, the start button was at the bottom of the array of target buttons. Hence, the task required a hand movement away from the subject. A distractor light produced negative priming only if it was closer to the subject than the prime trial target. If the distractor was farther away, it did not produce negative priming.

In a second experiment, the start button was moved to the top of the array. The task then required a hand movement *toward* the subject. Here, distractors farther from the subject produced negative priming, while closer distractors did not. Hence, negative priming in this task is "action centered": the distractor produces negative priming if it is within the range of the intended movement, but not if it is beyond that range.

Summary

Negative-priming effects have been demonstrated for a variety of materials: words, letters, drawings of objects, and unfamiliar shapes. They have also been demonstrated in various response modes: vocal naming, manual keypress, and reaching. Most important, negative priming occurs across quite different types of judgment: identification, categorization, matching, counting, and localization. While not all possible combinations of judgment, materials, and response mode have been tested, it seems reasonable to conclude that negative priming is a phenomenon of broad generality.

The generality of negative priming raises a number of questions, however. What is actually inhibited: response, perception, or something else? Does it depend on the demands of the task? Is there a single inhibitory control mechanism or many? The next section explores these questions further.

WHAT IS INHIBITED?

Response?

Negative priming in some experiments could be explained simply as withholding of the overt response that was elicited by an ignored distractor (see also the discussion of output interference in Brainerd, Chapter 4, and Reyna, Chapter 2, this volume). For example, if a subject ignores the word GREEN in the Stroop task, he or she might inhibit vocalizing the word "green." Similarly, in the localization task, the subject might inhibit the flexion of the finger on the corresponding key.

In other experiments, however, response inhibition per se cannot explain negative priming. Tipper et al. (1988) found just as much negative priming when prime and probe letters required opposite response modalities (vocal or manual) as when they required the same response modality (see also Tipper, Weaver, Kirkpatrick, & Lewis, 1991).

Neill, Lissner, and Beck (1990) also concluded that negative priming is not response inhibition, since negative priming in same/different matching occurred regardless of whether the prime target and probe target required the same response (Table 2). Response inhibition also cannot explain negative priming in experiments in which the same response is required for distractor-related probes and unrelated probes. For example, in lexical decision tasks, both conditions require a "word" response.

Neill, Valdes, and Terry (1992) applied this logic to demonstrate that negative priming in the localization task is not response inhibition. A target "O" appeared in one of four possible locations, as did a distractor "X." However, the target locations were mapped into two possible responses, such that subjects pressed one key for the two leftmost locations, and another key for the two rightmost locations. Reaction time to a probe target in the prime distractor location was slower than that to a probe target requiring the same response but in a neutral location (Table 3). Further, it is doubtful that any response inhibition occurred, since reaction time was actually faster to a neutral location requiring the same response as the distractor than to a neutral location requiring the other response.

Perception?

In some experiments, negative priming might be explained as the inhibition of a particular perceptual attribute. For example, ignoring a capital letter A or a picture of a dog might inhibit the perception of stimuli bearing the same shape. Or, in a localization task, ignoring a distractor at a particular location might inhibit the perception of other stimuli occurring at the same location.

In many experiments, however, the prime distractor bears little or no physical similarity to the probe target used to detect negative priming. For ex-

TABLE 3. Probe Localization Reaction Time (in ms) with 4-to-2 Mapping of Locations to Responses, with Examples of Arrays

	Prime–probe relation			
	Same response		Opposite response	
	Repeat	Neutral	Ignored	Neutral
Prime	_ O _ X	_ O _ X	_ Q _ X	_ O _ X
Probe	_ O _ _	O _ _ _	_ _ _ O	_ _ X _
Response	1	1	2	2
Reaction time	344	368	368	353

[a]Neill, Valdes, & Terry, 1992.

ample, in the Stroop task, the subject ignores a distractor *word;* this consequently slows a response to the denoted *color.* Hence, it is not just the perceptual processing of the distractor that is inhibited. Rather, the effect must occur
at a more abstract level of representation that relates the word and color.

Similarly, Tipper and Driver (1988) found negative priming between
pictures and corresponding words, and several studies have found negative
priming to generalize to semantic associates of pictures and words (Tipper,
1985; Tipper & Driver, 1988; Yee, 1991). Such results cannot be easily explained as inhibition of perceptual features of ignored stimuli.

On the other hand, some studies have found perceptual similarity to be
critical to negative priming: Neill (1991) reported an experiment in which
strings of five letters were presented in either upper- or lowercase. As in the
study by Neill, Lissner, and Beck (1990), subjects matched the second and
fourth letters as "same" or "different," ignoring the remaining distractor
letters. Negative priming occurred for same-case sequences (e.g.,
ABABA–DADAD, or ababa–dadad), but not for opposite-case sequences
(ABABA–dadad).

In the experiments by DeSchepper and Treisman (1991), subjects made
same/different judgments for novel shapes, which could have no preexisting
cognitive representations (Figure 3). Negative priming must therefore reflect
the perceptual shape characteristics. It would beg the issue to suggest that a
more abstract conceptual representation is formed on the first exposure to a
shape, since it is unclear what could define the representation other than the
shape's physical appearance.

Finally, it must be noted that negative priming in the localization task
does not result from shared identity, perceptual or abstract, between the
prime distractor and probe target. Rather, it is the shared perceptual attribute
of location that is critical.

Hence, in some studies, negative priming does not depend on physical
similarity between prime distractor and probe target; inhibition must therefore occur at a more abstract level of representation that relates physically different objects. In other studies, however, negative priming appears to be specific to the physical features of the ignored object.

Task-Relevant Information?

Why does negative priming sometimes depend on physical similarity
and sometimes not? A plausible speculation is that it depends on what information is required by the task. Some tasks require attention to physical characteristics like shape or location; other tasks require attention to more abstract levels of representation like name, meaning, or category.

Allport, Tipper, and Chmiel (1985, Experiment 2), found equivalent
negative priming of letter naming for opposite-case primes and probes and for
same-case primes and probes. Superficially, this result seems at odds with the

result reported by Neill (1991). However, the discrepancy is illuminating in view of the difference in task demands. In the experiment by Neill (1991), "same" matches were physically identical, and so it is likely that subjects relied on perceptual attributes for performance of the task. In contrast, naming is independent of letter case, and it is likely that the subjects of Allport et al. relied on more abstract information for their judgments.

Connelly, Hasher, and Kimble (1992) directly tested the hypothesis of task specificity in two experiments, in which target and distractor letters appeared in four possible locations. In both experiments, the target was defined by color (red or green), while the distractor appeared in the opposite color. In one experiment, subjects named the target letter; in the other, they responded to its location.

In the naming experiment, negative priming occurred for both color and location. That is, responses were slower to a probe target sharing either the same identity or same location as the prime distractor. Further, these two effects were additive, such that responses were especially slow to probes sharing both the same identity and same location as the prime distractor. In the localization experiment, negative priming was obtained only for location. Hence, there was no negative priming for the identity of an ignored object if identity was not relevant to the task.

It is intriguing that negative priming occurred for location in both experiments, roughly equal in magnitude, regardless of whether location was explicitly relevant to the task. This might reflect a special role for location, imputed by some theorists to "bind together" other, independent perceptual attributes (e.g., Nissen, 1985; Treisman & Gelade, 1980). Alternatively, it might reflect the faster processing of location than identity, as evidenced by the overall reaction-time differences between the two experiments. It is conceivable that task-irrelevant attributes are inhibited only if they are analyzed prior to the task-relevant attribute.

S–R Mapping?

Negative priming depends, in part, on the level of representation required by a task. The recognition of a stimulus might therefore be inhibited at that level of representation. However, there is another important process between recognizing a stimulus and making a response to that stimulus: retrieving the appropriate response to the recognized stimulus, or "S–R mapping." The rules for translating a stimulus into a response would, of course, vary directly with the demands of a given task.

Neill, Valdes, and Terry (1992; see also Valdes, 1993) investigated the importance of S–R mapping in negative priming, by varying stimulus–response compatibility in the localization task. One group of subjects received spatially reversed ("incompatible") response assignments, such that they pressed the rightmost key for the leftmost location, for example. Another group received spatially congruent ("compatible") assignments. As shown in Table 4, incompatible responses yielded more negative priming (52 ms) than did compatible responses (16 ms).

The significant interaction ($p < .01$) of negative priming with compatibility argues against either recognition or response alone as the locus of inhibition. That is, inhibition of recognizing the probe would add the same processing time, regardless of the subsequent response. Similarly, inhibition of a particular response would add the same amount to the response time, regardless of the stimulus. Given that compatibility affects the S–R mapping, but not recognition or response per se, the interaction with prime–probe relation suggests that negative priming *also* affects S–R mapping. (The reader may recognize the "additive factors logic" elucidated by Sternberg, 1969.)

In the above experiment, prime and probe trials had identical response assignments. Hence, it is unclear whether the magnification of negative priming for incompatible responses was due to the prime trial or the probe trial. In a follow-up experiment, we varied response assignments between trials. Target letters were either "S" or "O." Subjects were instructed to press the key in the *same* relative location for an S target (compatible), but to press the key in the *opposite* location for an O target (incompatible).

We had expected a straightforward effect of either prime compatibility, or probe compatibility, on negative priming. Much to our surprise, negative priming vanished altogether when response assignments were switched. (The

TABLE 4. Probe Localization Time (in ms), as a Function of Prime–Probe Relation, and S–R Compatibility of Prime–Probe Sequences, with Examples of Arrays[a]

	Repeat	Ignored	Neutral
	Prime–probe relation		
(Prime)	X _ O _	X _ O _	X _ O _
(Probe)	_ _ O X	O _ _ X	_ O _ X
S–R Compatibility			
Experiment 1			
Compatible/compatible	439	502	486
Incompatible/incompatible	585	791	739
Experiment 2			
Compatible/compatible	521	706	662
Compatible /incompatible	799	800	809
Incompatible/compatible	788	790	788
Incompatible/incompatible	650	798	762

[a]Experiment 1, from Neill, Valdes, & Terry, 1992; Experiment 2, previously unreported. (In Experiment 2, targets with compatible response assignments were "S" rather than "O.")

triple interaction of prime compatibility, probe compatibility, and prime–probe relation was significant, $p < .05$.) Negative priming occurred when prime and probe were both compatible (44 ms), or both incompatible (35 ms). However, as shown in Table 4, there was no negative priming in compatible–incompatible and incompatible–compatible sequences (–9 and 2 ms, respectively).

This experiment did not replicate the result previously reported by Neill, Valdes, and Terry (1992), in which negative priming was greater for incompatible–incompatible sequences than for compatible–compatible sequences. This may reflect the fact that subjects had to discriminate between targets, and had to remember which response assignment was appropriate to which target. In contrast, subjects in the earlier experiment had to remember only one response assignment, and in the compatible condition could take advantage of the natural tendency to respond in the direction of a target.

More important, this experiment indicates the importance of retaining the same S–R mapping between prime and probe trials. It may be noted that the disappearance of negative priming when assignments were switched cannot be attributed to the change of target stimuli: in other experiments with only compatible response assignments, negative priming was not affected by changes in target stimuli (Neill, Valdes, & Terry, 1992). Rather, it appears that negative priming applies to the specific mapping of an ignored stimulus to its corresponding response.

PARAMETERS OF NEGATIVE PRIMING

The research discussed so far has emphasized the generality of negative priming across a wide variety of tasks requiring selective attention. However, as discussed above, negative priming may not occur if response assignments are changed between prime and probe trials. Many other variables have also been found to affect the magnitude of negative priming.

Development of Negative Priming

A number of studies have demonstrated that the effects of attention require time to develop after the presentation of a relevant cue (e.g., Neely, 1976, 1977; Posner & Snyder, 1975). If negative priming reflects the operation of some inhibitory mechanism on distracting information, then we might similarly expect negative priming to build over time from the onset of a distractor stimulus. Indeed, since irrelevant stimuli do often interfere with task performance (as in the Stroop task), inhibition of a distractor must be preceded by some period of activation during which it may interfere with target processing.

SOA Effects   Several studies have demonstrated that negative priming does not occur immediately upon the presentation of a distractor stimulus, but rather requires time to develop. Some of these studies measure negative priming as a function of stimulus-onset asynchrony (SOA), that is, the time between onset of the prime stimuli and onset of a probe. Negative priming would be likely to develop within the period of time required for a prime target response. This response might interfere with responding to the probe, making it infeasible to test negative priming at short SOAs. Consequently, most SOA studies do not require an immediate response to the prime.

Lowe (1985) instructed subjects to "focus on" the color of a priming Stroop word presented for 50 ms, and then to identify the color of a probe Stroop word presented at an SOA of 50, 100, 200, or 400 ms. There was no negative priming at the shortest (50 ms) SOA, but negative priming was significant at the 100-ms and longer SOAs. Lowe established that the absence of negative priming at the 50-ms SOA was not caused by failure to process the prime (e.g., due to masking), because positive priming from the prime target color did occur at that duration (e.g., BLUE in *red* ink following YELLOW *red* ink yielded facilitation relative to unrelated stimuli).

Yee (1991, Experiment 2) found negative priming to increase with SOA in the lexical decision task. In her first experiment, previously discussed, subjects first responded to a geometric figure flanked by distractor words, and then to a word or nonword for a lexical decision judgment. In her second experiment, subjects did not respond immediately to the geometric figure. On some trials, subjects were signaled by a question mark that they should respond to the geometric figure; on other trials, they received a word or nonword for a lexical decision judgment. In either case, the signal to respond was presented at either a 500- or 600-ms SOA, relative to the onset of the flanking distractor words. (These intervals were selected because they bracketed the average prime reaction times in her first experiment.)

Yee found significant *positive* priming at the 500-ms SOA, which reversed to significant negative priming at the 600-ms SOA. It may be noted that the development of negative priming between 500 and 600 ms is considerably slower than in Lowe's experiments. However, the many procedural differences preclude any direct comparison: aside from the obvious differences in stimulus sets (many words vs. a few colors), Yee's distractors were presented 4.5° from fixation, flanking the prime trial targets, while Lowe's Stroop distractor words were foveal and integrated with the target colors. How such factors affect the accrual of inhibition remains to be investigated.

Speed/Accuracy Trade-off   Several studies have demonstrated that negative priming depends on whether subjects adopt a strict accuracy criterion, or adopt a lax criterion in order to achieve greater speed. Neill (1982) found a moderately strong ($r = .57$, $p < .01$) correlation over subjects between negative priming and an independent measure of reaction time. Neill and Westberry (1987) found negative priming when subjects were instructed to maintain strict accuracy, but positive priming when subjects were encouraged to sacrifice accuracy for greater speed. Similar results were found by Neumann and DeSchepper (1992), using a letter-naming task adapted from Tipper and Cranston (1985).

These results are most easily understood as reflecting the time course of developing inhibition in the prime trial. Initially, distractor information is highly activated (Figure 4A). Under instructions emphasizing speed, the subject may respond before the distractor information has been completely suppressed. If the distractor information is left more activated than the baseline of control condition responses (Figure 4B), then positive priming will occur for the corresponding probe. On the other hand, under strict accuracy instructions, distractor information may be more completely suppressed before responding (Figure 4C), yielding negative priming on the probe trial.

Persistence of Negative Priming

How long is distractor information inhibited? It seems implausible that irrelevant information is inhibited forever; eventually, all concepts would be inhibited! Inhibitory effects might decay over time, such that the mental representations of ignored objects spontaneously recover to some baseline level of availability. However, this is not logically necessary: it is conceivable that ignored concepts simply remain inhibited until they become task relevant and are then "disinhibited."

As discussed above, negative priming effects increase with delay from the onset of the prime distractor. However, one would not expect inhibition to

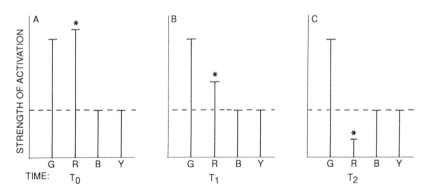

FIGURE 4. Hypothetical availability of responses to green (G), red (R), blue (BL), and yellow (Y). (A) Initial activation by Stroop word RED in *green* ink; (B) after partial suppression; (C) after complete suppression. (From Neill, 1989.)

increase indefinitely. In particular, there would seem to be little need to continue inhibiting the prime distractor after a response has been made to the prime target. Consequently, persistence of negative priming is often measured as a function of time between *response* to a prime target and onset of a probe (i.e., response–stimulus interval, or RSI). Some studies have also measured negative priming over trials intervening between prime and probe, or "lag."

RSI Effects   Neill and Westberry (1987) investigated the persistence of negative priming in the Stroop task by randomly varying RSI between trials. Negative priming occurred at 20, 520, and 1020 ms RSI, but not at 2020 ms RSI. Neill and Westberry concluded that inhibition "decays" fairly rapidly, dissipating within two seconds. Subsequent research suggested, however, that this conclusion was premature. Several studies have found considerably greater persistence of negative priming.

Tipper, Weaver, Cameron et al. (1991) manipulated RSI in both the picture-naming task (Tipper, 1985) and the localization task (Tipper et al., 1990). They found negative priming at RSIs of 1350, 3100, and 6600 ms, with no apparent decrease over time. Hasher, Stoltzfus, Zacks, and Rypma (1991) found roughly equivalent negative priming in two letter-naming experiments, despite different RSIs of 500 and 1200 ms. In a follow-up study, Stoltzfus, Hasher, Zacks, Ulivi, and Goldstein (1993) found nearly identical effects in experiments with 300- and 1700-ms RSIs.

Tipper, Weaver, Cameron, Brehaut, & Bastedo (1991) suggested that the Stroop task, used by Neill and Westberry (1987), might not be "typical" of selective-attention tasks. Consequently, Neill and Valdes (1992) investigated persistence of negative priming in the letter-matching task (Neill, Lissner, & Beck, 1990), using RSIs of 500, 1000, 2000, 4000, and 8000 ms. As shown in Figure 5, negative priming clearly diminished with longer SOAs, although it did appear to persist beyond two seconds.

Why have some studies (Neill & Valdes, 1992; Neill & Westberry, 1987) found a decay of negative priming, while others (Hasher et al., 1991; Stoltzfus et al., 1993; Tipper et al., 1991) have not? We noted that Tipper, Hasher, and their colleagues manipulated RSI as a between-subjects variable (actually, between experiments in Hasher's studies). Consequently, RSI between prime and probe was confounded with delays *prior* to the prime, as illustrated in Figure 6A. In contrast, Neill and colleagues manipulated RSI within subjects, completely randomized over trials. Hence, short RSIs were sometimes preceded by long delays, and *vice versa*, as shown in Figure 6B.

Neill, Valdes, Terry, and Gorfein (1992) measured negative priming as a function of RSI and the RSI *preceding* the prime (i.e., the delay between the trial $n - 2$ response and the $n - 1$ stimulus). We were also concerned that previously conflicting results might be attributable to different experimental tasks, so we chose to use a localization task similar to that employed by Tipper et al. (1991).

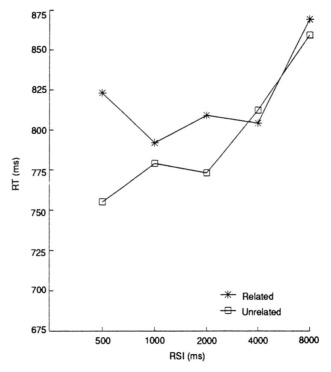

FIGURE 5. Mean reaction time of same/different judgments, as function of response–stimulus interval (RSI) and prime–probe relatedness. (From Neill & Valdes, 1992.)

The results, shown in Figure 7, are clear: when the preceding RSI is held constant, negative priming decreases with RSI. However, the effect of RSI is offset by the effect of the preceding RSI: negative priming did not differ significantly between the 500/500 and 4000/4000 conditions. In a follow-up experiment, we manipulated RSI within subjects but between blocks, deliberately confounding RSI with the preceding RSI as in the between-subject designs. As also shown in Figure 7, there was only a small, nonsignificant effect of RSI.

Why should delay *before* the prime affect negative priming? If distractor information is simply inhibited on the prime trial, and that inhibition passively diminishes over time, it is not at all obvious that the preprime delay should be relevant. We proposed an alternative theory of negative priming, emphasizing the role of the probe stimulus as a memory retrieval cue. We will elaborate further on this theory in a subsequent section. For now, we note that negative priming should persist over long periods if the prime distractor stimulus has not recently appeared in other trials as a target. This is most likely to be true in experiments that use a large stimulus set.

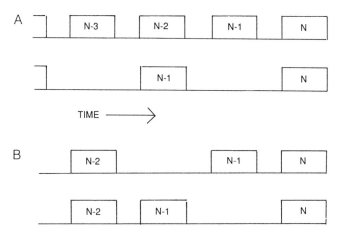

FIGURE 6. (A) Temporal sequences of trials when response–stimulus interval is blocked or manipulated between subjects. (B) Additional trial sequences when response–stimulus interval is randomized within subjects.

Lag Effects   Negative priming clearly persists over intervening trials. Tipper, Weaver, Cameron, et al. (1991, Experiment 2) found negative priming in the picture-naming task when an unrelated picture was named between the prime and probe trials. Similarly, we found negative priming of localization when a trial n probe appeared in the location of a trial $n - 2$ distractor (Neill, Valdes, & Terry, 1992).

DeSchepper and Treisman (1991) repeated distractors once in each block of 136 trials in their novel shape-matching task. They found that negative-priming effects tended to increase with the number of times that the distractor was ignored. Treisman and DeSchepper (1993) subsequently reported negative-priming effects persisting over more than 400 intervening trials. Thus, under some conditions, negative priming persists for a long time. It may be noted that the stimulus sets in these experiments were quite large, such that the critical test shapes appeared only once or twice in each block.

Capacity Limitations

A frequent objection to inhibitory theories of attention (as in Figure 1B) is that there are usually many more objects and events to be ignored than to which we respond. It might therefore seem more efficient to directly facilitate the processing of a small set of stimuli (cf. Figure 1A) than to inhibit the processing of many irrelevant stimuli. Such an argument presupposes that the mechanism underlying negative priming is limited in capacity, that is, it would be difficult for an inhibitory mechanism to act on a large number of stimulus representations within a short period of time.

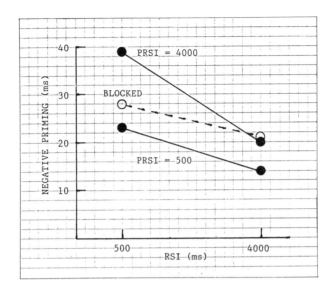

FIGURE 7.   Probe localization reaction time, as a function of response–stimulus interval (RSI) and previous response–stimulus interval (PRSI) (Neill, Valdes, Terry, & Gorfein, 1992).

However, as noted earlier, negative priming appears to be, at least in part, task dependent. At any particular time, *most* objects and events in our environment are irrelevant to immediate goals and intentions, and do not compete for the control of behavior. We do not spontaneously name the color of the sky, but obviously can if we are asked to do so. Similarly, subjects do not spontaneously name the color of a Stroop word (much less, twitch a corresponding finger), unless so instructed.

Inhibitory control of cognition would not require inhibition of processing *all* irrelevant stimuli, but rather just those stimuli that evoke responses that are incompatible with current goals, for example, when the Stroop distractor word evokes a response incompatible with the goal of naming the color.

Nonetheless, it is a valid question whether the mechanism underlying negative priming is limited in capacity, as is generally imputed to a facilitatory mechanism of attention (Broadbent, 1958; Kahneman, 1973; Posner & Snyder, 1975). Is there a limit to how much information can be inhibited? Research by Neumann (Neumann, Cherau, Hood, & Steinnagel, 1993; Neumann & DeSchepper, 1992) suggests strongly that there is.

Neumann and Deschepper (1992) investigated capacity limitations in a letter-naming task similar to that devised by Tipper and Cranston (1985). A prime trial included one, two, or three distractor letters. Negative priming decreased as the number of distractors increased. In that experiment, probe trials always had the same number of distractors as the prime trials. Neumann et al. (1993) found similar results when the number of probe-trial distractors was held constant.

Neumann and coauthors interpret these results as an inhibitory "fan effect" analogous to that postulated by Anderson (1976, 1983) for facilitatory priming. In Anderson's ACT theory, a limited-capacity activation "spreads" from activated nodes to associated nodes in the memory system. As the number of associations increases, the activation is spread more thinly, diluting the priming effects. Neumann suggests that a finite amount of inhibitory capacity is similarly spread across prime-trial distractors.

Neumann's interpretation presumes that inhibition is a divisible processing resource, such that all distractors receive a portion of the available inhibition. However, the results of Neumann and DeSchepper (1992) and Neumann et al. (1993) can alternatively be interpreted as a limit to the *number* of distractors that can be inhibited within a trial. The overall magnitude of negative priming would then reflect a probablistic mixture of inhibited and uninhibited distractors. The likelihood that a randomly selected probe target would match an inhibited distractor would, of course, decrease as the number of prime-trial distractors is increased.

Further research will be necessary to decide whether inhibition is continuous and divisible or, alternatively, discrete and item-by-item. For now, the more important observation is that many distractors cannot be inhibited as efficiently as can one. Thus, by definition, the mechanism that underlies negative priming is limited in capacity.

The previously discussed experiments by Yee (1991) are, however, somewhat problematic for this conclusion. Her prime-trial targets (geometric figures) were flanked by either one or two distractor words. Negative priming was significant *only* in the two-distractor condition, opposite to the results of Neumann and coauthors. In the next section, we speculate that negative priming may depend in part on how much interference occurs on prime trials. Thus, it is possible that Yee's one-distractor condition did not create sufficient interference to engage an inhibitory reaction.

Nonetheless, the discrepancy between Yee's results and those of Neumann and coauthors remains troublesome. Unfortunately, we have been unable to replicate Yee's results, and can throw no further light on the controversy.

Relation to Prime Interference

We have assumed that negative priming reflects the inhibition of irrelevant processing that otherwise interferes with relevant processing. There is ample evidence to support this general assertion, especially, as will be discussed further, that individuals who are more susceptible to distractor interference often show diminished negative-priming effects. However, this leaves open the question of how negative priming relates to greater or lesser interference within the individual.

We can envision two likely scenarios: first, an inhibitory mechanism might act on irrelevant stimuli prior to, or independently of, the actual interference caused by such stimuli. That is, inhibition may be *anticipatory,* serving to prevent, or at least limit, how much interference occurs. If so, negative priming should be inversely related to interference: applying a constant degree of inhibition to weakly activated distractor information would produce more negative priming than if applied to strongly activated information. Indeed, if the inhibition fails to outweigh the initial activation, then a strong distractor might even produce *positive* priming.

An alternative scenario is that inhibition is *reactive,* applied according to the amount of interference actually encountered. Since a weaker distractor would not create much interference, there would be little need to inhibit its processing. In contrast, a stronger distractor that creates more interference would require more inhibition, in order to enable relevant processing to proceed. Thus, negative priming would be directly associated with degree of interference.

The literature on this question is somewhat mixed, but tends to support the latter scenario. Neill and Lissner (1988) varied the proportion of congruent and incongruent trials in the previously described letter-matching task (Neill, Lissner, & Beck, 1990). As expected, incongruent letter strings (e.g., BABAB) produced slower reaction times when most trials were congruent (e.g, AAAAA) than when all trials were incongruent (cf. Logan & Zbrodoff, 1979; Zajano & Gorman, 1986). In addition, the incongruent letter strings produced more negative priming when they were mixed with congruent strings.

If inhibition were anticipatory, then negative priming should have occurred most strongly when subjects expected interference on all trials. Instead, it seems that relatively unexpected incongruent trials created more interference, in turn creating a greater need for inhibition. Thus, inhibition here appears to be reactive.

As discussed earlier, Neill, Valdes, and Terry (1992; see also Valdes, 1993) found increased negative priming in the localization task when subjects were given incompatible response assignments. We also measured interference effects by including some prime trials without a distractor. Not surprisingly, the presence of a distractor slowed responding more in the incompatible condition (73 ms) than in the compatible condition (30 ms). Here, too, increased interference appears to be associated with increased negative priming.

Valdes (1993; Valdes & Neill, 1993) investigated the relation between interference and negative priming, using the letter-identification task adapted from B. A. Eriksen and Eriksen (1974). In one experiment, Valdes varied the spatial separation between the flankers and target letters. As previously found by Eriksen and other researchers, flankers created significantly more interference when closer to the target. As shown in Table 5, "close" flankers also produced more negative priming than "far" flankers.

In this experiment, target letters were presented at fixation; consequently, proximity of flankers was necessarily confounded with retinal eccentricity. Accordingly, "far" flankers might simply be harder to identify, and so would cause less interference and less negative priming. Valdes controlled eccentricity in a second experiment, by presenting both the target and flankers on an imaginary circle, such that all stimuli were equidistant from fixation. Flankers close to the target still produced more negative priming than did distant flankers.

Other experiments, however, have found surprising independence of interference and negative-priming effects. A notable example is the previously discussed study by Driver and Tipper (1989), in which subjects counted the number of red characters in an array of red and black characters. In one experiment, the red targets were sometimes digits, which interfered with counting. In another experiment, the black distractors were sometimes digits, but they did not create any interference. Nonetheless, both experiments found roughly equivalent negative priming from the digits' identities. Thus, either red 2s or black 2s on a prime trial inhibited the count of *two* red items on the probe trial.

Francolini and Egeth (1980) interpreted the presence or absence of interference in this task as indicating that targets can be efficiently selected by color, such that different-color distractors are not identified. Many other re-

TABLE 5. Mean Reaction Times (in ms) for Letter
Identification as a Function of Trial Type and
Flanker Proximity[a]

Trial type	Flanker proximity	
	Close	Far
Prime trials		
Incongruent	686	677
Congruent	642	653
Interference	44	24
Probe trials		
Related	687	673
Unrelated	656	666
Negative Priming	31	7

[a]From Valdes, 1993.

searchers have similarly interpreted the absence of interference effects as evidence that unattended distractors are not identified (e.g., B. A. Eriksen & Eriksen, 1974; Kahneman & Henik, 1981). However, that such distractors still produce negative priming, even in the absence of interference, implies that they *are* identified.

Allport et al. (1985) also made this point in a letter-naming experiment, in which spatially separated distractor letters produced significant negative priming, despite the absence of significant interference effects. Allport (1989) argues that interference may reflect the ease of selection *after* distractor stimuli have been identified. Hence, presence versus absence of interference cannot be a reliable indicator of whether unattended stimuli are identified.

This argument also raises a more general point in regard to negative priming: prior to inhibition, some mechanism must select *which* information is irrelevant, and should be inhibited. (A similar point applies even if attention is facilitatory rather than inhibitory.) It may be easier to inhibit distracting information that is distinguishable from targets by color, or spatially separated from them, not because such information is more weakly activated, but because selection itself is easier.

Whereas Driver and Tipper (1989) found equivalent negative priming despite differences in interference, an experiment by Beech, Agar, and Baylis (1989) found differences in negative priming despite equivalent interference. In a variation of the Stroop task, distractors were either color words (RED, PINK, GREEN, and BLUE) or nonwords with the same initial pronunciations (REF, PIRF, GROIT, and BLOR). Words and nonwords produced equivalent interference relative to rows of colored Xs. However, the nonwords produced significant positive priming for related probe trials (e.g., "blue" following BLOR), while the color words produced negative priming.

The use of Xs as a baseline makes it impossible here to assess whether interference was perceptual, phonological, or semantic. Nonetheless, it seems likely that the positive priming from nonwords reflected a facilitation at the phonological level, priming the initial pronunciation of a color name. Negative priming from color words must then occur at a different level, probably conceptual. Thus, negative priming may be independent of interference when the effects occur at different levels of processing. Further, these results suggest that facilitation and inhibition may coexist at different levels.

Individual differences studies aside, experiments on the relation of negative priming to interference find either a positive relation (Neill & Lissner, 1988; Neill & Valdes, 1992; Neill, Valdes, & Terry, 1992; Valdes, 1993) or no relation (Beech, Agar, & Baylis ,1989; Driver & Tipper, 1989; see also Tipper, Weaver, Kirkpatrick, & Lewis, 1991). At the least, this suggests that negative priming is not wholly anticipatory, and perhaps partly reactive. However, more research is clearly needed to clarify the relation of negative priming to interference.

Relation to Probe Interference

In the Stroop task, if one has just inhibited responding to GREEN, one might expect the response "green" to be slowed regardless of whether the probe is a conflict stimulus (e.g., YELLOW in *green* ink) or a nonconflict stimulus (e.g., OOOOOO in *green* ink). Indeed, Neill (1982; Neill & Westberry, 1987) found equivalent negative priming for conflict and nonconflict probes. However, Lowe (1979) found *positive* priming for probes consisting of color patches, while probes consisting of random letters (e.g., OMTTV in *green* ink) produced negative priming when other probes were conflict words, but positive priming when other probes were color patches!

Lowe's results suggest that there is a "release from negative priming" if subjects do not expect to encounter interference on the probe trial, or if the probe stimulus is clearly distinguishable from a conflict word (i.e., a color patch). In this regard, it should be noted that the difference between Lowe's color patches and Neill's nonconflict stimuli is subtle: Lowe used four circular dots and Neill used strings of letter "ohs" varying in length (OOO, OOOO, OOOOO, OOOOOO). It would appear that the latter were sufficiently wordlike to prevent a release from negative priming.

Tipper and Cranston (1985) compared priming effects in their letter-naming task when the probe trial did or did not contain a distractor letter. As found by Lowe (1979), prime distractors produced negative priming when the probe contained a distractor, but positive priming when it did not (see also Allport, et al., 1985). Tipper and Cranston concluded that negative priming depends on whether subjects maintain a "selection state," in turn depending on whether interference is anticipated.

A series of four experiments by Moore (1993) confirm the dependence of negative priming on something like a selection state. In these experiments, subjects identified target letters I, O, S, and X by assigned keypress responses. A prime-trial target partially overlapped a distractor letter, distinguished by color. Probe trials were either "high-conflict" or "low-conflict." In high-conflict trials, the target letter again overlapped a distractor associated with an incompatible response. The four experiments differed only in what distractors were used in low-conflict trials: (1) other letters, not associated with a response; (2) a "pound" sign (#); (3) letter-sized fields of random dots; or (4) no distractor at all. In addition, Moore manipulated whether high- and low-conflict probes were randomly intermixed or blocked separately.

The results were straightforward: negative priming always occurred for high-conflict probes. Negative priming never occurred for low-conflict probes blocked separately. Negative priming never occurred for low-conflict probes with no distractor or with random-dot distractors. However, negative priming did occur for low-conflict probes with letter or pound sign distractors *if* they were randomly intermixed with high-conflict probes. Further, the magni-

tude of negative priming on such trials was equal to that found on high-conflict trials.

In computer simulations based on a neural network ("connectionist")
model, Houghton and Tipper (1994) found negative priming for probes with
distractors, but not for probes without. They attributed negative priming to
an increased vulnerability of the probe target to interference:

> The fact that the representation of the ignored distractor is suppressed at probe
> onset does not actually prevent that representation from rapidly reaching a significant
> activation level. What is slowing coherent response binding is the difficulty in selecting
> the distractor as the new target, which requires the suppression of a probe distractor
> which has an initial activation advantage. (p. 96)

It is not clear how this model would account for negative priming that
occurs when there is no interference on the probe trial. Indeed, the concept of
a "selection state" is not readily embodied in such a model. It could be argued
that a "neutral" distractor like a pound sign might cause some interference
even though it is not directly associated with a competing response. However,
some experiments, notably those on lexical decision (Fuentes & Tudela,
1992; Marcel, 1980; Yee, 1991), obtain negative priming without any distractors at all on probe trials.

Tipper et al. (1990, Experiment 5) report a failure to obtain any priming
effects in the localization task for probe trials without a distractor. However,
we have reported several experiments in which significant negative priming of
location occurred without probe-trial distractors (Neill, Valdes & Terry,
1992). In one experiment (Neill, Terry, & Valdes, 1994), we directly compared probe trials with and without distractors. The results are shown in
Table 6: there was somewhat more negative priming without probe distractors than with! (The interaction approached significance, $p < .10$.)

TABLE 6. Probe Localization Reaction Time (in ms) with or without Distractor
Present, as a Function of Prime–Probe Relation[a]

	Prime–probe relation		
Probe type	Repeat	Ignored	Neutral
With distractor			
(Prime)	X _ O _	X _ O _	X _ O _
(Probe)	_ _ O X	O _ _ X	_ O _ X
Reaction time	448	523	507
Without distractor			
(Prime)	X _ O _	X _ O _	X _ O _
(Probe)	_ _ O _	O _ _ _	_ O _ _
Reaction time	416	509	480

[a]From Neill, Terry, & Valdes, 1994.

These results clearly indicate that interference on probe trials is not a necessary condition for negative priming, and that negative priming cannot be explained as increased susceptibility to interference. Yet, presence or absence of distractors does affect negative priming in some experiments. Like the relation of negative priming to prime interference, the relation to probe interference requires further investigation.

Relation to Awareness

We will here address two aspects of awareness: first, subjects may or may not be aware of a relationship between the prime distractor and probe target. Second, subjects may or may not be aware of the prime distractor itself. How do these two aspects of awareness affect negative priming?

Awareness of Prime–Probe Relation In many experiments (particularly those by Tipper, Hasher, and their colleagues), subjects are asked afterward whether they noticed any relations between trials. Subjects who report noticing that the probe target sometimes matched the prime distractor are often replaced by new, naive subjects. Several experiments suggest that "aware" subjects may not exhibit negative-priming effects, and sometimes even show positive-priming effects (e.g., Driver & Baylis, 1993).

Hasher et al. (1991) analyzed the results of apparently aware subjects separately from unaware subjects. In their first experiment, with a 500-ms RSI, aware subjects showed approximately the same negative-priming effect as did the unaware subjects. However, in their second experiment, with a 1200-ms RSI, aware subjects showed a tendency (albeit nonsignificant) toward positive priming. Unaware subjects, meanwhile, showed negative priming similar to the first experiment. Hasher et al. suggested that aware subjects may attempt to anticipate the probe target and thereby over time reverse from negative to positive priming. They also noted that averaging over aware and unaware subjects would give the illusion of "decay" of negative priming over RSI.

In experiments reporting an effect of awareness (e.g., Driver & Baylis, 1993; Hasher et al., 1991), the "Ignored Repetition" and control conditions were usually tested in separate lists. Consequently, the same type of relationship between trials would recur successively over trials, as in the original study by Dalrymple-Alford and Budayr (1966). Under these conditions, it is not surprising that some subjects would notice the recurring relationship and attempt to predict the next target from the current distractor.

It should also be noted that the assessment of awareness in such studies is post hoc, and so the direction of causality becomes an issue. It is possible that some subjects notice a relationship and then deliberately recover each prime distractor to predict the probe. On the other hand, it is possible that negative priming is more short lived in some subjects, and these subjects are then more likely to notice that the recovered prime distractor matches the probe.

Neill and Valdes (1992, Experiment 3) attempted to manipulate awareness experimentally, by informing one group of subjects that "the irrelevant flankers sometimes appear as a target on the next trial." In addition, subjects were given a postexperiment recognition test in which subjects were asked to identify which possible relationships occurred in the experiment. Neither manipulated awareness nor self-reported awareness was related to the magnitude of negative priming or its decay over RSI. In this experiment, the probe was related to the prime distractor on a random 25% of trials. Under these conditions, subjects do not appear to notice the relation or use it to predict the probe targets.

Awareness of the Prime   A number of studies have reported positive priming by stimuli that are rendered unreportable by a pattern mask (e.g., Fowler, Wolford, Slade, & Tassinary, 1981; Marcel, 1983a; Neill, 1985). Marcel (1983b) has argued that pattern masking does not interrupt the perceptual processing of the stimulus but rather blocks the conscious awareness of such processing. Given that positive priming does not seem to require conscious awareness, we may ask a similar question regarding negative priming.

Allport et al. (1985, Experiments 4 and 5) presented a masking pattern after the priming stimuli in a picture-naming task. When the mask followed the prime by a relatively long stimulus-onset asynchrony (SOA), subjects could easily identify the prime stimuli. Under this condition, negative priming was obtained. However, when the mask followed at an SOA sufficiently short that subjects could not identify the prime stimuli, the effect reversed to positive priming. Marcel (1980) obtained a similar result in a different paradigm, which will be discussed in a later section.

Such results suggest that negative priming depends on conscious awareness, in contrast to positive priming. However, it is unclear whether awareness of the prime target or awareness of the distractor is necessary for negative priming to occur. There was no response to the prime target in Allport's short SOA condition because the target, too, was masked. It is possible that distractors were not inhibited simply because no response, overt or covert, was required on the prime trial.

Neill (1989; 1993) argued that negative priming blocks distracting information from conscious awareness, here equated with "working memory." If such information is already blocked by a masking pattern, inhibition is unnecessary. Thus, a masked distractor accompanying an unmasked target should not produce negative priming. We recently tested this hypothesis by masking only the prime-trial distractors in a letter-identification experiment. Pound signs (#) were used as pattern masks, which replaced the flanking letters at an SOA of 17, 33, 67, or 133 ms. As a control condition, the flankers remained unmasked on some prime trials.

As shown in Figure 8, priming appears to shift from positive to negative as SOA increases. The 18-ms positive priming at the shortest SOA and the 13-ms negative priming with no mask only approached significance (both $p <$ .10). However, the overall pattern clearly indicates that response to the prime target does not by itself cause inhibition of the distractors. (A linear trend analysis indicated that reaction time to related probes increased as SOA on prime trials increased, while reaction time to unrelated probes was essentially unaffected.)

Individual Differences

One of the most prolific areas of research in negative priming has been the identification of individual differences that are correlated with the effect. McDowd, Oseas-Kreger, and Filion (Chapter 11, this volume) review the ample research on aging effects. Briefly summarizing here, many studies have found diminished negative priming in the elderly relative to young adults (e.g., Hasher et al., 1991; McDowd & Oseas-Kreger, 1991; Tipper, 1991). Such results support the hypothesis that many cognitive deficits associated with aging reflect an inability to inhibit the intrusion of irrelevant information in working memory (Hasher & Zacks, 1988).

Many studies have found that children are also less able to ignore distracting information than are adults (see reviews by Day, 1975; Lane & Pearson, 1982). Comalli, Wapner, and Werner (1962) found that Stroop interference is greatest for children shortly after they learn to read (i.e., around age

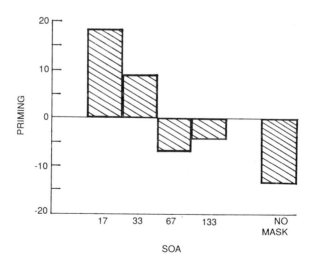

FIGURE 8.   Priming in a letter-identification task as a function of stimulus-onset ansynchrony between prime onset and mask.

6), and then decreases until adolescence. Interference remains fairly constant through adulthood until it increases again in old age.

Such results suggest that the ability to inhibit distracting information matures through adulthood (see also Harnishfeger, Chapter 6, this volume). Tipper, Bourque, Anderson, and Brehaut (1989) compared second graders and college students in the Stroop task and picture naming. Consistent with the developmental hypothesis, only the college students showed significant negative priming.

Diminished inhibitory control has also been implicated in schizophrenia (e.g., Frith, 1979; for a related discussion, see Lewandowsky & Li, Chapter 10, this volume). Beech and Claridge and their colleagues have amassed considerable support for this hypothesis. "Schizotypal" subjects, with a high frequency of schizophreniclike traits, showed positive priming by Stroop distractor words; in contrast, subjects low in schizotypy showed negative priming (Beech, Baylis, Smithson, & Claridge, 1989; Beech & Claridge, 1987). It is interesting to note that clinically diagnosed schizophrenics showed reduced negative priming but not an actual reversal (Beech, Powell, McWilliam, & Claridge, 1989). The authors speculate that the patients' medications may have ameliorated their symptoms.

In addition to developmental and clinical subgroups, consistent individual differences have also been demonstrated among normal young adults. The Cognitive Failures Questionnaire (Broadbent, Cooper, FitzGerald, & Parkes, 1982) measures self-reported failures in perception, memory, and motor function. Subjects estimate the frequency, from "Never" to "Very Often," of various lapses, for example: "Do you read something and find that you haven't been thinking about it and must read it again?" "Do you fail to notice signposts on the road?" "Do you find you forget people's names?" Such lapses are common for many individuals, but are much more frequent for some than for others.

Tipper and Baylis (1987, Experiment 1) required subjects to name the category of a target word, which was sometimes accompanied by a distractor word. Subjects with high CFQ scores exhibited significantly more interference from the distractor. In a second experiment, Tipper and Baylis compared negative-priming effects for the two groups. They found significant negative priming only for low-CFQ subjects, while high-CFQ subjects showed a nonsignificant trend toward positive priming. Such results suggest that individuals who are prone to cognitive lapses fail to adequately inhibit distracting information.

In general, diminished negative priming appears to be associated with more global cognitive deficits. This suggests (1) that the ability to inhibit distracting information is an important component of general cognitive functioning, and (2) that impairment of inhibitory control leaves an individual more susceptible to interference (cf. Gernsbacher & Faust, 1991, Chapter 9, this volume; Hasher & Zacks, 1988). This raises the question, however, of whether there are groups characterized by *too much* inhibitory control. While far from definitive, some studies of "absorption" support this possibility.

The Tellegen Absorption Scale was devised by Tellegen and Atkinson (1974) as a predictor of hypnotic susceptibility. It consists of a self-report questionnaire, with statements like, "When I listen to music, I can get so caught up in it that I don't notice anything else (TRUE/FALSE)." In general, the questions assess the degree to which one becomes "absorbed" in certain experiences to the exclusion of others. Tellegen and Atkinson interpret Absorption as "a disposition for having episodes 'total' attention that fully engage one's representational (i.e., perceptual, enactive, imaginative, and ideational) resources" (p. 268).

Westberry (1984) found that high absorbers, scoring more than one standard deviation above the scale mean, exhibited a remarkably large negative-priming effect (133 ms) in the Stroop task. In contrast, low absorbers (more than one standard deviation below the mean) exhibited only a small, nonsignificant effect (7 ms). This suggests, perhaps, that hypnotizability depends on the ability to inhibit awareness of one's immediate environment in order to be more under control of the hypnotist's suggestions.

In several memory experiments (e.g., Neill, Beck, Bottalico, & Molloy, 1990), we administered both the Absorption Scale and the Cognitive Failures Questionnaire to subjects in order to occupy them during the retention interval. We had expected that higher absorption scores would be related to lower CFQ scores, since the two measures are oppositely related to negative priming. Much to our surprise, we found a modest but significant positive correlation, r (79) = 0.33, p < .01. Apparently, some individuals become *too* absorbed in ongoing experiences.

Houghton and Tipper (1994) point out that it would be maladaptive to so thoroughly suppress an ignored object that one could not easily switch attention to it. They invoke the example of a bartender clearing glasses from a table: in order to reach for a glass, the remaining glasses must be ignored. Yet, efficient behavior requires that all glasses remain reasonably available for the control of action. There must be some optimum level of inhibition that enables both the momentary action toward an object and behavior toward multiple objects in succession.

Individual-differences studies should be particularly relevant to the question of whether there is a single inhibitory control mechanism (for further discussion of this issue, see McDowd et al., Chapter 11, this volume). If so, then negative priming should be highly correlated over different tasks. However, there are surprisingly few, if any, studies that have examined correlations between different negative-priming measures across individuals. On the other hand, comparisons of different developmental subgroups suggest that there may not be a single underlying inhibitory mechanism.

In particular, several studies have found essentially normal negative priming of location in the elderly and in children, despite diminished negative priming of identification. Connelly and Hasher (1993) found roughly equivalent negative priming of location for young and old subjects, even in a task requiring letter naming (see previous discussion of Connelly et al., 1992). Similarly, Tipper and McLaren (1990) found statistically equivalent negative priming of localization in first graders, sixth graders and college students.

Connelly and Hasher (1993) argue that negative priming of location and identity are mediated by two separate cortical visual pathways: one, the dorsal or occipitoparietal pathway, is specialized for processing spatial location; the other, the ventral or occipitotemporal pathway, is specialized for processing an object's identity (Ungerleider & Mishkin, 1982). That negative priming of location, but not identity, persists in the elderly is taken as evidence that the former pathway is spared by aging, while the latter is not.

Similarly, Tipper and McLaren suggest that "select-what, respond-where" mechanisms develop at an earlier age than do "select-where, respond-what mechanisms. Consequently, negative priming in target-localization tasks is present in children who have not yet developed the ability to inhibit distractor identities.

A caveat is necessary in regard to such conclusions, however. As noted in the earlier discussion of task specificity, localization tasks and identification tasks may differ on other variables in addition to the specific information required. In particular, localization is often faster and less error prone than identification. Different patterns of negative priming might reflect quantitative characteristics of the tasks rather than qualitatively different processing systems.

A new study by Sullivan and Faust (in press) is especially instructive in this regard: using a picture-naming task similar to Tipper (1991), they actually found slightly more negative priming of distractor identity in old subjects than in young subjects. In contrast to the previously cited studies, the overall level of performance was also nearly identical for young and old subjects. Thus, if task difficulty is equated, differences between age groups (and possibly between tasks) may vanish.

ENDOGENOUS NEGATIVE PRIMING

Just as selection is often necessary among external objects and events, selection is also required among the possible associations to an object or event. Much research indicates that multiple associations to a perceived object or event are retrieved automatically and in parallel. Some associations may be relevant to immediate goals and intentions, while other associations are not. For example, if one's goal is to draw a picture of a chair, its lines and surfaces are relevant, but its name ("chair") and category (furniture) are not. Effective action requires that irrelevant associations do not compete with relevant associations for the guidance of behavior.

In the experiments discussed to this point, prime-trial targets were accompanied by an irrelevant object or attribute that served as a distractor. Interference with task performance reflects the unintended processing of this irrelevant stimulus, and negative priming presumably results from the inhibition of further processing. Such effects can be described as *exogenous*, originating from distracting stimuli external to the subject (Figure 9A).

Negative priming can also be produced by an attended target stimulus rather than an ignored distractor. Such effects may be described as *endogenous*, originating from irrelevant internal associations to the relevant object. This may happen in two different ways: (1) the attended stimulus may directly evoke independent and incompatible mental representations (Figure 9B); (2) the relevant mental representation itself evokes irrelevant mental representations (Figure 9C). We discuss below two examples of endogenous negative priming.

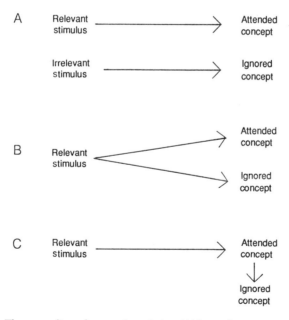

FIGURE 9. Three paradigms for negative priming: (A) ignored concept activated by an irrelevant stimulus (*exogenous*); (B) ignored concept activated by a relevant but ambiguous stimulus (*endogenous*); (C) ignored concept activated indirectly by association to an attended concept (*endogenous*).

Lexical Ambiguity

Many words in the English language are "polysemous," having two or more clearly distinct meanings. For example, BANK may refer to a financial institution, the shore of a river, or what an airplane does to change direction. However, in normal discourse, we are usually aware only of the meaning that is consistent with the context in which the word occurred.

Substantial research has been devoted to the issue of whether context constrains the initial mental representation of a polysemous word (such that only one meaning is activated), or, whether all meanings are initially activated in parallel, followed by selection of one meaning consistent with the context. While there is still some disagreement, the bulk of recent research supports the latter position. This does not mean that all meanings of an ambiguous word are *equally* activated; rather, a "horse race" of competing meanings is influenced by both the context and the relative frequency of each meaning (Neill, Hilliard, & Cooper, 1988; Simpson, 1984).

Neill (1989) argued that the simultaneous activation of word meanings creates a situation that is functionally equivalent to the Stroop Effect: even though there is no external distracting stimulus, lexical ambiguity creates two incompatible mental representations that compete for control of behavior. Consequently, the context-inappropriate meaning of a polysemous word should be inhibited, like the meaning of an externally presented distractor word. Several studies have, in fact, found negative-priming effects for the context-inappropriate meanings of fully attended but ambiguous words (Hekkanen, 1981; Marcel, 1980; Simpson & Kellas, 1989).

Marcel (1980) presented triplets of words in a lexical-decision task such that the second word was sometimes a homograph, following a word related to one of its meanings. The third "probe" word could be related to the same meaning of the homograph (e.g., MONEY–BANK–SAVE), related to the opposite meaning (MONEY–BANK–SHORE), or unrelated (MONEY–BANK–WRIST). In one condition, the second word was immediately followed by a pattern mask of random features such that subjects could not report its presence. Marcel also varied the interstimulus interval (ISI) between the second and third words.

In the unmasked condition, only the context-appropriate (same meaning) probes showed positive priming, consistent with previous studies (e.g., Schvaneveldt, Meyer, & Becker, 1976). At the short ISI (.6 s), opposite-meaning probes did not differ from unrelated probes. However, at the longer ISI (1.5 s), the opposite-meaning probes showed significant *negative* priming relative to unrelated probes. If the homograph had simply not activated its context-inappropriate meaning, corresponding probes should not have differed at all from unrelated probes. The most plausible explanation is then that the context-inappropriate meaning was initially activated and then quickly inhibited.

When the homograph was masked, Marcel found a different pattern of results: both meanings produced positive priming at both ISIs. Although subjects phenomenally experienced sequences like MONEY–######–SHORE, the masked word BANK nonetheless primed SHORE. This result is analogous to that of Allport et al. (1985), previously discussed, in which masking of an externally presented distractor reversed priming from negative to positive. Thus, like exogenous negative priming, endogenous negative priming depends on conscious awareness of the prime, whereas positive priming does not.

In the absence of any disambiguating context, subjects are often aware of only the more common meaning of a polysemous word. Accordingly, positive-priming effects are often greater for the more common meaning (e.g., BANK–SAVE) than for a less common meaning (e.g., BANK–RIVER) (e.g., Simpson, 1981). Although less common meanings are also activated by the ambiguous word, they appear to be inhibited soon after their activation (Simpson & Burgess, 1985). Burgess and Simpson (1988) obtained negative priming of subordinate meanings specifically when probes were presented to the right visual hemifield, indicating an inhibitory role of the left cerebral hemisphere in selection of meaning.

At the short delay, positive priming occurred for both meanings when probe words were presented in the right hemifield; however, positive priming occurred only for the dominant meaning in the left hemifield (Figure 10).By 750 ms, the pattern changed markedly: in the right hemifield, there was positive priming only for the dominant meaning, while the secondary meaning was inhibited relative to an unrelated word. Meanwhile, the left hemifield now showed positive priming for both meanings.

It appears that the left hemisphere has rapid access to both meanings of the ambiguous word, while the right hemisphere initially has access only to the subordinate meaning. By the time that the right hemisphere acquires the

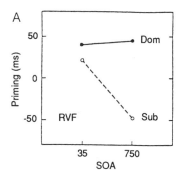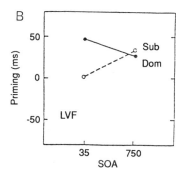

FIGURE 10.   Priming of dominant and subordinate meanings of homographs in (A) right visual field (RVF) and (B) left visual field (LVF) as a function of stimulus-onset asynchrony (SOA). (From Burgess & Simpson, 1988.)

secondary meaning, the left hemisphere has selected the dominant meaning and inhibited the subordinate one. Chiarello (1991) suggests that the right hemisphere maintains the alternative interpretation of the ambiguous word as a "backup," in case the one selected by the left hemisphere is wrong. Perhaps this is the mechanism by which we can understand puns and double-entendre jokes?

Although not tested directly, some evidence suggests that endogenous negative priming, like exogenous, may be reduced in schizophrenics. For example, Dick and McFarland (1978) found that for normal subjects, priming by homographs was determined most by whether probes were related to the context-appropriate meaning (cf. Marcel, 1980; Schvaneveldt et al., 1976). For schizophrenics, more priming occurred for the dominant (i.e., most frequent) meaning, regardless of the context in which the homograph appeared. Hence, "bizarre" associations sometimes evinced by schizophrenics may reflect an inability to inhibit dominant associations that are inappropriate to the context.

Intracategory Inhibition

Roediger and Neely (1982) review a variety of episodic and semantic memory phenomena in which semantically related cues inhibit the retrieval of target information. As one example, Watkins (1985) had subjects memorize a list of words belonging to various categories such as birds or kitchen utensils. Subjects were then given the category names as recall cues. Some of the category cues were accompanied by new (unstudied) instances of the category. Watkins found that recall of the studied category members was actually depressed by the presence of the additional category members.

A variety of theoretical explanations have been proposed for such "retrieval blocks" in recall and recognition memory. Bjork (1989) in particular has argued that inhibitory mechanisms play an important role in memory retrieval. An extensive review of inhibitory phenomena in memory is beyond the scope of this chapter. We will limit our discussion here to reaction-time experiments, which are more directly comparable to those that demonstrate exogenous negative-priming effects.

Same/Different Matching   Neill (1979) presented informative or uninformative warning signals to subjects, each followed by a pair of letters or digits to be matched as "same" or "different" (cf. Posner & Snyder, 1975). If the warning signal was a letter or digit, there was an 80% probability that the same character would appear in the subsequent match pair (e.g., A–AA or 2–23). On invalidly cued trials, the match pair was drawn from the same category as the warning signal (e.g., A–BB or 2–34) or from the opposite category (e.g., A –34 or 2–BB). On other trials, the warning signal was a neutral, uninformative plus sign.

Consistent with Posner and Snyder (1975), validly cued trials produced a significant "benefit" relative to the neutral condition, while invalidly cued trials produced a significant "cost." However, there was *more* cost for pairs drawn from the same category as the prime than for pairs drawn from the opposite category. Neill argued that the activation of same-category members could hamper the matching process in a manner analogous to the Stroop Effect. For example, if the prime "A" also activates the mental representation of "B," then AA might be mismatched as "different," or AB as "same." Subjects therefore suppress the intracategory associates to an expected stimulus.

In a follow-up experiment (Neill, 1979, Experiment 2), one group of subjects was given instructions to maintain strict accuracy, while another group was encouraged to sacrifice some accuracy for greater speed. Intracategory inhibition occurred only for the subjects who were instructed to maintain strict accuracy. The group given lax accuracy instructions showed *positive* priming of unexpected same-category pairs relative to opposite-category pairs. This result directly parallels the later finding by Neill and Westberry (1987) in the Stroop task. Thus, both endogenous and exogenous negative priming depend on task demands for accuracy versus speed.

Question Answering   Brown (1979) required subjects in several experiments to generate appropriate words in response to their definitions, preceded by either a correct word, a semantically related word, an orthographically related word, or an unrelated word. Subjects generated the correct word more slowly if they had been primed with a semantically related word relative to priming with an unrelated word. Brown interpreted these results as indicating an automatic "spread of inhibition" to associates of the prime, following an initial "spread of activation" as postulated by other theorists (e.g., Anderson, 1976; Collins & Loftus, 1975; Schvaneveldt & Meyer, 1973).

An experiment by Roediger, Neely, and Blaxton (1983) casts some doubt on Brown's interpretation. Subjects answered simple questions like, "Who was President during the Civil War?" In one condition, the question was preceded by one of four prime types; correct (*Abraham Lincoln*), related (*George Washington*), unrelated (*Colorado*), or neutral (*ready*). As found by Brown (1979), correct answers were slowest when the prime was related. However, in another condition in which the correct answer was never used as a prime, the related prime produced facilitation, or positive priming. If negative priming were due to a truly automatic spread of inhibition, it should not be affected by whether correct primes are included among the conditions. Hence, Brown's results may reflect subjects' strategic adaptation to the knowledge that the prime was a possible answer.

Picture Naming   In another experiment (Brown, 1979, Experiment 6), subjects named pictures preceded by a word prime. As in the previous experiments, the prime could be the correct name, a related word, or an unrelated word. Brown found slower picture naming when the prime was a related word than if it was unrelated. Thus, naming a picture of a dog would be slower if primed with CAT than if primed with SHOE. This result superficially resembles the results of Tipper (1985; Tipper & Driver, 1988) but the prime was attended rather than ignored. (Subjects were quite fast if primed with the correct word.)

Other researchers, however, have found positive priming of picture naming by related words (e.g., McCauley, Parmalee, Sperber, & Carr, 1980; Sperber, McCauley, Ragain, & Weil, 1979). Noting this discrepancy, McEvoy (1982) manipulated whether the prime word was itself a possible candidate for the picture's name. Parallel to the results of Roediger et al., she found negative priming by related primes only when primes sometimes correctly named the picture; related primes produced positive priming when correct names were not used as primes. McEvoy concluded that inhibition was not automatic, as postulated by Brown, but was rather an attentional, strategic adaptation similar to that argued by Neill (1979).

Lexical Decision   As noted earlier, an attended prime word usually facilitates recognizing a related word as a word per se. Dagenbach, Carr, and Barnhardt (1990) found, however, that an attended prime can inhibit lexical-decision judgments of semantically related words if the associations to the prime are not well learned. They first taught subjects the definitions of real but infrequent English words (e.g., *accipiter*: hawk). These words were then used in a lexical-decision task as primes for related words (e.g., EAGLE) or unrelated words. Afterward, subjects attempted to recall the definitions and then to recognize the definitions in a multiple-choice test.

Dagenbach et al. found that weakly learned primes, whose definitions were recognized but not recalled, slowed the responses to related words in the lexical-decision task. In contrast, better learned primes, whose definitions were both recalled and recognized, produced facilitation. Carr and Dagenbach (1990) suggest that the retrieval of weakly activated semantic codes may be enhanced by a "center-surround" mechanism of lateral inhibition such that related but inappropriate codes do not interfere with retrieval. Whereas Brown (1979) viewed "spread of inhibition" to be an automatic consequence of activation, Carr and Dagenbach argue that the inhibition is effortful and that it depends on the difficulty of retrieval.

Summary

Negative priming can be produced by an attended stimulus as well as by ignored stimuli. In the case of lexical ambiguity, negative priming occurs for incompatible associations to the attended word, as in Figure 9B. In the cases of intracategory inhibition, negative priming does not occur because the attended stimulus is ambiguous, but rather because the relevant associated concept is in turn associated to other concepts that may be irrelevant.

Several lines of evidence suggest that the inhibitory mechanism underlying such endogenous negative priming is similar to that which underlies exogenous negative priming. Both kinds of negative priming appear to depend on conscious awareness. That is, if the priming stimuli are rendered unreportable by pattern masking, positive priming occurs instead (Allport et al., 1985; Marcel, 1980). Both kinds of negative priming are affected by speed/accuracy demands such that negative priming under strict accuracy instructions may give way to positive priming under lax accuracy instructions (Neill, 1979; Neill & Westberry, 1987; Neumann & DeSchepper, 1992).

Finally, both kinds of negative priming show a qualitatively similar time course of development, such that widespread activation (positive priming) at short stimulus-onset asynchronies is followed by inhibition of associations that are incompatible with context and/or goals (Burgess & Simpson, 1988; Hekkanen, 1981; Lowe, 1985; Marcel, 1980; Yee, 1991). This last pattern of results especially emphasizes the importance of inhibition as a control mechanism that limits the interfering effects of automatically activated information.

THEORETICAL CONCEPTIONS OF NEGATIVE PRIMING

The existence of negative priming has been taken to demonstrate the importance of inhibitory mechanisms in cognition. While inhibitory mechanisms have only rarely been postulated in past cognitive theories, the occasional uses of "inhibition" have been inconsistent in their implications. We will briefly review several conceptions of inhibition that do not account for negative priming in addition to three that are more plausible.

What Negative Priming Is Not

Attenuation   Broadbent's (1958) original "filter" theory implied that information on unattended sensory channels could not be recognized. As such, the theory could not explain the occasional effects of unattended information such as noticing one's name in an unattended message (Moray, 1959). In an experiment with English–French bilinguals, Treisman (1964) had subjects repeat back ("shadow") an English message in one ear, ignoring an unrelated French message in the other. During the shadowing, the French message switched to a translation of the shadowed English message. If the French message lagged slightly behind the English message, most subjects noticed that the two messages had similar meanings.

Treisman suggested that unattended information is not completely excluded from processing but rather is "attenuated" or weakened. Under normal circumstances, such information is not recognized. However, subjects may lower their threshold for recognizing such information if it is related to an attended message or is otherwise especially salient (e.g., one's name). In such cases, the attenuated information would be sufficient for recognition to occur.

Treisman's concept of attenuation was applied specifically to sources of information, that is, sensory channels. As such, attenuation would account nicely for negative priming of distractor locations. However, since attenuation was hypothesized to be precategorical, an object in an unattended channel should not be difficult to recognize when it appears in an attended channel. Hence, attenuation does not account for negative priming of identity, especially not for negative priming of semantic associates. Treisman (1992) explicitly acknowledges that such results imply a postcategorical form of selection.

Processing "Cost"   Posner and Snyder (1975) applied a "cost/benefit" analysis to the effects of attentional priming. Given a predictive cue, responses to a validly cued stimulus are faster than to an uncued stimulus, that is, a "benefit." However, a predictive cue produces a "cost" to processing an unexpected stimulus relative to an uncued stimulus. Theoretically, a predictive cue directs attention to the expected stimulus (or its mental representation). Processing of an unexpected stimulus is then "inhibited" because attention must then be switched from the expected stimulus to the unexpected one.

"Inhibition" in this cost/benefit analysis is nonspecific and de facto; it does not reflect an operation directly on the unexpected information (Posner, 1982). As such, it does not explain negative priming. For example, suppose that attention is directed to the color *red*, ignoring the word GREEN. The concept "green" is then deprived of attention, but so are other concepts like "blue" and "yellow." That is, new stimuli should exhibit as much processing cost as does a recently ignored stimulus. Indeed, given that "green" has been more recently activated, it should still produce a processing benefit, positive priming, relative to the control condition.

Lateral Inhibition   Walley and Weiden (1973) proposed that selective attention operates by a mechanism of lateral inhibition analogous to the "center-surround" mechanism that sharpens contrast in sensory systems. They argued that processing channels are mutually inhibitory, such that increasing the activation of one channel would inhibit neighboring channels. Hence, attention to a particular object or attribute would result in a spread of inhibition to other objects or attributes. As previously discussed, Brown (1979) and Carr and Dagenbach (1990) have applied variations on this theme to explain intracategory inhibition effects.

The concept of *lateral* inhibition implies that some objects or attributes are more inhibited than others. In particular, lateral inhibition is strongest for channels that are close to the focus of excitation. This can account for intracategory inhibition, since intracategory associates to an attended stimulus may be "closer" to the activated portion of a semantic network. However, lateral inhibition cannot account for exogenous negative-priming effects, which do not depend on similarity to the *attended* stimulus.

Once again, consider negative priming in the Stroop task: attention to the color *red*, ignoring the distractor word GREEN, might well result in lateral inhibition of the concept "green." However, lateral inhibition spreading from the concept "red" would extend equally to other color concepts as well. (Given the appropriate counterbalancing of stimulus materials, we can ignore the fact that certain colors are "opponents.") Hence, the ignored color concept should be no more inhibited than are other color concepts. On the assumption that excitatory and inhibitory effects would be additive, we would again expect the ignored color concept to benefit from its recent activation, producing positive priming relative to other concepts.

Habituation   Several studies have demonstrated that constant repetition of the same distractor reduces its effectiveness as a distractor (Greenwald, 1972; Lorsch, Anderson, & Well, 1984; Reisberg, Baron, & Kemler, 1980). Greenwald also demonstrated slower responses to a target that had been repeated many times as a distractor, hence, a negative-priming effect. Lorsch et al. and Reisberg et al. interpreted these results as indicating "habituation" to the distractor, such that subjects were no longer responsive to it. Reisberg et al. suggested further that negative priming in the Stroop task (Neill, 1977) might reflect such habituation.

It seems unlikely, however, that habituation can account for many aspects of negative priming. For example, it is clear that negative priming often occurs at a conceptual level, for example, between the word GREEN and the color green, or between a picture of a dog and the word CAT. In contrast, habituation effects are usually dependent on perceptual similarity. It is also unclear why habituation would depend on instructional emphasis on accuracy versus speed (Neill, 1979; Neill & Westberry, 1987; Neumann & DeSchepper, 1992). Most important, negative-priming effects occur from a single stimulus exposure rather than from repeated exposures to the ignored stimulus.

It is unlikely that habituation occurs from a single exposure. If a prime-trial target is repeated, for example, then a strong facilitation occurs (e.g., Tipper, 1985; Tipper & Cranston, 1985). It has been suggested that a single exposure might be sufficient to cause habituation, or refractoriness, if attention is not directed to the activated concept (Cowan, 1988). Facilitation of a repeated target would then occur because attention to the target prevented its habituation. However, this overlooks the finding that pattern-masked stimuli produce positive priming (e.g., Allport et al. 1985; Fowler et al., 1981; Marcel, 1980, 1983b; Neill, 1985). It is awkward to argue that such stimuli are somehow "attended" even though subjects cannot report their presence.

What It Probably Is Not: Deactivation

Most theories of (positive) associative priming rely on a theoretical construct of *activation*. That is, a perceived object "activates" its representation in memory, making associated information more available for retrieval, judgment, and response (Anderson, 1976; Collins & Loftus, 1975; Meyer & Schvaneveldt, 1971; Neely, 1976, 1977; Posner & Snyder, 1975; Schvaneveldt & Meyer, 1973). Irrelevant stimuli cause interference, as in the Stroop task, presumably because their mental representations are activated automatically and compete for control of behavior.

The simplest conception of negative priming, then, is that activated mental representations are "deactivated" by an inhibitory mechanism if they conflict with immediate goals (Neill, 1979). From this perspective, both positive and negative priming reflect the degree to which a mental representation is activated either above or below some baseline level.

This conception, however, proves to be too simple. Most problematic is the finding that negative priming sometimes depends on whether there is interference on probe trials. As noted earlier, if one has inhibited the concept *green,* then the response "green" should be slowed regardless of whether a probe includes a distractor. Although this is sometimes found (e.g., Neill, 1982; Neill & Westberry, 1987), there may be a "release from negative priming" if the subject does not expect interference, or if the probe trial is sufficiently discriminable from trials in which interference would occur (Lowe, 1979; Moore, 1993; Tipper & Cranston, 1985).

Particularly troublesome for the deactivation hypothesis is that a prime distractor can cause positive priming for nonconflict probes, even though they cause negative priming for randomly intermixed conflict probes. Thus, once the inhibition is removed, a facilitation emerges. This suggests that facilitation and inhibition occur at separate levels of processing; at *some* level, activation persists even though it is not overtly manifested in positive priming.

What It Might Be: Blocking

Tipper and Cranston (1985) suggested that the representation of an ignored distractor is not deactivated but rather is blocked from access to response mechanisms. Thus, negative priming may occur even though the distractor representation remains highly activated. As long as a "selection state" is maintained, the distractor representation will continue to be blocked. If, however, the selection state is dropped, positive priming may occur from the persisting activation of the distractor representation.

Neill (1989, 1993) proposed a variation of this idea, based on the model of a production system. A production system consists of a declarative knowledge system, a procedural knowledge system, and a working memory (e.g., Anderson, 1983). An object or event would automatically activate associated concepts in the declarative knowledge system (*that* an object is red, is round, is called a "ball," is located two feet ahead of me, belongs to the category "toys," etc.). The function of attention in such a system would be to control what declarative knowledge is represented in working memory, blocking information that is incompatible with immediate goals (Figure 11).

Neill (1989; 1993) argued that conscious awareness reflects the selected contents of working memory. Thus, if a person's goal were to kick a ball, he or she would be particularly aware of its location and shape. The presence of this information in working memory would then enable the appropriate procedural knowledge, knowing *how* to move one's feet in order to kick the ball.

Both the deactivation hypothesis and the blocking hypothesis attribute negative priming to inhibition occurring on the priming trial. This inhibition, whether deactivation or blocking, carries forward to the probe trial, impeding the response to information related to the ignored distractor.

What It Might Be: Episodic Retrieval

Neill and Valdes (1991; Neill, Valdes, Terry, & Gorfein, 1992) proposed an alternative theory of negative priming based on Logan's (1988) "instance theory" of automatization. Logan has argued that performance improves on

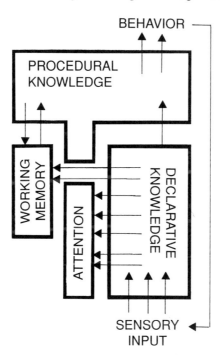

FIGURE 11. A production system model of attention: irrelevant declarative knowledge is blocked from access to working memory. (Adapted from Neill, 1989.)

tasks with practice because past instances of performance are stored in episodic memory. These processing episodes include information about the specific stimulus that was encountered and the response that was made to the stimulus. When presented with an unfamiliar stimulus, the subject must rely on slow, "algorithmic" processing to compute the appropriate response. As a stimulus becomes more familiar, the probability increases that the subject will quickly retrieve past processing episodes involving the same stimulus, bypassing the slower algorithmic processing.

What happens if the subject retrieves past processing episodes in which the current target stimulus had been ignored? We suggest that responding would be slowed, either because the "nonresponse" encoded in the episode would conflict with the appropriate response or because the subject would be forced to rely on the slower algorithmic processing. Whereas the deactivation and blocking hypotheses view negative priming as inhibition carried forward from the prime to the probe, the episodic retrieval hypothesis views it as a backward retrieval of the priming episode, cued by the probe target. Hence, "inhibition" may occur on the probe trial, not necessarily on the prime trial.

The episodic retrieval hypothesis is most strongly supported by the finding that negative priming depends on the delay *prior* to the prime trial as well as the delay between prime and probe (Neill, Valdes, Terry, & Gorfein, 1992). Murdock (1974) and Baddeley (1976) have argued persuasively that the likelihood of retrieving an episodic memory trace depends on its temporal discriminability from other memory traces. Applied to negative priming, the probability of retrieving the priming episode would decrease with delay to the probe. However, it would increase as the priming episode is made more discriminable from preceding episodes.

Baddeley (1976) argued that when retention intervals are blocked, discriminability between successive episodes is constant, regardless of retention interval. Thus, the probability of retrieving an item 20 s later when all items are separated by 20 s is the same as the probability of retrieving an item 5 s later when all items are separated by 5s. This would explain why negative priming appears to "decay" over time when delays are randomly intermixed (Neill & Valdes, 1992; Neill, Valdes, Terry, & Gorfein, 1992; Neill & Westberry, 1987) but not when they are blocked (Neill, Valdes, Terry, & Gorfein, 1992) or manipulated between subjects (Hasher et al., 1991; Stoltzfus et al., 1993; Tipper, Weaver, Cameron et al., 1991).

We assume that discriminability is most critical when stimuli are used repeatedly as both targets and distractors over the course of an experiment (as in most experiments by Neill and colleagues). Under such conditions, a past episode in which an item was ignored must compete with other episodes in which the item appeared as a target. Negative priming should then depend heavily on the discriminability of the priming episode. However, if an item has appeared only once before in the experiment, that episode is likely to be retrieved regardless of the delay.

Consistent with this speculation, studies with large stimulus sets have found negative-priming effects to persist over many intervening trials (De-Schepper & Treisman, 1991; Simpson & Kellas, 1989; Treisman & DeSchepper, 1993). Chiarello et al. (1993) directly examined the effect of stimulus set size in their previously discussed "crosswords" procedure. In one condition, a large set of words each appeared once in a related or unrelated prime–probe sequence, while in another condition a small set of words were repeated 32 times as distractors and/or targets over the experiment. Significant negative priming occurred only for the large stimulus set.

Neill, Valdes, Terry, and Gorfein (1992) discuss how episodic retrieval might account for other variables that affect negative priming, including speed/accuracy trade-off, pattern masking, number of distractors, and intervening trials. An episodic retrieval theory also necessitates a reevaluation of the relation of negative priming to effective cognitive functioning. Are groups characterized by cognitive deficits less likely to retrieve past processing episodes? Alternatively, do they fail to adequately encode *ignore this stimulus* in their processing episodes? The answers to such questions must await further research.

Regardless of whether the blocking hypothesis or the episodic retrieval hypothesis proves true, negative priming is probably more than just an accidental by-product of attention. As noted by Tipper, Weaver, Cameron et al. (1991), objects that are irrelevant in a natural context will probably remain irrelevant over some time. Hence, once an object has been ignored, it is usually adaptive to continue ignoring it. Either persisting inhibition or episodic retrieval would function to block further processing of the irrelevant object, preventing subsequent competition for the control of cognition and behavior. Thus, negative priming may provide the very mechanism by which we can sustain attention to a relevant source of information over time.

SUMMARY AND CONCLUSIONS

Responses to an object may be slower and/or less accurate if a related object has recently been ignored. This *negative-priming* effect has been demonstrated for many different kinds of stimulus materials, vocal and manual response modes, and a wide variety of judgments, including identification, classification, matching, counting, and localization.

Negative priming is not response inhibition. In some experiments, it pertains to the perceptual stimulus, but in other experiments, inhibition involves a higher, more abstract level of representation. Inhibited processing includes, but is not limited to, the level of representation explicitly required by the task. It is probably not the representation itself that is inhibited but rather the process of retrieving the response appropriate to that representation.

Negative priming requires time to develop, and dissipates over time after it is established. It may nevertheless persist over relatively long periods, even across many intervening trials. Negative priming appears to be limited in capacity, in that many distractors cannot be inhibited as effectively as one within a trial.

The relation of negative priming to interference is still unresolved: in general, conditions that increase interference also increase negative priming. Some studies, however, find negative priming to be independent of interference. Some studies suggest that negative priming depends on maintaining a "selection state" on probe trials; however, other studies find negative priming even when such a state is unlikely.

Negative priming is associated with effective cognitive functioning in "the real world." Individual-differences studies have found developmental, clinical, and personality variables that are related to negative priming. Diminished negative priming has been found in the elderly, children, schizophrenics, normal subjects prone to "cognitive failures," and "low absorbers."

Negative priming can be produced not only by ignored external objects (*exogenous* effects), but also by irrelevant associations to attended objects (*endogenous* effects). That both types of negative priming reflect a similar inhibitory mechanism is supported by findings that (1) both depend on instructional emphasis on accuracy versus speed, (2) both are reversed by pattern masking, and (3) both develop over time following an initial period of widespread activation (positive priming).

Negative priming cannot be attributed to previously hypothesized forms of inhibition, such as attenuation, processing "cost," lateral inhibition, or habituation. It does not appear to reflect an inhibitory "deactivation" of activated information in memory, as some studies suggest indicate persisting activation despite negative priming. Rather, activated information appears to be blocked from access to response mechanisms. It is unclear whether such blocking occurs when distracting information is initially encountered, or if it occurs when the subject retrieves past episodic memories of ignored information.

We hope that the reader is by now convinced that negative priming is widespread, is theoretically important, and has implications for effective cognitive functioning. We close here on the question of why negative priming is a "recent" phenomenon. Despite earlier demonstrations (e.g., Dalrymple-Alford & Budayr, 1966; Neill, 1977, 1979), it is only in the last few years that negative priming has become a major focus of empirical and theoretical discussion. Much of the current interest has undoubtedly been stimulated by the excellent work of Tipper and his colleagues since 1985, but why wasn't it discovered sooner?

We speculate that negative-priming research was delayed by the computer metaphor that underlay much of early cognitive theorizing (e.g., Neisser, 1967). Inhibitory mechanisms are ubiquitous in physiological, conditioning, and psychoanalytic theories, but they have little place in computer analogies (see Bjork, 1989; Bjorklund & Harnishfeger, Chapter 5, this volume, for a similar point). Computers do not suffer response competition caused by irrelevant stimuli. This is not to say that they do not encounter interference; retrieval of relevant information may be delayed by irrelevant information in memory. However, there is no need to inhibit the irrelevant information; search merely proceeds until the relevant information is located. The selected information then receives further processing: a facilitatory model of attention (cf. Figure 1A).

In recent years, the traditional computer metaphor has been supplemented by other metaphors, notably, the brain metaphor implied by neural network, or "connectionist" models (for a fuller discussion of the developments that have fueled recent interest in inhibitory mechanisms by cognitive psychologists, see Dempster, Chapter 1, this volume). Within such models, inhibitory processes play a major role. We do not intend here to endorse connectionist models of negative priming per se (see Neill & Klein, 1989, for discussion). However, as the standard computer metaphor wanes, cognitive psychologists may become more accepting of alternative conceptions of "how the mind works."

ACKNOWLEDGMENTS

We are indebted to Christine Chiarello, Frank Dempster, Lisa Maxfield, Cathleen Moore, Jim Neely, and Ewald Neumann, for their very helpful comments on the initial draft of this chapter.

REFERENCES

Allport, D. A. (1989). Visual attention. In M. I. Posner (Ed.), *Foundations of cognitive science* (pp. 631–682). Cambridge, MA: MIT Press.

Allport, D. A., Tipper, S. P., & Chmiel, N. R. J. (1985). Perceptual integration and postcategorical filtering. In M. I. Posner (Ed.), *Attention and performance XI* (pp. 107–132). Hillsdale, NJ: Erlbaum.

Anderson, J. R. (1976). *Language, memory, and thought*. Hillsdale, NJ: Erlbaum.

Anderson, J. R. (1983). *The architecture of cognition*. Cambridge, MA: Harvard University Press.

Baddeley, A. D. (1976). *The psychology of memory*. New York: Basic Books.

Beech, A., Agar, K., & Baylis, G. C. (1989). Reversing priming while maintaining interference. *Bulletin of the Psychonomic Society, 27,* 553–555.

Beech, A., Baylis, G. C., Smithson, P., & Claridge, G. (1989). Individual differences in schizotypy as reflected in measures of cognitive inhibition. *British Journal of Clinical Psychology, 28,* 117–129.

Beech, A., & Claridge, G. (1987). Individual differences in negative priming: Relations with schizotypal personality traits. *British Journal of Psychology, 78,* 349–356.

Beech, A., Powell, T., McWilliam, J., & Claridge, G. (1989). Evidence of reduced "cognitive inhibition" in schizophrenia. *British Journal of Clinical Psychology, 28,* 110–116.

Bjork, R. A. (1989). Retrieval inhibition as an adaptive mechanism in human memory. In H. L. Roediger, III & F. I. M. Craik (Eds.), *Varieties of memory and consciousness* (pp. 309–330). Hillsdale, NJ: Erlbaum.

Broadbent, D. E. (1958). *Perception and communication.* London: Pergamon.

Broadbent, D. E., Cooper, P. F., FitzGerald, P., & Parkes, K. R. (1982). The Cognitive Failures Questionnaire (CFQ) and its correlates. *British Journal of Clinical Psychology, 21,* 1–16.

Brown, A. S. (1979). Priming effects in semantic memory retrieval processes. *Journal of Experimental Psychology: Human Learning and Memory, 5,* 65–77.

Burgess, C., & Simpson, G. B. (1988). Cerebral mechanisms in the retrieval of ambiguous word meanings. *Brain and Language, 33,* 86–103.

Carr, T. H., & Dagenbach, D. (1990). Semantic priming and repetition priming from masked words: Evidence from a center-surround attentional mechanism in perceptual recognition. *Journal of Experimental Psychology: Learning, Memory, and Cognition, 16,* 341–350.

Chiarello, C. (1991). Interpretation of word meanings by the cerebral hemispheres: One is not enough. In P. Schwanenflugel (Ed.), *The psychology of word meanings.* (pp 251–278). Hillsdale, NJ: Erlbaum.

Chiarello, C., Maxfield, L., Richards, L., Stevenson, A., Hoffman, M., & Kahan, T. (1993, April). *Role of stimulus repetition in positive and negative priming from ignored distractors.* Paper presented at the meeting of the Eastern Psychological Association, Arlington, VA.

Collins, A. M., & Loftus, E. L. (1975). A spreading-activation theory of semantic processing. *Psychlogical Review, 82,* 407–428.

Comalli, P. E., Wapner, S., & Werner, H. (1962). Interference effects of Stroop color-wod test in children, adulthood and aging. *Journal of Genetic Psychology, 100,* 47–53.

Connelly, S. L., & Hasher, L. (1993). Aging and inhibition of spatial location. *Journal of Experimental Psychology: Human Perception and Performance, 19,* 1238–1250.

Connelly, S. L., Hasher, L., & Kimble, G. A. (1992, November). *The suppression of identity and location information.* Poster presented at the meeting of the Psychonomic Society, St. Louis, MO.

Cowan, N. (1988). Evolving conceptions of memory storage, selective attention, and their mutual constraints within the human information processing system. *Psychological Bulletin, 104,* 163–191.

Dagenbach, D., Carr, T. H., & Barnhardt, T. M. (1990). Inhibitory semantic priming of lexical decisions due to failure to retrieve weakly activated codes. *Journal of Experimental Psychology: Learning, Memory, and Cognition, 16,* 328–340.

Dalrymple-Alford, E. C., & Budayr, B. (1966). Examination of some aspects of the Stroop color-word test. *Perceptual & Motor Skills, 23,* 1211–1214.

Day, M. C. (1975). Developmental trends in scanning. In H. W. Reese (Ed.), *Advances in child development and behavior* (Vol. 10, pp. 153–193). New York: Academic Press.

DeSchepper, B., & Treisman, A. (1991, November). *Novel visual shapes in negative priming.* Paper presented at the meeting of the Psychonomic Society, San Francisco.

Deutsch, J. A., & Deutsch, D. (1963). Attention: Some theoretical considerations. *Psychological Review, 70,* 80–90.

Dick, M., & McFarland, C. E. (1978, March). *Context effects in sentence comprehension with schizophrenics.* Paper presented at the meeting of the Southeastern Psychological Association, Atlanta.

Driver, J., & Baylis, G. C. (1993). Cross-modal negative priming and interference in selective attention. *Bulletin of the Psychonomic Society, 31,* 45–48.

Driver, J., & Tipper, S. P. (1989). On the nonselectivity of "selective" seeing: Contrasts between interference and priming in selective attention. *Journal of Experimental Psychology: Human Perception and Performance, 15,* 304–314.

Eriksen, B. A., & Eriksen, C. W. (1974). Effects of noise letters upon the identification of a target letter in a nonsearch task. *Perception & Psychophysics, 16,* 143–149.

Eriksen, C. W., & Hoffman, J. E. (1973). The extent of processing noise elements during selective encoding from visual displays. *Perception & Psychophysics, 14,* 155–160.

Fowler, C. A., Wolford, G., Slade, R., & Tassinary, L. (1981). Lexical access with and without awareness. *Journal of Experimental Psychology: General, 110,* 341–362.

Francolini, C. M., & Egeth, H. E. (1980). On the nonautomaticity of "automatic" activation: Evidence of selective seeing. *Perception & Psychophysics, 27,* 331–342.

Frith, C. D. (1979). Consciousness, information processing, and schizophrenia. *British Journal of Psychiatry, 134,* 225–235.

Fuentes, L. J., & Tudela, P. (1992). Semantic processing of foveally and parafoveally presented words in a lexical decision task. *Quarterly Journal of Experimental Psychology, 45A,* 299–322.

Gernsbacher, M. A., & Faust, M. E. (1991). The mechanism of suppression: A component of general comprehension skill. *Journal of Experimental Psychology: Learning, Memory, and Cognition, 17,* 245–262.

Greenwald, A. G. (1972). Evidence of both perceptual filtering and response suppression for rejected messages in selective attention. *Journal of Experimental Psychology, 94,* 58–67.

Hasher, L., Stoltzfus, E. R., Zacks, L. T., & Rypma, B. (1991) Age and inhibition. *Journal of Experimental Psychology, 17,* 163–169.

Hasher, L., & Zacks, R. L. (1988). Working memory, comprehension, and aging: A review and a new view. In G. Bower (Ed.), *The psychology of learning and motivation* (Vol. 22, pp. 193–225). San Diego: Academic Press.

Hekkanen, S. T. (1981). The effects of context on the processing of ambiguous words (Doctoral dissertation, University of South Florida, 1981). *Dissertation Abstracts International, 42,* 1646B.

Houghton, G., & Tipper, S. P. (1994). A model of inhibitory mechanism in selective attention. In D. Dagenbach & T. Carr (Eds.), *Inhibitory mechanisms of attention, memory, and language* (pp. 53–112). San Diego: Academic Press.

Kahneman, D. (1973). *Attention and effort.* Englewood Cliffs, NJ: Prentice-Hall.

Kahneman, D., & Henik, A. M. (1981). Perceptual organization and attention. In M. Kubovy & J. R. Pomerantz (Eds.), *Perceptual organization* (pp. 181–211). Hillsdale, NJ: Erlbaum.

Kane, M., Hasher, L., Stoltzfus, E. R., Zacks, R. T., & Connelly, S. L. (1994) Inhibitory attentional mechanisms and aging. *Psychology & Aging, 9,* 103–112.

Lane, D. M., & Pearson, D. A. (1982). The development of selective attention. *Merrill-Palmer Quarterly, 28,* 317–337.

Logan, G. D. (1988). Toward an instance theory of automatization. *Psychological Review, 95,* 492–527.

Logan, G. D., & Zbrodoff, N. J. (1979). When it helps to be misled: Facilitative effects of increasing the frequency of conflicting stimuli in a Stroop-like task. *Memory & Cognition, 7,* 166–174.

Lorsch, E. P., Anderson, D. R., & Well, A. D. (1984). Effects of irrelevant information on speeded classification tasks: Interference is reduced by habituation. *Journal of Experimental Psychology: Human Perception and Performance, 10,* 850–864.

Lowe, D. G. (1979). Strategies, context, and the mechanism of response inhibition. *Memory & Cognition, 7,* 382–389.

Lowe, D. G. (1985). Further investigations of inhibitory mechanisms in attention. *Memory & Cognition, 13,* 74–80.

Marcel, A. J. (1980). Conscious and preconscious recognition of polysemous words: Locating the selective effects of prior verbal context. In R. S. Nickerson (Ed.), *Attention and performance VIII* (pp. 435–437). Hillsdale, NJ: Erlbaum.

Marcel, A. J. (1983a). Conscious and unconscious perception: Experiments on visual masking and word recognition. *Cognitive Psychology, 15,* 197–237.

Marcel, A. J. (1983b). Conscious and unconscious perception: An approach to the relations between phenomenal experience and perceptual processes. *Cognitive Psychology, 15,* 238–300.

McCauley, C., Parmalee, C. M., Sperber, R. D., & Carr, T. H. (1980). Early extraction of meaning from pictures and its relation to conscious identification. *Journal of Experimental Psychology: Human Perception and Performance, 6,* 265–276.

McDowd, J. M., & Oseas-Kreger, D. M. (1991). Aging, inhibitory processes, and negative priming. *Journal of Gerontology: Psychology Sciences, 46,* 340–345.

McEvoy, C. L. (1982). Facilitation and suppression in the retrieval of pictorial labels (Doctoral dissertation, University of South Florida, 1982). *Dissertation Abstracts International, 43,* 2373B.

Meyer, D. E., & Schvaneveldt, R. W. (1971). Facilitation in recognizing pairs of words: Evidence of a dependence between retrieval operations. *Journal of Experimental Psychology, 90,* 227–234.

Moore, C. (1993). *Negative priming effects depend on probe-trial conflict: Where has all the inhibition gone?* Manuscript submitted for publication.

Moray, N. (1959). Attention in dichotic listening: Affective cues and the influence of instructions. *Quarterly Journal of Experimental Psychology, 11,* 56–60.

Murdock, B. B. (1974). *Human memory: Theory and data.* Hillsdale, NJ: Erlbaum.

Neely, J. H. (1976). Semantic priming and retrieval from lexical memory: Evidence for facilitatory and inhibitory processes. *Memory & Cognition, 4,* 648–654.

Neely, J. H. (1977). Semantic priming and retrieval from semantic memory: Roles of inhibitionless spreading activation and limited-capacity attention. *Journal of Experimental Psychology: General, 196,* 227–234.

Neill, W. T. (1977). Inhibitory and facilitatory processes in selective attention. *Journal of Experimental Psychology: Human Perception and Performance, 3,* 444–450.

Neill, W. T. (1979). Switching attention within and between categories: Evidence for intracategory inhibition. *Memory & Cognition, 7,* 283–290.

Neill, W. T. (1982, March). *The suppression of distracting information in cognitive processing.* Paper presented at the meeting of the Southeastern Psychological Association, New Orleans.

Neill, W. T. (1985). Levels of processing in disruptive effects of prior information. *Memory & Cognition, 13,* 477–484.

Neill, W. T. (1989). Ambiguity and context: An activation-suppression model. In D. S. Gorfein (Ed.), *Resolving semantic ambiguity* (pp. 63–83). New York: Springer-Verlag.

Neill, W. T. (1991, August). *Consciousness and the inhibitory control of cognition.* Invited address to the meeting of the American Psychological Association, San Francisco.

Neill, W. T. (1993). Consciousness, not focal attention, is causally effective in human information processing: Commentary on Velmans (1991). *Behavioral and Brain Sciences, 16,* 406–407.

Neill, W. T., Beck, J. L., Bottalico, K. S., & Molloy, R. D. (1990). Effects of intentional versus incidental learning on explicit and implicit tests of memory. *Journal of Experimental Psychology: Learning, Memory, and Cognition, 16,* 457–463.

Neill, W. T., Hilliard, D. V., & Cooper, E.-A. (1988). The detection of lexical ambiguity: Evidence for context-sensitive parallel access. *Journal of Memory and Language, 27,* 279–287.

Neill, W. T., & Klein, R. M. (1989). Reflexions on modularity and connectionism. In D. S. Gorfein (Ed.), *Resolving semantic ambiguity* (pp. 276–293). New York: Springer-Verlag.

Neill, W. T., & Lissner, L. S. (1988, April). *Attention and selective inhibition in alphanumeric character matching.* Paper presented at the meeting of the Eastern Psychological Association, Buffalo, NY.

Neill, W. T., Lissner, L. S., & Beck, J. L. (1990). Negative priming in *same-different* matching: Further evidence for a central locus of inhibition. *Perception & Psychophysics, 48,* 398–400.

Neill, W. T., Terry, K. M., & Valdes, L. A. (1994). Negative priming without probe selection. *Psychonomic Bulletin & Review, 1,* 119–121.

Neill, W. T., & Valdes, L. A. (1992). The persistence of negative priming: Steady-state or decay? *Journal of Experimental Psychology: Learning, Memory, and Cognition, 18,* 565–576.

Neill, W. T., Valdes, L. A., & Terry, K. M. (1992, November). *Negative priming in target localization.* Paper presented at the meeting of the Psychonomic Society, St. Louis, MO.

Neill, W. T., Valdes, L. A., Terry, K. M., & Gorfein, D. S. (1992). The persistence of negative priming: II. Evidence for episodic trace retrieval. *Journal of Experimental Psychology: Learning, Memory, and Cognition, 18,* 993–1000.

Neill, W. T., & Westberry, R. L. (1987). Selective attention and the suppression of cognitive noise. *Journal of Experimental Psychology: Learning, Memory, and Cognition, 13,* 327–334.

Neisser, U. (1967). *Cognitive Psychology.* New York: Appleton-Century-Crofts.

Neumann, E., Cherau, J. F., Hood, K. L., & Steinnagel, S. L. (1993). Does inhibition spread in a manner analogous to spreading activation? *Memory, 1,* 81–105.

Neumann, E., & DeSchepper, B. G. (1992). An inhibition based fan effect: Evidence for an active suppression mechanism in selective attention. *Canadian Journal of Psychology, 46,* 1–40.

Nissen, M. J. (1985). Accessing features and objects: Is location special? In M. I. Posner & O. S. M. Marin (Eds.), *Attention and performance XI* (pp. 205–219). Hillsdale, NJ: Erlbaum.

Norman, D. A. (1968). Toward a theory of memory and attention. *Psychological Review, 75,* 522–536.

Posner, M. I. (1982). Cumulative development of attention theory. *American Psychologist, 37,* 168–179.

Posner, M. I., & Snyder, C. R. R. (1975). Facilitation and inhibition in the processing of signals. In P. M. A. Rabbitt & S. Dornic (Eds.), *Attention and performance V* (pp. 669–682). New York: Academic Press.

Reisberg, D., Baron, J., & Kemler, D. G. (1980). Overcoming Stroop interference: The effects of practice on distractor processing. *Journal of Experimental Psychology: Human Perception and Performance, 6,* 140–150.

Roediger, H. L., & Neely, J. H. (1982). Retrieval blocks in episodic and semantic memory. *Canadian Journal of Psychology, 36,* 213–242.

Roediger, H. L., Neely, J. H., & Blaxton, T. A. (1983). Inhibition from related primes in semantic memory retrieval: A reappraisal of Brown's (1979) paradigm. *Journal of Experimental Psychology: Learning, Memory, and Cognition, 9,* 478–485.

Schvaneveldt, R. W., & Meyer, D. E. (1973). Retrieval and comparison processes in semantic memory. In S. Kornblum (Eds.), *Attention and performance IV* (pp. 395–409). New York: Academic Press.

Schvaneveldt, R. W., Meyer, D. E., & Becker, C. A. (1976). Lexical ambiguity, semantic context and visual word recognition. *Journal of Experimental Psychology, 2,* 243–256.

Simpson, G. B. (1981). Meaning dominance and semantic context in the processing of lexical ambiguity. *Journal of Verbal Learning and Verbal Behavior, 20,* 120–136.

Simpson, G. B. (1984). Lexical ambiguity and its role in models of word recognition. *Psychological Bulletin, 96,* 316–340.

Simpson, G. B., & Burgess, C. (1985). Activation and selection processes in the recognition of ambiguous words. *Journal of Experimental Psychology: Human Perception and Performance, 11,* 28–39.

Simpson, G. B., & Kellas, G. (1989). Dynamic contextual processes and lexical access. In D. S. Gorfein (Ed.), *Resolving semantic ambiguity* (pp. 40–56). New York: Springer-Verlag.

Sperber, R. D., McCauley, C., Ragain, R. D., & Weil, C. (1979). Semantic priming effects on picture and word processing. *Memory & Cognition, 7,* 339–345.

Sternberg, S. (1969). The discovery of processing stages: Extensions of Donders' method. *Acta Psychologica, 30,* 276–315.

Stoltzfus, E. R., Hasher, L., Zacks, R. T., Ulivi, M. S., & Goldstein, D. (1993). Investigations of inhibition and interference in younger and older adults. *Journal of Gerontology, 48,* 179–188.

Stroop, J. R. (1935). Studies of interference in serial verbal reactions. *Journal of Experimental Psychology, 18,* 643–662.

Sullivan, M. P., & Faust, M. E. (in press). Evidence for identity inhibition during selective attention in old adults. *Psychology & Aging.*

Tellegen, A., & Atkinson, G. (1974). Openness to absorbing and self-altering experiences ("absorption"), a trait related to hypnotic susceptibility. *Journal of Abnormal Psychology, 83,* 268–277.

Tipper, S. P. (1985). The negative priming effect: Inhibitory priming by ignored objects. *Quarterly Journal of Experimental Psychology, 37A,* 571–590.

Tipper, S. P. (1991). Less attentional selectivity as a result of declining inhibition in older adults. *Bulletin of the Psychonomic Society, 29,* 45–47.

Tipper, S. P., & Baylis, G. C. (1987). Individual differences in selective attention: The relation of priming and interference to cognitive failure. *Personality and Individual Differences, 8,* 667–675.

Tipper, S. P., Bourque, T., Anderson, S., & Brehaut, J. (1989). Mechanisms of attention: A developmental study. *Journal of Experimental Child Psychology, 48,* 353–378.

Tipper, S. P., Brehaut, J. C., & Driver, J. (1990). Selection of moving and static objects for the control of spatially directed action. *Journal of Experimental Psychology: Human Perception and Performance, 16,* 492–504.

Tipper, S. P., & Cranston, M. (1985). Selective attention and priming: Inhibitory and facilitatory effects of ignored primes. *Quarterly Journal of Experimental Psychology, 37A,* 581–611.

Tipper, S. P., & Driver, J. (1988). Negative priming between pictures and words in a selective attention task: Evidence for semantic processing of ignored stimuli. *Memory & Cognition, 16,* 64–70.

Tipper, S. P., Lortie, C., & Baylis, G. C. (1992). Selective reaching: Evidence for action-centered attention. *Journal of Experimental Psychology: Human Perception and Performance, 18,* 891–905.

Tipper, S. P., MacQueen, G. M., & Brehaut, J. C. (1988). Negative priming between response modalities: Evidence for the central locus of inhibition in selective attention. *Perception & Psychophysics, 43,* 45–52.

Tipper, S. P., & McLaren, J. (1990). Evidence for efficient visual selectivity in children. In J. T. Enns (Ed.), *The development of attention: Research and theory* (pp. 197–210). Amsterdam: Elsevier/North-Holland.

Tipper, S. P., Weaver, B., Cameron, S., Brehaut, J. C., & Bastedo, J. (1991). Inhibitory mechanisms of attention in identification tasks: Time-course and disruption. *Journal of Experimental Psychology: Learning, Memory, and Cognition, 17,* 681–692.

Tipper, S. P., Weaver, B., Kirkpatrick, J., & Lewis, S. (1991). Inhibitory mechanisms of attention: Locus, stability, and relationship with distractor interference effects. *British Journal of Psychology, 82,* 507–520.

Treisman, A. M. (1964). Monitoring and storage of irrelevant messages in selective attention. *Journal of Verbal Learning and Verbal Behavior, 3,* 449–459.

Treisman, A. M. (1992). Perceiving and re-perceiving objects. *American Psychologist, 47,* 862–875.

Treisman, A. M., & DeSchepper, B. (1993, April). *Memory for novel visual shapes.* Paper presented at the meeting of the Association for Research in Vision and Opthalmology, Sarasota, FL.

Treisman, A. M., & Gelade, G. (1980). A feature-integration theory of attention. *Cognitive Psychology, 12,* 97–136.

Ungerleider, L. G., & Mishkin, M. (1982). Two cortical visual systems. In D. J. Ingle, M. A.,

Goodale, & R. J. W. Mansfield (Eds.), *Analysis of visual behavior* (pp. 549–586). Cambridge, MA: MIT Press.

Valdes, L. A. (1993). *The relation of negative priming to interference.* Doctoral dissertation, Adelphi University, Garden City, NY.

Valdes, L. A., & Neill, W. T. (1993, April). *Does negative priming depend on interference?* Paper presented at the meeting of the Eastern Psychological Association, Arlington, VA.

Van der Heijden, A. H. C. (1981). *Short term visual information processing.* London: Routledge & Kegan Paul.

Walley, R. E., & Weiden, T. D. (1973). Lateral inhibition and cognitive masking: A neuropsychological theory of attention. *Psychological Review, 80,* 284–302.

Watkins, M. J. (1975). Inhibition in recall with extralist "cues." *Journal of Verbal Learning and Verbal Behavior, 14,* 294–303.

Westberry, R. L. (1984). The nature of attentional control as a personality dimension (Doctoral dissertation, University of South Florida, 1983). *Dissertation Abstracts International, 45,* 1034B.

Yee, P. L. (1991). Semantic inhibition of ignored words during a figure classification task. *Quarterly Journal of Experimental Psychology, 43A,* 127–153.

Zajano, M. J., & Gorman, A. (1986). Stroop interference as a function of percentage of congruent items. *Perceptual and Motor Skills, 63,* 1087–1096.

8

Memory Interference and Misinformation Effects

Allison L. Titcomb and Valerie F. Reyna

Misinformation effects in memory have been extensively researched because of their theoretical and practical importance. Early studies seemed to show that memory for events was easily distorted by subsequent misinformation, a finding that inspired debate about the malleability of memory (e.g., Loftus, 1979). Such studies were also of practical relevance because misinformation manipulations were designed to mimic leading questions that might occur in the course of examining eyewitnesses. As is well known, verdicts often turn on such eyewitness testimony (Bell & Loftus, 1988, 1989). In this chapter, we review research on misinformation effects. Our review is divided into three major sections. The first section summarizes empirical findings; the second section details the major information-processing explanations for these findings; in the last section, we discuss newer theoretical perspectives.

As shall be seen, the misinformation procedure parallels classic interference paradigms (e.g., Schwartz & Reisberg, 1991), and similar theoretical controversies have arisen in both domains. (A detailed discussion of interference paradigms and theoretical controversies in connection with infant memory appears in Chapter 3 by Rovee-Collier & Boller, this volume.) Specifically, theorists have disagreed about whether misinformation effects are primarily due to storage failure, to retrieval failure, or, indeed, to memory at all. More recently, new distinctions have been introduced, including memory for the source of information, as opposed to its content, and memory for verbatim information, as opposed to gist (e.g., Lindsay & Johnson, 1989; Reyna, 1992; respectively). Therefore, misinformation research is a kind of microcosm of memory research generally, and it appears to encompass multiple memory phenomena.

MISINFORMATION EFFECTS: BASIC DESIGN AND FINDINGS

The original misinformation paradigm consists of three phases (Loftus, 1979). First, subjects are presented a sequence of events, such as a series of slides depicting a car accident. Subjects are then divided into two groups that differ only in the second phase. The misled group receives questions in which erroneous suggestions are embedded. For example, subjects might be questioned about a yield sign despite the fact that a stop sign was actually presented. The control group receives neutral questions. In the final phase, all subjects are given a forced-choice recognition test containing the original and misled items. The typical finding is that subjects in the misled group are more likely than those in the control group to select the misled item as having been initially presented (see Table 1).

This procedure resembles the well-known A-B, A-C transfer paradigm that dominated the psychology of forgetting for many years (Baddeley, 1976). This paradigm, shown in Table 2, usually involves learning an initial set of word pairs (A–B) followed by learning a second set that couples the original cue with a new response (A–C). Finally, memory is tested for the original response. The retroactive interference effect consists of poorer retention of the original response after transfer training has occurred. (Proactive interference, in which learning the first series of pairs interferes with learning the second series, also occurs.) Multiple explanations for these effects have been offered, including various retrieval and storage failure hypotheses (e.g., Baddeley, 1976; Schwartz & Reisberg, 1991).

The classic interpretation of the misinformation phenomenon (e.g., Loftus, 1979) has been of the storage-failure variety, namely, that misleading

TABLE 1. Comparison of Interference and Misinformation Paradigms

Condition	Time 1	Time 2	Recognition test
Retroactive interference			
Experimental	A–B	A–C	B vs. C
Misinformation effect			
Misled	Car stopped at yield sign	Car stopped at stop sign	Stop sign vs. yield sign

TABLE 2. Examples of Transfer Paradigms

Condition	List 1	List 2	Test
Retroactive interference			
Experimental	A–B	A–C	A–?
	opera–humid	opera–eager	opera–?
Control	A–B	C–D	A–?
	opera–humid	pastry–eager	opera–?
Proactive interference			
Experimental	A–B	C–B	C–?
	opera–humid	pastry–humid	pastry–?
Control	A–B	C–D	C–?
	opera–humid	pastry–eager	pastry–?

suggestions alter, or overwrite, original memories. In the numerous studies that have followed the original demonstrations, investigators have identified additional variables that modulate misinformation effects. Some of these findings have called into question the classic overwriting interpretation. We will now review these findings and, in a subsequent section, detail their theoretical implications.

Order Effects

The first result concerns the order in which test questions are posed. In the standard paradigm, all questions (both questions containing misleading information in phase 2 and test questions in phase 3) are presented in random order. Thus, although events are presented in a coherent order (a car is shown approaching an intersection, passing through the intersection, and, finally, colliding with a pedestrian), subjects are not questioned about these events in the order in which they occurred. Bekerian and Bowers (1983), however, tested subjects with questions either in random order or in the same order as the original event slides. Maintaining the same order of events for test items eliminated the misinformation effect, although random presentation replicated Loftus' findings. Bekerian and Bowers argued that memory for original information had not, in fact, been altered by misinformation. A follow-up study by Bowers and Bekerian (1984) replicated and extended these results by manipulating the order of questioning in phase 2 as well as the order of test items in phase 3. Random presentation of test questions was again associated with greater misinformation effects, but randomizing misleading questions produced smaller misinformation effects. Thus, Bowers and Bekerian argued that misinformation effects depend on the match between conditions at study and at retrieval, in contrast to the classic memory alteration view.

Order effects were also considered by Kroll, Ogawa, and Nieters (1988). In another variation of the standard paradigm, subjects saw the slide sequence twice and were tested after each sequence. After the initial event and first test, subjects were told they would be tested again, but only after "returning to the scene of the crime." Half of the subjects saw "return slides" in random order and half saw the slides in the same order as that shown first. When they saw the second set of slides in the same sequence, they were more likely to correct any mistakes made on the first test. Thus, the presence of order cues reduced misinformation effects. Again, the ability of the subjects to recover memories when the original order of events was reinstated seemed to imply that memory alteration had not occurred.

However, not all studies have failed to find misinformation effects by maintaining event order at test. Cohen and Faulkner (1989) used a recognition test that preserved the order of events in a film. They found that the younger misled subjects made 15% more errors than the control group and the elderly misled subjects made 29% more errors. In this case, preserving the order of events at test failed to eliminate misinformation effects.

Type of Memory Test

Other modifications of the standard paradigm that have challenged the alteration hypothesis focused on the alternatives offered to subjects during the memory test. As noted earlier, the standard recognition test (see Table 3) provided a forced choice between the correct item from the original event and the interfering item supplied during the second phase of the experiment. McCloskey and Zaragoza (1985) questioned these procedures on two grounds. First, subjects who did not fully encode the original information might have used the misled detail to "fill in the gap" of their memory for the event without any alteration occurring. Second, some subjects who remembered the original information may have selected the misleading detail at test because of social conformity. That is, subjects might simply be conforming to suggestions despite awareness that the items were incorrect.

In order to reduce these problems, McCloskey and Zaragoza developed a modified test that offered a choice between a novel item and the original

TABLE 3. Examples of Standard and Modified Tests

Condition	Original	Misinformation	Test
Standard			
Misled	Hammer	Wrench	Hammer vs. wrench
Control	Hammer	—	Hammer vs. wrench
Modified			
Misled	Hammer	Wrench	Hammer vs. screwdriver
Control	Hammer	—	Hammer vs. screwdriver

item (see Table 3). They argued that if memory were truly impaired, misled subjects should be more likely to select the novel item rather than the original. Furthermore, they reasoned that social conformity effects would be alleviated by deleting the suggested items from the test. Their procedure mirrored Loftus's three-phase sequence, although they used a new series of slides and a postevent narrative, rather than questions, to supply misleading details. They found no difference between control group performance (subjects who read "neutral" references to the details) and misled group performance. They concluded that misleading information had no effect on memory. Other measures of memory, such as cued recall (Zaragoza, McCloskey, & Jamis, 1987) and memory for source (see below; Zaragoza & Koshmider, 1989) also failed to yield significant effects.

Loftus, Donders, Hoffman, and Schooler (1989) compared response times and confidence levels for the standard and modified tests. They reasoned that, if misled subjects were attempting to resolve conflicts between competing memories, their response times for the standard test would be longer compared to controls. The modified test, in contrast, did not directly pit original and misinformation items against one another, and so should not elicit an increase in response time. On the other hand, if original memories were overwritten by misinformation, misled subjects should quickly and confidently select the misinformation item on the standard test, and should exhibit an increase in response time on the modified test because the "remembered" item was not offered.

Loftus et al. found the latter pattern of results: misled subjects took less time to respond when they answered incorrectly on the standard test, and their latencies and confidence were indistinguishable from those for correct responses to nonmisinformed items. However, misled subjects took longer than control subjects regardless of accuracy on the modified test. These results were replicated in a second experiment in which subjects were given more time to view the initial set of slides, increasing the chances that the original event had been encoded. Because subjects were quick to accept the misled item on the standard test and slow to choose when the misled item was omitted on the modified test, Loftus et al. concluded that it was unlikely that subjects were choosing between competing traces. Response times and confidence levels were instead compatible with the view that memories had been altered to reflect the misled item.

Although response times using the modified test revealed a subtle interference effect for misled subjects, the modified test has been criticized for a lack of sensitivity in detecting misinformation effects when simple choice data are used. Thus, subsequent modifications of the standard test have included Yes–No recognition tests of original details, misleading distractors, and novel distractors (e.g., Tversky & Tuchin, 1989). The rationale for separate Yes–No tests was that the modified test's forced choice between novel and original items could not distinguish between subjects who did not remember the initial event from those who rejected the novel item and selected the only other choice allowed. In other words, for the modified test, " . . . knowing what you did not see is just as good as knowing what you saw" (p. 89).

Tversky and Tuchin found that misled and control subjects were equally good at rejecting novel distractors, but that misled subjects were poorer at accepting original events and at rejecting misleading distractors. Therefore, the Yes–No test revealed that subjects were equally adept at rejecting unpresented items, but differed in their responses to original and misleading items. Thus, novelty effects could be distinguished from specific memory effects (see also Brainerd & Reyna, 1988, 1993). Because subjects showed decrements for original items (as well as increments for misleading distractors), Tversky and Tuchin interpreted their data as contradicting the notion that "nothing had happened to the original information" when misleading information was presented. However, they did not see their results as support for complete overwriting because some subjects accepted both original and misleading items.

Belli (1989) also used a Yes–No recognition test, but did not include misleading items in the test. He claimed, as did McCloskey and Zaragoza, that responses to misleading items were uninformative, and might elicit social conformity biases. According to Belli, responses to original and to novel items were sufficient to distinguish between two bases for responses. The first basis he called "misinformation acceptance," which applies if subjects, for whatever reasons, do not remember the original event. Thus, some percentage of subjects in the misled group might reject novel and original items simply because they accepted the misinformation, but not because of interference with original memories. Control subjects, who similarly failed to remember original events, would presumably guess when presented with either novel or original items. Therefore, misled subjects would perform above chance (and better than control subjects) on novel items, but would perform below chance (and worse than control subjects) on original items. On balance, Belli reasoned, if misinformation acceptance were the only basis for responses, misled and control subjects would perform at about the same level.

Misinformation interference, on the other hand, would apply if subjects had memories for original events (see also Reyna, Chapter 2, this volume). Naturally, control subjects who remembered the original event would reject the novel item and accept the original item. Misled subjects would also correctly reject the novel item, but if misinformation had interfered with their original memories, they would incorrectly reject the original item. In contrast to misinformation acceptance, then, overall performance for misled subjects would be lower than for control subjects.

In his first experiment, Belli found evidence for misinformation acceptance; overall performance for misled and control subjects did not differ significantly. He then introduced several changes, such as lengthening presentation times, that were designed to increase the chances that subjects would remember original events. After correcting for possible floor effects in original memories, Belli found significant misinformation interference in Experiment 2, in the sense that overall accuracy rates for misled subjects were lower than for control subjects. He noted, however, that misled subjects also exhibited misinformation acceptance because they rejected the novel items at a higher rate than did control subjects. Because he found evidence for misinformation acceptance, Belli concluded that mechanisms other than memory alteration could produce misinformation effects. He also pointed out that his results favoring memory interference were ambiguous because they could be interpreted as evidence of either memory impairment or source misattribution (i.e., misattributing narrative information to the original slides).

Results for Yes–No recognition tests can be compared to those for source monitoring tests (e.g., Johnson, Hashtroudi, & Lindsay, 1993; Lindsay, 1990; Lindsay & Johnson, 1989; Zaragoza & Koshmider, 1989). For example, Lindsay and Johnson (1989) administered a source monitoring test, in which subjects could indicate whether they had seen the misled item in the original picture, the narrative, both, or neither. They also administered a Yes–No recognition test. Although misled subjects were more likely to misjudge the misinformation as having appeared in the picture in the Yes–No task, they were no more likely than control subjects to attribute the misinformation to the picture in the source monitoring task. Lindsay and Johnson suggested that the source monitoring task alerted subjects to the possibility that misinformation could have come from a source other than the original event, thereby reducing its effect. Hence, subjects might well remember original and misled items, but be confused (on Yes–No tests) about their sources.

Lindsay (1990) found further support for the idea that source confusions increase misinformation effects. He presented two kinds of source monitoring conditions, easy and difficult. In the easy conditions (i.e., characteristics that made phase 1 distinctive from phase 2), misinformation failed to have an effect. However, under difficult source monitoring conditions (similar conditions for phase 1 and phase 2) subjects more often misreported seeing misled details in the original event. Because difficult monitoring conditions increased misinformation effects, these results suggest that source confusions might account for some misinformation errors even when discriminability between sources is not explicitly varied (for further discussion on this point, see Reyna, Chapter 2, this volume).

Modality Studies

In light of Lindsay's (1990) finding that differences between original and misleading events reduce misinformation effects, it is interesting to note that most studies have presented the original and misleading information in different modalities. Typically, original information is presented visually, such as in a series of slides concerning a burglary (e.g., McCloskey & Zaragoza, 1985), a single slide (Lindsay & Johnson, 1989), nature scenes (Chandler, 1989,

1991), or video clips (Loftus & Zanni, 1975; McSpadden, Schooler, & Loftus, 1988). Most studies have followed this visual presentation with some sort of verbal information (see Table 4), such as a narrative (e.g., McCloskey & Zaragoza, 1985) or a questionnaire (e.g., Loftus, Miller, & Burns, 1978). Zaragoza and Koshmider (1989) have argued that cross-modal presentation of original and misinformation items may give subjects "distinctive contextual and temporal cues to rely on in making their judgments" (p. 253). This would have the effect of decreasing misinformation effects because the context of misleading information could be distinguished from that of the original information. Consistent with this interpretation (which is reminiscent of Lindsay's, 1990, claims regarding source discriminability), Zaragoza and Koshmider failed to find misinformation effects. However, other studies that have kept modality of presentation constant have obtained significant misinformation effects. Chandler (1989, 1991), for instance, used visual stimuli in both phase 1 and 2, and found misinformation effects with a modified test.

Bowman and Zaragoza (1989) presented slides in phase 1 and 2 in Experiment 1 and verbal materials in both phases in Experiment 2. They found differences with the standard test, but not with the modified test. Toglia, Payne, and Anastasi (1991) also presented either visual materials or verbal materials in both phases. As in Bowman and Zaragoza, effects were larger with the standard test. The latter two studies also allow a comparison between modalities. In both, accuracy for control and misled subjects was higher in the verbal than in the visual conditions. Thus, although one might expect on the basis of discriminability that misinformation effects should be easier to obtain when modalities are the same, effects were actually less reliable, especially on the modified test. However, the number of studies is small, and these trends may be due to other aspects of the designs (e.g., delay between phases 1 and 2).

Context Studies

Much like modality, contextual cues can increase or decrease similarity between phases 1 and 2. Studies have varied the context in which subjects first experience the original event, the circumstances in which they receive misleading information, and the environment in which they are tested. These manipulations have ranged from room changes (e.g., Bonto & Payne, 1991) to changes in light levels in different phases of the experiment (Lindsay, 1990). Bonto and Payne (1991) had subjects move to different rooms in a psychology building during their experiment. They found no significant differences associated with context effects (although differences between misled and control subjects were larger when contexts were similar). Again, misinformation effects were obtained with the standard test, but not with the modified test (virtually no difference in performance in either context manipulation). Lindsay (1990) did find differences with context, but changes in

TABLE 4. Summary of Misinformation Studies Experimental Manipulations, Measures of Memory, and Results

Author	Original event	Postevent information	Timing of misinformation	Measure(s) of memory	Timing of test	Special manipulation	Results
Belli et al. (1992)	New slide sequence (44)[a]	Narrative	Immed., 1 week, 5 days	Modified recognition test	Immed., 1 week, 5 days	Used perceptually central details as critical items in slides and test	No difference w/immed. test, significant misinformation effect w/long-term retention interval
Belli (1993)	M & Z slide sequence[b] (79)	Narrative	Immed.	Modified recognition test (Final), interpolated test: Y/N, recall, confidence ratings	Immed.	Interpolated test added between narrative and final test	Misinformation effect on interpolated test but not final modified recognition test
Belli (1989)	M & Z slide sequence (79)	Narrative	Immed.	Y/N recognition test	Immed.	Y/N test including original and novel items	Misinformation effect after efforts were made to increase control level performance on the task
Belli, Lindsay, Gales, and McCarthy (1994)	M & Z slide sequence (79 and fewer)	Narrative	Immed.	Cued recall	Immed.	Used warnings, encouraged guessing, deleted commonly guessed items from last experiments	Significant misinformation effects, memory impairment evidence, but guessing and item biases had impact before they were controlled
Bonto and Payne (1991)	M & Z slide sequence (79)	Narrative	Immed.	Standard and modified recognition tests, response time	Immed.	Context changes, used different classrooms in a psychology building	Misinformation effect w/standard test, no effect w/modified test
Bowers and Bekerian (1984)	Loftus slide sequence (39)	Questions	Immed.	Standard recognition test	Immed.	Altered order of postevent questions and test questions (sequential and random)	Misinformation effect w/sequentially ordered phase 2; otherwise, effect found only w/random test
Bekerian and Bowers (1983)	Loftus slide sequence (24)	Questions	Immed.	Standard recognition test	Immed.	Altered order of slides at test (sequential and random)	Misinformation effect w/random test only
Toglia, Payne, and Anastasi (1991)	Nature scene slides (48)	Slides (48)	Immed.	Control, standard, and modified recognition of nature scenes, synonyms	Immed.	Influenced performance levels through manipulations of exposure time	Found misleading effect in each exp. condition, but effect varied depending on presentation rate and materials

(continues)

TABLE 4. *(continued)*

Author	Original event	Postevent information	Timing of misinformation	Measure(s) of memory	Timing of test	Special manipulation	Results
Ceci, Ross, and Toglia (1987)	Pictures plus narrative	Questions	1 day	Control, standard, and modified recognition tests	3 days	Varied time, age of subjects (ceiling effects with adults), presented information both verbally and pictorially, also used adult and child questioners	Reliable differences between standard and control groups; moderate performance w/modified test
Chandler (1991)	Nature scene slides (48)	Slides (48)	Immed.	Modified recognition test	Immed., 48 h	Pictorially presented information, tested pictorially as well; retroactive and proactive interference investigated	Found RI effect w/immed. condition but not delay; no PI effect
Chandler (1989)	Nature scene slides (48, 140)	Slides (48)	Immed.	Standard, modified recognition tests	Immed.	Varied similarity of pictures, changed presentation rate and study set size	Significant effects w/both tests; lower control performance associated w/smaller effect
Christiaansen and Ochalek (1983)	Diff. slide sequence (24)	Narrative	48 h	4-Alternative multiple choice test confidence ratings	48 h	Varied time of warning to subjects; immed./delay	Found difference for "biased" experimental group; no difference found if warned immed., delayed warning still was assoc. w/lower accuracy for exp. group
Cohen and Faulkner (1989)	Film	Narrative	Immed.	Exp. 2: recognition tests (18 multiple choice)	Immed.	Worked with subjects ranging from 25 to 82 years of age	Misinformation effects for all ages—older adults more likely to be influenced by misinformation—note that questions preserved the order of the events of the film
Davis and Schiffman (1985)	In vivo classroom experience (impromptu quasi experimental)	Questions	Immed. (misinf. contained in test)	Similar to Loftus's early work on misleading questions	Misled info. in test	Indefinite article vs. possessive pronoun	Higher "false alarm" rate w/possessive pronoun rather than with indefinite article (17.3% vs. 5.0%)

Study	Stimulus	Type	Timing	Test	Retention interval	Manipulation	Results
Dodson and Reisberg (1991)	M & Z slide sequence (79)	Narrative	Immed.	Initial accuracy test, Loftus's standard test, lexical decision task	Immed.	Used initial accuracy test before misleading narrative, tested Ss w/indirect test as well as standard test	Significant effect w/direct memory test, no differences w/indirect tests
Howe (1991)	Story	Questions or consistent or inconsistent statement	Immed.	Free recall	2 days, 9 days	Subjects were brought to criterion encoding level on the original informatio to accurately measure forgetting rates and apply mathematical model to distinguish storage from retrieval failure	Misinformation effects small but present; misled subjects exhibited higher rate of storage failures than of retrieval failures
Kroll, Ogawa, and Nieters (1988)	Diff. slide sequence (35)	Slides	Immed.	Y/N recognition test confidence ratings	Immed.	Random/sequential slide order and test order	Significant misinformation effect in Exp. 1 (random test question order)
Leippe, Romanczyk, and Manion (1991)	Actual personal experience	Questions	Immed. (misleading questions)	Free recall, 16 Y/N question, lineup recognition	Immed.	Three age groups (5/6, 9/10, college); actual experience w/researcher, involved memory for touch	Age differences; young children less likely than adults to be mislead by leading question re: touch & action; younger children gave less complete free recall responses and made more errors.
Lindsay and Johnson (1991)	Words presented on subjects left and right	Not misinformed	Immed.	Old/new recognition test, source monitoring test	Immed.	Subjects performed same or different orienting tasks w/word presentations on right and left	Subjects better discriminators when performing different orienting tasks rather than same task with different sets of words
Lindsay (1990)	M & Z slide sequence (79)	Audio tape plus written narrative	Immed. or 48 h	Cued recall	48 h	Discriminability of misinformation, high & low conditions	Found misleading information effect in low-discriminability condition
Lindsay and Johnson (1989)	Single slide from *Psychology Today*	Narrative	Immed.	Y/N recognition test, source monitoring test	Immed.	Type of test, instructions, degree of similarity	Misinformation effect w/Y/N recognition test but not w/source monitoring test

(continues)

TABLE 4. *(continued)*

Author	Original event	Postevent information	Timing of misinformation	Measure(s) of memory	Timing of test	Special manipulation	Results
Whaley (1988/1989)	M & Z slide sequence (39)	Narrative	Immed.	Standard and modified recognition tests	Immed.	Subjects took both standard and modified test	Accuracy on 2nd test depends on accuracy on 1st test; found misinformation effect w/standard test, not w/modified test
Loftus, Donders Hoffman, and Schooler (1989)	M & Z slide sequence (79)	Narrative	Immed.	Standard, modified recognition tests, response time, confidence ratings	Immed.	Measured response time; also varied narrative qualities by emphasizing physical appearance of different individuals (a maintenance man and a secretary)	Misinformation effect w/standard test, not w/modified test; control and misled subjects' response times different between tests
McSpadden, Schooler, and Loftus (1988)	Video tape sequence	Narrative	24 h	Cued recall	24 h	Tested guided memory techniques	Misinformation effect (misled condition less accurate)
Tousignant, Hall, and Loftus (1986)	Diff. slide sequence (24 pairs)	Narrative	Immed.	Standard recognition test, familiar or not, source judgments, reading rates, confidence ratings	Immed. (20 min. "delay")	Reading rates: measured "natural" rates, other experiments affected reading rates with differing instructions	Misinformation effect for test 1, slower reading rate assoc. w/better discrepancy detection, misinformed subjects faster and more confident on critical items
Loftus, Miller, and Burns (1978)	Loftus slide sequence (30)	Questions	Immed./delay (20 min, 1 day, 2 days, 1 week)	"Standard" recognition test, confidence ratings	20 min, 1 day, 2 days, 1 week	Misleading information in form of questionnaire	Different effect for misinformation at immed. presentation (monotonic decreasing effect) and delay (monotonic increasing); in other words, misleading information had a larger impact if presented just prior to the recognition test rather than just after the initial event
Loftus and Zanni (1975)	Film sequence	Questions	Immed.	Y/N recognition test	Immed.	Definite and indefinite article as variables in questions asked of subjects	Greater number of false recog. w/definite article

Study	Stimulus	Retention	Test	Retention	Features	Results
Bowman and Zaragoza (1989)	M & Z slides–Exp. 1 (76) Narrative–Exp. 2	Slides–Exp. 1 narrative–Exp. 2	Immed.	Standard and modified recognition tests	Immed.	Keep modality the same for original event and post-event	Misinformation effect w/standard test, not w/modified test; scores higher in general w/verbal materials
Zaragoza and Koshmider (1989)	M & Z slide sequence (79)	Narrative	Immed.	Standard recognition test "source" tests	Immed., 1 day	Attempted testing of Loftus's standard test, also used a version of source test	Significant effect w/standard test; no effect w/source test
Zaragoza, McCloskey, and Jamis (1987)	M & Z slide sequence	Narrative	Immed.	Cued recall, and standard recognition test	Immed.	Compared "cued recall" performance with standard test	Lack of misinformation effect in recall test; misinformation effect occurred with standard test
Zaragoza (1991)	Slides accompanied by narrative read aloud	Verbal summary read twice	Immed., 2 days	Standard and modified recognition tests, recall	Immed., 2 days	Worked with children ages 3–5	No differences between misled and control under any circumstances except with standard test; note that "no information" was provided in control condition
McCloskey and Zaragoza (1985)	M & Z slide sequence (79)	Narrative	Immed.	Modified recognition test	Immed.	Introduction of modified recognition test (target and new distractor)	No misinformation effect
Metcalfe (1990)	—	—	—	Standard and modified recognition tests	—	Simulated Loftus and M & Z experiments	Simulation: replicated McCloskey and Zaragoza and Loftus et al.'s results (significant difference w/standard test, no difference w/modified test)
Ryan and Geiselman (1991)	Films of crime scenario	Narrative	1 week	Recall, confidence ratings	Immed., 1 week	Looked at confidence and accuracy	Misled subjects more confident in incorrect than in correct responses
Tversky and Tuchin (1989)	M & Z slide sequence (78)	Narrative	Immed.	T/F recognition test, confidence ratings	Immed.	Y/N recognition task that included original, misleading and new items	Significant misinformation effects; misled confidence higher when incorrectly rejecting original, control group more accurate than misled (both groups equally good at rejecting new information)

[a] Number in parentheses indicates number of slides presented to subjects.

[b] McCloskey and Zaragoza's (1985) slide sequence and accompanying narrative.

context were coupled with other changes (e.g., in delay), and so effects are ambiguous. The lack of an isolable effect for context here parallels previous retroactive interference research that found few context effects when recognition tests were used (Baddeley, 1976).

Timing of Test

As the context studies again showed, immediate tests were less likely to detect misinformation effects. However, studies that incorporated long-term retention intervals have produced such effects. For example, Loftus et al. (1978), in a series of experiments, manipulated the time interval between the original event, misleading information, and final memory test. Their third experiment included delay intervals of 0 min, 20 min, 1 day, 2 days, and 1 week. Overall, longer intervals produced greater misinformation effects. Although Loftus et al. favored a storage-failure hypothesis (namely, that original events were altered or overwritten by misinformation), they acknowledged that original and misleading information might coexist in memory. In that case, misinformation effects could result from competition between traces.

Belli, Windschitl, McCarthy, and Winfrey (1992) examined the effect of delay using the modified test. They varied retention intervals from an immediate condition to one week. They replicated McCloskey and Zaragoza's findings under immediate conditions, but found poorer performance in misled subjects after a week. Belli et al. concluded that the sensitivity of the modified test to the effects of misleading information depended largely on delay. In particular, they argued that subjects' memories for original information were so strong under immediate conditions that they could successfully perform on the modified test despite interference from misinformation.

It should be noted that significant effects have been obtained on the modified test with short delays, albeit with different materials. Chandler (1991) found a significant effect with an immediate modified test, although she failed to find an effect after 48 h. Chandler did not manipulate the timing of the misleading information (as opposed to the timing of the memory test). Belli et al. (1992), who did find an effect of delay, presented both misleading information and the memory test after the delay. As we discuss later, effects of delayed memory tests depend on whether misleading information is also delayed. (The importance of the timing of postevent information is also stressed in Chapter 3, by Rovee-Collier & Boller, this volume.) Chandler may have found immediate differences also because, unlike earlier studies that presented a sequence of events, she presented similar nature scenes.

Nature of Misled Details

Timing also strengthened effects in other studies that manipulated the nature of the stimuli. In particular, Belli et al. (1992) questioned whether the peripheral location of the to-be-remembered details in McCloskey and Zaragoza's slides may have produced their null results. Consequently, they developed a new slide sequence that featured centrally presented details. Critical items, such as reading material (a book, newspaper, or magazine), playground equipment (slide, swings, or monkey bars), or a kitchen appliance (coffee maker, toaster, or blender) were used by a character in the series and occupied the central part of the field of view in the slide. They found robust misinformation effects for these salient details.

The concern about centrality was also expressed by Cassel and and Bjorklund (1992), who found that subjects recalled peripheral items (e.g., the color of a stolen bicycle) less frequently than they recalled thematically central items (e.g., who stole the bike). Cassel and Bjorklund suggested that these results were due to intrusions from "social or cultural prototypes of common objects" such as bicycle tires typically being black instead of red (the latter having been presented). Subjects were also more likely to be misled by suggestions regarding peripheral items compared with central ones. However, it should be noted that the term "centrality" was defined differently in the Belli et al. (1992) and Cassel and Bjorklund studies, so the results are not comparable.

Studies have also varied the extent to which subjects are misled about events. For example, Loftus and Palmer (1974) presented subjects with a film of a car accident, and asked them to estimate the speed of a car involved in the accident. However, the question regarding speed used the word "smashed" with one group of subjects and "hit" with the other group. Subjects responded to the former with higher speed estimates that were incorrect and, a week later, were more likely to mistakenly report broken glass at the scene of the accident. Similarly, Loftus and Zanni (1975) altered single words in the phase 2 questionnaire by referring to either "*a* broken headlight" or "*the* broken headlight." The indefinite article produced fewer false "yeses" and more "I don't know" responses. Thus, the degree to which questions are leading can alter the magnitude of misinformation effects.

There are, however, limits to subjects' susceptibility to misinformation. Loftus (1979) indicated that "blatantly incorrect" *misleading details* do not result in strong misinformation effects. In one experiment, slides were presented that depicted a thief lifting a red wallet out of a woman's purse. Shortly after seeing the slides, 98% of the subjects were misled that the wallet had been brown. However, all but two subjects selected *red* rather than *brown* on a memory test. Similarly, Loftus (1991) also reported that subjects were not susceptible to suggestions when the details involved were "blatant" rather than "non-blatant." The film used in this experiment depicted a shoplifting incident in which one of the stolen items was a candy bar. Regardless of whether the original detail was a Butterfinger or a Snickers bar, subjects easily rejected the incorrect alternative on the final test. Apparently, certain salient types of candy bars were resistant to interference.

Goodness of Event Encoding

As noted by Belli (1989), the nature of misinformation effects depends on whether subjects remember original information. From an information-processing perspective, however, remembering includes a variety of events, from encoding to retention. Most studies have not separated encoding failures from other sources of memory failure. However, studies have shown that misinformation effects can be obtained when original information has been successfully encoded. For example, Loftus et al. (1978) questioned whether subjects who had been misled about a yield sign had correctly encoded the initial stop sign. In a separate experiment, subjects saw the slide sequence and drew details on a diagram that represented the scene of the accident. Approximately half of the subjects correctly drew the traffic sign. Loftus et al. interpreted this as an indication that subjects did not have any trouble noticing and encoding the target sign. However, one could argue that half of the subjects might have failed to encode the critical item.

Indeed, as discussed earlier, an initial criticism of Loftus's design (McCloskey & Zaragoza, 1985) involved encoding. If subjects did not encode the original information, they might simply have used the misleading information to provide the missing piece in their memory. However, it has been pointed out by Belli et al. (1992), that even McCloskey and Zaragoza's critical event items ensured "less than perfect encoding" (p. 359). Because subjects might miss some critical details, this lack of encoding could preclude memory impairment for the obvious reason that there would be no memories to impair. In fact, Zaragoza and Koshmider (1989) supported this claim when they noted about their own experiment that ". . . it was necessary to focus subjects' attention on the critical item . . ." (p. 249). Subsequent studies have manipulated encoding levels and still found misinformation effects (e.g., Belli, 1989, 1993), indicating that encoding deficits are not the sole reason for misinformation effects.

Developmental Studies

Several studies that have incorporated the above-mentioned manipulations (e.g., encoding, order of testing, modified tests, delay intervals) have also examined developmental differences in the impact of misleading information (e.g., Cassel & Bjorklund, 1992; Ceci, Ross, & Toglia, 1987; Ceci, Toglia, & Ross, 1988; Howe, 1991; Warren & Hagood, in press). Children have shown misinformation effects but, like those with adults, effects are less reliable with the modified test (for a review, see Zaragoza, Dahlgren, & Muench, 1992).

There is some evidence that susceptibility to misinformation is greater in children and in older adults (although a number of studies have failed to find developmental differences; for a review, see Ceci & Bruck, 1993). For example, in a review of studies on aging and eyewitness memory, Adams-Price and Perlmutter (1992) suggest that older adults are more subject to schema-consistent (i.e., plausible) misinformation than are younger adults. Such developmental differences are consistent with contemporary interference theories, which generally assume that the ability to resist interference is lowest early and late in life (e.g., Bjorklund & Harnishfeger, 1990; Brainerd, Chapter 4, this volume; Dempster, 1992; Harnishfeger, Chapter 6, this volume; Hasher & Zacks, 1988; Reyna, Chapter 2, this volume).

A consistent trend across developmental studies is that the delay interval is of critical importance. Poole and White (1993) included one of the longest retention intervals in eyewitness memory research, two years. Over this period, children's error rates rose from 7% to 20%. In general, studies that find significant misinformation effects with children tend to present misleading information after a delay (see Reyna, Chapter 2, this volume).

However, interpretation of misinformation effects in children is especially subject to the criticism of encoding failure. That is, encoding failure is more likely for children than for adults, and so it is particularly important to control for levels of encoding in order to interpret developmental differences (Brainerd, Reyna, Howe, & Kingma, 1990). In one of the few studies in which such controls have been implemented, Howe (1991) equated initial encoding levels before measuring forgetting rates and found independence of age and misinformation effects.

THEORETICAL EXPLANATIONS OF MISINFORMATION EFFECTS

In summary, a number of researchers have investigated the conditions under which misinformation effects can be obtained, such as effects of the saliency of original and misleading details, similarities between the contexts in which details are presented (e.g., their modalities or sources), and various aspects of memory tests (e.g., the order of questions). The fact that variations in context, order of questions, and the like could reduce misinformation effects was typically interpreted as evidence against the memory alteration hypothesis.

In particular, McCloskey and Zaragoza (1985) questioned whether Loftus's misinformation effect was due to encoding failure or social conformity, as opposed to memory alteration. Therefore, they created the modified test, which offered a choice between novel and original items. In turn, other researchers criticized the sensitivity of the modified test in detecting changes in memory and provided alternative tests, such as Yes–No recognition tests (e.g., Belli, 1989; Tversky & Tuchin, 1989) and source monitoring tests (e.g., Lindsay & Johnson, 1989). Yes–No recognition tests and source monitoring tests have allowed researchers to distinguish more carefully among alternative explanations for misinformation effects, including misinformation acceptance, interference, and source misattribution or confusion. Factors such as discriminability between original and misleading contexts (effects of modalities, locations, order to test questions, etc.) have not produced consistent effects, however. Although effects of delay and so-called blatant memories suggest that memory strength might modulate misinformation effects, the nature of that effect (whether it is at storage, retrieval, or neither of these) is open to debate.

Information-processing explanations for misinformation effects fall into three categories: encoding failure, storage failure, and retrieval failure. Results regarding encoding failure are relatively clear. First, misinformation acceptance can occur because of encoding failure. Second, misinformation effects apparently also occur in the absence of encoding failure. Explaining the latter phenomenon has been problematic. Early explanations relied on concepts similar to those found in the older interference literature (Loftus, 1979). Storage-failure explanations, similar to unlearning explanations for forgetting, were contrasted with retrieval-failure explanations, such as trace competition or response competition (e.g., Chandler, 1989, 1991; Tversky & Tuchin, 1989). In addition, source confusions have been likened to list differentiation effects in interference theory (e.g., Bowman & Zaragoza, 1989; Lindsay & Johnson, 1989). More recently, a variety of storage and retrieval-failure explanations have been introduced. We will now summarize these explanations, and the evidence that bears on them.

Storage Failure

An early view was that misleading information entirely supersedes memory for the original event (overwriting). According to the principle of discrepancy detection, therefore, misinformation effects occurred to the extent that subjects did not remember the original information (e.g., Loftus & Hoffman, 1989). Explanations have since changed from a complete "overwriting" concept to a more inclusive definition: "Memory impairment could refer to a weakening of memory traces, or a clouding of memory, or an intrinsic impoverishment of memory. It could refer to . . . 'unlearning' . . . or to . . . 'disintegration' of features . . ." (Loftus & Hoffman, 1989, p. 101). Thus, memory impairments, in this sense, are storage failures because misleading information has altered or changed the memory trace of the original information.

Source misattribution, in which subjects fail to attribute a memory to its proper source, is a storage-failure explanation only in the sense that memory for source fails, rather than memory for the original event. In other words, subjects might remember the original information but mistakenly select the misleading detail as the item that they initially saw. Thus, misleading information might become attached to the wrong source "tag" in memory. Subjects might also simply be confused about the sources of their memories; for example, they might lack any clear memory about the sources of information, and assume that the misleading detail must have been in the original event. Such misinformation effects would be a function of *source monitoring* (e.g., Lindsay & Johnson, 1991), a judgment process "involved in the remembering of such things as where and when an event occurred, how it was perceived and who or what were involved in it" (p. 203).

The introduction of the concept of source monitoring has expanded theorists' ability to make distinctions among superficially similar misinformation effects, those due to misremembering information versus misremembering the sources of that information (see Reyna, Chapter 2, this volume). (Of course, the continued usefulness of such a concept will depend on the degree to which memory for source can be separated from memory for the event itself.) Research on source effects, like that on effects of modality and context, has also highlighted the issue of the distinctiveness of alternative memories. Effects of distinctiveness, however, have been contradictory.

For example, studies that have increased similarity between original and misleading contexts have sometimes produced reliable misinformation effects on modified tests (e.g., Chandler, 1991) and sometimes have not (e.g., Bowman & Zaragoza, 1989); variations in contextual similarity sometimes produce an effect (e.g., Lindsay, 1990) and sometimes do not (e.g., Bonto & Payne, 1991). In addition, some studies have reported results that oppose the distinctiveness hypothesis. Chandler (1993) increased temporal distinctiveness by lengthening the delay between original and "misleading" information (i.e., related distractors). Contrary to predictions by Lindsay (1990), higher discriminability produced larger misinformation effects. Although the role of contextual distinctiveness in misinformation effects is not yet fully understood, theorists must reckon with the fact that memory is not a wholesale phenomenon that either includes or excludes the substance of events as well as their source and other contextual details.

Other "changed trace" hypotheses (e.g., Chandler, 1991) have been proposed including blending (Belli, 1988; Chandler, 1989; Metcalfe, 1990) and convergence (Chandler, 1989). These are similar in that they posit a mingling of original and misleading information such that the new memory resembles both original and misled detail but matches neither. For example, Belli (1988) tested memory for color and Chandler (1989, 1991) tested memory for environmental scenery. This kind of misleading information allows for a continuum of responses along which subjects could store an intermediate value (e.g., a yellow-green color), as opposed to distinctive details for which a compromise value would be unlikely (i.e., a hammer and a screwdriver). Belli (1988), for example, found that subjects misrecognized blends of original and suggested colors.

Others, although not specifying any particular mechanism, have argued that storage-failure accounts remain viable (e.g., Belli, 1989; Belli et al., 1992; Lindsay & Johnson, 1989; Tousignant, Hall, & Loftus, 1986; Tversky &

Tuchin, 1989) because misinformation effects can be obtained despite the presence of such factors as maintaining the order of memory questions, presenting original and misleading information in the same modality, the use of modified tests, the use of immediate as opposed to delayed tests, and so on. Theorists generally acknowledge, however, that these effects cannot be uniquely attributed to storage failure, as opposed to one of the following retrieval explanations.

Retrieval Failure

Because of the lack of misinformation effects under enhanced retrieval conditions for original information, some researchers have favored retrieval-failure accounts. Such accounts include various coexistence hypotheses (that original and misleading traces coexist, but recency or the absence of cues for the original trace favors retrieval of misleading traces) (Bonto & Payne, 1991; Bowers & Bekerian, 1984; Chandler, 1991; Christiaansen & Ochalek, 1983; Tversky & Tuchin, 1989) and blocking (Chandler, 1991; but see Belli, 1993; Belli et al., 1994). Specifically, Bowers and Bekerian (1984; Bekerian & Bowers, 1983) describe a feature-matching process that facilitates access to original information by thematic cuing and access to the more recently presented misinformation when these cues are absent. Christiaansen and Ochalek (1983) speculate that accessibility to the newer information is increased because it has become part of an "organized schema, which can serve as a retrieval network" (p. 474).

However, Chandler (1991) presents evidence against memory alteration as well as coexistence. First, memory alteration is an unlikely explanation for her misinformation effects because the effects did not persist over a two-day interval. Second, the absence of proactive interference (in addition to retroactive interference) argues against a simple trace-competition hypothesis. In other words, original traces should have competed with misleading traces, as well as the other way around. Instead, she proposed a blocking hypothesis where retrieval of a competing trace prevents access to the other trace, as opposed to a more general retrieval-failure hypothesis that one of several coexisting traces is retrieved. However, Belli (1993) reported evidence against blocking, including that subjects who retrieved misleading memories on an interpolated test did not subsequently show bigger misinformation effects.

Nonmemory Explanations

In contrast to storage and retrieval failures in memory for the original event, some theorists favor "nonmemory" explanations for misinformation effects. Nonmemory factors include confidence, knowledge, and credibility of witnesses and interviewers, as well as the social compliance and conformity effects mentioned earlier (e.g., McCloskey & Zaragoza, 1985).

Wells and colleagues (Wells, 1993; Wells & Turtle, 1986, 1987) have focused on presentation factors related to eyewitness identification (e.g., the effect of lineup and photospread composition and format), but have also discussed the "malleability of certainty" (Wells, 1993) and the relation of certainty to accuracy (Wells, 1984). For example, an eyewitness, after tentatively identifying a person as a perpetrator of a crime, later finds out that the person was apprehended with stolen goods. This can inflate the eyewitness's certainty in the identification without any improvement in memory. This increased confidence can, in turn, influence jurors' judgments about the credibility of the eyewitness because of the well-documented public perception that confidence and accuracy are strongly related. In contrast to this "intuitive theory of eyewitness testimony" (Wells, 1993; Wells & Turtle, 1987), experimental work has revealed that confidence is not a reliable cue to accuracy (e.g., Loftus, 1979; Loftus et al., 1978, 1989).

Confidence of interviewers, as well as knowledgeability, can also predict the degree of misinformation effects. For example, Toglia, Ross, Ceci, and Hembrooke (1992) and Ceci et al. (1987) directly manipulated social compliance influences on children's suggestibility. They varied the credibility of an adult interviewer who, in introductory remarks before questioning, indicated familiarity or unfamiliarity with the story to which the children had been exposed. The results indicated that children were more frequently misled by a credible interviewer than by one whom they saw as uninformed (Toglia et al., 1992). They also varied the age of the interviewer who provided misleading information and found younger children to be less influenced by other children than by adults. Therefore, Ceci et al. (1987) and Toglia et al. (1992) concluded that "prestige factors" including age and perceived authority do influence misinformation effects, although they are not solely responsible for the effects.

Similar findings have been obtained in studies with adults. Smith and Ellsworth's (1987) subjects watched a film and were questioned either by a knowledgeable or naive interviewer. Misled subjects' error rates were worse when they perceived the interviewer to be knowledgeable. On the other hand, "naive" interrogators were unable to misinform subjects. Smith and Ellsworth proposed that misinformation effects could be explained by social factors. However, they noted that these social factors were particularly influential with "difficult" items. That is, items that were harder for subjects to remember were more subject to misinformation. Thus, social factors interacted with cognitive factors, such as memory strength.

Interpretation of Factors Affecting Misinformation

Because misinformation effects can be eliminated by changing the nature of testing, some investigators have concluded that retrieval failure best explains misinformation effects (e.g., Bekerian & Bowers, 1983; Bowers &

Bekerian, 1984). Although cues can facilitate recognition of original information, there is still evidence for impairment by misleading information (Cohen & Faulkner, 1989). For instance, studies using long delay intervals and centrally presented details result in effects even with the modified test. Efforts to ensure encoding and to reduce opportunities for social compliance have failed to eliminate misinformation effects. Finally, the interpretation of so-called retrieval cues is open to question. Reinstating the order of events, for example, especially in a recognition test, may help subjects redintegrate or *re-store* forgotten elements of a trace (e.g., Brainerd et al., 1990; Reyna, 1992). Recovery of memories, then, does not unambiguously imply that misinformation effects were the result of retrieval failure.

In conclusion, the mixed findings and assortment of explanations indicate that manipulations have been unable to disentangle the relative contributions of storage and retrieval failures. As Belli et al. (1992) point out, "misinformation effects . . . extend viability to all versions . . . including substitution" (p. 365). Indeed, different phenomena may be present in different studies. For example, delaying misleading information, which tends to consistently augment misinformation effects (e.g., Chandler, 1993) has been associated with smaller effects (e.g., Lindsay, 1990). What is needed is a theoretical approach that can consolidate this plethora of evidence under a unifying perspective.

Fuzzy-Trace Theory

Fuzzy-trace theory is a comprehensive theory of reasoning, remembering, and their relationship. We will not review the evidence for the theory (but see Reyna, 1992, Chapter 2, this volume) nor all of its assumptions (e.g., Reyna & Brainerd, 1991, 1992) here. There are, however, four tenets of the theory that are particularly relevant to the interpretation of misinformation effects. These tenets concern: (1) the nature of gist versus verbatim memory representations; (2) the independence of gist and verbatim memories; (3) the nature of forgetting (as the disintegration of traces); and (4) the differential forgetting rates for gist and verbatim memories. A number of researchers have used these tenets to explain misinformation effects in children and adults (e.g., Brainerd, in press; Brainerd & Ornstein, 1991; Cassel & Bjorklund, 1992; Ceci & Bruck, 1993; Poole & White, 1993, in press; Reyna, 1992, Chapter 2, this volume; Reyna & Kiernan, 1994; Warren & Hagood, in press).

As noted above, researchers have appealed to such knowledge structures as themes, schemas, or scripts to explain a variety of effects (e.g., of maintaining the original order of events). Cassel and Bjorklund (1992) and Ceci and Bruck (1993), in particular, have discussed the effects of different kinds of "misinformation," that which is compatible with knowledge structures versus contradictory details. Most memory researchers have stressed that memory for the substance of events is enhanced when subjects can rely on organized knowledge structures (e.g., Reyna & Kiernan, 1994; Schwartz & Reisberg, 1991).

However, memory for the substance of events may or may not be helpful in guarding against misinformation effects (e.g., Ceci & Bruck, 1993). As we have seen, misinformation manipulations typically involve specific details. So, for example, subjects might be misinformed about the tool used to break into an office (e.g., whether it was a hammer or a screwdriver, McCloskey & Zaragoza, 1985) or the color of a car involved in an accident (e.g., Loftus, Levidow, & Duensing, 1992). According to fuzzy-trace theory, the ability to misinform subjects about such details should depend on the nature of their memory for original events, gist or verbatim.

Traditionally, "gist," or memory for substance, has been distinguished from memory for exact surface details of experience. Psycholinguists, for instance, use the term "gist" to refer to the essence of semantic content, as opposed to verbatim memory for exact wording (e.g., Clark & Clark, 1977). In fuzzy-trace theory, this distinction has been extended to forms of information other than verbal, including numerical information (e.g., Reyna & Brainerd, 1993). When subjects experience an event, it is assumed that they lay down traces of both types, roughly in parallel (Reyna & Brainerd, 1992). Verbatim representations are not necessarily complete copies of experience; some information is not encoded, especially because encoding of verbatim information is susceptible to interference from cognitive outputs (Brainerd & Reyna, 1993; Reyna & Brainerd, 1989, 1993). If subjects have encoded verbatim representations of presented information, however, and those memories are accessible, subjects should be resistant to effects of misleading details. The specificity of verbatim representations, then, should reduce acceptance of contradictory details.

If subjects rely on gist, on the other hand, misleading details do not necessarily contradict subjects' memories. Therefore, subjects might accept such misinformation because it is compatible with the substance of what they remember. Furthermore, as Reyna (Chapter 2, this volume) discusses in some detail, gist and verbatim memories seem to be functionally independent. Thus, it is possible for subjects to accept misinformation, by relying on gist, despite accurate verbatim memories for original information (see also Reyna & Kiernan, 1994).

Which representation subjects rely on, verbatim or gist, depends on forgetting (e.g., Poole & White, 1993; Warren & Hagood, in press). An assumption of fuzzy-trace theory, one that has been amply documented in the psycholinguistic literature, is that forgetting rates are higher for verbatim (as opposed to gist) representations. Therefore, subjects are more likely to rely on verbatim representations immediately after original information is presented, but shift to gist after a delay (Reyna & Kiernan, in press).

Finally, in fuzzy-trace theory, forgetting is not an all-or-none loss of a trace. Instead, forgetting is the gradual disintegration of the features of a memory. As forgetting occurs, there are thresholds in the process of disintegration that can be identified as "retrieval failure" and "storage failure," respectively (Brainerd et al., 1990; Reyna, 1992). Traces that have fallen below the storage-failure threshold can, nevertheless, be redintegrated (or re-stored); estimates of the probabilities of restorage, retrieval relearning, and so on, have been made using Markov models (e.g., Brainerd et al., 1990). The key aspect of this assumption that we will invoke here is that pieces of a trace can become dissociated from one another as a result of forgetting.

From these four assumptions, it is possible to predict the kinds of interactions between original and misleading information that could be observed, as well as the effects of manipulations on those interactions. First, direct blocking between original and misleading details should be observed under immediate conditions. That is, when original and misleading information are presented close together in time, and memory is tested immediately thereafter, verbatim memories can directly compete with one another. Subjects might accept misleading information because they judge it to be more credible, or because they fail to remember the source of the original information. When verbatim memories for the events are both still accessible, however, their specificity forces an either–or choice between them. Chandler's (1991) data are clearly consistent with this account; blocking was detected on an immediate test, but disappeared after a delay.

After a delay, or an interpolated task that interferes with verbatim memory, however, original verbatim memories are gradually forgotten. Verbatim memory for misleading information (usually presented closer in time to the memory test) can support misinformation acceptance to the degree that original verbatim memories have faded. This is no more than the principle of discrepancy detection, except that verbatim memories are stipulated (the principle does not apply to verbatim and gist memories for the same event because they are not usually discrepant in misinformation research). Thus, intermediate delays between original information and the memory test (to avoid floor or ceiling effects for original memories) and more recent presentation of misleading information should favor observing a negative relation between the accuracy of original verbatim memories and the acceptance of misleading details. Most misinformation studies fit this kind of scenario. Delays are sufficient, or interpolated tasks are sufficiently interfering, that some forgetting of original verbatim information occurs: misinformation is accepted to the degree that original verbatim traces have faded (e.g., Cassel & Bjorklund, 1992; Ceci & Bruck, 1993; Titcomb & Reyna, 1993; Warren & Hagood, in press) or were never stably stored in the first place (e.g., Belli, 1989, Experiment 1). It is interesting to note that tests presented early after original information tend to "inoculate" children and adults against subsequent misinformation, in line with other research on fuzzy-trace theory (see Brainerd, in press; Warren & Hagood, in press).

It should be noted that storage failure for original verbatim traces is not necessary to obtain misinformation effects. Retrieval of gist, for example, can occur even under immediate testing conditions, given the right cuing conditions, despite accurate original verbatim memories (Ackerman, 1992; Brainerd & Reyna, in press; Reyna, Chapter 2, this volume; Reyna & Kiernan, 1994). It is plausible that subjects could similarly be cued to respond with misleading information, regardless of the state of their original memories. In that case a negative relation would not be obtained between misleading and original memories. Thus, the prevalence of larger misinformation effects with delay in both the adult and developmental literatures indicates that forgetting of original verbatim information is typically a feature of misinformation effects. But, research on retrieval effects in other domains suggests that it is possible to achieve misinformation effects that are not due to forgetting and, instead, are due to retrieval cues (Reyna, Chapter 2, this volume).

After long delays (e.g., two years in Poole & White, 1993), it is likely that verbatim information has been forgotten, and subjects have access to gist (although even gist is forgotten, but at a slower rate than verbatim information). The effort to make sense of one's experience or to assign guilt or innocence may foster the tendency to rely on an interpreted (or gistlike) account of events (e.g., Pennington & Hastie, 1993). If original and misleading information conflict substantively, for example, about thematically central events, the acceptance of one interpretation of events might depend on the rejection of the other interpretation, but this has not been explicitly investigated (but see Ceci & Bruck, 1993, for some interesting speculation). In the problem-solving literature, competition between alternative gist representations for problem information has been demonstrated (Reyna, Chapter 2, this volume).

Also after a delay, traces should become disintegrated so that it is possible to forget such aspects of an experience as its source, while remembering others. For example, it should be possible to remember the exact words of a quotation without necessarily remembering the exact circumstances of having learned it. Moreover, source as it has been instantiated in experiments is typically a verbatim aspect of an event (Reyna, Chapter 2, this volume). Therefore, as Reyna (Chapter 2, this volume) argues, source should be forgotten more quickly than the substance of information, which should lead to misinformation effects. Tests for the substance of events would be expected to produce different findings than tests that stressed verbatim information, as found by Lindsay and Johnson (1989). (However, this interpretation of the latter study is speculative because event vs. source tests, as well as central vs. peripheral questions [Cassel & Bjorklund, 1992] and general vs. specific questions [Poole & White, in press], do not map precisely onto the gist–verbatim distinction.)

Although forgetting causes traces to disintegrate, they can be redintegrated, for example, by repeated questioning (Brainerd & Ornstein, 1991). Thus, it is possible that source and event information can become redintegrated. Warren and Hagood (in press) replicated the repeated-questioning effect using a misinformation paradigm. After receiving the original and then the misleading information, subjects were given neutral questions about the original events. They showed significantly smaller misinformation effects, compared to subjects who had received no questions after the original event. Similarly, Belli (1993) found that misinformation effects were not detectable on a final memory test after an interpolated recall test for original events (Experiment 1).

Thus, the magnitude of misinformation effects has been linked to forgetting of original events (e.g., Brainerd, in press; Reyna, 1992). Delaying misleading information increases its impact because original information has been forgotten (e.g., Chandler, 1994). Delaying the memory test, as opposed to the misleading information, ultimately reduces misinformation effects, but this, too, is attributable to forgetting. Because forgetting curves are negatively accelerated, memory for original and misled items will converge after a delay, wiping out misinformation effects detected on earlier tests (e.g., Chandler, 1991; Reyna, Chapter 2, this volume).

When subjects receive immediate tests for original events, which reduces forgetting, later misinformation manipulations have smaller effects (Warren & Hagood, in press). Repeated questioning after a delay also combats the effects of forgetting: memory performance improves (and misinformation effects decrease) on repeated tests (e.g., Poole & White, 1993). Although one might speculate that repeated questioning could cause subjects to infer that their initial answers were incorrect (and therefore reduce the accuracy of subsequent recall), this does not seem to be the case (for reviews, see Brainerd, in press; Poole & White, in press). In short, the kinds of effects described in basic memory research have been replicated in the misinformation paradigm.

SUMMARY

Given the vast amount of research on misinformation effects in memory, it is necessary to (1) identify those factors that are known to contribute substantially to such effects and (2) develop theoretical explanations that take these factors into account. Our review identified three major classes of factors. First, memory strength for original events affects susceptibility to subsequent misinformation. Salient events that are easily remembered are difficult to misinform (e.g., Loftus, 1979, 1991). In addition, memory can be strengthened by immediate tests prior to misinformation and by repeated tests after misinformation (e.g., Warren & Hagood, in press). On the other hand, weaker memories, for example, after a delay, are easier to misinform (e.g., Reyna, Chapter 2, this volume). Memory can also be weak because subjects failed to encode original information. In that case, misinformation does not interfere with original memories (because they never existed), but subjects are more likely to accept misinformation (e.g., Belli, 1989).

The detection of misinformation effects, however, crucially depends on a second class of factors, the nature of memory tests. On standard tests, subjects choose between original and misled items. As McCloskey and Zaragoza (1985) argued, differences between misled and control groups might be due to social compliance or to failure to encode original events (i.e., misinformation acceptance). The modified test addressed these problems because it omitted the misled item; instead, subjects chose between original and novel items. Subjects could not comply because the misled item was not offered, and failure to encode original information would depress performance in both misled and control groups, making differences smaller (e.g., Chandler, 1989).

The sensitivity of the modified test was challenged, however. Research with children and adults showed that misinformation effects could be detected with the modified test, but effects were less reliable, compared with the standard test (e.g., Ceci & Bruck, 1993). As Brainerd and Reyna (1988) and Tversky and Tuchin (1989) noted, knowing what one had not seen (i.e., detecting novelty) was sufficient to select the correct item on the modified test. Belli (1989) and Tversky and Tuchin (1989) used Yes–No recognition tests to detect more subtle memory interference effects. Studies showed that misled subjects were more likely to reject original information, even when the misled item was not tested and even under enhanced encoding conditions (e.g.., Belli, 1989; Belli et al., 1992).

Yes–No recognition tests were also compared with tests that focus on the sources of information, and the latter elicited smaller misinformation effects (e.g., Lindsay & Johnson, 1989). Although source misattributions seems to contribute to misinformation effects (e.g., Belli, Lindsay, Gales, & McCarthy, in press), the underlying mechanisms for such effects are not fully understood. Source confusions ought to increase when original and misleading events are less discriminable (e.g., Lindsay, 1990). However, greater similarity between the contexts or modalities in which original and misled details were presented has not been reliably associated with larger misinformation effects (e.g., Bonto & Payne, 1991; Bowman & Zaragoza, 1989), and some findings have disconfirmed predictions based on distinctiveness (e.g., Chandler, 1994). Indeed, original and misled details are routinely presented in different modalities, and robust misinformation effects are obtained.

Finally, social factors also influence misinformation effects. The prestige or knowledge (and, perhaps, confidence) of those who present misinformation affect the degree to which such information is accepted (e.g., Ceci et al., 1987; Toglia et al., 1992). However misinformation effects remain when social compliance is minimized (e.g., by using the modified test) and when sources of misinformation have low or unknown credibility. Misled subjects report high confidence for erroneous memories, and measures that should detect conscious deliberation (e.g., response times) do not differ for misled versus control items (e.g., Belli et al., 1994; Loftus et al., 1989).

Thus, the literature indicates that, although social factors do play a role in misinformation acceptance, effects on memory seem to be real. Consistent with this conclusion, misinformation effects are associated with variations in memory strength. Although memorial factors have been identified that have consistent effects, by themselves, these factors do not allow us to distinguish between storage versus retrieval explanations. For example, reinstating the original order of events at test reduces misinformation effects, relative to randomized testing. This reduction in misinformation effects could occur because of improved retrieval conditions or because re-presentation of order information allows original traces to be redintegrated (e.g., Reyna, 1992). Hypotheses about storage impairment, ranging from overwriting to alteration, and varieties of retrieval explanations, including coexistence and blocking, are compatible with effects that have been observed. None of these explanations, however, encompasses all of the findings.

Although the literature on misinformation effects does not uniquely favor specific storage or retrieval explanations, other memory research with related paradigms provides a coherent framework for these effects. In particular, four tenets of fuzzy-trace theory can be used to organize these results: that gist and verbatim representations of events function independently, that these representations vary in specificity and in forgetting rates, and that forgetting consists of the disintegration of these representations (e.g., Reyna & Brainerd, 1992). Thus, misinformation effects resemble a collection of phenomena that have been distinguished in basic memory research (e.g., Brainerd et al., 1990). Specifically, the memory-strength effects that have been summarized here, of salience, delay, immediate testing, repeated testing, and so on, replicate well-known effects in the memory literature (e.g., Brainerd, in press).

For instance, susceptibility to misinformation (typically verbatim details) depends on factors affecting forgetting of original verbatim memories. Hence, factors that increase forgetting increase misinformation effects. Although gist representations of original events are accessible for longer periods of time, they lack specificity, and so they do not necessarily contradict misleading details. As original events are forgotten, elements such as source can become dissociated from other aspects of the events. To the degree that source memories are verbatim, they will be forgotten more rapidly than will the substance of events, producing confusions on later memory tests. Although models of forgetting indicate that verbatim memories can be redintegrated, even after long delays, the challenge in practice will be to distinguish actual memories that have been successfully redintegrated from reconstructions based on gist (Reyna, 1992; Titcomb & Reyna, 1992).

REFERENCES

Ackerman, B. P. (1992). The sources of children's errors in judging causal inferences. *Journal of Experimental Child Psychology, 54*, 90–119.

Adams-Price, C., & Perlmutter, M. (1992). Eyewitness memory and aging research: A case study in everyday memory. In R. L. West & J. D. Sinnott (Eds.), *Everyday memory and aging: Current research and methodology* (pp. 246–258). New York: Springer-Verlag.

Baddeley, A. (1976). *The psychology of memory.* New York: Basic Books.

Bekerian, D. A., & Bowers, J. A. (1983). Eyewitness testimony: Were we misled? *Journal of Experimental Psychology: Learning, Memory, and Cognition, 9,* 139–145.

Bell, B. E., & Loftus, E. F. (1988). Degree of detail of eyewitness testimony and mock juror judgments. *Journal of Applied Social Psychology, 18,* 1171–1192.

Bell, B. E., & Loftus, E. F. (1989). Trivial persuasion in the courtroom: The power of (a few) minor details. *Journal of Personality and Social Psychology, 56,* 669–679.

Belli, R. F. (1988). Color blend retrievals: Compromise memories or deliberate compromise responses? *Memory & Cognition, 16,* 314–326.

Belli, R. F. (1989). Influences of misleading postevent information: Misinformation interference and acceptance. *Journal of Experimental Psychology: General, 118,* 72–85.

Belli, R. F. (1993). Failures of interpolated tests in inducing memory impairment with final modified tests: Evidence unfavorable to the blocking hypothesis. *American Journal of Psychology, 106,* 407–427.

Belli, R. F., Lindsay, D. S., Gales, M. S., & McCarthy, T. T. (1994). Memory impairment and source misattribution in postevent misinformation experiments with short retention intervals. *Memory & Cognition, 22,* 40–54.

Belli, R. F., Windschitl, P. D., McCarthy, T. T., & Winfrey, S. E. (1992). Detecting memory impairment with a modified test procedure: Manipulating retention interval with centrally presented event items. *Journal of Experimental Psychology: Learning, Memory, and Cognition, 18,* 356–367.

Bjorklund, D. F., & Harnishfeger, K. K. (1990). The resources construct in cognitive development: Diverse sources of evidence and a theory of inefficient inhibition. *Developmental Review, 10,* 48–71.

Bonto, M. A., & Payne, D. G. (1991). Role of environmental context in eyewitness memory. *American Journal of Psychology, 104,* 117–134.

Bowers, J. M., & Bekerian, D. A. (1984). When will postevent information distort eyewitness testimony? *Journal of Applied Psychology, 69,* 466–472.

Bowman, L. L., & Zaragoza, M. S. (1989). Similarity of encoding context does not influence resistance to memory impairment following misinformation. *American Journal of Psychology, 102,* 249–264.

Brainerd, C. J. (in press). Children's forgetting, with implications for memory suggestibility. In N. L. Stein, P. A. Ornstein, B. Tversky, & C. J. Brainerd (Eds.), *Memory for everyday and emotional events.* Hillsdale, NJ: Erlbaum.

Brainerd, C. J., & Ornstein, P. A. (1991). Children's memory for witnessed events: The developmental backdrop. In J. Doris (Ed.), *The suggestibility of children's recollections* (pp. 10–20). Washington, DC: American Psychological Association.

Brainerd, C. J., & Reyna, V. F. (1988). Memory loci of suggestibility development: Comment on Ceci, Ross, and Toglia (1987). *Journal of Experimental Psychology: General, 117,* 197–200.

Brainerd, C. J., & Reyna, V. F. (1993). Memory independence and memory interference in cognitive development. *Psychological Review, 100,* 42–67.

Brainerd, C. J., & Reyna, V. F. (in press). Autosuggestibility in memory development. *Cognitive Psychology.*

Brainerd, C. J., Reyna, V. F., Howe, M. L., & Kingma, J. (1990). The development of forgetting and reminiscence. *Monographs of the Society for Research in Child Development, 55* (3–4, Serial No. 222).

Cassel, W. S., & Bjorklund, D. F. (1992). *Developmental patterns of eyewitness memory and suggestibility: An ecologically based short-term longitudinal study.* Manuscript submitted for publication.

Ceci, S. J., & Bruck, M. (1993). Suggestibility of the chile witness: A historical review and synthesis. *Psychological Bulletin, 113*, 403–439.

Ceci, S. J., Ross, D. F., & Toglia, M. P. (1987). Suggestibility of children's memory: Psycholegal implications. *Journal of Experimental Psychology: General, 116*, 38–49.

Ceci, S. J., Toglia, M. P., & Ross, D. F. (1988). On remembering . . . more or less: A trace strength interpretation of developmental differences in suggestibility. *Journal of Experimental Psychology: General, 117*, 201–203.

Chandler, C. C. (1989). Specific retroactive interference in modified recognition tests: Evidence for unknown cause of interference. *Journal of Experimental Psychology: Learning, Memory, and Cognition, 15*, 256–265.

Chandler, C. C. (1991). How memory for an event is influenced by related events: Interference in modified recognition tests. *Journal of Experimental Psychology: Learning, Memory, and Cognition, 17*, 115–125.

Chandler, C. C. (1994). Accessing related events increases retroactive interference in a matching recognition test. *Journal of Experimental Psychology: Learning, Memory, and Cognition, 19*, 967–974.

Christiaansen, R. E., & Ochalek, K. (1983). Editing misleading information from memory: Evidence for the coexistence of original and postevent information. *Memory & Cognition, 11*, 467–475.

Clark, H. H., & Clark, E. V. (1977). *Psychology and language.* New York: Harcourt Brace Jovanovich.

Cohen, G., & Faulkner, D. (1989). Age differences in source forgetting: Effects on reality monitoring and eyewitness testimony. *Psychology & Aging, 4*, 10–17.

Davis, J., & Schiffman, H. R. (1985). The influence of the wording of interrogatives on the accuracy of eyewitness recollections. *Bulletin of the Psychonomic Society, 23*, 394–396.

Dempster, F. N. (1992). The rise and fall of the inhibitory mechanism: Toward a unified theory of cognitive development and aging. *Developmental Review, 12*, 45–75.

Dodson, C., & Reisberg, D. (1991). Indirect testing of eyewitness memory: The (non)effect of misinformation. *Bulletin of the Psychonomic Society, 29*, 333–336.

Hasher, L., & Zacks, R. T. (1988). Working memory, comprehension, and aging: A review and a new view. In G. H. Bower (Ed.), *The psychology of learning and motivation* (Vol. 22, pp. 193–225). San Diego: Academic Press.

Howe, M. L. (1991). Misleading children's story recall: Forgetting and reminiscence of the facts. *Developmental Psychology, 27*, 746–762.

Kroll, N. E. A., Ogawa, K. H., & Nieters, J. E. (1988). Eyewitness memory and the importance of sequential information. *Bulletin of the Psychonomic Society, 26*, 395–398.

Johnson, M. K., Hashtroudi, S., & Lindsay, D. S. (1993). Source monitoring. *Psychological Bulletin, 114*, 3–28.

Leippe, M. R., Romanczyk, A., & Manion, A. P. (1991). Eyewitness memory for a touching experience: Accuracy differences between child and adult witnesses. *Journal of Applied Psychology, 76*, 367–379.

Lindsay, D. S. (1990). Misleading suggestions can impair eyewitness' ability to remember event details. *Journal of Experimental Psychology: Learning, Memory, and Cognition, 16*, 1077–1083.

Lindsay, D. S., & Johnson, M. F. (1989). The eyewitness suggestibility effect and memory for source. *Memory & Cognition, 17*, 349–358.

Lindsay, D. S., & Johnson, M. K. (1991). Recognition memory and source monitoring. *Bulletin of the Psychonomic Society, 29*, 203–205.

Loftus, E. F. (1979). *Eyewitness testimony.* Cambridge: Harvard University Press.

Loftus, E. F. (1991). Made in memory: Distortions in recollection after misleading information. In G. H. Bower (Ed.), *The psychology of learning and motivation: Advances in research and theory* (pp. 187–215). San Diego: Academic Press.

Loftus, E. F., Donders, K., Hoffman, H. G., & Schooler, J. W. (1989). Creating new memories that are quickly accessed and confidently held. *Memory & Cognition, 17*, 607–616.

Loftus, E. F., & Hoffman, H. G. (1989). Misinformation and memory: The creation of new memories. *Journal of Experimental Psychology: General, 118*, 100–104.

Loftus, E. F., Levidow, B., & Duensing, S. (1992). Who remembers best? Individual differences in memory for events that occurred in a science museum. *Applied Cognitive Psychology, 6*, 93–107.

Loftus, E. F., Miller, D. G., & Burns, H. J. (1978). Semantic integration of verbal information into visual memory. *Journal of Experimental Psychology, 4*, 19–31.

Loftus, E. F., & Palmer, J. C. (1974). Reconstruction of automobile destruction: An example of the interaction between language and memory. *Journal of Verbal Learning and Verbal Behavior, 13*, 585–589.

Loftus, E. F., & Zanni, G. (1975). Eyewitness testimony: The influence of the wording of a question. *Bulletin of the Psychonomic Society, 5*, 86–88.

McCloskey, M., & Zaragoza, M. S. (1985). Misleading postevent information and memory for events: Arguments and evidence against memory impairment hypotheses. *Journal of Experimental Psychology: General, 114*, 1–16.

McSpadden, M. D., Schooler, J. W., & Loftus, E. F. (1988). Here today, gone tomorrow: The appearance and disappearance of context effects. In G. M. Davies & D. M. Thomson (Eds.), *Memory in context: Context in memory* (pp. 215–229). Chichester: Wiley.

Metcalfe, J. (1990). Compostie holographic associative recall model (CHARM) and blended memories in eyewitness testimony. *Journal of Experimental Psychology: General, 119*, 145–160.

Pennington, N., & Hastie, R. (1993). The story model for juror decision making. In R. Hastie (Ed.), *Inside the juror: The psychology of juror decision making* (pp. 192–221). New York: Cambridge University Press.

Poole, C. A., & White, L. T. (1993). Two years later: Effects of question repetition and retention interval on the eyewitness testimony of children and adults. *Developmental Psychology, 29*, 844–853.

Poole, C. A., & White, L. T. (in press). Tell me again and again: Stability and change in the repeated testimonies of children and adults. In M. Zaragoza (Ed.), *Memory, suggestibility, and eyewitness testimony in children and adults.* New York: Harper & Row.

Reyna, V. F. (1992). Reasoning, remembering, and their relationship: Social, cognitive, and developmental issues. In M. Howe, C. J. Brainerd, & V. F. Reyna (Eds.) *Development of long-term retention* (pp. 103–132). New York: Springer-Verlag.

Reyna, V. F., & Brainerd, C. J. (1989). Output interference, generic resources, and cognitive development. *Journal of Experimental Child Psychology, 47*, 42–46.

Reyna, V. F., & Brainerd, C. J. (1991). Fuzzy-trace theory and children's acquisition of mathematical and scientific concepts. *Learning and Individual Differences, 3*, 27–59.

Reyna, V. F., & Brainerd, C. J. (1992). A fuzzy-trace theory of reasoning and remembering: Patterns, paradoxes, and parallelism. In A. F. Healy, S. A. Kosslyn, & R. M. Shifrin (Eds.), *From learning precesses to cognitive processes: Essays in honor of William K. Estes* (pp. 235–260). Hillsdale, NJ: Erlbaum.

Reyna, V. F., & Brainerd, C. J. (1993). Fuzzy memory and mathematics in the classroom. In G. M. Davies & R. H. Logie (Eds.), *Memory in everyday life* (pp. 91–119). London: North-Holland.

Reyna, V. F., & Kiernan, B. (1994). The development of gist versus verbatim memory in sentence recognition: Effects of lexical familiarity, semantic content, encoding instructions, and retention interval. *Developmental Psychology, 30*, 178–191.

Ryan, R. H., & Geiselman, R. E. (1991). Effects of biased information on the relationship between eyewitness confidence and accuracy. *Bulletin of the Psychonomic Society, 29*, 7–9.

Schwartz, R., & Reisberg, D. (1991). *Learning and memory.* New York: Norton.

Smith, V. L., & Ellsworth, P. C. (1987). The social psychology of eyewitness accuracy: Misleading questions and communicator expertise. *Journal of Applied Psychology, 72,* 294–300.

Titcomb, A. L., & Reyna, V. F. (1992, November). *Gist, verbatim memory, and suggestibility: Effects of different types of misinformation.* Poster presented at the meeting of the Society for Judgment and Decision Making, St. Louis, MO.

Titcomb, A. L., & Reyna, V. F. (1993, November). *Gist and verbatim misinformation: A fuzzy-trace theory analysis.* Poster presented at the meeting of the Society for Judgment and Decision Making, Washington, DC.

Toglia, M. P., Payne, D. G., & Anastasi, J. S. (1991, November). *Recognition level and the misinformation effect: A meta-analysis and empirical investigation.* Paper presented at the meeting of the Psychonomic Society, San Francisco.

Toglia, M. P., Ross, D. F., Ceci, S. J., & Hembrooke, H. (1992). The suggestibility of children's memory: A social-psychological and cognitive interpretation. In M. L. Howe, C. J. Brainerd, & V. F. Reyna (Eds.), *Development of long-term retention* (pp. 217–241). New York: Springer-Verlag.

Tousignant, J. P., Hall, D., & Loftus, E. F. (1986). Discrepancy detection and vulnerability to misleading postevent information. *Memory & Cognition, 14,* 329–338.

Tversky, B., & Tuchin, M. (1989). A reconciliation of the evidence on eyewitness testimony: Comments on McCloskey and Zaragoza. *Journal of Experimental Psychology: General, 118,* 86–91.

Warren, A. R., & Hagood, P. L. (in press). Effects of timing and type of questioning on eyewitness accuracy and suggestibility. In M. Zaragoza (Ed.), *Memory, suggestibility, and eyewitness testimony in children and adults.* New York: Harper & Row.

Wells, G. L. (1984). How adequate is human intuition for judging eyewitness testimony. In G. L. Wells & E. L. Loftus (Eds.), *Eyewitness testimony: Psychological perspectives* (pp. 256–272). New York: Cambridge University Press.

Wells, G. L. (1993). What do we know about eyewitness identification? *American Psychologist, 48,* 553–557.

Wells, G. L., & Turtle, J. W. (1986). Eyewitness identification: The importance of lineup models. *Psychological Bulletin, 99,* 320–329.

Wells, G. L., & Turtle, J. W. (1987). Eyewitness testimony research: Current knowledge and emergent controversies. *Canadian Journal of Behavioral Science, 19,* 363–388.

Whaley, R. (1989). Tests, testing, and the misinformation effect (Doctoral dissertation, University of Washington, 1988). *Dissertation Abstracts International, 50,* 1–B.

Zaragoza, M. S. (1991). Preschool children's susceptibility to memory impairment. In J. Doris (Ed.), *The suggestibility of children's recollections: Implications for eyewitness testimony* (pp. 27–39). Washington, DC: American Psychological Association.

Zaragoza, M. S., Dahlgren, D., & Muench, J. (1992). The role of memory impairment in children's suggestibility. In M. L. Howe, C. J. Brainerd, & V. F. Reyna (Eds.), *Development of long-term retention* (pp. 184–216). New York: Springer-Verlag.

Zaragoza, M. S., & Koshmider, J. W. (1989). Misled subjects may know more than their performance implies. *Journal of Experimental Psychology: Learning, Memory, and Cognition, 15,* 246–255.

Zaragoza, M. S., McCloskey, M., & Jamis, M. (1987). Misleading postevent information and recall of the original event: Further evidence against the memory impairment hypothesis. *Journal of Experimental Psychology: General, 13,* 36–44.

9

Skilled Suppression

Morton Ann Gernsbacher and Mark Faust

When information from two or more domains conflict, we often experience interference (see Dempster, 1992, for a review). The phenomenon of interference has long held intrigue for experimental psychologists. Many psychological theories revolve around the concept of interference. For example, retroactive and proactive interference have been imputed in many theories of learning and forgetting (Zechmeister & Nyberg, 1982), and disagreement over the locus of interference effects in selective-attention tasks (e.g., an early vs. late "bottleneck") distinguishes several theories of attention (Allport, Tipper, & Chmiel, 1985; Neill & Westberry, 1987; Yee, 1991). Recently, interference has been proposed as a powerful explanation for the cognitive changes associated with childhood development and adult aging (Bjorklund & Harnishfeger, 1990; Dempster, 1992, 1993; Harnishfeger, Chapter 6, this volume; Harnishfeger & Bjorklund, 1993; McDowd, Oseas-Kreger, & Filion, Chapter 11, and Reyna, Chapter 2, this volume).

In this chapter we explore the interference that often arises during comprehension. Consider, for example, the comprehension of a spoken or written sentence. Successful comprehension entails building a coherent mental representation from a string of serially presented words. Thus, at some level, individual words comprise a basis for building a mental representation of a sentence. However, even a brief examination of a dictionary documents that many English words are to some degree ambiguous; they have several, often distinct senses. Early "top-down" models of comprehension (e.g., Schank & Abelson, 1977) stressed the role of prior context; prior context constrained the semantic information that could be activated during word recognition, and thus the interference from different senses of a word was avoided.

Over the past decade, studies of ambiguous words heard or read in a sentence context have, for the most past, suggested the following pattern. Initially, multiple senses of an ambiguous word are activated to greater or lesser degrees; later, the meaning most contextually appropriate is selected (Conrad, 1974; Duffy, Morris, & Rayner, 1988; Merrill, Sperber, & McCauley, 1981; Onifer & Swinney, 1981; Swinney, 1979). Although several studies have challenged the generality of this proposal (Kellas, Paul, Martin, & Simpson, 1991; Tabossi, 1988a, 1988b), we assume that, on average, more information is activated during reading than is appropriate or relevant to comprehension of the text as a whole (Gernsbacher & Faust, 1991b). Thus, the potential for interference from contextually inappropriate information is a basic ingredient of our perspective on comprehension. We are not alone in this respect. Several other researchers have proposed models of comprehension that also include the potential for interference from inappropriate information (Hasher & Zacks, 1988; Just & Carpenter, 1992; Kintsch, 1988).

In this chapter we begin by describing how a mechanism of suppression can reduce the interference from inappropriate information; suppression dampens the activation of contextually inappropriate information. We then describe a series of studies that link the ability to successfully suppress inappropriate information (the facility to attenuate interference) to comprehension skill. We conclude by presenting the results of two experiments that demonstrate that the suppression effects we have examined before are susceptible to the probability of instances when suppression is needed. This finding suggests that our proposed mechanism of suppression is composed of at least some attentionally driven components.

THEORETICAL BACKGROUND

Our conception of suppression derives from the Structure Building Framework, which is a simple framework for understanding the cognitive processes and mechanisms involved in comprehension (Gernsbacher, 1990). According to the Structure Building Framework, the goal of comprehension is to build coherent mental representations or *structures*. The building blocks of these mental structures are what we refer to as memory nodes. Memory nodes represent previously comprehended information, perhaps in a distributed sense.

According to the Structure Building Framework, memory nodes are activated by incoming stimuli. Once activated, memory nodes transmit processing signals, which either enhance (increase) or suppress (dampen or decrease) other nodes' activation. Thus, once memory nodes are activated, two mechanisms control their level of activation: these mechanisms are suppression and enhancement. (For a related perspective on memory strength, see Brainerd's distinction between output interference and episodic activation in Chapter 4, this volume.) Memory nodes are enhanced when the information they represent is necessary for ongoing processing; they are suppressed when the information they represent is not necessary.

The notion that incoming stimuli activate memory representations is familiar. What is novel about the Structure Building Framework's proposal is that activated memory nodes transmit processing signals. This proposal more fully captures the analogy of neural activity—an analogy that inspires many models of cognition. This is because the familiar notion that incoming stimuli activate memory nodes captures only one aspect of the analogy, the electrical transmission of information (along axons); but the novel proposal that activated memory nodes also transmit processing signals completes the analogy. The transmission of processing signals (suppression and enhancement) parallels the chemical transmission of information (across synapses, via neurotransmitters).

The mechanisms of suppression and enhancement are crucial to successful language processing. Consider only the need for suppression: in many situations, irrelevant or inappropriate information is automatically activated, unconsciously retrieved, or naturally perceived. For instance, reading a string of letters activates phonological, semantic, and orthographic information (M. Coltheart, Davelaar, Jonasson, & Besner, 1977; Rosson, 1985). Indeed, laboratory experiments demonstrate that reading the letter string *rows* can activate the phonological sequence /roz/, which can activate the word *rose* (van Orden, 1987; van Orden, Johnston, & Hale, 1988). But to correctly understand a homophone (e.g., *rows*), the homophone's alternate forms (e.g., *rose)* must be suppressed.

Information from other modalities must also be suppressed. We often read in the presence of background noise, and we conduct conversations in the presence of visual stimuli. In these situations, we often experience interference across modalities. Laboratory experiments demonstrate that it is harder to read a word when it is written within a line-drawing of an object, and it is harder to name a line-drawn object if a word is written within it (Smith & McGee, 1980). But for successful language processing, irrelevant information from other modalities must be suppressed (Tipper & Driver, 1988).

Our previous research has illustrated the role of suppression in various language phenomena. These phenomena include **lexical access** (how we understand the meanings of words); **anaphoric reference** (how we understand to whom or what anaphors, such as pronouns, refer); **cataphoric reference** (how words that are marked by devices, such as spoken stress, gain a privileges status in comprehenders' mental structures); **surface information loss** (why seemingly superficial information, such as syntactic form, is forgotten more rapidly than seemingly more important information, such as thematic content; Gernsbacher, 1985); **syntactic parsing** (how we decode the grammatical form of sentences into meaning); and **general comprehension skill** (which is skill at comprehending linguistic as well as nonlinguistic media).

In addition to demonstrating the ubiquity of suppression, our previous research clarifies the nature of this mechanism. These experiments illustrate three critical principles of suppression:

Principle 1. Suppression is an active dampening of activation.
Principle 2. Suppression signals are transmitted by activated memory nodes.
Principle 3. Suppression is a general cognitive mechanism.

The experiments on lexical access and cataphoric reference (Gernsbacher & Faust, 1991b; Gernsbacher & Jescheniak, 1994) illustrate Principle 1: Suppression is an active dampening of activation. These experiments demonstrate that suppression differs from passive decay and from compensatory inhibition (the notion that some memory nodes must decrease in activation simply because others have increased).

The experiments on anaphoric and cataphoric reference (Gernsbacher, 1989; Gernsbacher & Hargreaves, 1988; Gernsbacher, Hargreaves, & Beeman, 1989; Gernsbacher & Shroyer, 1989) illustrate Principle 2: Suppression signals are transmitted by activated memory nodes. These experiments demonstrate that how strongly suppression signals are transmitted is a function of how marked the anaphoric and cataphoric devices are. The more marked the anaphoric or cataphoric devices are, the stronger the suppression signals will be.

The experiments on general comprehension skill (Gernsbacher & Faust, 1991a; Gernsbacher, Varner, & Faust, 1990) illustrate Principle 3: Suppression is a general cognitive mechanism. These experiments demonstrate that the same mechanism that suppresses inappropriate information during sentence comprehension could suppress inappropriate information during scene comprehension. Moreover, these experiments demonstrate that successful suppression underlies skilled comprehension. In the next part of this chapter we review these experiments. In the last part of this chapter, we present new data that demonstrate that employing the mechanism of suppression that we have identified in our previous work is a strategic skill.

SUCCESSFUL SUPPRESSION UNDERLIES SKILLED COMPREHENSION

According to many models of word understanding, when comprehenders first hear or read a word, information provided by that word activates various potential meanings. Then, constraints provided by lexical, semantic, syntactic, and other sources of information alter those meanings' levels of activation. Eventually, one meaning becomes most strongly activated. That is the meaning that comprehenders access and incorporate into their developing mental structures (these ideas are culled from the models of Becker, 1976; Kintsch, 1988; Marslen-Wilson & Welsh, 1978; McClelland & Rumelhart, 1981; Norris, 1986).

What the Structure Building Framework adds to these ideas is the proposal that suppression and enhancement modulate the different meanings' levels of activation. The role of the mechanism of suppression can be illustrated by examining how comprehenders access the appropriate meaning of ambiguous words (i.e., words such as *bugs* that have at least two diverse meanings). Immediately after comprehenders hear or read an ambiguous word, multiple meanings of the word are often activated. In fact, multiple meanings are often activated even though one meaning is strongly implied by the context (Conrad, 1974; Kintsch & Mross, 1985; Lucas, 1987; Seidenberg, Tanenhaus, Leiman, & Bienkowski, 1982; Tanenhaus, Leiman, & Seidenberg, 1979; Till, Mross, & Kintsch, 1988). For example, immediately after the word *spade* is heard or read, both the playing card meaning and the garden tool meaning are often momentarily activated. This occurs even when one meaning is strongly implied, for instance, even when the garden tool, not the playing card, meaning of *spade* is implied in the following sentence.

(1) He dug with the **spade.**

Successful comprehension must involve suppressing the contextually inappropriate meaning—the playing card meaning. In Gernsbacher et al. (1990), we discovered that skilled comprehenders are more successful in suppressing the inappropriate meanings of ambiguous words.

Skilled Comprehenders Are More Successful in Suppressing Inappropriate Meanings

In Gernsbacher et al. (1990; Experiment 4), we selected two samples of more-skilled and less-skilled comprehenders from the extreme thirds of a distribution of 270 University of Oregon students whom we had tested on the Multi-Media Comprehension Battery (Gernsbacher & Varner, 1988). The Multi-Media Comprehension Battery tests subjects' comprehension of written, auditorily presented, and nonverbal picture stories. When the more- and less-skilled comprehenders returned to the lab, they read short sentences; after each sentence, they saw a test word. Their task was to verify whether the test word fit the meaning of the sentence they just read. On 80 trials, the test word did indeed fit the sentence, but we were more interested in the 80 trials in which the test word did *not* fit the sentence. On half of those trials, the last word of the sentence was an ambiguous word, for example,

(2) He dug with the **spade**.

The test word on these trials was a meaning of the ambiguous word that was inappropriate to the context, for example, *ACE*. We measured how long subjects took to reject a test word like *ACE* after reading a sentence like (2). And we compared the latency with how long subjects took to reject *ACE* after reading the same sentence but with the last word replaced by an unambiguous word, for example.

(3) He dug with the **shovel**.

This comparison showed us how activated the inappropriate meaning of the ambiguous word was; the more time subjects took to reject *ACE* after the *spade* versus the *shovel* sentence, the more activated the inappropriate meaning must have been.

We presented the test words at two intervals: immediately (100 ms) after subjects finished reading each sentence, and after an 850-ms delay. We predicted that at the immediate test point, both the more- and less-skilled comprehenders would take longer to reject test words after ambiguous than after unambiguous words. For example, both groups would take longer to reject *ACE* after reading the *spade* sentence than after reading the *shovel* sentence. This prediction was based on the vast literature demonstrating that immediately after ambiguous words are read, contextually inappropriate meanings are often activated. We particularly expected the inappropriate meanings to be activated because our task required comprehenders to focus their attention on a subsequent word and try to integrate that word into the previous context (Glucksberg, Kreuz, & Rho, 1986; van Petten & Kutas, 1987).

Our novel predictions concerned what would happen after the delay. We predicted that after the delay, the difference between the more-skilled comprehenders' latencies to reject test words following ambiguous versus following unambiguous words would be reduced. This is because more-skilled comprehenders should be more able to successfully suppress the inappropriate meanings.

Figure 1 displays our 64 subjects' data, presented as estimated activation of the inappropriate meanings. We estimated activation of the inappropriate meanings by subtracting subjects' latencies to reject test words like *ACE* after reading ambiguous words like *spade* from their latencies to reject test words like *ACE* after reading unambiguous words like *shovel*.

As Figure 1 illustrates, immediately after comprehenders of both skill levels read the ambiguous words, the inappropriate meanings were highly activated. However, 850 ms after the more-skilled comprehenders read the ambiguous words, the inappropriate meanings were no longer reliably activated. We suggest that by this time the more-skilled comprehenders had successfully suppressed the inappropriate meanings. But for the less-skilled comprehenders, even after the delay, the inappropriate meanings were still highly activat-

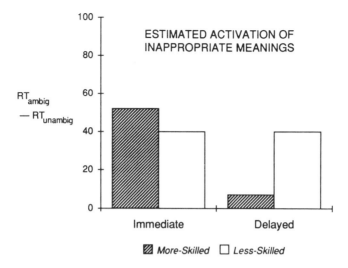

FIGURE 1. Estimated activation is the difference between subjects' latencies to reject test words like *ACE* after reading ambiguous words like *spade* versus unambiguous words like *shovel*. The more-skilled comprehenders are represented by hatching; the less-skilled comprehenders are represented by unfilled bars. Data from M. A. Gernsbacher, K. R. Varner, & M. E. Faust *Journal of Experimental Psychology: Learning, Memory, and Cognition* (1990; Experiment 4).

ed. In fact, they were as highly activated following the delay as they were immediately after reading the ambiguous words. These results support the hypothesis that skilled comprehenders are more successful in suppressing the inappropriate meanings of ambiguous words.

Skilled Comprehenders Are More Successful in Suppressing Incorrect Forms of Homophones

Reading a string of letters activates an array of information. Reading a letter string virtually always activates orthographic information—information about the individual letters in the string and their relative position to one another. Often, reading a letter string activates semantic information, lexical information, and phonological information. In fact, semantic, lexical, and phonological information is often activated even when the string does not compose an English word (M. Coltheart et al., 1977; Rosson, 1985).

Automatic activation of phonological information was the focus of our next experiment. By automatic activation of phonological information we mean the phenomenon in which reading the letter string (and homophone) *rows* activates the phonological sequence /roz/, which can activate *rose* (another form of the homophone). How do we know that a letter string often activates phonological information, which in turn activates other forms of homophones? Consider the following finding: comprehenders have difficulty quickly rejecting the word *rows* as not being an exemplar of the category *FLOWER* (van Orden, 1987; van Orden et al., 1988).

In order to successfully comprehend a written passage, these incorrect forms cannot remain activated. According to the Structure Building Framework, comprehension involves the mechanism of suppression. The same structure-building mechanism that suppresses the inappropriate meanings of ambiguous words could also suppress the incorrect forms of homophones. If this is the same mechanism, and if this general suppression mechanism underlies successful comprehension, then more-skilled comprehenders should be more successful in suppressing the incorrect forms of homophones.

Related evidence already supports this prediction. Consider the sentence:

(4) She **blue** up the balloon.

Six-year-olds are more likely to accept that sentence than are 10-year-olds, even when they clearly know the difference between *blue* and *blew* (Doctor & Coltheart, 1980; see also V. Coltheart, Laxon, Rickard, & Elton, 1988). If we assume that 10-year-olds are more skilled than 6-year-olds at comprehension, this finding suggests that more-skilled comprehenders are more successful in suppressing the incorrect forms of homophones that are often automatically activated.

We tested this hypothesis in Gernsbacher and Faust (1991a; Experiment 1). Our subjects were United States Air Force recruits who were selected from a sample of 455 subjects whom we tested with the Multi-Media Comprehension Battery. We selected 48 subjects from the top third of the distribution (those who scored the highest) and 48 subjects from the bottom third of the distribution (those who scored the lowest). When these more- and less-skilled comprehenders returned to the lab, they performed a laboratory task similar to the task we used in our previous research. They read short sentences, and following each sentence, they saw a test word. The subjects verified whether the test word fit the meaning of the sentence they just read. On 80 trials, the test word did indeed fit the sentence's meaning, but on 80 trials it did not. We were interested in those trials in which the test word did *not* fit the meaning.

On half of those trials, the last word of the sentence was one form of a homophone, for example,

(5) He had lots of **patients.**

On these trials, the test word was related to the homophone's other form, for example, the test word *CALM* is related to *patience.* We compared how long subjects took to reject *CALM* after reading sentence (5) with how long they took to reject *CALM* after reading the same sentence with the last word replaced by a nonhomophone, for example,

(6) He had lots of **students.**

This comparison showed us how activated the incorrect form was; the more time subjects took to reject *CALM* after the *patients* sentence versus after the *students* sentence, the more activated the *patients* form of the homophone must have been.[1]

We presented the test words at two intervals: immediately (100 ms) after subjects finished reading each sentence, and after 1-s delay. We predicted that at the immediate interval, comprehenders of both skill levels would take longer to reject test words following homophones than following nonhomophones. For example, both groups would take longer to reject *CALM* after reading the *patients* sentence than after reading the *students* sentence. This result would corroborate the results of van Orden (1987; van Orden et al., 1988). This result would also demonstrate that comprehenders of both skill levels often activate phonological information during reading. Our novel predictions concerned what would happen after the delay. We predicted that after the 1-s delay, the difference between the more-skilled comprehenders' latencies to reject test words following homophones versus following nonhomophones would be reduced, because more-skilled comprehenders should be more successful in suppressing the incorrect forms.

Figure 2 illustrates our 96 subjects' data, presented as estimated activation of the incorrect forms of the homophones. We estimated activation of the incorrect forms by subtracting subjects' latencies to reject test words like *CALM* after reading nonhomophones like *students* from their latencies to reject test words like *CALM* after reading homophones like *patients*. As Figure 2 illustrates, immediately after comprehenders of both skill levels read the homophones, the inappropriate forms were highly activated; in fact, they were almost equally activated for the more-skilled as for the less-skilled comprehenders. However, one second after the more-skilled comprehenders read the homophones, the incorrect forms were no longer reliably activated. We suggest that the more-skilled comprehenders had successfully suppressed the incorrect forms. But for the less-skilled comprehenders, even after the 1-s delay, the incorrect forms were still highly activated; in fact, they were as highly activated after 1 s as they were immediately after reading the words. These data support the hypothesis that more-skilled comprehenders are more successful in suppressing the incorrect forms of homophones.

---

[1]To ensure that the homophones would be familiar to our subjects, 25 students at the University of Oregon judged, without time pressure, whether the test words fit the meanings of our experimental and filler sentences. We used experimental sentences and test words only if 95% of our students agreed that the test words did *not* fit their sentences' meanings, and we used filler sentences and test words only if 95% of our students agreed that the test words *did* fit their sentences' meanings.

Skilled Comprehenders Are More Successful in Suppressing Typical-but-Absent Objects

According to the Structure Building Framework, many of the cognitive processes and mechanisms involved in comprehending language are involved in comprehending nonlinguistic stimuli, for instance, naturalistic scenes. Other researchers also consider scene perception as "comprehension" (Biederman, 1981; Friedman, 1979; Mandler & Johnson, 1976).

The mechanism of suppression seems critical to successful scene comprehension. Indeed, Biederman writes about the difficulty in "suppressing the interpretations of visual arrays that comprise scenes" (Biederman, Bickle, Teitelbaum, & Klatsky, 1988, p. 456). This difficulty is manifested in the following phenomenon: After briefly viewing a scene, subjects are more likely to incorrectly report that an object was present if that object is typically found in that type of scene. For instance, subjects are more likely to incorrectly report that a tractor was present in a farm scene than in a kitchen scene, and they are more likely to incorrectly report that a kettle was present in a kitchen scene than in a farm scene (Biederman, Glass, & Stacy, 1973; Biederman, Mezzanotte, & Rabinowitz, 1982; Biederman, Teitelbaum, & Mezzanotte, 1983; Palmer, 1975).

To successfully comprehend a scene, observers must suppress these typical-but-absent objects, just as readers and listeners must suppress the inappropriate meanings of ambiguous words and the incorrect forms of homophones.

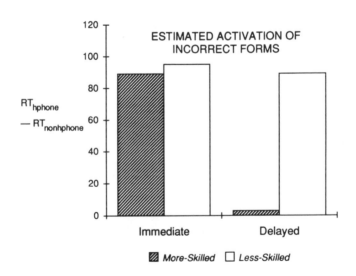

FIGURE 2. Estimated activation is the difference between subjects' latencies to reject test words like *CALM* after sentence final homophones like *patients* versus after sentence final non-homophones like *students*. Data from M. A. Gernsbacher & M. E. Faust. *Journal of Experimental Psychology: Learning, Memory, and Cognition* (1991; Experiment 1).

The same structure-building mechanism that suppresses the activation of inappropriate linguistic information could suppress the activation of inappropriate nonlinguistic information. If this is the same mechanism, and if this general suppression mechanism underlies skilled comprehension, then more-skilled comprehenders should be more successful in suppressing the activation of typical-but-absent objects when viewing scenes.

We tested this hypothesis (in Gernsbacher & Faust, 1991a; Experiment 2) using Biederman et al.'s (1988) stimuli. Biederman et al. (1988) replicated the phenomenon in which subjects incorrectly report that an object is present in a scene when the object is typical of that scene (for instance, subjects incorrectly report that a tractor was present in a farm scene). Instead of briefly viewing actual scenes, however, the subjects in Biederman et al.'s (1988) experiments viewed clock-face arrangements of objects, as illustrated in Figure 3. For instance, Figure 3A illustrates a clock-face arrangement of six objects normally found in a farm scene; *barn, pig, pitchfork, farmer, rooster,* and *ear of corn.* We refer to these clock-face arrangements as scenic arrays.

We presented all of Biederman et al.'s (1988) scenic arrays that comprised three, four, five, and six objects. However, we slightly modified Biederman et al.'s task so that it would better parallel our linguistic tasks. In our experiment, subjects first viewed a scenic array; then, they saw the name of a

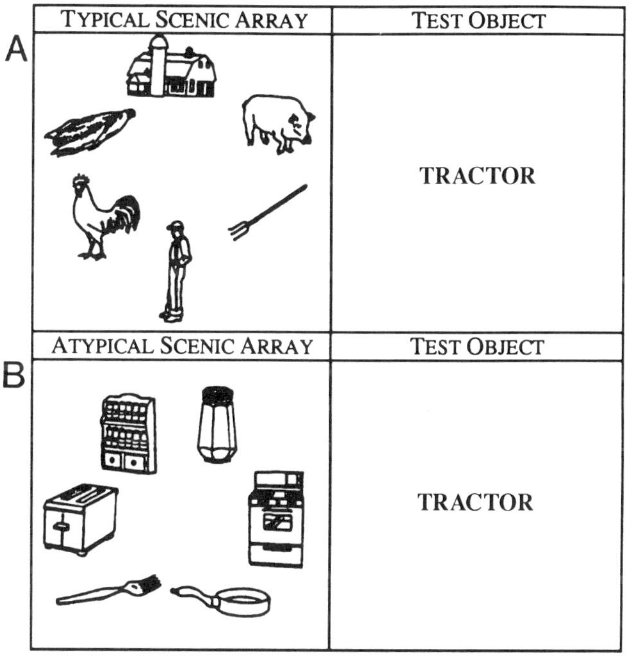

FIGURE 3. Example stimuli. From M. A. Gernsbacher & M. E. Faust. *Journal of Experimental Psychology: Learning, Memory, and Cognition* (1991; Experiment 2).

test object. Their task was to verify whether the named test object had been present in the array they just viewed. On 80 trials, the test object had been present, but in 80 it had not. In this experiment, we were interested in the trials in which the test object had *not* been present.

On half of these trials, the objects in the array were typical of a particular scene, for instance, objects that typically occur in a farm scene, as illustrated in Figure 3A. On these trials, the test object was something that also typically occurs in this type of scene, but it had not been present in the scenic array the subjects viewed. For instance, a *TRACTOR* typically occurs in a farm scene, but no *TRACTOR* occurs in the scenic array illustrated in Figure 3A.

We compared how long subjects took to reject *TRACTOR* after viewing the farm array with how long they took to reject *TRACTOR* after viewing another scenic array, for instance, objects belonging to a kitchen scene, as illustrated in Figure 3B. This comparison showed us how activated the typical-but-absent object was: the longer subjects took to reject *TRACTOR* after viewing the typical (*farm*) array versus the atypical (*kitchen*) array, the more activated the typical-but-absent object must have been.

We presented the names of the test objects at two intervals: immediately (50 ms) after subjects viewed each array, and after a 1-s delay. Figure 4 displays our 40 subjects' data, presented as estimated activation of the typical-but-absent objects. We estimated activation of the typical-but-absent objects by subtracting subjects' latencies to reject names of test objects like *TRAC-TOR* after viewing atypical (*kitchen*) arrays from their latencies to reject names of test objects like *TRACTOR* after viewing typical (*farm*) arrays. As Figure 4 illustrates, immediately after both the more- and less-skilled comprehenders viewed the scenic arrays, the typical-but-absent objects were highly activated. In fact, the typical-but-absent objects were about equally activated for the more- and the less-skilled comprehenders.

As Figure 4 also illustrates, 1 s after the more-skilled comprehenders viewed the scenic arrays, the typical-but-absent objects were no longer reliably activated. We suggest that the more-skilled comprehenders had successfully suppressed the typical-but-absent objects. But for the less-skilled comprehenders, even after the 1-s delay, the typical-but-absent objects were still highly activated; in fact, they were as activated after the 1-s delay as they were immediately after viewing the arrays. These results support the hypothesis that skilled comprehenders are more successful in suppressing typical-but-absent objects after they view scenic arrays.

Skilled Comprehenders Are More Successful in Suppressing Information across Modalities

To negotiate the environment, we must make sense of stimuli that originate from various modalities. We would be severely handicapped if we were

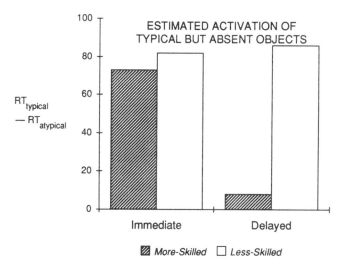

FIGURE 4.   Estimated activation is the difference between subjects' latencies to reject the names of test objects like *TRACTOR* after viewing typical arrays (of *farm* objects) versus atypical arrays (of *kitchen* objects). Data from M. A. Gernsbacher & M. E. Faust. *Journal of Experimental Psychology: Learning, Memory, and Cognition* (1991; Experiment 2).

skilled at only reading written words, or only listening to spoken words, or only comprehending graphic displays. Information originates from different modalities, often simultaneously. We read while listening to music, and we drive while carrying on a conversation.

Comprehenders often experience interference across modalities. For instance, it is harder to name a pictured object such as an *ashtray* if a letter string such as *INCH* is written across the picture, as illustrated in Figure 5A. The opposite is also true: it is harder to read a word such as *RIVER* if it is superimposed on a picture, as illustrated in Figure 5B (Smith & McGee, 1980).

Successful comprehension often requires suppressing information across modalities. The same structure-building mechanism that suppresses information within a modality could suppress information across modalities. If this is the same mechanism, and if this general suppression mechanism underlies skilled comprehension, then more-skilled comprehenders should be more successful in suppressing information across modalities.

We tested this hypothesis (in Gernsbacher & Faust, 1991a; Experiment 3) in the following way. Subjects first viewed a context display, which contained a line-drawn picture of a common object and a familiar word. For example, Figure 5A illustrates a picture of an *ashtray* with the word *INCH* written across it. Figure 5B illustrates the word *RIVER* superimposed on a picture of a *baseball player*. All context displays contained both a picture and a word.

After subjects viewed each context display, they were shown a test display. Each test display contained either another picture or another word. Half

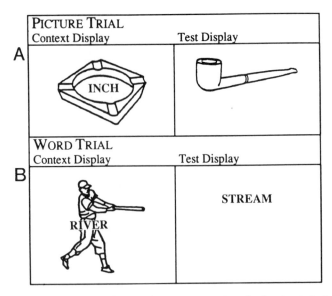

FIGURE 5. Example stimuli for filler trials. From M. A. Gernsbacher & M. E. Faust. *Journal of Experimental Psychology: Learning, Memory, and Cognition* (1991; Experiment 3).

the time, the test display contained another picture, and we referred to those trials as Picture trials; half the time, the test display contained another word, and we referred to those trials as Word trials. Subjects were told before each trial whether that trial would be a Picture trial or a Word trial.

Figure 5A illustrates a Picture trial. On Picture trials, subjects were told to focus on the picture in the context display and ignore the word. For example, for the Picture trial shown in Figure 5A, subjects should have focused on the *ashtray* and ignored the word *INCH*. Following each context display, subjects were shown a test display. On the Picture trials, the test display contained another picture. The subjects' task (on Picture trials) was to verify whether the picture shown in the test display was related to the picture shown in the context display. For the Picture trial shown in Figure 5A, subjects should have responded "yes," because the picture shown in the test display, the *pipe*, was related to the picture shown in the context display, the *ashtray*.

Figure 5B illustrates a Word trial. On Word trials, subjects were supposed to focus on the word in the context display and ignore the picture. For example, for the Word trial shown in Figure 5B, subjects should have focused on the word *RIVER* and ignored the *baseball player*. The test display on Word trials contained another word. The subjects' task was to verify whether the word written in the test display was related to the word written in the context display. For the Word trial shown in Figure 5B, subjects should have responded "yes," because the word written in the test display, *STREAM*, was related to the word written in the context display, *RIVER*.

On 40 Picture trials and 40 Word trials, the test display was related to what the subjects were to focus on in the context display, just as they are related in Figure 5. However, we were more interested in the 80 trials in which the test display was *unrelated* to what the subjects were supposed to focus on in the context display. On half of those trials, the test display was unrelated to what the subjects were to focus on in the context display, but it was related to what they were supposed to ignore.

For example, Figure 6A illustrates an experimental Picture trial. The context display contains a picture of a *hand* with the superimposed word *RAIN*. Because this is a Picture trial, subjects should have focused on the picture (the *hand*) and ignored the word. The test display is a picture of an *umbrella*. So the test display, the *umbrella*, is unrelated to what the subjects were supposed to focus on in the context display, the *hand*; therefore, the subjects

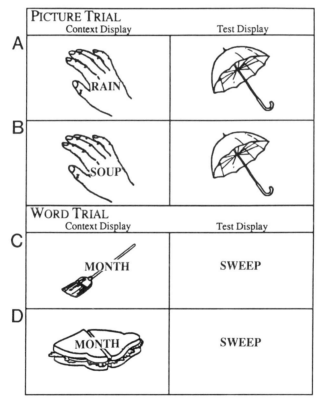

FIGURE 6. Example stimuli for experimental trials. From M. A. Gernsbacher & M. E. Faust. *Journal of Experimental Psychology: Learning, Memory, and Cognition* (1991; Experiment 3).

should have responded "no." But the test display is related to what the subjects were supposed to ignore, the word *RAIN*. We measured how long subjects took to reject the test display, the picture of the *umbrella*, after viewing the context display, the picture of the *hand* with the superimposed word *RAIN*. And we compared that with how long subjects took to reject the same test display, the picture of the *umbrella*, after viewing the same context display, the picture of the *hand*, but with another word superimposed, *SOUP*.

Experimental Word trials worked similarly, as illustrated by Figure 6C. When reading this Word trial context display, subjects should have focused on the word *MONTH* and ignored the surrounding picture of a *broom*. We measured how long subjects took to reject the word *SWEEP* after reading the word *MONTH* surrounded by the *broom*. And we compared that with how long subjects took to reject *SWEEP* after viewing the same context display with the picture of a *broom* replaced by a picture of a *sandwich* (as illustrated by Figure 6C).

As in our other experiments, we presented the test displays at two intervals: immediately (50 ms) after subjects viewed the context-setting display, and after a 1-s delay. Figure 7 displays our 160 subjects' data, presented as estimated activation of the to-be-ignored pictures/words. We estimated activation of the to-be-ignored pictures/words by subtracting subjects' latencies to reject test displays that were unrelated to ignored pictures/words from their latencies to reject test displays that were related to ignored pictures/words.[2] As Figure 7 illustrates, immediately after comprehenders of both skill levels saw the context displays, the ignored pictures/words were highly activated; in fact, they were almost equally activated for the more-skilled and the less-skilled comprehenders. However, 1 s after the more-skilled comprehenders saw the context displays, the ignored pictures/words were no longer reliably activated. We suggest that the more-skilled comprehenders had successfully suppressed them. However, even after the 1-s delay, the ignored pictures/words were still highly activated for the less-skilled comprehenders; in fact, they were as activated after 1 s as they were immediately (after 50 ms). These data support the hypothesis that more-skilled comprehenders are more successful in suppressing information across modalities.

In the experiments we have described, we found that more-skilled comprehenders were more successful in rejecting irrelevant or inappropriate information. We suggest that successful suppression underlies comprehension skill. A counterexplanation is that more-skilled comprehenders are more successful in suppressing inappropriate information because they more fully appreciate what is contextually appropriate. Perhaps they more successfully employ their enhancement mechanisms, not their suppression mechanisms. We tested that hypothesis in two further experiments.

---

[2]Although comprehenders of both skill levels responded more rapidly on Picture trials than on Word trials, there were no interactions with modality (Picture vs. Word). So, we have collapsed across this variable in our figures.

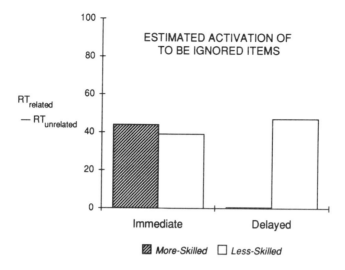

FIGURE 7. Estimated activation is the difference between subjects' latencies to reject test displays that were related versus unrelated to ignored pictures or words. Data from M. A. Gernsbacher & M. E. Faust. *Journal of Experimental Psychology: Learning, Memory, and Cognition* (1991; Experiment 3).

Skilled Comprehenders Do Not More Successfully Enhance Contextually Appropriate Meanings

According to the Structure Building Framework, comprehension requires enhancing the activation of memory nodes when those nodes are relevant to the structure being built. So, perhaps more-skilled comprehenders' enhancement mechanisms, not their suppression mechanisms, underlie their success at comprehension. By this logic, more-skilled comprehenders have less difficulty rejecting *ACE* after reading *He dug with the spade* because they more fully appreciate that the context of **digging** *with a spade* implies a garden tool, not a playing card.

This explanation seems unlikely given the repeated finding that more-skilled comprehenders are not more appreciative of predictable sentence contexts; in fact, laboratory research suggests just the opposite: less-skilled comprehenders often benefit *more* from predictable contexts more than do more-skilled comprehenders. For example, the word *dump* is predictable in the following context:

(7) The garbage men had loaded as much as they could onto the truck. They would have to drop off a load at the garbage **dump**.

In contrast, *dump* is less predictable in the following context:

(8) Albert didn't have the money he needed to buy the part to fix his car. Luckily, he found the part he wanted at the **dump.**

All comprehenders pronounce the word *dump* more rapidly when it occurs in the predictable context than when it occurs in the less predictable context; in other words, all comprehenders benefit from the predictable contexts. But less-skilled comprehenders benefit more than do more-skilled comprehenders (Perfetti & Roth, 1981).

We also evaluated this counterexplanation (in Gernsbacher & Faust, 1991a; Experiment 4) with adult comprehenders and a task similar to those we had used in our previous experiments. Subjects read short sentences, and following each sentence they saw a test word. As in our other experiments, the subjects' task was to verify whether the test word fit the meaning of the sentence they just read. However, in this experiment we were interested in the 80 trials in which the test word *did* indeed match the meaning of the sentence (and, therefore, the subjects should have responded "yes").

On half of those trials, the last word of the sentence was an ambiguous word, for example, *spade,* and the verb in the sentence was biased toward one meaning of the ambiguous word, for example,

(9) He **dug with** the spade.

The test word was related to the meaning of the ambiguous word that was biased by the verb, for example, *GARDEN.* In a comparison condition we presented the same sentence, but the biasing verb was replaced with a neutral verb, for example,

(10) He **picked up** the spade.

The *spade* in sentence (10) could be either a garden tool or a playing card.

We measured how rapidly subjects accepted test words after reading sentences with biasing verbs versus neutral verbs.[3] This comparison showed us how fully comprehenders could appreciate the biasing contexts: the faster subjects accepted *GARDEN* after reading the sentence with the biasing verb phrase *dug with* versus the neutral verb phrase *picked up,* the more fully they appreciated the biasing context.

We presented the test words at two intervals: immediately (100 ms) after subjects finished reading each sentence, and after a 1-s delay. We predicted that comprehenders of both skill levels would benefit from the biasing con-

---

[3]To ensure that the biased verbs were biased and the neutral verbs were neutral, 25 students at University of Oregon read all of the experimental and comparison sentences and made unspeeded judgments about the meanings of the ambiguous words. We used biased verbs only if 95% of our students selected the meaning of the ambiguous word that we intended, and we used neutral verbs only if our students were roughly split over which meaning we intended (e.g., when given the sentence *He picked up the spade,* approximately 50% chose *GARDEN TOOL* and approximately 50% chose *PLAYING CARD*).

texts; that is, both groups of comprehenders would accept test words more rapidly when the sentences contained biasing as opposed to neutral verbs. However, we were particularly interested in whether the more-skilled comprehenders would benefit more than the less-skilled comprehenders.

If more-skilled comprehenders are more successful in rejecting contextually inappropriate information (as we found in our previous experiments) simply because they are more appreciative of context, then the more-skilled comprehenders should have benefited more from the biasing contexts. In contrast, if more-skilled comprehenders are more successful in rejecting inappropriate information because they are more skilled in employing suppression, then the more-skilled comprehenders should not have benefited any more from the biasing contexts than the less-skilled comprehenders did. Based on previous literature, we predicted that the less-skilled comprehenders would benefit even more from the biasing contexts than the more-skilled comprehenders did.

Figure 8 displays our 120 subjects' data, presented as estimated activation of the biased meanings. We estimated activation of the biased meanings by subtracting subjects' latencies to accept test words like *GARDEN* after reading sentences with biasing verbs like **dug with** from their latencies to accept *GARDEN* after reading sentences with unbiased verbs like **picked up**. As Figure 8 illustrates, at both the immediate and delayed test intervals, the biased verbs led to greater activation, and this occurred for both more- and less-skilled comprehenders. Indeed, as Figure 8 also illustrates, at both test inter-

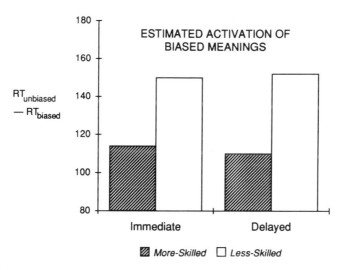

FIGURE 8. Estimated activation is the difference between subjects' latencies to accept test words like *GARDEN* after reading sentences with biasing verbs (*digging with*) versus neutral verbs (*picked up*). Data from M. A. Gernsbacher & M. E. Faust. *Journal of Experimental Psychology: Learning, Memory, and Cognition* (1991; Experiment 4).

vals, the less-skilled comprehenders benefited more from the biasing verbs than the more-skilled comprehenders benefited. These data do not support the hypothesis that more-skilled comprehenders are more skillful in suppressing inappropriate information because they more fully appreciate what is contextually appropriate.

Skilled Comprehenders Are Not Necessarily More Successful in Enhancing Typical Objects in Scenes

Just as sentence comprehension often requires enhancing appropriate or relevant information, scene comprehension might also require enhancing relevant information (i.e., information present in the visual array). In Gernsbacher and Faust (1991a; Experiment 2) we found that more-skilled comprehenders were more successful in suppressing the typical-but-absent objects presented in scenic arrays. Perhaps more-skilled comprehenders' enhancement mechanisms, not their suppression mechanisms, underlie their success in suppressing the typical-but-absent objects presented in scenic arrays. By this logic, more-skilled comprehenders have less difficulty rejecting *TRACTOR* after viewing an array of farm objects in which a tractor is *not* present because more-skilled comprehenders more fully comprehend the objects that are present in the scenic array.

We tested this hypothesis (in Gernsbacher & Faust, 1991a; Experiment 5) in the following way. Subjects first viewed a scenic array of objects, and then they read the name of a test object. For instance, subjects first viewed the scenic array illustrated in Figure 9A, and then they saw the test object, *TRACTOR*. The subjects' task was to verify whether the test object had been present in the array they just viewed. On 80 trials, the test object had not been present, but on 80 it had. In this experiment, we were interested in the trials in which the test object *had* been present (and, therefore, the subjects should have responded "yes").

On half of those trials, the other objects in the array were typical of the scene in which the test object typically occurs. For example, the other objects in the array shown in Figure 9A typically occur in a farm scene, just as a *tractor* does. In a comparison condition, the other objects were atypical of the scene in which the test object typically occurs. For example, the other objects in the array shown in Figure 9B do not typically occur in a farm scene.

We compared how rapidly subjects accepted *TRACTOR* after viewing it in an array of typical objects with how rapidly they accepted *TRACTOR* after viewing it in an array of atypical objects. This comparison showed us how fully comprehenders could appreciate the typical contexts: the faster subjects were to accept *TRACTOR* after viewing the array of typical versus atypical objects, the more fully the subjects must have appreciated the context.

We presented the names of the test objects at two intervals: immediately (50 ms) after subjects finished viewing each scenic array, and after a 1-s delay.

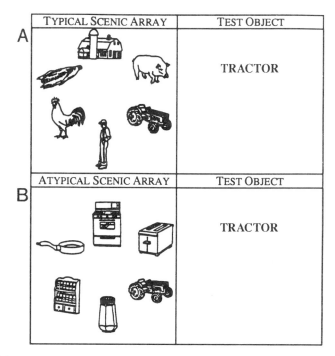

FIGURE 9. Example stimuli for experimental trials. From M. A. Gernsbacher & M. E. Faust. *Journal of Experimental Psychology: Learning, Memory, and Cognition* (1991; Experiment 5).

We expected that comprehenders of both skill levels would benefit from the typical contexts. That is, both groups of comprehenders would accept test objects more rapidly when the arrays contained typical objects as opposed to atypical objects. This result would corroborate Biederman et al. (1988).

However, we were interested in whether the more-skilled comprehenders would benefit more from the typical contexts. If more-skilled comprehenders are more successful in rejecting contextually inappropriate information (as we found in our previous experiments) simply because they are more appreciative of context, then they should have benefited more from the typical contexts. In contrast, if more-skilled comprehenders are more successful in rejecting inappropriate information because they are more skilled in employing suppression, then the more-skilled comprehenders should not have benefited any more from the typical contexts than the less-skilled comprehenders did.

Figure 10 displays our 40 subjects' data, presented as estimated activation of the typical-and-present objects. We estimated activation of the typical-and-present objects by subtracting subjects' latencies to accept test objects like *TRACTOR* after viewing a *tractor* in a typical (*farm*) array from their latencies to accept *TRACTOR* after viewing a *tractor* in an atypical (*kitchen*)

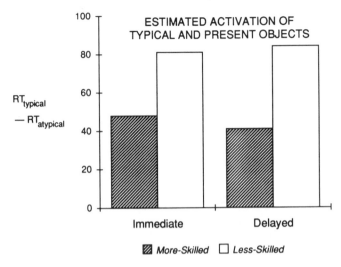

FIGURE 10. Estimated activation is the difference between subjects' latencies to accept test objects like *TRACTOR* after viewing those test objects in typical (*farm*) versus atypical (*kitchen*) arrays. Data from M. A. Gernsbacher & M. E. Faust. *Journal of Experimental Psychology: Learning, Memory, and Cognition* (1991; Experiment 5).

array. As Figure 10 illustrates, at both the immediate and delayed test intervals, the typical contexts led to greater activation, and this occurred for comprehenders of both skill levels. Indeed, as Figure 10 also illustrates, the less-skilled comprehenders benefited more from the typical contexts than did the ᵐore-skilled comprehenders. These data do not support the hypothesis that more-skilled comprehenders are more skillful in suppressing inappropriate information because they more fully appreciate what is contextually appropriate.

This dissociation between enhancement and suppression is suggested by data collected from other populations who might have comprehension difficulty. For instance, 1 s after reading a sentence such as, *The man moved the piano,* less-skilled fifth-grade readers show activation of a semantically associated but contextually less-relevant word, such as *music,* as well as activation of contextually relevant words, such as *heavy;* in contrast, 1 s after reading the same sentence, more-skilled fifth-grade readers show activation of only contextually relevant words (Merrill et al., 1981). This result suggests that less-skilled fifth-grade readers are not deficient in activating contextually appropriate information (e.g., the sense of a piano being heavy), yet they are deficient in suppressing contextually irrelevant semantic associates (e.g., the conception of a piano as a musical instrument).

Some older adults might also be characterized by less-efficient suppression mechanisms but relatively healthy enhancement mechanisms. Elderly adults show little deficit in traditional semantic priming tasks, yet they show difficulty in "negative-priming" tasks. After younger adults focus on one object and ignore another, they are less able to identify the object they ignored (hence the term, "negative priming"). For example, after younger adults focus on a green *A* superimposed on a red *B,* they are less able to identify a red *B* if it appears on the next display. Presumably, the younger adults have efficiently suppressed the object they were supposed to ignore (e.g., the red *B).* However, older adults do not experience this negative-priming effect, suggesting that they less efficiently suppressed the to-be-ignored item (Hasher, Stoltzfus, Zacks, & Rypma, 1991; McDowd, Oseas-Kreger, & Filicon, Chapter 11, this volume; Neill, Valdes, & Terry, Chapter 7, this volume).

Finally, consider a population whose members experience grave difficulties in many everyday cognitive tasks: schizophrenics. Among other difficulties, schizophrenics are notoriously inefficient at maintaining the same topic while speaking, suggesting that they suffer from less-efficient suppression mechanisms; however, they are notoriously hyperactive in their semantic associations, suggesting that they do not suffer from less-efficient enhancement mechanisms (Chapman & Chapman, 1973). (For a more complete discussion of susceptibility to interference among schizophrenics, see Lewandowsky and Li, Chapter 10, this volume.)

SUPPRESSION IS SUSCEPTIBLE TO PROBABILITY

According to the Structure Building Framework, memory nodes are automatically activated by incoming stimuli. Once activated, memory nodes transmit processing signals: they send signals to suppress other memory nodes when the information represented by those other nodes is less relevant to the structure being developed. And they send signals to enhance other memory nodes when the information represented by those other nodes is more relevant.

This simple conception implies that suppression operates relatively automatically. According to this conception, suppression signals are obligatorily sent, based on some criterion, for instance, a similarity criterion. The literature on cognitive processes differentiates between this type of automatic mental activity from processes that are more attentional (Keele & Neill, 1978; Posner & Snyder, 1975a, 1975b). Is suppression an automatic mental activity or is the deployment of suppression signals a function of attention?

Automatic versus attentional mechanisms have been claimed to be distinguishable in the laboratory by manipulating the probability of a particular type of trial occurring within an experiment. The logic of a probability manipulation is this: if a certain type of experimental trial occurs only rarely, subjects might not even notice that type of trial. But if a certain type of trial occurs frequently, subjects might attend to that type of trial at some level of conscious or even unconscious awareness.

Consider the following experimental task: subjects see pairs of letter strings, appearing side by side (e.g., *DORTZ BLAUGH*). The subjects' task is to decide whether each member of the pair is a word. On some trials, both members are words, and on some of the trials in which both members are words, the two words are semantically related, for example, *BREAD BUTTER* . A classic finding is that the second letter string is recognized more rapidly when it appears in a pair of related words; for example, *BUTTER* is recognized more rapidly when it appears in the related-word pair *BREAD BUTTER* than when it appears in the unrelated-word pair *NURSE BUTTER* (Meyer & Schvaneveldt, 1971).

Now consider the following manipulation: in one condition, only 1/8 of the word pairs are related (*BREAD BUTTER*), and the majority (7/8) are unrelated (*NURSE BUTTER*); in another condition 1/2 are related, and 1/2 are unrelated; and in a third condition, the majority (7/8) of the word pairs are related, and only 1/8 are unrelated. With this manipulation, subjects recognize the second word of the pair more rapidly if the pair is related (just as other experiments have shown), and the advantage of the relatedness between the two words in a pair is a function of the probability of a related-word pair appearing in the experiment. When only 1/8 of the word pairs in the experiment are related, the advantage is smallest; when 7/8 of the word pairs are related, the advantage is largest. The high probability of related pairs affects subjects' processing and responses (Tweedy, Lapinski, & Schvaneveldt, 1977).

In other experiments, subjects also respond differently when there is a high versus low probability of a certain type of experimental trial. For instance, in experiments in which subjects perform a letter-matching task, subjects are shown pairs of letters, and they decide rapidly whether the members of the pair match (either physically, e.g., *A* and *A*, or in name, e.g., *a* and *A)*. In Posner and Snyder's (1975b) experiment, the letter pairs were preceded by three types of cues: an informative cue, which was one of the letters of the pair (e.g., the cue was *A*, and the pair was *AA*), a neutral cue (a plus sign), or an uninformative cue, which was a letter that did not match either member of the pair (e.g., the cue was *B*, and the pair was *AA*). Posner and Snyder (1975b) varied the probability of the cue being informative. It was informative on 20%, 50%, or 80% of the trials. Subjects were fastest when the cue was informative, and when the informative cue occurred 80% of the time.

However, subjects do not always respond differently when there is a high versus a low probability of a particular type of trial. For instance, in an experiment in which subjects have to decide whether each member of a pair of letter strings is a word, subjects typically respond more rapidly to the related-word pairs (e.g., *BREAD BUTTER*) when there is a high probability of related-word pairs. However, subjects are affected by the proportion manipulation only if they have enough time to process the first word of the pair; without adequate time for processing the first word, a 1/8 versus 1/2 versus

7/8 ratio of related- to unrelated-word pairs is ineffective (den Heyer, Briand, & Dannenbring, 1983).

Consider another experimental situation in which subjects were unaffected by a proportion manipulation. In Simpson and Burgess (1985), subjects first read an ambiguous prime word, such as *BANK*. After 750 ms, each prime word disappeared, and the subjects saw a test word, such as *MONEY*. The subjects made a lexical decision to each test word. On some trials, the test words were related to the most-frequent meaning of the ambiguous prime words. For example, *MONEY* is related to the most-frequent meaning of *BANK*. On other trials, the test words were related to a less-frequent meaning of the ambiguous prime words. For example, *RIVER* is related to a less-frequent meaning of the ambiguous prime word *BANK*. These relations are illustrated in Table 1.

Simpson and Burgess (1985) measured how rapidly subjects responded to the test words (*MONEY* or *RIVER*) when the prime words were ambiguous (*BANK*) versus when they were unambiguous (e.g., *RIDDLE*), as illustrated in Table 1. Simpson and Burgess (1985) also manipulated the probability that the test words were related to the less- versus more-frequent meanings of the ambiguous prime words. In one condition, test words were related to the less-frequent meaning on the majority, 80%, of the trials, and on only 20% of the trials were the test words related to the more-frequent meanings. In a second condition, the test words were related to the less- versus more-frequent meanings on an equal number of the trials (50%). In a third condition, the test words were related to the less-frequent meanings on only 20% of the trials, and they were related to the more-frequent meanings on 80% of the trials.

Simpson and Burgess (1985) found that the probability manipulation was ineffective. Regardless of the probability that the test words would be related to the less- versus more-frequent meanings, subjects recognized (made lexical decisions to) the more-frequent meanings (*MONEY*) more rapidly than they recognized the less-frequent meanings (*RIVER*). Thus, even when

TABLE 1. Example Stimuli[a]

Context word	Test words	
	River	Money
Bank	Related to LESS-frequent meaning	Related to MORE-frequent meaning
Riddle	Unrelated to either meaning	Unrelated to either meaning

[a]From Simpson & Burgess, 1985.

the test words were related to the less-frequent meanings on 80% of the trials, subjects still recognized the more-frequent meanings more rapidly than they recognized the less-frequent meanings (just as they did when the test words had an equal probability of being related to the less- versus more-frequent meanings). In fact, in a fourth condition, subjects were informed that many of the prime words would be ambiguous and that 80% of the test words would be related to those prime words' less-frequent meanings. But even with this informative warning, subjects still did not recognize the less-frequent meanings more rapidly than they recognized the more-frequent meanings. These data suggest that subjects could not improve their recognition of the less-frequent meanings of ambiguous words.

In the last set of experiments that we discuss here, we used a probability manipulation to investigate further the cognitive mechanism of suppression. In Gernsbacher et al. (1990), we demonstrated that correctly understanding a sentence that contains an ambiguous word requires a suppression of the meanings of that ambiguous word that are not implied by the sentence's context. For example, correctly understanding the sentence. *He dug with the spade*, requires suppression of the meaning of *spade* that is associated with playing cards. Is this suppression of contextually inappropriate meanings of ambiguous words susceptible to the proportion of trials on which suppression is needed?

Successful Suppression of Contextually Inappropriate Meanings Is Affected by Probability

In this experiment, subjects read short sentences, and after each sentence they saw a test word. Their task was to verify whether the test word fit the meaning of the sentence they just read. On 60 trials, the test word did indeed fit the sentence, but we were more interested in the 60 trials in which the test word did *not* fit the sentence. In these 60 trials, the sentence final word was either an ambiguous word (e.g., *spade*) or an unambiguous word (e.g., *shovel*). We manipulated the proportion of trials in which the sentence final word was ambiguous or unambiguous. In the High-Proportion condition, the sentence final word was ambiguous on the majority, 67%, of the trials and unambiguous on only 33% of the trials. In the Low-Proportion condition, the sentence final word was ambiguous on only 33% of the trials and unambiguous on the majority, 67%, of the trials. The design of this experiment is illustrated in Table 2.

The test word on both types of trials was related to a meaning of the ambiguous word that was inappropriate to the context, for example, *ACE*. All the test words were presented 1000 ms after the offset of the sentence final words, and the proportion variable was manipulated between subjects. Rejecting a test word like *ACE* following an ambiguous sentence final word like *spade* requires suppressing the inappropriate meaning. Rejecting *ACE* follow-

TABLE 2. Experimental Design

	Context sentence	Test word	# of trials	Proportion	Trial type
Gernsbacher,	He dug with the **spade**.	ACE	40	50%	Suppression
Varner, and	He dug with the **shovel**.	ACE	40	50%	No suppression
Faust (1990)					
Low-Proportion	He dug with the **spade**.	ACE	20	33%	Suppression
condition	He dug with the **shovel**.	ACE	40	67%	No suppression
High-Propostion	He dug with the **spade**.	ACE	40	67%	Suppression
condition	He dug with the **shovel**	ACE	20	33%	No suppression

ing an unambiguous sentence final word like *shovel* does not require this suppression. If subjects' suppression of inappropriate meanings is susceptible to the probability of trials on which suppression is needed, then subjects should be more likely to suppress the contextually inappropriate meanings in the High-Proportion condition than in the Low-Proportion condition.

Figure 11 displays our 202 subjects' data, presented as estimated activation of the inappropriate meanings. We estimated activation of the inappropriate meanings by subtracting subjects' latencies to reject test words like *ACE* after reading ambiguous words like *spade* from their latencies to reject test words like *ACE* after reading unambiguous words like *shovel*. In Figure

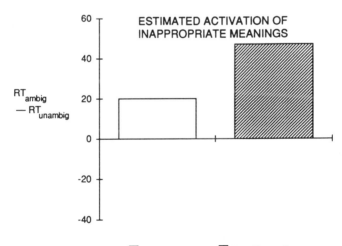

FIGURE 11. Data from the ambiguous word proportionality manipulation experiment. Estimated activation is the difference between subjects' latencies to reject test words like *ACE* after reading ambiguous words like *spade* versus unambiguous words like *shovel*.

11, the data provided by the subjects tested in the High-Proportion condition are represented by the unfilled bars, and the data provided by subjects tested in the Low-Proportion condition are represented by the hatched bars.

As Figure 11 illustrates, the inappropriate meanings remained more activated in the Low-Proportion condition than they did in the High-Proportion condition. This finding suggests that subjects were more inclined to suppress the contextually inappropriate meanings in the High-Proportion condition.

Successful Suppression of Incorrect Forms of Homophones Is Affected by Probability

In Gernsbacher and Faust (1991a), we demonstrated that correctly understanding a sentence that contains a homophone requires suppressing the other forms of that homophone that are not implied by the sentence's context. For example, correctly understanding the sentence, *He had lots of patients,* requires suppressing the homophone *patience.* In a recent experiment, subjects read short sentences, and after each sentence they saw a test word. Their task was to verify whether the test word fit the meaning of the sentence they just read. On 60 trials, the test word did indeed fit the meaning of the sentence, but we were more interested in the 60 trials in which the test word did *not* fit the meaning of the sentence. These were our experimental sentences.

We manipulated how many of these 60 experimental sentences had sentence final words that were homophones versus nonhomophones, for example, *He had lots of **patients*** versus *He had lots of **students.*** In the High-Proportion condition, 67% of the 60 experimental sentences contained homophonic sentence final words, and only 33% of the experimental sentences had nonhomophonic sentence final words. In the Low-Proportion condition, only 33% of the 60 experimental sentences contained homophonic sentence final words, and 67% had nonhomophonic sentence final words. The design of this experiment is summarized in Table 3.

The test words for all the experimental sentences were related to a meaning of the homophone's other form, for example, *CALM.* All the test

TABLE 3. Experimental Design

	Context sentence	Test word	# of trials	Proportion	Trial type
Gernsbacher and Faust (1991b)	He had lots of **patients.**	CALM	40	50%	Suppression
	He had lots of **students.**	CALM	40	50%	No suppression
Low-Proportion condition	He had lots of **patients.**	CALM	20	33%	Suppression
	He had lots of **students.**	CALM	40	67%	No suppression
High-Proportion condition	He had lots of **patients.**	CALM	40	67%	Suppression
	He had lots of **students.**	CALM	20	33%	No suppression

words were presented 1000 ms after the offset of the sentence final words, and the proportion variable was manipulated between subjects. Rejecting a test word like *CALM* following a homophonic sentence final word like *patience* requires suppressing the incorrect form. Rejecting *CALM* following a nonhomophonic sentence final word like *students* does not require this suppression. If subjects' suppression of the incorrect forms of homophones is susceptible to the probability of trials on which suppression is needed, then our subjects should have been more likely to suppress the incorrect forms in the High-Proportion condition than in the Low-Proportion condition.

Figure 12 displays our 200 subjects' data, presented as estimated activation of the homophones' incorrect forms. We estimated activation of the homophones' incorrect forms by subtracting subjects' latencies to reject test words like *CALM* after reading nonhomophones like *students* from their latencies to reject test words like *CALM* after reading homophones like *patients*. In Figure 12, the data provided by the subjects tested in the High-Proportion condition are represented by the unfilled bars, and the data provided by the subjects tested in the Low-Proportion condition are represented by the hatched bars.

As Figure 12 illustrates, the incorrect forms remained more activated in the Low-Proportion condition than they did in the High-Proportion condition. This finding suggests that subjects were more inclined to suppress the homophones' incorrect forms in the High-Proportion condition than they were in the Low-Proportion condition.

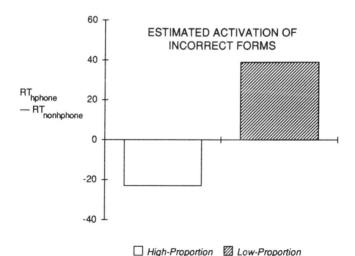

FIGURE 12.   Data from the homophone proportionality manipulation experiment. Estimated activation is the difference between subjects' latencies to reject test words like *CALM* after sentence final homophones like *patients* versus sentence final nonhomophones like *students*.

CONCLUSIONS

We began this chapter by briefly sketching our conception of suppression. We envision suppression as an active dampening of activation. We propose that suppression differs from passive decay. We also propose that successful suppression underlies skilled comprehension. We then presented several experiments that demonstrated that skilled comprehenders are more successful in suppressing inappropriate, incorrect, absent, or to-be-ignored information. And we presented some further experiments that demonstrated that skilled comprehenders are not better at rejecting inappropriate or related-but-absent information simply because they more keenly recognize what is appropriate or related.

In the last part of our chapter we discussed whether the mechanism of suppression that we have identified to underlie skilled comprehension is susceptible to probability. We presented two new experiments that demonstrated that successful suppression of the contextually inappropriate meanings of ambiguous words and successful suppression of the incorrect forms of homophones are susceptible to the probability of trials on which suppression is needed. These new data suggest that our conception of suppression is mediated somewhat by the demands of the experimental context. It remains for our further investigation to discern where skilled suppression during comprehension falls on the continuum of automatic versus more attentionally demanding cognitive processes.

ACKNOWLEDGMENTS

Much of the research we report here was supported by grants from the Air Force Office of Sponsored Research (AFOSR 89-0258, 89-0305, and 91-0323) and the National Institutes of Health (RO1 NS01376, KO4 NS2996).

REFERENCES

Allport, D. A., Tipper, S. P., & Chmiel, N. R. (1985). Perceptual integration and postcategorical filtering. In M. I. Posner & O. S. M. Marin (Eds.), *Attention and performance XI* (pp. 107–132). Hillsdale, NJ: Erlbaum.

Becker, C. A. (1976). Semantic context and word frequency effects in visual word recognition. *Journal of Experimental Psychology: Human Perception and Performance, 2,* 556–566.

Biederman, I. (1981). On the semantics of a glance at a scene. In M. Kubovy & J. R. Pomerantz (Eds.), *Perceptual organization* (pp. 213–252). Hillsdale, NJ: Erlbaum.

Biederman, I., Bickle, T. W., Teitelbaum, R. C., & Klatsky, G. J. (1988). Object search in non-scene displays. *Journal of Experimental Psychology: Learning, Memory, and Cognition. 14,* 456–467.

Biederman, I., Glass, A. L., & Stacy, E. W., Jr. (1973). Searching for objects in real world scenes. *Journal of Experimental Psychology, 97,* 22–27.

Biederman, I., Mezzanotte, R. J., & Rabinowitz, J. C. (1982). Scene perception: Detecting and judging objects undergoing relational violations. *Cognitive Psychology, 14,* 143–177.

Biederman, I., Teitelbaum, R. C., & Mezzanotte, R. J. (1983). Scene perception: A failure to find a benefit of prior expectancy or familiarity. *Journal of Experimental Psychology: Learning, Memory, and Cognition, 9,* 411–429.

Bjorklund, D. F., & Harnishfeger, K. K. (1990). The resources construct in cognitive development: Diverse sources of evidence and a theory of inefficient inhibition. *Developmental Review, 10,* 48–71.

Chapman, L., & Chapman, J. (1973). *Disordered thought in schizophrenia.* New York: Appleton-Century-Crofts.

Coltheart, M., Davelaar, E., Jonasson, J. T., & Besner, D. (1977). Access to the internal lexicon. In S. Dornic (Ed.), *Attention and performance VI* (pp. 535–555). New York: Academic Press.

Coltheart, V., Laxon, V., Rickard, M., & Elton, C. (1988). Phonological recoding in reading for meaning by adults and children. *Journal of Experimental Psychology: Learning, Memory, and Cognition, 14,* 387–397.

Conrad, C. (1974). Context effects in sentence comprehension: A study of the subjective lexicon. *Memory & Cognition, 2,* 130–138.

Dempster, F. N. (1992). The rise and fall of the inhibitory mechanism: Toward a unified theory of cognitive development and aging. *Developmental Review, 12,* 45–75.

Dempster, F. N. (1993). Resistance to interference: Developmental changes in a basic processing mechanism. In M. L. Howe & R. Pasnak (Eds.), *Emerging themes in cognitive development* (pp.1–27). New York: Springer-Verlag.

den Heyer, K., Briand, K., & Dannenbring, G. L. (1983). Strategic factors in a lexical-decision task: Evidence for automatic and attention-driven processes. *Memory & Cognition, 11,* 374–381.

Doctor, E. A., & Coltheart, M. (1980). Children's use of phonological encoding when reading for meaning. *Memory & Cognition, 8,* 195–209.

Duffy, S. A., Morris, R. K., & Rayner, K. (1988). Lexical Ambiguity and fixation times in reading. *Journal of Memory and Language, 27,* 429–446.

Friedman, A. (1979). Framing pictures: The role of knowledge in automatized encoding and memory for gist. *Journal of Experimental Psychology: General, 108,* 316–355.

Gernsbacher, M. A. (1985). Surface information loss in comprehension. *Cognitive Psychology, 17,* 324–363.

Gernsbacher, M. A. (1989). Mechanisms that improve referential access. *Cognition, 32,* 99–156.

Gernsbacher, M. A. (1990). *Language comprehension as structure building.* Hillsdale, NJ: Erlbaum.

Gernsbacher, M. A., & Faust, M. E. (1991a). The mechanism of suppression: A component of general comprehension skill. *Journal of Experimental Psychology: Learning, Memory, and Cognition, 17,* 245–262.

Gernsbacher, M. A., & Faust, M. (1991b). The role of suppression in sentence comprehension. In G. B. Simpson (Ed.), *Understanding word and sentence* (pp. 97–128). Amsterdam: North-Holland.

Gernsbacher, M. A., & Hargreaves, D. (1988). Accessing sentence participants: The advantage of first mention. *Journal of Memory and Language, 27,* 699–717.

Gernsbacher, M. A., Hargreaves, D., & Beeman, M. (1989). Building and accessing clausal representations: The advantage of first mention versus the advantage of clause recency. *Journal of Memory and Language, 28,* 735–755.

Gernsbacher, M. A., & Jescheniak, J. D. (1994). *Cataphoric devices in spoken discourse.* Manuscript submitted for publication.

Gernsbacher, M. A., & Shroyer, S. (1989). The cataphoric use of the indefinite *this* in spoken narratives. *Memory & Cognition, 17,* 536–540.

Gernsbacher, M. A., & Varner, K. R. (1988). *The multi-media comprehension battery* (Tech. Rep. No. 88-03). Eugene: University of Oregon, Institute of Cognitive and Decision Sciences.

Gernsbacher, M. A., Varner, K. R., & Faust, M. (1990). Investigating differences in general comprehension skill. *Journal of Experimental Psychology: Learning, Memory, and Cognition, 16,* 430–445.

Glucksberg, S., Kreuz, R. J., & Rho, S. H. (1986). Context can constrain lexical access: Implications for models of language comprehension. *Journal of Experimental Psychology: Learning, Memory, and Cognition, 12,* 323–335.

Harnishfeger, K. K., & Bjorklund, D. F. (1993). The ontogeny of inhibition mechanisms: A renewed approach to cognitive development. In M. L. Howe & R. Pasnak (Eds.), *Emerging themes in cognitive development* (pp. 28–49). New York: Springer-Verlag.

Hasher, L., Stoltzfus, E. R., Zacks, R., & Rypma, B. (1991). Age and inhibition. *Journal of Experimental Psychology: Learning, Memory, and Cognition, 17,* 163–169.

Hasher, L., & Zacks, R. T. (1988). Working memory, comprehension, and aging: A review and a new view. In G. H. Bower (Ed.), *The psychology of learning and motivation* (Vol. 22, pp. 193–225). San Diego: Academic Press.

Just, M. A., & Carpenter, P. A. (1992). A capacity theory of comprehension: Individual differences in working memory. *Psychological Review, 99,* 122–149.

Keele, S. W., & Neill, W. T. (1978). Mechanisms of attention. In E. C. Carterette & M. P. Friedman (Eds.), *Handbook of perception* (pp. 3–47). New York: Academic Press.

Kellas, G., Paul, S. T., Martin, M., & Simpson, G. B. (1991). Contextual feature activation and meaning access. In G. B. Simpson (Ed.), *Understanding word and sentence* (pp. 47–71). New York: Elsevier.

Kintsch, W. (1988). The role of knowledge in discourse comprehension: A construction-integration model. *Psychological Review, 95,* 163–182.

Kintsch, W., & Mross, E. F. (1985). Context effects in word identification. *Journal of Memory and Language, 24,* 336–349.

Lucas, M. (1987). Frequency effects on the processing of ambiguous words in sentence context. *Language and Speech, 30,* 25–46.

Mandler, J. M., & Johnson, N. (1976). Some of the thousand words a picture is worth. *Journal of Experimental Psychology: Human Learning and Memory, 2,* 529–540.

Marslen-Wilson, W., & Welsh, A. (1978). Processing interactions and lexical access during word recognition in continuous speech. *Cognition, 10,* 29–63.

McClelland, J. L., & Rumelhart, D. E. (1981). An interactive activation model of context effects in letter perception: Part 1. An account of basic findings. *Psychological Review, 88,* 375–407.

Merrill, E. C., Sperber, R. D., & McCauley, C. (1981). Differences in semantic encoding as a function of reading comprehension skill. *Memory & Cognition, 9,* 618–624.

Meyer, D. E., & Schvaneveldt, R. W. (1971). Facilitation in recognizing pairs of words: Evidence of a dependence between retrieval operations. *Journal of Experimental Psychology, 90,* 227–234.

Neill, W. T., & Westberry, R. L. (1987). Selective attention and the suppression of cognitive noise. *Journal of Experimental Psychology: Learning, Memory, and Cognition, 13,* 327–334.

Norris, D. (1986). Word recognition: Context effects without priming. *Cognition, 22,* 93–136.

Onifer, W., & Swinney, D. A. (1981). Accessing lexical ambiguities during sentence comprehension: Effects of frequency of meaning and contextual bias. *Memory & Cognition, 9,* 225–236.

Palmer, S. E. (1975). The effects of contextual scenes on the perception of objects. *Memory & Cognition, 3,* 519–526.

Perfetti, C. A., & Roth, S. (1981). Some of the interactive processes in reading and their role in reading skill. In A. M. Lesgold & C. A. Perfetti (Eds.), *Interactive processes in reading* (pp. 269–297). Hillsdale, NJ: Erlbaum.

Posner, M. I., & Snyder, C. R. R. (1975a). Attention and cognitive control. In R. L. Solso (Ed.), *Information processing and cognition: The Loyola symposium* (pp. 55–85). Hillsdale, NJ: Erlbaum.

Posner, M. I., & Snyder, C. R. R. (1975b). Facilitation and inhibition in the processing of signals. In P. M. A. Rabbitt & S. Dornic (Eds.), *Attention and performance V* (pp. 669–682). New York: Academic Press.

Rosson, M. B. (1985). The interaction of pronunciation rules and lexical representations in reading aloud. *Memory & Cognition, 13*, 90–99.

Schank, R. C., & Abelson, R. P. (1977). *Scripts, plans, goals and understanding*. Hillsdale, NJ: Erlbaum.

Seidenberg, M. S., Tanenhaus, M. K., Leiman, J. M., & Bienkowski, M. (1982). Automatic access of the meanings of ambiguous words in context: Some limitations of knowledge-based processing. *Cognitive Psychology, 14*, 489–537.

Simpson, G. B., & Burgess, C. (1985). Activation and selection processes in the recognition of ambiguous words. *Journal of Experimental Psychology: Human Perception and Performance, 11*, 28–39.

Smith, M. C., & McGee, L. E. (1980). Tracing the time course of picture-word processing. *Journal of Experimental Psychology: General, 109*, 373–392.

Swinney, D. A. (1979). Lexical access during sentence comprehension: (Re)consideration of context effects. *Journal of Verbal Learning and Verbal Behavior, 18*, 645–659.

Tabossi, P. (1988a). Accessing lexical ambiguity in different types of sentential contexts. *Journal of Memory and Language, 27*, 324–340.

Tabossi, P. (1988b). Effects of context on the immediate interpretation of unambiguous nouns. *Journal of Experimental Psychology: Learning, Memory, and Cognition, 14*, 153–162.

Tanenhaus, M. K., Leiman, J. M., & Seidenberg, M. S. (1979). Evidence for multiple stages in the processing of ambiguous words in syntactic contexts. *Journal of Verbal Learning and Verbal Behavior, 18*, 427–440.

Till, R. E., Mross, E. F., & Kintsch, W. (1988). Time course of priming for associate and inference words in a discourse context. *Memory & Cognition, 16*, 283–299.

Tipper, S. P., & Driver, J. (1988). Negative priming between pictures and words in a selective attention task: Evidence for semantic processing of ignored stimuli. *Memory & Cognition, 16*, 64–70.

Tweedy, J. R., Lapinsky, R. H., & Schvaneveldt, R. W. (1977). Semantic-context effects on word recognition: Influence of varying the proposition of items presented in an appropriate context. *Memory & Cognition, 5*, 84–89.

van Orden, G. C. (1987). A rows is a rose: Spelling, sound, and reading. *Memory & Cognition, 15*, 181–198.

van Orden, G. C., Johnston, J. C., & Hale, B. L. (1988). Word identification in reading proceeds from spelling to sound to meaning. *Journal of Experimental Psychology: Learning, Memory, and Cognition, 14*, 371–386.

van Petten, C., & Kutas, M. (1987). Ambiguous words in context: An event-related potential analysis of the time course of meaning activation. *Journal of Memory and Language, 26*, 188–208.

Yee, P. L. (1991). Semantic inhibition of ignored words during a figure classification task. *Quarterly Journal of Experimental Psychology, 43A*, 127–153.

Zechmeister, E. B., & Nyberg, S. E. (1982). *Human memory: An introduction to research and theory*. Monterey CA: Brooks/Cole.

10

Catastrophic Interference in Neural Networks
Causes, Solutions, and Data

Stephan Lewandowsky and Shu-Chen Li

A thumbnail sketch of the history of interference research during the last several decades would identify three distinct stages, each tied to major paradigm shifts in cognitive psychology as a whole. The 1950s and 1960s were the heyday of the verbal learning approach, which examined forgetting in terms of S–R associations, transfer surfaces, paired associates, and the like. During the 1970s, the field rapidly embraced the information-processing approach, with its new emphasis on dividing simple S–R relations into distinct stages of processing and distinct memory stores. In most information-processing models, forgetting and interference were represented by a variety of putative processes, such as displacement, failure to engage the correct type of rehearsal, failure to access information in the absence of the proper retrieval cue, and so on. Some twenty years later, the focus of the field has arguably shifted again, this time in part because of the advent of connectionist networks that have rapidly become the tool of choice for many cognitive scientists (see Dempster, Chapter 1, this volume for a related perspective on the history of interference research).

Several reasons can be cited for the growing enthusiasm for connectionist networks, also variously known as neural nets or PDP models. First, unlike information-processing models, they can claim some biological plausibility owing to their apparent structural similarity to the human brain. Second, and perhaps more important, connectionist networks, together with the closely allied distributed memory models, have provided elegant accounts of a number of basic aspects of human cognition, such as letter and word recognition (McClelland & Rumelhart, 1981; Rumelhart & McClelland, 1982), word pronunciation (Seidenberg & McClelland, 1989), children's acquisition of past tense (Rumelhart & McClelland, 1986), memory for serial order (Lewandowsky & Murdock, 1989), Stroop interference (Cohen, Dunbar, & McClelland, 1990), base-rate neglect in categorization tasks (Gluck & Bower, 1988), and numerous other categorization phenomena (e.g., Kurschke, 1992).

Most of these cases are related by several common threads. First, prior attempts to derive explanations of the same phenomena within the traditional information-processing framework had been arguably less successful or less elegant. Second, applications of neural networks have often spurred empirical tests (e.g., Besner, 1990; Lewandowsky & Hockley, 1987) or exploration of novel predictions (e.g., Li & Lewandowsky, 1993). Third, although publication of the original network sometimes engendered rejoinders, critiques, and follow-up articles, the stimulation of controversy can also be viewed as an indication of progress and success (cf. Lewandowsky, 1993). Finally, networks have often served to integrate diverse phenomena that, on the surface, have little in common. A particularly compelling example is Metcalfe's (1993) recent model that unifies Korsakoff's syndrome, feeling-of-knowing judgments, and release from proactive interference under a common theoretical umbrella. In similar spirit, this chapter attempts to illuminate the relationships between seemingly diverse tasks, concepts, and applications.

A CONNECTIONIST MODEL OF COGNITIVE DEFICITS IN SCHIZOPHRENIA

The utility of the network approach is best illustrated by a more detailed presentation of a particular case. Cohen and Servan-Schreiber (1992) presented a model of the cognitive deficits and biological abnormalities observed in schizophrenia, which tied together numerous concepts that turn out to be relevant in the interference domain, such as the utilization of context, the nature and origin of individual differences, and the biological underpinnings of behavior.

Although schizophrenia is marked by a wide variety of behavioral disturbances, including social deficiencies not relevant here, remarkable consistencies can be identified at the biological and at the information-processing levels of analysis. At the information-processing level, schizophrenics can be characterized as being unable to choose the behavior appropriate for the particular context; hence, they exhibit the attentional deficits that, since its recognition as an illness, have been associated with schizophrenia (e.g., Bleuler, 1911, cited in Cohen & Servan-Schreiber, 1992). Thus, schizophrenics show disproportionate interference in the Stroop task (see also Neill, Valdes, & Terry, Chapter 7, this volume), in which the ink color of an incompatible color word must be named (e.g., respond "blue" to *red* printed in blue ink). Similarly, schizophrenics have difficulty with the continuous performance task (CPT), in which a target letter has to be detected within a sequence of context stimuli. One version of this task, the CPT-double, requires recognition of the consecutive reoccurrence of any letter in the sequence, thus confronting schizophrenics with the particular difficulty of having to use a variable context to determine the appropriate response (Cohen & Servan-Schreiber, 1992, p. 47).

Turning to the biological level of analysis, the most enduring and most widely accepted hypothesis of the causes of schizophrenia points to a reduction of the effects of dopamine in prefrontal cortex. This hypothesis has been supported by the chemical specificity of neuroleptics used to treat schizophrenia; by the psychotropic effects of drugs that affect dopamine activity in the central nervous system; and by postmortem studies of schizophrenics (Cohen & Servan-Schreiber, 1992, p. 51). Prefrontal cortex, in turn, has been identified as playing a role in retaining the context necessary for the selection and control of actions. Support for this notion derives from a variety of findings, including the identification of prefrontal cells that are active in response to particular context demands, the losses of contextual abilities associated with prefrontal lesions, and observations of cerebral blood flow (Cohen & Servan-Schreiber, 1992, p. 50).

Given the apparent prominence of prefrontal cortex in both schizophrenia and utilization of context, Cohen and Servan-Schreiber (1992) were able to propose an integration of the two levels of analysis—biological and information-processing—within a single connectionist architecture. The networks included a separate context module that governed the selection of appropriate behaviors, analogous to one of the presumed functions of prefrontal cortex. The response properties of that context module, in turn, could be disrupted, through adjustment of a single simulation parameter, in a fashion analogous to the presumed disturbance of the dopamine system in schizophrenia. Cohen and Servan-Schreiber applied networks of this type to three different tasks, Stroop interference, CPT-double, and lexical disambiguation, which, despite their surface dissimilarities, are conceptually related because all require efficient use of context.

For simplicity of exposition, we focus here on the CPT-double task, in which the subject must detect the repetition of a letter in a random sequence of stimuli. Table 1 contrasts the results of a behavioral experiment (Cornblatt, Lenzenweger, & Erlenmeyer-Kimling, 1989) with those of a stimulation of the CPT-double. (Details of this and all other simulations are reported in the Appendix.)

Schizophrenics differ from normals primarily in their dramatically elevated miss rate, an effect that is mimicked by the neural network through adjustment of a "gain" parameter. Full explanation of that parameter must be deferred until the workings of neural nets have been presented in more detail; at this point it suffices to state that gain refers to the ability of quasi-neuronal units in the context module to respond to their (quasi-synaptic) input. Hence, adjustment of gain can be considered a simulation analog to the presumed effects of dopamine in prefrontal cortex, and the simulation results therefore support the notion that a disrupted ability to utilize context underlies the cognitive deficits observed in schizophrenia. Finally, taken together with the other simulations reported by Cohen and Servan-Schreiber (1992), the results show how simple connectionist networks can capture and relate previously unconnected levels of analysis, and can faithfully reproduce data from behavioral experimentation.

Moreover, an immediate connection exists between Cohen and Servan-Schreiber's (1992) model and the focus of the present volume: Dempster (1991, Chapter 1, this volume), in a review of the literature, suggested that the frontal lobes play an important role in resisting interference, as shown by an analysis of individual differences, the behavior of patients with frontal lobe lesions, and so on (see also Chapter 5 by Bjorklund & Harnishfeger and Chapter 6 by Harnishfeger, this volume). It follows that Cohen and Servan-Schreiber's (1992) model, with its claim to simulating the functioning of the frontal lobes, should also constitute the theoretical tool of choice to examine individual differences in interference and inhibition. Alas, interference and forgetting have often been considered to be the Achilles' heel of connectionism.

TABLE 1. Behavioral Data and Simulation Results for the CPT-Double Task Comparing Normals and Schizophrenics (or Simulation Analogue)

Response	Empirical data		Simulation results	
	Normals	Schizophrenics	Normal gain	Reduced gain
Misses	.17	.46	.20	.49
False alarms	.05	.08	.05	.09

CATASTROPHIC INTERFERENCE

The implausible forgetting characteristics of most networks were first demonstrated by McCloskey and Cohen (1989) and Ratcliff (1990). McCloskey and Cohen (1989) discovered that, in the type of network used by Cohen and Servan-Schreiber (1992), memory for a first list of paired associates was virtually eradicated by a single study trial on a second list of competing associations. That is, in a simulation of the classic A–B/A–C paradigm (e.g., Barnes & Underwood, 1959), performance on A–B pairs dropped from 100% correct to near 0% after a single trial on the competing A–C pairs, which contrasts sharply with the ability of human subjects to remember roughly 50% of first-list pairs even after 20 interfering trials.

Similarly, Ratcliff (1990) demonstrated that networks could not perform above chance in a simple recognition task, owing to extensive interfer-

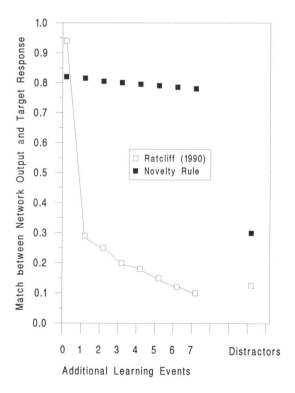

FIGURE 1. Catastrophic interference observed by Ratcliff (1990) and its reduction when the novelty rule is applied.

ence between items. Figure 1, adapted from Ratcliff's simulations, shows the extremely steep drop in performance associated with learning of additional list items. (Data from the novelty rule will be discussed later.)

Immediately after presentation of a study item (0 additional learning events), the model is capable of correct recognition, indicated in the figure by a high match between the model's output and the just-studied item. Moreover, as required for intact discrimination, the model gives low match values to distractor items that had not been studied (far right of the graph). When the recognition test is repeated after study of only one additional item, performance drops dramatically: there is little difference between the network's responses to the first old item (studied just previously) and a nonstudied distractor. Finally, after seven additional learning episodes, recognition of the first item is completely eliminated and indistinguishable from the response to the distractors.

This rapid forgetting has been termed catastrophic interference and has engendered a flurry of subsequent corrective research activity (e.g., French, 1991; Hetherington & Seidenberg, 1989; Kortge, 1990; Lewandowsky, 1991; McRae & Hetherington, 1993). Because the forgetting problem can be shown to derive from the same fundamental properties that also produce several desirable properties of connectionist nets, an understanding of catastrophic interference, and ways of reducing it, deserves to be more than an esoteric topic for debate among modelers. In the remainder of this chapter, we discuss how networks retrieve and acquire information, how those processes necessarily give rise to (potentially catastrophic) forgetting, how the extent of that forgetting can be reduced by a variety of modifications, and how these in turn affect the models' predictive capabilities. A final set of simulations extends variants of the earlier Cohen and Servan-Schreiber (1992) models to the interference domain.

WEIGHTED CONNECTIONS AND RETRIEVAL IN CONNECTIONIST NETWORKS

Connectionist networks typically store information in a *distributed* and *composite* fashion. Following notation proposed by Shiffrin and Murnane (1991), the former property implies that information for a given item is distributed across a large number of individual components, known as connections or weights. The latter property implies that each weight, in turn, contributes to retention of all items in memory. These two properties are best identified by considering a simple model, known as the linear associator, in some depth.

Figure 2 shows the architecture of a linear associator with three input and two output units in two different ways, each emphasizing a different characteristic of the model. (A) underscores the connectivity of the network

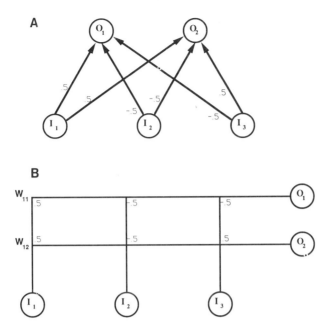

FIGURE 2. Two ways to represent the architecture of a simple linear associator. Weights are indicated next to each connection between input and output units.

and the fact that it consists of layers of units and weights, whereas (B) underscores the matrix structure of the weights. In both (A) and (B), when the network is given an input (by applying some pattern of activation to the bottom units) the weighted connections compute a response that is instantiated as some pattern of activation across the two output units O_1 and O_2.

The values of the weights shown in the figure correspond to the state of the network after study of two associations, allowing examination of the model's retrieval properties before discussing the learning process. Suppose the test pattern {1, 0 −1} is presented, which corresponds to activating input unit I_1 with the value 1, I_2 with 0, and I_3 with −1. The input is fed from each unit along all weighted connections, such that each output node will receive, and sum, signals from its incoming connections. Consider the output unit O_1. According to the weights shown in the figure, the unit will receive .5 of whatever activation was applied to input unit I_1 and, correspondingly, −.5 of I_2, and −.5 of I_3. The input pattern {1, 0, −1} thus yields an activation of unity for output unit O_1 (.5 × 1 + −.5 × 0 + −.5 × −1). The activation of O_2, computed in an analogous fashion, turns out to be zero. Hence, the response to the retrieval cue {1, 0 −1} is the output pattern {1, 0}. Now consider presentation of an alternate set of inputs, consisting of the pattern {0, −1, 1}. Using the weights in Figure 2, the network responds with the pattern {0, 1}. With the additional assumption that input and output patterns are isomorphic to patterns of psychologically relevant *features* of concepts, this network can be said to contain the associations between two pairs of words.

This simple model fulfills the criteria of a distributed and composite associative memory. It is *associative* because two associations can be reliably retrieved, with the cue {1, 0, −1} giving rise to the response {1, 0} and the cue {0, −1, 1} yielding {0, 1}. It is *distributed,* because a given association is stored across a number of weights, each of which contributes a small part to the total information. Consider the response term of the first association: The activation of O_1 is the result of partial contributions from *three* weights (with values .5, −.5, and −.5). Finally, the network is a *composite* model because all weights are involved in the storage of all associations. Consider the weights that connect I_3 to the output units. Both weights are involved in retrieval, regardless of whether the input activation of I_3 is −1 (for the first input cue) or +1 (for the second association).

The way in which associations are stored in connectionist models turns out to be at the heart of some of their more attractive properties, as well as being the cause of their susceptibility to catastrophic interference. Consider first the clearly desirable ability to generalize, that is, to provide an approximation of a previously learned response even when the retrieval cue is distorted.

Returning to the linear associator in Figure 2, focus on the version shown in (B). Suppose the input pattern for the first association is distorted somewhat, such that it now is {.5, 1, −1} instead of the original {1, 0, −1}. Clearly, when presented with that input, the network can no longer give the desired response {1, 0}. However, because only a subset of connections is affected by the altered input, an approximation to the initial response is still obtained, which in the present case turns out to be {.75, −.25}. Although different from the original response, that output is still far closer to it than to the alternate response {0, 1}. It is only when the input is distorted further, for example by presenting {0, 0, −1}, that the output no longer clearly resembles the appropriate response.

In one way or another, this ability to generalize underlies many successful network applications. Knapp and Anderson's (1984) model of categorization and prototype formation was founded almost entirely on the generalization properties outlined in the foregoing. Similarly, Seidenberg and McClelland's (1989) word pronunciation model relied on generalization to extract rules applicable to the pronunciation of regular words. And in the CPT-double example presented at the outset (Cohen & Servan-Schreiber, 1992), generalization allowed the network to learn detection of the repetition of *any* letter in the sequence, as opposed to the recognition of specific static combinations.

Clearly, generalization is an important property of most connectionist network applications. Hence, it must be of concern that the distributed representations that produce generalization, through their involvement in the learning process, also seemingly promote the occurrence of catastrophic interference.

LEARNING IN CONNECTIONIST NETWORKS

We have given an example to show that a network can store and retrieve multiple associations and can generalize in a plausible fashion if it is assumed that the weights have somehow taken on the required values during learning. Several learning algorithms exist to ensure that this weight pattern is obtained; most prominent among them is the *delta rule* (e.g., Rumelhart, Hinton, & Williams, 1986; Stone, 1986). The delta rule states that weights are iteratively adjusted in order to minimize the discrepancy, or *error,* between the network's current output and a desired target response. At each learning trial, the cue pattern that is to be associated with the response is presented, the current output from the network is computed, and the error (discrepancy) between that output and the desired response is used to adjust all weights in the necessary direction. Across learning trials, the error approaches zero as the weights continue to be adjusted until they give rise to the exact desired responses (for the purposes of this chapter we consistently assume that such weight pattern exists). In addition to governing learning, the delta rule is also involved in producing forgetting. An analysis of the forgetting process identifies three distinct cases of (potentially catastrophic) interference.

Case I: Response Competition and Catastrophic Interference

Return once again to Figure 2. Suppose that the linear associator is now given another association to learn, consisting of the earlier cue {1, 0, –1} in conjunction with the *different* target response {1, 1}. In behavioral terms, this corresponds to the well-known A–B/A–C paradigm in which, after learning a first list of paired associates to perfection, the subject is given a second list involving the same stimuli paired with different responses (e.g., Barnes & Underwood, 1959).

Analysis of the Delta Rule   How does the linear associator accommodate learning of a competing association? We know that, with the weight pattern shown in Figure 2, presentation of the cue {1, 0, –1} yields the output {1, 0}. The network can therefore be said to have mastered the A–B phase of an interference experiment involving lists of paired associates. Now suppose a single A–C association is to be acquired, consisting of the earlier input pattern {1, 0, –1} in conjunction with a new target vector {1, 1}. *Vector* is the technical label for any array of numbers and will be used to refer to patterns of activation.

When presented with the input vector {1, 0, −1}, the output of the network {1, 0}, considered correct until now, differs from the newly desired target {1, 1}. Specifically, the *delta* or error vector on the first competing learning trial, formed by taking the difference between desired and actual output, is {0, 1}. The delta vector, in turn, is used to update each weight by adding to its current value some fraction of the product of error and input:

$$\Delta w_{ij} = k \delta_j a_i,$$

where k is a learning parameter (typically assuming values in the range .0001–.1), δ_j is the error signal received from the jth output unit, and a_i is the input activation received from the ith input unit. Two implications of this equation should be apparent: first, a weight update occurs only if the error signal is nonzero and, second, a weight is updated only if it receives nonzero input.

Consider the left-most column of weights in Figure 2(B). For the top weight (w_{11}), the error signal (δ_j) is zero, hence obviating the need for an update. For the bottom weight (w_{12}), on the other hand, the error signal is 1, and the activation (a_i) received from the left-most input unit (I_1) is also 1. Suppose the learning parameter k has been arbitrarily set to the value .1: the Δw_{ij} for the bottom weight (w_{12}) would be .1, thus changing its value to .6 for the next trial.

Once all weights have been updated in this fashion, the next learning trial commences with repeated presentation of the stimulus. In the present case, the new output from the network would be {1, .1}: clearly, that output is still far from the desired target {1, 1}, but the discrepancy has already been reduced, with a new delta vector of {0, 9}. At the end of learning, the delta vector will be zero and the network's output will be identical to the newly desired target. The final weight pattern, listing the three columns of connections from left to right, will be {.5, 1}, {−.5, −.5}, and {−.5, 0}.

We have shown that the delta rule enables the linear associator to acquire a new association: every time the pattern {1, 0, −1} is now presented, the network responds, as desired, with {1, 1}. However, that response is now the only one available from the network upon presentation of the cue; the initial association, involving the output {1, 0}, has been forgotten. Given the constraints of this example, no set of circumstances exists that would allow retrieval of the exact initial response. Hence, catastrophic interference has occurred.

Weight Spaces   The inevitability of catastrophic interference can be understood by visualizing learning as movement through *weight space*. Consider an even simpler version of the linear associator, one in which two input units map into a single output unit via two weights. Suppose that a single association must be learned. We know from the preceding section that the delta learning rule would iteratively adjust the two weights until the desired output has been associated with the stimulus. Now suppose that each weight maps into a value along an ordinate or an abscissa, such that the model's current state can be represented by a position in this two-dimensional weight space. Suppose furthermore that the total magnitude of the error, best defined as the sum of all squared elements of the delta vector, is represented by a third, vertical axis, such that height is inversely related to the extent of learning. We can then understand learning to represent the model's descent along an error surface in this three-dimensional space. Learning ceases once the lowest point (ideally 0 height) on that surface has been reached, which corresponds to that conjunction of weights that yields the correct response.

Now let a topographic map of the United States represent weight space. Let Colorado be the starting point, and let Oklahoma be the solution space. Because the error-driven learning minimizes error (corresponding to altitude in this analogy) the model will leave Colorado and gravitate toward Oklahoma, until a point is reached at which any further movement would only increase altitude and, hence, error. Now suppose that a new response is associated with the same imaginary stimulus, and that the correct response is now represented by, say, California. In our analogy, this would be tantamount to raising the altitude of Oklahoma above that of California: because Oklahoma no longer corresponds to the correct response, the error would suddenly be enormous. Again, the error-driven learning will drive the model toward the new solution space; however, this will also cause complete forgetting of the previous response. By the time California is reached, the model is far away from Oklahoma, exactly as it was at the outset of learning.

The analogy clarifies two points. First, catastrophic interference is a direct consequence of distributed, composite representations. Because all responses are represented by the same set of weights (latitude and longitude in the analogy), any new learning must affect retention of existing information. Second, complete *catastrophic* forgetting is inevitable because the model cannot simultaneously be in Oklahoma *and* California. Put more formally, because the solution spaces do not overlap, only one or the other, but not both, responses can be retained by the network.

Does this imply that connectionist networks, quite unlike humans, are incapable of acquiring and retaining competing information? The intriguing answer to this question is both encouraging and bleak at the same time. It is encouraging because, with little effort, modifications can be made that, in principle, allow competing associations to be learned. It is bleak because, once these modifications have been made, further examination of the learning process reveals that the catastrophic interference problem is even more pervasive and pernicious than might appear at first glance.

Case II: Sequential Learning and Catastrophic Interference

Figure 3 shows an expanded version of the linear associator. It differs from the network used in the previous example by an additional two weights, currently set to zero, and an additional input unit.

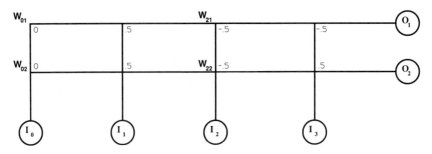

FIGURE 3. Extended version of the linear associator, with an additional column of weights to represent context.

The presence of the additional input unit, said to represent "context," allows differentiation between two lists of associations. For example, the input pattern from the preceding example could be expanded to $\{0, 1, 0, -1\}$ for the first-list response $\{1, 0\}$, whereas the competing response $\{1, 1\}$ might be associated with the expanded input pattern $\{1, 1, 0, -1\}$. In consequence, although both responses are to be associated with, virtually, the same input pattern, each response can be retrieved selectively by cueing the appropriate list using the additional input unit. For the network in Figure 3, selective retrieval requires that the two additional weights in the left-most column are set to $0(w_{01}$, top) and $1(w_{02}$, bottom).

This is encouraging news: With only a slight, and by all accounts reasonable, change in the representation of the input, the linear associator can store and retrieve two competing associations. Indeed, an expanded version of this revised representation of input underlies the "context module" that Cohen and Servan-Schreiber (1992) identified as crucial in performance on several tasks; it now appears that a "context module" of this type might also form a possible basis for list differentiation and, hence, reduction of interference.

In terms of an abstract graphical weight space analogy, the introduction of context allows the solution spaces for the two associations to overlap. In consequence, a common set of weights exists that can satisfy the constraints imposed by both associations but that nonetheless allows selective retrieval. McCloskey and Cohen (1989) showed that under these circumstances catastrophic interference can be avoided. However, a particularly pernicious problem remains: there is no guarantee that the delta learning rule will converge on the desired set of weights, even though it does exist in principle. Consider the expanded network in Figure 3. The weights shown there, including the zeros on the additional pair of connections, currently represent the association between the first input pattern $\{0, 1, 0, -1\}$ and the corresponding response $\{1, 0\}$, but not the competing association involving $\{1, 1, 0, -1\}$ and

{1, 1}. Now suppose that the competing association is to be learned, using a value of .1 for the learning parameter k. On the first learning trial, the delta vector will be {0, 1}, thus sending a strong error signal to the bottom row of weights. Because the new, left-most input unit (I_0) is set to unity for the second association, the critical bottom-left weight (w_{02}) is updated by +.1. Although that update is in the required direction (recall that we earlier identified 1 as the desired final value of that weight), the presence of an error signal and a nonzero input for some of the *other* weights in the bottom row implies that they, too, will be updated. Specifically, after the first learning trial, the bottom row of weights will be {.1, .6, –.5, .4}, and at the end of learning the final pattern will be {.333, .833, –.5, .167}. Clearly, the network will then have acquired the association between {1, 1, 0, –1} and {1, 1}. However, computation of the response to the original cue {0, 1, 0, –1} reveals that the network has also, at least partially, forgotten the first association. That response is now {1, .667}, as opposed to the originally learned {1, 0}.

What happened? Although a common solution space accommodating both associations was known to exist, the network failed to find it. Instead, the model moved from a solution space satisfying only the first constraint to another one that satisfied *only* the second constraint. Figure 4 provides an abstract representation of why this occurred.[1]

---

[1]A weight-space analysis of Case II was provided earlier by McCloskey and Cohen (1989).

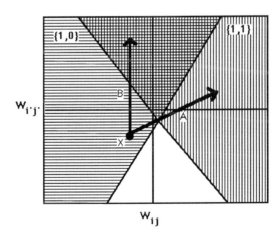

FIGURE 4. Arbitrary two-dimensional weight space representing two solution spaces for the responses {1, 0} and {1, 1}, a starting point (X), and two possible paths (A and B) that can be followed during learning. Path A leads to catastrophic interference, path B allows simultaneous retention of both responses.

The figure shows an *arbitrary* weight space, involving two weights w_{ij} and $w_{i'j'}$, together with two partially overlapping solution spaces. At the outset of the preceding example, the network (only two of its weights are shown in the figure) can be considered to be somewhere in the solution space for the first association. To provide a connection with the present problem, that space is labeled {1, 0} in Figure 4, and is shown to contain some arbitrary point X denoting the initial state of the model. When the second association is presented for learning, the delta rule propels the model along the path labeled A in the figure (the third dimension, representing the magnitude of error, is not shown), until the alternate solution space {1, 1} is entered. It is clear from the figure that the network has then departed the initial solution space {1, 0}.

Why, then, does the model follow path A, which involves forgetting of the first association, when it could have followed path B to the common solution space? The answer involves an analysis of the training regime used in this example. By presenting only the second association for training, the network satisfied that constraint only, and did so in the quickest way possible. In the present case, this involved adjusting *all* weights (w_{ij} and $w_{i'j'}$ in Figure 4) simultaneously. A different path, somewhere in between A and B , would have been followed to the common solution space only if *both* associations had been presented for training in alternating order. It is only by alternating between desired responses, and hence error signals, that the delta rule can satisfy both constraints simultaneously.

It follows that the existence of a common solution space, although necessary to avoid catastrophic interference, by itself is not sufficient to eliminate forgetting. Indeed, catastrophic interference can occur whenever any set of stimuli (even if they do not involve competing responses) is learned in *sequential* fashion, one after the other, rather than in alternating fashion by cycling through all stimuli on each learning trial. Hence, the catastrophic interference problem is often referred to as the sequential learning problem (e.g., Hetherington & Seidenberg, 1989). The magnitude of the problem should now be apparent: catastrophic forgetting is not merely a problem of "interference" between competing stimuli, in the way that people have difficulty differentiating between first-list and second-list responses, but represents a fundamental aspect of the ahistoric nature of learning in connectionist networks. Thus, whereas children acquire arithmetic facts in sequential order, such that "1 + 1 = 2" is, presumably, learned at a younger age than "23 + 7 = 30," connectionist networks fail to retain the earlier information under an equivalent training regime (McCloskey & Cohen, 1989).

Given the severity of the problem and the interest in connectionism, it is not surprising that several solutions to catastrophic interference have been put forward. It turns out that, in one way or another, most of these solutions eliminate interference by attempting to achieve within the network what the modeler can achieve outside the model by carefully selecting special input and output patterns.[2] To illustrate, consider one final example.

Case III: Orthogonality and Catastrophic Interference

An important property of the delta learning rule, briefly mentioned earlier, is that only those weights that receive an input signal are updated. Weights connected to an input unit that is never activated are not updated. For confirmation, consider the third column of weights (w_{21} and w_{22}) in the linear associator in Figure 3. Because the corresponding input unit (I_2) is set to zero for both associations, those weights remain the same throughout learning. Now suppose that, instead of learning the second association from above, the network in Figure 3 is given the pattern {0, 0, 1, 0}, which is to be paired with the response {0, 1}. Note that the input pattern involves a nonzero activation only for that input unit (I_2) that does not contribute to the other associations. By tracing weight updates in the usual fashion, it can be shown that this novel response is learned without interfering with information already stored in the weight matrix. The pattern of weights at the end of learning is shown in Figure 5, and Figure 6 illustrates graphically the reasons for the absence of interference.

Figure 6 again shows the solution space for the first association, labeled {1, 0}, together with the starting point X. An additional weight, $w_{i^*j^*}$, is represented on the vertical axis. Suppose that this third weight is not involved in retention of the initially stored information: in that case, as shown in the figure by the three-dimensional wedgelike structure, the solution space for the first association is unbounded in the third dimension. Hence, if subsequent

---

[2]One exception that deserves mention is a recent model by Kruschke (1992), which avoids interference by creating quasi-localized representations with little overlap between items.

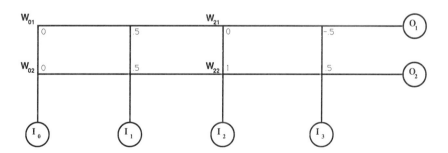

FIGURE 5. Final weight pattern in the linear associator after learning of an orthogonal association.

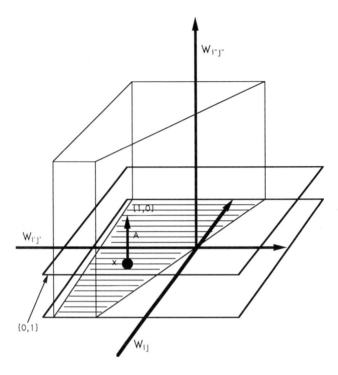

FIGURE 6. Arbitrary three-dimensional weight space illustrating the reasons for an absence of interference if patterns are orthogonal. Three-dimensional wedge structure represents solution space for {1, 0}, which is unbounded in the third dimension. Solution space for the pattern {0, 1} is a plane unbounded in the first two dimensions. Sequential learning does not lead to interference because different weights are involved in retaining the two patterns.

learning involves updating of only $w_{i''j''}$, the network will follow path A in the figure, and learn the new response {0, 1} by entering its solution space, an unbounded plane parallel to the other two axes, without leaving the initial solution space.

In general, interference between sequentially learned patterns is minimal, or indeed absent, if the input vectors are *orthogonal* to each other. Two vectors are said to be orthogonal if the pairwise products of elements across the two vectors sum to zero. Consider the patterns {0, 0, 1, 0} and {0, 1, 0, −1}: the sum of their pairwise products ($0 \times 0 + 0 \times 1 + 1 \times 0 + 0 \times -1$) is zero; hence the patterns are orthogonal and did not interfere with each other. Now consider the patterns {0, 1, 0, −1} and {1, 1, 0, −1} used for Case II: the sum of their pairwise products is 2, the patterns are not orthogonal, and, hence, they interfered with each other.

A demonstration of the effectiveness of orthogonalization of input patterns is shown in Figure 7. These results are from a simulation of the

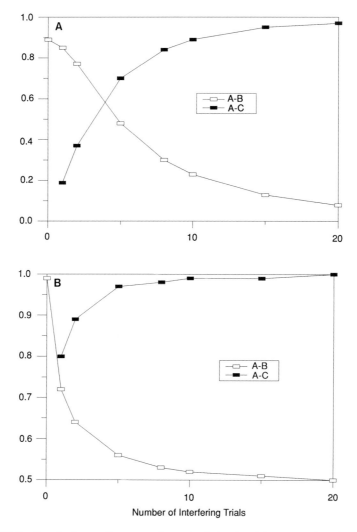

FIGURE 7. Results from a linear associator simulation involving approximately orthogonal (A) and nonorthogonal (B) random stimulus and response vectors. Different baselines reflect different expected similarities between random pairs of vectors. Data taken from Lewandowsky (1991).

A–B/A–C paradigm (Lewandowsky, 1991). The model underlying these simulations was a linear associator identical to the networks used in the present examples, except that a larger number of units and weights was involved. It is clear from comparison of the panels that orthogonal vectors (A) engender considerably less rapid forgetting than nonorthogonal vectors (B).

One limitation associated with reducing interference by changing the nature of the input patterns is that not all learning problems can be represented by orthogonal vectors. For example, if two competing lists are to be differentiated by context units, as in the earlier Case II, then all items *within* a given list necessarily share the same activation pattern on those context units. In consequence, items within a list are no longer orthogonal to each other. Lewandowsky's (1991) simulation in Figure 7 did not involve context units to differentiate between lists because input patterns were to remain orthogonal. Hence, although steepness of forgetting differed between (A) and (B), loss of information after the maximal number of interfering trials was complete for the reasons cited in connection with Case I.

The challenge, then, is somehow to achieve orthogonality even though the input patterns themselves may not be orthogonal. As counterintuitive as this may appear at first glance, several solutions to catastrophic interference have been proposed that follow an internal orthogonalization approach.

SOLUTIONS TO CATASTROPHIC INTERFERENCE

The linear associator contains a single layer of weights (Figure 2A clarifies how weights can be considered to form a "layer") that connects input with output units. Single-layer networks have known performance limitations (cf. McClelland & Rumelhart, 1988, p. 123) and, in practice, are used less frequently than multilayer networks. For example, the Cohen and Servan-Schreiber (1992) models described at the outset involved a multilayer *back-propagation* network.

Multilayer networks share numerous properties with the linear associator. In particular, the earlier discussion of the delta rule, catastrophic interference, and solution spaces also applies, with only minor changes, to back-propagation networks. However, multilayer networks have several additional unique properties, some of which are relevant here. Figure 8 displays the architecture of a back-propagation network with four input units, three hidden units, and four output units.

As before, the input units are activated by a cue vector, and the weighted connections compute a response pattern across the output units. However, unlike the linear associator, the back-propagation network computes the response in *two* steps, by first feeding activation from the input to the hidden layer, and from there to the output layer. During learning, an extended version of the delta rule (Rumelhart et al., 1986) is used to update the weight pattern, by "back-propagating" the error, for both layers of connections.

A necessary feature of multilayer networks is that the activation of a given unit at the hidden or output layer is a *nonlinear* function of the input received from all weights. In the case of back-propagation networks, the activation function usually is logistic:

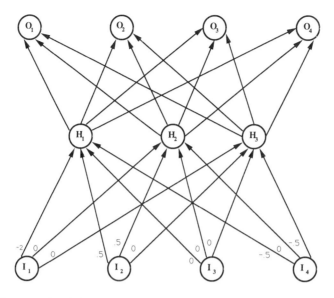

FIGURE 8. Typical multilayer back-propagation architecture, with input units, hidden units, and output units.

$$a_i = 1/[1 + e^{-g \times net_i + bias}],$$

where net_i refers to the total summed input, *bias* refers to a constant that represents the inherent propensity of a unit to be active (or not to be active in the case of a negative bias), and *g*, finally, refers to the *gain* parameter that Cohen and Servan-Schreiber (1992) manipulated to mimic the effects of a disturbance of the prefrontal dopamine system. Figure 9 illustrates the logistic activation function, for a constant unity bias, together with the effects of changes in the gain parameter. It can be seen that a reduction in gain flattens the activation profile of the unit, such that its response to a given (positive) input is attenuated. If one recalls that Cohen and Servan-Schreiber (1992) modeled schizophrenia by reducing gain of the context units in exactly that way, the impaired utilization of context (see simulation results in Table 1) can be recognized as a consequence of an attenuated output of those units.

It turns out that the nonlinearity of the activation function, in a curiously indirect fashion, is essential to avoiding catastrophic interference. If the units had a *linear* activation function (as in the linear associator, where a unit's activation is simply the sum of its inputs), *any* arbitrary multilayer network could be mathematically re-expressed as an equivalent single-layer linear associator (e.g., Jordan, 1986, p. 397). It is only with a nonlinear activation function that multiple layers of connections become meaningful. It is the presence of an intermediate layer of hidden units, in turn, that enables the

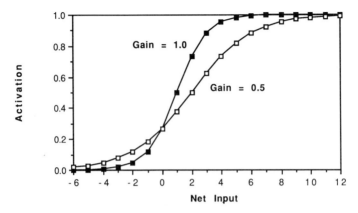

FIGURE 9. Nonlinear logistic activation function of units in a back-propagation network for two values of gain.

network to build a distinct internal representation, which may differ considerably from the structure of the input and may thus be less susceptible to interference.

To illustrate, consider the following hypothetical example involving the weights in Figure 8. Assume that the two familiar patterns {0, 1, 0, −1} and {1, 1, 0, −1} are to be associated with two arbitrary responses whose exact nature is irrelevant here. We know from the preceding discussion that the two input patterns are not orthogonal and hence can be expected to interfere with each other. Now observe what happens at the hidden layer upon presentation of those two vectors: given the weights shown in the figure, the first pattern yields hidden activations of {1, 0, 1} and the second one yields {−1, 0, 1}.[3] Using the earlier definition, the two patterns *at the hidden layer* are orthogonal, despite the fact that the input vectors are, by the same definition, not orthogonal. It follows that interference, at least concerning the updating of the second layer of weights between hidden and output units, should be minimized.

Although interference between nonorthogonal inputs can thus be reduced by abstraction of the proper internal representations, the delta rule, similar to the earlier Case II, does not necessarily converge on the required set of weights. Indeed, McCloskey and Cohen's (1989) and Ratcliff's (1990) earliest demonstrations of catastrophic interference used back-propagation models nearly identical to the one shown in Figure 8. Hence, although multiple layers of connections provide the conditions necessary for a reduction of in-

---

[3]For reasons of tractability, the example ignores the nonlinearity of the units' activation profiles. To reinforce the fact that this example serves illustrative purposes only, and is indeed mathematically incorrect, the second set of weights has not been specified in the figure.

terference, modifications to the standard learning algorithm are nonetheless required to ensure that a less interference-prone weight pattern is established.

Novelty Rule

Kortge (1990) proposed a novelty-driven modification of delta learning that reduces catastrophic interference by focusing only on the novel aspects of a to-be-learned pattern. Instead of learning each item "from scratch," only those components that *differ* from previously acquired information are learned. In consequence, only those weights that have not been previously dedicated to the storage of information are updated, thus leading to dissimilar internal representations even in the presence of correlated input.

Specifically, during learning, the input pattern is replaced by a *novelty vector*, which captures the yet-to-be-learned components of the stimulus. Weight updates are then computed as follows:

$$\Delta w_{ij} = k \delta_j \ d_i,$$

where the δ_j's correspond to the standard error signals applicable to that layer of weights. In contrast to the earlier equation stating the delta rule, in which the error signal was multiplied by the activation (a_i) received along a weight, under the novelty rule the error signal is multiplied by the corresponding element of the novelty vector (d_i). The novelty vector, in turn, is defined as follows: for the first layer of weights (connecting input units to hidden units), the vector is taken to be the target pattern minus the current output from the network, and is thus isomorphic to the usual delta vector. For the second layer of weights, the novelty vector is taken to be the activation pattern of the hidden units obtained by feeding the input novelty vector through the first layer.

The effectiveness of this scheme can be ascertained by returning to Figure 1, which shows the performance of the novelty rule in comparison to the "catastrophic" simulation results obtained by Ratcliff (1990). It is quite clear that under the novelty rule there is virtually no forgetting when additional list items are acquired, similar to the way in which humans are capable of retaining nearly all words on a brief list for subsequent recognition. An additional demonstration of the effectiveness of the novelty rule in a prototype learning task was provided by Lewandowsky (in press).

At present, however, the novelty rule applies only to so-called auto-encoder networks, in which the target response is identical to the input. This limitation derives from the way in which novelty vectors are computed: the novelty vector for the first layer of weights is taken to be the difference between target and output pattern, which can meaningfully apply only to situations in which the desired output equals the input. In behavioral terms, this corresponds mainly to variants of episodic recognition tasks, such as those examined by Ratcliff (1990) and Kortge (1990).

Activation Sharpening

Unlike the preceding approach, sharpened back-propagation (French, 1991) is a way of reducing interference in back-propagation networks with no limitations imposed on the learning situation. The remainder of this chapter therefore focuses on sharpening. Similar to the novelty rule, activation sharpening forces the representations at the hidden layer to become more distinct. Specifically, the technique introduces dependence among hidden units during learning by raising the activation (a) of some of the most active hidden units by some proportion α, while decreasing the activation of all other units, such that:

$$a_{new} = a_{old} + \alpha(1 - a_{old}) \qquad \text{for the most active units}$$

$$a_{new} = a_{old} - \alpha a_{old} \qquad \text{for all others.}$$

At each learning trial, the input activations are first forwarded to the hidden layer, and the pattern of hidden-unit activations is recorded. Some number s (usually $1 \leq s < 4$) of the most active units are then sharpened, and the difference between that new activation pattern (all $a_{new}s$) and the earlier activations of the hidden units ($a_{old}s$) is used as error signal to update the weights between input and hidden layer. Following that sharpening pass, back-propagation resumes in the usual fashion for both layers of weights.

As demonstrated by French (1991), this algorithm leads to the emergence of internal representations that have only a few highly activated units at the hidden layer. Because the identity of these "sharpened" units likely differs across stimuli, interference is reduced. French showed that the number of relearning trials required after the interfering acquisition of a single association was dramatically affected by activation sharpening. Whereas standard back-propagation required some 330 trials to relearn an association chosen from an initially studied set, the number of trials dropped to 81 and 53, respectively, when one and two nodes were sharpened. Similarly, Lewandowsky (in press) showed that sharpened back-propagation is more robust to interference in a prototype learning situation than is unmodified back-propagation.

ROBUST CONNECTIONIST NETWORKS

At the outset, we presented a connectionist model that manipulated the utilization of context to explain cognitive deficits in schizophrenia. Because context, by affording list discrimination and the like, is of central importance to interference and forgetting, the chapter traced the role of context within an examination of catastrophic interference (Case II), and showed that by itself the representation of context does not eliminate excessive forgetting. Instead, we demonstrated that context must be used in conjunction with other modifications before interference is reduced. Having introduced the necessary tools and concepts, we now turn to a more detailed examination of various theoretical and empirical questions surrounding the Cohen and Servan-Schreiber (1992) model.

Gains versus Losses in Robust Networks

Applications of robust networks have been largely limited to the narrow problem area for which they were designed, namely, the elimination of catastrophic forgetting. Given that the distributed and composite architecture that gives rise to catastrophic interference also underlies the networks' more attractive properties, it seems possible that robust networks may lose some predictive power together with their susceptibility to forgetting. If this were the case, little would have been gained by activation sharpening or use of the novelty rule, and networks would continue to suffer from the consequences of undue interference, albeit in a more indirect way.

A partial resolution to this problem is provided by the simulation results shown in Table 2. The simulation compared the standard back-propagation network of Cohen and Servan-Schreiber (1992) to an activation-sharpened version in the CPT-double task. The only difference between the two networks was that, during learning, the sharpened network created dissimilar representations at the hidden layer.

It is clear from the results that the predictions of sharpened back-propagation need not differ from those of the standard network: with a slight adjustment of parameter values (see Appendix for details), the predictions of activation sharpening are within one percentage point, on average, of those of the unmodified model. If parameter values are instead held constant for both networks (parenthesized results in Table 2), the *qualitative* pattern remains unchanged; sharpened back-propagation still predicts a disproportionate in-

TABLE 2. Simulation Results for the CPT-Double Task Comparing Standard Back-Propagation and Activation Sharpening

Response	Standard back-propagation		Activation sharpening	
	Normal gain	Reduced gain	Normal gain	Reduced gain
Misses	.20	.49	.22 (.24)[a]	.49 (.79)
False alarms	.05	.09	.07 (.13)	.09 (.15)

[a]Values in parentheses are obtained with same parameter values as in standard back-propagation.

crease in the miss rate under reduced gain of the context units, although the effect is grossly overestimated.

These results reinforce the generality of a related investigation of catastrophic forgetting. Lewandowsky (in press) examined several different robust networks and found that, in general, their ability to generalize was indistinguishable from the generalization properties of standard back-propagation. The preliminary conclusion appears warranted that robust networks need not lose any explanatory power in exchange for a reduction in interference. Although a common architecture underlies the entire range of behaviors of neural networks, interference can be selectively reduced without negating the advantages of distributed and composite representations.

The reasons for this are best illustrated, at an intuitive level, by returning to Figure 4. The only difference between catastrophic forgetting and complete absence of interference is the path through weight space taken by the model during learning and, by implication, the final weight pattern. Interference-reduction techniques ensure that the network sticks to path B during learning, and therefore alter the nature of the final weight pattern. It follows that the network's predictions will be changed only to the extent that they are tied to a highly specific set of weights. Fortunately, in most situations, numerous different weight patterns exist that satisfy the same set of constraints, in the same way that an infinite set of values of X_1 and X_2 can satisfy $Y = aX_1 + bX_2$.[4] Hence, in the situations and networks examined to date, reduction of interference was achievable at no measurable predictive cost.

Consider again the Cohen and Servan-Schreiber (1992) model of cognitive deficits in schizophrenia. Notwithstanding the central role of context in interference, the authors did not extend their context-based model to forgetting situations, most likely in the knowledge that catastrophic interference would dominate the outcome. Now, having demonstrated the applicability of activation sharpening to Cohen and Servan-Schreiber's model, and having ensured that little explanatory loss is associated with a reduction of interference, a robust version of their network may well be capable of modeling forgetting and interference in schizophrenics.

Forgetting and Interference in Schizophrenia

The apparent consensus in the literature is that nearly all schizophrenics exhibit impaired memory and more rapid forgetting than matched controls. The loss is particularly pronounced in tests of long-term memory (e.g., Tamlyn et al., 1992). In most cases, the stated reasons for the memory loss are directly compatible with Cohen and Servan-Schreiber's (1992) views: for example, the causal involvement of the frontal lobes has been invoked in numerous

---

[4]If a third term, X_3, is introduced, the obvious pairwise constraint on X_1 and X_2 can be removed and the two, in isolation, can be considered independent.

studies (e.g., Gold, Randolph, Carpenter, & Goldberg, 1992; Schwartz, Deutsch, Cohen, Warden, & Deutsch, 1991; see also Dempster, 1991); other results have pointed to the impaired ability to utilize context during memory retrieval (Manschreck, Maher, Rosenthal, & Berner, 1991); and finally, largely *intact* memory has been observed for patients with those types of schizophrenia that are arguably less associated with frontal lobe dysfunction (Shoqeirat & Mayes, 1988).

Taken together, these results provide a clear empirical bench mark for the Cohen and Servan-Schreiber (1992) network. Assuming the activation-sharpened model starts out with reasonable forgetting characteristics, a reduction in gain should significantly accelerate that forgetting, analogous to the increased interference observed in most schizophrenics. Note that if successful, this simulation would extend the scope of the model to a problem area for which it was not initially designed.

Figure 10 illustrates the behavior of an activation-sharpened back-propagation network in a retroactive interference situation, using context units in the input patterns to differentiate between lists, in the standard A–B/A–C paradigm.[5] In (A) is shown the results for gain set equal to unity (corresponding to normal subjects) and (B) shows the results for gain set to 0.5 (corresponding to schizophrenic subjects).

Several comments about the results are in order. First, activation sharpening clearly helps eliminate catastrophic interference. Forgetting of A–B pairs in (A) is not unduly precipitous; indeed, the rate of forgetting mirrors typical behavioral data (e.g., Barnes & Underwood, 1959). This in itself is a novel result because previous tests of activation sharpening involved only relearning (savings) tasks (French, 1991) or sequential recognitionlike tasks (Lewandowsky, in press). Second, as shown in the bottom panel, forgetting becomes steeper if gain is reduced during interpolated learning, quite as expected from the schizophrenia literature.

This simulation was designed so as to maximize comparability to others in the catastrophic interference domain; hence, a separate context module was absent, and gain was reduced for *all* output units. This stands in contrast to the Cohen and Servan-Schreiber (1992) models in which the effects of gain were limited to a context module. The next simulation therefore included a separate context module.

Context was represented by a set of output units whose target response was equal to the context portion of the input patterns, and hence identical for all items within a list (but differed between lists). Output patterns, like the in-

---

[5]We are not aware of any directly relevant comparison data (i.e., A–B/A–C paradigm) involving schizophrenics. We nonetheless chose to stimulate the retroaction paradigm because it has frequently been used to demonstrate catastrophic interference and because the literature leaves little room for doubt that schizophrenics would suffer greater interference than would normals.

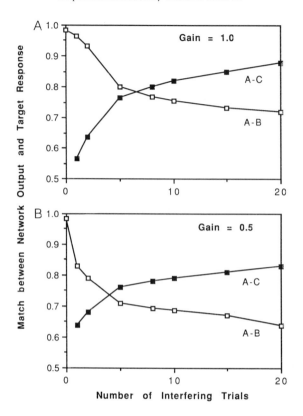

FIGURE 10. Results from a simulation of the A–B/A–C paradigm using an activation-sharpened version of Cohen and Servan-Schreiber's (1992) model. (A) represents normal subjects (gain = 1.0), (B) schizophrenics (gain = 0.5). Gain is manipulated for all output units.

put vectors, thus conformed to the structure outlined in the earlier Case II, with four units dedicated to list context and the remainder to each individual item. During interpolated learning, gain was manipulated only for the output units in the context module.

The results of this simulation are shown in Figure 11. As before, it is clear from comparison of the panels that forgetting is accelerated if gain (of the context units only) is reduced, in this case to 0.25.

Together, the simulations demonstrate that properly modified networks can overcome catastrophic forgetting. Moreover, the results underscore the generality of Cohen and Servan-Schreiber's (1992) account of cognitive deficits in schizophrenia. Although their model was not designed for this situation, it nonetheless provided a good illustration of how forgetting differs between schizophrenics and normals. Lest one think that this success was entirely due to modeling "tricks," it must be kept in mind that the use of gain to differentiate between normals and schizophrenics, and the importance of a

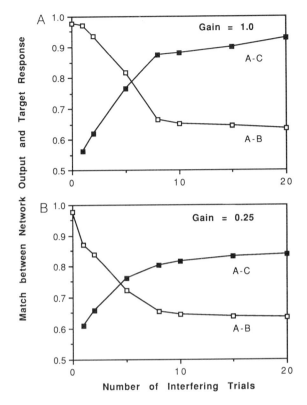

FIGURE 11. Results from a simulation of the A–B/A–C paradigm using an activation-sharpened version of Cohen and Servan-Schreiber's (1992) model. (A) represents normal subjects (gain = 1.0), (B) schizophrenics (gain = 0.25). Gain is manipulated only for the context units at the output level.

separate context module, was derived from a biologically based analysis of the role of frontal cortex in schizophrenia.

One remaining issue concerns the ability of the connectionist approach to predict interesting new results. Critics of modeling and connectionism have often cited the perceived dearth of predictions as a reason for abandoning computational models (e.g., Watkins, 1990). We therefore close by presenting two further applications of the Cohen and Servan-Schreiber model; one that explores a prediction borne out by existing data, and one that explores a prediction that, to our knowledge, has yet to be put to an empirical test.

Shoqeirat and Mayes (1988) showed that a group of schizophrenics with generally mild memory impairments could match the memory performance, and forgetting rates, of normal control subjects if given extra study time. Figure 12 shows the results of a simulation that explored this finding. All parameters remained unchanged from the previous simulation (e.g., gain =

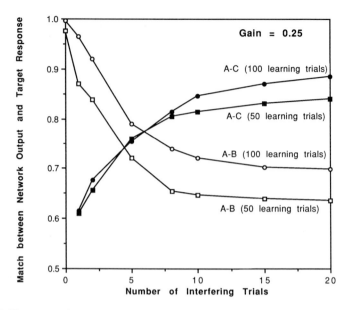

FIGURE 12. Results from a simulation of the A–B/A–C paradigm with gain set to 0.25 (corresponding to schizophrenic subjects) and different amounts of first-list learning.

0.25), except that the number of learning trials on the first list was increased to 100. Clearly, the additional study opportunities slowed forgetting of A–B pairs; indeed, the forgetting rate after 100 learning trials does not differ from "normal" forgetting (gain = 1.0; Figure 11A), exactly as would be expected from the results of Shoqeirat and Mayes.

Finally, the activation-sharpened network predicts that schizophrenics, owing to their reduced ability to use context, should benefit *less* from manipulations that facilitate list discrimination. That is, whereas the performance of normal subjects would be expected to increase if lists were better differentiated (e.g., by changing environmental context), no such benefit should result for the schizophrenics. In an exploratory simulation, "enriching" the context pattern by ensuring that it consisted primarily of 1s (recall that 0s do not lead to weight updates) reduced the forgetting rate for the A–B list when gain = 1.0 (normal subjects), but had little or no effect on forgetting if gain of the context units was reduced (schizophrenics). This prediction is arguably counterintuitive because, without the aid of a computational model, one might equally well expect that enriching the context would enable the schizophrenics to improve their performance. To our knowledge, the corresponding behavioral experiment has not been conducted, and the viability of the network's prediction must therefore remain unclear. What is clear, however, is that a connectionist network served to derive an arguably counterintuitive prediction.

CONCLUSIONS

Implausible forgetting characteristics have been identified as one of the main problems of neural networks. This chapter explored the causes underlying "catastrophic" forgetting, and discussed two techniques to solve the problem. One of those techniques, activation sharpening, was applied to an existing connectionist model of cognitive deficits in schizophrenia. The revised model was shown to have reasonable forgetting characteristics and, at the same time, accounted for the impaired memory and accelerated forgetting observed in most schizophrenics.

Our principal conclusions are twofold. First, although interference manipulations necessarily present difficulties for the inherently ahistorical learning rule of connectionist nets, techniques exist that can reduce interference without losing predictive power elsewhere. Second, appropriately modified networks can be successfully applied to forgetting paradigms, including those involving individual differences. We feel that the connectionist approach to learning, memory, *and forgetting,* continues to hold promise.

APPENDIX

All simulations involved the standard back-propagation architecture, with fully interconnected layers of input units, hidden units, and output units. Asymmetric binary (0|1) vectors were used to represent input and output patterns. Momentum was set to 0.9 throughout.

Simulation of CPT-Double (Table 1)

The procedure of Cohen and Servan-Schreiber (1992, pp. 75–76) was followed as closely as possible. The network involved 22 input units, 30 hidden units, and 11 output units. One of the output units served as response unit, with a target value of unity to indicate detection of the repetition of a stimulus, and a target value of zero to indicate absence of repetition. The remaining 10 output units indicated the perceived identity of the letter on a given trial. Twelve of the input units represented visual features of the stimulus letter for a given trial, using a coding scheme adapted from Cohen and Servan-Schreiber (1992, p. 75). The remaining 10 input units served as context units, and were set equal to the activation pattern of the 10 output units representing letter identity from the *preceding* trial.

At the outset, all weights were initialized to uniform random values in the range −1 to +1. The network was trained using a random sequence of 32,000 trials, one-third of which (target trials) involved repetition of a letter. The learning rate was 0.05, and the fixed bias of the logistic activation function was −4.0.

Testing involved 1000 trials, a random third of which involved repetition of letters. On each trial, independent random Gaussian noise with standard deviation (σ) 0.185 was added to the net input of each hidden and output unit before the final set of output activations was computed. Network performance was assessed by recording the activation of the response unit and classifying it as being above or below a threshold value (θ). Activations above θ were counted as indicating the perceived repetition of a letter, activations below θ as the perceived absence of repetition. Misses (and false alarms) were computed as the relevant proportion of test trials with response unit activations below (above) θ when letters were (were not) repeated.

The value of θ was 0.46 for the control condition (mimicking normal subjects) in which gain remained at unity. For the experimental condition (mimicking schizophrenics), θ was 0.425 and the gain of the 10-letter identification units at the output layer was reduced to 0.5.

Activation-Sharpened Simulation of CPT-Double (Table 2)

The training regime and representational details were identical to those of the preceding simulation, except that the activation of one hidden unit was sharpened (using a factor of 0.2) during learning. Sharpening was implemented using the description given by French (1991). When the remaining parameters were set to the same values as before, the results greatly overestimated the miss rate for the reduced gain condition (see parenthesized results in Table 2). To restore comparability of results with the preceding simulation, the following parameter values were required: $\sigma = 0.125$; $\theta = 0.59$ for gain = 1.0; $\theta = 0.52$ for reduced gain (0.715).

Interference Simulation with Gain Affecting All Output Units (Figure 10)

The network consisted of 20 input units, 20 hidden units, and 8 output units. One of the hidden units was activation sharpened during learning using a sharpening factor of 0.2. Each list consisted of 8 pairs of input and output patterns. Patterns were randomly chosen, subject to the constraint that 10 of the input units were the same for all stimulus members within a list (but differed between lists). The remaining 10 input units were free to vary within a list, but were repeated in the other list. In conformance to the A–B/A–C paradigm, output patterns differed between lists as well as within lists.

At the outset, all weights were initialized to uniform values in the range −0.3 to +0.3. Learning rate was 0.1, and the fixed bias of the activation function was set to zero. Original learning was conducted for 70 trials (each involving presentation of all 8 pairs). Interpolated learning was carried to 20 trials, and was identical to original learning except that these trials were interspersed throughout. On each test trial, input patterns from *both* lists were presented as retrieval cues one at a time, and the output from the network was compared to the corresponding target on the appropriate list (using the cosine as a match measure; Goebel & Lewandowsky, 1991). Data represent the average match across pairs and across the five replications. Test trials did not involve any weight updates. Gain was set to unity for the control condition, and to 0.5 for the schizophrenia-analogue condition. The reduction in gain was applied to *all* output units.

Interference Simulation with Gain Affecting Only Context Module (Figures 11 and 12)

This simulation differed from the preceding one only in the structure of input and output. There were now 14 input units, 4 of which were devoted to representing list context. Similarly, 4 of the 12 output units were also devoted to indicate list membership. During learning, the target activations for those four output context units were identical to the input context. Hence, the network learned to produce not only the response member of a pair, but also learned to identify the list it belonged to, exactly as required of subjects in the MMFR procedure (Barnes & Underwood, 1959). To maintain a comparable level of performance at the end of original learning, there were 50 learning trials for the first list (except for one of the conditions shown in Figure 12). Gain was set to unity for the control condition, and to 0.25 for the schizophrenia-analogue condition. The reduction in gain was applied to only those 4 output units that indicated list membership.

ACKNOWLEDGMENTS

The authors wish to thank the editors of this volume for numerous helpful comments on earlier versions of this chapter. Thanks are also due to William E. Hockley, John K. Kruschke, and Bennet B. Murdock for their comments.

REFERENCES

Barnes, J. M., & Underwood, B. J. (1959). "Fate" of first-learned associations in transfer theory. *Journal of Experimental Psychology, 58,* 97–105.

Besner, D. (1990, November). *Word recognition and connectionism: More words, definitely a lexicon.* Paper presented at the annual meeting of the Psychonomic Society, New Orleans, LA.

Bleuler, E. (1911). Dementia praecox, or the group of schizophrenias. New York: International Universities Press.

Cohen, J. D., Dunbar, K., & McClelland, J. L. (1990). On the control of automatic processes: A parallel distributed processing account of the stroop effect. *Psychological Review, 97,* 332–361.

Cohen, J. D., & Servan-Schreiber, D. (1992). Context, cortex, and dopamine: A connectionist approach to behavior and biology in schizophrenia. *Psychological Review, 99,* 45–77.

Cornblatt, B., Lenzenweger, M. F., & Erlenmeyer-Kimling, L. (1989). A continuous performance test, identical pairs version: II. Contrasting attentional profiles in schizophrenic and depressed patients. *Psychiatry Research, 29*, 65–85.

Dempster, F. N. (1991). Inhibitory processes: A neglected dimension of intelligence. *Intelligence, 15*, 157–173.

French, R. M. (1991). Using semi-distributed representations to overcome catastrophic forgetting in connectionist networks. In *Proceedings of the 13th Annual Conference of the Cognitive Science Society* (pp. 173–178). Hillsdale, NJ: Erlbaum.

Gluck, M. A., & Bower, G. H. (1988). From conditioning to category learning: An adaptive network model. *Journal of Experimental Psychology: General, 117*, 227–247.

Goebel, R. P., & Lewandowsky, S. (1991). Retrieval measures in distributed memory models. In W. E. Hockley & S. Lewandowsky (Eds.), *Relating theory and data: Essays on human memory in honor of Bennet B. Murdock* (pp. 509–527). Hillsdale, NJ: Erlbaum.

Gold, J. M., Randolph, C., Carpenter, C. J., & Goldberg, T. E. (1992). Forms of memory failure in schizophrenia. *Journal of Abnormal Psychology, 101*, 487–494.

Hetherington, P. A., & Seidenberg, M. S. (1989). Is there "catastrophic interference" in connectionist networks? In *Proceedings of the 11th Annual Conference of the Cognitive Science Society* (pp. 26–33). Hillsdale, NJ: Erlbaum.

Jordan, M. I. (1986). An introduction to linear algebra in parallel distributed processing. In D. E. Rumelhart, J. L. McClelland, & the PDP Research Group (Eds.), *Parallel distributed processing: Vol. 1: Foundations* (pp. 365–422). Cambridge, MA: MIT Press.

Knapp, A. G., & Anderson, J. A. (1984). Theory of categorization based on distributed memory storage. *Journal of Experimental Psychology: Learning, Memory, and Cognition, 10*, 616–637.

Kortge, C. A. (1990). Episodic memory in connectionist networks. In *Proceedings of the 12th Annual Conference of the Cognitive Science Society* (pp. 764–771). Hillsdale, NJ: Erlbaum.

Kruschke, J. K. (1992). ALCOVE: An exemplar-based connectionist model of category learning. *Psychological Review, 99*, 22–44.

Lewandowsky, S. (1991). Gradual unlearning and catastrophic interference: A comparison of distributed architectures. In W. E. Hockley & S. Lewandowsky (Eds.), *Relating theory and data: Essays on human memory in honor of Bennet B. Murdock* (pp. 445–476). Hillsdale, NJ: Erlbaum.

Lewandowsky, S. (1993). The rewards and hazards of computer simulations. *Psychological Science, 4*, 236–243.

Lewandowsky, S. (in press). The relation between catastrophic interference and generalization in connectionist networks. *Journal of Biological Systems*.

Lewandowsky, S., & Hockley, W. E. (1987). Does CHARM need depth? Similarity and levels of processing effects in cued recall. *Journal of Experimental Psychology: Learning, Memory, and Cognition, 13*, 443–455.

Lewandowsky, S., & Murdock, B. B. (1989). Memory for serial order. *Psychological Review, 96*, 25–57.

Li, S.-C., & Lewandowsky, S. (1993). Intra-list distractors and recall direction: Constraints on models of memory for serial order. *Journal of Experimental Psychology: Learning, Memory, and Cognition, 18*, 895–908.

Manschreck, T. C., Maher, B. A., Rosenthal, J. E., & Berner, J. (1991). reduced primacy and related features in schizophrenia. *Schizophrenia Research, 5*, 35–41.

McClelland, J. L., & Rumelhart, D. E. (1981). An interactive activation model of context effects in letter perception: Part 1. An account of basic findings. *Psychological Review, 88*, 375–407.

McClelland, J. L., & Rumelhart, D. E. (1988). *Explorations in parallel distributed processing*. Cambridge, MA: MIT Press.

McCloskey, M., & Cohen, N. J. (1989). Catastrophic interference in connectionist networks: The sequential learning problem. In G. H. Bower (Ed.), *The psychology of learning and motivation* (Vol. 24, pp. 109–164). San Diego: Academic Press.

McRae, K., & Hetherington, P. A. (1993, June). *Catastrophic interference is eliminated in pretrained networks.* Paper presented at the annual meeting of the Cognitive Science Society, Boulder, CO.

Metcalfe, J. (1993). Novelty monitoring, metacognition, and control in a composite holographic associative recall model: Implications for Korsakoff amnesia. *Psychological Review, 100,* 3–22.

Ratcliff, R. (1990). Connectionist models of recognition memory: Constraints imposed by learning and forgetting functions. *Psychological Review, 97,* 285–308.

Rumelhart, D. E., Hinton, G. E., & Williams, R. J. (1986). Learning internal representations by error propagation. In D. E. Rumelhart, J. L. McClelland, & the PDP Research Group (Eds.), *Parallel distributed processing: Vol. 1: Foundations* (pp. 318–362). Cambridge, MA: MIT Press.

Rumelhart, D. E., & McClelland, J. L. (1982). An interactive activation model of context effects in letter perception: Part 2. The contextual enhancement effect and some tests and extensions of the model. *Psychological Review, 89,* 60–94.

Rumelhart, D. E., & McClelland, J. L. (1986). On learning the past tenses of English verbs. In D. E. Rumelhart, J. L. McClelland, & the PDP Research Group (Eds.), *Parallel distributed processing: Vol. 2: Psychological and biological models* (pp. 216–271). Cambridge, MA: MIT Press.

Schwartz, B. L., Deutsch, L. H., Cohen, C., Warden, D., & Deutsch, S. I. (1991). Memory for temporal order in schizophrenia. *Biological Psychiatry, 29,* 329–339.

Seidenberg, M. S., & McClelland, J. L. (1989). A distributed, developmental model of word recognition and naming. *Psychological Review, 96,* 523–568.

Shiffrin, R. M., & Murnane, K. (1991). Composition, distribution, and interference in memory. In W. E. Hockley & S. Lewandowsky (Eds.), *Relating theory and data: Essays on human memory in honor of Bennet B. Murdock* (pp. 331–346). Hillsdale, NJ: Erlbaum.

Shoqeirat, M. A., & Mayes, A. R. (1988). Spatiotemporal memory and rate of forgetting in acute schizophrenics. *Psychological Medicine, 18,* 843–853.

Stone, G. O. (1986). An analysis of the delta rule and the learning of statistical associations. In D. E. Rumelhart, J. L. McClelland, & the PDP Research Group (Eds.), *Parallel distributed processing: Vol. 1. Foundations* (pp. 444–459). Cambridge, MA: MIT Press.

Tamlyn, D., McKenna, P. J., Mortimer, A. M. Lund, C. E., Hammond, S., & Baddeley, A. D. (1992). Memory impairment in schizophrenia: Its extent, affiliations and neuropsychological character. *Psychological Medicine, 22,* 101–115.

Watkins, M. J. (1990). Mediationism and the obfuscation of memory. *American Psychologist, 45,* 328–335.

11

Inhibitory Processes in Cognition and Aging

Joan M. McDowd, Deborah M. Oseas-Kreger,
and Diane L. Filion

INTRODUCTION

Age-related declines in cognitive functioning have been observed in a variety of domains, ranging from deficits in classic learning tasks to deficits in higher level problem solving. By way of summary, Craik and Salthouse (1992) have identified six "core topics" in cognition that are vulnerable to the effects of aging: attention, memory, knowledge representation, reasoning ability, spatial ability, and language (Craik & Salthouse, 1992, p. vii). Many of the studies from these domains point to a difficulty on the part of older adults in focusing attention on only the most relevant information for the task at hand. One hypothesis about this deficit is that declines in processing efficiency on the part of older adults may represent a decline in inhibitory function in the selective processing of information. Indeed, Hasher and Zacks (1988) have stated that with age, "the efficiency of the inhibitory processes that underlie selective attention is reduced" (p. 219). McDowd and Oseas-Kreger (1991) suggested that "the ability to inhibit processing of irrelevant information is compromised with increasing age" (p. P340). Dempster (1992) has also proposed "that resistance to interference (i.e., the capacity for inhibition) is a major factor in cognitive development and aging" (p. 46) (see also Harnishfeger, Chapter 6, and Reyna, Chapter 2, this volume). The present review examines the hypothesis that declines in inhibitory function are indeed implicated in age differences in cognitive functioning.

The notion that inhibitory function may be compromised in aging is not a new idea (see Dempster, Chapter 2, this volume). It is evident in the work of Pavlov (cited in Gakkel & Zinina, 1953), Birren (1959a,b), Jakubczak (1967), Solyom (1968), and Frolkis and Bezrukov (1979). Birren (1959a,b) pointed to a number of lines of evidence to support the hypothesis that aging affects inhibitory function. He cited studies showing that in verbal fluency tasks, older adults were more likely to stray from the task of generating words starting with the same letter, being unable to inhibit semantic associations that did not fit the task instructions. He also pointed to work showing older adults to be slower in learning tasks that required them to override past habits. Birren (1959b) suggested that this inhibitory deficit may manifest itself "in all behavior where withholding, modifying, or extinction of previously learned responses is required" (p. 161). He made the further claim that his hypothesis "has heuristic value for many reported age differences in acquisition and extinction of responses, psychophysical judgments and speed of response in relation to stimulus intensities, and many other kinds of behavior subserved by the central nervous system" (1959a, p. 37). However, he also recognized that "there is clearly the task of demonstrating whether or not" the inhibitory deficit hypothesis is true (1959b, p. 161).

Although relatively little attention has been given to evaluating the inhibitory deficit hypothesis in the last three decades or so, there is now a resurgence of interest in inhibition and its role in cognition. One reason is that inhibition may be a primitive in central nervous system functioning. It is observed at many levels of the nervous system, from neurons and neurotransmitters to muscles and motor action (see Bjorklund & Harnishfeger, Chapter 5, this volume). In principle, then, changes in inhibitory function could have far-reaching effects. Altered information processing in the form of less suppression of irrelevant information could produce the age-related deficits in selective attention, memory, reasoning and problem solving, and language abilities that Craik and Salthouse (1992) identified as core topics in cognitive aging. Hasher and Zacks (1988) have applied this hypothesis to age differences in working memory with some success; McDowd (1990; Sugar & McDowd, 1992) has done the same with age differences in selective attention. Thus the inhibitory deficit hypothesis of cognitive aging holds some promise for explaining a variety of age-related changes in cognitive functioning; whether or not it will fulfill this promise remains to be seen. Similar statements have been made about cognitive development during childhood (Harnishfeger, Chapter 6, this volume).

The present chapter critically reviews a number of studies that have implications for the inhibitory decline hypothesis. Table 1 presents a summary of the evidence reviewed here. The literature has been grouped under three major headings: sensory processing, learning, and semantic activation. To preview, studies of sensory processing suggest that older adults are less adept at protecting the early phases of information processing from interruption by subsequent stimuli. In addition, older adults may be less selective regarding the stimuli they respond to and process. In learning paradigms, older adults are slower to learn that a given stimulus is irrelevant to the task at hand. And finally, a variety of data suggest that the maintenance and spread of semantic activation is less optimally controlled in old as compared to young adults.

All of these findings have lent credence to the notion of an age-related decline in inhibitory function. However, a number of interpretive issues are relevant to evaluating the data. For example, Birren (1959b) concluded that older adults have an inhibitory deficit based on a study showing that older adults were slower to learn a task that involved negative transfer from tasks learned previously. Birren's assumption was that slower learning on the part of older adults was due to a reduced ability to withhold, modify, or inhibit a previously learned response. However, it is also true that older adults are slower to learn in a variety of situations, not just those requiring inhibition. Perhaps it is difficulty with any new learning and not inhibitory deficits that produced slower learning in the studies Birren cited. There are a number of age changes in cognitive functioning that may interact with or compound any deficits produced by changes in inhibitory functioning, and their contribution to performance must also be recognized. This is one of several issues that needs to be addressed before an inhibitory deficit is unambiguously implicated in the aging of cognitive function.

These issues are raised throughout our review, and can be summarized as follows. (1) Careful task analyses must be conducted and task components specified in order to make *a priori* predictions about the role of inhibitory processes in task performance. (2) Other age-related phenomena that may be contributing to task performance need to be recognized and controlled in studies in which they may confound the inhibitory effects. (3) Specification of the mechanism by which inhibitory processes function is essential to further understand the ways in which aging may affect cognition. (4) Related to the issue of mechanism is the fact that a variety of paradigms have been used to assess inhibition without much thought about whether all these "inhibitions" are in fact the same phenomenon. (Analogous concerns are expressed by Harnishfeger, Chapter 6, this volume). It seems unlikely that they are; already Connelly and Hasher (1993) have suggested multiple inhibitory mechanisms in the processing of visual information. Eccles (1969) indicated multiple inhibitory mechanisms and transmitter substances at the most basic levels of

TABLE 1. Summary of Evidence in Support of the Inhibitory Deficit Hypothesis of Cognitive Aging

Domain	Summary of findings	Age effects	Reference(s)
Sensory processing	Older adults show less evidence of differential sensory processing based on stimulus relevance	Reduced prepulse inhibition (PPI) and equivalent PPI with relevant and irrelevant stimuli	Filion and McDowd (1993)
		Less differential processing of relevant and irrelevant stimuli	McDowd, Oseas-Kreger, and Filion (1993)
Learning	Older organisms have reduced ability to learn that a stimulus is irrelevant	Less evidence of latent inhibition	Misanin et al. (1983, 1985)
			Bailey et al. (1984); Brennan et al. (1984); D. W. Harrison and Isaac (1985); Lloyd and Levine (1984); McDowd and Filion (1992)
		Slower rates of habituation	
Semantic activation	Older adults activate and maintain activation of more semantic information in the stimulus array	Greater interference of nontarget information	Connelly et al. (1991); Shaw (1991)
		Increased verbosity	Gold et al. (1988)
		Continued activation of expected information	Hartman and Hasher (1991)
		Incorrect inferences go uncorrected	Hamm and Hasher (1992)
		Personal information intrudes	Hashtroudi et al. (1990)
		Less suppression of multiple word meanings	Johnson et al. (1993)
		No negative priming with language stimuli	Hasher et al. (1991); McDowd and Oseas-Kreger (1991); Tipper (1991)

central nervous system functioning. One or more inhibitory mechanisms may be at work in the nervous system, any of which may or may not be influenced by the aging process. Thus, it appears that some caution is warranted in the context of any global inhibitory deficit theory of cognitive aging, and a number of issues are best kept in mind as the inhibitory decline hypothesis is evaluated.

SENSORY PROCESSES

In the stream of information-processing events, environmental stimuli impinging on an individual are first detected by the sensory receptors and then communicated to the central nervous system where they are analyzed and interpreted. However, not all information available in the environment is actively processed by the nervous system. In fact, not all of the stimulation that reaches the sense organs actually reaches the brain. Because the momentary processing capacity of the central nervous system is limited, selective attention allows that processing capacity to be focused on only a subset of the information available for processing. The interaction of selective attention and sensory processes can have both central and peripheral origins. For example, at the peripheral level, attention can be directed to sensory input by turning one's eyes or ears toward the stimulus. At the central level, an individual's current goals and activities determine which sensory input is most relevant and should be given priority for processing. In this way the information-processing system is protected from overload by the variety of stimuli impinging on the sense organs. In the sections that follow, inhibition of the startle eyeblink is discussed as reflecting a sensory gating process that allows selective stimulus processing.

Incoming sensory information is also registered in the autonomic nervous system. If a significant event is detected in the environment, the sympathetic nervous system acts to increase heart rate, increase sweat gland activity, and stimulate the flow of epinephrine in the bloodstream in preparation for action. In the context of selective-attention tasks, the relative magnitudes of these physiological changes in response to stimuli have been shown to reflect the direction of attention of the subject. Thus autonomic nervous system activity in response to sensory input also interacts with attentional processes, and measures of this activity provide another index of attentional functioning. Patterns of autonomic orienting to stimuli designated as relevant or irrelevant are yet another measure of the impact of attention on sensory processes that we discuss.

Inhibition of the Startle Eyeblink

The startle eyeblink is part of a general, automatic, involuntary, brain-stem-mediated (Davis, 1984) reflex, which is elicited by relatively strong stimuli with abrupt onsets. Prepulse inhibition (PPI) of the startle reflex occurs when a relatively weak nonstartling stimulus (prepulse) precedes the onset of a startle-eliciting stimulus by a "lead interval" of approximately 500 ms or less. In such cases, the magnitude of the elicited startle reflex is significantly reduced and sometimes even completely suppressed (Anthony, 1985; Graham, 1975; Hoffman & Ison, 1980). In humans, it has been hypothesized that PPI acts to protect early stimulus processing such that when a prepulse is detected and is processed, a gating process is also initiated that momentarily decreases or buffers other sensory stimulation until the processing of the prepulse has been completed (Graham, 1980). Thus, inhibition of the startle eyeblink is viewed as an index of sensory gating, a basic inhibitory process that regulates sensory input to the brain, filters irrelevant information, and allows the early stages of processing of relevant information to occur without disruption (Braff & Geyer, 1990). Sensory gating provides a buffer for incoming information, allows selective stimulus processing, and prevents sensory overload. The view that startle inhibition serves to "protect" the processing of the prepulse stimulus from disruption is also consistent with recent research that has shown the PPI effect in humans to be increased when subjects are instructed to focus their attention on the prepulse (Acocella & Blumenthal, 1990; Delpezzo & Hoffman, 1980; Filion, Dawson, & Schell, 1993; Hackley & Graham, 1987; Hackley, Woldorff, & Hillyard, 1987). Thus attention directed to a task-relevant or significant prepulse may act to increase the level of protection provided to the processing of that prepulse.

In the first study to examine the effects of aging on sensory gating, younger and older adults were presented with trials consisting of either a brief air puff to the eye alone or an innocuous tone (the prepulse) followed by the air puff shortly (less than 500 ms) after tone onset (Harbin & Berg, 1983). The results showed that for both younger and older adults, the air puff alone elicited large startle eyeblinks, that the nonstartling prepulse produced significant inhibition of the eyeblink response, and that there were no age differences in the magnitude of these effects. Subsequent work has, however, produced some interesting age differences in the pattern of inhibitory functioning. For example, Filion and McDowd (1993) recently conducted a study to examine PPI and its attentional modulation in groups of young and older adults. This study employed an "attention-to-prepulse" paradigm in order to examine both voluntary and involuntary attentional effects on PPI. In this study, subjects were presented with two prepulse types, high- and low-pitched tones, and instructed to attend to one type and ignore the other. These tones then served as prepulses for a startle-eliciting air puff presented at the subject's neck, just under the chin. The prediction was that the instruction to attend to one class of tones should increase protection of processing of that class, whereas instructions to ignore should result in less protection of processing of that class of tones. The results of this study revealed that the younger subjects (mean age = 18.8 years) showed significantly greater PPI to the attended than to the ignored prepulse. That is, attending to the prepulse resulted in greater protection of its processing via inhibition of the startle response relative to the level of inhibition observed during a to-be-ignored prepulse. The older adults (mean age = 73.7 years), on the other hand, showed equivalent levels of PPI to the two prepulse types, and compared to young adults, showed reduced startle inhibition to the to-be-attended but not to the to-be-ignored stimuli. This pattern of results suggests a lessened ability on the part of the older adults to mobilize volitional attentional processes and thereby increase the level of protection provided to the processing of task-relevant stimuli. Again, this decline in inhibitory function and reduced selectivity of processing are likely to have a negative impact on the efficiency of information processing. However, the significance for other aspects of cognition of this PPI deficit remains to be documented. We have observed a positive correlation between the magnitude of PPI and the magnitude of negative priming (a reaction-time-based measure of inhibitory function discussed later in this chapter), suggesting that the PPI deficit may indicate a more general inhibitory dysfunction.

The Orienting Response

The autonomic orienting response is another physiological index of cognitive processing. The orienting response (OR) is a complex pattern of skeletal, physiological, and behavioral changes that is elicited by any novel, unexpected, complex, signal, or significant stimulus that conveys information about the environment. These changes typically involve momentary increases in cephalic blood flow and pupil dilation, decreases in heart rate and peripheral blood volume, and head turning toward the source of the environmental event. One of the most widely studied components of the more generalized OR is the skin conductance response, a momentary increase in the electrical conductivity of the skin associated with increased eccrine sweat gland activity in the fingertips.

The orienting response is an important element in several theoretical models of attention and memory (e.g., Kahneman, 1973; Öhman, 1979; Pribram & McGinness, 1975). The first detailed theory of the relationship of the orienting response to information processing was developed by Sokolov (1963). He proposed that the orienting response was a part of an attentional mechanism that prepares the organism for more efficient information processing. Sokolov viewed the function of the orienting response as producing heightened sensitivity to environmental stimulation, resulting in enhanced intake and processing of information. Kahneman (1973) extended this view and proposed that orienting is associated with the allocation of effort or limited processing resources. According to Kahneman, an orienting response reflects two processes associated with the allocation of these processing resources. The first process is described as the effort to more intensely investigate any stimulus that is evaluated as novel or significant. In this case, the orienting response reflects a change in the organism's resource "allocation policy" for the purpose of investigating the stimulus. The second process is described as a brief increase in arousal that occurs in anticipation of future stimulation, and that varies with the amount of processing resources available to the organism for subsequent allocation. According to this model, a stimulus elicits a surge of effort, or an allocation of processing resources, which is then accompanied by the autonomic manifestations of arousal characterizing the orienting response. Consistent with Kahneman's view, several recent studies have demonstrated a relationship between elicitation of the OR and the capture of attention (e.g., Dawson, Filion, & Schell, 1989; Filion, Dawson, Schell, & Hazlett, 1991).

The concept of attention as a pool of undifferentiated processing resources has been resoundingly criticized (e.g., Light, 1991; Navon, 1984; Salthouse, 1985, 1991). Specific weaknesses of resource models of attention have been enumerated, including the lack of a precise definition or mechanism for resources and lack of an independent measure of resources (see Dempster, Chapter 1, this volume). For an attentional interpretation of the orienting response, however, all that is required is to accept that orienting reflects the engagement of an attentional mechanism (Sokolov, 1963), and that this engagement can take place in a graded fashion. Our further assumption is that an inhibitory mechanism modulates the engagement of the attentional mechanism and the magnitude of the attentional orienting response. Thus, deficits in inhibitory function will produce consistently large ORs.

Based on these assumptions, we recently carried out a series of experiments using the skin conductance OR to study age-related changes in the efficiency of inhibitory function. McDowd, Oseas-Kreger, and Filion (1993) presented younger and older adults with a series of intermixed to-be-attended and to-be-ignored stimuli that differed in terms of sensory modality (half of the subjects attended to tones while ignoring lights, with the instruction reversed for the remaining subjects). Consistent with the inhibitory decline hypothesis, younger adults showed smaller and fewer responses to the to-be-ignored stimuli than to the to-be-attended stimuli. However, the pattern of results for the older adults was more complex. Older adults who were instructed to attend to the tones and ignore the lights showed a pattern of responding quite similar to the younger adults, namely, larger ORs to the attended than to the ignored stimuli. However, the older adults instructed to attend to the lights and ignore the tones showed similar patterns of responding to the two stimulus types. This result suggests a modality effect influencing age differences in selective attention; for older adults, irrelevant auditory stimuli may be more difficult to inhibit than irrelevant visual stimuli.

A methodological artifact complicating interpretation of the McDowd, Oseas-Kreger, and Filion (1993) study was that tones elicited a larger initial OR than did lights. Thus the difference in responding may have been a result of the salience of the stimuli and the associated initial response differences, not a function of inhibitory processes. In a second experiment designed to follow up on this modality effect, auditory and visual stimulus characteristics were modified in an attempt to equate initial levels of responsivity. Each younger and older adult subject was presented with three stimulus types: a to-be-attended stimulus, a to-be-ignored stimulus presented in the same sensory modality as the attended stimulus, and a to-be-ignored stimulus presented to a different sensory modality. For example, a subject may have been instructed to attend to high-pitched tones, ignore low-pitched tones, and ignore a light. These three stimuli were presented sequentially in an unpredictable order. In this experiment, initial levels of responsivity were equivalent across the three stimulus types. The results of interest again revealed efficient attending for younger subjects: regardless of attended-stimulus modality, ORs were largest to the to-be-attended stimulus, smaller to the same-modality distractor, and smallest to the different-modality distractor. For the older adults, the same pattern of results in terms of the ordering of OR magnitude was obtained, but only when the to-be-attended stimulus was a tone. When the to-be-attended stimulus was a light, older adults showed larger ORs (and thus more attentional processing) to the targets than to the distractors, but showed comparable OR magnitude to the same-modality and different-modality distractors. That is, they were less able to take advantage of modality of input to guide attentional processing when the different-modality distractor was a tone than when it was a light. Again, it appears more difficult for older adults to inhibit the processing of irrelevant acoustic stimuli than to inhibit the processing of irrelevant visual stimuli. The data from this second experiment indicate that this pattern of results is not due to differential responsivity to the two stimulus modalities. Although the explanation remains unclear, it appears that auditory stimuli may pose a particular challenge to the inhibitory mechanisms of older adults.

LEARNING

Learning reflects the malleability of the human information processing system as it is altered by the effects of experience; it subsumes the processes by which we acquire information about the significance of stimuli in the environment. At a basic level, learning may be described as acquiring knowledge about which information is relevant and which is not relevant for a given set of circumstances. In this way, learning processes contribute to efficient information processing by focusing attention on relevant information and suppressing attention to irrelevant information.

Two learning paradigms are considered in the following sections: habituation and latent inhibition. In both paradigms learning involves differential responding to significant and insignificant stimulus events. For our purposes, the extent to which individuals inhibit processing insignificant events is of special interest.

Habituation of the Orienting Response

Habituation of the orienting response "is widely considered as an elementary form of learning" (Stephenson & Siddle, 1983, p. 183). After repeated presentations of a stimulus that no longer provides information, the organism ceases to attend to it. In our view, inhibitory mechanisms modulate the engagement of the attentional mechanism. Accordingly, habituation of the OR may be interpreted as an inhibitory mechanism. Consistent with this view, Waters and Wright (1979) hypothesized that " . . . habituation of the phasic orienting response is a mechanism whereby irrelevant, inconsequential stimuli are 'gated out' of attention" (p. 110). Thus, if an individual's inhibitory processes are compromised, he/she should be slower to habituate to irrelevant stimuli. In an explicit test of this hypothesis, McDowd and Filion (1992) reported a study in which groups of younger and older adults were instructed either to attend to or to ignore a series of tones. The results revealed that the younger adults instructed to ignore the tones habituated significantly more quickly than the younger adults who were instructed to attend to the tones. In contrast, the older adults in the attend and ignore groups showed nearly identical habituation patterns, and were significantly slower to habituate across the experimental session. A similar pattern was reported by Eisenstein, Eisenstein, Bonheim, and Welch (1990) who found age to be the best predictor of habituation rates of skin conductance responses to shock stimuli among males aged 18–39, concluding that "the younger the subject the faster the habituation rate, the older the subject the slower the habituation rate." Thus inhibitory learning appears to be slowed with advancing age.

The animal literature on aging and habituation reports results similar to those found in the human literature. For example, in support of an age-related decrease in habituation, Bailey, Castellucci, Koester, and Chen (1984) studied the siphon withdrawal reflex in young and old aplysia and concluded that "aging impairs the long-term retention of habituation. . . ." D. W. Harrison and Isaac (1985) reported that older squirrel monkeys were slower to habituate to irrelevant auditory stimuli than were younger monkeys. In addition, several animal studies have assessed habituation in terms of exploratory behavior. Animals who have become familiar with and thus habituated to their environments engage in less exploratory behavior. Brennan, Allen, Aleman, Azmitia, and Quartermain (1984) studied exploratory behavior in aging mice and reported that, unlike younger animals, older mice exhibited no between-session habituation. Lloyd and Levine (1984) reported disturbances in the ability of older cats to habituate to repeated stimuli.

These results suggest that there may be an age-related decrease in the ability to inhibit responding to irrelevant stimuli, and suggest that habituation paradigms may provide useful measures of this important aspect of inhibitory function. However, a careful examination of the existing literature suggests that the subtleties of the relationship between aging and habituation need to be better understood. For example, several studies from the 1960s examining age effects on classical conditioning reported that older adults were faster to habituate than younger adults (e.g., Botwinick & Kornetsky, 1960; Kimble & Pennypacker, 1963). However, it may be that in some cases this pattern of results was an artifact of differences in initial levels of responding. There are also a number of animal studies demonstrating that the habituation rates of older animals were either equal to (e.g., J. M. Harrison, 1984; Le Bourg, 1983; Parsons, Fagan, & Spear, 1973) or faster than (e.g., Rinaldi & Thompson, 1985) those of younger animals. As in the human studies, in some of these studies the older subjects had lower levels of initial responsivity than the younger subjects (e.g., Parsons et al., 1973). As an additional complication, one of the studies reported a gender difference in habituation rate (Rinaldi & Thompson, 1985). These studies clearly indicate that further research is needed in order to understand the impact of increasing age on habituation processes. The effect of age on habituation rates in nonhumans appears to be dependent on many factors such as gender, the behavior being tested (behavioral orienting, startle responding, exploratory behavior), and the subjects' initial levels of responsivity.

Latent Inhibition

The latent inhibition (LI) paradigm is a learning paradigm believed to measure a basic, automatic inhibitory function. LI is "the detrimental effect of passive, non-reinforced pre-exposure of a stimulus on the subsequent ability of an organism to form new associations to that stimulus" (Lubow, 1989, p. 1). Much of the work examining the latent inhibition phenomenon in aging has been done with animals. In the latent inhibition paradigm, one group of animals is preexposed to several presentations of a target stimulus in a random and unpredictable manner. A comparison group of animals is given no such preexposure. In a subsequent test phase, animals in both groups are required to learn a new association between the preexposed target stimulus and some other event. The typical result is that the group that was preexposed to the stimulus is less successful in learning the new association. The interpretation of this result is that because of the random presentation of the target stimulus in the preexposure phase, the animals inhibit the processing of that stimulus. This inhibition then is detrimental to their performance in the second phase, which requires that they form an association to the inhibited target stimulus.

Studies of LI in humans also involve two groups of subjects engaged in a learning task. In a study by Baruch, Hemsley, and Gray (1988), one group of subjects experienced a preexposure phase in which they listened to a list of nonsense syllables and counted the number of repetitions of a target series of syllables. Superimposed over the syllable list was the occasional presentation (one every 6-8 seconds) of a 1.25-s white noise stimulus. The subjects were told nothing about the white noise; the instructions specified only that they should listen to the syllable list and count the number of repetitions of the target series. This phase lasted about three min; the white noise was presented 26 times. Following the preexposure phase, the second phase of the experiment was conducted. Two groups of subjects participated in the second phase, those that had been in the preexposure phase and a comparison group who had not experienced the preexposure phase. Both groups were presented with a series of nonsense syllables with superimposed white noise bursts. Their instructions in this phase were to listen to the auditory presentation while at the same time carefully watching a digital scoreboard. They were further informed that the point total on the scoreboard would change at irregular intervals during the auditory presentation and that there was a relationship between what they were hearing and the timing of the changes on the scoreboard. Their task was to discover the nature of this relationship and to indicate which aspect of the auditory presentation was associated with the incrementing of the points on the scoreboard. In fact, it was the white noise that predicted the incrementing of points on the scoreboard. Subjects who had not participated in the preexposure phase learned the association quickly; subjects who had been preexposed to random presentations of the white noise stimulus were less likely to successfully learn the association. The interpretation of this finding is that in the preexposure phase, the random presentation of the white noise stimulus produces a subsequent inhibition of processing of that stimulus. The (latent) inhibition of processing produces the learning deficits observed in the test phase. If inhibitory function is compromised in some population, the prediction for this paradigm would be for reduced latent inhibition; that is, preexposed and nonpreexposed groups should show similar learning. An important aspect of the LI paradigm is that an inhibitory deficit results in *better* than normal performance: an individual with decreased inhibitory function will learn the new association more quickly than will an individual with normal inhibitory function.

The only developmental studies of LI with humans involve children of various ages (see Lubow, 1989, for a review). However, there is some work with aging rats in the context of conditioned taste aversion. For example, Misanin and colleagues (Misanin, Blatt, & Hinderliter, 1985; Misanin, Guanowsky, & Riccio, 1983; Peterson, Valliere, Misanin, & Hinderliter, 1985) varied the duration of preexposure and the preexposure–test interval in five separate experiments involving conditioned taste aversion. Together, the results of these studies show that in very old rats latent inhibition is only weakly present or absent altogether. This pattern of results is consistent with the notion of an age-related weakening of inhibitory function. At this stage of our knowledge the results of LI studies with older organisms are provocative, but it is obvious that more empirical work is needed.

SEMANTIC ACTIVATION

Network models of long-term memory assume that information is organized as a system of interconnected elements, called nodes. A node is the fundamental unit in the semantic network, and represents a word and its meaning, a concept, or an idea. Nodes are interconnected via associative links that vary in strength (see Brainerd, Chapter 4, this volume). For example, bread and butter are fairly strongly linked, whereas bread and knife may be only weakly linked. At any given moment in time, nodes vary in their level of activation. That is, when a word or an idea is encountered, the corresponding node is temporarily activated, and this activation spreads to other linked items and activates associated words or concepts. Thus, activation reflects the status of network nodes: activated nodes are those that comprise the current contents of short-term or working memory. In other words, nodes that receive activation either directly or via associative links are those that are currently included in information processing.

In the sections that follow, the role of attention in determining the direction and breadth of activation within the semantic network is examined. A variety of paradigms are considered here: reading, selective attention, working memory, language comprehension, language production, and negative priming. Efficient performance within each paradigm requires that target information in the stimulus array is activated, while irrelevant information is suppressed. The activation of irrelevant semantic information, which intrudes on the processing of target information, is an inhibitory deficit in the control of activation.

Reading

In two experiments examining the impact of distracting material on reading performance in younger and older adults, Connelly, Hasher, and Zacks (1991) asked subjects to read aloud a series of passages, some of which contained distracting material in a different font interspersed with the relevant text. The distracting material was either meaningless, meaningful but unrelated to the passage, or meaningful and related to the passage. After reading each passage, subjects answered four multiple-choice comprehension questions. Results indicated that for both younger and older adults, the presence of distracting text significantly increased reading time. However, only the older adults were more slowed by the related distracting text than by the unrelated distracting text; younger adults showed comparable performance in these two conditions. This pattern of results indicates that for the older adults only, the to-be-ignored distractor text was processed to the level of semantic activation. Inhibitory processes apparently failed to adequately suppress the activation of irrelevant information.

In addition to age differences in reading speed, age differences in comprehension accuracy point to a more negative effect of the distracting material for the older adults. However, this comprehension difference was not consistently observed across Connelly et al.'s two experiments. These data suggest that less efficient inhibitory mechanisms in older adults enabled the distracting but meaningful information to enter working memory and interfere with speed of performance (and, in one case, accuracy) on the reading task (Connelly et al., 1991).

Selective Attention

In addition to reading and comprehension paradigms, the flanker paradigm has also been employed to examine age differences in the ability to inhibit semantic activation of irrelevant information (e.g., Shaw, 1991). Figure 1 shows sample stimuli from Shaw's (1991) study. Subjects were instructed to attend only to the center target word, and to ignore the flanking words. They were to respond by pressing one key if the target word was a member of the category "metal" and another key if the target word was a member of the category "furniture." The target words were flanked above and below with distracting words that were either (1) the same word as the target word; (2) from the same category as the target word; (3) a neutral word; or (4) a word from the other relevant category. Shaw reasoned that those individuals who are less

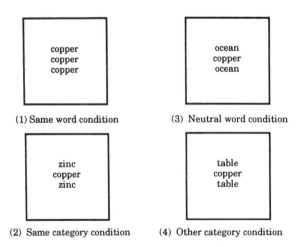

FIGURE 1.   Sample stimuli for a semantic flanker task, patterned after Shaw (1991).

able to suppress the processing of distracting words would be more influenced by the flankers, and the direction of this influence could be either facilitatory as in the case of the same category condition, or inhibitory, as in the case of the other category condition. This latter condition is similar to the Stroop task in which the distracting stimulus on a given trial is linked to a possible but incorrect response, a condition which typically produces slowed response times. Thus, fast and accurate performance in the other-category condition is especially dependent on inhibitory function and may be particularly sensitive to aging.

Response times in each of the four conditions were measured in a sample of 16 young adults and 16 older adults. Derived inhibition scores were calculated by subtracting neutral word response times from other-category response times. Facilitation scores were calculated by subtracting same-category response times from neutral word response times. Shaw's results indicate comparable facilitation effects for younger and older adults, but inferior inhibitory function on the part of older adults who were significantly more slowed by the other-category condition than were younger adults. This finding supports the notion that meaning from distracting information receives activation and affects the speed of processing (both positively and negatively) of target information. Shaw's data also indicate that older adults may benefit just as much as younger adults from the processing of distracting information when the task allows it, but that the costs are greater for older adults when the distracting information interferes with the target task.

Hartley (1993) used variants of the Stroop color-word task to examine selective attention and aging. In the "color block" version, a visual cue indicated the screen location at which a colored rectangle would appear. A color name (printed in black) was presented above or below the rectangle. The subject's task was always to name the color of the rectangle, ignoring the printed word. A second, "color-word" version involved standard Stroop stimuli: color names printed in various colors. Again, the subject's task was to name the *color* of the word, ignoring the printed word. In both task versions, the to-be-ignored information could be congruent with the target color (the word "blue" presented above a blue rectangle or the word "blue" presented in blue print), or incongruent (the word "blue" presented above a red rectangle or the word "blue" presented in red print). Relative to congruent conditions, subjects are typically slowed in the incongruent condition where any processing of the to-be-ignored information may activate the incorrect response and slow the execution of the correct response. This reaction time difference defines the Stroop effect. It is assumed that those less adept at suppressing the distracting information are then more prone to errors and are significantly slowed. The inhibitory deficit hypothesis predicts that if older adults are less able to suppress distracting information, then the magnitude of the Stroop effect should be greater for them than for younger adults.

Based on previous work showing that age differences in performance are typically small when attention and suppression can be allocated on the basis of spatial location, Hartley predicted small age differences in the Stroop effect for the color-block version of his tasks. Other work, suggesting that age differences are significantly larger when attention must be directed to one *aspect* of stimulus processing among others prompted Hartley to predict larger age differences in the magnitude of the Stroop effect for the color-word task version. His data supported these predictions. The magnitude of the Stroop effect was comparable for younger and older adults in the color-block task, but significantly larger for older compared to younger adults in the color-word task. Network models of memory would hold that the irrelevant words received activation, which interfered with task performance, particularly for older adults. These results further suggest that older adults are more impaired in situations requiring inhibition of one line of processing than in situations requiring inhibition of processing at one location in space. Thus, the inhibitory deficit is not a global one, but rather varies as a function of the task.

An important issue for interpreting results of selective-attention tasks concerns the relative contributions of both inhibitory *and* facilitatory processes. In order to implicate altered inhibitory function as primarily responsible for age deficits, facilitatory processes must be shown to be relatively insensitive to age. Indeed, Shaw (1991) reported comparable effects of facilitation conditions for younger and older adults, but impaired inhibitory function on the part of older adults. Hartley's (1993) data are similar to Shaw's (1991) findings in that older adults appear to have difficulty suppressing activation of the semantic attributes of a stimulus array, suggesting an inhibitory deficit. Unlike Shaw's study, however, Hartley did not include a neutral condition against which to measure the facilitatory effects of his congruent conditions. Hartley does seem to have considered facilitatory effects, stating that for the color-block task version, "to the extent that the word can be filtered out, the response should not be facilitated when the color and color word agree" (Hartley, 1993, p. 372). His observation of a significant Stroop effect in both task conditions, however, suggests that the color word is only imperfectly filtered out and facilitation might be observed in both tasks. Given the larger Stroop effect in the color-word task version, we might also predict larger facilitatory effects relative to the color-block task version. The interesting question that remains, then, is whether this facilitation is comparable for young and old adults in the two task conditions.

Working Memory

Much of the recent attention received by the inhibitory deficit hypothesis stems from Hasher and Zacks' (1988) "new view" of age differences in working memory capacity as resulting from age deficits in inhibitory functioning. They hypothesize that inhibitory processes play an important role in cognitive processes such as memory and language comprehension across the life-span. For example, in the case of working memory, inhibitory processes may serve to limit the contents of working memory to goal-oriented information. Their hypothesis suggests that reduced efficiency of inhibitory processes leads to increased activation of irrelevant thoughts that intrude into working memory. The presence of these "off-goal" thoughts in working memory then interferes with and impairs current goal-directed behavior (for an analogous perspective on age-related improvements in inhibitory function, see Bjorklund & Harnishfeger, Chapter 5, and Harnishfeger, Chapter 6, this volume). They also suggest that age-related deficits in comprehension and memory may be a result of age-related declines in the efficiency of these inhibitory processes, citing evidence from studies of memory and selective attention, which "suggests that the behavior of older adults is consistent with the expectations that stem from a diminished inhibition view" (p. 216) of cognitive aging. What follows here is a review of several working memory and language studies relevant to Hasher and Zacks' inhibitory deficit hypothesis, which have appeared since their 1988 review.

One study that supports the notion of an important influence of age-related inhibitory deficits on the contents of working memory was conducted by Hartman and Hasher (1991). In this study, subjects were required to generate a final word for each of a series of sentences (e.g., She ladled the soup into her . . .). In most cases, the subjects generated the most probable ending for the sentence (e.g., bowl). Following the generation task, the subject's generated ending was either confirmed by the actual presentation of the most probable ending, or disconfirmed when a plausible but unexpected ending was presented (e.g., lap). The subjects were asked to remember the identity of the final word that was *actually* presented during the experiment. The results of an implicit memory test indicated that the older adults showed equivalent repetition priming for both the confirmed (i.e., actually presented) and disconfirmed (i.e., initially generated but not actually presented) endings, while the younger adults demonstrated repetition priming only for the confirmed endings. These findings were interpreted as evidence that inhibitory deficits in older adults cause previously relevant ideas to remain activated in working memory even after they are determined to be no longer relevant to the task at hand. Hartman and Hasher also report a correlation between the tendency to maintain activation of disconfirmed words and a measure of Stroop interference among older adults, suggesting that the continued activation is related to an inhibitory deficit. Whether this continued activation of information actually contributes to age differences in explicit memory performance, however, remains to be seen. Still needed is more direct support for the negative impact of altered inhibitory processes on memory functioning.

Another study (Hamm & Hasher, 1992) is also consistent with the hypothesis that inefficient inhibitory mechanisms in older adults cause much difficulty in abandoning ideas that are no longer contextually appropriate. Older and younger adults read passages of text that first suggested either a target inference or an incorrect, competing inference, before finally confirming the target inference. For each passage, a speeded decision task occurred either midway through or immediately following the passage. This decision task asked whether a series of words was consistent with the subject's current interpretation of the passage. Results of this study indicated that older adults were more likely than younger adults to accept a competing incorrect inference as being consistent with their interpretation, even *after* the passage had been disambiguated. These findings were taken as evidence that inhibitory processes fail to quickly narrow down the range of interpretations for older adults. Consequently, older adults continued to entertain a broader range of possible interpretations while reading the passages of text. With respect to the implications of reduced inhibitory efficiency on comprehension ability, Hamm and Hasher (1992) suggest that the broader range of activated ideas may lead to increased rates of forgetting for older adults. That is, the increase in number of activated ideas may produce more competition and associative interference and consequently reduce the speed and accuracy of retrieval for older adults. Again, this aspect of the hypothesis needs further empirical support.

Language Comprehension

As discussed earlier in the section on selective attention, a fundamental assumption of the inhibitory deficit hypothesis is that facilitatory function remains relatively intact across the life-span. Strong tests of the hypothesis would seem to require measures of both inhibitory and facilitatory function. However, even when studies show comparable facilitation processes in younger and older groups, patterns of data are often interpreted only in terms of altered inhibitory function. One recent study of language comprehension explicitly examined both inhibitory *and* facilitatory processes. Johnson, McDowd, and MacDonald (1993) used a paradigm employed by Gernsbacher (Gernsbacher & Faust, 1991, Chapter 9, this volume), who has developed a model of language comprehension involving the processes of facilitation and suppression. The experimental task involves the presentation of a short sentence (e.g., He won the match) followed by a test word (e.g., fire). Subjects make a Yes–No decision about whether the target word fits the meaning of the preceding sentence. According to Gernsbacher's model, when the subject first is presented with the sentence, both meanings of the word *match* (game, fire-starter) are activated, and the context-incorrect meaning must be suppressed or inhibited in order to correctly answer No. The speed with which an individual can process these types of sentences and respond to the target word are compared to a neutral condition (e.g., He won the title—fire) as an index of the efficiency of inhibitory processes. (See also Gernsbacher and Faust, Chapter 9, this volume.)

Facilitation conditions involve a similar comparison. Sentences with neutral verbs (e.g., She thought about the match) are followed by a word that could be consistent with the sentence (e.g., fire). The time taken to respond Yes to this target word is compared to the condition in which the verb biases, or facilitates, the processing of just one interpretation of the sentence final word (e.g., She blew out the match—fire). The speeding of response time in the biased condition is taken as an index of the efficiency of facilitatory processes.

In the Johnson et al. (1993) study, groups of young and old adults were auditorily presented with sentences such as those described above, followed by a visually presented target word that either did or did not match the meaning of the sentence. Half of the target words in each condition were presented 100 ms after the last word in the sentence; the other half were presented 850 ms after the last word in the sentence. The results indicate that in a comparison of control and inhibition conditions at the short 100-ms delay, younger and older adults were comparably slowed, but at the later, 850-ms delay, older adults were differentially slowed in the inhibition condition compared to younger adults. These results suggest that at the later delay, younger adults had inhibited the incorrect meaning of the polysemous word (e.g., match) and were able to respond rapidly based on the correct meaning of the word. The interpretation of the older adults' data is that they were less successful in inhibiting the incorrect meaning of the ambiguous word, and so were slowed in responding to the target word. In contrast, data from the facilitation conditions show comparable patterns of responding in younger and older adults at both the early and later delays. Together, these results suggest that in the context of language comprehension, facilitatory processes are relatively unaffected by age, whereas inhibitory processes show an age-related decline in efficiency. This pattern of results supports the inhibitory deficit hypothesis is an important way: inhibitory processes are implicated in cognitive aging, whereas facilitatory processes are not. However, additional tests of this finding should be conducted in other paradigms to test its generality.

Intrusion of Idiosyncratic Information

Additional studies suggesting an age difference in inhibitory efficiency indicate that older adults often allow personal memories to enter working memory, even when they are not immediately relevant to the task at hand (Hashtroudi, Johnson, & Chrosniak, 1990). In a study examining age differences in memory for perceived and imagined events, Hashtroudi et al. had subjects either listen to a detailed description of an activity and imagine themselves carrying out that activity (e.g., packing a picnic basket) or actually carry out the activity. In the case of the picnic basket example for the latter condition, all the typical items were provided and the subject actually packed the basket. Following a delay of 1–2 days after the initial encoding, younger and older adults completed a questionnaire regarding qualitative characteristics of their memory for the activities. Older adults were more likely than younger adults to say that their memories included personal thoughts and feelings in both experienced and imagined situations. In addition, recall performance demonstrated that the older adults had better memory for these thoughts and feelings but poorer memory for perceptual details of both perceived and imagined events than the younger adults. In their discussion, the authors note that their results are consistent with the inhibitory framework outlined by Hasher and Zacks (1988). That is, one interpretation of their data is that the failure of older adults to inhibit personal information from entering working memory may have interfered with the encoding and retrieval of objective information (Hashtroudi et al., 1990).

An age-related increase in the intrusion of personal thoughts and memories is also observed in speech production. A pair of studies of verbosity in older adults suggests that they are more likely than younger adults to produce off-target or personally relevant speech (Gold, Andres, Arbuckle, & Schwartzman, 1988). Subjects were interviewed, given a variety of psychological tests to complete, and classified by interviewers into one of three categories of verbosity: " *extreme talker* (very verbose, speech consists of sequences of loosely associated topics, much extraneous information), *controlled talker* (chatty, talks a great deal but sticks more or less to the point even though much extra information is given), and *nontalker* (only answers questions asked and volunteers little extraneous information)" (Gold et al., 1988, p. P28, italics ours). Data analyses in their first study indicated that those individuals categorized as extreme talkers were significantly older than the other two groups. These findings provide additional support for an age-related vulnerability to the intrusion of personal information into consciousness. However, some caution should be exercised in the interpretation of these results. Classification of verbosity level involved a subjective assessment on the part of the interviewer. In addition, besides chronological age, increased experience of stress and extroversion were also factors that significantly differentiated the verbosity groups.

Following this first study, a second study reported by Gold et al. (1988) revealed a somewhat more complex picture of the relationship between age and verbosity. In a regression analysis of a second sample of adults, although the role of stress and extroversion were replicated from the first study, age was eliminated as a significant predictor of verbosity when scores representing longitudinal changes in performance on nonverbal ability measures similar to fluid intelligence were included. That is, "verbosity appears to be related not to age but to decreases in nonverbal intellectual ability" (Gold et al., 1988, pp. P31–P32). Gold et al. conclude that "this pattern of results suggests that failure to maintain focus in speech could reflect the particular combination of a significant loss of nonverbal intellectual ability and intact, well-developed, and practiced verbal skills" (p. P32).

The stable association of the experience of stress and personality factors with verbosity is also interesting. Gold et al. suggest that "verbosity could be a relatively benign behavioral variant, occurring in elderly people who have certain personality and social characteristics and serving to maintain constancy of identity. Alternatively, the pattern of poorer cognitive functioning associated with verbosity could be indicative of central nervous system impairment" (p. P32). This latter possibility is most relevant to the inhibitory deficit hypothesis. Intact attentional functioning is vital to good performance on fluid ability measures (e.g., Stankov, 1988); perhaps age-related declines in inhibitory function underlie both declines in fluid abilities and increases in verbosity.

Important interpretive issues remain, however, for the Gold et al. and the Hashtroudi et al. data. For example, Hashtroudi et al. observed more frequent personal thoughts and feelings in the recall protocols of older adults than among younger adults, and a coincident reduction in memory for perceptual details on the part of older adults. The inference that the former produced the latter may not be warranted. Missing, for example, is any evidence for age-invariant memory performance in the *absence* of greater personal thoughts and feelings. That is, the literature is replete with examples of poorer recall on the part of older adults, especially for details. Before the inhibitory deficit hypothesis can be applied convincingly to the Hashtroudi et al. (1990) findings, a stronger link between increased personal thoughts and declining memory performance must be established. Some evidence in favor of increasingly idiosyncratic encoding of information might be found in the literature on aging and subjective organization in free recall. Organizational processes are typically assessed by analyzing the clustering of items at recall based on some common property such as taxonomic category. More idiosyncratic clustering, known as subjective organization, occurs when the organization of items at recall is consistent across recall trials, but the basis of that organization is not immediately apparent, at least to the experimenter. Declining inhibitory function might be predicted to increase the likelihood of subjective organization in that the intrusion of idiosyncratic interpretations of information may lead to an obscure linking of items in memory. Burke and Light (1981) have reviewed a number of studies of age differences in organizational processes in free recall, and concluded that the evidence on subjective organization is mixed. None of the studies they review, however, was designed to examine organization in recall in light of the inhibitory deficit hypothesis. They do conclude that "older adults show less organization in free recall" (Burke and Light, 1981, p. 518) and it may be that this difference is due at least in part to an age-related increase in subjective organization.

More recently, Light (1992) reviewed a number of paradigms in which the intrusion of idiosyncratic information might be expected to have an effect, but found little evidence for age differences. For example, she concluded that there is "little indication that word associations are more variable or idiosyncratic in the old" (p. 133). Further, Light concluded that the organization of semantic information in memory appears to be similar in younger and older adults and this information is typically brought to bear on language and memory tasks in similar ways. In support of this claim, Light (1992) reported another study in which subjects read a narrative about the events in an individual's life. Analyses of intrusion error data from free recall and recognition tests revealed a similar pattern of results for old and young adults. In sum, Light's review provides little evidence that idiosyncratic intrusions disrupt the performance of older adults. Nevertheless, Hasher and Zacks' (1988) argument that reduced efficiency of inhibitory processes leads to increased processing of "non-goal-path information, such as personally relevant thoughts, contextually inappropriate interpretations of words or phrases having multiple meanings, and daydreams" (p. 212) would seem to predict that idiosyncratic interpretations of information should alter organizational processes in memory. Thus, this prediction should be subjected to direct empirical test.

More evidence for the inhibitory deficit hypothesis of age-related memory declines might also come from experiments showing a significant relationship between some measure of inhibitory function and the measure of memory function of interest. Gold and colleagues (Arbuckle & Gold, 1993) have taken a step in this direction with their recent work showing that their measures of verbosity are correlated with performance on a set of cognitive tasks designed to assess inhibitory function (Wisconsin Card Sorting task, word fluency, Trailmaking B). No such relationship was observed between verbosity and cognitive tasks presumed to be unrelated to inhibitory function (digit span, Logical Memory, figure copying). Their conclusion is that verbosity may reflect a more general deficit in the inhibition of irrelevant information. It is more direct tests such as these that will advance our understanding of age differences in cognitive functioning.

In addition to these limitations, to date there is no independent evidence that it is a failure of inhibitory function that leads to the observed increase in memory for personal thoughts and feelings (e.g., Hashtroudi et al., 1990) or in verbosity (e.g., Gold et al., 1988). That is, the definition of "goal-oriented information" or even the perceived goal of the task itself may differ for the researcher and the research subject. Although Hasher and Zacks (1988) recognize that the "interests, values, beliefs, and goals (of older adults) may be different from those of younger adults" (p. 212), they do not seem to consider the possibility that it is these differences themselves, and not altered inhibitory function, that may be producing age differences in working memory tasks. For them, differing goals may actually *produce* inefficient inhibitory function: "consider what might happen if inhibitory mechanisms malfunction or become inefficient, as might occur whenever central neural functioning is slowed and/or when goals differ from the determination of objective meaning" (p. 212). It does not seem appropriate in this case to describe inhibitory processes as malfunctioning or inefficient; rather, the individual may simply have different goals or intentions.

It is also possible that differing goals and altered inhibitory function may interact. One chain of events Hasher and Zacks (1988) envision is as follows: altered inhibitory function allows the entry and maintenance of off-goal information into working memory. At retrieval, the activation of both relevant and irrelevant information increases the likelihood of retrieval interference and retrieval failures. Repeated experience with retrieval difficulty leads to a compensatory reliance on easily accessed information; older adults are more likely to activate and make use of overlearned or personally relevant information in retrieval situations. This then becomes a retrieval strategy that older adults may employ on a regular basis. The evidence they cite in support of these possibilities, however, does not rule out the alternative account suggested here, that differing goals may be independent of any inhibitory deficits. In addition, Light, Valencia-Laver, and Zavis (1991) report data that are at odds with the notion that overlearned or stereotypic information is more easily accessed for older adults. In their study examining priming of typical and atypical category instances, they observed no age differences in the pattern of priming effects with typical and atypical exemplars, suggesting that atypical exemplars are not less accessible for the older adults. The Light et al. study, however, was not designed to test the inhibitory deficit hypothesis. It would have been interesting to have measures of working memory on their subjects; given their result, the inhibitory deficit hypothesis would have to predict equivalent working memory in the two groups. Thus, the importance of the Light et al. finding for the inhibitory deficit hypothesis remains to be seen.

Another alternative to an inhibitory deficit account of age changes in semantic activation processes comes from the possibility that older adults have a richer or more elaborated knowledge structure. In this case, then, a given stimulus may elicit a broader range of activated information, which may in turn enter working memory. If so, then performance differences may be an outcome of differences in the richness of knowledge structures and not a result of declining inhibitory function. One strategy for assessing this alternative would involve groups of young adults that differ in some knowledge base, such as novices and experts (e.g., lay people and physicians). Memory tests using materials designed to access the knowledge base of the experts might then be administered. If these materials produce a pattern of results like that observed for older adults in the studies just reviewed, it would argue against a pure inhibitory deficit account of these studies. For the inhibitory deficit hypothesis to hold, it must be demonstrated that younger adults also activate as broad a range of information as do older adults, but subsequently inhibit that information, preventing entrance into working memory and the associated retrieval interference. In the Hashtroudi et al. experiment, for example, the inhibitory deficit hypothesis would predict that at encoding, personal thoughts and feelings occurred to both young and old adults, but only the young adults inhibited them and so prevented them from interfering with retrieval processes. There is some evidence that this is the case; initial ratings of thoughts and feelings about events immediately after their presentation did not differ between age groups. At recall, however, older adults reported more thoughts and feelings than did younger subjects. Whether they did so because personal information was more salient, more accessible, more important, or more interesting to them, or because it comprised the bulk of the information that was still available for recall remains in question. For the notion of an inhibitory deficit to remain viable in this case, these alternatives must be sorted out and eliminated.

In addition to these concerns, there is one piece of evidence that runs counter to Hasher and Zacks' (1988) hypothesis that reduced inhibitory function allows more off-goal information into working memory. Giambra (1989) examined the occurrence of "task-unrelated thoughts" (TUTs) during boring vigilance tasks. If TUTs are more frequent among older adults, their occurrence could account for age differences in detection accuracy commonly observed in vigilance tasks. Giambra (1989) reported five experiments measuring the frequency of TUTs during relatively lengthy vigilance tasks. For example, in a visual detection task lasting just over an hour, subjects were asked to press a key each time a task-unrelated thought ended. Under these conditions, older adults reported significantly fewer TUTs than did younger adults. In a second experiment, subjects were asked every 25 s for just over an hour whether or not a TUT had occurred in the last 25 s interval. In a third and fourth experiment, preexperimental activities were controlled for 2 h prior to the experiment in an effort to control for the availability of task-unrelated thoughts. In no case did older adults report more TUTs than younger adults; in fact they continued to report significantly fewer TUTs than younger adults. A final experiment manipulated the level of intellectual stimulation of the pretask activities and also manipulated the information-processing demands of the vigilance task itself. Older adults again reported significantly fewer TUTs. Accuracy on the vigilance task in all cases exceeded 93%, so it is unlikely that vigilance task demands exceeded the capacity of older adults. Thus, it cannot be argued that they did not have any capacity "left over" for task-unrelated thoughts.

By way of explanation, Giambra suggested that older adults engage in less nonconscious processing of thoughts that might then surface in boring situations like vigilance tasks than do younger adults. This view is directly counter to the inhibitory deficit account of Hasher and Zacks (1988). Indeed, Giambra's results are not easily integrated with most of the data reviewed here. McDowd and Birren (1990) suggested that one way to reconcile these apparently contradictory sets of data is to consider the rate of occurrence of thoughts as well as their task relatedness. The question then concerns the proportion of subjects' thoughts that are unrelated to the task. Another possibility is that the demand characteristics of the situation prevent a valid assessment of the frequency of task-unrelated thoughts.

To summarize, a number of studies of working memory and language have provided data that are consistent with the hypothesis of an age-related decline in the integrity of inhibitory processes. In general, the findings have suggested that older adults are more verbose and likely to produce off-target speech, that they fail to inhibit the intrusions of irrelevant personal information, and that they continue to maintain a greater range of activated ideas in working memory, even when deemed irrelevant to the task at hand. A number of cautions have been outlined, which must be addressed before these data can be interpreted as favoring the inhibitory deficit hypothesis. These include ruling out the possible confound of differing goals and priorities among older adults, as well as the possible confound of a richer knowledge base leading to greater semantic activation among older adults.

Negative Priming

One performance measure that is believed to index inhibitory function has been termed "negative priming" (Tipper, 1985). Negative priming is a measure of the efficiency with which an individual inhibits attention to a distracting stimulus while focusing attention on a target stimulus. The negative-priming paradigm typically involves the presentation of two competing stimuli; the subject is instructed to select one stimulus for processing and ignore the other. Reaction time for processing the target stimulus is the dependent measure. If a previously ignored distractor stimulus is subsequently represented as a to-be-attended stimulus, processing of that stimulus is slower than if there had been no prior presentation. This slowing is attributed to the extra time required to access the just-inhibited stimulus, and is taken as a measure of inhibitory strength. A strongly inhibited stimulus will take relatively longer to access than a weakly inhibited stimulus. It is interesting to note that like LI, one of the useful aspects of the negative-priming paradigm is that an inhibitory *deficit* results in *better* than normal performance. An individual with decreased inhibitory function will actually respond faster in the negative-priming condition than will an individual with normal inhibitory function. This is an important advantage of this paradigm over the multitude of others that reliably result in poorer performance on the part of older adults, important for distinguishing deficits in inhibitory function from any generalized cognitive slowing present in older adults. (Negative priming is the focus of Chapter 7 by Neill, Valdes, and Terry, this volume.)

In order to investigate the hypothesis of weaker inhibition with advancing age, a number of studies have compared the amount of negative priming demonstrated by older and younger adults (Hasher, Stoltzfus, Zacks & Rypma, 1991; McDowd & Oseas-Kreger, 1991; Tipper, 1991). If older adults suffer from a deficit in the ability to inhibit irrelevant information, they should demonstrate a reduced amount of negative priming in comparison to that shown by younger adults. Tipper (1991) investigated the degree of negative priming in older adults using a selective-attention task involving spatially separated line drawings (see Figure 2). Subjects were presented with pairs of line drawings using a tachistoscope. The target stimulus was located at a central fixation point, and a distracting stimulus was present either to the left or right of the central stimulus. Each trial consisted of an initial "prime" display in which the subjects were instructed to remember the central stimulus for later recall while ignoring the stimulus off to the side. After a brief interval, a subsequent "probe" display was presented. In this case the subjects were instructed to name aloud the picture in the central position, again ignoring stimuli located at either side. Each pair of prime–probe displays served as one trial. The

FIGURE 2. Sample stimuli for a negative-priming experiment, patterned after Tipper (1991). On each trial, subjects must name the target picture (shown here as solid lines) and ignore the distractor picture (shown here in dashed lines). On alternate trials, they must name a picture that is unrelated to those in the previous pair (control condition), or name a picture that is identical to the just-ignored picture (negative priming condition).

identities of the pictures in the probe displays were manipulated to produce either a control trial or a negative-priming trial. Negative priming was then assessed by the amount of slowing of naming latencies in the negative-priming condition relative to the control condition.

Tipper (1991) found no evidence of negative priming in older adults. In fact, older adults demonstrated significant facilitatory priming instead. That is, not only are older adults less efficient at inhibiting distractor information, but they apparently process it to a level that allows performance to be speeded rather than slowed. This pattern of results may be another example of broader semantic activation on the part of older adults, and is in marked contrast to the significant negative-priming effect demonstrated by younger adults (see Tipper, Borque, Anderson, & Brehaut, 1989). Tipper (1991) concluded that older adults experience weakened inhibitory mechanisms, and thus fail to produce the negative-priming effect expected with efficient inhibitory function.

In a study by McDowd and Oseas-Kreger (1991), a comparison was made between the amount of negative priming shown by groups of older and younger adults in a task requiring subjects to name a red letter while ignoring a partially superimposed green letter (see Figure 3). In contrast to the task used by Tipper (1991) in which each trial was composed of discrete prime–probe pairs, this task presented the stimuli in a continuous format, where the probe display for one trial served as the prime display for the subsequent trial.

Results indicated that the negative-priming effect was significant only for younger adults. However, there was a large main effect of age; older adults were considerably slower overall than the younger adults. In order to rule out the possibility that the results were a consequence of the slower initial reading speeds of the older adults, a median split analysis was performed

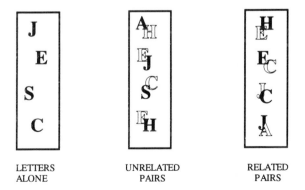

FIGURE 3. Sample stimuli from McDowd and Oseas-Kreger (1991). Red letters (shown here as solid) were to be named; green letters (shown here in outline) were to be ignored.

on the data. This analysis indicated that the slowest younger adults (who had slower baseline reading speeds than the fastest older adults) still demonstrated a significant negative-priming effect, while the fastest older adults did not. Thus, the slower baseline reading speeds of the older adults were not responsible for the age differences in the magnitude of the negative-priming effect.

Hasher et al. (1991) examined age differences in negative priming in two experiments using a continuous-trials identification task with spatially separated letter pairs. Again, the subject's task was to name the letter presented in red and ignore the letter presented in green (or vice versa). In both experiments, younger adults showed significant negative priming, but older adults did not. Hasher et al. also investigated the notion that the absence of negative priming in older adults results from an age-related "slowing" of inhibitory processes. This possibility is consistent with a variety of studies that have showed older adults to be slower on a wide range of tasks (e.g., Salthouse, 1985). Thus, in the first experiment, the interval between a subject's response to the prime display and the presentation of the probe display (RSI) was fixed at 500 ms, while the second experiment used an RSI of 1200 ms. The use of a longer RSI in the second experiment was an effort to replicate earlier findings that the magnitude of negative priming in younger adults dissipates over RSIs of 520 ms to 2020 ms (Neill & Westberry, 1987). In addition, the longer interval would provide "an opportunity for an inhibitory system that is slow or inefficient, or both, to build up to detectable levels of activity" (Hasher et al., 1991, p. 166).

The results of the two experiments indicated that at both the 500-ms RSI and the 1200-ms RSI, the older adults failed to demonstrate negative priming. In contrast, the younger adults demonstrated negative priming at both intervals. These findings were interpreted as evidence that the inhibitory mechanisms of older adults are not merely slowed, but are in fact weaker than they are in younger adults (Hasher et al., 1991). More recently, Stoltzfus, Hasher, Zacks, Ulivi, and Goldstein (1993) examined negative priming in younger and older adults using RSIs of 300 ms and 1700 ms. At both delays, younger adults showed significant negative priming, whereas at neither delay did older adults show the negative-priming effect.

The studies that have been reviewed thus far have all used tasks that require subjects to select target information on the basis of color, and respond to the identity of the target. A distinction has been made between these types of tasks and those that require subjects to select target information based on identity and respond to the location of the target. It has been suggested that the latter form of selective attention is more representative of real-life situations (Tipper, Brehaut, & Driver, 1990; Tipper, Weaver, Kirkpatrick, & Lewis, 1991). As an example of such a situation, consider what occurs when choosing a desired item at the grocery store. An individual first selects an item based on identity, and then must respond spatially to the location of the item in order to retrieve it and place it into the shopping cart.

Performance on a negative-priming task in which response to the target stimulus is made on the basis of spatial location has been reported by Tipper et al. (1991). This task involves the presentation of target and distractor stimuli each in one of four spatial locations on a computer screen (see Figure 4). A trial consists of a prime display followed by a probe display, with each display consisting of one "X" and one "O" each presented at one of the four spatial locations. The subject's task for each display is to press a key corresponding to the location of the O as rapidly as possible while simply ignoring the X. Negative priming is measured on those prime–probe pairs in which the O in the probe display appears in the same location as the to-be-ignored X had appeared on the prime display. Any slowing observed in this condition relative to a comparison condition in which the location of X's and O's within a prime–probe pair are unrelated is interpreted as due to the momentary inhibition of the location associated with the X, which then had to be overcome in order to respond to the target O on the subsequent display. Weakened inhibitory function results in a reduction in the magnitude of this slowing.

Connelly and Hasher (1993) report a series of three experiments in which they examined negative priming in young and older adults using a task requiring inhibition on the basis of spatial location like that just described, as well as a task requiring inhibition on the basis of identity. The location version of the task required subjects to press a key corresponding to the location of a target "O" and inhibit responding to a distractor "+." In the identity version of the task subjects were required to name a target letter presented in red and ignore a distractor letter presented in green (or vice versa). An additional version of the task involving both identity and location suppression was also reported (Experiment 3), which allowed an examination of the separate and perhaps additive effects of the two types of suppression. Stimuli were presented in prime–probe pairs, and subjects were allowed to control the pacing of

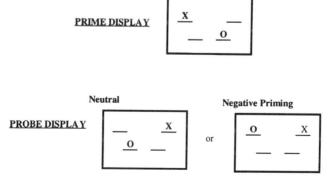

FIGURE 4.   Sample displays like those used for location tasks in Connelly and Hasher (1993) and McDowd, Filion, and Baylis (1992).

pair presentation. That is, between each set of prime and probe trials, stimulus presentation paused until the subject initiated the next trial set with a key-press.

The results of the Connelly and Hasher (1993) experiments replicated earlier work showing significant negative priming for younger adults in the identity task, but no negative priming for older adults. However, they reported *equivalent* negative priming for younger and older adults in the location task. This pattern of results was replicated in a further experiment combining identity and location suppression. The data from young adults indicate that the two types of suppression appear to be additive. Older adults, however, showed no more negative priming in conditions involving both location and identity than was present in the location suppression conditions alone. Thus, a critical factor in determining the presence of age differences in inhibitory function appears to be what it is that must be suppressed. Again, selective processing based on spatial location appears to be preserved in aging.

In a further study of negative priming with location information, Mueller and Baylis (1993) used a task similar to the O/X location task described above, but which was performed in three-dimensional space. The experimental apparatus was a 51 cm × 51 cm stimulus board consisting of 10 translucent keys, each separated by 13 cm both horizontally and vertically from adjacent keys (see Figure 5). Nine keys were arranged in a 3 × 3 grid; the tenth key was located directly beneath the middle key in the first row. The board was tilted toward the subject at a 35° angle above horizontal.

Beneath each of the nine keys was a red LED, a green LED, and a microswitch for recording reaction times. The tenth key at the bottom of the board was illuminated with a yellow LED. The task required that the subject

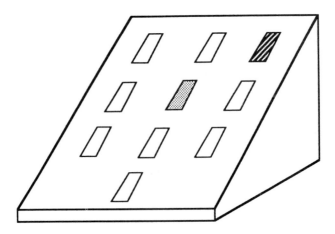

FIGURE 5. Design of experimental apparatus used by Mueller and Baylis (1993). As pictured here, the red target light is shown in stripes and the green distractor light is shown as dotted.

initiate a trial by pressing the illuminated yellow key. As the yellow key was pressed the light would go out, and 500 ms later one or two of the remaining nine lights would light up. The subject's task was to reach out and press the key lighted by a red LED, and to ignore all other lights. On some trials both a red and a green light were illuminated. Subjects were instructed to ignore the green key and press the red key as rapidly as possible. The lights remained illuminated until the subject made a response. 1000 ms after the subject's response the yellow key would be illuminated signaling the beginning of another sequence, again initiated by the subject. In conditions involving the presentation of both red and green lights, the relationship between the location of targets and distractions on adjacent trials could be unrelated (control condition) or related (negative-priming condition). In the unrelated condition, the locations of target and distractor on trial n were distinct from their respective locations in trial $n -1$. In the related condition, the location of a target red light on trial n was the same as the location of the distractor green light on trial $n -1$.

Mueller and Baylis (1993) assessed both interference and negative priming in younger and older adults. Interference was measured by comparing the target-alone condition with the unrelated condition. Although both younger and older adults were slowed by the presence of a green distractor light (when it appeared between the yellow home key and the target key), the magnitude of the interference was comparable in the two age groups. That is, older adults were not more sensitive to the presence of distracting information in this task. Negative priming was assessed by comparing the unrelated and related conditions. Both older and younger adults were slowed in the related condition relative to the unrelated condition, and the magnitude of this negative priming was similar in the two age groups. In fact, data from this task provided no evidence to suggest that older adults experienced a decline in inhibitory efficiency. Given previous findings, however (e.g., Connelly & Hasher, 1993; Hasher et al., 1991; McDowd & Oseas-Kreger, 1991; Tipper, 1991), this result may be limited to selection tasks involving primarily spatial information processing.

Another factor that may be critical in determining the magnitude of age differences in negative priming is task pacing. Whereas Connelly and Hasher (1993) and Mueller and Baylis (1993) observed equivalent negative priming for younger and older adults in their self-paced location suppression task, McDowd, Filion, and Baylis (1992) observed an interaction between age and the magnitude of negative priming in their forced-pace location suppression task. The McDowd et al. task required subjects to press a key corresponding to the location of a target "O" and to inhibit responding to the location of the distractor "X." Trials were presented in prime–probe pairs, but a constant, computer-controlled, 3-s interval between pairs of trials was included instead of offering subjects the opportunity to initiate the next set of trials. Under these conditions, although both old and young show significant negative priming, older adults show less location suppression than do younger adults. Exactly what it is about self-paced presentation conditions that allows older adults to improve their performance remains for further research.

In sum, the magnitude of negative priming in groups of older adults has been shown to be reduced in comparison to the amount of negative priming demonstrated by younger adults (Hasher et al., 1991; McDowd & Oseas-Kreger, 1991; Stoltzfus et al., 1993; Tipper, 1991). The data suggest that the efficiency with which inhibitory mechanisms can operate is influenced by the nature of the selection process (e.g., location vs. identity) and the pacing of the task (e.g., self-paced vs. forced pace). More specifically, age differences are most apparent with tasks requiring subjects to inhibit the identity of distracting stimuli and when forced-paced conditions are employed (Connelly & Hasher, 1993; McDowd, Filion, & Baylis, 1992). The presence of an age-related cognitive slowing appears not to be a causal factor in the absence of negative priming in older adults, as suggested by between-subject, between-experiment comparisons (Hasher et al., 1991; Stoltzfus et al., 1993), and by median split data (McDowd & Oseas-Kreger, 1991). Taken together, these findings lend support to the hypothesis of an age-related decline in the ability to inhibit *the identity* of irrelevant information when that information is in the form of pictures or words. This pattern of results may be another example of older adults' greater tendency to activate and maintain activation of more semantic information in the stimulus array compared to young adults. It is also interesting to note that inhibition in a location task like those described above appears to be preserved in aging, at least when the subject controls task pacing. Thus, the hypothesized age-related inhibitory deficit is not a global deficit; the evidence suggests that it is subject to important boundary conditions.

CONCLUSIONS AND FUTURE DIRECTIONS

What now is the status of the inhibitory deficit hypothesis of cognitive aging? In this chapter we have reviewed various paradigms that have been used to assess that hypothesis. Taken together, available data suggest that at several levels of information processing in the nervous system, older adults show evidence of a deficit in inhibitory function. Although the evidence is not unequivocal, the following generalization can be made: older adults are less selective information processors than are younger adults. In a variety of situations ranging from elicitation of a brain-stem reflex to the execution of higher language functions, in which both relevant and irrelevant information is available for processing, older adults are more likely to process both classes of information, rather than restricting processing to the most relevant information. The theoretical notion of an inhibitory deficit has been applied with some success in accounting for empirical observations, both in direct tests with models that specifically invoke inhibitory function (e.g., prepulse inhibition, latent inhibition, negative priming) and less direct tests with tasks for which inhibitory processes are assumed to be relevant (e.g., autonomic orienting, habituation, measures of verbosity). However, a number of empirical and theoretical issues remain to be addressed.

One important issue is the question of global versus specific deficits. An important contribution to theory building in cognitive aging would be "to tease apart the various types of interference and determine their specific contributions to age differences" (Dempster, 1992, p. 66). One approach might be to develop a taxonomy of variables that influence age differences in inhibitory function to create a descriptive framework for sorting results (see also Harnishfeger, Chapter 6, this volume). In the realm of negative priming, for example, Connelly and Hasher (1993) have suggested that this taxonomy might include selective responding on the basis of target stimulus identity versus responding on the basis of target stimulus location. In their work, only the identity condition produced age differences in inhibitory function. Hartley's (1993) work similarly shows age equivalence for selection and suppression based on spatial location but an age deficit when selecting only one among several possible streams of information processing. Thus selecting, suppressing, and responding on the basis of spatial location appears to be one task characteristic that is unaffected by aging.

The work of McDowd, Filion, and Baylis (1992) suggests that the taxonomy of relevant variables might also include factors related to stimulus pacing. Age-related inhibitory deficits appear to be absent when stimuli are presented in such a manner that the subject has some control over the pacing of trials. The modality differences reported in the McDowd, Oseas-Kreger, and Filion (1993) orienting study may also reflect important task variables that affect inhibitory function. These findings, while provocative, need to be replicated and perhaps extended to other paradigms.

In addition to providing a descriptive framework, a taxonomy of task variables might also provide some insight into the types of mechanisms that are responsible for observed age differences and similarities. Already there is evidence that Dempster's (1991) "guess . . . that there is a family of inhibitory mechanisms, each specialized to deal with somewhat different processing demands" has merit (p. 168). For example, Connelly and Hasher (1993) cite evidence for separate visual sensory pathways underlying the processing of identity and location information. The inference is that one of these pathways (the identity pathway) might be more negatively affected by aging than the other (the location pathway). If so, this might account for greater age-related inhibitory declines for identity compared to location information. Whether or not the two pathways involve the same or different mechanisms of inhibition, however, remains to be determined.

Hartley's (1993) account of age similarities and differences in selection and suppression processes focuses on two attention systems in the brain, the anterior attention system and the posterior attention system (Posner & Peterson, 1990). He cites behavioral and neuroanatomical evidence suggesting that these two systems age at different rates. The posterior system (parietal cortex, the pulvinar nucleus of the thalamus, the superior colliculus) is responsible for directing attention in space and appears to remain intact across the adult years. The anterior system (primarily frontal cortex), on the other hand, responsible for selecting one of several possible streams of information processing, suffers age-related changes in morphology and function. Along with Connelly and Hasher's multiple visual pathway account, these models suggest that one or more inhibitory mechanisms may be at work in the nervous system, any of which may or may not be influenced by the aging process.

A second issue to be resolved (if the inhibitory deficit hypothesis is to play a role in understanding cognitive aging) involves the demonstration of a direct link between declines in inhibitory function and declines in other aspects of cognition. For example, Connelly et al. (1991) reported that the presence of distracting information set in a different font than the target information slowed reading times in older adults more than in younger adults. However, comprehension scores were not consistently affected by the distracting information. Thus, even though the older adults exhibited reduced inhibition, comprehension was not always impaired. Similarly, McDowd and colleagues (Filion & McDowd, 1993; McDowd & Filion, 1992; McDowd, Oseas-Kreger, & Filion, 1993) have shown with psychophysiological indices that older adults are less efficient in their allocation of attention, but the implications of this difference for other cognitive processes such as comprehension and memory needs also to be demonstrated. In addition, Stoltzfus et al. (1993) have suggested that older adults can select relevant information without suppressing irrelevant information. Indeed, older adults can perform the task of naming target letters, words, or pictures in the presence of distractor stimuli, yet they do not show evidence of suppression processes associated with the negative-priming effect. Observed age differences, then, explain little if their relation to other aspects of cognitive functioning is unspecified or undocumented.

A final issue concerns the observation that, in some cases, an inhibitory deficit may in fact be an advantage. This "deficit" speeds response time in negative-priming tasks (relative to individual baselines) and produces faster learning in latent inhibition tasks. In language tasks, the inclusion or intrusion of personal information or anecdotes may make conversations even *more* interesting. The point is that the costs and benefits of changes in inhibitory function vary as a function of task characteristics. In short, the implications of altered inhibitory function are not all negative.

ACKNOWLEDGMENTS

Preparation of this work was supported in part by NIA Grant AG07991, which is gratefully acknowledged. This chapter has benefited from useful discussions with James Birren, Deborah Burke, and Elizabeth Zelinski. Thanks are also due to Frank Dempster and Charles Brainerd for their comments on earlier drafts of this manuscript. We dedicate this chapter to James E. Birren, with respect and admiration.

REFERENCES

Acocella, C. M., & Blumenthal, T. D. (1990). Directed attention influences the modification of startle reflex probability. *Psychological Reports, 66,* 275–285.

Anthony, B. J. (1985). *In the blink of an eye: Implications of reflex modification for information processing.* Greenwich, CT: JAI Press.

Arbuckle, T. Y., & Gold, D. P. (1993). Aging, inhibition, and verbosity. *Journal of Gerontology: Psychological Sciences, 48,* P225–P232.

Bailey, C. H., Castellucci, V. F., Koester, J., & Chen, M. (1984). Behavioral changes in aging. Aplysia: A model system for studying the cellular basis of age-impaired learning, memory, and arousal. *Behavioral and Neural Biology, 38,* 70–81.

Baruch, I., Hemsley, D. R., & Gray, J. A. (1988). Latent inhibition and "psychotic proneness" in normal subjects. *Personality and Individual Differences, 9,* 777–784.

Birren, J. E. (1959a). Principles of research on aging. In J. E. Birren (Ed.), *Handbook of aging and the individual* (pp. 3–42). Chicago: University of Chicago Press.

Birren, J. E. (1959b). Sensation, perception and modification of behavior in relation to the process of aging. In J. E. Birren, H. A. Imus, & W. F. Windle (Eds.), *The process of aging in the nervous system* (pp. 143–165). Springfield, IL: Charles C. Thomas.

Botwinick, J., & Kornetsky, C. (1960). Age differences in the acquisition and extinction of the GSR. *Journal of Gerontology, 15,* 190–192.

Braff, D. L., & Geyer, M. A. (1990). Sensorimotor gating and schizophrenia: Human and animal model studies. *Archives of General Psychiatry, 47,* 181–188.

Brennan, M. J., Allen, D., Aleman, D., Azmitia, E. C., & Quartermain, D. (1984). Age differences in within-session habituation of exploratory behavior: Effects of stimulus complexity. *Behavioral and Neural Biology, 42,* 61–72.

Burke, D. M., & Light, L. L. (1981). Memory and aging: The role of retrieval processes. *Psychological Bulletin, 90,* 513–546.

Connelly, S. L., & Hasher, L. (1993). Aging and the inhibition of spatial location. *Journal of Experimental Psychology: Human Perception and Performance, 19,* 1238–1250.

Connelly, S. L., Hasher, L., & Zacks, R. T. (1991). Age and reading: The impact of distraction. *Psychology & Aging, 6,* 533–541.

Craik, F. I. M., & Salthouse, T. A. (1992). *Handbook of aging and cognition.* Hillsdale, NJ: Erlbaum.

Davis, M. (1984). *The mammalian startle response.* New York: Plenum.

Dawson, M. E., Filion, D. L., & Schell, A. M. (1989). Is the elicitation of the orienting response associated with the allocation of resources? *Psychophysiology, 26,* 560–572.

Delpezzo, E. M., & Hoffman, H. S. (1980). Attentional factors in the inhibition of a reflex by a visual prestimulus. *Science, 210,* 673–674.

Dempster, F. N. (1991). Inhibitory processes: A neglected dimension of intelligence. *Intelligence, 15,* 157–173.

Dempster, F. N. (1992). The rise and fall of the inhibitory mechanism: Toward a unified theory of cognitive development and aging. *Developmental Review, 12,* 45–75.

Eccles, J. C. (1969). *The inhibitory pathways of the central nervous system.* Springfield, IL: Charles C. Thomas.

Eisenstein, E. M., Eisenstein, D., Bonheim, P., & Welch, E. A. (1990). Habituation of the galvanic skin response in adult males as a function of age. *Physiology & Behavior, 48,* 169–173.

Filion, D. L., Dawson, M. E., & Schell, A. M. (1993). Modification of the acoustic startle-reflex eyeblink: A tool for investigating early and late attentional processes. *Biological Psychology, 35,* 185–200.

Filion, D. L., Dawson, M. E., Schell, A. M., & Hazlett, E. A. (1991). The relationship between the skin conductance orienting response and the allocation of processing resources. *Psychophysiology, 28,* 410–425.

Filion, D. L., & McDowd, J. M. (1993). *Startle eyeblink modification measures of inhibitory function in aging.* Manuscript submitted for publication.

Frolkis, V. V., & Bezrukov, V. V. (1979). *Aging of the central nervous system, Interdisciplinary topics in gerontology.* New York: Karger.

Gakkel, L. B., & Zinina, N. V. (1953). Changes of higher nerve function in people over 60 years of age (English translation). *Fiziologicheskii Zhurnal SSSR im I.M. Sechenova, 39,* 533–539.

Gernsbacher, M. A., & Faust, M. E. (1991). The mechanism of suppression: A component of general comprehension skill. *Journal of Experimental Psychology: Learning, Memory, and Cognition, 17,* 245–262.

Giambra, L. M. (1989). Task-unrelated-thought frequency as a function of age: A laboratory study. *Psychology & Aging, 4,* 136–143.

Gold, D., Andres, D., Arbuckle, T., & Schwartzman, A. (1988). Measurement and correlates of verbosity in elderly people. *Journal of Gerontology, 43,* 27–33.

Graham, F. K. (1975). The more or less startling effects of weak prestimulation. *Psychophysiology, 12,* 238–248.

Graham, F. K. (1980). *Control of reflex blink excitability.* New York: Academic Press.

Hackley, S. A., & Graham, F. K. (1987). Effects of attending selectively to the spatial position of reflex-eliciting and reflex-modulating stimuli. *Journal of Experimental Psychology, 13,* 411–424.

Hackley, S. A., Woldorff, M., & Hillyard, S.A. (1987). Combined use of microreflexes and event-related brain potentials as measures of auditory selective attention. *Psychophysiology, 24,* 632–647.

Hamm, V. P., & Hasher, L. (1992). Age and the availability of inferences. *Psychology & Aging, 6,* 56–64.

Harbin, T. J., & Berg, W. K. (1983). The effects of age and prestimulus duration upon reflexinhibition. *Psychophysiology, 20,* 603–610.

Harrison, D. W., & Isaac, W. (1985). Disruption and habituation of stable fixed-interval behavior in younger and older monkeys. *Physiology & Behavior, 32,* 341–344.

Harrison, J. M. (1984). Effects of age on some behavioral characteristics of novel auditory stimuli in the rat. *Experimental Aging Research, 9,* 35–39.

Hartley, A. A. (1993). Evidence for the selective preservation of spatial selective attention in old age. *Psychology & Aging, 8,* 371–379.

Hartman, M., & Hasher, L. (1991). Aging and suppression: Memory for previously irrelevant information. *Psychology & Aging, 6,* 587–594.

Hasher, L., Stoltzfus, E. R., Zacks, R. T., & Rypma, B. (1991). Age and inhibition. *Journal of Experimental Psychology: Learning, Memory, and Cognition, 17,* 163–169.

Hasher, L., & Zacks, R. (1988). Working memory, comprehension, and aging: A review and a new view. In G. Bower (Ed.), *The psychology of learning and motivation* (pp. 193–325). San Diego: Academic Press.

Hashtroudi, S., Johnson, M. K., & Chrosniak, L. D. (1990). Aging and qualitative characteristics of memories for perceived and imagined complex events. *Psychology & Aging, 5,* 119–126.

Hoffman, H. S., & Ison, J. R. (1980). Reflex modification in the domain of startle: 1. Some empirical findings and their implications for how the nervous system processes sensory input. *Psychological Review, 87,* 175–189.

Jakubczak, L. F. (1967). Psychophysiological aging. *Gerontology, 7,* 67–72.

Johnson, S. L., McDowd, J. M., and MacDonald, M. C. (1993). *Suppression and facilitation in sentence comprehension and aging.* Manuscript in preparation.

Kahneman, D. (1973). *Attention and effort.* Englewood Cliffs, NJ: Prentice-Hall.

Kimble, G. A., & Pennypacker, H. S. (1963). Eyelid conditioning in young and aged subjects. *Journal of Genetic Psychology, 103,* 283–289.

Le Bourg, E. (1983). Aging and habituation of the tarsal response in Drosophila melanogaster. *Gerontology, 29,* 388–393.

Light, L. L. (1991). Memory and aging: Four hypotheses in search of data. *Annual Review of Psychology, 42,* 333–376.

Light, L. L. (1992). The organization of memory in old age. In F. I. M. Craik & T. A. Salthouse (Eds.), *The handbook of aging and cognition* (pp. 111–165). Hillsdale, NJ: Erlbaum.

Light, L. L., Valencia-Laver, D., & Zavis, D. (1991). Instantiation of general terms in young and older adults. *Psychology & Aging, 6,* 337–351.

Lloyd, R. L., & Levine, M. S. (1984). Behavioral alterations in aged cats. *Society for Neuroscience Abstracts, 10,* 450.

Lubow, R. E. (1989). *Latent inhibition and conditioned attention theory.* Cambridge, UK: Cambridge University Press.

McDowd, J. M. (1990). *Aging, selective attention, and inhibitory processes.* Paper presented at the annual meeting of the Western Psychological Association, Los Angeles.

McDowd, J. M., & Birren, J. E. (1990). Aging and attentional processes. In J. E. Birren & K. W. Schaie (Eds.), *Handbook of the psychology of aging* (pp. 222–233). San Diego: Academic Press.

McDowd, J. M., & Filion, D. L. (1992). Aging, selective attention, and inhibitory processes: A psychophysiological approach. *Psychology & Aging, 7,* 65–71.

McDowd, J. M., Filion, D. L., & Baylis, G. C. (1992). *Aging and negative priming: The role of spatial location and stimulus pacing.* Poster presented at the Cognitive Aging Conference, Atlanta, GA.

McDowd, J. M., & Oseas-Kreger, D. M. (1991). Aging, inhibitory processes, and negative priming. *Journal of Gerontology, 46,* 340–345.

McDowd, J. M., Oseas-Kreger, D. M., & Filion, D. L. (1993). *Orienting and habituation as measures of inhibitory function in aging.* Manuscript submitted for publication.

Misanin, J. R., Blatt, L. A., & Hinderliter, C. F. (1985). Age dependency in neophobia: its influence on taste aversion learning and the flavor preexposure effect in rats. *Animal Learning and Behavior, 13,* 69–76.

Misanin, J. R., Guanowsky, V., & Riccio, D. C. (1983). The effects of CS preexposure on conditioned taste aversion in young and adult rats. *Physiology & Behavior, 30,* 859–862.

Mueller, P. M., & Baylis, G. C. (1993). *The effect of normal aging and Alzheimer's disease on attention: Inter-trial priming effects.* Manuscript in revision.

Navon, D. (1984). Resources—A theoretical soupstone? *Psychological Review, 91,* 216–234.

Neill, W. T., & Westberry, R. L. (1987). Selective attention and the suppression of cognitive noise. *Journal of Experimental Psychology: Learning, Memory, and Cognition, 13,* 327–334.

Öhman, A. (1979). *The orienting response, attention, and learning: An information processing perspective.* Hillsdale, NJ: Erlbaum.

Parsons, P. J., Fagan, T., & Spear, N. E. (1973). Short-term retention of habituation in the rat: a developmental study from infancy to old age. *Journal of Comparative and Physiological Psychology, 84,* 545–553.

Peterson, C. S., Valliere, W. A., Misanin, J. R., & Hinderliter, C. F. (1985). Age differences in the potentiation of taste aversion by odor cues. *Physiological Psychology, 13,* 103–106.

Posner, M. I., & Peterson, S. E. (1990). The attention system of the human brain. *Annual Review of Neuroscience, 13,* 25–42.

Pribram, K. H., & McGinness, D. (1975). Arousal, activation, and effort in the control of attention. *Psychological Review, 82,* 116–146.

Rinaldi, P. C., & Thompson, R. F. (1985). Age, sex and strain comparison of habituation of the startle response in the rat. *Physiology & Behavior, 35,* 9–13.

Salthouse, T. A. (1985). *A theory of cognitive aging.* North-Holland: Elsevier.

Salthouse, T. A. (1991). *Theoretical perspectives on cognitive aging.* Hillsdale, NJ: Erlbaum.

Shaw, R. J. (1991). Age-related increases in the effects of automatic semantic activation. *Psychology & Aging, 6,* 595–604.

Sokolov, E. N. (1963). *Perception and the conditioned reflex.* New York: Pergamon.

Solyom, L. (1968). The role of inhibition in senile and arteriosclerotic brain disease. *Comprehensive Psychiatry, 9,* 507–516.

Stankov, L. (1988). Aging, attention, and intelligence. *Psychology & Aging, 3,* 59–74.

Stephenson, D., & Siddle, D. (1983). Theories of habituation. In D. Siddle (Ed.), *Orienting and habituation: Perspectives in human research* (pp. 183–236). New York: Wiley.

Stoltzfus, E. R., Hasher, L., Zacks, R. T., Ulivi, M. S., & Goldstein, D. (1993). Investigations of inhibition and interference in younger and older adults. *Journal of Gerontology: Psychological Sciences, 48,* P179–P188.

Sugar, J. A., & McDowd, J. M. (1992). Memory, learning, and attention, In J. E. Birren, R. B. Sloane, & G. D. Cohen (Eds.), *Handbook of mental health and aging* (pp. 307–337). San Diego: Academic Press.

Tipper, S. P. (1985). The negative priming effect: Inhibitory priming by ignored objects. *Quarterly Journal of Experimental Psychology: Human Experimental Psychology, 37A,* 571–590.

Tipper, S. P. (1991). Less attentional selectivity as a result of declining inhibition in older adults. *Bulletin of the Psychonomic Society, 29,* 45–47.

Tipper, S. P., Bourque, T. A., Anderson, S. H., & Brehaut, J. C. (1989). Mechanisms of attention: A developmental study. *Journal of Experimental Child Psychology, 48,* 353–378.

Tipper, S. P., Brehaut, J. C., & Driver, J. (1990). Selection of moving and static objects for the control of spatially directed action. *Journal of Experimental Psychology: Human Perception and Performance, 16,* 492–504.

Tipper, S. P., Weaver, B., Kirkpatrick, J., & Lewis, S. (1991). Inhibitory mechanisms of attention: Locus, stability, and relationship with distractor interference effects. *British Journal of Psychology, 82,* 507–520.

Waters, W. F., & Wright, D. C. (1979). Maintenance and habituation of the phasic orienting response to competing stimuli in selective attention. In H. D. Kimmel, E. H. van Olst, & J. H. Orlebeke (Eds.), *The orienting reflex in humans* (pp. 101–121). Hillsdale, NJ: Erlbaum.

12

New Perspectives on Interference and Inhibition in Cognition
Final Comments

Frank N. Dempster and Charles J. Brainerd

As we survey the chapters in this volume, we are struck by the diversity of topics and research agendas that are represented. They range from efforts to understand the history of research on interference (Dempster's historical introduction) and human evolution (Bjorklund & Harnishfeger's inquiry into the evolution of inhibition) to a most recent development—namely, neural network models (Lewandowsky & Li's study of catastrophic interference). Between these extremes are work on infancy (Rovee-Collier & Boller's analysis of interference in infant memory), cognitive development (Harnishfeger's model of inefficient inhibition), and cognitive aging (McDowd, Oseas-Kreger, & Filion's study of reduced inhibition in the elderly). Some new ideas have been presented that link interference and inhibition to fundamental processes of cognition—specifically, selective attention (Neill, Valdes, & Terry's chapter), comprehension (Gernsbacher & Faust's chapter), reasoning (Reyna's chapter), recall (Brainerd's analysis of cognitive triage), and memory suggestibility (Titcomb & Reyna's account of misinformation effects). Thus, there is diversity with respect to substantive issues, paradigms, the types of interference and inhibition studied, and the ages of the subjects that are studied. Clearly, the range of application of modern psychological concepts of interference and inhibition is very broad indeed.

In retrospect, then, our original objective in planning this volume, which was to present a variety of different perspectives, has been realized. We believe this is the best way of documenting the potential centrality of interference and inhibition concepts in modern research on human cognition. Although such diversity might seem daunting at first, there are some unifying themes that we will identify and discuss in the present chapter. We conclude the chapter by noting some unresolved issues that suggest directions for future research.

UNIFYING THEMES

Surely the major unifying theme of these chapters is that the ability to resist interference is a hallmark of effective, mature cognition. To be sure, some failures to inhibit irrelevant, misleading, or post-event information appear to be adaptive, particularly in infants (Rovee-Collier & Boller) and older adults (McDowd et al.) On the whole, however, the ability to resist interference seems to play a crucial role in the execution of a variety of cognitive processes, including selective attention (Harnishfeger; Neill et al.), comprehension (Gernsbacher & Faust), reasoning (Reyna), and recall (Brainerd). In current theoretical work in these areas, resistance to interference, and its counterpart the capacity for inhibition, seems to be attaining a status once held by such familiar explanatory concepts as activation resources, strategies, logical operations, and knowledge base. As a consequence, the concepts of interference and inhibition have enabled researchers to develop a more balanced view of cognition. Strategies, knowledge base, and other "high-cognitive" explanations are not so much wrong as they are incomplete. Effective thinking and remembering require more than strategies and knowledge, they also require a capacity for controlling interference from extraneous sources. Likewise, a complete picture of cognitive development would seem to require an understanding that resistance to interference varies with age.

In our opinion, resistance to interference and inhibition are basic processes that are part of a larger "back-to-basics" movement that is underway in some areas of cognitive psychology. By a basic process, we mean a mechanism that is mediated largely or entirely by some biologically determined aspect of the brain and nervous system. In this respect, resistance to interference and inhibition are like activation resources. But they are unlike strategies, logical operations, and other familiar high-cognitive concepts (e.g., metacognition). It is these latter concepts, of course, that have dominated the psychology of memory and reasoning for the past quarter-century (for reviews see Pressley, 1994). For us, a fundamental limitation of such concepts is that they beg the question of why some people perform better than others. Research shows that some individuals are more strategic or more metacognitive in certain situations than others. How did they get that way? A basic process, such as resistance to interference, may provide an answer. For example, ineffective problem solving strategies, such as those that may be used to solve controlling variables problems (e.g., Linn, 1978) or verbal analogy problems (e.g., Marr & Sternberg, 1986) are commonly ones in which irrelevant information is not resisted. Hence, achieving some critical level of interference resistance may be a necessary precondition for the emergence of particular strategies (see also Dempster, 1991; 1992).

The concept of resistance to interference also places the activation resource hypothesis in perspective and helps us to interpret this important idea. There is a growing sense that inhibitory as well as excitatory (i.e., activation) mechanisms are needed to provide a more complete picture of cognition. Evidence presented in four of the chapters in this volume (Brainerd, Gernsbacher & Faust, Lewandowsky & Li, and Reyna) provide detailed pictures of how activation processes and interference or inhibition interact in specific domains. For example, the optimization model of recall (Brainerd) assumes that a word's memory strength in a free recall task is modulated by the dynamic interaction between episodic activation, which facilitates recall, and output interference, which inhibits recall. More generally, these developments enrich simple activation resource hypotheses, such as the capacity increase hypothesis, and allow them to explain a broader range of findings. Developmental changes in capacity are inferred from a variety of indices, including memory span, but what appear to be changes in capacity may actually be changes in the ability to resist interference.

Another theme that binds the chapters together is the notion that there are a number of distinct forms of interference and inhibition that influence cognition. Proactive and retroactive interference figure in the Dempster and Rovee-Collier and Boller chapters; contextual interference is discussed in the chapter by Gernsbacher and Faust; interference between verbatim and gist traces is considered in the chapters by Reyna and Titcomb and Reyna; and Brainerd explores the effects of two types of output interference. Among the different kinds of inhibition that are examined are cognitive and behavioral (Bjorklund & Harnishfeger's and Harnishfeger's chapters), inhibition of location information versus inhibition of identity information (the McDowd et al. chapter), reactive inhibition (the Neill et al. chapter), suppression or the active dampening of activation (the Gernsbacher & Faust chapter), and context differentiation (the Lewandowsky & Li chapter). It is also clear that the behavioral expression of interference is influenced by a variety of methodological variables, such as the timing and nature of the interpolated information (Rovee-Collier & Boller), the degree of original learning (Brainerd), the type of test used (Reyna), and social factors (Titcomb & Reyna). In light of the evidence, consistent with proposals in Harnishfeger and McDowd et al.'s chapters, there is a family of inhibitory mechanisms, each specialized to manage somewhat different types of interference (see also Dempster, 1991; 1993).

Although this very complexity may, again, seem rather disconcerting, it may be an inevitable consequence of the deep involvement of interference and inhibition in so many aspects of cognition. This complexity also serves to illustrate how far modern interference concepts have evolved beyond classical interference theory. As a specific example, although classical interference theory was concerned with just two forms of interference, proactive and retroactive, most recent work emphasizes that one of the most serious forms of interference is *coactive*. Coactive interference occurs when two or more contiguous events compete with one another, as is often the case in attention, comprehension, and reasoning.

UNRESOLVED ISSUES AND AVENUES
FOR FUTURE RESEARCH

We believe that research on interference and inhibition should soon address two fundamental issues. The first is the relationship between interference and inhibition. This question never arose in classical interference theory because most investigators used the term "inhibition" to refer to observed decrements in performance and the term "interference" to refer to processes that caused those decrements. So, therefore, whenever there were substantial amounts of inhibition, there were necessarily substantial amounts of interference. For modern theorists, however, "inhibition" and "interference" are both theoretical concepts. Thus, the relationship between the two requires interpretation and that, in turn, requires independent behavioral measures of each. Such data as are available suggest that the relationship may be far from straightforward. For instance, it has been reported that groups of subjects who show less inhibition do not always show more interference (Beech, Baylis, Smithson, & Claridge, 1989; Kane, Hasher, Stoltzfus, Zacks, & Connelly, 1994; Stoltzfus, Hasher, Zacks, Ulivi, & Goldstein, 1993), but it has also been reported that the two are negatively correlated (Beech et al., 1989; Beech & Claridge, 1987). In addition, some studies of negative priming, a widely used measure of inhibition, have failed to find any relationship between inhibition and interference (Neill et al.'s chapter).

If there are distinct forms of interference, then the relationship between interference and inhibition will probably depend on the type of interference. For example, there does not appear to be any relationship between inhibition and interference in concurrent selection tasks (cf. Stoltzfus et al., 1993). In addition, some evidence suggests that inhibition is not the only mechanism for resisting interference. For example, studies have shown that interference can be reduced, if not altogether eliminated, by certain forms of processing, including gist processing (Reyna's chapter), processing that effectively differentiates task relevant from task irrelevant information (Andre, Anderson, & Watts, 1976; Lewandowsky & Li's chapter; Perlmutter, 1991), and by predictive relations that help stimuli retrieve unique responses (Bower, Thompson-Schill, & Tulving, 1994).

The second issue that research on interference and inhibition will have to address is the core assumption that resistance to interference (or inhibition) is implicated in most aspects of cognition, including comprehension and reasoning. If that belief is misplaced, modern research on interference and inhibition, like classical interference theory, might fail the test of relevance (see Dempster, Chapter 1). At present, evidence bearing on this issue is mixed. For example, on the one hand, Gernsbacher and Faust (1991) found that more-skilled comprehenders and less-skilled comprehenders did not differ significantly in their performance on the Air Force Qualifying Exam or on tests that measured general knowledge, administrative ability, and mechanical ability, even though these less-skilled subjects were plagued "by less-efficient suppression mechanisms." Similarly, Connelly, Hasher, and Zacks (1991) found that comprehension scores of adults were not consistently affected by the presence of distracting, potentially interfering, information, and, even though the older adults exhibited reduced inhibition, comprehension was not always impaired.

On the other hand, significant negative correlations have been reported between scores on the WAIS and perseverative errors on the Wisconsin Card Sorting Test (a well-accepted measure of interference), and between general intelligence scores and Stroop interference. In both cases, however, the correlations were modest, although restricted ranges may have been a factor (see Dempster, 1991, for a review). Similar findings have been obtained in four other studies. In one, Smith and Baron (1981) found a positive correlation between intelligence, as measured by the Scholastic Aptitude Test and Raven's Progressive Matrices, and resistance to interference in a speeded classification task containing an irrelevant dimension. In another study, "distractibility" was measured in a speeded visual search task by comparing performance in the presence and absence of extraneous auditory and visual stimuli. Although general measures of mental ability were administered under normal (no distraction) conditions, highly distractible subjects scored, on average, 9.4 percentile points lower than the less distractible subjects (Aks & Coren, 1990). Finally, in two studies with college students (Dempster, 1985; Dempster & Cooney, 1982), estimates of susceptibility to Brown-Peterson interference were negatively correlated with reading comprehension as measured by a variety of indices, including the SAT Verbal, SAT Reading, and ACT Social Science and Natural Science Reading Tests. Some recent efforts to replicate these findings, however, have met with limited success (Hau, 1994; J. McIntyre, personal communication, October 17, 1993).

In short, some data show a link between resistance to interference and inhibition and suggest that differences in interference sensitivity contribute to individual differences in cognitive processing, but other research does not. In addition, some research suggests that a variety of clinical syndromes and educational classifications, including attention–conduct disorder, psychopathology, obsessive–compulsive disorder, schizophrenia, mental retardation, and reading and learning disabilities are characterized, to some extent, by failures to inhibit irrelevant or inappropriate behaviors or cognition or by failures to resist interference from inappropriate stimuli. Moreover, many of these failures appear to be related to frontal-lobe dysfunction (for reviews, see Dempster, 1991; Harnishfeger & Bjorklund, 1994).

In closing, we believe that the chapters in this volume represent a new generation of potentially revolutionary theories and models of cognition. Although it is always difficult to chart the course of future research, it appears that the concepts of interference and inhibition are now deeply rooted not only in the cognitive mainstream but in developmental research as well. Thus, we are confident that many of the ideas presented in this volume will continue to contribute substantially to our growing knowledge about cognition well into the next century.

REFERENCES

Aks, D. J., & Coren, S. (1990). Is susceptibility to distraction related to mental ability? *Journal of Educational Psychology, 82,* 388–390.

Andre, T., Anderson, R. C., & Watts, G. H. (1976). Item-specific interference and list discrimination in free recall. *Journal of General Psychology, 72,* 533–543.

Beech, A., Baylis, G., Smithson, P., & Claridge, G. (1989). Individual differences in schizotypy as reflected in measures of cognitive inhibition. *British Journal of Clinical Psychology, 28,* 117–129.

Beech, A., & Claridge, G. (1987). Individual differences in negative priming: Relations with schizotypal personality traits. *British Journal of Psychology, 28,* 110–116.

Bower, G. H., Thompson-Schill, S., & Tulving, E. (1994). Reducing retroactive interference: An interference analysis. *Journal of Experimental Psychology: Learning, Memory, and Cognition, 20,* 51–66.

Connelly, S. L., Hasher, L., & Zacks, R. T. (1991). Age and reading: The impact of distraction. *Psychology and Aging, 6,* 533–541.

Dempster, F. N. (1985). Proactive interference in sentence recall: Topic similarity effects and individual differences. *Memory & Cognition, 13,* 81–89.

Dempster, F. N. (1991). Inhibition processes: A neglected dimension of intelligence. *Intelligence, 15,* 157–173.

Dempster, F. N. (1992). The rise and fall of the inhibitory mechanism: Toward a unified theory of cognitive development and aging. *Developmental Review, 12,* 45–75.

Dempster, F. N. (1993). Resistance to interference: Developmental changes in a basic processing dimension. In M. L. Howe & R. Pasnak (Eds.), *Emerging themes in cognitive development, Vol. 1: Foundations* (pp. 3–27). New York: Springer-Verlag.

Dempster, F. N., & Cooney, J. B. (1982). Individual differences in digit span, susceptibility to proactive interference, and aptitude/achievement test scores. *Intelligence, 6,* 399–416.

Gernsbacher, M. A., & Faust, M. E. (1991). The mechanism of suppression: A component of general comprehension skill. *Journal of Experimental Psychology: Learning, Memory, and Cognition, 17,* 245–262.

Harnishfeger, K. K., & Bjorklund, D. F. (1994). A developmental perspective on individual differences in inhibition. *Learning and Individual Differences.*

Hau, R. (1994). *Establishing reliability and loci of effect for individual differences in susceptibility to proactive interference.* Unpublished master's thesis, University of Manitoba, Winnipeg, Manitoba.

Kane, M. J., Hasher, L., Stoltzfus, E. R., Zacks, R. T., & Connelly, S. L. (1994). Inhibitory attentional mechanisms and aging. *Psychology and Aging, 9,* 103–112.

Linn, M. C. (1978). Influence of cognitive style and training on tasks requiring the separation of variables schema. *Child Development, 49,* 874–877.

Marr, D. B., & Sternberg, R. J. (1986). Analogical reasoning with novel concepts: Differential attention of intellectually gifted and nongifted children to relevant and irrelevant novel stimuli. *Cognitive Development, 1,* 53–72.

Perlmutter, L. C. (1991). Choice enhances performance in non-insulin dependent diabetics and controls. *Journal of Gerontology: Psychological Sciences, 46,* 218–223.

Pressley, M. (1994). Embracing complexity: Studying good information processing and how it might develop. *Learning and Individual Differences.*

Smith, J. D., & Baron, J. (1981). Individual differences in the classification of stimuli by dimensions. *Journal of Experimental Psychology: Human Perception and Performance, 7,* 1132–1145.

Stoltzfus, E. R., Hasher, L., Zacks, R. T., Ulivi, M. S., & Goldstein, D. (1993). Investigations of inhibition and interference in younger and older adults. *Journal of Gerontology: Psychological Sciences, 48,* P179–P188.

Author Index

Abelson, R. P., 296
Ackerman, B. P., 38, 40, 41, 42, 43, 44, 48, 54, 56, 72, 82, 99, 287, 290
Acocella, C. M., 368
Acredolo, C., 53, 56
Adams-Price, C., 279, 290
Adler, S.A., 72, 75, 82, 85, 96,102
Agar, K., 232
Ahlquist, J. E., 156
Ainsworth, M. D. S., 147,164
Aks, D. J. , 405
Alba, J., 31, 38, 56
Aleksandrowicz, D. R., 176, 199
Aleman, D., 372
Alexander, R. D., 159
Allen, M., 105, 106, 107, 109, 137, 372
Allport, D. A., 219, 220, 232, 233, 236, 243, 247, 249, 295
Amabile, T. A., 72, 74, 75, 85, 99
Ames, E.W., 64, 103
Anastasi, J., 270, 271, 294
Anderson, D. R., !44, 249
Anderson, J. A., 336
Anderson, J. R., 7, 8 ,10, 63, 99, 229, 245, 250
Anderson, R. C., 7
Anderson, S. H., 144, 193, 204, 238, 389
Andre, T., 405
Andres, D., 382
Anthony, B. J., 368
Arbuckle, T. Y., 382, 384
Arenberg, D., 16
Armstrong, E., 158
Aron, M., 71, 83, 103
Atkinson, G., 239
Ausubel, D. P., 6, 7, 11

Baddeley, A. D., 191, 192, 264, 252, 276, 291, 352
Baer, R. A., 153
Bailey, C. H. 366, 372
Baillargeon, R., 14
Baker-Ward, L., 113, 137, 138
Bandura, A., 147
Banks, J., 53, 56
Barclay, J. D., 31, 56
Barnes, J. M., 333, 337, 353, 359
Barnhardt, T. M., 246
Baron, J., 249
Baruch, I., 373
Bastedo, J., 211, 225
Battig, W. F., 105, 106, 107, 109, 137
Baylis, G. C., 189, 204, 212, 216, 232, 235, 238, 392, 393, 394, 395
Beach, F. A., 161
Beal, C. R., 39, 42, 43, 48, 56
Beck, J. L., 213, 218, 219, 225, 230, 239
Becker, C. A., 242, 299
Beech, A. R., 143, 150, 232, 238, 404
Beeman, M., 298
Beier, J. A., 68,103
Bekerian, D., 265, 271, 282, 283, 284, 291
Bell, B., 263, 291
Bell, M. A., 152
Belli, R. F., 44, 56, 93, 99, 268, 269, 271, 276, 277, 278, 281, 282, 284, 286, 288, 289, 291
Bentler, P. M., 185, 199
Berg, W. K., 368
Bergstrom, J. A., 4
Berk, L. E., 164
Berner, J., 353
Bernholtz, J. E., 129, 137

Subject Index

421

Forgetting (*cont.*)
  retrieval-based, 62–63
  storage-based, 62–63, 72
Fuzzy-trace theory, 17–18, 29, 34, 38, 48,
    119, 179–181, 284–286, 290, 293–294

Gain parameter, 332, 347–348, 351–356,
    358–359

Homophones, 297, 301–304, 322–324

Infants, 13–14, 61–99, 146, 149, 184, 152,
    263, 401–402
Inhibition, 3–4, 6, 12–1, 20–21, 62, 98,
    143–144, 146,163, 217–218, 298,
    363–387, 389–391, 394–396, 401–406
  and aging, 145–146, 181–182, 363–396,
    401
  behavioral, 141, 147, 175, 182, 184–186,
    190, 198, 403
  development of, 15–19, 83–84, 145–147,
    152–153, 175–199, 401
  evolution of, 141–142, 153–169, 401
  inefficient inhibition theory, 16–18, 178,
    401
  ntracategory, 244–246
  latent, 373–375
  lateral, 178, 248–249
  mechanisms, 19, 141–143, 145–169,
    175–179
  of aggression, 143–144, 148, 153, 166–168
  of sexual responding, 144, 148, 153,
    166–168
Input pattern, 335–336, 340, 343–344, 346,
    348, 353, 357
Integration, 63, 76, 85–86, 88, 93, 99
Interference, 29–30, 34–36, 49, 52, 54–55,
    105, 120–121, 176, 188–189,
    191–192, 198, 263–265, 267–269,
    272, 276–277, 279–280, 282, 285,
    289, 291–293, 295–296, 329–334,
    337, 342, 344–345, 348, 350–353,
    357, 393–395, 401–406
  Brown-Peterson, 5–12, 405
  catastrophic, 20, 329, 333–334, 336–339,
    342, 346–348, 351–352, 401
  classical interference theory, 3–9, 11, 21,
    404–405
  coactive, 404
  gist, 15, 34–35, 38, 41–42, 45–49, 54, 403
  hypothesis, 118, 108
  misinformation, 268–269, 291

output, 36–37, 119–120, 129, 131, 135,
    179–181, 297, 403
probe, 232–235
prime, 229–232
proactive, 5–7, 9, 11–12, 14, 16, 21,
    61–64, 66–87, 89–97, 151, 264–265,
    272, 282, 295, 403–404
resistance (susceptibility) to, 14–21, 137,
    158, 178–179, 183, 189–190, 193,
    199, 317, 402–403, 405–406
retroactive, 4–7, 10–12, 16, 21, 61–62,
    68–69, 72, 85, 95, 97, 264–265, 272,
    276–282, 292, 295, 403–404
stroop, 330–331, 405
verbatim, 15, 34–37, 42, 45–49, 54, 403
Intertrial sharpening, 110–111, 113, 117,
    122, 135, 166

Linear association, 334–338, 345–347

Memory, 178, 184, 191, 363–364, 383,
    402–403
alteration, 265–267, 269, 276, 279–280,
    282, 290
and reasoning, 29–31, 46–48, 50, 53–55,
    403
blend, 96
capacity, 16, 77, 191, 378
dependency, 33, 47, 49
development, 105, 130, 136
gist, 30–42, 45, 47–50, 53–55
impairment, 269, 278, 280, 291, 293–294
independence, 33, 45, 47
intrusions, 178, 189, 381–84, 387
long-term, 69, 73, 93, 96, 375
necessity, 30
modification, 77, 79, 82, 86, 90–91, 94, 96
nodes, 296–298, 317
primacy, 110–113
recall, 17, 105–120, 122–126, 129–137,
    267, 271, 273–275, 277, 288,
    292–294, 359, 383, 402–403
recency, 109–110, 135
short-term, 48, 64–65, 93
specificity, 71, 99
strength, 105–107, 112–113, 115–116,
    119–121, 123, 127, 130, 132–136,
    145–146, 158, 280, 283. 288, 290,
    403
test, 266, 271–275, 276–277, 279, 286,
    288–289, 290
verbatim, 30–36, 38–45, 47–50, 53–55,